Lecture Notes in Artificial Intelligence 10035

Subseries of Lecture Notes in Computer Science

LNAI Series Editors

Randy Goebel
University of Alberta, Edmonton, Canada
Yuzuru Tanaka
Hokkaido University, Sapporo, Japan
Wolfgang Wahlster
DFKI and Saarland University, Saarbrücken, Germany

LNAI Founding Series Editor

Joerg Siekmann
DFKI and Saarland University, Saarbrücken, Germany

More information about this series at http://www.springer.com/series/1244

Maosong Sun · Xuanjing Huang
Hongfei Lin · Zhiyuan Liu
Yang Liu (Eds.)

Chinese Computational Linguistics and Natural Language Processing Based on Naturally Annotated Big Data

15th China National Conference, CCL 2016, and
4th International Symposium, NLP-NABD 2016
Yantai, China, October 15–16, 2016
Proceedings

Springer

Editors
Maosong Sun
Tsinghua University
Beijing
China

Zhiyuan Liu
Tsinghua University
Beijing
China

Xuanjing Huang
Fudan University
Shanghai
China

Yang Liu
Tsinghua University
Beijing
China

Hongfei Lin
Dalian University of Technology
Dalian
China

ISSN 0302-9743   ISSN 1611-3349 (electronic)
Lecture Notes in Artificial Intelligence
ISBN 978-3-319-47673-5   ISBN 978-3-319-47674-2 (eBook)
DOI 10.1007/978-3-319-47674-2

Library of Congress Control Number: 2016954126

LNCS Sublibrary: SL7 – Artificial Intelligence

This Springer imprint is published by Springer Nature
The registered company is Springer International Publishing AG
The registered company address is: Gewerbestrasse 11, 6330 Cham, Switzerland

Preface

Welcome to the proceedings of the 15th China National Conference on Computational Linguistics (15th CCL) and the Fourth International Symposium on Natural Language Processing Based on Naturally Annotated Big Data (4th NLP-NABD). The conference and symposium were hosted by Ludong University located in Yantai City, Shandong Province, China.

CCL is an annual conference (bi-annual before 2013) that started in 1991. It is the flagship conference of the Chinese Information Processing Society of China (CIPS), which is the largest NLP scholar and expert community in China. CCL is a premier nationwide forum for disseminating new scholarly and technological work in computational linguistics, with a major emphasis on computer processing of the languages in China such as Mandarin, Tibetan, Mongolian, and Uyghur.

Affiliated with the 15th CCL, the Fourth International Symposium on Natural Language Processing Based on Naturally Annotated Big Data (NLP-NABD) covered all the NLP topics, with particular focus on methodologies and techniques relating to naturally annotated big data. In contrast to manually annotated data such as treebanks that are constructed for specific NLP tasks, naturally annotated data come into existence through users' normal activities, such as writing, conversation, and interactions on the Web. Although the original purposes of these data typically were unrelated to NLP, they can nonetheless be purposefully exploited by computational linguists to acquire linguistic knowledge. For example, punctuation marks in Chinese text can help word boundaries identification, social tags in social media can provide signals for keyword extraction, and categories listed in Wikipedia can benefit text classification. The natural annotation can be explicit, as in the aforementioned examples, or implicit, as in Hearst patterns (e.g., "Beijing and other cities" implies "Beijing is a city"). This symposium focuses on numerous research challenges ranging from very large scale unsupervised/semi-supervised machine leaning (deep learning, for instance) of naturally annotated big data to integration of the learned resources and models with existing handcrafted "core" resources and "core" language computing models. NLP-NABD 2016 was supported by the National Key Basic Research Program of China (i.e., "973" Program) "Theory and Methods for Cyber-Physical-Human Space-Oriented Web Chinese Information Processing" under grant no. 2014CB340500 and the Major Project of the National Social Science Foundation of China under grant no. 13&ZD190.

The Program Committee selected 101 papers (64 Chinese papers and 37 English papers) out of 307 submissions from China, Hong Kong (region), Singapore, and USA for publication. The total accepted rate is 32.9 %. The 37 English papers cover the following topics:

- Semantics (3)
- Machine translation (5)
- Multilinguality in NLP (6)
- Knowledge graph and information extraction (5)

- Linguistic resource annotation and evaluation (2)
- Information retrieval and question answering (2)
- Text classification and summarization (5)
- Social computing and sentiment analysis (5)
- NLP applications (4)

The final program for the 15th CCL and the fourth NLP-NABD was the result of a great deal of work by many dedicated colleagues. We want to thank, first of all, the authors who submitted their papers, and thus contributed to the creation of the high-quality program that allowed us to look forward to an exciting joint conference. We are deeply indebted to all the Program Committee members for providing high-quality and insightful reviews under a tight schedule. We are extremely grateful to the sponsors of the conference. Finally, we extend a special word of thanks to all the colleagues of the Organizing Committee and secretariat for their hard work in organizing the conference, and to Springer for their assistance in publishing the proceedings in due time.

We thank the Program and Organizing Committees for helping to make the conference successful, and we hope all the participants enjoyed a remarkable visit to Yantai, a historical and beautiful seaside city in East China.

August 2016

Maosong Sun
Tat-Seng Chua
Xuanjing Huang
Hongfei Lin
Jian-Yun Nie
Jun Zhao

Organization

General Chairs

Bo Zhang   Tsinghua University, China
Sheng Li   Harbin Institute of Technology, China

Program Committee

15th CCL Program Chair

Maosong Sun   Tsinghua University, China
Tat-Seng Chua   National University of Singapore, Singapore

15th CCL Program Co-chairs

Xuanjing Huang   Fudan University, China
Hongfei Lin   Dalian University of Technology, China

15th CCL Area Co-chairs

Linguistics and Cognitive Science

Yulin Yuan   Peking University, China
Weiguang Qu   Nanjing Normal University, China

Fundamental Theory and Methods of Computational Linguistics

Baobao Chang   Peking University, China
Yue Zhang   Singapore University of Technology and Design, Singapore

Information Retrieval and Question Answering

Bin Wang   Institute of Information Engineering, CAS, China
Ben He   University of Chinese Academy of Sciences, China

Text Classification and Summarization

Xiaojun Wan   Peking University, China
Fei Liu   University of Central Florida, USA

Knowledge Graph and Information Extraction

Xianpei Han   Institute of Software, CAS, China
Wenjie Li   Polytechnic University of Hong Kong, SAR China

Machine Translation

Tiejun Zhao   Harbin Institute of Technology, China
Hui Huang   University of Macau, China

Minority Language Information Processing

Xiaobing Zhao   Minzu University of China, China
Jirimutu   Delihi IT Co., Ltd., China

Language Resource and Evaluation

Ru Li   Shanxi University, China
Li Zhou   University of Maryland, Baltimore County, USA

Social Computing and Sentiment Analysis

Minlie Huang   Tsinghua University, China
Lun-Wei Ku   Academia Sinica, Taiwan

NLP Applications

Xiaojie Wang   Beijing University of Posts and Telecommunications, China
Qin Lu   Polytechnic University of Hong Kong, SAR China

15th CCL Technical Committee

Rangjia Cai   Qinghai Normal University, China
Dongfeng Cai   Shenyang Aerospace University, China
Baobao Chang   Peking University, China
Xiaohe Chen   Nanjing Normal University, China
Xueqi Cheng   Institute of Computing Technology, CAS, China
Key-Sun Choi   KAIST, Korea
Li Deng   Microsoft Research, USA
Alexander Gelbukh   National Polytechnic Institute, Mexico
Josef van Genabith   Dublin City University, Ireland
Randy Goebel   University of Alberta, Canada
Tingting He   Central China Normal University, China
Isahara Hitoshi   Toyohashi University of Technology, Japan
Heyan Huang   Beijing Polytechnic University, China
Xuanjing Huang   Fudan University, China
Donghong Ji   Wuhan University, China
Turgen Ibrahim   Xinjiang University, China
Shiyong Kang   Ludong University, China
Sadao Kurohashi   Kyoto University, Japan
Kiong Lee   ISO TC37, Korea
Hang Li   Huawei, Hong Kong, SAR China
Ru Li   Shanxi University, China
Dekang Lin   NATURALI Inc., China

Qun Liu	Dublin City University, Ireland
	Institute of Computing Technology, CAS, China
Shaoming Liu	Fuji Xerox, Japan
Ting Liu	Harbin Institute of Technology, China
Qin Lu	Polytechnic University of Hong Kong, SAR China
Wolfgang Menzel	University of Hamburg, Germany
Jian-Yun Nie	University of Montreal, Canada
Yanqiu Shao	Beijing Language and Culture University, China
Xiaodong Shi	Xiamen University, China
Rou Song	Beijing Language and Culture University, China
Jian Su	Institute for Infocomm Research, Singapore
Benjamin Ka Yin Tsou	City University of Hong Kong, SAR China
Haifeng Wang	Baidu, China
Fei Xia	University of Washington, USA
Feiyu Xu	DFKI, Germany
Nianwen Xue	Brandeis University, USA
Erhong Yang	Beijing Language and Culture University, China
Tianfang Yao	Shanghai Jiaotong University, China
Shiwen Yu	Peking University, China
Quan Zhang	Institute of Acoustics, CAS, China
Jun Zhao	Institute of Automation, CAS, China
Guodong Zhou	Soochow University, China
Ming Zhou	Microsoft Research Asia, China
Jingbo Zhu	Northeast University, China
Ping Xue	Research & Technology, the Boeing Company, USA

4th NLP-NABD Program Chairs

Maosong Sun	Tsinghua University, China
Jian-Yun Nie	University of Montreal, Canada
Jun Zhao	Institute of Automation, CAS, China

4th NLP-NABD Technical Committee Members

Key-Sun Choi	KAIST, Korea
Li Deng	Microsoft Research, USA
Alexander Gelbukh	National Polytechnic Institute, Mexico
Josef van Genabith	Dublin City University, Ireland
Randy Goebel	University of Alberta, Canada
Isahara Hitoshi	Toyohashi University of Technology, Japan
Xuanjing Huang	Fudan University, China
Donghong Ji	Wuhan University, China
Sadao Kurohashi	Kyoto University, Japan
Kiong Lee	ISO TC37, Korea
Hang Li	Huawei, Hong Kong, SAR China

Hongfei Lin	Dalian Polytechnic University, China
Qun Liu	Dublin City University, Ireland
	Institute of Computing, CAS, China
Shaoming Liu	Fuji Xerox, Japan
Ting Liu	Harbin Institute of Technology, China
Yang Liu	Tsinghua University, China
Qin Lu	Polytechnic University of Hong Kong, SAR China
Wolfgang Menzel	University of Hamburg, Germany
Hwee Tou Ng	National University of Singapore, Singapore
Jian-Yun Nie	University of Montreal, Canada
Jian Su	Institute for Infocomm Research, Singapore
Zhifang Sui	Peking University, China
Le Sun	Institute of Software, CAS, China
Benjamin Ka Yin Tsou	City University of Hong Kong, SAR China
Fei Xia	University of Washington, USA
Feiyu Xu	DFKI, Germany
Nianwen Xue	Brandeis University, USA
Jun Zhao	Institute of Automation, CAS, China
Guodong Zhou	Soochow University, China
Ming Zhou	Microsoft Research Asia, China
Ping Xue	Research & Technology, the Boeing Company, USA

15th CCL and 4th NLP-NABD Local Arrangements Chairs

| Shiyong Kang | Ludong University, China |
| Yang Liu | Tsinghua University, China |

15th CCL and 4th NLP-NABD System Demonstration Chair

| Yiqun Liu | Tsinghua University, China |

15th CCL and 4th NLP-NABD Publications Chairs

| Zhiyuan Liu | Tsinghua University, China |
| Xin Zhao | Renmin University of China, China |

15th CCL and 4th NLP-NABD Publicity Chairs

| Shiqi Zhao | Baidu Inc., China |
| Haofen Wang | East China University of Science and Technology, China |

15th CCL and 4th NLP-NABD Sponsorship Chairs

| Wanxiang Che | Harbin Institute of Technology, China |
| Kang Liu | Institute of Automation, CAS, China |

15th CCL and 4th NLP-NABD Organizers

Chinese Information Processing Society of China

Tsinghua University

Ludong University

Publishers

Lecture Notes in Artificial Intelligence,
Springer

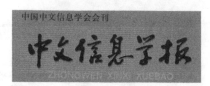

Journal of Chinese Information Processing

Science China

清华大学学报（自然科学版）
Journal of Tsinghua University (Science and Technology)

Journal of Tsinghua University
(Science and Technology)

Sponsoring Institutions

Platinum

Gold

Silver

Bronze

Contents

Knowledge Graph and Information Extraction

Linguistic Resource Annotation and Evaluation

Information Retrieval and Question Answering

Text Classification and Summarization

Social Computing and Sentiment Analysis

NLP Applications

Semantics

Improving Chinese Semantic Role Labeling with English Proposition Bank

Tianshi Li[1,2], Qi Li[1,2], and BaoBao Chang[1,2(✉)]

[1] Key Laboratory of Computational Linguistics, Ministry of Education,
School of Electronics Engineering and Computer Science,
Peking University, Beijing 100871, China
lts_417@hotmail.com, {qi.li,chbb}@pku.edu.cn
[2] Collaborative Innovation Center for Language Ability, Xuzhou 221009, China

Abstract. Most researches to SRL focus on English. It is still a challenge to improve the SRL performance of other language. In this paper, we introduce a two-pass approach to do Chinese SRL with a Recurrent Neural Network (RNN) model. We use English Proposition Bank (EPB) to improve the performance of Chinese SRL. Experimental result shows a significant improvement over the state-of-the-art methods on Chinese Proposition Bank (CPB), which reaches 78.39 % F1 score.

Keywords: Chinese semantic role labeling · Two-pass approach · Recurrent neural network · English resource

1 Introduction

Semantic Role Labeling (SRL) aims to recognize the arguments for a given predicate and assign semantic roles to them. Figure 1 shows an example of SRL. *John* is the agent of the predicate *married* denoting that he is the man who got married, *his neighbor* is the patient of *married* denoting who John married. Both of the agent and patient are the sematic roles of *married*.

SRL can be formalized as a sequence labeling task, and we use IOBES tagging schema to tag the semantic roles. According to this tagging schema, argument identification consists of tagging all tokens of a sentence with IOBES tags (Inside, Outside, Begin, End, Single) relative to a given predicate. Figure 1 shows an example.

Most SRL approaches use supervised learning model and thus heavily rely on semantically annotated corpora. For the Chinese dataset English Proposition Bank (CPB) [1], it contains over 80,000 verb instances for 11,000 verb types. However, it is still not enough using only CPB to solve the whole Chinese SRL task. For the English standard benchmark dataset in English Proposition Bank (EPB) [2], it contains nearly 100 thousand annotated sentences. Given that manually annotating SRL corpus is labor-intensive and expensive, how to improve the monolingual SRL performance with merging different language resources is thus an important issue deserving to explore.

© Springer International Publishing AG 2016
M. Sun et al. (Eds.): CCL and NLP-NABD 2016, LNAI 10035, pp. 3–11, 2016.
DOI: 10.1007/978-3-319-47674-2_1

Chinese	约翰	娶	他的	邻居
English	John	married	his	neighbor
Role	(Agent)	Predicate	(Patient	)
	(ARG0)	REL	(ARG1	)
IOBES	S-ARG0	REL	B-ARG1	E-ARG1

Fig. 1. An Chinese sentence with semantic labels. REL denotes the given predicate.

Chinese Role	ARG0	REL	ARGM-LOC
Chinese	你	去	哪里
English	where	you	go
English Role	ARGM-LOC	ARG0	REL

Fig. 2. A Chinese-English parallel sentence pair with semantic labels and word alignment.

In this paper, we propose a simple but effective two-pass training approach based on recurrent neural network (RNN) with bidirectional long-short-term memory (LSTM), aiming at improving the Chinese SRL performance using English semantic role labeled corpus. The main points are as follows: By representation learning, Chinese SRL corpus and English SRL corpus are mapped into an uniform semantic representation space. This makes it possible to merge the corpora of two languages and train a single SRL model across languages. On the basis of the cross language SRL model, we further train the SRL model specific to Chinese. Our approach requires neither parallel SRL corpus nor machine translation of the corpus. Experiments show that our approach outperforms current state-of-art systems for Chinese SRL task.

2   Related Work

SRL task was firstly proposed in the work of Gildea and Jurafsky [3] and a large body of work has been devoted to this task since then. Traditional SRL approaches normally use a lot of handcrafted features. Koomen et al. [8] get the best performance among all traditional approaches on English SRL task, they used different parse tree information with lots of traditional features. Most Chinese SRL work adopted similar strategies, although using a much smaller training corpus. Xue and Palmer [10] and Xue [11] stands for first through and systematic Chinese SRL research. Sun et al. [12] performed Chinese SRL with shallow parsing, which took partial parses as inputs. Yang and Zong [13] proposed multipredicate SRL, which showed improvements both on English and Chinese Proposition Bank. Recently, to reduce the heavy burden of feature engineering, deep learning models like CNNs and RNNs have been introduced into

SRL task. Collobert and Weston [9] proposed a Convolutional Neural Network (CNN) on English. For Chinese SRL, Wang et al. [14] used bidirectional LSTM and outperformed previous traditional models. Different from previous work, we focus on how to use English semantic role labeled corpora to improve the performance of Chinese SRL.

3 Two-Pass Training Approach

3.1 Basic Idea

Generally, semantics is believed to be more language general than syntax. Especially in SRL corpus, many sematic roles are same or have similar meanings across languages. In this paper, we focus on Chinese and English SRL corpus. In Fig. 2, although words and word order are different between Chinese and English, the semantic roles are the same. We call these language independent roles as common semantic roles, such as ARG0, and call the roles which only appear in the Chinese SRL corpus as non-common semantic roles, such as ARGM-CND[1]. Table 1 shows that over 60 % types of Chinese roles can be found in English and the total number of common roles accounts for 98.35 % on the whole CPB. Similar result applys for the English side, the total number of common roles account for 88.54 % on whole EPB. Intuitively, adding EPB to train set is helpful for improving the performance of Chinese common role labeling.

Table 1. Statistics for Chinese common roles and non-common roles on CPB.

Chinese roles	Common	Non-common
Type numbers	11	7
Total numbers	79748	1335
Example	ARG0	ARGM-CND
Meaning	Agent	Condition

Although the semantic similarity between Chinese and English, there is still a gap between the linguistic structure and syntax of Chinese and English corpus. To cross this gap, we propose to project these corpus into a same vector space by means of bilingual embedding. Progress in bilingual representation learning [4,7] shows that words in different languages can be projected into the same vector space as distributed vector embeddings. Moreover, these word embeddings are shown to have the ability of capturing semantic coherence across languages [5,6]. With bilingual embedding, words with similar meanings in different languages are projected into close position in the shared vector space.

With these considerations, we propose a two-pass training approach as follows: First, we merge and randomly shuffle CPB and EPB, keep the common

---

[1] Conditional clause is seen as a semantic role in the Chinese but not in the English.

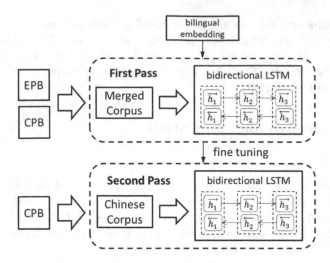

Fig. 3. The two-pass training model.

semantic roles and remove the non-common semantic roles. We use bilingual parallel corpus to learn bilingual word embedding. Using these merged corpus and bilingual embedding, we train an RNN model for all common semantic roles. We ignore the Chinese non-common roles in first pass because these roles are rare and language-specific. Second, for CPB only, we learn both Chinese common roles and Chinese non-common roles together, using the same RNN model in the first pass. We utilize the parameters (including the bilingual word embedding) we get in the first pass as the initialization of the RNN model in second pass. Our approach can be illustrated in Fig. 3.

3.2   Bilingual Word Representation

In our approach, we utilize bilingual compositional vector model (BiCVM) [6] to learn our bilingual word embedding. BiCVM learns to assign similar embeddings to aligned sentences and dissimilar ones to sentence which are not aligned while not requiring word alignments. We chose BiCVM for the reason that SRL is a task based on the whole sentence and BiCVM can catch more semantic knowledge on sentence level across aligned parallel sentences between two languages.

3.3   Basic SRL Model

Given a sentence s, we first compute its representation sequence z. Here $z_t = \sigma(Wa_t)$ denotes the representation of the t-th word in s. a_t is the feature embedding of current word t which concatenates bilingual embeddings (word t, word $t-1$, word $t+1$ and the predicate), POS tag embeddings (word t, word $t-1$, word $t+1$) and distant feature (the distant from word t to the predicate). $W \in \mathbb{R}^{n_1 \times n_0}$, n_0 is the length of a_t, σ is the sigmoid function.

Then we use the bidirectional LSTM, the two LSTMs process the input sequence z from both forward and backward directions. We use the bidirectional LSTM because it is a sequence labeling model which can easily catch semantic information and works well in monolingual SRL task [14]. We can compute LSTM layer at each word t as follows:

$$\widetilde{C}_t = \tanh(W_c z_t + U_c h_{t-1} + b_c) \tag{1}$$

$$g_j = \sigma(W_j z_t + U_j h_{t-1} + b_j) \tag{2}$$

$$C_t = g_i \odot \widetilde{C}_t + g_f \odot C_{t-1} \tag{3}$$

$$h_t = g_o \odot C_t \tag{4}$$

where C_t is the memory cell of position t, $\widetilde{C}_t$ computes the candidate value for C_t, h_t is the output state of position t, $j \in \{i, f, o\}$, $g_i \backslash g_f \backslash g_o$ is input\forget\output gate of LSTM. $W_c, W_j \in \mathbb{R}^{n_2 \times n_1}$, $U_c, U_j \in \mathbb{R}^{n_2 \times n_2}$. $\odot$ indicates elementwise vector multiplication. For the t-th word, we get both a forward hidden state $\overrightarrow{h_t}$ and a backward hidden state $\overleftarrow{h_t}$ from the bidirectional LSTM. These hidden states are then concatenated together into a merged hidden state $hid_t = [\overrightarrow{h_t}^{\mathrm{T}}; \overleftarrow{h_t}^{\mathrm{T}}]^{\mathrm{T}}$.

At last, we put hid_t into a softmax layer to generate final output, each dimension of output corresponds to the score of a certain semantic role label in IOBES schema.

3.4 Training Criteria

Given training examples:

$$T = (x^{(i)}, y^{(i)}) \tag{5}$$

where $x^{(i)}$ denotes the i-th training sentence, $y^{(i)}$ is the correct sequence labels of $x^{(i)}$. $y_t^{(i)} = k$ means the t-th word has the k-th semantic role label in IOBES schema. We can define the score of i-th sentence as follows:

$$s(x^{(i)}, y^{(i)}, \theta) = \sum_{t=1}^{N_i} o_{t y_t^{(i)}} \tag{6}$$

where N_i is the length of the i-th sentence, $o_{t y_t^{(i)}}$ is the value of the correct label in the output layer for the t-th word in the i-th sentence, θ is an ensemble of all the parameters in the whole network.

We use maximum log likelihood method to training all examples. For a single example, the log likelihood is:

$$\begin{aligned}
\log p(y^{(i)}|x^{(i)}, \theta) &= \log \frac{\exp(s(x^{(i)}, y^{(i)}, \theta))}{\sum_{y'} \exp(s(x^{(i)}, y', \theta))} \\
&= s(x^{(i)}, y^{(i)}, \theta) - \log \sum_{y'} \exp(s(x^{(i)}, y', \theta))
\end{aligned} \tag{7}$$

where y' ranges from all the valid paths of tags.

The full log likelihood of the whole training corpus is as follows:

$$J_{MLE}(\theta) = \sum_i \log p(y^{(i)}|x^{(i)}, \theta) \tag{8}$$

We use stochastic gradient ascent in the experiments.

4   Experiments

4.1   Experiment Settings

To comparison with previous work, we conduct experiments on the standard benchmark dataset CPB, follow the same data setting as previous work [11,14]. For English dataset, we use the training set of CoNLL-2005 dataset (based on EPB), the same data setting as Li and Chang [15]. For training the bilingual word embedding, we use PKU bilingual corpus[2].

Table 2. Results comparison on CPB test set.

Method	F1 (%)
Xue (2008)	71.90
Yang and Zong (2014)	75.31
Sun et al. (2010)	76.46
Wang (2015)	77.59
Our approaches	
Random (one-pass)	76.29
BiCVM (one-pass)	76.97
BiCVM + EPB (two-pass)	**78.39**

For the SRL model, the parameters are set as follows: the dimension of bilingual word embedding is 50; the dimension of POS tag embedding is 20; the dimension of distant feature embedding is 20; n_1 is 200; n_2 is 100; the number of bidirectional LSTM layer is 1; the learning rate in both first pass and second pass is 10^{-3}; the hyper-parameter λ in the objective function is 10^{-3}; Using early stop strategy to get the best result on development set, the training epochs in the first pass is set to 12, the training epochs in the second pass is set to 6.

---

[2] PKU bilingual corpus is developed by Peking University, it is a English-Chinese parallel corpus. It contains 807,500 aligned English-Chinese sentence pairs and is available by licensing.

4.2 SRL Results

Table 2 shows the Chinese SRL results on CPB. *one-pass* denotes training a bidirectional LSTM model on CPB for both Chinese common roles and non-common roles, *two-pass* denotes our two-pass approach described in Sect. 3.1. *random* denotes that the word embedding is randomized initialized, *BiCVM* in Table 2 denotes that we use the bilingual word embedding described in Sect. 3.2 instead of randomized initialization. We don't do experiment with monolingual word embedding because it is beyond our focus in this paper. *EPB* in Table 2 denotes that we use EPB in the first pass training during the two-pass approach.

Compared with randomized initialization of word embedding in one-pass approach, using bilingual embedding has a slight improvement. While compared with one-pass training approach, our two-pass approach improves a lot and establishes a new state-of-the-art result in Chinese SRL with 78.39.

Figure 4 shows the effectiveness of EPB for both Chinese common roles and non-common roles. From Fig. 4, EPB is helpful for most Chinese roles, especially none of common role's performance decreases after adding EPB. This proves that our strategy of using EPB is successful, our approach exactly capture the common semantic role information between Chinese and English. The performance on Chinese non-common roles is inconsistent, because these roles are language-specific and EPB can't definitely improve the performance of these roles.

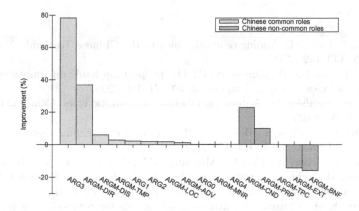

Fig. 4. Improvement of all Chinese semantic roles on CPB test set for two-pass approach compared with one-pass approach (randomized initialization). The 11 yellow columns denote to Chinese common roles in test set, the 5 blue columns denote to Chinese non-common roles in test set. (Color figure online)

4.3 Translation Equivalent Regularizer

Furthermore, we try to make the embedding of the words, which has translation equivalent relation between Chinese and English, more closer in vector space in the first pass training. For each word t (either Chinese or English) in merging corpus, we define a translation equivalence regularizer which equals to $\|x_t - \sum_j a_{tj}x_j\|$. Here, x_t is the embedding of the word t, x_j is the embedding of the word j which has translation equivalent with word t, a_{tj} is the translation probability[3] from word t to word j. However, after adding the regularizer, the result gets 78.31 on CPB test set, doesn't outperform the best result we gets before. This is possibly because translation equivalence regularizer leads to overfitting in the first pass training.

5 Conclusion

In this paper, we introduce a two-pass approach with bidirectional LSTM, using EPB to improve the performance on Chinese SRL. Our approach doesn't need any parallel annotated SRL corpus, heavy job of feature engineering. And our approach can apply to other languages. Our approach achieves the state-of-the-art results on the Chinese SRL task. In future work, we plan to project different language sentences into same semantic space in a better way.

Acknowledgments. This work is supported by National Key Basic Research Program of China (2014CB340504) and National Natural Science Foundation of China (61273318).

References

1. Xue, N., Palmer, M.: Adding semantic roles to the Chinese Treebank. Nat. Lang. Eng. **15**, 143–172 (2009)
2. Palmer, M., Gildea, D., Kingsbury, P.: The proposition bank: an annotated corpus of semantic roles. Comput. Linguist. J. **31**, 71–106 (2005)
3. Gildea, D., Jurafsky, D.: Automatic labeling of semantic roles. Comput. Linguist. **28**, 245–288 (2002)
4. Klementiev, A., Titov, I., Bhattarai, B.: Inducing crosslingual distributed representations of words. In: COLING (2012)
5. Zou, W.Y., Socher, R., Cer, D., Manning, C.D.: Bilingual word embeddings for phrase-based machine translation. In: The 2013 Conference on Empirical Methods in Natural Language Processing (EMNLP), pp. 1393–1398 (2013)
6. Hermann, K.M., Blunsom, P.: Multilingual models for compositional distributed semantics. In: ACL, pp. 58–68 (2014)
7. Chandar, S., Lauly, S., Larochelle, H., Khapra, M.M., Ravindran, B., Raykar, V.C., Saha, A.: An autoencoder approach to learning bilingual word representations. In: NIPS, pp. 1853–1861 (2014)
8. Koomen, P., Punyakanok, V., Roth, D., Yih, W.T.: Generalized inference with multiple semantic role labeling systems. In: The Ninth Conference on Computational Natural Language Learning, pp. 181–184. Association for Computational Linguistics (2005)

---

[3] We use GIZA++ to get the translation probability from PKU bilingual corpus, GIZA++ can be download in http://code.google.com/p/giza-pp/downloads/list.

9. Collobert, R., Weston, J.: A unified architecture for natural language processing: deep neural networks with multitask learning. In: The 25th International Conference on Machine Learning, pp. 160–167. ACM (2008)
10. Xue, N., Palmer, M.: Automatic semantic role labeling for Chinese verbs. In: IJCAI, vol. 5, pp. 1160–1165. Citeseer (2005)
11. Xue, N.: Labeling Chinese predicates with semantic roles. Comput. Linguist. **34**, 225–255 (2008)
12. Sun, W.: Semantics-driven shallow parsing for Chinese semantic role labeling. In: ACL, pp. 103–108 (2010)
13. Yang, H., Zong, C.: Multipredicate semantic role labeling. In: The 2014 Conference on Empirical Methods in Natural Language Processing (EMNLP), pp. 363–373 (2014)
14. Wang, Z., Jiang, T., Chang, B., Sui, Z.: Chinese semantic role labeling with bidirectional recurrent neural networks. In: The 2015 Conference on Empirical Methods in Natural Language Processing (EMNLP), pp. 1626–1631 (2015)
15. Li, T., Chang, B.: Semantic role labeling using recursive neural network. In: Chinese Computational Linguistics and Natural Language Processing Based on Naturally Annotated Big Data, pp. 66–76 (2015)

Transition-Based Chinese Semantic Dependency Graph Parsing

Yuxuan Wang[✉], Jiang Guo, Wanxiang Che, and Ting Liu

School of Computer Science and Technology,
Harbin Institute of Technology, Harbin 150001, China
{yxwang,jguo,car,tliu}@ir.hit.edu.cn

Abstract. Chinese semantic dependency graph is extended from semantic dependency tree, which uses directed acyclic graphs to capture richer latent semantics of sentences. In this paper, we propose two approaches for Chinese semantic dependency graph parsing. In the first approach, we build a non-projective transition-based dependency parser with the SWAP-based algorithm. Then we use a classifier to add arc candidates generated by rules to the tree, forming a graph. In the second approach, we build a transition-based graph parser directly using a variant of the list-based transition system. For both approaches, neural networks are adopted to represent the parsing states. Both approaches yield significantly better results than the top systems in the SemEval-2016 Task 9: *Chinese Semantic Dependency Parsing*.

1 Introduction

Given a complete sentence, semantic dependency parsing aims at determining all the word pairs related to each other semantically and assigning specific predefined semantic relations. The results of semantic dependency parsing can be highly beneficial for question answering (*who did what to whom when and where*).

Chinese semantic dependency graphs are directed acyclic graphs (DAG) extended from traditional tree-structured representation of Chinese sentences. This graph structure can capture richer latent semantics. The goal of SemEval-2016 Task 9: *Chinese Semantic Dependency Parsing* is to identify such semantic structures from a corpus of Chinese sentences.[1] The task provides two distinguished corpora in the NEWS domain and the TEXTBOOKS domain. An example of semantic dependency graph is presented in Fig. 1. We can see that 他 (he) has two head words, respectively 离开 (leave) and 去 (go) with the *Agent* (Agt) relation in the graph representation. More detailed information about the corpora will be reported in Sect. 4.

Transition-based dependency parsing has become increasingly popular in NLP because of its speed and accurate performance. This kind of parser construct dependency trees by using a sequence of transition actions over input sentences. They are mostly used to produce dependency trees, rather than graphs, or more accurately DAG in *Chinese Semantic Dependency Parsing*.

---

[1] http://alt.qcri.org/semeval2016/task9/.

© Springer International Publishing AG 2016
M. Sun et al. (Eds.): CCL and NLP-NABD 2016, LNAI 10035, pp. 12–24, 2016.
DOI: 10.1007/978-3-319-47674-2_2

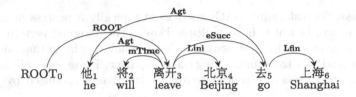

Fig. 1. An example of semantic dependency graph.

To address the challenge of DAG parsing, we investigate two approaches in this work. Our first approach has two stages. First, we adopt a set of linguistic-motivated rules to transform graphs to trees, based on which a traditional non-projective transition-based parser is trained. Then, we use a classifier to recover the extra arcs from a candidate arc set generated also by rules and add them to the parser's output to form dependency graphs. A similar approach was studied in [23], which applied pseudo-projective transformations [20] to transform non-projective dependencies to projective ones, and then use a dependency graph parser to parse projective graphs. This approach typically requires inconvenient pre-process and post-process.

We further propose a transition-based dependency graph parser that produce DAG directly for Chinese sentences. This parser is a variant of the list-based algorithm of [4], which was designed to parse dependency trees. In order to handle dependency graphs, we change the preconditions of the transitions to allow some words to have multiple head words. We have also tried to simplify the transition action set to investigate the relation between the parser performance and the number of transition actions. Extensive experiments show that both of our approaches obtain significantly better results compared with the top participated systems in the SemEval-2016 Task 9: *Chinese Semantic Dependency Parsing*.

2   Methods

Since most existing current dependency parsers only deal with dependency trees, it is a challenge to produce graphs with transition-based parser. To begin with, we propose a hybrid system which combines a traditional dependency tree parser and a binary classifier for complementing extra arcs. Then we propose a transition-based dependency parser that produce dependency graphs directly.

2.1   Tree-Based Method

In our first approach, we separate the task into two steps. In the first step, we use a traditional transition-based dependency parser to parse preprocessed semantic dependency trees. Then an SVM classifier is used to identify extra arcs that will be added to the parser results from candidate arc set created by rules.

Pre-process. Transforming DAGs to trees is typically a process of removing extra arcs of words which have multiple heads. We designed certain rules to remove such extra arcs in given semantic dependency graphs so that we can get semantic dependency trees for training the tree parser. These rules will be reused in the future to re-generate candidate arc set from trees produced by the tree parser.

These rules require human knowledge and are summarized by observing semantic dependency graphs in training data. We present them in the Appendix. Our rules can cover 95.5 % graph situations in the NEWS corpus and 95.0 % in the TEXTBOOKS corpus. The uncovered ones are basically all irregular situations, under which we hold the closest arc of the multi-head words.

For example, in causative sentences, a noun can be the object of the causative verb as well as the subject of the following verb, which introduces multiple heads to it. Figure 2 shows an instance of this situation. For this kind of graph, we remove the dependency arcs between the noun and the following verb (介绍 (introduce) $\xrightarrow{Agt}$ 张先生 (Mr.Zhang)).

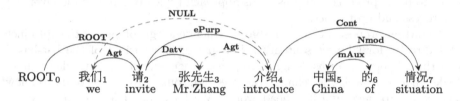

Fig. 2. A pre-process and post-process example of semantic dependency graph. (Color figure online)

After dependency parsing, these rules are used again to re-generate candidate arcs from parsing results. For every verb pair with an arc between them, we find all noun children of the head verb "请 (invite)", and add arcs from the child verb "介绍 (introduce)" to these nouns to the candidate arc set (the two dashed arcs). According to the gold-standard graph, the label of the red arc is *Agt*, while the label of the blue one is NULL, meaning it should not be added to the final semantic dependency graph.

Dependency Parser. The semantic dependency trees transformed from DAGs are not necessarily projective. So we adopt the SWAP-based algorithm [19], which can parse non-projective trees with a time complexity that is quadratic in the worst case but still linear in the best case.

[3] proposed a transition-based dependency parser using neural networks as the classifier, which solved several problems caused by traditional sparse indicator features and yielded good results. Following their footsteps, we train a neural network classifier for use in a greedy, transition-based dependency parser. Their feature templates are used as the basic features in our experiment.

SVM Classifier for Post-process. The preprocessing rules mentioned above are used reversely to generate the training samples of SVM classifier from pre-processed semantic dependency trees. Labels of these samples include all possible relations of extra arcs and one *NULL* label indicating that the corresponding candidate arc should not be added to the tree. The features primarily include words, POS tags and distances. The specific feature templates are presented in [8].

2.2 Dependency Graph Parser

The above method is a compromise to the tree parser, which still requires careful pre-process and post-process. Moreover, for new dependency relation sets, the preprocessing rules need to be redesigned. We then present a transition-based dependency graph parser, which parses dependency graphs directly. In the SWAP-based algorithm [19], we have to precompute the *projective order* which indicates when the SWAP transition appears while generating oracle transition sequences. However, the coocurrence of non-projectivity and multiple heads makes it hard to compute the *projective order*. Here, we base our graph parser on the *list-based arc-eager algorithm* that was originally introduced to parse non-projective trees [4]. By simply modifying the preconditions of transitions, we make it capable of parsing dependency graphs. The specific preconditions are introduced in the next section.

We use a tuple $(\sigma, \delta, \beta, A)$ to represent each of the parsing state, where σ is a stack holding processed words, δ is a stack holding words popped out of σ that will be pushed back in the future, and β is a buffer holding unprocessed words. A is a set of labeled dependency arcs. We use index i to represent word w_i, and the index 0 represents the root of the graph w_0. It's important to notice that in this task all the roots w_0 of DAGs are required to have only one child. The initial state is $([0], [\ ], [1, \cdots, n], \emptyset)$, while the terminal state is $(\sigma, \delta, [\ ], A)$. During the parsing, arcs will only be generated between top element of σ, w_i, and the first element of β, w_j. The transition is generated by consulting the gold-standard trees during training and a neural network classifier during decoding.

Transition System 1. The transitions of the dependency graph parser is listed in Table 1, while corresponding preconditions are described in Table 2. LEFT$_l$-* and RIGHT$_l$-* add an arc with label l from w_j to w_i, and vice versa. These transitions are performed only when one of w_i and w_j is the head of the other. Otherwise, NO-* will be performed. *-SHIFT is performed when no dependency exists between w_j and any word in σ other than w_i, which pushes all words in δ and w_j into σ. *-REDUCE is performed only when w_i has head and is not the head or child of any word in β, which pops w_i out of σ. *-PASS is performed when neither *-SHIFT nor *-REDUCE can be performed, which moves w_i to the front of δ. $(i \xrightarrow{l} j)$ is used to denote an arc from w_i to w_j with label l. $(i \rightarrow j)$ and $(i \rightarrow^* j)$ indicate that w_i is a head and an ancestor of w_j respectively.

The preconditions of LEFT$_l$-*, RIGHT$_l$-* and *-REDUCE are different from [4]'s algorithm. For LEFT$_l$-* and RIGHT$_l$-*, it's necessary to make sure no word

Table 1. Transitions in the *list-based arc-eager algorithm*.

Transitions	Current state $\Rightarrow$ Next state
LEFT$_l$-REDUCE	$([\sigma|i], \delta, [j|\beta], A) \Rightarrow (\sigma, \delta, [j|\beta], A \cup \{(i \xleftarrow{l} j)\})$
RIGHT$_l$-SHIFT	$([\sigma|i], \delta, [j|\beta], A) \Rightarrow ([\sigma|i|\delta|j], [\,], \beta, A \cup \{(i \xrightarrow{l} j)\})$
NO-SHIFT	$([\sigma|i], \delta, [j|\beta], A) \Rightarrow ([\sigma|i|\delta|j], [\,], \beta, A)$
NO-REDUCE	$([\sigma|i], \delta, [j|\beta], A) \Rightarrow (\sigma, \delta, [j|\beta], A)$
LEFT$_l$-PASS	$([\sigma|i], \delta, [j|\beta], A) \Rightarrow (\sigma, [i|\delta], [j|\beta], A \cup \{(i \xleftarrow{l} j)\})$
RIGHT$_l$-PASS	$([\sigma|i], \delta, [j|\beta], A) \Rightarrow (\sigma, [i|\delta], [j|\beta], A \cup \{(i \xrightarrow{l} j)\})$
NO-PASS	$([\sigma|i], \delta, [j|\beta], A) \Rightarrow (\sigma, [i|\delta], [j|\beta], A)$

Table 2. Preconditions of transitions in Table 1.

Transitions	Preconditions
LEFT$_l$-*	$[i \neq 0] \land \neg[(i \rightarrow^* j) \in A]$
RIGHT$_l$-*	$\neg[(j \rightarrow^* i) \in A]$
*-SHIFT	$\neg[\exists k \in \sigma.(k \neq i) \land ((k \rightarrow j) \lor (k \leftarrow j))]$
*-REDUCE	$[\exists h.(h \rightarrow i) \in A] \land \neg[\exists k \in \beta.(i \rightarrow k) \lor (i \leftarrow k)]$

Table 3. A transition sequence for dependency graph in Fig. 1 generated by *list-based arc-eager algorithm* with gold-standard graph.

State	Transition	σ	δ	β	A
0	Initialization	$[0]$	$[\,]$	$[1|\beta]$	$\emptyset$
1	NO-SHIFT	$[\sigma|1]$	$[\,]$	$[2|\beta]$	
2	NO-SHIFT	$[\sigma|2]$	$[\,]$	$[3|\beta]$	
3	LEFT-REDUCE	$[\sigma|1]$	$[\,]$	$[3|\beta]$	$A \cup \{2 \leftarrow \mathrm{mTime} - 3\}$
4	LEFT-PASS	$[\sigma|0]$	$[1]$	$[3|\beta]$	$A \cup \{1 \leftarrow \mathrm{Agt} - 3\}$
5	RIGHT-SHIFT	$[\sigma|3]$	$[\,]$	$[4|\beta]$	$A \cup \{0 - \mathrm{ROOT} \rightarrow 3\}$
6	RIGHT-SHIFT	$[\sigma|4]$	$[\,]$	$[5|\beta]$	$A \cup \{3 - \mathrm{Lini} \rightarrow 4\}$
7	NO-REDUCE	$[\sigma|3]$	$[\,]$	$[5|\beta]$	
8	RIGHT-PASS	$[\sigma|1]$	$[3]$	$[5|\beta]$	$A \cup \{3 - \mathrm{eSucc} \rightarrow 5\}$
9	LEFT-REDUCE	$[\sigma|0]$	$[3]$	$[5|\beta]$	$A \cup \{1 \leftarrow \mathrm{Agt} - 5\}$
10	NO-SHIFT	$[\sigma|5]$	$[\,]$	$[6|\beta]$	
11	RIGHT-SHIFT	$[\sigma|6]$	$[\,]$	$[\,]$	$A \cup \{5 - \mathrm{Lfin} \rightarrow 6\}$

has multiple heads in their tree parser, which is not required in our graph parser. For *-REDUCE, we have to confirm that all of w_i's heads and children are found before removing it from σ. While they only need to check w_i's children, since w_i already has and can only have one head in tree structure.

A transition sequence for the sentence in Fig. 1 generated by the *list-based arc-eager algorithm* is presented in Table 3. In state 4, w_1 is moved from σ

to δ because it has another head w_5 in β, and the arc between them will be generated in the future (state 9). In state 8, the transition is RIGHT-PASS rather than RIGHT-SHIFT because w_5 still has a child w_1 in σ, w_3 is moved to δ so that the arc between w_5 and w_1 can be generated (state 9). In states 3, 7 and 9, w_2, w_4 and w_1 are popped out of σ respectively because all of their children and heads have been generated.

Transition System 2. In order to improve the performance of our parser, we adopt another list-based arc-eager algorithm [5] which has less transitions which is referred to as *simplified list-based algorithm* henceforth (Table 4).

Table 4. Transitions and corresponding preconditions in the *simplified list-based algorithm*.

Transitions	Change of state & Preconditions
LEFT-POP$_l$	$([\sigma\|i], \delta, [j\|\beta], A) \Rightarrow (\sigma, \delta, [j\|\beta], A \cup \{(i \overset{l}{\leftarrow} j)\})$ $[i \neq 0] \wedge \neg[(i \rightarrow^* j) \in A] \wedge \neg[\exists k \in \beta.(i \rightarrow k) \vee (i \leftarrow k)]$
LEFT-ARC$_l$	$([\sigma\|i], \delta, [j\|\beta], A) \Rightarrow (\sigma, [i\|\delta], [j\|\beta], A \cup \{(i \overset{l}{\leftarrow} j)\})$ $[i \neq 0] \wedge \neg[(i \rightarrow^* j) \in A]$
RIGHT-ARC$_l$	$([\sigma\|i], \delta, [j\|\beta], A) \Rightarrow (\sigma, [i\|\delta], [j\|\beta], A \cup \{(i \overset{l}{\rightarrow} j)\})$ $\neg[(i \rightarrow^* j) \in A]$
SHIFT	$(\sigma, \delta, [j\|\beta], A) \quad \Rightarrow ([\sigma\|\delta\|j], [\,], \beta, A)$ $\sigma = [\,] \vee \neg[\exists k \in \sigma.(k \rightarrow j) \vee (k \leftarrow j)]$
PASS	$([\sigma\|i], \delta, [j\|\beta], A) \Rightarrow (\sigma, [i\|\delta], [j\|\beta], A)$ default transition

LEFT-ARC$_l$, LEFT-POP$_l$, RIGHT-ARC$_l$, SHIFT and PASS are transitions LEFT$_l$-PASS, LEFT$_l$-REDUCE, RIGHT$_l$-PASS, NO-SHIFT and NO-PASS in system 1 respectively. While RIGHT$_l$-SHIFT and NO-REDUCE are discarded. In labeled parsing task like semantic dependency parsing, the number of transitions that generate arcs (LEFT$_l$-*, RIGHT$_l$-*) equals to the number of label classes. Thus the number of transitions is reduced by a quarter for our task.

A transition sequence generated by *simplified list-based algorithm* for the same semantic dependency graph in Fig. 1 is presented in Table 5. Since RIGHT-SHIFT is discarded, a RIGHT-ARC and a SHIFT is used to replace it in the simplified algorithm, resulting in an extra transition for each RIGHT-SHIFT (states 5 and 6, states 7 and 8). Since NO-REDUCE is discarded, the word that should be popped out of σ stays, which generate an extra PASS every time it is moved to δ (state 9). Generally speaking, we reduce the number of transitions at the price of longer transition sequences.

Table 5. A transition sequence for dependency graph in Fig. 1 generated by *simplified list-based algorithm* with gold-standard graph.

State	Transition	σ	δ	β	A
0	Initialization	[0]	[ ]	$[1|\beta]$	$\emptyset$
1	SHIFT	$[\sigma|1]$	[ ]	$[2|\beta]$	
2	SHIFT	$[\sigma|2]$	[ ]	$[3|\beta]$	
3	LEFT-POP	$[\sigma|1]$	[ ]	$[3|\beta]$	$A \cup \{2 \leftarrow \text{mTime} - 3\}$
4	LEFT-ARC	$[\sigma|0]$	[1]	$[3|\beta]$	$A \cup \{1 \leftarrow \text{Agt} - 3\}$
5	RIGHT-ARC	[ ]	[0, 1]	$[3|\beta]$	$A \cup \{0 - \text{ROOT} \rightarrow 3\}$
6	SHIFT	$[\sigma|3]$	[ ]	$[4|\beta]$	
7	RIGHT-ARC	$[\sigma|1]$	[3]	$[4|\beta]$	$A \cup \{3 - \text{Lini} \rightarrow 4\}$
8	SHIFT	$[\sigma|4]$	[ ]	$[5|\beta]$	
9	PASS	$[\sigma|3]$	[4]	$[5|\beta]$	
10	RIGHT-ARC	$[\sigma|1]$	[3, 4]	$[5|\beta]$	$A \cup \{3 - \text{eSucc} \rightarrow 5\}$
11	LEFT-POP	$[\sigma|0]$	[3, 4]	$[5|\beta]$	$A \cup \{1 \leftarrow \text{Agt} - 5\}$
12	SHIFT	$[\sigma|5]$	[ ]	$[6|\beta]$	
13	RIGHT-ARC	$[\sigma|4]$	[5]	$[6|\beta]$	$A \cup \{5 - \text{Lfin} \rightarrow 6\}$

Feature Templates. Our feature templates are generally adapted from [3]. Considering the difference between dependency graphs and dependency trees, we add additional features regarding the heads of words on top of σ and in the front positions of β. The complete feature templates are presented in Table 6.

Table 6. Feature templates.

Baseline features
$S_0w, S_1w, B_0w, B_1w, P_0w, lc(S_0)w, rc(S_0)w, lh(S_0)w, rh(S_0)w, lc(B_0)w, lh(B_0)w,$
$llc(S_0)w, rrc(S_0)w, llh(S_0)w, rrh(S_0)w, llc(B_0)w, llh(B_0)w; S_0p, S_1p, B_0p, B_1p, P_0p,$
$lc(S_0)p, rc(S_0)p, lh(S_0)p, rh(S_0)p, lc(B_0)p, lh(B_0)p, llc(S_0)p, rrc(S_0)p, llh(S_0)p,$
$rrh(S_0)p, llc(B_0)p, llh(B_0)p; lc(S_0)l, rc(S_0)l, lh(S_0)l, rh(S_0)l, lc(B_0)l, lh(B_0)l,$
$llc(S_0)l, rrc(S_0)l, llh(S_0)l, rrh(S_0)l, llc(B_0)l, llh(B_0)l$

Valency & Distance
$S_0v_{lc}, S_0v_{rc}, S_0v_{lh}, S_0v_{rh}, B_0v_{lc}, B_0v_{lh}; d(S_0, B_0)$

Cluster
$S_0c, S_1c, B_0c, B_1c, P_0c, lc(S_0)c, rc(S_0)c, lh(S_0)c, rh(S_0)c, lc(B_0)c,$
$lh(B_0)c, llc(S_0)c, rrc(S_0)c, llh(S_0)c, rrh(S_0)c, llc(B_0)c, llh(B_0)c$
(w - word; p - POS-tag; l - dependency label; $v_{lc}, v_{rc}, v_{lh}, v_{rh}$ - valency; d - distance; c - cluster) S_i - word in σ; B_i - word in β; P_i - word in δ; lc, rc, lh, rh - left/rightmost child/head; llc, rrc, llh, rrh - leftmost of leftmost/rightmost of rightmost child/head.

Besides these baseline features, we add some non-local features including *valency, distance* and *cluster*. The numbers of left and right modifiers to a given head are identified as *left valency* and *right valency* respectively [30]. We extend the definition to graphs and use *left head valency* and *right head valency* to denote the numbers of left and right heads to a given modifier respectively. And the original valencies are then referred to as *left child valency* and *right child valency*. Brown Clustering [1] is a form of hierarchical clustering of words based on the contexts in which they occur and have proved beneficial for neural parsing [11]. We use pre-trained Brown clusters for each word involved in the baseline features. All of these new features are represented as embeddings and then pass through the neural network.

3 Experiments

3.1 Datasets

The SemEval-2016 Task 9 provides two distinguished corpora in the domain of NEWS and TEXTBOOKS. Detailed statics are presented in Table 7. The non-local dependencies [25] in the table refers to the dependency arcs which make dependency trees collapsed.

Table 7. Statics of the corpora.

	NEWS				TEXTBOOKS			
	#sent	#word	#g-sent	#n-rate	#sent	#word	#g-sent	#n-rate
Train	8,301	250,249	3,615	4.8%	10,754	128,095	2,506	5.0%
Dev	534	15,325	223	4.2%	1,535	18,257	363	5.1%
Test	1,233	34,305	364	2.9%	3,073	36,097	707	5.0%

(#g-sent is graph sentence number; #n-rate is non-local dependency rate.)

The evaluation measures of this task are on two granularity, dependency arc and the complete sentence. Labeled and unlabeled precision and recall with respect to predicted dependencies are used as evaluation measures. Since non-local dependencies are extremely difficult to discover, they are evaluated separately. For sentence level, labeled and unlabeled exact matches are used to measure sentence parsing accuracy. These metrics are abbreviated as:

- Labeled precision (LP), recall (LR), F1 (LF) and F1 score for non-local dependencies (NLF);
- Unlabeled precision (UP), recall (UR), F1 (UF) and F1 score for non-local dependencies (NUF);
- Labeled and unlabeled exact match (LM, UM).

When ranking systems, average F1 (LF) on testing sets are main references.

3.2   Results

The following hyper-parameters are used in all of our neural models: basic embedding size (for words, POS tags and dependency labels) $d = 50$, hidden layer size $h = 400$, dropout rate $p_d = 0.5$, regularization parameter $\lambda = 10^{-8}$, initial learning rate of Adagrad $\eta = 0.01$.

The initial word embeddings and Brown clusters are trained using Xinhua portion of the Chinese Gigawords. We use 20-dimensional vector for cluster, and 10 for valency and distance. The number of Brown clusters are set to 256. The numbers of training samples for the SVM classifier in NEWS corpus and TEXTBOOKS corpus are 1,869,819 (6,748 positive) and 248,716 (3,542 positive) respectively. We use the liblinear toolkit [10] for training linear-kernel SVM classifiers. We conduct experiments with baseline features alone and with all features (baseline features, valency, distance and cluster) in both approaches. Tables 8 and 9 show the results of our systems and other participating systems. The detailed description of other participating systems are presented in [2].

Table 8. Results of our systems and other participating systems in NEWS corpus

System	LP	LR	LF	UP	UR	UF	NLF	NUF	LM	UM
IHS-RD-Belarus	58.78	59.33	59.06	77.28	78.01	77.64	40.84	60.2	12.73	20.60
OCLSP (lbpg)	55.64	58.89	57.22	72.87	77.11	74.93	45.57	58.03	12.25	18.73
OCLSP (lbpgs)	58.38	57.25	57.81	76.28	74.81	75.54	41.56	54.34	12.57	20.11
OCLSP (lbpg75)	57.88	57.67	57.78	75.55	75.26	75.4	48.89	58.28	12.57	19.79
OSU CHGCG	55.52	55.85	55.69	73.51	73.94	73.72	**49.23**	60.71	5.03	11.35
Tree+SVM (base)	61.08	60.60	60.84	78.60	77.98	78.29	41.43	**63.62**	13.95	22.87
List-based (base)	60.44	59.85	60.14	77.69	76.94	77.31	46.80	62.50	13.46	22.38
Simplified (base)	60.65	60.09	60.37	77.98	77.25	77.61	43.41	59.31	13.06	21.65
Tree+SVM (all)	**61.47**	**61.01**	**61.24**	**79.19**	**78.60**	**78.89**	40.89	62.89	**14.36**	**23.03**
List-based (all)	61.02	60.40	60.71	78.26	77.47	77.86	47.01	61.90	13.06	22.47
Simplified (all)	61.13	60.40	60.76	78.42	77.48	77.95	46.34	61.93	13.22	22.47

Table 9. Results of our systems and other participating systems in TEXT corpus

System	LP	LR	LF	UP	UR	UF	NLF	NUF	LM	UM
IHS-RD-Belarus	68.71	68.46	68.59	82.56	82.26	82.41	50.57	64.58	16.82	40.12
OCLSP (lbpg)	63.34	67.89	65.54	76.73	82.24	79.39	51.75	63.21	11.49	27.60
OCLSP (lbpgs)	67.35	65.11	66.21	81.22	78.52	79.85	47.79	55.51	12.82	33.29
OCLSP (lbpg75)	66.43	66.43	66.38	79.97	79.85	79.91	**57.51**	63.87	12.56	32.09
OSU CHGCG	65.36	64.98	65.17	79.06	78.60	78.83	54.70	65.71	11.36	32.02
Tree+SVM (base)	71.17	70.00	70.58	83.96	82.58	83.26	49.69	**68.56**	20.31	44.81
List-based (base)	70.05	68.58	69.31	82.42	80.68	81.54	53.57	63.96	19.23	41.46
Simplified (base)	70.63	69.19	69.90	82.59	80.91	81.74	54.24	64.55	20.08	42.01
Tree+SVM (all)	**71.35**	**70.19**	**70.76**	**84.23**	**82.87**	**83.54**	49.17	68.69	20.37	**45.10**
List-based (all)	70.76	69.34	70.04	82.85	81.19	82.01	55.59	65.55	20.31	42.56
Simplified (all)	71.01	69.59	70.29	82.87	81.22	82.04	54.48	65.59	**20.53**	42.43

3.3 Discussions

The labeled F1 scores of our three systems with baseline features are higher than other participating systems. The first approach (Tree+SVM) has the best performance in LF and UF but worst in NLF. However, its NUF is higher than others. It is mainly due to the low precision of the SVM classifier, resulting from the small amount of the positive training samples. Some of the labels only occur very few times, making it difficult to predict the dependency labels of the extra arcs precisely. However, in the second approach (dependency graph parser), with lower NUF, we present much higher NLF scores, showing the high precision of dependency label prediction. This is because the labeling part is trained with all samples rather than non-local samples alone in dependency graph parser.

All of our systems perform better with richer non-local features. It is important to notice that the NUF and NLF of the first approach do not benefit from richer features which improve the non-local scores of the second approach a lot. This is probably because richer features only help improve the performance of tree parsing which do not provide non-local information. This is an advantage of our dependency graph parser, since we can improve the performance of entire structure prediction and non-local dependency prediction at the same time by using richer features.

With respect to non-local arcs, the *list-based arc-eager algorithm* works better than *simplified list-based algorithm* in most situations. This is because we reduce the number of transitions at the price of lengthening transition sequences in the *simplified list-based algorithm*. Longer transition sequences make it harder to discover non-local informations (NUF and NLF). However, smaller transition set provides higher precision for the entire structure prediction (UF and LF).

Generally speaking, although the first approach (Tree+SVM) performs better in LF and UF, it requires extra human knowledge to design preprocessing rules. So for new dependency relation sets, we have to redesign the rules manually in the first approach. Also its NLF is limited by the tree parser's performance. However, our dependency graph parser in the second approach can parse dependency graphs completely automatically and does not require extra human knowledge.

4 Related Works

Transition-based dependency parsing [13,19,20,28,29] makes structural predictions with a deterministic shift-reduce process. Most of these parsers are designed to parse dependency trees. [23] presented a transition-based approach to DAG parsing on the work of [20] on pseudo-projective transformations. Since their parser can only parse projective dependency graphs, their approach requires pre-process and post-process. [17] presented a DAG parser by extending the maximum spanning tree dependency framework of their early work in 2005, which is a graph-based dependency parser. Other parsing approaches that produce dependency graphs [6,18,22] are generally based on linguistically-motivated lexicalized grammar formalisms, such as HPSG, CCG and LFG.

Since [12]'s first attempt to use neural networks in a broad-coverage Penn Treebank parser, applying neural networks to dependency parsing and representing the states with dense embedding vectors has been more and more popular [3,24,26,27,31]. Recently, [9] proposed a technique for learning representations of parsing states in transition-based dependency parser with stack LSTM and yielded state-of-the-art performance.

Semantic dependency parsing integrates dependency structure and semantic information in the sentence based on dependency grammar [21]. [14] were the first to use dependency grammar in semantic analysis. Then [7] proposed Stanford typed dependencies representations. [15,16] were the first to work on Chinese semantic dependency, and have manually annotated a corpus in the scale of one million words. HIT semantic dependency is established by Research Center for Social Computing and Information Retrieval in Harbin Institute of Technology in 2011. [8] refined the HIT dependency scheme with stronger linguistic theories, yielding a dependency scheme with more clear hierarchy.

5   Conclusion

We present two transition-based approaches for DAG parsing, and studied two kinds of transition set for the latter one. All of our systems yield significantly better LF than other participating systems in SemEval-2016 Task 9. We further provide extensive analysis and show the advantages and disadvantages of both approaches.

From the experiments, we can see that the performance of our graph parser can be further improved by using richer features. Therefore, our approach is expected to benefit from the recently proposed LSTM-based architectures [9]. We leave it to our future work.

Appendix

Preprocessing rules used in our first approach:

- In a causative sentence, we remove the dependency arc between the following verb and the noun;
- For multi-head situation caused by dependency arc between a noun and a pronoun, we remove this arc to eliminate the situation;
- For multi-head situation caused by reverse relation between a noun and a verb, we remove this arc to eliminate the situation;
- For multi-head situation caused by possessor relation between two nouns, we remove this arc to eliminate the situation.

References

1. Brown, P.F., Desouza, P.V., Mercer, R.L., Pietra, V.J.D., Lai, J.C.: Class-based n-gram models of natural language. Comput. Linguist. **18**(4), 467–479 (1992)
2. Che, W., Shao, Y., Liu, T., Ding, Y.: SemEval-2016 task 9: Chinese semantic dependency parsing. In: Proceedings of the 10th International Workshop on Semantic Evaluation (SemEval 2016), San Diego, US (2016, forthcoming)
3. Chen, D., Manning, C.: A fast and accurate dependency parser using neural networks. In: Proceedings of EMNLP, pp. 740–750 (2014)
4. Choi, J.D., McCallum, A.: Transition-based dependency parsing with selectional branching. In: Proceedings of ACL, pp. 1052–1062 (2013)
5. Choi, J.D., Palmer, M.: Getting the most out of transition-based dependency parsing. In: Proceedings of ACL, pp. 687–692. ACL (2011)
6. Clark, S., Hockenmaier, J., Steedman, M.: Building deep dependency structures with a wide-coverage CCG parser. In: Proceedings of ACL, pp. 327–334. ACL (2002)
7. De Marneffe, M.C., Manning, C.D.: The Stanford typed dependencies representation. In: Proceedings of the Workshop on Cross-Framework and Cross-Domain Parser Evaluation, COLING 2008, pp. 1–8 (2008)
8. Ding, Y., Shao, Y., Che, W., Liu, T.: Dependency graph based Chinese semantic parsing. In: Sun, M., Liu, Y., Zhao, J. (eds.) NLP-NABD 2014 and CCL 2014. LNCS, vol. 8801, pp. 58–69. Springer, Heidelberg (2014)
9. Dyer, C., Ballesteros, M., Ling, W., Matthews, A., Smith, N.A.: Transition-based dependency parsing with stack long short-term memory. In: Proceedings of ACL and IJCNLP, pp. 334–343 (2015)
10. Fan, R.E., Chang, K.W., Hsieh, C.J., Wang, X.R., Lin, C.J.: LIBLINEAR: a library for large linear classification. JMLR **9**, 1871–1874 (2008)
11. Guo, J., Che, W., Yarowsky, D., Wang, H., Liu, T.: Cross-lingual dependency parsing based on distributed representations. In: Proceedings of the 53rd Annual Meeting of the Association for Computational Linguistics and the 7th International Joint Conference on Natural Language Processing, vol. 1(Long Papers), pp. 1234–1244, July 2015
12. Henderson, J.: Discriminative training of a neural network statistical parser. In: Proceedings of ACL, p. 95. Association for Computational Linguistics (2004)
13. Huang, L., Sagae, K.: Dynamic programming for linear-time incremental parsing. In: Proceedings of ACL, pp. 1077–1086. ACL (2010)
14. Johansson, R., Nugues, P.: Dependency-based syntactic-semantic analysis with PropBank and NomBank. In: Proceedings of CoNLL, pp. 183–187. ACL (2008)
15. Li, M., Li, J., Dong, Z., Wang, Z., Lu, D.: Building a large Chinese corpus annotated with semantic dependency. In: Proceedings of SIGHAN, pp. 84–91. ACL (2003)
16. Li, M., Li, J., Wang, Z., Lu, D.: A statistical model for parsing semantic dependency relations in a Chinese sentence. Chin. J. Comput. **27**(12), 1679–1687 (2004)
17. McDonald, R.T., Pereira, F.C.: Online learning of approximate dependency parsing algorithms. In: Proceedings of EACL, pp. 81–88 (2006)
18. Miyao, Y., Tsujii, J.: Probabilistic disambiguation models for wide-coverage HPSG parsing. In: Proceedings of ACL, pp. 83–90. ACL (2005)
19. Nivre, J.: Non-projective dependency parsing in expected linear time. In: Proceedings of ACL and IJCNLP, pp. 351–359 (2009)
20. Nivre, J., Hall, J., Nilsson, J., Eryigit, G., Marinov, S.: Labeled pseudo-projective dependency parsing with support vector machines. In: Proceedings of CoNLL, pp. 221–225. ACL (2006)

21. Robinson, J.J.: Dependency structures and transformational rules. Language **46**, 259–285 (1970)
22. Sagae, K., Miyao, Y., Tsujii, J.: HPSG parsing with shallow dependency constraints. In: ACL, vol. 45, p. 624 (2007)
23. Sagae, K., Tsujii, J.: Shift-reduce dependency DAG parsing. In: Proceedings of ICCL, pp. 753–760. ACL (2008)
24. Stenetorp, P.: Transition-based dependency parsing using recursive neural networks. In: Deep Learning Workshop at NIPS (2013)
25. Sun, W., Du, Y., Kou, X., Ding, S., Wan, X.: Grammatical relations in Chinese: GB-ground extraction and data-driven parsing. In: ACL (1), pp. 436–456 (2014)
26. Titov, I., Henderson, J.: Constituent parsing with incremental sigmoid belief networks. In: ACL, vol. 45, p. 632 (2007)
27. Weiss, D., Alberti, C., Collins, M., Petrov, S.: Structured training for neural network transition-based parsing. In: Proceedings of ACL and IJCNLP, pp. 323–333 (2015)
28. Yamada, H., Matsumoto, Y.: Statistical dependency analysis with support vector machines. In: Proceedings of IWPT, pp. 195–206 (2003)
29. Zhang, Y., Clark, S.: A tale of two parsers: investigating and combining graph-based and transition-based dependency parsing using beam-search. In: Proceedings of the Conference on EMNLP, pp. 562–571. ACL (2008)
30. Zhang, Y., Nivre, J.: Transition-based dependency parsing with rich non-local features. In: Proceedings of ACL, pp. 188–193 (2011)
31. Zhou, H., Zhang, Y., Chen, J.: A neural probabilistic structured-prediction model for transition-based dependency parsing. In: Proceedings of ACL, pp. 1213–1222 (2015)

Improved Graph-Based Dependency Parsing via Hierarchical LSTM Networks

Wenhui Wang[1,2] and Baobao Chang[1,2(✉)]

[1] Key Laboratory of Computational Linguistics, Ministry of Education,
School of Electronics Engineering and Computer Science,
Peking University, No. 5 Yiheyuan Road, Haidian District, Beijing 100871, China
{wangwenhui,chbb}@pku.edu.cn
[2] Collaborative Innovation Center for Language Ability, Xuzhou 221009, China

Abstract. In this paper, we propose a neural graph-based dependency parsing model which utilizes hierarchical LSTM networks on character level and word level to learn word representations, allowing our model to avoid the problem of limited-vocabulary and capture both distributional and compositional semantic information. Our model achieves state-of-the-art accuracy on Chinese Penn Treebank and competitive accuracy on English Penn Treebank with only first-order features. Moreover, our model shows effectiveness in recovering dependencies involving out-of-vocabulary words.

Keywords: Graph-based dependency parsing · Hierarchical LSTM

1 Introduction

Dependency parsing is a fundamental task for language processing which has been investigated for decades. Among a variety of dependency parsing models, graph-based models are attractive for their ability of scoring the parsing decisions on a whole-tree basis. Recently, neural network models have been successfully introduced into graph-based dependency parsing and obtained state-of-the-art results. [16] presented a simple feed-forward network model which uses only atomic features such as word unigrams and POS tag unigrams. [18] proposed utilizing word representations learned by Bidirectional LSTM network to support parsing decisions and further improved their model by segment embeddings.

Effective as these models are, above models have a strong limitation in vocabulary due to its standard lookup-based word representations, which lead to difficulty in recovering dependencies involving out-of-vocabulary words. On the other hand, this standard lookup-based word representations capture only distributional semantics of words, which in essence encodes useful information in the surrounding contexts of the concerned word. However, for a more complete word representation, compositional semantics of a word would be necessary as well, which can be derived by combining meaning of word parts. This is especially important for languages like Chinese. The characters making up words bear meanings of their own and usually determine the meanings of words to a certain extent.

© Springer International Publishing AG 2016
M. Sun et al. (Eds.): CCL and NLP-NABD 2016, LNAI 10035, pp. 25–32, 2016.
DOI: 10.1007/978-3-319-47674-2_3

In this paper, we propose to utilize a hierarchical LSTM-based network model to graph-based dependency parsing. Our model includes two levels of Bidirectional LSTM network: one at the character level and one at the word level. The character-level LSTM aims to capture compositional semantics of word, which is then combined with the standard lookup-based word embedding to produce a more complete representation of word. The introduction of compositional representation also makes our model more robust to OOV words which are usually not well represented by the lookup-based word embeddings. The word-level LSTM aims to enrich the word representation and capture potential long range contextual information to support parsing decisions.

Character-level information has already been explored in transition-based dependency parsing. [5] proposed replacing lookup-based word representations with character-based representations which obtained by Bidirectional LSTM. They show that character-level information is helpful for morphologically rich language. However, simply using character-based representations results in their model performing poorly for English and Chinese. Different from their work, lookup-based word representations and character-based representations are combined and a word-level Bidirectional LSTM is further utilized to capture richer contextual information in our work. The combined word representation used in our work captures both distributional and compositional semantic information.

We evaluate our model on the English Penn Treebank and Chinese Penn Treebank, our model achieves state-of-the-art accuracy on Chinese Penn Treebank and competitive accuracy on English Penn Treebank.

2   Neural Network Model

In this section, we describe the architecture and the training of our neural network model in detail.

2.1   Word Representation

Given an input sentence $s = w_1, \ldots, w_n$ together with the corresponding POS tags $p_1, \ldots, p_n$, a hierarchical LSTM network is utilized to learn word representations, which is summarized in Fig. 1. A character-level Bidirectional LSTM is used to compute character-based embeddings of words. We then concatenate four vectors: the forward character-level LSTM hidden vector ($\overrightarrow{c}$); the backward character-level LSTM hidden vector ($\overleftarrow{c}$); the word embedding ($e(w_i)$) and the POS tag embedding ($e(p_i)$). A linear transformation w_e is performed and passed though an element-wise activation function g (ReLU is used as our activation function):

$$x_i = g(w_e[\overrightarrow{c}; \overleftarrow{c}; e(w_i); e(p_i)] + b_e) \tag{1}$$

A word-level Bidirectional LSTM is utilized to enrich word vector representations. Each output vector (v_i) of word-level Bidirectional LSTM is used to

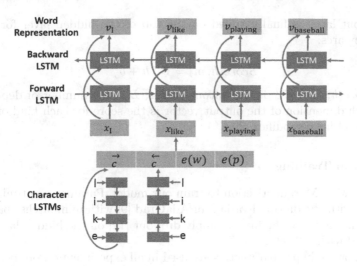

Fig. 1. Illustration for learning word representations based on hierarchical LSTM networks. $e(w)$ and $e(p)$ stand for the word embedding and POS tag embedding for this word.

represent words in sentence. Hierarchical LSTM networks allow each word representation v_i to capture information regarding the character level, the word form and POS tag, as well as the sentential context it appears in. In addition, combining character-level information allows our model to avoid the problem of out-of-vocabulary words.

2.2 Score Model

A neural network model is utilized to score dependency arcs. We use the same architecture and the same features as [18].

For a dependency pair (h, m), [18] utilize feature embeddings including the word representations for head word h and the modifier word m, distance between them (distance features are encoded as randomly initialized embeddings), and segment embeddings for the dependency pair (h, m). A sentence is divided into three parts (*prefix, infix* and *suffix*) by head word h and modifier word m, these parts are called segments. An extra forward LSTM layer is placed on top of the word representations and segment embeddings are learned by using subtraction between the forward LSTM hidden vectors.

All feature embeddings are mapped to the hidden layer. Direction-specific transformation is utilized to model edge direction:

$$h = g\Big(\sum_i W_{h_i}^d a_i + b_h^d \Big) \qquad (2)$$

where a_i is the feature embedding, $W_{h_i}^d$ and b_h^d are bound with index $d \in \{0, 1\}$ which indicates the direction between head and modifier.

A output layer is finally added on the top of the hidden layer for scoring dependency arcs:

$$Score(h, m) = W_o^d h + b_o^d \tag{3}$$

where $Score(h, m) \in \mathbb{R}^L$ is the output vector, L is the number of dependency types. Each dimension of the output vector is the score for each kind of dependency type of head-modifier pair.

2.3   Neural Training

We use the Max-Margin criterion to train our model. Parameter optimization is performed with the diagonal variant of AdaGrad [9] with minibatchs (batch size = 20). To mitigate overfitting, we apply dropout [12] on the hidden layer of the score model with 0.2 rate.

The following hyper-parameters are used in all experiments: word embedding size = 100, POS tag embedding size = 50, character embedding size = 50, hidden layer size = 200, character-level LSTM hidden vector size = 50, word-level LSTM hidden vector size = 100, character-level LSTM layers = 1, word-level LSTM layers = 2, regularization parameter $\lambda = 10^{-4}$.

We initialized the parameters using pretrained word embeddings[1]. Following [10] and [18], we use a variant of the skip n-gram model introduced by [13] on Gigaword corpus [11]. We also experimented with randomly initialized embeddings, where embeddings are uniformly sampled from range $[-0.3, 0.3]$. All other parameters are uniformly sampled from range $[-0.05, 0.05]$.

3   Experiments

In this section, we present our experimental setup and the main results of our work.

3.1   Experiments Setup

We conduct our experiments on the English Penn Treebank (PTB) [1] and the Chinese Penn Treebank (CTB) [2] datasets.

For English, we evaluated on the standard Wall Street Journal (WSJ) part of the Penn Treebank. Dependencies generated from version $3.3.0^2$ of the Stanford converter [15], we call it Penn-SD In the following section. We followed standard practice and used sections 2–21 for training, section 22 for development, and section 23 for testing. The Stanford POS Tagger [17] with ten-way jackknifing of the training data is used for assigning POS tags (accuracy $\approx$97.2 %).

---

[1] In our experiments, all words occurring less than 10 times in the corpus are treated as unknown words.

[2] http://nlp.stanford.edu/software/lex-parser.shtml.

For Chinese, we adopt the same split of CTB5 as described in [21]. Dependencies are converted using the Penn2Malt[3] tool with the head-finding rules of [21]. And following [21,23], we use gold segmentation and POS tags for the input.

3.2   Experiments Results

We first compare our model with previous state-of-the-art models on Chinese. Following previous work, UAS (unlabeled attachment scores) and LAS (labeled attachment scores) are calculated by excluding punctuation[4]. Table 1 lists the performances of our model as well as previous state-of-the-art models on CTB5. As we can see, word representations combining character-level information do improve model's performance compared with [18]. Moreover, the LAS of our model achieves state-of-the-art accuracy.

Table 1. Comparison with previous state-of-the-art models on CTB5.

Method	CTB5	
	UAS	LAS
Zhang and Nivre [23]	86.0	84.4
Bernd Bohnet [6]	87.5	85.9
Zhang and McDonald [22]	**87.96**	86.34
Dyer et al. [10]	87.2	85.7
Ballesteros et al. [5]	85.30	83.72
Wang and Chang [18]	87.55	86.23
Our model	87.77	**86.42**

Table 2. Comparison with previous state-of-the-art models on Penn-SD.

Method	Penn-SD	
	UAS	LAS
Zhang and McDonald [22]	93.01	90.64
Dyer et al. [10]	93.1	90.9
Weiss et al. [19]	93.99	92.05
Ballesteros et al. [5]	91.63	89.44
Andor et al. [3]	**94.41**	**92.55**
Wang and Chang [18]	94.08	91.82
Our model	94.13	91.85

We then compare our model with previous state-of-the-art models on English. Table 2 lists the performances of our model as well as previous state-of-the-art

---

[3] http://stp.lingfil.uu.se/nivre/research/Penn2Malt.html.

[4] Following previous work, a token is a punctuation if its POS tag is { "" : , .}.

models on Penn-SD. As we can see, the improvement on Penn-SD is lower than CTB5. On one hand, the OOV rate of Penn-SD (2.2 %) is much lower than CTB5 (10.4 %). On the other hand, character-level information of English reflects more morphological information which is also encoded in treebank POS tags, while character-level information of Chinese supplements semantic information within words to support parsing decisions. Moreover, our model outperforms [5] by a substantial margin on both Chinese and English since our word representations capture richer information rather than simple character-level information.

To show the effectiveness of our model in recovering dependencies involving out-of-vocabulary words, we compare the UAS and LAS of out-of-vocabulary words between our hierarchical LSTM network model and bidirecitonal LSTM network model proposed by [18] on CTB5. As shown in Table 3, incorporating character-level information makes our model achieve better UAS and LAS of out-of-vocabulary words. We observed a 3.96 % rise in UAS and 5.88 % rise in LAS respectively on recovering dependencies involving out-of-vocabulary words. A t-test on the difference shows the improvement is statistically significant.

We further examine POS tags and character-level information that account for the performance of our parser. As shown in Table 4, our basic model uses only lookup-based word representations and shows the worst performance. Using character-level information and POS tags do improve our basic model and lets our model achieve competitive accuracy. Moreover, we find that character-level information makes greater improvement when POS tags are not provided. Again we observe a much bigger improvement in Chinese than in English when introducing the character-level representation of words. In addition, although using character-level information could improve model to a certain extent, POS tags is still necessary for dependency parsing. It seems that the introduction of POS information contributes more in Chinese than in English as well. This is, however, not strictly comparable, since we use gold standard POS tag for Chinese and automatically generated POS tag for English as most previous work did.

Table 3. Accuracy and significant test in recovering dependencies involving out-of-vocabulary words.

	HiLSTM	BiLSTM	Significant test
UAS	84.42	80.46	$t = 1.96$, $p < 0.05$
LAS	81.72	75.84	$t = 3.91$, $p < 10^{-4}$

Table 4. The impact of POS tags and character-level information on CTB5 and Penn-SD.

Method	Penn-SD		CTB5	
	UAS	LAS	UAS	LAS
Basic model	92.81	90.18	79.33	75.55
+character	93.63	91.12	82.99	79.64
+POS	94.08	91.82	87.55	86.23
+POS+character	94.13	91.85	87.77	86.42

We also test out model without pre-trained word embeddings, our model achieves 93.52 % UAS/91.23 % LAS on Penn-SD and 86.62 % UAS/85.11 % LAS on CTB5. Using pre-trained word embeddings can obtain around 0.6 %~1.1 % improvement.

4 Conclusion

In this paper, we propose a hierarchical LSTM network model for graph-based dependency parsing. Word-level and character-level LSTM networks are utilized to capture information regarding the character level, the word form and POS tag, as well as the sentential context it appears in, which allows for a improvement on Chinese and lets our model achieve state-of-the-art accuracy. Moreover, our model is still a first-order model using standard Eisner algorithm for decoding, the computational cost remains at a lowest level among graph-based models.

As further work, we will improve our model to generate nonprojective trees and test our model on morphologically rich languages which are often nonprojective dependencies.

Acknowledgments. This work is supported by National Key Basic Research Program of China under Grant No. 2014CB340504 and National Natural Science Foundation of China under Grant No. 61273318. The Corresponding author of this paper is Baobao Chang.

References

1. Marcus, M.P., Marcinkiewicz, M.A., Santorini, B.: Building a large annotated corpus of English: The Penn Treebank. Comput. Linguist. **19**(2), 313–330 (1993)
2. Xue, N., Xia, F., Chiou, F.-D., Palmer, M.: The penn Chinese treebank: phrase structure annotation of a large corpus. Nat. Lang. Eng. **11**(02), 207–238 (2005)
3. Andor, D., Alberti, C., Weiss, D., Severyn, A., Presta, A., Ganchev, K., Petrov, S., Collins, M.: Globally normalized transition-based neural networks. In: Proceedings of the 54rd Annual Meeting of the Association for Computational Linguistics (2016)
4. Ballesteros, M., Dyer, C., Smith, N.A.: Improved transition-based parsing by modeling characters instead of words with LSTMs. Computer Science (2015a)
5. Ballesteros, M., Dyer, C., Smith, N.A.: Improved transition-based parsing by modeling characters instead of words with LSTMs. In: Proceedings of the Conference on Empirical Methods in Natural Language Processing, EMNLP, Lisbon, Portugal, 17–21 September 2015, pp. 349–359 (2015)
6. Kuhn, J., Bohnet, B.: The best of both worlds: a graph-based completion model for transition-based parsers. In: Conference of the European Chapter of the Association for Computational Linguistics
7. Chen, D., Manning, C.D.: A fast and accurate dependency parser using neural networks. In: Proceedings of the Conference on Empirical Methods in Natural Language Processing, pp. 740–750 (2014)
8. Cross, J., Huang, L.: Incremental parsing with minimal features using bi-directional LSTM. In: Proceedings of the 54rd Annual Meeting of the Association for Computational Linguistics (2016)

9. Duchi, J., Hazan, E., Singer, Y.: Adaptive subgradient methods for online learning and stochastic optimization. J. Mach. Learn. Res. **12**, 2121–2159 (2011)

10. Dyer, C., Ballesteros, M., Ling, W., Matthews, A., Smith, N.A.: Transition-based dependency parsing with stack long short-term memory. In: Proceedings of the 53rd Annual Meeting of the Association for Computational Linguistics, pp. 334–343 (2015)

11. Graff, D., Kong, J., Chen, K., Maeda, K.: English Gigaword. Linguistic Data Consortium, Philadelphia (2003)

12. Hinton, G.E., Srivastava, N., Krizhevsky, A., Sutskever, I., Salakhutdinov, R.R.: Improving neural networks by preventing co-adaptation of feature detectors (2012). arXiv preprint arXiv:1207.0580

13. Ling, W., Dyer, C., Black, A., Trancoso, I.: Two/too simple adaptations of word2vec for syntax problems. In: Proceedings of the 2015 Conference of the North American Chapter of the Association for Computational Linguistics: Human Language Technologies (2015a)

14. Ling, W., Dyer, C., Black, A.W., Trancoso, I., Fermandez, R., Amir, S., Marujo, L., Luís, T.: Compositional character models for open vocabulary word representation. In: Proceedings of the Conference on Empirical Methods in Natural Language Processing, EMNLP, pp. 1520–1530 (2015b)

15. De Marneffe, M.C., Maccartney, B., Manning, C.D.: Generating typed dependency parses from phrase structure parses. LREC **6**, 449–454 (2006)

16. Pei, W., Ge, T., Chang, B.: An effective neural network model for graph-based dependency parsing. In: Proceedings of the 53rd Annual Meeting of the Association for Computational Linguistics, pp. 313–322 (2015)

17. Toutanova, K., Klein, D., Manning, C.D., Singer, Y.: Feature-rich part-of-speech tagging with a cyclic dependency network. In: Proceedings of the Conference of the North American Chapter of the Association for Computational Linguistics on Human Language Technology-Volume 1, pp. 173–180. Association for Computational Linguistics (2003)

18. Wang, W., Chang, B.: Graph-based dependency parsing with bidirectional LSTM. In: Proceedings of the 54rd Annual Meeting of the Association for Computational Linguistics (2016)

19. Weiss, D., Alberti, C., Collins, M., Petrov, S.: Structured training for neural network transition-based parsing. In: Proceedings of the 53rd Annual Meeting of the Association for Computational Linguistics (2015)

20. Yamada, H., Matsumoto, Y.: Statistical dependency analysis with support vector machines. In: Proceedings of IWPT, vol. 3, pp. 195–206 (2003)

21. Zhang, Y., Clark, S.: A tale of two parsers: investigating and combining graph-based and transition-based dependency parsing. In: Conference on Empirical Methods in Natural Language Processing, pp. 562–571 (2008)

22. Zhang, H., McDonald, R.T.: Enforcing structural diversity in cube-pruned dependency parsing. In: Proceedings of the 52nd Annual Meeting of the Association for Computational Linguistics, pp. 656–661 (2014)

23. Zhang, Y., Nivre, J.: Transition-based dependency parsing with rich non-local features. In: The 49th Annual Meeting of the Association for Computational Linguistics: Human Language Technologies, pp. 188–193 (2011)

24. Zhang, Y., Weiss, D.: Stack-propagation: improved representation learning for syntax. In: Proceedings of the 54rd Annual Meeting of the Association for Computational Linguistics (2016)

Machine Translation

Error Analysis of English-Chinese Machine Translation

Fei Fang[1], Shili Ge[1,2(✉)], and Rou Song[2]

[1] School of English for International Business,
Guangdong University of Foreign Studies, Guangzhou 510420, China
fangfei562@126.com, geshili@gdufs.edu.cn
[2] Guangdong Collaborative Innovation Center
for Language Research and Service, Guangzhou 510420, China
songrou@126.com

Abstract. In order to explore a practical way of improving machine translation (MT) quality, the error types and distribution of MT results have to be analyzed first. This paper analyzed English-Chinese MT errors from the perspective of naming-telling clause (NT clause, hereafter). Two types of text were input to get the MT output: one was to input the whole original English sentences into an MT engine; the other was to parse English sentences into English NT clauses, and then input these clauses into the MT engine in order. The errors of MT output are categorized into three classes: incorrect lexical choices, structural errors and component omissions. Structural errors are further divided into SV-structure errors and non-SV-structure errors. The analyzed data shows firstly, the major errors are structural errors, in which non-SV-structural errors account for a larger proportion; secondly, translation errors decrease significantly after English sentences are parsed into NT clauses. This result reveals that non-SV clauses are the main source of MT errors, and suggests that English long sentences should be parsed into NT clauses before they are translated.

Keywords: Machine translation · Error analysis · NT clauses · SV clauses · Non-SV clauses

1 Categorization of Errors in Machine Translation

The past 60 years has witnessed great progress in machine translation. Nowadays, online automatic translation systems play a vital role in rough reading of foreign-language texts, which has become the necessary function of word processing systems and information retrieval systems. However, as for the need of intensive reading, there still exist many problems in automatic machine translation, especially in the translation of long sentences.

In the field of machine translation, there are two widely-used evaluation methods: manual evaluation and objective evaluation (also known as automatic evaluation). According to Koehn [1], the former is a method that evaluates outputs of machine translation systems by subjective judgments; the latter evaluates MT outputs automatically according to a certain mathematical model. Neither of them can show the source of MT errors, not to mention the improvement of long sentence translation.

© Springer International Publishing AG 2016
M. Sun et al. (Eds.): CCL and NLP-NABD 2016, LNAI 10035, pp. 35–49, 2016.
DOI: 10.1007/978-3-319-47674-2_4

According to Zhao et al. [2], translation errors can be divided into 7 types: (1) incorrect words, (2) missing content words, (3) wrong word order, (4) translation with meaning contrary to the original, (5) errors of named entity, (6) errors of numerals and quantifiers/temporal words and (7) other errors. That paper comes to the conclusion that the first 3 types, especially incorrect words and wrong word order, accounts for the largest proportion. This analysis is correct, but it does not explain the objective phenomenon that MT has a poorer performance in long-sentence translation than in short-sentence translation. Still it fails to reveal the causes of the errors. Thus the analysis provides no direct benefit for the quality improvement of long sentence machine translation.

The paper explores the results of English-Chinese machine translation, categorizing errors in machine translation into 3 types: incorrect lexical choices, structural errors and component omissions. Examples are employed to illustrate the significant influence of the complexity of naming-telling clause (NT clause, hereafter) in English sentences on the performance of machine translation and to suggest the possibility that parsing long English sentences into NT clauses will reduce errors. The paper is expected to offer some inspirations for breaking through the bottleneck of automatic long sentence translation.

As for the categories in machine translation errors, our ideas are as follows:

The aim of translation is to keep the semantic consistency between the source text and the target text. As semantics has its own constructions, so we can examine the correctness of forms of semantic structures, including errors like additions, omissions, mistaken usages, wrong types of semantic structures and wrong word choices in leaf nodes of semantic structures. Giving that additions rarely occur, we can categorize translation errors into 3 types: omissions of semantic structures (component omissions), errors of semantic structures in form or type (structural errors) and errors of word choice (incorrect lexical choices).

The semantic structure mentioned in this paper is in view of a higher and more abstract level, which includes the referential component plus its statement (subject-predicate), the modifier plus its modified (attribute-head or the adverbial-head), the action plus its object (verb-object), the action plus its supplementary instructions (verb-complement), preposition plus its object (preposition-object), conjunctive and its logical arguments and so on. Particularly, if the antecedent and consequent of a certain structure are transposed, it will be classified into errors of structural type, naming the structural error, equivalent to the wrong word order proposed by Zhao et al. [2]; but the structural error we refer to includes not only the wrong word order but also other errors. For example, some construction should be translated into attribute-head construction but the MT output is a structure of adverbial-head, or there is confusion of logical arguments on whether they are the referential or the statement on the two sides of coordinate conjunctions, etc. In this paper, component omissions are generally the type of missing content words proposed by Zhao et al. [2]. Incorrect lexical choices are mostly incorrect words proposed by Zhao et al. [2]. Yet, if prepositions, conjunctions, or any verbs are omitted or mistranslated, causing structural errors, they are classified into errors of structural types. As for the rest 4 types proposed by Zhao et al. [2], they can also be classified into the 3 types mentioned above.

To illustrate semantic structure more clearly, we offer the following example of semantic structure in the form of a semantic tree.

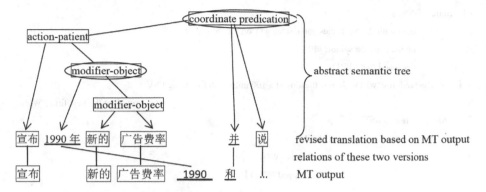

Fig. 1. Error analysis of machine translation from the perspective of semantic structure

Original English text: (It) announced new advertising rates for 1990 and said
The MT output: 宣布新的广告费率1990和
The revised translation: 宣布1990年新的广告费率并说
The comparison of semantic structures:

In Fig. 1, the last line is Chinese MT output; the line above it is the manually revised translation based on the MT output. From Fig. 1, we can see that "1990" should be translated into "1990 年". So, it is an incorrect lexical choice which is annotated by underlined words. Besides, "1990年" is the modifier of "新的广告费率", but "1990" is placed after "新的广告费率" in the MT output, unable to show its modifier-object structure. It is also a structural error marked with ellipses on nodes of the semantic tree. "and", here showing the coordination of two predicate components, should be translated into "并", not "和" which shows the coordination of referential components. It is not only an incorrect lexical choice but also a structural error, therefore marked with an underline and an ellipse respectively. "said" should be translated into "说", which does not occur in the MT output. This kind of error, i.e., component omission, is marked with dots.

2   NT Clause, SV Clause and Non-SV Clause

Song and Ge [3] define an NT clause as the structure consisting of a naming and a telling. A naming is a referential component and a telling is the description or post-modification component of the naming. In English language there are 8 specific relationships between a naming and its telling: subject and predicate, the referential component and its seven types of telling, including relative clauses, past participial phrases, present participial phrase, infinitive phrase, adjective phrases, declarative prepositional phrases and the explanatory noun phrases.

Example 1: *Documents filed with the Securities and Exchange Commission on the pending spinoff disclosed that Cray Research Inc. will withdraw the almost $ 100 million in financing it is providing the new firm if Mr. Cray leaves or if the product-design project he heads is scrapped.*

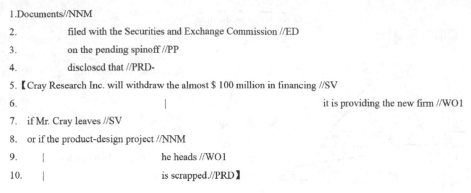

1.Documents//NNM

2.   filed with the Securities and Exchange Commission //ED

3.   on the pending spinoff //PP

4.   disclosed that //PRD-

5. 【Cray Research Inc. will withdraw the almost $ 100 million in financing //SV

6. | it is providing the new firm //WO1

7. if Mr. Cray leaves //SV

8. or if the product-design project //NNM

9. | he heads //WO1

10. | is scrapped.//PRD 】

Fig. 2. Newline-indented schema of Example 1

For the sake of visual cognition, we represent the relation between naming and telling in an English sentence with specific method called newline-indented schema by Song [4]. The specific method is: when a naming and its telling are not subject-predicate relation, or they are non-adjacent subject-predicate relation, we place the telling part in a new line and indent it after its naming part.

In Fig. 2, the first line and the eighth line except the conjunction "or" and "if " are referential components, i.e. naming, annotated with NNM; the fifth and seventh lines are subject-predicate NT clauses, annotated with SV; in the remaining six lines, the second line is past participial phrases, typed ED; the third line is a prepositional phrase, typed PP; in the fourth line, the finite verb acts as predicate of the first line, but lacking the object, so typed PRD-; "Documents" in the first line acts as the naming of these three tellings, so they are indented to its right end in the new lines. The sixth line is a relative clause, and its antecedent is "the almost $100 million in financing" in the fifth line and is the direct object of the relative clause, which is suggested by the WO1 in the sixth line. The sixth line is indented to the right end of its antecedent and a vertical bar is used to mark the left end of the antecedent, signaling the beginning of the naming. The types of the ninth line and the tenth line can be inferred from the above expla- nation. A pair of black square brackets is employed to mark the object clause ranging from the fifth line to the tenth line, which belongs to the fourth line.

In Fig. 2, each naming is placed on the upper-left side of its telling, thus sequences of NT clauses of this English sentence can be constructed mechanically as follows. These NT clauses are numbered according to the line number of their tellings.

2. Documents + filed with the Securities and Exchange Commission //ED
3. Documents + on the pending spinoff //PP
4. Documents + disclosed that //PRD-
5. Cray Research Inc. will withdraw the almost $100 million in financing //SV
6. the almost $100 million in financing +it is providing the new firm //WO1
7. if Mr. Cray leaves //SV
9. the product-design project + he heads //WO
10. or if the product-design project + is scrapped.//PRD

NT clauses can be used for the basic structure of categorizing translation errors. NT clause is classified into two types. One is adjacent subject-predicate structures, called SV clauses, while the other one is non-adjacent subject-predicate structures or non-subject-predicate structures, called non-SV clauses. Therefore, the structural error can be classified into SV-structure error and non-SV-structure error. The reason that we distinguish these two types is the different difficulty levels they occur in machine translation. The former structure (subject-predicate NT clauses) accords with syntax of clauses and the subject and predicate are adjacent, which can be handled effectively by either rule method or statistical method; however, the latter does not accord with the syntax of normal English clauses, and non-adjacent subject-predicate structures or non-subject-predicate structures as they are, the above two traditional methods may be confronted with great difficulty.

By using the newline-indented schema, we have annotated NT-clause structure for several thousands of English sentences from the Wall Street Journal in Penn Treebank and have a more detailed test on 253 English sentences among them. Two ways are adopted for machine translation in the paper. One is that we input these whole English sentences into *Baidu Translate*, a popular machine translation engine in China, and amend the MT outputs manually. Then, through comparing the MT outputs with the manually amended texts, we classify and tag the errors in MT outputs. The other way is very similar to the former one, only with a difference that the whole English sentences are parsed into English NT clauses in advance, and these English NT clauses are then translated separately. The errors are tagged according to three types we mentioned above, and the structural errors among them are divided into SV-structure errors and non-SV-structure errors. Examples will be given in Sect. 3 to illustrate the specific procedure of these two ways. In Sect. 4, we categorize and compare errors occurring in MT outputs which are obtained through these two different ways. Section 5 will list conclusions drawn from the comparison.

3   Analysis of Errors in English-Chinese Machine Translation

Example 2: *Newsweek, trying to keep pace with rival Time magazine, announced new advertising rates for 1990 and said it will introduce a new incentive plan for advertisers.*

The alignment of the translated Chinese word sequences and the original English text are as follows (Fig. 3):

①Newsweek , ②trying to③keep pace④with ⑤rival   ⑥Time magazine , ⑦announced
①新闻周刊 , ②试图   ③并驾齐驱④与   ⑤竞争对手⑥时代杂志   ，   ⑦宣布了

⑧new ⑨advertising rates ⑩for 1990⑪and ⑫said ⑬it ⑭will   ⑮introduce
⑧新的 ⑨广告费率   ⑩1990 年⑪并   ⑫说   ⑬它⑭将   ⑮引入

⑯a   ⑰new ⑱incentive ⑲plan ⑳for   ㉑advertisers .
⑯一个⑰新的⑱激励   ⑲计划⑳为   ㉑广告主

Fig. 3. Alignment of English and Chinese in words of Example 2

MT output:

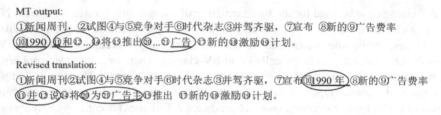

Revised translation:

Fig. 4. MT output and revised translation of Example 2

MT output and revised translation are as follows:

In Fig. 4, in order to save printing space, words where structural errors occur are directly enclosed with ellipses, which is different with the practice in Fig. 1 of the semantic tree that ellipses are placed on nodes of the semantic tree; incorrect lexical choices are still underlined under the words; component omissions are marked with dots on corresponding MT output texts.

There are errors in 3 phrases of the MT output:

(1) "1900" should be translated into "1990 年(year)". Numerals can be functioned as dates or years in English without any addition, but in Chinese, these characters "日(date), 月(month) and 年(year)" should be added after the numerals. So it belongs to incorrect lexical choices. Besides, "1990年(for 1990)" is the modifier of "新的广告费率(new advertising rates)", but "1990" is placed after "新的广告费率" in the MT output, which is ungrammatical Chinese structure.

(2) "and said" should be translated into "并说", but the machine translates it into "和(and)". Even though "and" has two corresponding meanings of "和" and "并" in Chinese, "和" is used for the coordination of the referential components while "并" signifies for the coordination of statements. Here the context contains two statements, thus "and" should be translated into "并". This point belongs to incorrect lexical choices. Besides, it also belongs to errors of structural type. Furthermore, the meaning of "said" is omitted in the Chinese text, so this belongs to component omission.

(3) "for advertisers" should be translated into "为广告商", but the machine translates it into "广告", which signals the omission of beneficiary argument "为(for)". "广告商(advertisers)" is translated into "广告(advertisement)", which belongs to incorrect lexical choices. Besides "为广告商(for advertiser)" is an adverbial and should be placed before its modified predicate "推出新的激励计划 (announced a new incentive plan)". The post-position of the adverbial "广告" makes the translated text hard to understand. So this also belongs to structural errors.

To sum up, we can make a calculation that there are 3 structural errors, 3 incorrect lexical choices and 2 component omissions.

In order to analyze the causes for these errors, we parse the original sentence into NT clauses by showing with a newline-indented schema as follows, and original words of errors in the MT output are underlined, where the different line types will be explained soon:

In Fig. 5, the third line and the fourth line where errors occur are both predicates of the first line. These two lines are also tellings of the first line. The difficulty of

Newsweek ,//NNM

> trying to keep pace with rival Time magazine ,//ING
> announced new advertising rates for 1990 //PRD
> <u>and said</u>//PRD-

>> it will introduce a new incentive plan <u>for advertisers</u> .//SV

Fig. 5. Newline-indented schema of Example 2

translation increases because of the two pairs of subjects and predicates being non-adjacent. Besides, the conjunction "and" before the predicate of the fourth line also increase the difficulty of machine translation. The fifth line is a NT clause of subject-predicate type and is not long, but is placed at the end of the whole sentence without any punctuation before it, so translation errors before it would be propagated into it. Therefore, there is no surprise that errors occur in this simple clause.

The above analysis of reasons for translation errors enlightens us to think that if we parse long English sentences into NT-clause sequences, errors in machine translation may decline. In order to verify the assumption, we parse this long English sentence into 4 NT clauses and make simple mechanical changes to let every NT clauses be grammatically correct clauses with a subject-predicate structure. Then we input these NT clauses into machine translation system, and the results are as follows:

(1)

The NT clauses: ①Newsweek②(trying|tries) to③keep pace④with⑤rival⑥Time magazine

Note: "(trying|tries)" means shifting the present participle *trying* into finite verb *tries*.

The MT output: ①新闻周刊杂志②试图④与⑤对手⑥...   ③并驾齐驱
The revised translation: ①新闻周刊 ②企图④与⑤对手⑥时代杂志③并驾齐驱
Analysis of errors: "⑥时代杂志" is omitted in the sentence.

(2)

The NT clauses: ①Newsweek⑦announced⑧new⑨advertising rates⑩for 1990
The MT output: ①新闻周刊 ⑦宣布   ⑧新的   ⑨广告费率   ⑩为1990
The revised translation: ①新闻周刊 ⑦宣布 ⑩1990年⑧新的 ⑨广告费率
Analysis of errors: there still occurs an incorrect lexical choice and a structural error "for 1990".

(3)

The NT clauses: ①Newsweek (and) ⑫said

Note: (and) means temporarily deleting the conjunction *and* between the naming and the telling before translation.

The MT output: ①新闻周刊⑫说

No error.

(4)

The NT clauses: ⑬ it ⑭ will ⑮ introduce ⑯ a ⑰ new ⑱ incentive ⑲ plan ⑳ for ㉑ advertisers

The MT output: ⑬它⑭将⑳为㉑广告主⑮引入⑯一个⑰新的⑱激励⑲计划
No error.

Total errors: 1 structural error, 1 incorrect lexical choice and 1 component omissions.

Compared with errors in the MT output of the original whole sentence, the errors in MT output of NT clauses are with 2 structural errors, 2 incorrect lexical choices and 1 component omission less.

In order to show the comparison between the two results, in the above newline-indented schema, namely, in Fig. 4, we underline words and phrases where errors occur in MT output of the original whole sentence with bold underlines while wave lines are used to mark words and phrases where errors occur in MT output of NT clauses, and bold wave lines to mark words and phrases where errors occur in MT outputs of both ways.

Example 3: *About 160 workers at a factory that made paper for the Kent filters were exposed to asbestos in the 1950s.*

The alignment of the translated Chinese word sequences and the original English text as follows (Fig. 6):

①About②160③workers④at⑤a   ⑥factory⑦that⑧made paper⑨for⑩the Kent
①大约 ②160 名③工人④在⑤一家⑥工厂里⑦   ⑧造纸   ⑨为⑩肯特

⑪filters   ⑫were exposed to⑬asbestos⑭ in⑮the 1950s.
⑪过滤嘴 ⑫接触过   ⑬石棉 ⑭在⑮20 世纪 50 年代。

Fig. 6. Alignment of English and Chinese in words of example 3

MT output:
①大约②160 名③工人④在⑤一家⑥工厂⑧制造的造纸厂⑯的⑨..⑩肯特⑪过滤器 ⑭在⑮20 世纪 50 年代⑫暴露于⑬石棉。
Revised translation:
①大约②160 名③工人④在⑨为⑩肯特⑪过滤器⑧造纸⑯的⑤一家⑥工厂⑭在⑮20 世纪 50 年代⑫暴露于⑬石棉。

Fig. 7. MT output and revised translation of example 3

MT output and revised translation are as follows:
Errors in MT output are as follows:

All errors occur in the relative clause "that made paper for the Kent filter". The verb-object structure "made paper" is translated into a modifier-head structure "制造的造纸厂的" in Chinese. So the above error belongs to structural errors. "for the Kent filter" is translated into "肯特过滤器". First of all, the preposition "for" is omitted; then, the prepositional phrase "为肯特过滤器(for the Kent filter)" functioning as adverbial should be placed before the verb phrase "造纸(made paper)". This error belongs to structural errors.

To sum up, there are 2 structural errors and 1 component omission in MT output.

The newline-indented schema of Example 3 are as follows:

About 160 workers at a factory//NNM

| that <u>made paper for the Kent filters</u>//WS

      were exposed to asbestos in the 1950s.//PRD

Fig. 8. Newline-indented schema of Example 3

In Fig. 8, errors occur in the non-subject-predicate NT clause in the second line, because the relative clause of "a factory" is inserted into the middle of the subject and the predicate. Position adjustment is needed because there is a prepositional phrase functioning as adverbial in the relative clause, which increase the difficulty of machine translation. We parse the whole sentence into 2 NT clauses, make simple mechanical changes that make them into normal subject-predicate clause and input them into the machine translation system separately. Results are as follows:

(1)

The NT clause:

①About②160③workers④at⑤a⑥factory⑫were exposed to⑬asbestos⑭in⑮the 1950s

The MT output:

⑭在⑮20世纪50年代⑤一家⑥工厂①大约②160名③工人⑫暴露在⑬石棉中

(2)

The NT clause: ⑤the ⑥factory (that) ⑧made paper⑨for⑩the Kent ⑪filters

Note: (that) means temporally deleting the relative pronoun *that* between the naming and the telling.

The MT output: ⑤这家⑥工厂⑨为⑩肯特⑪过滤器⑧制造了纸

Both of these two clauses have no errors.

Compared with the MT output of the original sentence, according to Fig. 7, we can see there is a reduction of 2 structural errors and 1 component omission.

Example 4: *The survival of spinoff Cray Computer Corp. as a fledgling in the supercomputer business appears to depend heavily on the creativity – and longevity – of its chairman and chief designer.*

The alignment of the translated Chinese word sequences and the original English text is as follows (Fig. 9):

①The survival②of③spinoff ④Cray Computer Corp.⑤as ⑥a ⑦fledgling
①生存　　　②的③分拆　④克雷计算机公司　⑤作为⑥一个⑦新生儿

⑧in ⑨the supercomputer business⑩appears to⑪depend⑫heavily⑬on
⑧在⑨超级计算机事业　⑩似乎　⑪依赖　⑫严重地⑬于

⑭the creativity -- ⑮and⑯longevity –⑰of⑱its　⑲chairman⑳and㉑chief designer
⑭创造力　　⑮和 ⑯寿命　⑰的⑱它的 ⑲主席　⑳和 ㉑首席设计师

Fig. 9. Alignment of English and Chinese in words of Example 4

MT output and revised translation are as follows (Fig. 10):

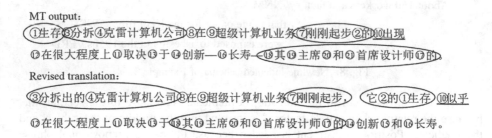

Fig. 10. MT output and revised translation of Example 4

Errors in MT output are as follows:

(1) "spinoff Cray Computer Corp." should be translated into a modifier-head structure "分拆出的克雷计算机公司" in Chinese, but here it is translated into a verb-object structure "分拆克雷计算机公司", which belongs to structural errors.

(2) it is correct to translate "the survival" into "生存", but as the head noun, in Chinese it should be placed after its attribute "分拆出的克雷计算机公司的". It is placed before its attribute in the MT output, so it is a structural error.

(3) "as a fledgling in the supercomputer business" is the post-modifier of "spinoff Cray Computer Corp.". It is acceptable to translate "as a fledgling in the super-computer business" into an adverbial-verb structure "在超级计算机事业中刚刚起步" as a statement of "spinoff Cray Computer Corp.", but in MT output, the addition of "的" in Chinese makes the adverbial-verb structure shift into a modifier-head structure. It is a structural error.

(4) "of its chairman and chief designer" is the attribute of the head noun "the creativity – and longevity –", so when translated into Chinese, it should be placed before its head noun. It is a structural error.

(5) "appear" has two meanings: "出现" and "似乎" in Chinese, but according to the context, it should be translated into "似乎", while "出现" in MT output, so it is an incorrect lexical choice.

From the above analysis, there are 4 structural errors and 1 incorrect lexical choice in the MT output.

The newline-indented schema of example 4 are as follows:

In Fig. 11, errors occur in the naming of the first line and the telling of the second and the third lines. The results are as follow after the sentence is parsed into NT clauses and inputted into machine translation system.

The survival of spinoff Cray Computer Corp. //NNM

        as a fledgling in the supercomputer business//PPM

          appears to depend heavily on the creativity -- and longevity –of its chairman and chief designer.//PRD

Fig. 11. Newline-indented schema of Example 4

(1)

The NT clause: ③spinoff④Cray Computer Corp. [is]⑤as⑥a⑦fledgling⑧in⑨the supercomputer business

Note: [is] is added to make the sentence accord with grammatical rules.

The MT output: ③分拆 ④克雷计算机公司⑧在⑨超级计算机业务⑦刚刚起步

The revised translation:③分拆出的④克雷计算机公司⑧在⑨超级计算机业务中⑦刚刚起步

Analysis of errors: there is still 1 structural error.

(2)

The NT clause:

①The survival②of③spinoff④Cray Computer Corp⑩appears to⑪depend⑫heavily⑬on⑭the creativity -- ⑮and⑯longevity –⑰of⑱its⑲chairman⑳and㉑chief designer

The MT output:

③分拆④克雷计算机公司②的①生存⑩似乎⑫很大程度上⑪取决⑬于⑭创造力⑮和⑯寿命，⑱其⑲主席⑳和㉑首席设计师⑰...

The revised translation：

③分拆出的④克雷计算机公司②的①生存⑩似乎⑫很大程度上⑪取决⑬于⑱其⑲主席⑳和㉑首席设计师⑰的⑭创造力⑮和⑯寿命

Analysis of errors: there is still 1 structural error and component omission.

Compared with the original result of MT output, there is a reduction of 2 structural errors and 1 incorrect lexical choice. The compared results show that making the subject and the predicate adjacent can strengthen the bondage of their meanings, thus the parsing of NT clauses also can help eliminate incorrect lexical choices.

4 Statistics and Analysis of Errors in English-Chinese Machine Translation

4.1 Analysis of Error Types

We use the method described above to carry on manual evaluation in English-Chinese machine translation. So far, 243 English sentences have been manually evaluated, including 6232 English word tokens in 682 NT clauses. Total amount of errors in MT outputs is 606 in whole sentence translation. According to our categorization, the proportion of error types in MT output among the 243 English sentences is presented in the pie chart below.

According to the data in Fig. 12, we can see the specific proportion of each error type. The structural error accounts for 47 %, in which the proportions of SV-structure errors and non-SV-structure errors are respectively 20 % and 27 %. Incorrect lexical choices take up 37 %, and component omissions 16 %. Then we can see that structural errors nearly takes up about a half of all errors, in which non-SV-structure errors are more than SV-structure errors obviously.

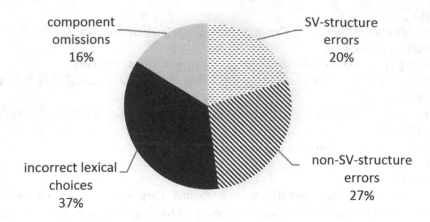

Fig. 12. Distribution of error types

Statistic data in Table 1 show the distribution of SV-structure errors and non-SV-structure errors among SV clauses and non-SV clauses. According to data in Table 1, non-SV-structure errors are 1.39 times as many as SV-structure errors. The causes for the majority of non-SV-structure errors can be attribute to these two aspects: firstly, the ratio of the number of non-SV clauses and SV clauses is 1.02: 1 which is not a very large number; secondly, a more important cause is that structural errors in each non-SV clause are greatly more than those in each SV clause, with the ratio of 1.33: 1. Therefore, we can conclude that non-SV clauses are main source of errors.

Table 1. The distribution of structural errors

Type of clause	Number of clauses	Number of structural errors	Average number of structural errors in one clause
SV clause	337	119	0.36
Non-SV clause	345	166	0.48
Non-SV/SV	1.02	1.39	1.33

4.2 Comparison Between Whole Sentence Translation and NT Clause Translation

When parsing the English sentences which have errors in the MT output of whole sentence translation, into NT clauses and then inputting them into Baidu Translate, we obtain the result of MT output of these NT clauses and the distribution of errors. The Table 2 is a comparative result of errors before and after parsing.

According to the data in Table 2, structural errors and component omission decline by about one half, and incorrect lexical choices decline by 10 %. The total reduction is one third. Non-SV-structure errors decline much more than SV-structure errors. We maintain that there are two causes for the reduction. Firstly, when English sentences (especially long ones) are parsed into NT clause, their naming and telling are linked

Table 2. Comparison of the error amount between two ways of translation

Error number	Error type					
	Structural errors			Incorrect lexical choices	Component omissions	Total
	SV-structure errors	Non-SV-structure errors	Total			
Before parsing	119	166	285	222	99	606
After parsing	72	71	143	199	60	402
The reduction	47	95	144	23	39	204
The reduced percentage	39.5 %	57.2 %	50.5 %	10.4 %	49.4 %	33.7 %

together, which can strengthen syntactic and semantic constraint, thus largely eliminating ambiguity of phrases; secondly, that sentences are shortened after parsing also helps reduce incorrect lexical choices and omissions.

4.3 Correlation Between the NT Clause Number in a Sentence and the Error Number in Its Whole-Sentence Translation

Based on preliminary observation of machine translated results, we predict that machine translation has a better performance in short sentences than in long sentences. In order to verify this predication, we analyze data of the number of NT clauses in English sentences and the distribution of errors among them respectively. The following line chart shows the relationship between these two variables.

In Fig. 13, the horizontal axis represents the numbers of NT clauses in sentences and numbers in brackets represent the total amount of sentences which contain each number of NT clauses in our investigation. The vertical axis represents the average number of errors. So the line in the figure represents the correlation between the number of NT clauses and the average number of errors in sentences. The line shows a positive correlation between these two variables when the number of NT clauses ranges from 1 to 5 in sentences, which is consistent with our predication.

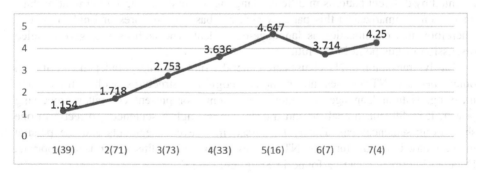

Fig. 13. Correlation between the NT clause number in a sentence and the error number in its whole-sentence translation

The line in Fig. 13 shows that errors occurring in sentences with 6–7 NT clauses are less than errors in sentences with 4–5 NT clauses, which apparently contradicts with our previous predication. As to causes for this phenomena, we think that compared with sentences containing 1–5 NT clauses, the number of sentences with 6–7 NT clauses is too small to be used as statistics data. Deeper causes for this phenomena need further studies.

5 Discussion

This paper applied the theory of NT clauses to the analysis of results of English-Chinese machine translation, and conclusions are made as follows.

Firstly, the majority of errors in machine translation is structural errors. These structural errors mainly exist in non-SV clauses including non-adjacent subject-predicate structures and adjacent or non-adjacent non-subject-predicate structures.

Secondly, as non-SV structures exist largely in long English sentences, so the above conclusion reveals the cause for the bottleneck of English long-sentence translation. Furthermore, the conclusion above suggests that English long sentences should be parsed into NT clauses before being translated. The suggested model has been proposed by Song and Ge [3], and examples in Sect. 3 and data in Sect. 4 of this paper support the suggestion. Definitely parsing long sentences of English will bring loss, and assembling NT clauses of Chinese into Chinese text after translation will also bring loss. These losses are not discussed in the paper. However, firstly parsing and assembling are tasks made in monolingual category, so their difficulties are apparently lower than tasks made in bilingual category; secondly, as NT clauses are generally simple and short and if units in training corpus are all NT clauses, the quality of clause translation is expected to be further improved. Therefore, this model is worthy of further exploration.

Thirdly, the relationship between naming and telling, based on cognitive structures, is common to human language. All languages may be parsed into sequences of NT clauses according to relationships of naming and telling. On this point, the method adopted in this paper is language-independent. However, naming and telling are represented by different patterns in different languages. Eight naming-telling relationships have been summarized in this paper, which are based on features of English syntax. Therefore, this classification is language-dependent. The authors will give detailed discussion of this point in the future.

Lastly, translation of NT clauses are generally (not absolutely) independent of each other, because NT clauses are complete cognitive structures with self-sufficient meaning. Natural language is context dependent. For present computer processing power, it is difficult to analyze and translate long English sentences correctly in one shot. Long sentences can usually be parsed into several segments and the parsing method based on structures of NT clauses advocated in this paper is appropriate. Detailed information can be found in Song and Ge [3].

Acknowledgements. This research is supported by the 2016 Key Project of the National Languages Committee (ZDI135-30), Innovative School Project in Higher Education of Guangdong, China (GWTP-LH-2015-10), the Science and Technology Project of Guangdong Province, China (2016A040403113), National Natural Science Foundation of China (61171129) and the fund of Center for Translation Studies, Guangdong University of Foreign Studies (CTS2014-13).

References

1. Koehn, P.: Statistic Machine Translation. Publishing House of Electronic Industry, Beijing (2012). (Trans. by Zong, C., Zhang, X.)
2. Zhao, H., Xie, J., Lv, Y., Yu, H., Zhang, H., Liu, Q.: Common error analysis of machine translation output. In: The Ninth China Workshop on Machine Translation, Kunming (2013)
3. Song, R., Ge, S.: English-Chinese translation unit and translation model for discourse-based machine translation. J. Chin. Inf. Process. **29**, 125–135 (2015)
4. Song, R.: Stream model of generalized topic structure in Chinese text. Chin. Lang. **6**, 483–494 (2013)

I Can Guess What You Mean: A Monolingual Query Enhancement for Machine Translation

Chenxi Pang[1,2], Hai Zhao[1,2(✉)], and Zhongyi Li[1,2]

[1] Department of Computer Science and Engineering,
Shanghai Jiao Tong University, Shanghai 200240, China
{pangchenxi,rival2710}@sjtu.edu.cn, zhaohai@cs.sjtu.edu.cn
[2] Key Laboratory of Shanghai Education Commission for Intelligent Interaction
and Cognitive Engineering, Shanghai Jiao Tong University, Shanghai 200240, China

Abstract. We introduce a monolingual query method with additional webpage data to improve the translation quality for more and more official use requirement of statistical machine translation outputs. The motivation behind this method is that we can improve the readability of sentence once for all if we replace translation sentences with the most related sentences generated by human. Based on vector space representations for translated sentences, we perform a query on search engine for additional reference text data. Then we rank all translation sentences to make necessary replacement from the query results. Various vector representations for sentence, TFIDF, latent semantic indexing, and neural network word embedding, are conducted and the experimental results show an alternative solution to enhance the current machine translation with a performance improvement about 0.5 BLEU in French-to-English task and 0.7 BLEU in English-to-Chinese task.

1 Introduction

Research on statistical machine translation (SMT) has achieved remarkable progress on various ways [1–15]. Huge effort has been paid to improve quality and confidence of translation sentences to make them more similar to human translation. These works include automatic translation quality measure [16–18], preordering [19–21], neural network based SMT training and decoding [22–25]. However, most SMT system outputs can only serve as an assistant role for nearly all applications even though many translation sentences may be amazingly and natively accurate. For most cases, people can guess what the translation outputs mean, but feel hard to officially use them in any way. Here is a translation

H. Zhao—This paper was partially supported by Cai Yuanpei Program (CSC No. 201304490199 and No. 201304490171), National Natural Science Foundation of China (No. 61170114 and No. 61272248), National Basic Research Program of China (No. 2013CB329401), Major Basic Research Program of Shanghai Science and Technology Committee (No. 15JC1400103), Art and Science Interdisciplinary Funds of Shanghai Jiao Tong University (No. 14JCRZ04), and Key Project of National Society Science Foundation of China (No. 15-ZDA041).

© Springer International Publishing AG 2016
M. Sun et al. (Eds.): CCL and NLP-NABD 2016, LNAI 10035, pp. 50–63, 2016.
DOI: 10.1007/978-3-319-47674-2_5

example in Table 1. Without knowing any knowledge about the source language or source sentence, readers can easily guess the true meaning of the translation sentence despite it is not a perfect sentence and such a guess indeed matches the true meaning of the respective source sentence.

Table 1. A translation example

source sentence	我会在明天之前完成要求的任务
machine translation	*I'll be tomorrow before the completion of the tasks required*
human translation	*I will finish the required task by tomorrow.*

The example in Table 1 shows that there is still a gap between machine translation and human translation that results in machine translation sentence can not be officially used. At least, to our best knowledge, no reports are obtained to show that there is an application case for official use of SMT outputs, such as this paper itself being fully translated from its Chinese source only using an SMT system but without any human polishing Work (We cannot run such a risk!). It is even worse that the gap will still exist in the near future. As the current research on SMT is not likely to reach such an ideal aim to eliminate the gap, we propose to directly use human-generated sentences to replace those poorly translated ones. The motivation can be explained still from the above example in Table 1, if one can speculate the meaning of a sentence with improper word order or word usage, then it is quite possible to retrieve more accurate or authentic expression from a human-generated text dataset, only if it is large enough. Such a database will be referred to the relevant dataset hereafter in this paper.

In this work, we use the retrieval results from web search engine as search engine database is supposed to be the largest corpus that computational linguistician can ever find. However, our preliminary experiments show that even the most powerful search engine would fail to provide sufficient text data for every sentences in this task. Therefore we will limit our process only to a small number of machine translation sentences that are much more possible to find matching sentences in the retrieval results.

A lot of works are about post editing and even manual labor is used to produce better quality machine translations. Both rule-based and statistical automatic post editing methods have been proposed over the years [26–32], but most of them focus on evaluating a specific method and have a common trait that the reported methods are only suitable for very limited cases. There are two major differences between this work and all previous post-editing like methods. The first is that there is no any 'editing' operation inside our work, our approach just makes full replacement for a translated sentence if necessary. The second is that our method does not rely on the source side of machine translation and any specific language characteristics, which has been an obvious advantage other than all previous methods. In fact, all relevant data are automatically retrieved from web search engine. All languages are treated equally without discrimination so it has the potential to be generally used.

2   Our Model

Searching from the Internet for each translation sentence output by an SMT system, we look forward to finding a well-formed sentence that expresses the same or similar meaning. Usually, these translation sentences may be quite long and few retrieval results will return as searching all words inside them. Therefore instead of full long sentence replacing, we separate sentences that have few retrieval results into short ones and then carry out replacing based on these shorter sentences. All our later process will be based on translation sentences and these short sentences, which will be referred to *segments* hereafter.

After stop words are filtered out, all words in each sentence or segment will be separately put into search engine to collect returned webpages and a relevant sentence dataset S will be obtained by putting all sentences inside webpages together. We also build a relevant segment dataset SG by spliting all sentence in dataset S into segments and let W denote the set of all word types in S. Every sentence will be compared to the sentence in S to find the most similar sentence for possible whole sentence replacement at first, and every segment in the sentence will be compared to the segment in SG for possible segment replacement of the sentence if the previous process fails to achieve a reasonable result.

Vector space model (VSM) is a classical tool for representing text as a vector. For a sentence $s_i = w_1 w_2 ... w_m$ in S, its vector representation v_i is:

$$v_i = (v_{i1}, v_{i2}, ..., v_{in}),$$

and each dimension v_{ij} is related to a separate word. The value of v_{ij} in the vector is non-zero if w_i occurs in the segment. We consider a typical similarity or distance measures between vectors, Euclidean, as the following:

$$sim_2(x, y) = \sqrt{\sum_{i=1}^{n}(x_i - y_i)^2} \qquad (1)$$

There are multiple strategies to build sentence vector from word vectors. The following will give a list of vector representation formalizations for sentences and segments, including TFIDF, Latent Semantic Indexing and Neural network word embedding.

2.1   TFIDF

TFIDF, short for term frequency-inverse document frequency, is a numerical statistic to indicate how important a word is to a document in a collection or corpus. The TFIDF value increases proportionally to the number of times a word appears in the document, but is offset by the frequency of the word in the corpus, which helps to adjust for the fact that some words appear more frequently in general. The obvious shortcoming of TFIDF is the ignorance of word order information is ignored.

We use the following detailed formalizations to calculate TFIDF value of word w_i in sentence s_j, where $count_{s_j}(w_i)$ is how many times word w_i occurs in sentence s_j, $|s_j|$ is the sentence length or the number of words inside sentence s_j, $|s|$ is the sentence size and $count_s(w_i)$ is the number of sentences that contains word w_i.

$$TF = \frac{count_{s_j}(w_i)}{|s_j|}, \tag{2}$$

$$IDF = \log(\frac{|s|}{count_s(w_i) + 1}), \tag{3}$$

$$TFIDF = TF \cdot IDF \tag{4}$$

For each sentence, we construct a one-hot vector with its TFIDF values. To make the representation more smoothing, we set an empirical threshold, TFIDF values below this threshold will be forced to set to zero and dismissed. Then we select part of remain words in the sentence to construct TFIDF vector of the sentence.

2.2 Latent Semantic Indexing

Latent semantic indexing (LSI) or latent semantic analysis (LSA) is an indexing and retrieval method that uses singular value decomposition (SVD) to identify patterns in the relationships between terms and concepts contained in an unstructured collection of text [33]. LSI is based on the principle that words that are used in the same contexts tend to have similar meanings. A key feature of LSI is its ability to extract the conceptual content of text by establishing associations between those words that occur in similar contexts.

The LSI model for this work will be based on our previous TFIDF vectors. The initial matrix for LSI is from all sentences of S in which the i-th column is TFIDF vector of i-th sentence. Then SVD is used to obtain vectors with certain number of topics, which will be regarded as sentence vectors.

2.3 NN Word Embedding

In recent works, learning vector representations of words using neural network has been proved effective for various natural language processing tasks. Mikolov proposed two models, Continuous Bag-of-Words Model (CBOW) and Continuous Skip-gram Model (Skip-gram), for computing continuous vector representations of words from very large data sets by using efficient NNs without hidden layer [34,35]. After the model is trained, the word vectors are supposed to be mapped into a vector space, semantically similar words have similar vector representations and their word vector have a similar position in the vector space.

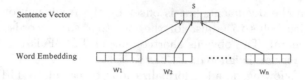

Fig. 1. A framework for learning sentence vector without word order information.

Sentence Representation Without Word Order Information. After we have vector representations for each word in sentence our task is to compare different sentence pairs, we need to consider how to combine word vectors for sentence representation and model sentence at last. The most intuitive method is to sum or calculate average of all the word vectors in the sentence[1].

$$v_s = \sum_{k=1}^{n} tfidf_{w_k} \cdot v_{w_k} \tag{5}$$

Figure 1 just illustrates such a simple strategy that utilizes the TFIDF weighted average of all word vectors as sentence vector, where n is number of words in sentence, and $tfidf_{w_k}$ is the corresponding TFIDF values.

Note that all the above process can be either applied to sentences or segments so that we can obtain vector representations for both. Once sentence or segment vector has been computed, their similarity or distance can be directly computed through predefined measures.

Segment Vector with Sentence Context. Besides the above word order free integration from word vectors, we still consider an effective method that may introduce useful word order information for sentence vector building. The motivation is simple, as machine translation system outputs sentences according to target language model constraints, the original word order in the translated sentences should still make sense to some extent. Therefore our exact query purpose is to find a human-generated sentence that has the most word overlapping and least word order change compared to the original machine translation sentence.

Le and Mikolov [37] proposed an unsupervised learning algorithm that learns vector representations for variable length pieces of texts by adding paragraph vector as an additional feature for the word embedding learning framework, which has shown effective in text classification and sentiment analysis tasks. The paragraph vector and word vectors are averaged or concatenated to predict the next word given many contexts sampled from the paragraph.

Figure 2 illustrates Le and Mikolov's method, which is adopted for our task. The sentence vector will be integrated into the word embedding learning.

---

[1] We are aware that there are many other effective method such as [36] who used a parse tree and matrix-vector operations to retain word order information. However, this work is about machine translation sentence processing, we need robust and simple strategy to handle various possible defective sentences.

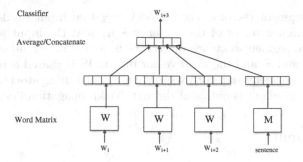

Fig. 2. Word embedding incorporated with sentence vector.

Every sentence sen_j is mapped to unique vector, represented by a column in a matrix M. The column is indexed by the position of the sentence in the relevant sentence dataset S. Every word is also mapped to a unique vector, represented by a column in a matrix W. The column is indexed by position of the word in the vocabulary. The sentence vector and word vectors are averaged or concatenated to predict the next word given many contexts sampled from the sentence.

However, while applying this method to segments we still lose the contextual information of other segments in the same sentence. Therefore we propose a combinational approach to help ease such a drawback by adding a sentence vector for segment vector learning as shown in Fig. 3.

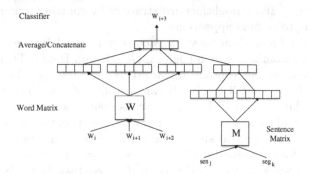

Fig. 3. Integrating sentence vector for learning segment vector. The input words (w_i, w_{i+1}, w_{i+2}) are mapped to columns of the matrix W and input sentence (sen_j) and segment (seg_k) are mapped to vectors via matrix M. The segment vector acts as a memory of what missing from the current context and the sentence vector acts as a memory that remembers what missing from other segments.

Segment and sentence vectors are weighted averaged to a context vector to contribute to the prediction task of the next word:

$$v = \alpha v_{seg_k} + (1 - \alpha)v_{sen_j} \tag{6}$$

where v_{seg_k} is segment vector of the segment seg_k that input words are located and v_{sen_j} is sentence vector of the sentence sen_j that the input segment seg_k are located. The segment-sentence matrix M is shared across all segments and sentence in SG and S, and the word vector matrix W is shared across all words in W. Sentence, segment and word vectors are trained using stochastic gradient descent and the gradient is obtained through backpropagation [38].

3   Experiments

3.1   Experimental Settings

We conduct experiments on the French-to-English translation task. The baselines of the IWSLT2014 evaluation campaign are followed. The dataset with $186k$ sentence pairs are used to train a phrase-based MT system, and dev2010 and tst2010 are selected as development data and evaluation data. We also conduct experiments on the English-to-Chinese machine translation tasks. MultiUN parallel corpus [39,40] with $200k$ sentence pairs is used to train a phrase-based MT system. We run GIZA++ [41] on the training corpus in both directions [42] to obtain the word alignment for each sentence pair and MERT [43] for tuning on the development data. Using the SRILM Toolkits [44] with interpolated Kneser-Ney smoothing, we train a 5-gram language model for the tasks on the target side of its training data. In our experiments, the translation performances are measured by case-sensitive BLEU4 metric with a single reference.

There are many methods to separate sentence to segments (short sentences)[2], We adopt a simply and straightforward strategy by splitting sentence into segments according to comma appearance.

We retrieve 500 records at most for each sentence and 1000 records at most for each segment from two search engines, Google and Baidu. Then we remove all sentences that do not contain any word in the sentence. Our preliminary experiments indicate that if the Euclidean distance of two 100-dimension sentence vectors is larger than 2, then these two sentences are nearly irrelevant. So after filtering out all these sentences, we put all the rest sentences together as our relevant sentence dataset and split all sentences into segments as our relevant segment dataset for later process. There are many ways of word segmentation [47] and two different ways are used in English-to-Chinese task for these Chinese sentence corpus and datasets, one is done by Stanford Word Segmenter [48,49] and another is done by trivially splitting each character into single-character words.

We construct a 20 dimension vector for both TFIDF and LSI model. Word embedding is done on both English and Chinese Wikipedia corpus via CBOW model. 5 previous words and 5 next words are used as context and corresponding vectors are concatenated to predict the next word. Each word is projected to

---

[2] A sophisticated approach is cutting sentence into several relative independent parts according to parse tree of sentence [45,46], which can be regarded as a further improvement over the current simple segmentation strategy.

a 100-dimension vector and all sentences and segments are also mapped to a 100-dimension vector.

In the replacement process, we use the following formalization:

$$P_{sen} = \log(\prod_{i=1}^{t} p(w_i|w_{i-4}w_{i-3}w_{i-2}w_{i-1})) \tag{7}$$

to calculate the 5-gram value of all the translation sentences, where $p(w_i|w_{i-4}...w_{i-1})$ is the conditional probability of w_i given previous four words. Intuitively, the higher the 5-gram language model score is, the better the translation sentence is. Therefore we only focus on those sentences with language model scores lower than -1.3 (it is empirically determined according to BLEU scores over development set) and replacement operations will be only done over them.

3.2 Results

The experiments are done as we measure the similarity between sentences and then proceed replacement. For Euclidean distance, we set a threshold value of sentence similarity from 0 to 2 with interval 0.5 and sentences will be adopted only if the similarity is lower than the threshold. Too high Euclidean distance threshold will let too many sentences replaced, even some already very good sentences, while too low Euclidean distance threshold will result in no replacement of sentence. For Euclidean distance, the smaller the distance is, the higher similarity between sentences is. The results are given in Table 2.

Table 2. BLEU scores in terms of Euclidean distance, where WE and SEG-SEN correspond to word-embedding and segment-sentence respectively.

Word vector	Sentence vector	French-to-English					English-to-Chinese				
		0	0.5	1.0	1.5	2.0	0	0.5	1.0	1.5	2.0
TFIDF		31.82	**31.89**	30.68	27.58	26.51	26.46	**26.51**	25.38	21.77	18.46
LSI		31.82	**31.93**	30.77	27.72	26.59	26.46	**26.59**	25.41	22.63	18.65
WE	TFIDF-weight	31.82	**32.22**	31.91	29.07	28.26	26.46	**26.85**	26.52	23.81	21.46
WE	SEG-SEN	31.82	**32.34**	32.08	30.25	28.63	26.46	**27.03**	26.85	23.89	22.05

We compare the results from different vector representations with the baseline in terms of BLEU scores. It is well known that the translation quality of MT system highly depends on the language model and MT systems could generate very good translations if there is a strong LM. Original translation sentence have already preserve enough semantic and word order information. However in our TFIDF model, we only focus on word occurrence and ignore all of these information. As shown in Table 3, when we try to remain some useful semantic information in our LSI model, we can improve translation quality slightly. In our word embedding model, we suppose to preserve both semantic and word order

Table 3. Comparisions among different similarity calculation methods. BLEU score is the best result of corresponding method.

Word vector	Sentence vector	French-to-English	English-to-Chinese
TFIDF		**31.89**	**26.51**
LSI		**31.93**	**26.59**
Word embedding	TFIDF-weight	**32.22**	**26.85**
Word embedding	Sengment-sentence	**32.34**	**27.03**
Baseline		**31.82**	**26.46**

information that contained in translation sentence by adding sentence into our word embedding framework.

Our experiments indicate that our word embedding models outperform traditional model and achieve a better translation quality. Word embedding with both segment and sentence is better than sentence representation without word order information as it supposed to remain word and segment order information. An improvement in BLEU score also proves that our model successes in preserving semantic and order information of translation sentence and the refined sentences preserve the same meaning of the original one from another aspect.

We also investigate the impact of different Chinese word segmentation over the SMT performance. Table 4 indicates that single-character segmentation slightly outperforms Stanford Word Segmenter and achieve about 0.1 BLEU score improvement in word embedding with segment-sentence method. Here, single character segmentation means just trivially segment each Chinese character as a word without truly considering they are words.

The improvement over BLEU scores indicates that the corresponding sentence replacement is helpful, and the returned sentences have successfully approached the meaning of those corresponding translation sentences as BLEU score improvement has demonstrated that the returned sentences are more closed to the reference sentence than the respective translation sentence.

Table 4. Comparisions among different word segmentation methods. BLEU score is the best result of corresponding method with Euclidean distance.

Word vector	Sentence vector	Standford-word-segmenter	Single-character-segmenter
TFIDF		**26.51**	**26.33**
LSI		**26.59**	**26.47**
Word embedding	TFIDF-weight	**26.85**	**26.89**
Word embedding	Sengment-sentence	**27.03**	**27.13**
Baseline		**26.46**	

3.3 Discussion

Our experiment has processed about 13 % and 15 % translation sentences in French-to-English and English-to-Chinese experiment, about 9 % and 10 % among them are originally the same as human translation sentences, the reference sentence is exactly the same as the returned results by search engines. However, we have set a good start, for all these processed sentences, they can be officially used in any way only if we carefully limit the processed sentences onto a small range to guarantee the accuracy. With the process of the proposed method, we have automatically put all machine translation sentences into two parts, one part is still from SMT system outputs, but the other part is right from human translation. If we can access larger and larger relevant dataset such as much more webpages crawled by search engines, then we can enlarge the portion of human translation part more and more.

The above has already shown that our process brings about BLEU improvement, but our work is more than the higher score, as we introduce human-generated sentences to replace those poorly machine translations. As well known, BLEU score is more reliable a metric only for lower quality translation matching. Effective and accurate translation for one source sentence can be multiple. We observe all non-reference-matching replacements by our model, they are exactly accurate translation for the corresponding source sentences. However, BLEU scores for these part are not 100 % as it simply gives matching rate on n-grams but not semantic equivalence.

The following shows a series examples how our model replaces and improves those machine translation sentences. Sometimes, our methods are lucky enough as the example in Table 5. The search engine just returns exactly the same sentence as the reference sentence, which has been shown 2/3 replacements are so lucky. Of course, this also shows that both the selected search engine and our query methods work effectively so that they can jointly return the right reference sentences.

However, it is impossible to always retrieve reference sentence for every machine translation sentence. Many times, our methods just come up with a sentence quite similar with translation sentence. Table 6 demonstrates such a case. It is actually very hard for readers to understand the meaning of machine translation sentence which suffers from unrecognized word order and out-of-vocabulary word (OOV) problem.

The proposed method is an approximate search, so it is quite robust for such malfunctions inside machine translation sentences. The result shown in Table 6 just demonstrates that OOV word has been perfectly handled according to the query-replacement process in an English-to-Chinese translation example.

Readers can guess the general meaning of the translation sentence from words contained in the sentence, but can not understand its full true meaning or convince that this is a complete sentence. However, this difficulty can be partially solved by our methods and Table 7 shows such a translation example. Our methods find a segment from our relevant segment dataset that is semantically similar with the second segment of translation sentence and also a segment that is the

Table 5. A-hole-in-one example. Underlines indicates words that are improperly translated. For words in translation and retrieval sentences, the same color and font indicate that the translation is nearly exactas the alignment part in reference sentence, while the same color but different font indicate closed but inaccurate meaning that are translated.

	French-to-English	English-to-Chinese
source sentence	*la plupart sont complètement ignorés par notre ' moi du souvenir ' .*	*Namibia will deal with perpetrators of terrorist acts according to the ordinary criminal law.*
translation sentence	most are completely ignored by our ' me the memory . '	纳米比亚 将 涉及 普通 刑法 的 恐怖 行为 的 实施者 。
reference sentence	most of them are completely ignored by the remembering self .	纳米比亚 将 根据 一般 刑法 处理 从事 恐怖 行为者 。
retrieval sentence	most of them are completely ignored by the remembering self .	纳米比亚 将 根据 一般 刑法 处理 从事 恐怖 行为者 。

Table 6. A standard replace, similar but different, where OOV words are well handled.

	French-to-English	English-to-Chinese
source sentence	*c'est très difficile d'évaluer correctement son bien-être . j'espère vous avoir montré combien cela est difficile .*	*the production of sanitary napkins, another basic reproductive health commodity, is also hampered by restrictions on imports of raw materials.*
translation sentence	it's very difficult to evaluate properly its well-being . I hope I've shown you how much this is hard .	另 一 个 基本 生殖 保健 商品 ， 也受到限制， 卫生 napkins 的 生产 原料 进口 。
reference sentence	it is very difficult to think straight about well-being , and I hope I have given you a sense of how difficult it is .	另外 一 种 基本 的 生殖 健康 商品 ， 即 卫生巾 的 生产 也 由于 原料 的 进口 受到 限制 而 遭到 损害 。
retrieval sentence	it's very difficult to *evaluate its well-being properly* . I hope I've *shown you how hard it is.*	另 一 种 基本 生殖 保健 用品 卫生巾 的 生产 也 由于 对 原材料 进口 的 限制 而 受到 影响 。

same as the first translation sentence segment. Even through our retrieval sentence is not completely the same with reference sentence, but it has been easy enough to let readers full understand the sentence. In fact, the returned sentence is semantically consistent with the source sentence.

We also find that our methods perform well in some English-to-Chinese translation sentences that need reordering. As shown in Table 8, the only difference between machine translation sentence and reference sentence is word order. Though failing to make the foreign name translation, our retrieval sentence successfully recovers the right word order for target language.

Table 7. An example about incomplete translation.

source sentence	*presque toutes les techniques pour produire aujourd'hui de l'électricité , en dehors desénergies renouvelables et du nucléaire , rejettent du CO2 .*	*Cuba has been engaged in a process of institutional and economic reforms for almost 10 years now.*
translation sentence	*almost all the techniques to* produce today of electricity , *outside of renewable energies and nuclear , dismiss CO2 .*	近 10 年 来 ， 古巴 一直 在 **体制 的 进程** 和 经济 改革 。
reference sentence	almost every way we make electricity today , except for the emerging renewables and nuclear , puts out CO2 .	古巴 进行 体制 改革 和 经济 改革 迄今 已 差不多 十 年 。
retrieval sentence	*almost all the techniques to produce electricity today ,* except renewable energies and nuclear , *dismiss CO2 .*	近 10 年 来 ， 古巴 一直 在 **实行** 体制 改革 和 经济 的 改革 。

Table 8. An example for word reording.

source sentence	*Samuel Zbogar, Secretary of State, Ministry of Foreign Affairs of Slovenia*
translation sentence	Samuel Zbogar 外交部 国务 秘书 斯洛文尼亚
reference sentence	斯洛文尼亚 外交部 国务 秘书 塞缪尔·日博加尔
retrieval sentence	斯洛文尼亚 外交部 国务 秘书 Samuel Zbogar

4 Conclusion

We have proposed a simple and effective method to enhance machine translation by replacing them with human translation sentences and expect to make them available for later official use. Our relevant sentences are queried from search engine and TFIDF, LSI, NN word embedding and specially designed segment vectors are used to calculate the similarity between sentences. The results show that our approach indeed gives better translation performance. In addition, this work shows a convenient start to improve the quality of machine translation by the roots.

References

1. Huang, S., Chen, H., Dai, X.-Y., Chen, J.: Non-linear learning for statistical machine translation. In: ACL, pp. 825–835 (2015)
2. Yu, H., Zhu, X.: Recurrent neural network based rule sequence model for statistical machine translation. In: ACL, pp. 132–138 (2015)

3. Lu, S., Chen, Z., Xu, B.: Learning new semi-supervised deep auto-encoder features for statistical machine translation. In: ACL, pp. 122–132 (2014)
4. Xiong, D., Zhang, M.: A sense-based translation model for statistical machine translation. In: ACL, pp. 1459–1469 (2014)
5. Neubig, G., Duh, K.: On the elements of an accurate tree-to-string machine translation system. In: ACL, pp. 143–149 (2014)
6. Riezler, S., Simianer, P., Haas, C.: Response-based learning for grounded machine translation. In: ACL, pp. 881–891 (2014)
7. Wang, R., Zhao, H., Lu, B.-L.: Bilingual continuous-space language model growing for statistical machine translation, pp. 1209–1220. IEEE (2015)
8. Zhang, J., Utiyama, M., Sumita, E., Zhao, H.: Learning local word reorderings for hierarchical phrase-based statistical machine translation. Mach. Transl. 1–18 (2016)
9. Wang, R., Utiyama, M., Goto, I., Sumita, E., Zhao, H., Lu, B.-L.: Converting continuous-space language models into N-gram language models with efficient bilingual pruning for statistical machine translation. ACM (2016)
10. Wang, R., Zhao, H., Ploux, S., Lu, B.-L., Utiyama, M.: A Bilingual Graph-Based Semantic Model for Statistical Machine Translation
11. Zang, S., Zhao, H., Wu, C., Wang, R.: A novel word reordering method for statistical machine translation. In: FSKD, pp. 843–848 (2015)
12. Zhang, J., Utiyama, M., Sumita, E., Zhao, H.: Learning word reorderings for hierarchical phrase-based statistical machine translation. In: ACL-IJCNLP, pp. 542–548 (2015)
13. Wang, R., Zhao, H., Lu, B.-L., Utiyama, M., Sumita, E.: Neural network based bilingual language model growing for statistical machine translation. In: EMNLP, pp. 189–195 (2014)
14. Zhang, J., Utiyama, M., Sumita, E., Zhao, H.: Learning hierarchical translation spans. In: EMNLP, pp. 183–188 (2014)
15. Wang, R., Utiyama, M., Goto, I., Sumita, E., Zhao, H., Lu, B.-L.: Converting continuous-space language models into N-gram language models for statistical machine translation. In: EMNLP, pp. 845–850 (2013)
16. Papineni, K., Roukos, S., Ward, T., Zhu, W.-J.: BLEU: a method for automatic evaluation of machine translation. In: ACL, pp. 311–318 (2002)
17. Guzmán, F., Joty, S., Màrquez, L., Nakov, P.: Pairwise neural machine translation evaluation. In: ACL, pp. 805–814 (2015)
18. Graham, Y.: Improving evaluation of machine translation quality estimation. In: ACL, pp. 1804–1813 (2015)
19. Miceli-Barone, A.V., Attardi, G.: Non-projective dependency-based pre-reordering with recurrent neural network for machine translation. In: ACL, pp. 846–856 (2015)
20. Zhang, J., Utiyama, M., Sumita, E., Zhao, H.: Learning word reorderings for hierarchical phrase-based statistical machine translation. In: ACL, pp. 542–548 (2015)
21. Nakagawa, T.: Efficient top-down BTG parsing for machine translation preordering. In: ACL, pp. 208–218 (2015)
22. Bengio, Y., Ducharme, R., Vincent, P., Jauvin, C.: A neural probabilistic language model. JMLR **3**, 1137–1155 (2003)
23. Vaswani, A., Zhao, Y., Fossum, V., Chiang, D.: Decoding with large-scale neural language models improves translation. In: EMNLP, pp. 1387–1392 (2013)
24. Devlin, J., Zbib, R., Huang, Z., Lamar, T., Schwartz, R., Makhoul, J.: Fast and robust neural network joint models for statistical machine translation. In: ACL, pp. 1370–1380 (2014)

25. Liu, S., Yang, N., Li, M., Zhou, M.: A recursive recurrent neural network for statistical machine translation. In: ACL, pp. 1491–1500 (2014)

26. Simard, M., Ueffing, N., Isabelle, P., Kuhn, R.: Rule-based translation with statistical phrase-based post-editing. In: SMT, pp. 203–206 (2007)

27. Dugast, L., Senellart, J., Koehn, P.: Statistical post-editing on SYSTRAN's rule-based translation system. In: SMT, pp. 220–223 (2007)

28. Simard, M., Goutte, C., Isabelle, P.: Statistical phrase-based post-editing. In: NAACL, pp. 508–515 (2007)

29. Isabelle, P., Goutte, C., Simard, M.: Domain adaptation of MT systems through automatic post-editing. In: MT Summit, pp. 255–261 (2007)

30. Lagarda, A.-L., Alabau, V., Casacuberta, F., Silva, R., Diaz-de-Liano, E.: Statistical post-editing of a rule-based machine translation system. In: ACL, pp. 217–220 (2009)

31. Béchara, H., Ma, Y., van Genabith, J.: Statistical post-editing for a statistical MT system. In: MT Summit, pp. 308–315 (2011)

32. Huang, Z., Devlin, J., Matsoukas, S.: BBN's Systems for the Chinese-English Subtask of the NTCIR-10 PatentMT Evaluation

33. Deerwester, S.S., Dumals, T., Furnas, G.W., Landauer, T.K., Harshman, R.: Indexing by Latent semantic analysis. JASIS **41**, 391–407 (1990)

34. Tomas, M., Chen, K., Corrado, G., Dean, J.: Efficient Estimation of Word Representations in Vector Space (2013). arXiv preprint arXiv:1301.3781

35. Mikolov, T., Sutskever, I., Chen, K., Corrado, G.S., Dean, J.: Distributed representations of words and phrases and their compositionality. In: NIPS, pp. 3111–3119 (2013)

36. Huang, E., Socher, R., Manning, C., Ng, A.: Improving word representations via global context and multiple word prototypes. In: ACL, pp. 873–882 (2012)

37. Le, Q.V., Tomas, M.: Distributed representations of sentences and documents. Eprint Arxiv, pp. 1188–1196 (2014)

38. Werbos, P.J.: Backpropagation through time: what it does and how to do it, pp. 1550–1560. IEEE (1990)

39. Eisele, A., Chen, Y.: MultiUN: a multilingual corpus from United Nation documents. In: LREC, pp. 2868–2872 (2010)

40. Tiedemann, J.: Parallel data, tools and interfaces in OPUS. In: LREC (2012)

41. Och, F.J., Ney, H.: A systematic comparison of various statistical alignment models. Comput. Linguist. **29**(1), 19–51 (2003)

42. Koehn, P.F., Och, J., Marcu, D.: Statistical phrase-based translation. In: NAACL, pp. 127–133 (2003)

43. Och, F.J.: Minimum error rate training in statistical machine translation. In: ACL, pp. 701–711 (2003)

44. Stolcke, A.: SRILM - an extensible language modeling toolkit. In: ICSLP, pp. 901–904 (2002)

45. Soricut, R., Marcu, D.: Sentence level discourse parsing using syntactic and lexical information. In: ACL, pp. 149–156 (2003)

46. Zhang, Z., Zhao, H., Qin, L.: Probabilistic graph-based dependency parsing with convolutional neural network. In: ACL, pp. 1382–1392 (2016)

47. Cai, D., Zhao, H.: Neural word segmentation learning for Chinese. In: ACL, pp. 409–420 (2016)

48. Tseng, H., Chang, P., Andrew, G.: A conditional random field word segmenter. In: SIGHAN, Daniel Jurafsky and Christopher Manning (2005)

49. Chang, P.-C., Galley, M., Manning, C.: Optimizing Chinese word segmentation for machine translation performance. In: WMT, pp. 224–232 (2008)

Keeping the Meanings of the Source Text: An Introduction to Yes Translate

Xiaoheng Zhang[(⊠)]

Department of Chinese and Bilingual Studies,
Hong Kong Polytechnic University, Kowloon, Hong Kong
ctxzhang@polyu.edu.hk

Abstract. The primary task of language translation is to faithfully pass the meaning(s) of the source text to the target language. Unfortunately, meanings often get lost or distorted in machine translation, including state-of-the-art Google Translate and Baidu Translate. Yes Translate is a Chinese-English translation tool to be maximally loyal to the source text while maintaining adequate fluency. This is implementable by avoiding risky actions of word deleting, adding and re-ordering. The tool is supported by an 116,000-words Dictionary. In an experiment on natural news articles freely selected by themselves, 10 postgraduate students with good command of Chinese and English all agreed or strongly agreed that the general meaning of the translation by Yes Translate was correct and understandable. And 9 out of the 10 students agreed or strongly agreed that the general meaning of each sentence was correct.

Keywords: Machine translation · Meanings · Yes translate · YES-CEDICT

1 Introduction

The basic goal of translation is to faithfully convey the intended meaning(s) of the author in one language to the reader in a different language. However, there is large room for improvement in this aspect in machine transition (MT) (Bhattacharyya 2015, p. 30), which is true even to the most popular and state-of-the-art systems such as Google Translate and Baidu Translate, as demonstrated by the following example.

The source text is a Chinese article from Yahoo News (Yahoo 2016). Due to limitation of space, only the title and one paragraph is presented here, as shown in Fig. 1.

English translations by Google and Baidu are shown in Figs. 2 and 3.

There are several problems in the translations.

(1) Loss of words and their meanings. For example, in Baidu's translation of the second sentence in the paragraph, Chinese word "符合" (in line with) in the source text is simply ignored. Another example is an error made by both Google and Baidu. The meaning of one of the two occurrences of word "難民" (refugee) in the original title is missing in the translation, while the function of the space in the Chinese title is also neglected, bringing more confusion to the reader.

© Springer International Publishing AG 2016
M. Sun et al. (Eds.): CCL and NLP-NABD 2016, LNAI 10035, pp. 64–75, 2016.
DOI: 10.1007/978-3-319-47674-2_6

教宗訪希臘難民營　帶走12敘利亞難民返梵蒂岡
星島日報 – 2016年4月17日星期日上午11:33.

...

教宗是於一星期前決定應梵蒂岡一名官員建議，收容3個敘利亞家庭。教宗解釋，他接納建議，是因為符合他到訪萊斯沃斯島的精神。他說：「這好比滴了一個水滴到大海，但這個小水滴已令到大海變得不一樣。」

...

Fig. 1. Source text in Chinese

Pope to visit Greece 12 Syrian refugees camps took back the Vatican
Sing Tao Daily - April 17, 2016 11:33 Sunday morning.

...

Vatican Pope decided should an official recommendation, accommodating three families in Syria a week ago. Pope explained that he accepted the proposal, because in line with the spirit of his visit Lesbos. He said: "It's like a drop of water onto the sea, but the sea have caused the water droplets become different."

...

Fig. 2. Translation by Google Translate (https://translate.google.com.hk/, May 28, 2016)

The Pope's visit to the Greek camp took 12 refugees from Syria back to the Vatican
Sing Tao Daily - April 17, 2016 Sunday morning 11:33.

...

The Pope is in a week before the decision should be a Vatican official suggested that the 3 Syria family housing. The Pope explained that he accepted the proposal because he visited with the spirit of lesbos. He said: "this is like a drop of water to the sea, but the small water droplets have made the sea become different. "

...

Fig. 3. Translation by Baidu Translate (http://translate.baidu.com/, May 28, 2016)

(2) Loss of the intended meaning of a word. For example, in the first sentence of Google's translation, when clicking word "should" on Google Translate, we can see that it corresponds to word "應" in the source text. That is obviously wrong translation. And, to make it worse, the correct translation (such as "accept") is not available on the candidate list. Baidu makes similar mistakes.

(3) Adding words with non-intended meanings. For example, in the title of the article, Google Translate added a "to" before "visit" to form "Pope to visit Greece…", meaning the visit was going to happen, while actually it had already happened. In addition, Google and Baidu both incorrectly use plural "droplets", while the source text indicates a single drop (by both 一個水滴 and 這個小水滴).

(4) Improper words order. For example, in the last sentence of Google's translation, improper movement of words has generated "but the sea have caused the water droplets become different", contrary to the intended meaning of "but the water droplet has caused the sea become different." of the source text. And in Google's translation of the title, "12 Syrian refugees" has been moved to a wrong location. The correct place is after "took". Google also incorrectly moved "Vatican" away from its modification of "an official" to modify the pope in the first sentence.

A post-edited version of the translation by Google is presented in Fig. 4.

> Pope visited Greece refugee camps and took 12 Syrian refugees back to the Vatican
> Sing Tao Daily - April 17, 2016 11:33 Sunday morning.
> ...
> Pope decided to accept a Vatican official's recommendation of accommodating three families from Syria a week ago. Pope explained that he accepted the proposal, because it was in line with the spirit of his visit to Lesbos. He said: "It's like a drop of water onto the sea, but the water droplet has caused the sea become different."
> ...

Fig. 4. A post-edited version of the translation by Google

In the following sections, we will introduce Yes Translate, a Chinese-English translation tool aiming to be maximally loyal to the meanings of the source text while maintaining adequate fluency, and be free from the above-mentioned problems.

2   System Design Considerations

The purpose is to build a Chinese-English bidirectional machine translation (MT) tool for general purposes. We selected English and Chinese because we are more familiar with these two languages and use them more frequently. According to the Internet World Stats (2016), English and Chinese are by far the two most popular languages on the Web. Their Internet users are 872,950,266 and 704,484,396 respectively, followed by a large gap before the 3rd-place Spanish with 256,787,878 users. We are working on Chinese-to-English translation first because a large Chinese-English dictionary of over 110,000 words and phrases is available (Zhang et al. 2015).

Keeping source text meanings in machine translation is implementable by avoiding risky actions of word deleting, adding and re-ordering, and by employing more reliable methods.

Every word in the source text will be taken into consideration, not ignored without good reasons. For the example of the previous section, the meanings of word "符合" (in line with) and all uses of "難民" (refugee) will be kept in the translation, while the function of the space in the Chinese title is kept as a mark between two phrases.

All possible meanings and functions of a word or phrase will be maintained. For the example of word "應", in addition to "should", "accept" is added to the translation candidate list. Possible translations of a word will be sorted according to frequency of use. For example, in CC-CEDICT, the first sense/definition of 届 is "arrive". However, on corpus 现代汉语语料库 (http://www.cncorpus.org/index.aspx), the first 20 entries of the concordance are all in the form of "第 (number) 届". Hence we should put its corresponding English translation to the top. We need a frequency list of each meaning (or translation) of each word (translation unit). And if the context is also considered, the correctness rate may be further improved. For example, word "将" has two frequently used functions of "representing a future tense" and "indicating the following is the object of an action". From the Chinese corpus, we can see that if "将" is followed by a verb then "will" is a more possible translation, and object indicating is more likely when followed by a noun phrase. For example, "将吃完饭" and "将饭吃完" will be translated into "will finish eating food" and "(object:) food finish eating" respectively, while Google Translate output "The meal"(将吃完饭) and "will eat rice." (将饭吃完). That means optimization can be achieved using big data and other resources.

Addition of words or letters with non-intended meaning should be avoided. For the news article in Sect. 1, it is better not to add a "to" before "visit" in the title of the article, or add an "s" at the end of "droplet" in the last sentence.

Movement of words is not allowed when it may incorrectly change the meaning of the sentence. Then for the pope's news, we will have the correct translation of "but the water drop has caused the sea become different.", "took 12 Syrian refugees back to the Vatican" and "a Vatican official's recommendation". Moving a word or not may require different expressions. For example, Chinese word "之后" is often translated to "after" in English. Phrase "3年之后" is translated into "after 3 years". It involves moving word 之后 (after) to the front of 3年 (3 years), which may be risky for the computer if 3年 is replaced by a more complicated phrase. If the word is kept in its original position, then "3年之后我去英国 (after 3 years I went to UK)" will be translated into "3 years after I went to UK", which is more likely to mean "3 years after my going to UK". A safer option is to translate 之后 into "later" or "afterwards", or add a comma after "after", then "3年之后我去英国" will be translated into "3 years later I went to UK", "3 years afterwards I went to UK" or "3 years after, I went to UK", all can convey the correct meaning without words movement.

The output text may be more similar to the source text in word order, however that does not prevent passing the correct meanings to the target language, as shown by the feasibility of simultaneous interpretation and sight translation.

Translation (in both direction) is carried out sentence by sentence in order of the original text. Starting from the beginning of a sentence, the computer will repeat two processing stages:

(1) Select the next translation element in the source text. Here we employ the maximum-length-first word segmentation method. This is implemented by sorting the bilingual dictionary by word (and phrase) lengths in descending order, before matching with the source text.

(2) Select a translation of the element in the target language. If there are more than one meaning (or translation) of the element, the most possible (frequently used and reliable) one is presented, while the rest are preserved in a backup candidate list for the user to select once the translation presented is not consistent with the context.

There are three levels of goals:

(1) Keeping all the possible meanings (most important)
(2) Using correct grammar
(3) Achieving native speaker fluency

We would first of all focus on successful convey of meaning, because that is the basic requirement of the reader. All the possible meanings of the author should be well kept in the translation output, for the reader's reference. The feasibility of the design is high, because if the source text is understandable to its readers, so will a translation honestly keeping all its meanings (be understandable) to its readers in the target language.

3   Implementation and Improvement

3.1   Implementation

Yes Translate is implemented in the form of a web site for convenience of accessibility. The initial state is shown in Fig. 5.

To translate a text from Chinese to English or vice visa, simply type or paste it in the source text window on the left, then click a translating button at the top (English-to-Simplified Chinese, English-to-Traditional Chinese, Simplified Chinese to English, and Traditional Chinese to English), and the translation will appear in the target text widow on the right hand side. And in addition to the PC version, a mobile phone version is available, with the source and target text windows arranged in a vertical mode.

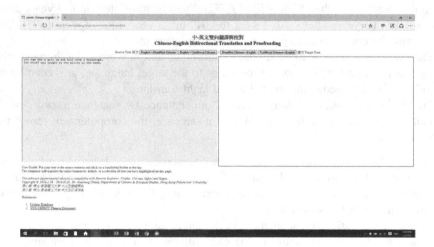

Fig. 5.   The initial state of Yes Translate

Internally, Yes Translate has four components: the Chinese-English dictionary (or called translation memory), the English-Chinese dictionary (translation memory), the translation engine and the user interface.

Both the Chinese-English dictionary and the English-Chinese dictionary are developed from the latest version of YES-CEDICT (Zhang and Li 2016), which includes over 116,000 word entries, covering the following (except a small number of characters not displayable on the computer):

- All the 5,000 words of the new word list of HSK (Hanyu Shuipin Kaoshi), the official Chinese Proficiency Test of China mainland (Hanban 2012);
- All the 8,000 words of the new word list of TOCFL (Test of Chinese as a Foreign Language), the official Chinese proficiency test of Taiwan (National Taiwan Normal University 2013);
- All 113,935 headwords in CC-CEDICT, the most popular downloadable Chinese dictionary on the Web (MDBG 2016);
- All 11,408 characters in the Complete List of Chinese Characters Used by the Media in 2013 (2013 年度媒体用字总表, National Language Commission of China 2014);
- All 13,000 plus characters in the latest version of the Xinhua Dictionary (Linguistic Institute of the Chinese Academy of Social Sciences 2011);
- All 13,000 plus characters in the latest version of the Contemporary Chinese Dictionary (Linguistic Institute of the Chinese Academy of Social Sciences, 2012).

Other references include the Oxford Chinese Dictionary (Kleeman and Yu 2010), ABC Chinese-English Comprehensive Dictionary (DeFrancis 2003), the List of Frequently-used Words of Modern Chinese (in frequency order, National Language Commission of China, 2008), big data (such as corpora on the Web), Google Translate, Baidu Translate as well as our working experiences.

An entry in the English-Chinese dictionary (translation memory) has the contents of English word (or phrase), translation in Simplified Chinese, translation in Traditional Chinese and linguistic labels, and the entries are sorted by the length of the English words descendingly. An entry in the Chinese-English dictionary (translation memory) has the contents of Simplified Chinese, Traditional Chinese, translation in English and linguistic labels, and the entries are sorted by the length of the Chinese words descendingly. Linguistic labels include marks of part of speech, time, voice, plurality, etc.

If a word has multiple meanings (or translations), the meanings are sorted according to their frequency of use. For example, in CC-CEDICT, Chinese word 不满 is defined as:/resentful/discontented/dissatisfied/. But in Google Translate, the frequency order is/dissatisfied/discontented/resentful/. Hence, the frequency order is adopted.

Some translations are added to the existing words in the dictionary for MT purpose. For example, Chinese word 只有 is often translated to "only" referring to the only condition for something to happen, such as "我们只有努力才能成功" (We will succeed only by working hard). We have added the possible phrasal meaning of "only have", such as in "我们只有一个地球." (We only have one earth.)

Capitalization of the first letter of a sentence in the English target text is fulfilled in a simple way: the initial letter of a word is capitalized if it is preceded by a next line (/n) or a full stop (.) character.

No repeating English translation will appear in the option list. For example, to look after the variant words of 裏 and 裡 in traditional Chinese-to-English translation, there are

inside 里 裏
inside 里 裡
lining 里 裏
lining 里 裡

among the entries of simplified Chinese里in the Chinese-English dictionary. In simplified Chinese to English translation. only

inside 里
lining 里

will appear in the optional list.

Due to limitation of space here, more technical details will be reported in a separate paper.

3.2   Improvement

Substantial improvement of the software has been achieved by continuous tests on real-life Chinese texts. In the recent months, we have used Yes Translate to translate the complete government work report by Premier Li (2016), some paragraphs from the Bible and a large number of news articles from China Mainland, Taiwan, Hong Kong and other places on Google, Baidu, BBC, VOA, etc. Weak points of translation revealed by the tests are carefully analyzed and effectively solved.

For example, Yes Translate used to translate Chinese word 把 into English "handle" or "hold", while in real life, it is most frequently used as a preposition in the "把 + O+V" expressions (with particle 把 marking the beginning of an object noun phrase followed by the verb phrase), which are very common in Chinese but not used in English. Translating an "S + 把+O + V" sentence to "S + V+O" sentence is likely to lose emphasis on the object. A more serious risk is caused by incorrect detecting of the boundaries of the following noun phrase or the verb phrase, which is more likely to happen when the object is long. For instance, Google Translate translates:

"把去北京的人带回香港。" into a mess of

"The man went back to Hong Kong to Beijing."

To solve this problem, we have added a new entry to the dictionary to translate 把 into an "O + V" marker, avoiding movement of the object NP. A much better translation is generated for the pervious sentence:

"(object + vt:) Go (to) Beijing ('s) people bring back to Hong Kong."

By human intelligence, the reader should have no difficulty finding out the O-V boundary between "people" and "bring". Word 将 can be processed in a similar way when functioning as 把. Translate to "(object + vt:)" when followed by a noun, and into "will" when followed by a verb, while keeping the other possibilities on the option list.

的 is the most frequently used word in modern Chinese. It can be translated into "of", "that", "'s" etc. in English. For instance, "我们老师的办公室" (the office **of** our teacher), and "我将要读的书" "the book **that** I will read". Both "of" and "that" involve movement of the attributive, which can be risky. Translation with "'s" follows the same word order of Chinese. And "'s" is not limited to express possession, e.g., "a master's degree", "block sb.'s path", "New Year's Day", "a lifetime's absence", "father's elder brother's wife", etc. Hence, it seems safer to use ('s) before a more reliable grammar parser is available. The previous two sentences will then be translated into "our teacher's office", and "I will read's book". The second sentence may not sound grammatically correct, but its meaning is more accurate than Google's translation: "I am going to read the book".

4   Evaluation

Yes Translate is on the Web for testing. The initial results are very encouraging.

4.1   Translation of the Pope's News Article

Figure 6 is a translation by Yes Translate of the news article on Pope's visit to the refugee camp.

Comparing with the translation of Google and Baidu, the meanings of the source text are better preserved by Yes Translate. And assistance to post-editing is available: If a translation element has more than one option, it is presented in the form of an interactive link, which, when clicked, will display the candidate list of translations for the reader to select. For example, the word "should" in the first sentence is obviously inconsistent with the context. When clicked, it will present "should, answer, accepted, etc.", among which "accept" is selected. Similarly, verb "suggest" has been changed into a noun form, as shown in Fig. 7.

The pope visit Greece refugee camp   take away 12 Syria refugee return (to) Vatican City

Sing Tao Daily - 2016 year April 17 date Sunday morning 11:33.

…

The pope be in one week before, decide should Vatican City one name officer suggest , house 3 Syria family . The pope explain , he accept suggest , be because satisfy he visit Lesbos Island ('s) spirit . He say : " this be just like drop (completed) a drop of water to (the) sea , but this small drop of water already make (the) sea become different . "

…

Fig. 6. Translation by Yes translate (May 28, 2016, http://www.mypolyuweb.hk/ctxzhang/ yesmt/)

The pope visit Greece refugee camp   take away 12 Syria refugee return (to)
Vatican City

Sing Tao Daily - 2016 year April 17 date Sunday morning 11:33.

...

The pope be in one week before, decide accept Vatican City one name officer
suggestion , house 3 Syria family . The pope explain , he accept suggestion
, be because satisfy he visit Lesbos Island ('s) spirit . He say : " this
be just like drop (completed) a drop of water to (the) sea , but this small
drop of water already make (the) sea become different . "

...

Fig. 7. Improvement by computer assisted proofing

With minimum editing, the text has become more accurate and intelligible, though a number of grammar errors still exist.

4.2   Evaluation by Students

In this experiment, 10 postgraduate students from our class of "Computer Tools for the Language Professionals" were asked to select a simplified or traditional Chinese news article of their own interest from the Web, and translate it into English with Yes Translate. Then personally proofread the translation and fill the questionnaire. The results are summarized in Table 1.

Table 1. Evaluation of Yes translate's translation by 10 students

	1	2	3	4	5	Average mark
	Strongly disagree	Disagree	Neutral	Agree	Strongly agree	
1 General meaning of the text correct and understandable				7	3	4.3
2 General meaning of each sentence correct			1	8	1	4
3 Grammar is OK		1	2	4	3	3.9
4 Writing is OK			1	3	6	4.5
5 The tool is useful				3	7	4.7

The accuracy of the translation is quite exciting. Of all the 10 students, 7 agree and 3 strongly agree that the general meaning of the English translation is correct and understandable. The average mark is (7*4 + 3*5)/10 = 4.3, of a full mark of 5. And 9 out of the 10 students agree or strongly agree that the general meaning of each sentence is correct. The fluency of the translation is roughly OK, as reflected by the marks of grammar and writing, though the marks may be lower if we changed "OK" into "good" in questions 3 and 4. Finally all students agree or strongly agree that the tool is useful, with an impressive average mark of 4.7.

4.3 Evaluation by the Computer

A small-scaled evaluation in BLEU and NIST has been performed on Asiya-Online (http://asiya.lsi.upc.edu/demo/asiya_online.php). Data for the source and reference texts are 5 articles from VOA Chinese-English bilingual news of July 25 to 27, 2016 (on http://www.voachinese.com/z/2404.html). There are totally 1,722 characters in the Chinese source file, and 967 words in the English Reference file. Table 2 presents the BLEU and NIST values of system translations by Google Translate, Baidu Translate and Yes Translate.

The BLEU and NIST values of Yes are much lower than Google and Baidu. And all three systems score less than 50 % of the full marks of BLEU (1) and NIST (10). Possible reasons include

- The Yes translation text is much longer than the reference text, (1312-967)/ 967 = 35.7 %.
- Yes uses expressions which are not used in traditional English, for example "('s)", "(completed)", "(object + vt:)", etc.
- Frequently used function words such as "the", "a" and "an" are often missing in Yes.

Yes Translate is still very young. Formal development of the software started less than 7 months ago. There is large room for improvement.

As a matter of fact, there are excellent translations which have been scored unbelievably low BLEU and NIST marks. For instance, the Bible in Basic English on the bible website at http://www.o-bible.com/kjv.html is a high-quality translation. However, according to our experiment on Asiya-Online with the King James Version for reference, the BLEU value given to Chapter 1 of Genesis in the Basic English version is 0.4565, below half the full mark of 1.

Table 2. BLEU and NIST values of translations by Google, Baidu and Yes.

	BLEU	NIST	Words
Google	0.1496	4.4727	922
Baidu	0.1462	4.1836	979
Yes	0.0175	1.7821	1312

5 Conclusion and Further Development

Meanings of the source text often get lost or distorted by machine translation tools, including leader products such as Google Translate and Baidu Translate. Yes Translate is a Chinese-English translation tool to be maximally loyal to the source text while maintaining adequate fluency. In an experiment on 10 students with good command of Chinese and English, all agreed or strongly agreed that the general meaning of the English translation by Yes Translate was correct and understandable. And 9 out of the 10 students agreed or strongly agreed that the general meaning of each sentence was correct.

Other important features of Yes Translate are its effective support to post-editing, and the client-side work mode. That means no continuous connection to the server is required. The size of the whole website is 12.6 MB, very handy for a machine translation system.

There is large space for further improvement. Some sentences are still translated without accurate meanings. The mistakes are mostly caused by incorrect word segmentation, for example,

一张/人手/大小的试纸 (One sheet (of paper) **manpower** size ('s) test paper),/在理/论方面 (**Reasonable** theory aspect),国际债权/方向/希腊发放更多的救助款项 (International creditor's rights (law) **direction** Greece provide more ('s) aid funds).

Ambiguous word segmentations in the form of "cc" vs "c/c" is limited to the two characters, hence can be properly represented by putting both word "cc" and phrase "c/c" in the dictionary. For example, both "人手, manpower" and "人手, human hands" are included.

Ambiguity in the form of "cc/c" vs "c/cc" can be dealt with in a similar way. For example, the error segmentation of/在理/论方面 can be avoided by adding phrase"在理论, in theory" to the translation dictionary. Unfortunately, there are too many words starting with 理 which may follow 在, including 在理论…, 在理解…, 在理想…, etc. And the ambiguous chain can be longer than two words, e.g. /在理/大校/园 [/在/理大/校园/].

It seems more cost-effective to delete entry 在理 from the dictionary. Then 在理 will be translated into "in reason", which is also acceptable. However, some words are too popular to delete, e.g., 十分, 有力, in spite of the existence of expressions like 十分钟, 有力不从心的时刻.

A better method is to further improve word segmentation. For example, we can take advantage of the feature that, comparing with "十分 (ten seconds/marks)", "十分 (very)" is more likely to be followed by an adjective or adverb. Another method is to combine forward word segmentation processing and backward processing, and mark the inconsistent parts for post-editing choices. But that will slow down the translation substantially.

However, word segmentation can never be 100 % correct (Zhang and Sun 2012). When probability is involved, there is space of missing the correct choice. A more ideal way is to promote word segmented writing (Chen 1996; Zhang 1998) like English, but that will take a very long period of time. Yes Translate is already capable to process word-segmented text. For example, "在 理大 校园" is translated to "at PolyU campus".

Another aspect for further improvement is grammar and fluency of the output. Grammar errors are mainly caused by the lack of physical marks in the Chinese language to represent differences in time, voice, number, phrase structures, etc., and due to the limited time we have been working on this project.

We will continue to improve Yes Translate on real-life texts, especially daily news articles on various topics. Yes Translate is mainly data-driven, improvement of the system heavily relies on improvement of the dictionary.

Work is now focused on the Chinese-English part. The next step is to improve English-Chinese machine translation.

Acknowledgements. The project has been partially supported by a University research fund (Account Code: 4-ZZEW). The author is also very grateful to the three anonymous reviewers, whose valuable comments helped in the revision of the paper.

References

Bhattacharyya, P.: Machine Translation. CRC Press, Taylor and Francis, Boca Raton (2015)

Chen, L.: Word segmentation in written Chinese (汉语书面语的分词问题———一个有关全民的信息化问题). J. Chin. Inf. Process. 10(1) (1996)

DeFrancis, J.: ABC Chinese-English Comprehensive Dictionary. Hanyu Dacidian Press, Shanghai (2003)

Hanban: New HSK Word List (新汉语水平考试词汇表). Hanban, Beijing (2012). http://www.chinesetest.cn/godownload.do

Internet World Stats: "INTERNET WORLD USERS BY LANGUAGE (2016). http://www.internetworldstats.com/stats7.htm

Kleeman, J., Yu, H.: The Oxford Chinese Dictionary. Oxford University Press, Oxford (2010)

Li, K. (李克强): Government Work Report 2016 (政府工作报告2016). http://www.gov.cn/guowuyuan/2016-03/05/content_5049372.htm (2016)

Linguistic Institute of the Chinese Academy of Social Sciences: Xinhua Dictionary (Xinhua Zidian, 新华字典). The Commercial Press, Beijing (2011)

Linguistic Institute of the Chinese Academy of Social Sciences: Contemporary Chinese Dictionary (Xiandai Hanyu Cidian, 现代汉语词典). The Commercial Press, Beijing (2012)

MDBG: CC-CEDICT Chinese to English Dictionary. http://www.mdbg.net/chindict/chindict.php?page=cedict. (Downloaded on January 23, 2016)

National Language Commission of China (国家语委): The List of Frequently-used Words of Modern Chinese (现代汉语常用词表(草案)). The Commercial Press, Beijing (2008)

National Language Commission of China: Language Situation in China: 2014. (中国语言生活状况报告 (2014)). Commercial Press, Beijing (2014)

National Taiwan Normal University: New Word List of TOCFL (Test of Chinese as a Foreign Language) (2013). http://www.tw.org/tocfl/

Yahoo: 教宗訪希臘難民營　帶走12敘利亞難民返梵蒂岡 (2016). https://hk.news.yahoo.com/教宗訪希臘難民營-帶走12敘利亞難民返梵蒂岡-033300795.html

Zhang, K., Sun, M.: Unified framework of performing Chinese word segmentation and part-of-speech tagging. China Commun. (中国通信) 9(03), 1–9 (2012)

Zhang, X.: Written Chinese word-segmentation revisited: ten advantages of word-segmented writing. J. Chin. Inf. Process. (中文信息学报) 12(3), 57–63 (1998)

Zhang, X., Li, X.: Computer-assisted revision of the YES-CEDICT Chinese dictionary (《一二三汉英大词典》的计算机辅助修订). In: Li, X., Xu, J. (eds.) (李晓琪,徐娟主编), Digital Teaching of Chinese Language 2016 (数字化汉语教学 2016). Tsinghua University Press, Beijing (2016, to appear)

Zhang, X., Li, X., Lun, C.: A brief introduction to the YES-CEDICT Chinese dictionary. J. Mod. Chin. Lang. Educ. 4(1), 27–31 (2015). http://xuebao.eblcu.com/

Sentence Alignment Method Based on Maximum Entropy Model Using Anchor Sentences

Chao Che[✉], Wenwen Guo, and Jianxin Zhang

Key Laboratory of Advanced Design and Intelligent Computing
(Dalian University), Ministry of Education, Dalian, China
chechao101@163.com

Abstract. The paper proposes a sentence alignment method based on maximum entropy model using anchor sentences to align ancient and modern Chinese sentences in historical classics. The method selects the sentence pairs with the same phrases at the beginning or the end of the sentence or with the same time phrases as anchor sentence pairs, which are employed to divide the paragraph into several sections. Then, the sentences in each section are aligned using dynamic programming algorithm according to the entropy calculated by maximum entropy model. The maximum entropy model employs improved Chinese co-occurrence character feature, length feature and sentence alignment mode feature. The Chinese co-occurrence characters feature is improved by giving different weights to characters in different position based on the contribution to align sentences. In the experiment performed on *ShiJi*, the precision and recall of the proposed method reaches 95.9 % and 95.6 % respectively, which outperforms other sentence alignment methods significantly.

Keywords: Anchor sentences · Maximum entropy model · Chinese co-occurrence character · Sentence alignment

1 Introduction

History classics are the wisdom crystallization of the Chinese nation and the root of the modern culture. Translating history classics into English is one of direct and effective means to introduce the outstanding Chinese culture to the world. Due to the lack of ancient corpus and language process method of ancient Chinese, directly translating into English is very difficult. Therefore, we try to extract the term translation in the historical books using the modern Chinese as bridge, which may achieve good results with the help of rich resources of modern Chinese. The extraction method of term translation is based on parallel corpus between modern Chinese and ancient Chinese. Therefore, this paper presents a sentence alignment method, to provide the parallel corpus between ancient and modern Chinese for term translation of historical classics, taking *Shiji* [1] for example.

The sentence alignment methods can be classified into three types: statistical method, lexical method and the combined method. The statistical method originally proposed by Brown [2] and Gale [3] is based on the fact: longer sentences in source

© Springer International Publishing AG 2016
M. Sun et al. (Eds.): CCL and NLP-NABD 2016, LNAI 10035, pp. 76–85, 2016.
DOI: 10.1007/978-3-319-47674-2_7

language tend to be translated into longer sentences in target language, and shorter sentences tend to be translated into shorter sentences. The statistical method align sentence on the basis of sentence length. The lexical method use special symbols and special words (such as punctuations, mathematical symbols, the named entity etc.), cognate information or lexicon to align the sentences [4–6]. The combined method employs both length and lexical information. For example, Wu [7] combined the sentence length with lexical information and achieved 92.1 % accuracy on Chinese-English Hong Kong Hansard corpus.

Although the research of sentence alignment has been conducted for a long period of time, the research of sentence alignment between ancient and modern Chinese is still in initial stage. At present, the log-linear model and statistical method are employed to align sentences in ancient and modern corpus in [8, 9]. In this paper, we employ maximum entropy model based anchor sentences to align ancient and modern sentences in historical classics. According to the characteristics of history books, we select anchor sentences and improve Chinese co-occurrence characters characteristic function.

2 A Sentence Alignment Method Based on Maximum Entropy Model Using Anchor Sentences

In the sentence alignment method, we firstly select two kinds of sentences as anchor [10, 11], one type of sentence with the same phrases in begin or the end, the other type is *1–1* mode sentence pair containing the same time phrases. The anchor sentences are employed to divide the paragraph into several sections. Then, the entropy of ancient and modern sentences is calculated using maximum entropy model. At last, the sentences in each section are aligned by dynamic programming algorithm [12].

2.1 Selection of Anchor Sentences

The anchor sentences are implemented to control the alignment errors in a small range to prevent the spread of error. In theory, any kind of sentence pair can become anchors. But for the consideration of simplicity in practice, we only consider *1–1* mode sentences as anchor sentences [13], which accounts for a large majority of all the alignment modes. Thus, we select two kinds of *1–1* mode sentence pairs in ancient and modern Chinese as the anchor sentences.

(1) Sentence pairs begin or end with the same phrases

Through the observation of *Shiji* in ancient and modern Chinese, we find that some aligned sentences have same phrases at the beginning and the end of the sentence, while the non-aligned sentences do not have the characteristic. Obviously the sentences with the same phrases at the beginning and the end can be used as anchor sentences. Two points should be noted: ① Ancient modal words does not make sense, so the modal words at the beginning and the end of ancient sentences are removed, including "维" (wei), "而" (er), "何" (he), "乎" (hu), etc. ② Some of the ancient Chinese words are replaced by the modern Chinese characters. Some characters have the same

Table 1. Sentences with the same time phrases

Ancient Chinese	Modern Chinese	β
出子 六年 三父等复共令人贼杀出子	出子 六年 三父等人又合伙派人谋杀出子	0. 73
四年 晋伐秦取少梁	四年 晋伐秦占领少梁	0. 875
景公 四年 晋栾书弑其君厉公	景公 四年 晋国的栾书杀其国君厉公	0. 92
五年 晋卿中行范氏反晋	五年 晋卿中行氏范氏反叛晋国	1
十三年 初有史以纪事民多化者	十三年 开始设史官记事人民越来越开化	0. 58

meaning in both modern Chinese and ancient Chinese, the characters need to be replaced. For example, "於是" (yushi) in ancient Chinese is replaced by "于是" (yushi) in modern, "曰" (yue) is replaced by "说" (shuo).

(2) Sentence pairs with the same time phrases

Shiji is a biographical history book, which records the history by biography. Each biography is recorded in chronological order, so there are a large number of time phrases in the sentence of *Shiji*. Time phrases containing "年" (nian) is more typical while the time phrases in ancient and modern Chinese are the same, sentence pairs with the same time phrases can be regarded as anchor sentences. In our training corpus, there are 341 pairs of sentences containing the same time phrases among 2798 pairs, some of which are shown in Table 1, (β is the ratio of Chinese co-occurrence characters and the number of ancient sentence character)

The sentence pairs aligned to each other usually have big β. There are little anchor sentences with the small β. In the training corpus, there are only 10 β of sentences less than or equal to 0.6. So the pair of sentences with $\beta \leq 0.6$ can't been regarded as anchor. We find the anchor sentences with the same time phrases in following steps:

① Calculate the sentence number rate $\alpha = M/N$, in which, N is the number of sentences in ancient paragraph, M is the number of sentences in corresponding modern paragraph.

② Assume the *i-th* ancient sentences contains time phrases with "年" (nian), *j-th* modern sentence is the possible translation corresponds to the *i-th* ancient sentences. $j = \alpha * i + k$, sets $k = [\pm 1, 0, \pm 2]$ from experience.

③ Calculate the value of β for each sentence pairs and regard the maximal value as β_{max}. Remove the sentence pairs with $\beta_{max} \leq 0.6$.

④ Determine whether the sentence pair is *1–1* alignment mode. Seeking all possible entropy with different alignment modes. If the entropy of $s_i - t_u$ with *1–1* mode is the optimal solution, then $s_i - t_u$ can be regarded as anchor sentences. The sentence pairs of different alignment modes needed to be calculated are shown in Table 2.

⑤ Repeat above step, find anchor sentences until the end of the paragraph.

Table 2. Sentence combinations needed seek entropy

Alignment mode	Sentence combinations
1–1	$s_i - t_u$
1–2	$s_i - t_{u-1}, t_u \ s_i - t_u, t_{u+1}$
2–1	$s_{i-1}, s_i - t_u \ s_i, s_{i+1} - t_u$
2–2	$s_{i-1}, s_i - t_{u-1}, t_u \ s_{i-1}, s_i - t_u, t_{u+1}$
	$s_i, s_{i+1} - t_{u-1}, t_u \ s_i, s_{i+1} - t_u, t_{u+1}$

2.2 Maximum Entropy Model

For bilingual sentence alignment, the integration of multiple characteristic functions can get good results. The maximum entropy model makes use of sentence length, alignment mode, Chinese co-occurrence character. Sentence alignment process is to compute the entropy of ancient and modern sentences. And the formula is shown in Eq. (1).

$$\arg \max e(s, t) = \arg \max [\lambda_m h_m(s, t)]$$
$$= \arg \max [\lambda_1 L(s, t) + \lambda_2 M(s, t) + \lambda_3 H(s, t)] \tag{1}$$

In which, $L(s, t)$ is the length feature function, $M(s, t)$ is the alignment mode feature function, $H(s, t)$ is the Chinese co-occurrence characters feature function.

Chinese Co-occurrence Characters. Through observation on corpus, we find that two sentences with more co-occurrence Chinese characters, the greater the chance of alignment. In the real corpus, there are some the same Chinese characters in ancient sentence and the corresponding modern sentence, there are also the co-occurrence of Chinese characters in the surrounding sentences. If the Chinese co-occurrence characters are used in the sentence alignment, it is in ancient sentence and the corresponding modern sentence far more than in the surrounding sentence pairs. In order to verify whether the Chinese co-occurrence characters can be used, we have selected 50 ancient sentences from manual alignment corpus to calculate similarity β, the results shown in Fig. 1.

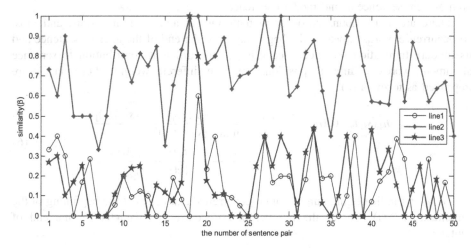

Fig. 1. The similarity of Chinese co-occurrence characters in align and unaligned sentences

In Fig. 1, line 1 denotes the similarity between ancient sentence and the sentence before its corresponding modern Chinese translation, line 2 is the similarity between ancient sentence and its corresponding translation, line 3 denotes the similarity between ancient and the sentence after its corresponding translation. From Fig. 1 we can see the fact that the similarities between the aligned sentences is much bigger than the unaligned ones. Wang [14] puts forward an algorithm to calculate the co-occurrence character feature in the alignment between China and Japan, shown as formula (2). We improve the formula by giving different weights to characters in different position based on the contribution to sentences alignment especially begin and the end of a sentence.

$$H(s,t) = \begin{cases} 0 & 0-1 \, or \, 1-0 \\ h_1(s_i, t_u : 0,0) & 1-1 \\ h_1(s_i, t_u : 0,0) + h_2(s_i, t_u; s_j, 0) & 2-1 \\ h_1(s_i, t_u : 0,0) + h_3(s_i, t_u; 0, t_v) & 1-2 \\ h_1(s_i, t_u : 0,0) + h_1(0, 0; s_j, t_v) & 2-2 \end{cases} \tag{2}$$

Formula (3) indicates the similarity between s_i and t_u. Formula (4) is the similarity increased by the characters that appear in s_j and do not appear in s_i. Formula (5) indicates the similarity increased by the characters that appear in t_v and do not appear in t_u.

$$h_1(s_i, t_u : 0,0) = \frac{c(s_i \cap t_u)}{\min(c(s_i), \ c(t_u))} \tag{3}$$

$$h_2(s_i, t_u : s_j, 0) = \frac{c(s_j \cap t_u) - c(s_i \cap s_j \cap t_u)}{c(s_j)} \tag{4}$$

$$h_3(s_i, t_u : 0, t_v) = \frac{c(s_i \cap t_v) - c(s_i \cap t_u \cap t_v)}{c(t_v)} \tag{5}$$

$c(s_i)$ denotes the character number in ancient sentence s_i, $c(t_u)$ denotes the number in modern sentence t_u, $c(s_i \cap t_u)$ denotes the number of the co-occurrence characters in both ancient sentence s_i and modern sentence t_u.

There are many nouns co-occur in both ancient and modern corpus, and most co-occurrence words appear at the beginning or at the end of the ancient sentence and its modern translation sentence. According to the different contribution to sentence alignment, words at different positions are gave different weights. Formula (3) are improved as formula (6).

$$h_1(s_i, t_u : 0,0) = \frac{\lambda_1[c(s_i \cap t_u) - c_b(s_i \cap t_u) - c_e(s_i \cap t_u)]}{\min(c(s_i), c(t_u))} + \frac{\lambda_2 c_b(s_i \cap t_u) + \lambda_3 c_e(s_i \cap t_u)}{\min(c(s_i), c(t_u))} \tag{6}$$

$c_b(s_i \cap t_u)$ indicates the number of co-occurrence characters at the beginning of the sentence. $c_e(s_i \cap t_u)$ denotes the number of co-occurrence characters at the end of sentence.

Sentence Length. The alignment method employs sentence lengths based on the fact: longer sentences in source language tend to be translated into longer sentences in target language, and shorter sentences tend to be translated into shorter sentences [2]. In the study of the Gale and Church [3], each character in a language will corresponds to certain random number of characters in another language. The character number is independent identically distributed, complying with normal distribution.

The sentence length is denoted by the number of Chinese characters. In our experiment, l_2 is the length of the modern sentence, l_1 indicates the length of the ancient sentence. We fit the length ratio l_2/l_1 in the corpora of ancient and modern Chinese sentences to normal distribution, fitting results is shown in Fig. 2.

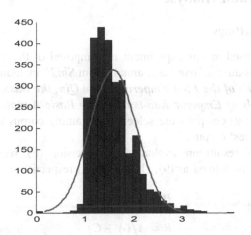

Fig. 2. Normal distribution curve of length ratio

In Fig. 2, we find the length ratio l_2/l_1 obeys normal distribution $c \approx 1.588 s^2 = 2.007$. Given $\delta = (l_2 - l_1 \cdot c)/\sqrt{l_1 \cdot s^2}$, δ meets the standard normal distribution [15]. Sentence length feature is computed using the formula (7) [8].

$$L(s,t) = -100 \times \log_2\left(1 - 1\bigg/\sqrt{2\pi}\int_{-\infty}^{\delta} e^{-\frac{z^2}{2}}dz\right) \tag{7}$$

Alignment Mode Analyzing the parallel corpora of *Shiji*, we get the probability of different alignment modes in Table 3.

In the alignment, we consider only the six modes including *1–0, 0–1, 1–1, 1–2, 2–1, 2–2*. If m ancient Chinese sentences align n modern Chinese sentences, we call the alignment as m-n alignment mode. The alignment mode feature $M(s,t)$ is calculated using the formula (8) [9].

$$M(s,t) = -100 \log(\Pr(m - n)) \tag{8}$$

Table 3. Alignment mode statistics

Mode(m-n)	Frequency	Probability
1–0 or 0–1	4	0.14 %
1–1	2522	90.14 %
1-2	132	4.72 %
2–1	112	4.00 %
2–2	8	0.29 %
others	20	0.71 %

3   Experiments and Analysis

3.1   Experiment Settings

The parallel corpus used in this experiment is composed of the ancient Chinese and modern Chinese translation of five basic annals from *ShiJi,* including *Basic Annals of Qin, the Basic Annals of the First Emperor of the Qin, the Basic Annals of Hsiang Yu, the Basic Annals of Emperor Kao-tsu* and *the Basic Annals of Empress Lü* as corpus [16]. 2798 sentences pairs are selected as training corpus and 1341 sentences pairs are selected as test corpus.

The experimental results are evaluated by precision (P), recall ratio(R), and F measure. R, P and F is defined as (9), (10) and (11) respectively.

$$P = A/(A+B) \tag{9}$$

$$R = A/(A+C) \tag{10}$$

$$F = 2 \times (RP/(R+P)) \tag{11}$$

In which, A is the number of sentence correct aligned, B is the number of sentence wrong aligned, C is the number of sentence not correct aligned.

In the experiment, we employ different combination of features to do sentence alignment and the results are showed in Table 4. CC denotes Chinese co-occurrence characters feature presented by Wang [14], improved Chinese co-occurrence characters feature proposed by this paper is denoted by ICC. A denotes anchor sentences feature.

Table 4. The experimental results using different features

Length	Mode	CC	ICC	A	P	R	F
+					78.6 %	51.2 %	62.0 %
			+		80.3 %	52.8 %	63.7 %
				+	84.2 %	56.4 %	67.5 %
+	+				89.8 %	89.0 %	89.4 %
	+		+		90.2 %	90.0 %	90.1 %
+	+		+		93.5 %	93.3 %	93.4 %
+	+		+	+	95.9 %	95.6 %	95.7 %

3.2   Analysis

Many factors affect the alignment results. According to the characteristics of the method, we analyze the results from the following three aspects.

(1) Anchor sentences

The anchor sentences, which are the sentence pairs with the same phrase at the beginning and the end of the sentences, have similar effects with the improved Chinese co-occurrence characters feature. The anchor sentences require aligned entirely correct, so the accuracy of using anchor sentence is higher than using Chinese co-occurrence characters.

Sentences with time phrases describe events including person names, place names or time etc. These phrases often have the same representation in ancient and modern Chinese, and there are more co-occurrence Chinese characters. Therefore similarity can be identified as a measure to determine anchor sentences.

One disadvantage of the anchor sentences is the uneven distribution. Therefore, the anchor sentences take effect obviously in some paragraphs, while do not work in other paragraphs. For example, the paragraph from "十三年，向寿伐韩，取武始" to "五十年十月，武安君白起有罪，为士伍，迁阴密" in *Basic Annals of Qin*, has 35 time parses with "年" (nian), including 77 sentences. Clearly the role of anchor sentence in this paragraph will be very obvious.

(2) Chinese co-occurrence character

As shown in Table 4, when only a feature is used, the co-occurrence characters features obtains the best result. The improved co-occurrence characters feature that gives different weights to co-occurrence characters in different position perform even better. When only using co-occurrence characters feature, the alignment is conducted according to the similarity between the two sentences. Chinese characters appear relatively random, so the similarity in different sentences pairs may be the same or not very different. However, if the position of co-occurrence character can be considered, accuracy is increased by 3.9 % as shown in Table 4. The improved accuracy mainly from the sentences with same characters at the beginning or the end of the sentence as shown in Table 5.

(3) Length Feature

The length feature intends to match sentences whose length ratio is around 1.588, and it is easy to cause a mismatch for distribution on both ends of the peak. Due to the symmetry of normal distribution, the length feature cannot work well in both wings of the normal distribution, slightly different will cause the mismatch.

Table 5. Aligned sentences with same characters at the beginning or the end of sentences

Ancient	Modern sentences
女脩织，…生子大业。	女脩织布时，…生下儿子大业。
其玄孙曰费昌，…或在夷狄	费氏的玄孙叫费昌。…，有些住在夷狄。
项梁前使项 羽别攻襄城，	项梁在这之前派项羽另率一军攻打襄城

4 Conclusion

In this paper, we conduct a preliminary study of sentence alignment in historical classics, and achieve satisfactory results using the maximum entropy model based on the anchor sentences. Since the sentence alignment method is based on the characteristic of Chinese characters, the application of the method has many limitations. In the future research, we will study a widely used alignment model not limited to ancient Chinese.

Acknowledgements. This work is supported by the National Natural Science Foundation of China (No. 61402068) and Support Program of Outstanding Young Scholar in Liaoning Universities. (No. LJQ2015004).

References

1. Sima, Q.: (Han dynasty): Shiji. Zhong Hua Book Company, Beijing (2006)
2. Brown, P.F., Lai, J.C., Mercer, R.L.: Aligning sentences in parallel corpora. In: Proceedings of 29th Annual Conference of the Association for Computational Linguistics, ACL 1991, pp. 169–176, Stroudsburg, PA, USA (1991)
3. Gale, W.A., Church, K.W.: A program for aligning sentences in bilingual corpora. In: Proceedings of 29th Annual Conference of the Association for Computational Linguistics, MIT, MA, USA, vol. 19(1), pp. 75–102 (1993)
4. Kay, M., Roscheisen, M.: Text-translation alignment. Comput. Linguist. **19**(1), 121–142 (1993)
5. Chen, S.F.: Aligning sentences in bilingual corpora using lexical information. In: Proceedings of 31st Annual Meeting of the Association for Computational Linguistics, pp. 9–16. ACL, Stroudsburg (1993)
6. Simard, M., Foster, G.F., Isabelle, P.: Using cognates to align sentences in bilingual corpora. In: Proceedings of the 1993 Conference of the Centre for Advanced Studies on Collaborative research, pp. 1071–1082. IBM Press, Indianapolis (1993)
7. Wu, D.K.: Aligning a parallel English-Chinese corpus statistically with lexical criteria. In: Proceedings of the 32nd Annual Conference of the Association for Computational Linguistics, pp. 80–87. ACL, Stroudsburg, USA (1994)
8. Liu, Y., Wang, N.: Research on classical and modern Chinese sentence alignment. Comput. Appl. Softw. **30**(11), 127–130 (2013)
9. Lin, Z.: Alignment for Ancient-Modern Chinese Bi-text. Beijing University of Posts and Telecommunications, Beijing (2007)
10. Zhou, Y.Q.: Maximum Entropy Method and its Applications in Natural Language Processing. Fudan University, Shanghai (2004)
11. Berger, A.L., Pietra, V.J.D., Pietra, S.A.D.: A maximum entropy approach to natural language processing. In: Proceedings of the 34th Annual Conference of the Association for Computational Linguistics, pp. 39–71. ACL, Stroudsburg (1996)
12. Cormen, T.H., Leiserson, C.E., Rivest, R.L., Stein, C.: Introduction to Algorithms, pp. 323–369. MIT Press, Cambridge (2001)
13. Tian, S.W., Turgun, I., Yu, L., et al.: Chinese-Uyhur sentence alignment based on hybrid strategy. computer. Science **37**(4), 215–218 (2010)

14. Wang, X., Ren, F.: Chinese-Japanese clause alignment. In: Gelbukh, A. (ed.) CICLing 2015. LNCS, vol. 9042, pp. 400–412. Springer, Heidelberg (2005). doi:10.1007/978-3-540-30586-6_43
15. Zhu, G.J., Guo, D.W., Liu, X.: Probability Theory and Mathematical Statistics. National Defence Industry Press, Beijing (2010)
16. Watson, B.: Records of the Grand Historian: Qin Dynasty. Chinese University of Hong Kong Press, Hong Kong (1993)

Using Collaborative Training Method to Build Vietnamese Dependency Treebank

Guoke Qiu[1], Jianyi Guo[1(✉)], Zhengtao Yu[2], Yantuan Xian[2], and Cunli Mao[2]

[1] The School of Information Engineering and Automation, Kunming University of Science and Technology, Kunming 650500, Yunnan, China gjade86@hotmail.com
[2] The Key Laboratory of Intelligent Information Processing, Kunming University of Science and Technology, Kunming 650500, Yunnan, China

Abstract. For the difficulty of marking Vietnamese dependency tree, this paper proposed the method which combined MST algorithm and improved Nivre algorithm to build Vietnamese dependency treebank. The method took full advantage of the characteristics of collaborative training. Firstly, we built a bit samples. Secondly, we used the samples to build two weak learners with two fully redundant views. Then, we marked a large number of unmarked samples mutually. Next, we selected the samples of high trust to relearn and built a dependency parsing system. Finally, we used 5000 Vietnamese sentences marked manually to do tenfold cross-test and obtained the accuracy of 76.33 %. Experimental results showed that the proposed method in this paper could take full advantage of unmarked corpus to effectively improve the quality of dependency treebank.

Keywords: Dependency treebank · Vietnamese · Collaborative training · Dependency parsing

1 Introduction

Vietnam is a close neighbour of China. The mutual translation will play an important role for exchanges between the two countries. A large-scale dependency treebank can provide strong support for machine translation and other upper applications. Therefore, building Vietnamese dependency treebank has an important practical significance. Currently, the construction of dependency treebank for English and other large languages has got some achievements. But research about Vietnamese is still relatively less and there are a lack of large-scale Vietnamese dependency treebanks.

This work was supported in part by the National Natural Science Foundation of China (Grant Nos. 61262041, 61363044 and 61472168) and the key project of National Natural Science Foundation of Yunnan province (Grant No. 2013FA030).

© Springer International Publishing AG 2016
M. Sun et al. (Eds.): CCL and NLP-NABD 2016, LNAI 10035, pp. 86–100, 2016.
DOI: 10.1007/978-3-319-47674-2_8

Currently, in the field of Vietnamese information processing, there are some research achievements in morphology and bilingual alignment method [1–3]. But research on building dependency treebank is relatively inadequate. With the rapid development of statistical learning, today more and more researchers use this method to study language information processing. Among them, Lai and others used the idea of span and statistical learning to solve the problem of Chinese dependency parsing in 2001 [4]. Yamada and others converted the English sentences in the Penn Treebank to the dependency structure completely in 2003. Then they used the statistical learning method to analyze these sentences and finally achieved the accuracy of 90.3 % [5]. Ma Jinshan built the SVM dependency parsing model through using the marked Chinese dependency treebank in 2004 and finally solved the Chinese dependency parsing [6]. These methods above mainly relied on supervised learning of dependency treebank resource to achieve dependency parsing. Nguyen and others converted ten thousand phrase trees in the Penn Treebank to dependency trees in 2013 [7]. But the scale was still relatively small.

The foundation of dependency parsing is the construction of dependency treebank. However, marking dependency treebank is very difficult and currently there isn't a mature dependency parser. For the construction of Vietnamese dependency treebank, marking it manually is very difficult and this process requires a lot of manpower and other material resource. Moreover, in reality there is a lot of unmarked crude corpus and the corpus has not undergone any processing. Therefore, how to use the corpus to build Vietnamese dependency treebank effectively has become an important issue for Vietnamese dependency parsing.

Based on the features of Vietnamese, this paper proposed the method which combined the maximum spanning tree (MST) algorithm with the improved Nivre algorithm to build Vietnamese dependency treebank. The method was aimed to explore how to use unmarked crude corpus effectively with the help of collaborative training. Firstly, we selected some Vietnamese sentences marked manually as the initial training corpus and used them to build two weak learners. Secondly, we used a large number of unmarked Vietnamese sentences to mark each other and extracted a sample of high trust to train and update on the two learners repeatedly. Finally, we achieved building a Vietnamese dependency treebank of high accuracy successfully. Experimental results showed that the proposed method in this paper improved the UAS, LAS, RA and the accuracy of other aspects more significantly than other methods.

2 Related Theories

2.1 The Maximum Spanning Tree (MST) Algorithm

Dependency-tree parsing as the search for the maximum spanning tree (MST) in a graph was proposed by McDonald et al. [8]. This formulation leads to efficient parsing algorithms for both projective and non-projective dependency trees with the Eisner algorithm [9] and the Chu-Liu-Edmonds algorithm [10, 11] respectively. The formulation works by defining the score of a dependency tree to be the sum of edge scores:

$$s(x, \ y) = \sum_{(i,j) \ \in \ y} s(i,j)$$

where x = x1 ⋯xn is an input sentence and y a dependency tree for x. We can view y as a set of tree edges and write $(i,j) \in y$ to indicate an edge in y from word xi to word xj.

We call this first-order dependency parsing since scores are restricted to a single edge in the dependency tree. The score of an edge is in turn computed as the inner product of a high-dimensional feature representation of the edge with a corresponding weight vector:

$$s(i,j) = \mathbf{w} \cdot \mathbf{f}(i,j)$$

This is a standard linear classifier in which the weight vector w are the parameters to be learned during training. We should note that f(i,j) can be based on arbitrary features of the edge and the input sequence x.

Given a directed graph G = (V, E), the maximum spanning tree (MST) problem is to find the highest scoring subgraph of G that satisfies the tree constraint over the vertices V. By defining a graph in which the words in a sentence are the vertices and there is a directed edge between all words with a score as calculated above, McDonald et al. [8] showed that dependency parsing is equivalent to finding the MST in this graph. Furthermore, it was shown that this formulation can lead to state-of-the-art results when combined with discriminative learning algorithms. Although the MST formulation applies to any directed graph, our feature representations and one of the parsing algorithms (Eisner's) rely on a linear ordering of the vertices, namely the order of the words in the sentence.

In this paper, we expressed the dependency tree of a Vietnamese sentence $S = \{s_1, s_2, \ldots, s_n\}$ as a directed graph $G = (V, E)$, where the words in the sentence constituted a set of vertexs of G and $E \subseteq [1 : n] \times [1 : n]$ represented the dependency. If there was a directed connection from vertex i to vertex j in the dependency tree, there was a directed edge between i and j. The weight of each directed edge was defined as $score(i, j, y)$, which represented the probability of j depending on I and y was a dependency type. The weight of a dependency tree was the sum of the weights of all directed edges. Therefore, this dependency parsing method would convert looking for the best result into searching for the maximum spanning tree in the directed graph $G = (V, E)$:

$$T = \mathop{\arg\max}_{G \ = \ (V,E)} \sum_{(i,j) \in E} score(i,j,y)$$

2.2   The Improved Nivre Algorithm

The Nivre algorithm is based on the process of state transition. The algorithm can obtain the model of dependency parsing through training. The model can predict the next state according to the current state and the features of input sentences and previous decisions.

During the dependency parsing, the analyzer transfers greedily from a primitive state to a subsequent state according to the forecast sets of the model until it reaches the end state.

For the deterministic Nivre algorithm, the division about the Reduce operation and the Shift operation is not very accurate. In order to solve this problem, the paper proposed an improved Nivre algorithm.

In the Nivre algorithm, a parser can be expressed as a triad <S,I,A>, Where S and I are stacks. The input sequence to be parsed is stored in I. A is a set and it can be used to store the determinate dependency items in the process of parsing. Given an input sequence Sen, the parser is firstly initialized as $<nil, Sen, \varnothing >$. The parser analyzes the dependency between the top element t of stack S and the top element n of stack I. Then, the parser takes appropriate action to move the elements and control the algorithm iteration until stack I is empty. At the moment, the parser stops iterating and outputs the dependency sequences of set A. The Nivre algorithm defines a total of four operations:

(1) Right. If t depends on n in the current triad $<t|S, n|I, A >$, the item t->n is added into set A and the top element t of stack S is popped up. Finally, the triad becomes $<S, n|I, A \cup \{(t \rightarrow n)\} >$.

(2) Left. If n depends on t in the current triad $<t|S, n|I, A >$, the item n->t is added into set A and the element n is pushed into stack S. Finally, the triad becomes $<n|t|S, I, A \cup \{(n \rightarrow t)\} >$.

  If there isn't any dependency between n and t, the improved Nivre algorithm makes a clear definition about the Reduce operation and the Shift operation.

(3) Reduce. If there isn't any dependency between n and t, t has a parent node in its left side and there is a dependency between its parent node and n, the parser pops up t from stack S. Finally, the triad becomes $<S, n|I, A >$.

(4) Shift. When the Right, Left and Reduce can't be met, n is pushed into stack S. Finally, the triad becomes $<n|t|S, I, A >$.

2.3   The Bottom-up Algorithm and the Top-Down Algorithm

The Bottom-Up Computation (BUC) algorithm is a bottom-up approach [12]. BUC processes the partitions starting from a single attribute and moves towards the apex of the lattice. BUC relies on APRIORI-like pruning to reduce the computation space. BUC is a divide and conquer strategy, and partitioning is its major cost. BUC can be used to compute either a full data cube or an iceberg cube. Due to its pruning power, BUC works especially well at computing iceberg cubes for sparse database tables. As well, BUC is not memory intensive. When the database is dense, the dividing into partitions costs more and the pruning is less effective, so the overall performance of BUC degrades. According to extensive studies, BUC is faster than TDC in most cases [13].

As the name implies, the Top-Down Computation (TDC) algorithm (Findlater and Hamilton 2003) is a top-down approach that starts from the least aggregated group-bys at the top of the lattice and works its way down to the most aggregated group-bys at the bottom. Each underlined group-by is also an ordering, i.e., a child group-by that permits the shared computation of its parent and other ancestor group-bys during the pass in which it is being computed. Using orderings, the number of passes over the database can be reduced. TDC uses orderings to cover all group-bys. To cover the 2^m group-bys of an m dimensional data cube, 2^{m-1} orderings are required (Findlater and Hamilton 2003). When processing an ordering, TDC simultaneously aggregates all group-bys that are prefixes of it. Shared computation is the main advantage of TDC. The main disadvantage of TDC is weak pruning, i.e., it is relatively poor at identifying cases where pruning is possible.

2.4   Basic Principle of Collaborative Training

Cooperative training was proposed by Blum and Mitchell in 1998. This method assumes that the data set has two fully redundant views, that is to say the data set has several attribute sets to meet the following two conditions: Firstly, the training data of each attribute set is enough to describe the problem and each attribute set can obtain a weak learner through learning. Secondly, any two attribute sets are independent conditionally in the process of marking.

Firstly, cooperative training requires some marked samples to train their classifiers in both views respectively. Secondly, each classifier selects some samples of high confidence from unmarked samples. Next, the selected samples are added into another classifier to train after being marked, so that the classifier can use the newly added marked samples to train and update. Finally, the two classifiers update and iterate constantly until the parameters of the model converge. Research has shown that when the assumption about fully redundant views is established, cooperative training can effectively use unmarked samples to improve training performance. The standard collaborative training method is shown in Fig. 1, where X1 and X2 respectively represent the corresponding samples of view 1 and view 2.

input:	the data set L about marked samples
	the data set U about unmarked samples
process:	randomly select u samples as U ' from U
	K iterations
	use L and X1 to train the learner h1
	use L and X2 to train the learner h2
	use h1 to mark P positive samples and n negative samples of U '
	use h2 to mark P positive samples and n negative samples of U '
	add the samples marked in the previous step into L
	randomly select 2P + 2n samples from U and add them into U '

Fig. 1. The standard collaborative training method

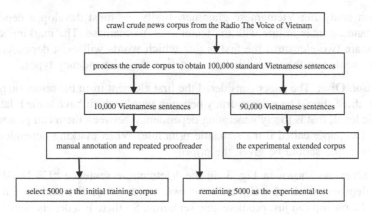

Fig. 2. The selecting and processing of corpus

3 Related Work

3.1 Selecting and Processing of Corpus

Corpus is a very important concept in the field of natural language processing. The selection of corpus is very important for the construction of treebank. Because corpus is important for both annotation and experiment.

In this paper, the corpus originally came from some crude news corpus crawled from the Radio The Voice of Vietnam (Abbreviation: VOV). The news corpus was covered with politics, economy, military, sports, entertainment and other aspects, thus ensuring a diversity of experimental data. The next step was to process the original crude data manually to obtain 100,000 standard Vietnamese sentences. Then 10,000 Vietnamese sentences among them were selected to do manual annotation and repeated proofreader in order to obtain the initial training corpus and experimental test corpus. Either of them was a small Vietnamese dependency treebank and they both contained 5000 marked Vietnamese sentences. The remaining 90,000 unmarked Vietnamese sentences were used as the experimental extended corpus. The selecting and processing of corpus was shown in Fig. 2.

3.2 Marking Vietnamese Dependency

The formulation of marking standard is not only the first step to build treebank but also one of the most important work. The marking standard of high quality should be able to accurately reflect the inherent regular pattern of language and lay a good foundation for the next research. Meanwhile, in order to facilitate users to understand the marking standard, it is also crucial of improving the marking quality and manual proofreader efficiency. In addition, the appropriate standard will play a positive role for training and testing data.

Through analyzing Vietnamese grammar, firstly we must develop a dependency marking standard table in line with the features of Vietnamese. The marking standard should contain two elements: the first is that which words will exist dependency in a Vietnamese sentence; the second is how to define their dependency types.

For Question One: The paper considered the first element from the semantic point. In a sentence, there should be a dependency between words which have some relationship in semantic level, that is to say generating dependency between them can promote new semantic. The paper called it the semantic principle. When marking dependency, the semantic principle should be given the priority.

Example One: As shown in Fig. 3, in the Vietnamese sentence **"Cô là (she) một (is) xinh đẹp(beautiful) cô gái(girl)"**, the two words **"một (is) and cô gái (girl)"** generate relationship can just promote new semantic. So there is a dependency between the two words.

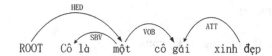

Fig. 3. A dependency marking example

Secondly, in a sentence, some words play a leading role for the expression of the sentence. They are essential in the sentence, so they are key words. However, some words play a auxiliary role in the sentence, only modifying the key words, even removing them will not affect the expression of the sentence, so they are minor words. When marking dependency, it should be ensure that the key words must be located in the core of the dependency. The minor words should depend on the key words. The paper called it the trunk principle. So that it is easy to extract the main components of a sentence in subsequent applications through the dependency. Vietnamese dependency parsing is mainly led by the predicate and analyzes the relationship between the predicate and other components.

Example Two: In the Vietnamese sentence **"cảm_ơn (thank) các_anh_chị (you) của (is) thịnh_tình (heart) tiếp_đãi (hospitality)"**, the words **"cảm_ơn (thank) and tiếp_đãi (hospitality)"** are the key words of the sentence. Other words only modify them. So, there should be a dependency between the two words.

For Question Two: The paper defined their dependency type, that is to say the paper built a Vietnamese dependency marking standard table. In order to cover various grammatical phenomena more accurately, but not lead to the problem of marking difficulty and sparse data because of excessive dependency types, the paper developed 14 kinds of dependency marking standard in line with the features of Vietnamese through analyzing Vietnamese grammar. They were shown in Table 1.

Table 1. Vietnamese dependency marking standard table

Dependency type	Tag	Description	Example
Subject-predicate	SBV	Subject-verb	I give him an apple (I <- to)
Verb-object	VOB	Verb-object	I gie him an apple (to -> apple)
Indirect-object	IOB	Indirect-object	I give him an apple (to -> him)
Fronting-object	FOB	Fronting-object	He eats any fruit (fruit <- eat)
Double	DBL	Double	My mother called me to eat dinner (called -> I)
Attribute	ATT	Attribute	Little poplar (small <- poplar)
Adverbial	ADV	Adverbial	Very quick (very <- quick)
Complement	CMP	Complement	End to eat dinner (eat -> end)
Coordinate	COO	Coordinate	Tree and grass (tree -> grass)
Preposition-object	POB	Preposition-object	In the room (in -> inside)
Left adjunct	LAD	Left adjunct	Tree and grass (and <- grass)
Right adjunct	RAD	Right adjunct	Students (students -> s)
Independent structure	IS	Independent structure	Two sentences are structurally independent
Head	ROOT	Head	The core of the whole sentence

3.3 Construction of Initial Corpus

According to the above table, the paper marked 5000 Vietnamese sentences manually as the initial corpus. The annotation storage and structure of the dependencies was shown in Table 2.

Table 2. annotation storage and structure of dependencies of the initial corpus

Vietnamese word	Part-of-speech	The location of dependency node	Dependency
Thủy	N	2	SBV
thủ	V	0	ROOT
tàu	N	2	FOB
sẽ	R	5	ADV
giao	V	2	VOB
lưu	V	5	VOB
thể	R	6	ADV
thao	N	6	DOB
...	...	...	...

3.4 Feature Selection

After a deep research about Vietnamese, it is found that the structure of Vietnamese is relatively simple. Therefore, the paper selected the current word W0, its previous word W-1, its front second word W-2, the next word W1, the next second word W2 and the part-of-speech of the current word POS0, the part-of-speech of its previous word

Table 3. Feature selection

1	W_n	Word in different locations: n = −2, −1, 0, 1, 2
2	POS_n	Part-of-speech in different locations: n = −2, −1, 0, 1, 2

POS-1, the part-of-speech of its front second word POS-2, the part-of-speech of the next word POS1, the part-of-speech of the next second word POS2 as the features. The feature selection was shown in Table 3.

The selection way fully took into account the features of Vietnamese and it had a better coverage on them. Because it not only met the basic needs but also effectively avoided the sparse data due to excessive feature selection.

4 Using Collaborative Training to Build Vietnamese Dependency Treebank

The main idea of building Vietnamese dependency treebank based on collaborative training is to build two learner models and do collaborative learning. This paper proposed the method which combined the MST algorithm [8] and the improved Nivre algorithm [14] to build two weak learner models. In the process of collaborative training, this paper used the K-Best algorithm to select one learner's forecast results, and regarded the results of high confidence as the input of the other learner to train and update repeatedly until the parameters of the learner models converged.

4.1 Confidence Judgment Criterion

After having the initial training corpus, the next problem to be considered was how to use a large number of unmarked samples effectively for collaborative training. In the process of predicting unmarked samples, the confidence judgment criterion was particularly important. In order to measure the forecast results, we used the K-Best algorithm to determine the confidence. If the K weight scores of forecast results were closer, it showed that the confidence was lower. If the weight difference of forecast results was greater, the results were more accurate. Then we chose the forecast result of the highest weight score as the marked result of Vietnamese sentence.

This paper used the following three methods to calculate confidence:

Method One: the score difference sum's reciprocal of any two different results in K-Best results:

$$H = \frac{1}{\sum_{i=1}^{k-1} \sum_{j=i+1}^{k} (score_i - score_j)} \tag{1}$$

where $score_i$ and $score_j$ were the scores of weak learners to the i-th and j-th sentences' forecast results.

Method Two: the growth rate' reciprocal of 1-Best with respect to 2-Best in K-Best results:

$$H = \frac{score_2}{score_1 - score_2} \tag{2}$$

Method three: the entropy of K results:

$$H = \sum_{i=1}^{k} -p_i \log p_i \tag{3}$$

$$p_i = \frac{score_i}{\sum_{j=1}^{k} score_j}$$

Method one and Method two showed that the difference of forecast results was greater, the confidence was more higher. Method three used the entropy to determine the confidence.

4.2 Collaborative Training Combining MST Algorithm with Improved Nivre Algorithm

Models of MST and Nivre are both data-driven models. So McDonald and Nivre proposed a combination method [15] which regarded the forecast results of one model as the training corpus of the other to promote their mutual learning of the two models.

Firstly, the paper used some of the initial corpus samples marked previously to obtain two weak dependency parsing learners S1 and S2 through training as two fully redundant views. The learner S1 was based on the MST algorithm. The learner S2 was based on the improved Nivre algorithm. Secondly, the paper randomly selected some of unmarked Vietnamese sentences as set A and set B from many unmarked samples. Then the paper respectively used the set A and the set B to predict Vietnamese dependency. The paper regarded 100 unmarked Vietnamese sentences as a unit and used the learner S1 to predict the 100 sentences. Next, the paper used the formula 1 to select 20 sentences of high confidence to mark, and then added these marked sentences into the learner S2 to train and update. Conversely, the paper also regareded 100 unmarked Vietnamese sentences as a unit and used the learner S2 to predict these 100 sentences. Next, the paper used the formula 1 to select 20 sentences of high confidence to mark, and then added these marked sentences into the learner S1 to train and update. This cycle repeated until the parameters of the learner S1 and the learner S2 became unchanged. The process of collaborative training was shown in Fig. 4.

After the parameters of the training model converged, the paper used the two learners to do Vietnamese dependency parsing for a large number of unmarked Vietnamese sentences and build Vietnamese dependency treebank. In the process of building Vietnamese dependency treebank, if the forecast results of the two learners were consistent, the results were correct. If the results were inconsistent, the paper used the formula 2 and the formula 3 to calculate confidence.

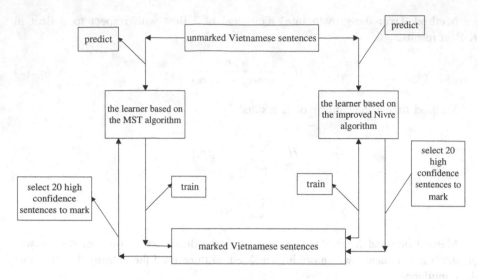

Fig. 4. The process of collaborative training

Finally, the paper used the formula 1, the formula 2 and the formula 3 to respectively calculate their average score for the forecast results of the two learners and the paper selected a higher score as the correct prediction. The paper used the model to do Vietnamese dependency parsing for 90,000 unmarked Vietnamese sentences. Then the paper also used the model to do Vietnamese dependency parsing for 5000 Vietnamese sentences in the test corpus and ultimately build a large-scale Vietnamese dependency treebank.

5   Experimental Results and Analysis

5.1   Experimental Evaluation Method

In the experiments, the paper used the Unlabeled Attachment Score (UAS), the Labeled Attachment Score (LAS) and the Root Accuracy (RA) as the evaluation standard of the final built dependency treebank. They were defined as follows:

$$UAS = \frac{\text{the number of words whose arcs are correct}}{\text{the number of all words}} * 100\%$$

$$LAS = \frac{\text{the number of words whose dependency arcs and dependencies are both correct}}{\text{the number of all words}} * 100\%$$

$$RA = \frac{\text{the number of sentences whose roots are correct}}{\text{the number of all sentences}} * 100\%$$

5.2   Experimental Design

In order to prove that the collaborative training can use a large number of unmarked Vietnamese sentences corpus effectively and improve the accuracy of dependency treebank, the paper designed three groups of comparative experiments to respectively build Vietnamese dependency treebank and compared the experimental results of different methods.

The First Comparative Experiment: Firstly, the paper used the three algorithms based on the maximum entropy to design experiments to build Vietnamese dependency treebank. They were respectively the Bottom-Up algorithm, the Top-Down algorithm and the MST algorithm. It was easy to find that the MST algorithm in USA, LAS and RA was the highest after the comparison of the experimental results. The first comparative experimental results were shown in Table 4.

Table 4. The first comparative experimental results

Method	Training corpus	Extended unmarked corpus	Test corpus	UAS %	LAS %	RA %
The Bottom-Up algorithm	5000	90000	5000	70.62	67.32	75.45
The Top-Down algorithm	5000	90000	5000	72.25	68.30	77.35
The MST algorithm	5000	90000	5000	75.25	71.01	79.68

The Second Comparative Experiment: Secondly, the paper used the improved Nivre algorithm to design experiments to build Vietnamese dependency treebank. Its experimental result in USA, LAS and RA was higher than that of the MST algorithm. Therefore, in order to take full advantage of these two algorithms and enhance their complementarity, the paper used the combination of the MST algorithm and the improved Nivre algorithm through collaborative training to build Vietnamese dependency treebank.

The Third Comparative Experiment: Finally, the paper used the collaborative training to design experiments to build Vietnamese dependency treebank. In this experiment, the paper expanded 90000 Vietnamese sentences corpus. It was easy to find that the UAS, LAS and RA of the dependency treebank based on collaborative training had been significantly improved compared with the improved Nivre algorithm after the comparison of the experimental results. In addition, we compared the collaborative training method with the latest Chinese-Vietnamese bilingual-word-alignment-corpus-based method. It was easy to find that the UAS, LAS and RA of the dependency treebank based on the former were all higher than the latter. It fully proved the effectiveness of the collaborative training method. The second and third comparative experimental results were shown in Table 5.

Table 5. The second and third comparative experimental results

Method	Training corpus	Extended unmarked corpus	Test corpus	UAS %	LAS %	RA %
The MST algorithm	5000	90000	5000	75.25	71.01	79.68
The improved Nivre algorithm	5000	90000	5000	78.35	72.32	80.76
The latest Chinese-Vietnamese bilingual-word-alignment-corpus-based method	5000	90000	5000	78.93	74.22	83.32
The collaborative training method	5000	90000	5000	80.36	76.33	83.56

5.3 Experimental Results Analysis

After careful analysis of the experimental results, it was easy to find that the accuracy of Vietnamese dependency treebank based on the collaborative training method in UAS, LAS and RA was the highest. Because the MST algorithm uses the dependency tree of the whole sentence for training and utilizes the maximum spanning tree to search for the optimal dependency tree in the process of building dependency treebank. The intermediate results of parsing cannot be applied to the subsequent analysis, leading to the low accuracy. However, the improved Nivre algorithm is based on state transition process for training and it searches for the partial optimum transfer status until the whole sentence parsing ends in the process of building dependency treebank. So the improved Nivre algorithm has the features of locality and greed and this is the reason why it has low accuracy.

However, the collaborative training method the paper proposed makes full use of the complementarity of the MST algorithm and the improved Nivre algorithm. It regards the forecast results of one model as the input of the other. When the analysis accuracy of the two models differs little, the combined model can improve the accuracy of UAS, LAS and RA significantly. In this paper, the final built dependency treebank contained 100,000 Vietnamese sentences and it eventually obtained the accuracy of 76.33 %. Compared with other methods to build Vietnamese dependency treebank, the final built dependency treebank in this paper had a larger scale and higher accuracy.

Because of the complex language features, more grammar rules and types of dependency in Vietnamese, there would be inevitably some errors in the final built treebank. Although these errors were less, they were difficult to find. So the repeated manual correction for the final built dependency treebank was necessary and this work had a great significance for improving the quality of the final built dependency treebank.

6 Conclusion and Future Work

In case that the sample corpus was relatively less, we studied the three algorithms based on the maximum entropy and the improved Nivre algorithm in depth and found that only using one algorithm to build Vietnamese dependency treebank was not very satisfactory. Therefore, the paper proposed the method which combined the MST algorithm and the improved Nivre algorithm to build Vietnamese dependency treebank. The method was based on the idea of collaborative training. Experimental results showed that the proposed method had a better effect than only using an algorithm. It also had a stable parsing performance and could effectively improve the accuracy of the final built dependency treebank. The Vietnamese dependency treebank resource was relatively inadequate. But the proposed method in this paper could effectively use unmarked Vietnamese sentences to build Vietnamese dependency treebank. The method solved the experimental difficulty due to the lack of sample corpus. At the same time, the method avoided the process of manually marking Vietnamese dependency treebank and fully saved the time of manpower and other material resource.

After a detailed study, it is not difficult to find such a grammatical phenomenon in Vietnamese. In some Vietnamese sentences, some words represent a development trend of things. But these words doesn't make much sense for the expression of the whole sentence. Moreover, there isn't any dependency between these words and other ingredients of the sentence. For example, there is a Vietnamese sentence **"Hoa (Flower) đang (is) dần (slowly) dần (slowly) nở (open) ra.".** In the sentence, **"ra"** is such a word. It represents a development trend that the flower is slowly open. In this case, the parsed dependencies based on the proposed method in this paper must be wrong. Moreover, this type of error is difficult to find through manual correction. So in the future work, we will do further research about how to remove these wrong dependencies in the process of building dependency treebank. If these dependencies are removed, the accuracy of the dependency treebank can also be significantly improved.

In addition, we will combine more methods to build Vietnamese dependency treebank through collaborative training and compare these methods with the proposed method in this paper. Our ultimate goal is to build a more-fusion-method, higher-accuracy and more-larger-scale Vietnamese dependency treebank.

References

1. Le-Hong, P., Nguyen, T.M.H.: Part-of-speech induction for Vietnamese. In: Huynh, V.N., Denoeux, T., Tran, D.H., Le, A.C., Pham, B.S. (eds.) KSE 2013, Part II. AISC, vol. 245, pp. 273–286. Springer, Heidelberg (2014)
2. Le-Hong, P., Nguyen, T.M.H., Rossignol, M., Roussanaly, A.: An empirical study of maximum entropy approach for part-of-speech tagging of Vietnamese texts. In: Actes du Traitement Automatique des Langues Naturelles (TALN-2010), Montreal, Canada (2010)
3. Dinh, Q.T., Nguyen, T.M H., Vu, X.L., Rossignol, M., Le-Hong, P., Nguyen, C.T.: Word segmentation of Vietnamese texts: a comparison of approaches. In: Proceedings of the Sixth International Conference on Language Resources and Evaluation, Marrakech, Morocco (2008)
4. Lai, T.B.Y., Huang, C.N., Zhou, M., Miao, J.B., Siu, K.C.: Span-based statistical dependency parsing of Chinese. In: Proceedings of NLPRS, pp. 677–684 (2001)
5. Yamada, H., Matsumoto, Y.: Statistical dependency analysis with support vector machines. In: Proceedings of the 8th International Workshop on Parsing Technologies (IWPT), pp. 195–206 (2003)

6. Ma, J.S., Zhang, Y., Liu, T., Li, S.: A statistical dependency parser of Chinese under small training data. In: Workshop: Beyond Shallow Analyses-Formalisms and Statistical Modeling for Deep Analyses, IJCNLP-2004, San Ya, pp. 113–118 (2004)
7. Thi, L.N., Vietnam, H.N., Minh, H.N.T., Le Hong, P.: Building a treebank for Vietnamese dependency parsing. In: IEEE RIVF International Conference on Computing and Communication Technologies - Research, Innovation, and Vision for the Future (RIVF), 10–13 November 2013
8. McDonald, R.: Non-projective dependency parsing using spanning tree algorithms, pp. 523–530. Association for Computational Linguistics (2005)
9. Eisner, J.: Three new probabilistic models for dependency parsing: an exploration. In: Proceedings of the COLING (1996)
10. Chu, Y.J., Liu, T.H.: On the shortest arborescence of a directed graph. Sci. Sinica **14**, 1396–1400 (1965)
11. Edmonds, J.: Optimum branchings. J. Res. Natl. Bur. Stand. **71B**, 233–240 (1967)
12. Beyer, K., Ramakrishnan, R.: Bottom-up computation of sparse and iceberg cubes. In: Proceedings of the 1999 ACM SIGMOD International Conference on Management of Data, Philadelphia, pp. 359–370 (1999)
13. Findlater, L., Hamilton, H.J.: Iceberg-cube algorithms: an empirical evaluation on synthetic and real data. Intell. Data Anal. **7**(2), 77–97 (2003)
14. Nivre, J., Scholz, M.: Deterministic dependency parsing of English text. In: Proceedings of the 20th International Conference on Computational Linguistics (COLING), pp. 64–70 (2004)
15. Nivre, J., McDonald, R.: Integrating graphbased and transition-based dependency parsers. In: Proceedings of ACL, pp. 950–958 (2008)

Multilinguality in NLP

"Multilinguality in PDF"

A Novel Approach to Improve the Mongolian Language Model Using Intermediate Characters

Xiaofei Yan, Feilong Bao[✉], Hongxi Wei, and Xiangdong Su

College of Computer Science, Inner Mongolia University,
Hohhot 010021, China
Xiaofeiyan_h@sina.com,
{csfeilong,cswhx,cssxd}@imu.edu.cn

Abstract. In Mongolian language, there is a phenomenon that many words have the same presentation form but represent different words with different codes. Since typists usually input the words according to their representation forms and cannot distinguish the codes sometimes, there are lots of coding errors occurred in Mongolian corpus. It results in statistic and retrieval very difficult on such a Mongolian corpus. To solve this problem, this paper proposed a method which merges the words with same presentation forms by Intermediate characters, then use the corpus in Intermediate characters form to build Mongolian language model. Experimental result shows that the proposed method can reduce the perplexity and the word error rate for the 3-gram language model by 41 % and 30 % respectively when comparing model trained on the corpus without processing. The proposed approach significantly improves the performance of Mongolian language model and greatly enhances the accuracy of Mongolian speech recognition.

Keywords: Mongolian language · Intermediate characters · N-gram language model · Speech recognition

1 Introduction

Mongolian language has a wide influence in the world. It is used in China, Mongolia, Russia and other countries where the pronunciations are almost the same but the writing forms are different from each other. The Mongolian language used in China is called "Traditional Mongolian". The corresponding Mongolian language used in Mongolia is called "Cyrillic Mongolian", which letters are borrowed from the alphabets of Russian. In this paper, the Mongolian language particularly refers to the traditional Mongolian language.

In the traditional Mongolian language, its alphabet contains 35 letters and each letter has several different presentation forms. The concrete presentation forms are determined by their positions (initial, medial or final) occurred in words. It leads to a phenomenon that many Mongolian words have the some presentation forms with different codes. In fact, most people only input the words according to their presentation forms without considering their codes. Therefore, the words bearing the same

© Springer International Publishing AG 2016
M. Sun et al. (Eds.): CCL and NLP-NABD 2016, LNAI 10035, pp. 103–113, 2016.
DOI: 10.1007/978-3-319-47674-2_9

presentation forms with different codes may be incorrect in the Mongolian text. It results in the statistical information from the corresponding Mongolian corpus is inaccurate and weakens the performance of the language model in Mongolian information processing, such as speech recognition [1], information retrieval [2], machine translation [3] and so on.

Table 1. Example of the same presentation forms

No	Presentation form	Position in word	Nominal form	Keyboard mapping	Code
1	ᠠ / ᠠ	medial, final	ᠠ	a	1820
			ᠡ	e	1821
			ᠨ	n	1828
2	᠊	final	ᠠ	a	1820
			ᠡ	e	1821
3	ᠣ / ᠥ	medial, final	ᠣ	q	1823
			ᠣ	v	1824
			ᠣ	o	1825
			ᠣ	u	1826
			ᠣ	w	1838
4	ᠣ / ᠥ	initial, medial	ᠣ	q	1823
			ᠣ	v	1824
5	ᠣ / ᠣ / ᠥ / ᠥ	initial, medial, final	ᠣ	o	1825
			ᠣ	u	1826
6	ᠢ / ᠢ	medial, final	ᠢ	i	1822
			ᠢ	y	1836
7	ᠲ / ᠲ	initial, medial	ᠲ	t	1832
			ᠳ	d	1833
8	ᠬ/ ᠬ/ ᠬ /ᠬ ᠬ/ ᠬ/ ᠬ	initial, medial	ᠬ	h	182c
			ᠭ	g	182d
9	ᠵ	medial	ᠵ	j	1835
			ᠴ	i	1832
10	ᠸ	medial	ᠸ	w	1838
			ᠠ	q	1823

To solve the above problem, several correction approaches were proposed in the literature. Jun [4] and Su et al. [5] adopted language model to correct the coding errors. Sloglo [6] proposed a correction method based on the finite automata. Jiang [7] used a rule-based approach to deal with the correction problem. However, these approaches can only correct part of the coding errors, and the words that do not follow the spelling rules or out of vocabulary (OOV) cannot be corrected.

This paper proposes a novel approach by using a kind of Intermediate characters to express the words being the same presentation forms with the different codes. In detail of our approach, the words can be converted into same forms by the Intermediate characters. Then, the language models (without processing, in Intermediate characters) were constructed. And these language models are compared by perplexity and accuracy of Mongolian speech recognition. Experimental results show that the proposed approach not only greatly reduced the perplexity of the N-gram language model, but also greatly reduced the word error rate (WER) of Mongolian speech recognition.

The rest of the paper is organized as follows. Section 2 presents the characteristics of Mongolian encoding. Section 3 describes the Mongolian Intermediate characters. Section 4 gives the Mongolian language model based on the Intermediate characters. Section 5 briefly introduces the process of speech recognition. Section 6 shows the experimental results. Section 7 draws the conclusion.

2 Characteristics of Mongolian Encoding

Mongolian characters contain two character types: nominal characters and presentation characters. According to Universal Coded Character Set (UCS) ISO/IEC 10646 and PRC National Standard GB 13000-2010, Mongolian character set only includes the nominal characters, and the units larger than one letter or less than one letter are not encoded. Generally, Mongolian letter set refers to the nominal characters (also known as nominal form). It is suitable for Mongolian writing, transmission, processing, storage, displaying. A few coding standards that created by some commercial companies use the presentation characters to encode Mongolian words [8].

Mongolian letter set contains 35 nominal characters and 58 presentation forms. Each nominal characters has several presentation forms according to its positions in words [8]. Table 1 shows Mongolian nominal characters and its corresponding presentation forms. From Table 1, we can see that some characters have different nominal forms but same presentation forms.

There is a phenomenon that many words have correct presentation forms but with the incorrect Mongolian code in Mongolian corpus. The reasons are twofold: first, the pronunciations of some letters are often confused in Mongolian dialects, such as the vowels "u" and "v", the vowels "o" and "u", the consonants "t" and "d", and thus Mongolian people living this regions often make many typo errors in text; second, some typists only care about whether the presentation forms of the words are correct or not, rather than the codes of these words, and freely replace the correct letter with another one with same presentation forms. The typo errors in Mongolian corpus makes it difficult for us to count, retrieval of the text, as well as training Mongolian language model. We use an example to illustrate this.

	undusuden(36187)	**undusuten(24708)**	undvsvden(7902)	undvsvdan(5141)
	ondosoden(2403)	undusudan(1989)	undusutan(1895)	undqsqden(1828)
	undvsvten(1181)	ondvsvdan(976)	untusuten(915)	undusudee(869)
	ondqsqden(860)	undvsvdaa(840)	ondvsvden(788)	untusutee(723)
	uedvsvden(706)	undqsqdan(661)	untvsvtan(658)	ondosoten(650)
	undvsuden(622)	undusvden(510)	uedvsvdee(474)	undusudaa(450)
	uadvsvdan(406)	uadqsqden(363)	undvsudan(281)	undvsvtan(259)
correct spelling :	uedqsqdan(256)	ondqsqdan(245)	uadusudee(240)	uedvsvdan(235)
undusuten	uedusuden(230)	uadusudan(217)	oedvsvdan(199)	oetvsvten(193)
	uadqsqdan(189)	untvsvten(187)	undusvdan(177)	ondosodan(160)
	undqsuden(158)	undqsvden(136)	ondvsoden(132)	ondvsvten(128)
	ondosotan(128)	undvsqden(128)	uetqsqtea(123)	undusoden(118)
	oetvsvtan(115)	undvsuten(114)	undqsqtan(113)	undqsqten(106)
	uadvsvden(106)	uadvsvdaa(100)		

Fig. 1. Different spelling and frequency about the same Mongolian word "⟨Mongolian script⟩"

For the Mongolian word "⟨Mongolian script⟩" (meaning: minority), its keyboard mapping is "undusuten". According to the analysis on a Mongolian corpus including 76 million Mongolian words, this word appears 102532 times, and only 24708 times of its codes are correctly. The other 78124 ones are typed as other words with the same presentation forms. Actually, there are 291 words that have the same presentation forms as the word "⟨Mongolian script⟩" (meaning: minority). Figure 1 shows the Mongolian word "⟨Mongolian script⟩" (meaning: minority) and its typos whose frequency is greater than 100 in the corpus.

3   Mongolian Intermediate Characters

This paper puts forward a novel method to represent the Mongolian words according to the characteristics of Mongolian presentation forms. This method uses Latin characters to represent the nominal letters, and the nominal characters with same presentation forms are represented by the same Latin characters. These Latin characters are called Intermediate characters. In some cases, a nominal character is converted into multiple Intermediate characters depending on its positions in words. That is, the words in same presentation forms are mapping to the same Intermediate characters string. It is worth pointing out that a string of Latin characters can only correspond to a string of Intermediate characters and a string of Intermediate characters can correspond to one or multiple strings of Latin characters with some presentation forms.

In experiment, we compare the language models built on the Mongolian corpus without processing and the corresponding Mongolian corpus represented in Intermediate characters.

In this paper, we use the regular expression to convert Mongolian words into Intermediate characters form. This takes the advantages of regular expression that the rules can be easily expressed by regular expressions. At the same time, we integrate some rules to correct the spelling errors. In this paper, we summarize 116 transformation and correction rules of Intermediate characters. We do the related statistics that these

Table 2. Normalize rules on different nominal form with same presentation characters

No	Match regular expressions (RE)	Replace RE	Priority	Interpretation
1	(g|h)([eiouIU])	G$2	4	When "g" and "h" are in initial of the word and the next letter is "e","i", "o", "u", it uses "G" to replace "g" and "h"
2	^[_'"'&*\^]{0,}(u|o)([[:ANY:]])	U$2	4	When "u" and "o" are in initial of the word, they will be replaced with "U"
3	^[_'"'&*\^]{0,}(w|v)([[:ANY:]])	V$2	4	When "w" and "v" are in initial of the word, they will be replaced with "V"
4	([^ghG])['"]{0,}(a|e)['"]{0,}$	$1A	5	When the previous character is "non-g" or "non-h", "a" and "e" in the final of word will be replaced with "A"
5	([^ghG])['"]{0,}(a|e)([[:ANY:]])	$1A$3	4	When the previous character is "non-g" or "non-h", "a" and "e" will be replaced with "A"
6	([[:VOW:]])['"]{0,}(yi|ii)([[:ANY:]])	$1I$3	5	When the previous character is a vowel, "yi" and "ii" will be replaced with "I"
7	([[:VOW:]])['"]{0,}y['"]{0,}([[:CSNT-W:]])	$1I$2	4	When the previous character is a vowel and the next character is consonant of "non-W", "y" is replaced with "I"
8	([[:VOW:]])['"]{0,}h['"]{0,}([[:CSNT:]])	$1 g$2	4	When the previous character is a vowel and the next character is consonant, "h" is replaced with "g"
9	([nmlNrsd])['"]{0,}aaa([[:ANY:]])	$1 ha$2	6	When the previous character is "n", "m", "l", "N","r", "s", "d"; "aaa" will be replaced with "ha"
10	([[:ANY:]])ng['"]{0,}([[:CSNT:]])	$1 N$2	4	When the next character is a consonant, "ng" will be replaced with "N"

rules can cover most of the Mongolian word. Table 2 shows part of these rules. " _'"'&*^ " represents the Mongolian control character; ":ANY:" represents of any Mongolian letter; ":VOW: " represents all vowels; ":CSNT:" means all consonants; "G", "U", "V", "A", "I" and other characters represent Intermediate forms which are defined. In Table 2, No 1–7 is the Intermediate characters conversion rule and No 8–10 is the correct rule. For example, the 291 Mongolian words having the same presentation forms as Mongolian words "ᠲᠣᠭᠣᠯᠣᠭᠤᠨ" (meaning: minority) will be converted into the same Intermediate characters string "UnTOsOTAn".

4 Language Model Establishment

Language model is a mathematical model to describe the inherent laws of natural language. It is the core of computational linguistics. In theory, the structure of language model is to induce, discover, and obtain the inherent laws of natural language in statistical and structural aspects. Language model are crucial components in many Natural Language Processing (NLP) applications, such as speech recognition, handwriting recognition, machine translation, information retrieval and so on.

N-gram language model [9] has been widely used in statistical language model. The probability of a Mongolian word sequence $w = w_1 w_2 \ldots \ldots w_m$ can be written in the form of conditional probability:

$$p(w) = p(w_1 w_2 \ldots \ldots w_m) = \prod_{i=1}^{m} p(w_i | w_1^{i-1}) \approx \prod_{i=1}^{m} p\left(w_i | w_{i-n+1}^{i-1}\right) \tag{1}$$

The probability of the m-th words w_m depends on all the words $w_1 w_2 \ldots \ldots w_{m-1}$. We can now use this model to estimate the probability of seeing sentences in the corpus by providing a simple independence assumption based on the Markov assumption [10]. Corresponding to the language model, the current word is only related to the previous n−1 words. From the Eq. (1), we can see that the target of language model is how to estimate the conditional probability of the next word in the list using $p(w_i | w_{i-n+1}^{i-1})$. The most commonly probability estimation method we used is the maximum likelihood estimation (MLE).

$$p\left(w_i | w_{i-n+1}^{i-1}\right) = \frac{c(w_{i-n+1}^{i})}{c(w_{i-n+1}^{i-1})} \tag{2}$$

$c(*)$ means the total count of the N-gram in the corpus. However, a drawback of the MLE is that the N-tuple corpus which does not appear in the training set will be given zero-Probability. This is not allowed in the NLP. Smoothing algorithm can be used to solve this kind of zero-Probabilities problem. In this paper, we us the Kneser-Ney smoothing algorithm [11].

Based on the Intermediate characters to build language model, the Mongolian word sequence $w = w_1 w_2 \ldots \ldots w_m$ are converted into its corresponding Intermediate characters $w' = w_1' w_2' \ldots \ldots w_m'$. We can use N-gram probabilities to approximate this as:

$$p\left(w'\right) = p\left(w_1' w_2' \ldots \ldots w_m'\right) \approx \prod_{i=1}^{m} p\left(w_i' | w_{i-n+1}'^{i-1}\right) \tag{3}$$

5 Mongolian Speech Recognition

Speech recognition allows the machine to turn the speech signal into text or commands through the process of identification and understanding [12]. The process of speech recognition mainly includes pre-processing, feature extraction, model training, decoding, post-processing. Its basic structure is shown in Fig. 2. Pro-processing consists of pre-filtering, sampling, quantization, adding window, endpoint detection, and pre-emphasis towards the speech signal. Feature extraction is to effectively extract the features form the speech signal. Speech decoding is to look for the maximum probability of the output word sequences toward the speech signal, which greatly relies on the acoustic model, language model and pronunciation dictionary and is carried out by Viterbi algorithm [15]. For the speech feature $x = x_1x_2\ldots\ldots$ and its corresponding word sequence $w = w_1, w_2\ldots\ldots$, the formula of speech recognition based on the maximum a post-probability (MAP) is shown as follows:

$$\hat{w} = argmax_w\{p(w|x)\} \approx argmax_w\{p(x|w)p(w)\} \tag{4}$$

Form the Eq. (4), we just need to calculate the maximum product of $p(x|w)$ and $p(w)$. $p(x|w)$ is the probability of speech feature vector sequence x under the condition of word sequence w, which is determined by the acoustic model. $p(w)$ is the probability of a word sequence w, which is determined by the language model.

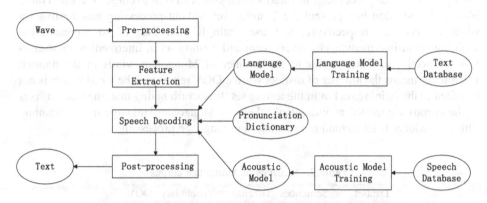

Fig. 2. The structure of automatic speech recognition

Currently, mainstream technology is that use the N-gram and recurrent neural network (RNN) [13, 14] to build language model, combining with deep neural network (DNN) and hidden Markov model (HMM) for acoustic model. This paper uses the language model of 3-gram and the acoustic model of DNN or LSTM in Mongolian speech recognition. The language model (without processing, in Intermediate characters) was respectively created, compared in perplexity experiments and speech recognition experiments.

6 Experiment

In this paper, the performance of the language model was verified on the Mongolian corpus through a series of experiments, including the perplexity experiments and speech recognition experiments. The evaluation metrics are perplexity (PPL) of language model and WER of speech recognition.

6.1 Perplexity

6.1.1 Data

The datasets is constructed by the page content coming from mgyxw.net, mongol. people.com.cn, holvoo.net and more than 20 other websites. Part of those website uses the Mongolian menksoft encoding and the other uses the Mongolian standard encoding. In order to unify coding, the text of Mongolian menksoft encoding was converted into Mongolian standard encoding. The correct rate reached over 99 % by using the Mongolian conversion toolkit (http://mtg.mglip.com) which was developed by Inner Mongolia University. The Mongolian corpus used for constructing the language model is about 1.2G in data size. In this paper, 10-fold cross-validation method was used to evaluate the experimental performance. Table 3 lists the details of the training set and testing set (without processing, in Intermediate characters) in average. We use Train_ Mon and Test_Mon to represent the Training set without processing and Testing set without processing respectively, and use Train_IC and Test_IC to represent the Training set in Intermediate characters form and Testing set in Intermediate characters form respectively. Tokens refer to the number of Mongolian words in the dataset; vocabulary means the number of distinct words; OOV represents the word which is not included in the training set but in the testing set. It is worth noting that, the case suffixes in the corpus are treated as individual tokens in Mongolian language model training. This is a widely used technique in Mongolian language processing.

Table 3. Statistics of Mongolian corpus

Dataset	Sentences	Tokens	Vocabulary	OOV
Train_Mon	3033075	70886970	1778571	
Train_IC	3033075	70886970	**1033450**	
Test_Mon	337008	7886050	444289	123504
Test_IC	337008	7886050	**263301**	**70439**

In Table 3, the number of vocabulary relatively reduced by 41.89 % in train-ing set and 40.74 % in testing set. The OOV of testing set decreased 42.97 %. The reduction of vocabulary was due to Mongolian spaces which were incorrectly used. For example, case suffix "ᠠᠨ" (correspond to the keyboard: "-bar") and its stem should have been continuously wrote with the Mongolian space (correspond to the keyboard: "-") in the text. However, some text use the common spaces instead of Mongolian space in front of many case suffixes and possessive suffixes. The vocabulary of the corpus in Intermediate characters form is greatly reduced compared to that of the corpus without processing. The reduction ratio of vocabulary and OOV can be seen that many Mongolian words have same presentation forms but different codes.

6.1.2 Evaluation of Language Model

Perplexity is a common metric to measure the performance of a language model. The perplexity PPT (T) of the model $p(w_i|w_{i-n+1}^{i-1})$ is defined as follows:

$$PPT(T) = 2^{H_p(T)} = 2^{-\frac{1}{W_T}\log_2 P(T)} \tag{5}$$

where $H_p(T)$ represents the cross entropy for the testing data T in the model $p(w_i|w_{i-n+1}^{i-1})$. It is a basic criterion for evaluating language model performance that the lower perplexity is, the better performance of the language model is.

Table 4. The perplexity of Mongolian language model

Model	Perplexity PPT(T)		
	1-gram	2-gram	3-gram
Trained on Train_Mon and tested on Test_Mon	6130.706	609.0156	238.1425
Trained on Train_IC and tested on Test_IC	**2887.565**	**349.8624**	**139.3985**

Table 4 shows the performance of N-gram language model using SRILM toolkit [16]. We trained 1-gram, 2-gram and 3-gram language model toward the corpus without processing and the corresponding Mongolian Intermediate characters, respectively. It can be seen from Table 4, the perplexity of 1-gram, 2-gram and 3-gram language model was relatively reduced by 52.9 %, 41.98 % and 41.46 % respectively when the training corpus represented in Intermediate characters form. It is clear that the performance of the Mongolian language model has been significantly improved by our proposed approach.

6.2 Speech Recognition

6.2.1 Dataset
This experiment takes the Kaldi [17] speech recognition system as the platform using state-of-the-art acoustic models trained on the Mongolian corpus. The dataset contains approximately 78 h of speech, in which 70 h of speech (62794 sentences) is used to train the acoustic model training and which 8 h of speech (6987 sentences) acts as testing set. The pronunciation dictionary consists of 38235 words.

Mongolian corpus used for constructing the language model is the same as experiment 6.1. In addition, this experiment is performed on the basis of perplexity experiment.

6.2.2 Evaluation of Speech Recognition
When testing, the acoustic model of speech recognition system is kept unchanged and the language model is changed to calculate, compare the WER in the experiment. The evaluation metric is WER defined as follows:

$$WER = (I + D + S)/N \tag{6}$$

where I, D, S are the numbers of numeric insertions, deletions and substitutions, respectively. N is the total number of numeric entities in the corpus.

Table 5. The WER under different Mongolian language model

Model	Word error rate WER/%		
	1-gram	2-gram	3-gram
Baseline DNN (Trained on Train_Mon and tested on Test_Mon)	30.66	16.47	12.37
DNN (Trained on Train_IC and tested on Test_IC)	**27.01**	**12.37**	**7.83**
LSTM (Trained on Train_Mon and tested on Test_Mon)	20.0	10.35	9.05
LSTM (Trained on Train_IC and tested on Test_IC)	**18.06**	**8.11**	**5.97**

In Mongolian speech recognition, we compared the WER for the 1-gram, 2-gram and 3-gram language model toward the corpus without processing and the corresponding Mongolian Intermediate characters, respectively. Experimental results are shown in Table 5. We can see that the WER in testing set with the language model trained on the dataset Train_IC is significant lower than that with the language model trained on the dataset Train_Mon. Meanwhile, the WER of DNN+3-gram model [18] and LSTM+3-gram model has been respectively reduced by 36.7 %, 34.03 % using Intermediate characters, greatly improving the performance of Mongolian speech recognition. It also proves that converting the training corpus into Intermediate characters form can make the language model performs better.

7 Conclusion

This paper presents a method that combining different presentation form using Intermediate characters to build Mongolian language model. The experimental results show that this method decreases the vocabulary by 41 % and reduce the perplexity of 3-gram language model by 41.46 %. Meanwhile, the WER for the 3-gram language model decrease around 30 % when comparing with the language model trained without processing in the Mongolian speech recognition. This approach not only effectively improves the performance of Mongolian language model, but also greatly enhances the accuracy of Mongolian speech recognition. It is of great significance to related technological development of Mongolian natural language processing.

In future, we will investigate the processing approach of this kind of word in order to improve the retrieval and statistics performance of the Mongolian words.

Acknowledgements. This research was partially supported by the China National Nature Science Foundation (No. 61263037 and No. 61563040), Inner Mongolia nature science foundation (No. 2014BS0604) and the program of high-level talents of Inner Mongolia University.

References

1. Bao, F., Gao, G., Yan, X., Wang, W.: Segmentation-based Mongolian LVCSR approach. In: 2013 IEEE International Conference on Acoustics, Speech and Signal Processing (ICASSP), pp. 8136–8139 (2013)
2. Gao, G., Jin, W., Long, F.: Mongolian text retrieval: language specialities and IR model. J. Comput. Inf. Syst. 1561–1568 (2009)
3. Bao, F., Gao, G., Yan, X., Wang, H.: Language model for cyrillic mongolian to traditional Mongolian conversion. In: Li, J., Ji, H., Zhao, D., Feng, Y. (eds.) NLPCC 2015. CCIS, vol. 9362, pp. 13–18. Springer, Heidelberg (2013). doi:10.1007/978-3-642-41644-6_2
4. Jun, Z.: Design and Implementation of Mongolian Word Analyzing and Correcting Based on Statistical Language Method. Inner Mongolia University, Hohhot (2007)
5. Su, C., Hou, H., Yang, P., Yuan, H.: Based on the statistical translation framework of the Monglian automatic spelling correction method. J. Chin. Inf. Proces. 175–179 (2013)
6. Sloglo: A proofreading algorithm of Mongolian text based on nondeterministic finite automata. J. Chin. Inf. Proces. 110–115 (2009)
7. Jiang, B.: Research on Rule-Based the Method of Mongolian Automatic Correction. Inner Mongolia University, Hohhot (2014)
8. GB 25914-2010: Information technology of traditional Mongolian nominal characters, presentation characters and control characters using the rules, 10 January 2011
9. Zong, C.: Natural Language Processing, 2nd edn., pp. 83–104. Tsinghua University Press, Beijing (2013)
10. Jurafsky, D., Martin, J.: Speech and Language Processing, 2nd edn. Prentice Hall, Upper Saddle River (2009)
11. Frankie, J.: Modified Kneser-Ney smoothing of n-gram models. RIACS Technical report (2000)
12. Meng, J., Zhang, J., Zhao, H.: Overview of the speech recognition technology. In: International Conference on Computational and Information Sciences (2012)
13. Mikolov, T., Karafiat, M., Burget, L., et al.: Recurrent neural network based language model. In: Proceedings of 11th Annual Conference of the International Speech Communication Association, Makuhari, Japan, pp. 1045–1048 (2010)
14. Mikolov, T., Kombrink, S., Burget, L., et al.: Extensions of recurrent neural network language model. In: Proceedings of the IEEE International Conference on Acoustics, Speech and Signal Processing, Prague, Czech Republic, pp. 5528–5531 (2011)
15. Forney Jr., G.D.: The Viterbi algorithm. Proc. IEEE **61**(3), 268–278 (1973)
16. Stolcke, A., et al.: SRILM –an extensible language modeling toolkit. In: Proceedings of the International Conference on Spoken Language Processing, vol. 2, Denver, pp. 901–904 (2002)
17. Povey, D., Ghoshal, A., Boulianne, G., Burget, L., Glembek, O., Goel, N., Hannemann, M., Motlicek, P., Qian, Y., Schwarz, P., Silovsky, J., Stemmer, G., Vesely, K.: The Kaldi speech recognition toolkit. In: IEEE 2011 Workshop on Automatic Speech Recognition and Understanding. IEEE Signal Processing Society (2011)
18. Zhang, H., Bao, F., Gao, G.: Mongolian speech recognition based on deep neural networks. In: Sun, M., Liu, Z., Zhang, M., Liu, Y. (eds.) CCL 2015. Lecture Notes in Artificial Intelligence (LNAI), vol. 9427, pp. 180–188. Springer, Heidelberg (2015). doi:10.1007/978-3-319-25816-4_15

Improved Joint Kazakh POS Tagging and Chunking

Hao Wu[1,2(✉)] and Gulila Altenbek[1,2(✉)]

[1] College of Information Science and Engineering,
Xinjiang University, Urumqi, China
{18299151954, glaxd2014}@163.com
[2] The Base of Kazakh and Kirghiz Language of National Language Resource
Monitoring and Research Centre Minority Languages, Urumqi, China

Abstract. This paper describes a mixing model of joint POS tagging and chunking for Kazakh where partial optimal solution provide feature information for joint model. A improved beam-search algorithm use dynamic beam instead of unified beam to obtain search space of small-but-excellent during both training and decoding phases of the model. Moreover we can statistical induction the information of chunk to disambiguation of multi-category words and experiment shows the precision is improved from 81.6 % to 87.7 % by information of chunk.

Keywords: Mixing model · Joint model · Dynamic beam · Multi-category words

1 Introduction

The tasks of Kazakh part-of-speech (POS) tagging and chunking have been widely investigated since the early stages of NLP research. Meanwhile, this task is a the key techniques needed for automatic text categorization, topic extraction patent information retrieval and other text understanding tasks and is very important for to the practice on information retrieval, machine translation, dictionary compiling, and other natural language processing tasks. At the present stage, the Kazakh part-of-speech (POS) tagging and chunking is needed before Kazakh corpus annotation and further processing at a later stage and is an important part of Kazakh Language Processing. The realization of the tasks will definitely promote the research of linguistics and translation theory of the languages of minorties. Typically, POS tagging and chunking are modeled in a pipelined way. However, the pipelined method is prone to error propagation. The state-of-the-art accuracy of Kazakh POS tagging is about 89.3 % [1], which is much lower than that of English (about 97 %) [2] and Chinese (about 93.5). Moreover POS tagging errors cannot be corrected by tagging and structure of chunk.

In order to avoid error propagation and make use of chunk information for POS tagging, POS tagging and chunking can be viewed as a single task: given a raw Kazakh input sentence, the joint POS tagger considers all possible tagged and sequences, and chooses the overall best output. A major challenge for such a joint system is the large search space faced by the decoder. To deal with the increased search space, we adopt a

© Springer International Publishing AG 2016
M. Sun et al. (Eds.): CCL and NLP-NABD 2016, LNAI 10035, pp. 114–124, 2016.
DOI: 10.1007/978-3-319-47674-2_10

recently proposed beam-search extension to shift-reduce joint model [5–8], which enables the model to pack equivalent tagger states, improving both speed and accuracy.

In this paper, we propose the mixing model which is acquire partial optimal solution to provide some feature in order to the joint model. For example, we obtain the unlabeled chunk to provide the coarse structure of sentence firstly. Moreover for further improving both speed and accuracy of decoder, we propose the search space dynamic beam to obtain the small-but-excellent as far as possible. This provides the rich feature information, leading to large improvements over using either the generative model or the discriminative model in term of POS tagging (the mixing model achieves 89.1 % precision on the Xingjiang Daily Tagging set, compared to figures of 81.4 % and 86.1 % for the HMM molde and ME Models). In term of chunking, the precision is large improvements over using either CRF model or ME model. The remaining part of the paper is organized as follows. Section 2 gives a brief introduction to the foregoing method of POS tagging and chunk and propose the mixing model. Section 3 describes the perceptron algorithm and decode process. Section 4 describes the disambiguation of multi-category words and the setting of feature. Section 5 presents experimental results and empirical analyses. Section 6 conclude the paper.

2 The Analyze Models

2.1 The Pipelined Method

Given an input sentence $x = w1...wn$, we denote its POS tagging sequence by $t = t_1...t_n$, where $ti \in T$, $1 \le i \le n$, and T is the POS tagging set. A chunk sequence is denoted by $d = \{(b, e, ct): 0 \le h \le n, 0 < m \le n, ct \in CT\}$, where CT is the chunk tags set, (b, e) represents a chunk $(wb...we)$ whose first word of chunk is wb and last word is we. The pipelined method treats POS tagging and chunking as two cascaded problems. First, an optimal POS tagging sequence $\hat{t}$ is determined.

$$\hat{t} = \arg \max t \, Score_{pos}(x, t) \tag{1}$$

In a perceptron, the score of a tag sequence is:

$$Score_{pos}(x, t) = w_{pos} \cdot f_{pos}(x, t) \tag{2}$$

where $f_{pos}(x, t)$ refers to the feature vector and w_{pos} is the corresponding weight vector. Then, an optimal chunking $\hat{ct}$ is determined based on x and $\hat{t}$.

$$\hat{ct} = \arg \max_{ct} Score_{cnk}(x, ct) \tag{3}$$

Similar to POS tagging, the score a chunking sequence is

$$Score_{cnk}(x, \hat{t}, ct) = w_{cnk} \cdot f_{cnk}(x, \hat{t}, ct) \tag{4}$$

2.2 The Joint Models

In the joint method [5–8], we aim to simultaneously solve the two problems.

$$(\hat{t}, \hat{ct}) = \arg \max t, ct \; Score_{joint}(x, t, ct) \tag{5}$$

Under the linear model, the score of a tagged sentence sequence is:

$$Score_{joint}(x, t, ct) = Score_{pos}(x, t) + Score_{cnk}(x, t, ct) = w_{pos \oplus cnk} \cdot f_{pos \oplus cnk}(x, t, d) \tag{6}$$

For simplicity, we denote

$$w_{pos} \cdot f_{pos}(x, t) + w_{cnk} \cdot f_{cnk}(x, \hat{t}, ct) = w_{pos \oplus cnk} \cdot f_{pos \oplus cnk}(x, t, d)$$

where $w_{pos \oplus cnk}$ means the concatenation of weights of feature.

Under the joint model, the weights of POS and chunk features, $w_{pos \oplus cnk}$ are simultaneously learned. We expect that POS and chunk features can interact each other to determine an optimal joint result.

2.3 The Mixing Model

In Sect. 2.1, we know that POS tagging and chunking are modeled in a pipelined way. However, the pipelined method is prone to error propagation. The state-of-the-art accuracy of Kazakh POS tagging is about 89.3 %, which is much lower than that of English and Chinese. Simultaneously, Joint approach is that since the shift-reduce model processes an input sentence in a right-to-left manner [9], it cannot exploit look-ahead POS tags, which a pipeline shift-reduce parser can consider, to determine the next action. In experiment, the ablation of the features including look-ahead POS results about 1.1 % decrease in POS tagging performance on the development set, suggesting that the look-ahead POS information is indispensable to achieve the state-of-the-art performance.

In order to make up for shortcomings pipelined method and joint method, we combine the two approaches. First, before we analyze the sentence, we use the method of segmentation with perceptron algorithm (Zhang and Clark [10]) to identify sentence chunks (not give a label). We follow the convention of word-based chunking, and define the set of chunks tags as {B, E, M, S}. The tags B, E, M represent the character being the beginning, end, and middle of a multiple-word chunk, respectively, and the tags S represents the character being a single-word chunk.

For example: ۇستەلM/مەن M/ارقالىE/ورىندىقB (table and chair).

Then we have improved shift-reduce process [9], and show in Fig. 1. Note that the transfer system is composed of four states and four actions. Four states, respectively, comprise one queue, two linked list and a stack, the input is assumed to sentence, and the word waiting to be processed are stored in first queue, the first linked list holds the partial POS tagging that are built during the labeling process, the chunk of none tag waiting to be processed are stored in second linked list, the s tack holds the partial POS tagging and chunk that are built during the labeling process.

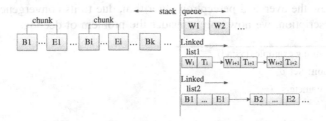

Fig. 1. The improved shift-reduce process

The main shift-reduce actions are:

- SHIFT1, which choose the next word from queue to POS tagging, then pushes the word-POS pair in the queue onto the first linked list;
- SHIFT2, which pushes the first word-POS pair in the linked list onto the stack;
- REDUCE, which predict the position of word in chunk (start, middle and end). If the word is start of chunk, predict tag of chunk according the feature. Otherwise the word merge with top element of stack.
- TERMINATE, which check the linked list 2 is empty.

3 Learning and Decoding Algorithm

3.1 Linear Models for NLP

We follow the framework outlined in Collins [2, 3]. The task is to learn a mapping from inputs $x \in \chi$ to outputs $y \in y$. For example, χ might be a set of sentences, with being a set of possible POS tagging. We assume:

- Training examples (x_i, y_i) $i = 1 \ldots n$
- A function GEN which enumerates a set of candidates GEN(x) for an input x.
- A representation Φ mapping each $(x, y) \in \chi \times y$ to a feature vector $\Phi(x, y) \in R^d$.
- A parameter vector $\bar{\alpha} \in R^d$.
- The components GEN, Φ and $\bar{\alpha}$ define a mapping from an input x to an output F(x) through

$$F(x) = \arg \max_{y \in GEN(x)} \Phi(x, y) \cdot \bar{\alpha} \qquad (7)$$

Where $\Phi(x, y)$ $\bar{\alpha}$ is the inner product $\sum_s \alpha_s \Phi_s(x, y)$, The learning task is to set the parameter values $\bar{\alpha}$ using the training examples as evidence. The decoding algorithm is a method for searching for the arg max in Eq. 7.

3.2 The Perceptron Algorithm

In the 3.1 section, we assume the $\bar{\alpha}$ is the parameter vector in the model. Each element in $\bar{\alpha}$ gives a weight to its corresponding element in $\Phi(x, y)$, which is the count of a particular feature over the whole sentence y. We calculate the $\bar{\alpha}$ value by supervised learning, using the averaged perceptron algorithm [10–12], given in Algorithm 1.

After review the averaged perceptron algorithm, due to its convergence properties have a full description, we now only consider the problem of decode.

Inputs: Training examples $(x_i; y_i)$

Initialization: Set $\bar{\alpha} = 0$

Output: Parameters $\bar{\alpha}$

Algorithm:

For $t = 1 \dots T, i = 1 \dots n$

   Calculate $z_i = \arg\max_{z \in GEN(x_i)} \Phi(x_i, z) \cdot \bar{\alpha}$

   if $(z_i \neq y_i)$ then $\bar{\alpha} = \bar{\alpha} + \Phi(x_i, y_i) - \Phi(x_i, z_i)$

Algorithm 1. Averaged perceptron algorithm

Variables: state item item = (S,Q), where
      S is stack and Q is incoming queue;
      the agenda agenda;
      list of state items next;
Algorithm:
for item $\in$ agenda:
   if item.score = agenda.bestScore and
   item.isFinished:
   rval = item
      break
      next = []
      for move $\in$ item.legalMoves:
         next.push(item.TakeAction(move))
agenda = next.getBBest()
Outputs: rval

Algorithm 2. Beam-search algorithm

3.3   Decode Algorithm

In Sect. 3.2, we introduced the averaged perceptron algorithm. Note that the most complex step of the method is finding $zi = \arg\max_{y \in GEN(x)} \Phi(x, y) \cdot \bar{\alpha}$ and this is precisely the decoding problem [14, 15]. In this section, we will introduce an improved beam-search algorithm to improve decode performance.

Beam Search Algorithm. First of all, we apply beam-search [4, 9, 10], keeping the B highest scoring state items in an agenda during the shift-reduce process. The agenda is initialized with a state item containing the starting state, i.e. an empty stack and three queue consisting of all word, partial word-POS pairs and all chunk of unlabeled from the sentence. At each stage in the decoding process, existing items from the agenda are progressed by applying legal shift-reduce actions. From all newly generated state items, the B highest scoring are put back on the agenda. The decoding process is terminated when the highest scored state item in the agenda reaches the final state. If multiple state items have the same highest score, shift-reduce process terminates if any of them are finished. The algorithm is shown in Algorithm 2.

Optimized Beam-Search Algorithm. In the averaged beam-search algorithm, choose the B highest scoring state items in an agenda during the shift-reduce process. For uniform B, we select the appropriate value of B is difficult. If we choose the value of B is too large, while decoding accuracy has improved, but the decoding speed is greatly reduced. The value of B is too small, the opposite effect. Therefore we designed a dynamic value B to solve the above problems.

At each step in the decoding process, outputs a set of prediction $\{<(t_1(x), r_1), \ldots, (t_1(x), r_k)>, r_i \geq r_{i+1}\}$, where $t_i(x)$ is a possible outcome of each shift action, r_i is a score of result. Suppose that $(<r_1/r_i = Br>, Br \geq 1)$, where Br is a relative score. Note that with a larger value of Br, I have a less possibility to as a gold prediction. Therefore we filter out the result of slim chance by setting a reasonable threshold. Moreover, the closer that the value of Br is to 1, the word have greater possibility is a multi-category words in the word tagging process. Hence, we can set a threshold and mark each words of relative value within the threshold for the disambiguation of multi-category words. For chunking, we summary rule to constrain the search space of our models due to their high complexity.

4 A Full Description of the Tagging Approach

This section gives a full description of the tagging approach. We first describe the disambiguation of multi-category words, and then move on to the baseline feature set for the mixing model.

4.1 Disambiguation of Multi-category Words

In the Sect. 3.3, we introduce the relative score Br and mark each words of relative value within the threshold. For mark words, we regard it as a multi-category words. Next, we will introduce the main process disambiguation of multi-category words by using the information of chunking [13].

First of all, we extract the structure of basic chunk from the corpus as a set of rule.

For example, we statistical induction the structure of noun phrase shown in following:

(1)ەر وقىتۇشىلار   (Male teachers,   n + n)

(2)ۇستەل جانە ورىندىق   (table and chair,   n + conj + n)

(3)مەن جانە ونىڭ   (he and me,   pron + conj + pron)

(4)مەنىڭ كىتاپ   (my book,   pron + n)

(5)گۇل ادەمى   (beautiful flower,   adj + n)

(6)قارتتار قۇرمەت ەتۇ   (respect senior,   v + n)

(7)العان نارسەلەرىنە ٴراسىمىات تا گۇلدەۇ(pleased with hold the flower, adj + adv + n)

(8) قول ارىا   (push cart,   v + n)

(9)گۇل تال 5   (five flower,   num + n)

We now assume w_i is a marked word, $a_1 \cdot a_2$ is ambiguity tag of w_i and t_k is a tag of current chunk that contains the word w_i. Moreover the C_1, C_2 represent the corresponding structure of a_1 and a_2. Then find t_k corresponding rule sets, traverse the set to check C_1 and C_2 whether or not it was in the set. Next we operate in three steps:

1. If there is only one in the set, we think that it is POS tagging of w_i.
2. If neither of them not in the set, we mark the word and the chunk as wrong recognition, then to further identify them by ME (Maximum Entropy) model. For the word, we can use the information of chunk from the context.
3. If all of them in the set, the word will tagged by ME model again. For the two score of each part-of-speech, you might multiply them together. Choose the part-of-speech of the biggest product as tagging of the word.

4.2 Features

For this paper, we wanted to compare the results of a perceptron model with a generative model for a comparable feature set. Unlike in [11], there is no look-ahead statistic, so we modified the feature set from those papers to explicitly include the next unlabeled chunk and POS tag of the next word. But for the neighboring chunk, we think that it have less correlation between the last word of first chunk and first word of second chunk, therefore we have not choose it as feature. Otherwise the features are basically the same as in those papers. To concisely present the baseline feature set, let us establish a notation. All of the labels that we will include in our feature sets. Note that we recognize POS and chunk to choose different feature. In terms of feature extraction, we according feature template to choose features set. For POS tagging:

(1) If Wi is first word of the chunk and the chunk and previous chunk is more than one word, the POS tagging feature template shown in Fig. 2(a).
(2) If Wi is last word of the chunk and the chunk and next chunk is more than one word, the POS tagging feature template shown in Fig. 2(b).
(3) If the chunk is only a word. The POS tagging feature template shown in Fig. 2(c).

For chunking: We set the feature template in Fig. 2(d).

In those feature template, The current word the symbols S0 represent the current word, S1, S2, and S3 represent the top three nodes on the stack, the symbols N0, N1 and represent the first two words in the incoming linked list1, and symbols P1 and P1 represent the top two chunk on the stack. L0, L1, L2 represents following two unlabeled chunk of the current word. w represents word, c represents structure of chunk, t represents the tag for a word or a chunk.

(a)

Unigrams	S_0w, S_0t, N_0w, N_0t, N_1w, N_1t, P_0t, P_0c, P_0w, P_1t, P_1c, L_1c, L_1w, L_2w.
Bigrams	S_0wN_0w, S_0wN_0c, N_0wN_1w, N_0tN_1w, N_0tN_1t, P_0tS_0w, P_0cS_0w, P_0wS_0w, P_0tL_1c, P_0tL_1w, P_1tL_1c, P_0wL_1c, P_0cL_1c
Trigrams	$P_0tS_0wN_0w$, $P_0wS_0wN_0t$, $P_0cS_0wN_0t$, $S_0wN_0tL_1c$, $P_0tN_0wN_1w$, $P_0cN_0wN_1w$, $N_0wN_1wL_1c$, $N_0wN_1wL_1w$

(b)

Unigrams	S_0w, S_0t, S_1w, S_1t, S_2w, S_2t, P_0t, P_0c, P_0w, P_1t, P_1c, L_1c, L_1w, L_2w.
Bigrams	S_0wS_1w, S_0wS_1t, S_1wS_2w, S_1tS_2w, S_1tS_2t, P_0tS_0w, P_0cS_0w, P_0wS_0w, P_0tL_1c, P_0tL_1w, P_1tL_1c, P_0wL_1c, P_0cL_1c
Trigrams	$P_0tS_0wS_1w$, $P_0wS_0wS_1t$, $P_0cS_0wS_1t$, $S_0wS_1tL_1c$, $P_0tS_1wN_1w$, $P_0cS_1wN_1w$, $S_1wS_2wL_1c$, $S_1wS_2wL_1w$

(c)

Unigrams	S_0w, S_0t, P_0t, P_0c, P_0w, P_1t, P_1c, L_1c, L_1w, L_2w.
Bigrams	S_0wS_0t, P_0tS_0t, P_0tS_0w, P_0cS_0w, P_0wS_0w, P_0tL_1c, P_0tL_1w, P_1tL_1c, P_0wL_1c
Trigrams	$P_0tS_0wS_0t$, $P_0wS_0wS_0t$, $P_0cS_0wS0_1t$, $S_0wS_1tL_1c$, $P_0tP_0wP_0c$, $P_0cL_1wL_1c$, $P_0tP_0cL_1c$, $P_0tP_0cL_1w$

(d)

Unigrams	P_0t, P_0c, P_0w, P_1t, P_1c, L_0c, L_0w, L_1c, L_1w, L_2w.
Bigrams	L_0wL_0c, P_0tL_0c, P_0tL_0w, P_0cL_0w, P_0cL_0c, P_0tL_1c, P_1tL_1c, P_0cL_1c
Trigrams	$P_0tL_0wL_0c$, $P_0cL_0wL_0c$, $P_0cP_0tL_0c$, $P_0tP_1tL_0c$, $P_0cP_1tL_0c$, $P_0tP_1cL_1c$, $P_1tP_1cL_1c$

Fig. 2. Feature template

5 Empirical Result

5.1 Experimental Settings

The experimental corpus from annotated Xingjiang Daily (Kazakh language version), including political, economic, cultural, sports, entertainment, military. The total corpus include 40233 sentences, 231208 words and 83026 chunks.

Precision, recall and F which is used to identify the results of the evaluation. For the Kazak POS tagging result, we evaluate the different tag respectively. Then the evaluation function is defined as follows:

- a = number of correct tagging Then: $P(\text{Precision}) = \frac{a}{a+c} \times 100\%$
- b = number of undiscerned tagging $R(\text{Recall}) = \left(\frac{a}{a+b}\right) \times 100\%$
- c = number of wrong tagging F-measure = $\left(\frac{2 \times P \times R}{P+R}\right) \times 100\%$

5.2 Pipelined Model and Joint Model Performance

First of all, we evaluate the performance of our pipelined model and joint model annotator described in Sect. 2. The result of pipelined model shown in Table 1. For joint model, based on our preliminary experiments, we both set the beam size to 16 and 32 for the joint annotator, the result shown in Table 2. Compare to the Tables 1 and 2, we can see that joint model leading to large improvements over pipelined model. Only observe the Table 2, 32 beam size compare to 16 beam size, while the precision improved about 0.6 %, the speed decreased approximately 50 %.

Table 1. Result of pipelined model

	Precision (%)	Recall (%)	F (%)
POS tagging	89.3	80.5	84.7
Chunking	78.6	71.2	74.7

Table 2. Result of beam size is 16 and 32 for the joint model

Beam size	16		32	
	Precision (%)	Speed (s)	Precision (%)	Speed (s)
POS tagging	90.6	40.4 sentence	91.2	23.6 sentence
Chunking	81.6		82.4	

5.3 Development Results

In this paper, we propose the dynamic beam to control the search space. For dynamic beam, we should set the appropriate threshold to improving the efficiency of decoder. In this experiment, we set the threshold to 2, 3, 4, 5, 6, 7, 8, 9 for compare with the performance of annotator in different threshold. The dynamic beam curves of the mixing models are shown in Fig. 3. From the Fig. 4,we integrated consideration the precision and the decode speed choose 6 as the threshold. In addition, we conduct a large number of experiment which discern multi-category words to confirm the threshold of best performance. From the Figure, we obtain the best threshold is 3.5.

In this experiment, recognition rate of multi-category words is improved greatly in the POS tagging. Moreover for output word as error, we correct its tagging and push it into corpus. From the Table 3, we contrast it with previous work to know that chunk provides the rich information, leading to recognition rate of multi-category words large improvements whether in precision or F-measure.

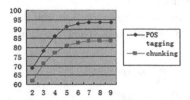

Fig. 3. Accuracies for joint POS tagging and chunking using dynamic beam threshold 2, 3, 4, 5, 6, 7, 8, 9 respectively.

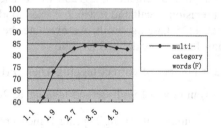

Fig. 4. F-measure for discern multi-category words using the threshold 1.1, 1.5, 1.9, 2.3, 2.7, 3.1, 3.5, 3.9, 4.3 respectively.

5.4 Final Results and Analysis

For show the final result, we contrast previous work with mixing model. First of all, we test the POS tagging and chunking which utilize joint model and mixing model respectively. The contrast result shown in the Table. For the chunking, our result contrast with the result of shown in Table 4.

Table 3. Contrast pipelined method with mixing model for recognition rate of multi-category words

	Precision (%)	Recall (%)	F (%)
Pipeline method	81.6	75.8	78.6
Mixing model	87.7	81.3	84.3

Table 4. Compare result of mixing model with result of joint model

Beam size	Joint method			Mixing model		
	Precision (%)	Recall (%)	F (%)	Precision (%)	Recall (%)	F (%)
POS tagging	90.6	83.4	86.9	92.1	88.5	90.3
Chunking	81.6	76.5	79	83.4	80.8	82.1

It is noteworthy that we obtained the first positive result that the mixing model does improve POS tagging about 2.8 %, while, remove 6.1 % improved in multi-category words, otherwise only have 1.8 % improved. But for the chunking, this is our mixing model is considered to have improved the chunking accuracy over the pipelined tagger about 4.8. Therefore we should consider peculiarity of broader and more in-depth to perfect the feature of POS in order to obtain best performance.

6 Conclusion

We proposed a joint POS tagging and chunking mixing model, which achieved a considerable reduction in error rate compared to a baseline two stage system. We used a single linear model for combined POS tagging and chunking, and chose the generalized perceptron algorithm for joint training. And beam search for efficient decoding and propose the dynamic beam to improve the performance of decode. Moreover the search space is reduction greatly and precision of multi-category words is improved by set the appropriate threshold. We statistical induction the structural relationship of between the chunk and the word to obtain broader and more in depth feature.

The joint system takes features only from partal context. There may be additional features that are particularly useful to the joint system. Open features, such as knowledge of numbers and relationships from semantic networks [12], have been reported to improve the accuracy of segmentation and POS tagging. Therefore, given the flexibility of the feature-based linear model, an obvious next step is the study of open features in the joint POS tagger and chunk recognition.

References

1. Altenbek, G., Wang, X., Haisha, G.: Identification of basic phrases for Kazakh language using maximum entropy model. In: COLING, Dublin, pp. 1007–1014 (2014)
2. Collins, M.: Discriminative training methods for hidden Markov models: theory and experiments with perceptron algorithms. In: Proceedings of the ACL-2002 Conference on Empirical methods in Natural Language Processing, vol. 10, pp. 1–8. Association for Computational Linguistics, Philadelphia, July 2002

3. Collins, M.: Parameter estimation for statistical parsing models: theory and practice of distribution free methods. In: Bunt, H., Carroll, J., Satta, G. (eds.) New Developments in Parsing Technology, pp. 19–55. Springer, Netherlands (2004)

4. Zhang, Y., Clark, S.: Syntactic processing using the generalized perceptron and beam search. Comput. Linguist. **37**(1), 105–151 (2011)

5. Hatori, J., Matsuzaki, T., Miyao, Y., Tsujii, J.: Incremental joint POS tagging and dependency parsing in Chinese. In: IJCNLP, pp. 1216–1224 (2011)

6. Hatori, J., Matsuzaki, T., Miyao, Y., Tsujii, J.: Incremental joint approach to word segmentation, POS tagging, and dependency parsing in Chinese. In: Meeting of the Association for Computational Linguistics: Long Papers, Jeju, vol. 1, pp. 1045–1053 (2012)

7. Saraclar, M., Roark, B.: Joint discriminative language modeling and utterance classification. In: CASSP, vol. 1, pp. 561–564 (2005)

8. Wang, Z., Xue, N.: Joint POS tagging and transition-based constituent parsing in Chinese with non-local features. In: ACL, Maryland, vol. 1, pp. 733–742 (2014)

9. Zhang, Y., Clark, S.: Transition-based parsing of the Chinese treebank using a global discriminative model. In: International Conference on Parsing Technologies, pp. 162–171. Association for Computational Linguistics, Paris (2009)

10. Zhang, Y., Clark, S.: Chinese Segmentation with a word-based perceptron algorithm. In: ACL 2007, Proceedings of the, Meeting of the Association for Computational Linguistics, Prague, Czech Republic, 23–30 June 2007

11. Collins, M., Roark, B.: Incremental parsing with the perceptron algorithm. In: Meeting of the Association for Computational Linguistics, Barcelona, 21–26 July 2004, pp. 111—118 (2004)

12. Freund, Y., Schapire, R.E.: Large margin classification using the perceptron algorithm. Mach. Learn. **37**(3), 277–296 (1999)

13. Collins, M., Duffy, N.: New ranking algorithms for parsing and tagging: kernels over discrete structures, and the voted perceptron. In: Meeting on Association for Computational Linguistics, pp. 263–270. Association for Computational Linguistics, Philadelphia (2002)

14. DauméIII, H., Marcu, D.: Learning as search optimization: approximate large margin methods for structured prediction. In: ICML, Bonn, pp. 169–176 (2009)

15. Shi, B.Y.: A dual-layer CRF based joint decoding method for cascade segmentation and labelling tasks. In: Proceedings of IJCAI, pp. 1707–1712 (2012)

Coping with Problems of Unicoded Traditional Mongolian

Boli Wang[1], Xiaodong Shi[1,2,3(✉)], and Yidong Chen[1]

[1] Department of Cognitive Science, Xiamen University, Xiamen, China
mandel@xmu.edu.cn
[2] Collaborative Innovation Center for Peaceful Development of Cross-Strait Relations,
Xiamen University, Xiamen, China
[3] Fujian Province Key Laboratory for Brain-Inspired Computing, Xiamen University,
Xiamen, China

Abstract. Traditional Mongolian Unicode Encoding has serious problems as several pairs of vowels with the same glyphs but different pronunciations are coded differently. We expose the severity of the problem by examples from our Mongolian corpus and propose two ways to alleviate the problem: first, developing a publicly available Mongolian input method that can help users to choose the correct encoding and second, a normalization method to solve the data sparseness problems caused by the proliferation of homographs. Experiments in search engines and statistical machine translation show that our methods are effective.

Keywords: Traditional Mongolian script · Homographs · Input method · Normalization

1 Introduction

Although traditional Mongolian script was standardized in ISO/IEC 10646 and Unicode in 1999, Unicoded traditional Mongolian is still not the prevalent encoding among the various forms of Mongolian encodings used in China[1], where traditional Mongolian script is the national standard, as opposed to the Cyrillic alphabet used in Outer Mongolia. This situation is due to several reasons, one of which is that there was no support for Unicoded traditional Mongolian from the major OS vendors until the release of Windows Vista in 2007. However, the way traditional Mongolian is standardized in Unicode presents many obstacles to its effective use and handling by the computer and the paper is an attempt to remedy the problems caused by the Unicode encoding of traditional Mongolian.

As far as we know, characters with the same glyph appearance have the same internal Unicode encoding in all languages except traditional Mongolian script, where the vowels *o* and *e* have the same glyph[2] (see [2]) but different encodings (U+1823, U+1824), and

---

[1] The authors can scarcely find a Unicoded traditional Mongolian web site in the year 2014, although things began to change starting from the year 2015.

[2] ᠠ ·

© Springer International Publishing AG 2016
M. Sun et al. (Eds.): CCL and NLP-NABD 2016, LNAI 10035, pp. 125–131, 2016.
DOI: 10.1007/978-3-319-47674-2_11

oe and *ue* also have the same glyph[3] but are coded as (U+1825, U+1826) [3], cf. the Chinese character 行 which has different pronunciations (xíng, háng) and meanings but has the unique Unicode code point (U+884C). Another problem is that the consonant *ang* (U+1829, normally transliterated as *ng*[4]) is redundantly encoded as its glyph is often the same as the consonants *na* (U+1828) and *ga* (U+182D) joined together (thus also transliterated as *ng*). This creates lots of problems, as many words with identical glyphs but different Unicode encodings, henceforth called *homographs*, are generated by the computer users using various input methods. Table 1 lists some of the homographs we find in our publicly available Unicode Mongolian web corpus[5] with 150 million words:

Table 1. Some common Mongolian words with exact glyphs but different encodings in the corpus

Word / gloss	Homographs (transliteration and frequency)*
Mongolia	*munḡḡlul* 3496535 *munḡgul* 388308 **monggol** 171610 *monggul* 71666 *monḡglol* 5714 *munggul* 4519 *munḡgol* 2107 *monḡglul* 383 *mong3gol* 224 *monggul* 103 *monggol* 7
game	**nagadum** 1781301 *nagadom* 19666 *nagaduem* 4068
song	**daguu** 1258831 *dagou* 86530 *dagoo* 51920 *daguo* 20100

*Italic homographs are *incorrect*. The transliteration scheme used are ours (the specification is available on http://mandel.cloudtranslation.cc/moncode_en.html). Number 1–3 in the homographs means free variation selector 1–3 which is used to select a specific presentation form of a Mongolian letter (Unicode 2015).

The first entry, *munḡglul* (meaning **Mongolia**) is the most frequent encoding in the corpus, however, it is spelled wrong (the correct one is *monḡgol*)! This is an unfortunate state of affairs, as when shown on the computer screen or printed on the paper, the homographs appear the same, but internally they are different, thus resulting in great

---

[3]

[4] To emphasize the letter *ang* is one code point, we transliterate it as *nḡ*. It is often pronounced as [ŋ].

[5] http://cloudtranslation.cc/corpus_minority.html.

headaches for many NLP applications (e.g. for search engines[6]). However, As Andrew West pointed out[7], the Mongolian Unicode standard is here to stay, and we can only live with it now.

We propose two ways to alleviate the problems caused by the current Mongolian Unicode standard [11]: first we developed a Unicode input method for Mongolian which shows the transliteration and thus helps users to select the correct homograph; second, for the bulk of existing Unicoded Mongolian, we normalize the corpus using an automatically compiled homograph table and the **vowel harmony principle** [1, 6, 10]. To test the effectiveness of our normalization method, we do experiments on our publicly accessible search engine[8] which supports Mongolian and the results show significant improvement on recall. Experiments on statistical Mongolian-Chinese machine translation also result in an absolute improvement of 5.70 BLEU score [9].

2 Yunmeng: A New Unicode Mongolian Input Method

The most widely used Mongolian input methods in China is Menksoft Mongolian IME [7] but it is not based on Unicode (this fact alone shows that Mongolian Unicode Encoding is problematic). There are researches on Unicode Mongolian Input method, e.g. [5, 8], but few free Unicoded Mongolian Input software have emerged from the researches.

We have implemented *Yunmeng*, a Mongolian Input based on the Unicode standard. We designed a transliteration scheme compatible with Unicode code standard and the specification is available online. Control characters such as three Mongolian Free Variation Selectors are supported. There are 3 salient characteristics of the Yunmeng input method:

1. To input Mongolian, one only needs to remember the pronunciations of the Mongolian vowels and consonants. No keyboard layout is required.
2. Both letter-by-letter and word-by-word input modes are supported. To input a Mongolian word, just type its shortened transliteration which consists of its first syllable and all the consonants of the remaining syllables, e.g. the word *monggol*'s shortened transliteration is *monggl*. In fact, as soon as its prefix *mongg* is typed, the first candidate is shown correctly. See Fig. 1 for details.
3. The transliteration can be shown along with the traditional Mongolian script. This helps the user to choose the correct encodings. And if an encoding fails to satisfy the vowel harmony (it basically says that all the vowels in a word are either of masculine or feminine gender. The neuter vowel *i* is compatible with both the masculine and the feminine gender), it's highlighted to the user as a possible incorrect encoding. Again refer to Fig. 1 for examples.

---

[6] Prof. Garudi of Inner Mongolia Normal University, personal communication.
[7] Personal communication.
[8] http://search.cloudtranslation.cc/.

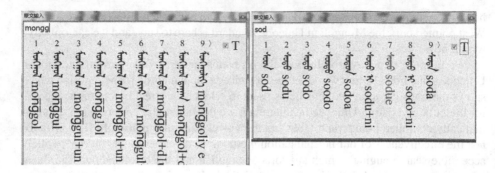

Fig. 1. Yunmeng input interface for words *monggol* and *sodo*.

The Yunmeng input software is freely available for downloading[9]. This input method can help to reduce the incorrect homographs caused by the current Unicode Mongolian encoding.

3   Normalization of the Mongolian Corpus in Unicode

As can be seen from Table 1, there are lots of wrongly encoded Mongolian words in the corpus. This makes the vocabulary unnecessarily large and severe data sparseness will result. If no pre-processing is done, basic NLP processing tasks such as tagging, parsing, machine translation, searching, etc., will suffer a lot in accuracy. The obvious answer is of course **normalization**, that is, to convert a wrongly spelled Mongolian word to its correct normal form.

Now the problem is, how can we find all the (correct or wrong) homographs of a word? It's out of the question to compile the homograph table (like Table 1) manually. There are simply too many variant spellings/encodings which appear the same.

The second problem is, suppose we have gotten such a table, how can we determine which homograph is the correct one? Frequency information cannot be used reliably here as we have seen from Table 1 that the most used form of the word *monggol* is the wrong one!

Our solutions are outlined below:

- For problem 1, we can resort to glyph similarity comparison algorithms to find the homographs that look the same. See [4] for a review for graph matching algorithms.
- For problem 2, as long as the application is not concerned with the morphology of the Mongolian words, it actually does not matter whether a correct homograph can be chosen or not. We can simply pick the most frequent (albeit perhaps wrong) one as the normalized encoding, although word encodings violating the vowel harmony should certainly be discarded. For example, word-based or phrase-based statistical machine translation normally does not need morphological analysis. However, if morphological information is required, then manual work is unavoidable.

---

[9] http://uread.superfection.com/software/uread_mongolian.rar.

In our current implementation of the homograph mining algorithm, we require that their glyphs be exactly the same if two word encodings are regarded as homographs. This is an unnecessarily *strict* requirement because it will find fewer homographs than our naked eyes can recognize, but it serves our purpose here. The algorithm is outlined below[10],[11].

Algorithm 1. Homograph mining.

```
foreach word in Vocabulary
    foreach generated homograph candidate according to the
    letter equivalence table10
        if glyph_same(word, candidate)11
        then {
            put the pair into a equivalent group
            if one of the pair already has equivalent groups
            then merge the generated group with others
        }
```

We find 84611 homograph equivalent groups for our 150-million-word corpus! To appreciate this result, here we just give an example of these groups (Yunmeng transliterations, of the Mongolian word shown at the footnote[12]):

For automatic normalization for use in search engines and statistical machine translation, we simply choose the most frequent variation as the normalized encoding (upon applying vowel harmony), if our small normalization table compiled manually does not show which encoding is the correct one. We report our experiments of the normalization in the next section.

---

[10] The letters *o* and *u* are regarded *equivalent* letters. We collected 22 such equivalent pairs and they form the letter equivalence table. Note that equivalent letters do not always have same glyphs in all positions, e.g. some letters are only equivalent at the medial positions.

[11] We rely on the Microsoft Uniscribe engine to generate the correct glyphs. However, as [1] points out, even if Microsoft failed to generate some of the correct glyphs.

[12] oendosoeden uentusutan uentusueten uentuesuten uentuesuetan uentuesueten
uentosotan uendusutan uendusuten uendusudan uendusuden uendusuetan
uendusueten uendusueden uendoesoden uendoesoeten uenduesodan uenduesoden
uenduesuten uenduesudan uenduesuden uenduesuetan uenduesueten
uenduesuedan uenduesueden uendosotan uendosodan uendosoden uendosueten
uendosueden oentoesoeten oentosotan oendusudan oendusuden oendusoeden
oendoesoeten oendoesoedan oendoesoeden oenduesueten oenduesoeten
oendosoden uendluesueten uendluesudlan oenduesuedlen uendlusudlan
uendluesuedlen

4   Efficacy of the Normalization

To test the effectiveness of the normalization, we do experiments both on our search engine which supports Mongolian, and on statistical Mongolian-Chinese machine translation:

- For the search engine, we do normalization on both the query and documents.
- For the machine translation, we also do normalization on both training and testing data.

The result of the search engine experiment is reported in Table 2. We randomly choose a few words with various frequencies and search these words in the Google search engine and ours[13]. Because there are many Mongolian sites still not indexed by our search engine[14], for meaningful comparison, we restrict Google search results using the "site:" directive.

Table 2. Effects of Mongolian normalization on search engine results

Word and frequency	Google hits	Our search engine hits before normalization	Our search engine hits after normalization
᠊ᠣᠨᠢᠶᠠᠯ (2)	18	6	**16128**
᠊ᠠᠢᠭᠨᠢᠪᠠᠭᠧ (15)	1	1	**1**
᠊ᠠᠣᠢᠪᠡᠢᠨ (33)	17	28	**283**
᠊ᠠᠣᠢᠬᠷᠢᠪᠧ (166)	125	78	**209**

It can be seen that the recall of the search engine is boosted significantly. It is safe to say that we have made a big step toward solving the search problem that has been plaguing the Unicoded Mongolian for many years!

The result on statistical Mongolian-Chinese machine translation is shown in Table 3. The system used is an in-house phrase-based machine translation system. The training data are the China laws and government reports, with 59 k parallel sentences, and only one reference translation is provided for test data. It can be seen that an absolute improvement of 5.70 BLEU-4 score can be achieved on average upon normalization.

Table 3. Effects of Mongolian normalization on machine translation

	Size (sentences)	BLEU before normalization	BLEU after normalization
Training data	59 K		
Test data1 (government report)	266	38.44	**46.07**
Test data2 (leader's speech)	122	50.28	**56.54**
Test data3 (law)	123	57.19	**60.41**
Average improvement			**+5.70**

---

[13] Google's powerful engine can index pdf files, while ours does not yet.

[14] For this experiment, we only indexed two popular Mongolian website: www.mgyxw.net and mgl.nmg.gov.cn.

The new Mongolian-Chinese machine translation system with normalization is also available online[15].

5   Conclusion

We discussed the *homograph plague* problem that has defied the widespread use and application of Unicoded traditional Mongolian for many years, and we propose a new input method called **Yunmeng** and a normalization algorithm to deal with it. Experiments on search engines and statistical machine translation showed great improvements.

Acknowledgements. The work done in this paper is partially supported by the Research Fund for the Doctoral Program of Higher Education of China (No. 20130121110040), National High-Tech R&D Program of China (No. 2012BAH14F03), and the Special Fund Project of Ministry of Education of China (Intelligent Conversion System from Simplified to Traditional Chinese Characters). We thank Dr. Yanlong He for kindly providing the Mongolian-Chinese test corpus for the statistical machine translation experiment.

References

1. Batjargal, B., Khaltarkhuu, G., Kimura, F., Maeda, A.: A study of traditional Mongolian script encodings and rendering: use of unicode in OpenType fonts. Int. J. Asian Lang. Proc. **21**(1), 23–44 (2011)
2. Chinggaltai: A Grammar of the Mongol Language. Frederick Ungar Publishing Co, New York (1963)
3. Choijinzhab: Mongolian Encoding. Inner Mongolia University Press, Hohhot. (确精扎布: 蒙古文编码. 内蒙古大学出版社, 呼和浩特) (2000). (in Chinese) http://www.babelstone.co.uk/Mongolian/MGWBM.html
4. Conte, D., Foggia, P., Sansone, C., Vento, M.: Thirty years of graph matching in pattern recognition. Int. J. Pattern Recogn. Artif. Intell. **18**(03), 265–298 (2004)
5. Daoerji, F., Fengshan, B., Huijuan, W.U.: Research on Mongolian input method in unicode. J. Chin. Inf. Process. **24**(6), 120–124+128 (2010). (in Chinese)
6. Goldsmith, J.: Vowel harmony in Khalkha Mongolian, Yaka, Finnish and Hungarian. Phonology **2**(01), 253–275 (1985)
7. MünggeGal: Menksoft Mongolian IME. http://www.menksoft.com/
8. Ochir, Wang, G.F.: Corpus and Mongolian inputting methods. In: International Conference on Chinese Computing 2005, Singapore (2005)
9. Papineni, K., Roukos, S., Ward, T., Zhu, W. J.: BLEU: a method for automatic evaluation of machine translation. In: Proceedings of 40th Annual Meeting on Association for Computational Linguistics, pp. 311–318. Association for Computational Linguistics (2002)
10. Poppe, N.: Grammar of Written Mongolian. Otto Harrassowitz Verlag, Wiesbaden (1974)
11. The Unicode Consortium: The Unicode Standard, Version 8.0.0 (2015). http://www.unicode.org/versions/Unicode8.0.0/

---

[15] http://cloudtranslation.cc/mt.

Tibetan Person Attributes Extraction
Based on BP Neural Network

Lili Guo[1,2] and Yuan Sun[1,2(✉)]

[1] School of Information Engineering, Minzu University of China, Beijing, China
guolili0305@163.com, tracy.yuan.sun@gmail.com
[2] Minority Languages Branch,
National Language Resource and Monitoring Research Center,
Beijing 100081, China

Abstract. At present, Tibetan information is quickly connected with modernization and information, which results the expansive development of Tibetan information on the network. In the face of the massive network information, extracting the information that people want is an urgent problem to be solved. Currently, Chinese person attributes extraction studies have some good results, but there is still much space to Tibetan person attributes extraction. The paper uses person attribute keywords, case-auxiliary word, verbs and other related meaningful words as features to vector, constructs the error BP neural network model and utilizes this model to identification and classification for Tibetan person attributes, and achieved good results. This research has a very important role in the search engine, information security, machine translation and many other applications.

Keywords: Tibetan · Person attributes extraction · BP neural network

1 Introduction

With the rapid development of Internet, a large number of electronic text information resources appear in front of people, and more and more online information in the form of multiple languages is released. At the same time, how to get the needed information quickly and accurately becomes a major problem. There is an urgent need for some automated tools to help people quickly find the information that you really need in the mass of information resources. According to incomplete statistics, the number of people uses the Tibetan language as much as 4.22 million. It is mainly distributed in China's Tibet autonomous region, Gansu, Qinghai, Sichuan and Yunnan and other Tibetan areas [1]. Research on Tibetan person attributes extraction can promote communication between nationalities, enhance mutual understanding between nationalities and drive the development of Tibetan economy, science and technology, culture and other fields to better serve the Tibetan people. Therefore, electronic and information processing of the Tibetan text becomes the focus of contemporary social issues.

In the early 1980s, National Institute of the Chinese Academy Social Sciences Zhang Lianshengtried to sort Tibetan vocabulary by computer, opened the precedent of Tibetan text processing. However, due to the form of Tibetan and English and Chinese

M. Sun et al. (Eds.): CCL and NLP-NABD 2016, LNAI 10035, pp. 132–142, 2016.
DOI: 10.1007/978-3-319-47674-2_12

is very different, so in the computer operating system platform will be difficult to develop. Some Tibetan studies so far has been a great progress. In Tibetan text resources and literature classification, text statistics [2] and entropy value calculation [3], Tibetan speech recognition and word segmentation method [4] other fields have a considerable part of the progress. These are good foreshadowing roles and the accumulation of relevant knowledge to study of Tibetan attributes extraction in this paper. The ultimate goal of information extraction is to turn the useful information in unstructured text into a structured text. The origin of information extraction technology is text understanding. But it is not fully to understand an entire text, but on the part relevant information of the document for analysis. In Tibetan person attributes extraction is the same understanding. The first Tibetan corpus are obtained from the Tibetan websites, and in this paper, the sentence which contains the Tibetan person attributes is selected from the Tibetan corpus as the preprocessing data. In this paper, we select the person's father, birth place, gender, occupation and so on as the information point that needs to be extracted.

Person attributes extraction is an important part in information processing technology, and it is becoming a more and more hot topic. Tibetan person attributes extraction is still in its infancy, there is still a lot of work to be done. Typical methods in English are based on the feature vector method [5, 6] and based on kernel function method [7, 8]. There are two methods for the specific application of research in the Chinese language [9, 10]. At present, there are many methods used in information processing, among which the machine learning algorithm is used to train and test is the most popular method. Vahideh Sadat Sadeghi, Khashayar Yaghmaie [11] uses a neural network that a combination as the input parameters to extract the edge characteristics of the vowel letters. Joachim Schenk and Gerhard Rigoll [12] used the neural network to feature extraction, and then applied to the standard HMM method, to improve the feature recognition of online handwritten research. Deng Bo et al. [13] introduced the lexical semantic matching technology to extract the Chinese entity relation on the basis of using pattern matching technology in Chinese information processing. Zelenko [14] early used the method to study the relationship between kernel extraction fields. Culotta [15] defined the kernel function based on the dependency tree and used the SVM classifier to extract the relationship by some conversion rules. Zhang et al. [16] designed a kind of compound convolution tree kernel function to carry on the relation extraction.

In Tibetan attributes extraction, there is very little research work. Natural language processing method used in Chinese can be used in Tibetan information processing [17]. However, the actual process of using must consider problems that Tibetan and Chinese compared to have a larger gap in the study of natural language processing. If this key issue has been resolved, Tibetan natural language processing technology will be further developed. At present the biggest difficulty is the lack of Tibetan corpus. According to the characteristics of the Tibetan language, this paper uses person feature keywords, case-marking, verbs and other related meaningful words to carry on the vector as the input to BP neural network [19] and extract results as output, training via BP learning arithmetic [20]. In the experiment, the vector of Tibetan corpus, neural network structure design, learning rate, training algorithm and other related parameters were adjusted to get the best results.

2   Person Attributes Extraction Based on BP Neural Network

At present, BP neural network is the most representative and widely used model in artificial neural network model, which has the ability of self-learning, self-organization, self-adaptation and strong nonlinear mapping [18]. BP neural network has become a important tool for classification problems such as face recognition, character recognition and signal processing, etc. The entity relation extraction method based on BP neural network is usually transformed into classification problem, and the design of neural network structure is one of the key problems. The Tibetan corpus is obtained by configured crawler system from a Tibetan website, then selected articles about introducing the person introduction and processed these sentences such as artificial segmentation, marking word class. The tagged corpus select the relevant features to vector as input data, and reused to build neural network model identification and classification. The extraction process is illustrated in Fig. 1.

2.1   Tibetan Corpus Processing

The Tibetan corpus is obtained by configured crawler system from a Tibetan website, such as Wikipedia (Tibetan Edition), Kangba media network, China Tibetan middle school network, etc., then selected articles about introducing the person introduction and processed these sentences such as artificial segmentation, marking word class, as shown in example 1–4. Among them, we choose 9,216 sentences with the person attributes, using 6,000 sentences as the training data, and the 3,216 sentence as the test data. Finally, the labeled corpus to vector is used as the input data to train neural network model.

Example 1:<e1> རྫོང་དུ་ར་རྣ་ས/nh</e1>-ནི་/v<e2>ས/n</e2>- རབས་ཤིག་ཡིན་/v/w

Example 2: <e1>གཙང་སྐྱིད་ཉེ་ད་ཀ་རྣམ་པའི་རྒྱུ་ཚན/nh</e1>-ནི་/v<e2>གུང་ཚོ/n</e2>-ཡིན་/v/w

Example 3: <e1>འཕྲོ་མགོན་འདི་ཞི་/nh</e1>-ནི་/v<e2>ཚོ་༡༢༢༤པ་ཞིང་ཚོ་ལུག་/nt</e2>-ལ་/k ཁ་བྱུང་ས/v/w

Example 4: <e1>སྐྱེ་བཙན་རྒྱས་ཚོ་/nh</e1>-ནི་/v<e2>རྒྱལ་ཚོ/n</e2>-ཡིན་/v-ལ/w

Vectoring of characteristics mainly uses keyword characteristics, annotation combination characteristics and marked characteristics of words nearby. High frequency keywords appear in a certain attribute category, with a high degree of recognition. There are many different Tibetan and Chinese and English. Tibetan is a post-predicate sentence. Verbs are the core of a sentence in Tibetan. The case-marking of verb nearby is rich semantic role information. To a certain extent, the case-marking reflects the relationship [1] between the predicate and the subject in the sentence, and the appearance of these markers has certain rules. The case-marking is an important effect for Tibetan attributes extraction. So the case-marking and named entity marking in combination may be helpful to the classification effect. The marking characteristics of

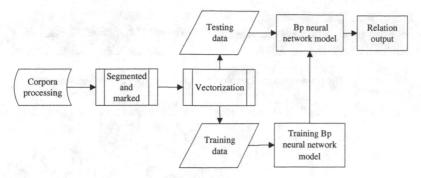

Fig. 1. Extraction flow chart

keywords nearby have a certain effect on improving the classification performance like the role of entity words.

The pos tagging adopts "Modern Tibetan lexical category tag set specification for information processing" of "The national language resource monitoring and research center of minority language center", where the "/nh" said the name, "/t" said the time, "/ns" said the name, "/n" means the common noun, "/k" said case markers, "/v" for verb.

2.2 BP Neural Network

Each layer of the BP neural network is made up of a lot of nerve cells. Each layer of neurons receives the input from the previous layer, and outputs the calculated results to the next layer by the transfer function. If the error of the output value of the output layer and the actual output value is less than a predetermined value, the error will back propagation. By adjusting the connection weights and thresholds of each layer, the error between the calculated value and the actual value is gradually reduced until the error reaches the predetermined requirements. This algorithm has become an error back propagation algorithm. The neural network model based on BP algorithm is the BP neural network model.

The artificial neural network is similar to the neural system of the human brain, which is composed of a large number of artificial neural cells. BP neural network model, as shown in Fig. 2, includes the input layer, hidden layer and output layer. The paper uses person attribute keywords, case-auxiliary word, verbs and other related meaningful words as features to vector. Through different experiments, the data of input layer selects a 12-dimensional vector: $x = (x_1, x_2, x_3 \cdots x_{12})$. $w = (w_1, w_2, w_3 \cdots w_{12})$ is the connection strength with the hidden layer connected to it and that means weight. Each of the inputs of the artificial nerve cell is associated with a weight, which will determine the overall positivity of the neural network. The sum of the input values being multiplied by the corresponding weights is the sum of the neurons input. If the sum exceeds a certain threshold θ_i, the cell is activated, the cell output signal $y_i = f(\sum wx - \theta_i)$. The function $f(\sum wx - \theta_i)$ is called activation function or transfer function and connected to the input and output of the nerve cell. It has a variety of

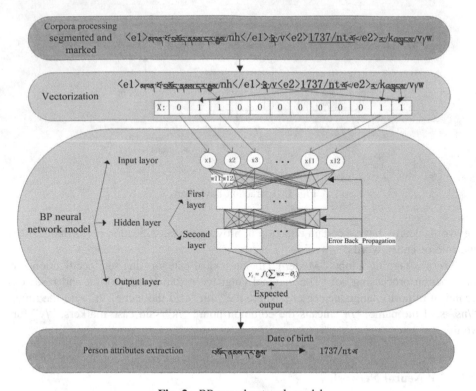

Fig. 2. BP neural network model

types, often using S type logarithmic or tangent function and linear function. In this paper, we use S function as transfer function.

The hidden layer is composed of any number of neurons. In this paper, we use two layer of hidden layer to distinguish the person attributes. The number of hidden layer nodes is determined according to the experience of the previous design and the experiment. The number of hidden layer nodes is directly related to Requirements for solving problems and the number of the input and output. In addition, too many hidden layer nodes can lead to long learning time, while too few nodes may identify the low ability of the sample without learning. The initial value of hidden layer nodes (L) is determined by one of the following two formulas [21].

$$L = \sqrt{m+n} + a \tag{1}$$

$$L = \sqrt{0.43mn + 0.12n^2 + 2.54m + 0.77n + 0.35 + 0.51} \tag{2}$$

Among them, n and m are the number of input nodes and the number of output nodes, and a is a constant of $0 \sim 10$. In this paper, the number of input node m is 12, the number of output node n is 1. The number of two hidden layer nodes selected 12 neurons.

In addition to the input layer, hidden layer and output layer neurons need to activate the function. In this paper, the hidden layer uses Sigmoid function, and the output layer utilizes a linear function. Training network has two kinds of modes: one by one mode and the batch mode. In one by one mode, each input is applied to the network, and the weights and thresholds are updated. Batch mode variable does not need to set the training function for each layer's weights and thresholds, but only need to specify a training function for the entire network and is relatively easy to use. Many improved fast training algorithms can only use the batch mode, so this paper uses the batch mode to train the network's function. Training functions have trainlm algorithm, trainrp algorithm, trainbfg algorithm, traingdx algorithm, etc. In this paper, we use the traingdx algorithm which is suitable for simulation classification. Learning speed parameter can't be selected too large, otherwise the algorithm does not converge. Learning speed parameter can't too small to make the training process too long. Generally people choose the value to between 0.01 to 0.1. This paper uses 0.01. The training target error is 0.01.

3   Simulation Results and Analysis

The corpus of each attribute is divided into 3 parts, with 6,000 sentences as the training data, the 3,126 sentence as the test data. Performance evaluation of extraction can use the evaluation methods of information retrieval. The recall (R) can be roughly seen as a measure for the proportion of correctly extracted information, and the precision (P) is a measure of the correct amount of information extracted. There is an inverse relationship between recall and precision, that is to say, the increase of the precision will lead to the decrease of the recall, and vice versa. Evaluation of a performance should also consider the recall rate and precision, but at the same time comparing the two values will not achieve a clear effect. In this paper, the F value is used to evaluate the performance of the final system. In this way, we can see that the algorithm is good or bad with a numerical value. A value closer to 1 the better the result.

The results of the experiment are shown in Table 1. The F value of the father, mother, gender and other attributes is relatively high, and the nationality and occupation and other attributes of the F value is relatively low. The key words such as father, mother and gender are more obvious and have high recognition, and the characteristics of nationality and occupation have some difficulty in the stage of feature vector. So the relative correct rate is lower.

During the experiment, the best experimental results are obtained by adjusting Feature vector, activation function, training algorithm, learning speed and so on to achieve the highest accuracy rate. In this paper, two hidden layers are used to construct the neural network model. Each hidden layer contains 10 neurons. Activation function selects sigmoid function. The algorithm of training neural network uses traingdx algorithm. Learning speed is set to 0.01. The training target error is set to 0.01.

In the experiment, with MATLAB simulation results are shown in Fig. 3 Training error reduction diagram. With the increase of the iteration number, the value of the validation performance is reduced. The best validation performance is 0.0697 at epoch 100.

Table 1. Tibetan attributes extraction results

Attribute class	Precision (%)	Recall (%)	F (%)
Father	91.05	89.32	90.18
Mother	89.26	86.24	87.69
Date of birth	86.28	84.25	85.25
Place of birth	87.94	84.18	86.00
Gender	88.56	86.04	87.28
Death day	82.65	78.91	80.73
Nationality	81.21	78.47	79.82
Occupation	79.89	75.49	77.58

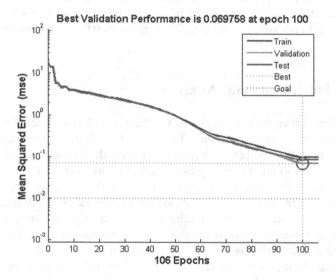

Fig. 3. Training error reduction diagram

Figure 4 shows the changes in the gradient, validation checks and learning rate. The values of the gradient, verification checks and learning rate are 1.2863, 6, 0.0415, when the iteration is constant.

Figure 5 shows the linear regression of training, validation, testing and the three together. Linear regression function is $output = 0.98 * t \arg et + 0.13$.

Figure 6 is a comparison of forecast and actual classification by BP neural network model. The green represents the label of the prediction category. The red indicates an annotated label before the testing. The one to eight represents the eight attributes person.

Figure 7 is the percentage of the error and the absolute error. A very small part of the prediction error is relatively large.

BP neural network to extract Tibetan person attributes as shown in Table 2. It provides support for search engine, information security, machine translation and other researches.

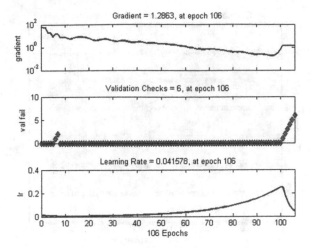

Fig. 4. Training status chart

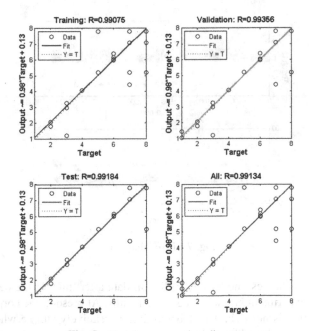

Fig. 5. Training regression diagram

4 Summary

This paper introduces a kind of using BP neural network method for Tibetan person attributes extraction. The design and training of BP neural network model is the main part. In the training process, each implementation will produce different neural network

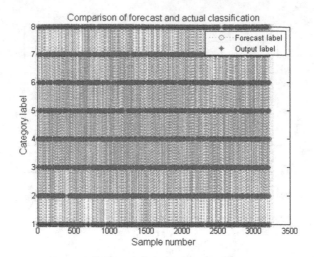

Fig. 6. Comparison of forecast and actual classification (Color figure online)

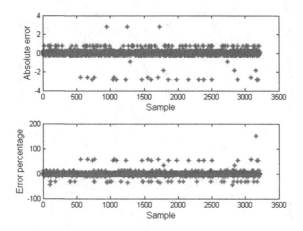

Fig. 7. Error diagram

models. It chooses the best model for prediction data after training the neural network model. And the experiment has achieved good results. At present, the corpus of person attributes extraction is not rich. The Tibetan data is relatively simple when compared with the test data of the Chinese in the experiment. And the number of labels, the expansion of the corpus content and inspection work is still further improved. The experimental results in a certain extent are obtained. In the study of Tibetan person attributes extraction is still great room for improvement. It provides support for search engine, information security, machine translation and other researches.

Table 2. Results of Song zanganbu's attributes extraction

Attribute class	Extract attribute value	Sentences that contain attributes
Father	རྗེ་གནམ་རེ་སྲོང་བཙན་	སྲོང་བཙན་སྒམ་པོའི་ཡབ་ནི་རྗེ་གནམ་རེ་སྲོང་བཙན་ ཡིན།
Mother	འབྲི་བཟའ་ཐོད་དཀར་ཙེ་སྲོང་བཟའ་	སྲོང་བཙན་སྒམ་པོའི་ཡུམ་ནི་འབྲི་བཟའ་ཐོད་དཀར་ ཙེ་སྲོང་བཟའ་ཡིན།
Date of birth	བོད་མེ་སྤྲང་ (༥༢༩) ལོར་	སྲོང་བཙན་སྒམ་པོ་ནི་བོད་མེ་སྤྲང་ (༥༢༩) ལོར་ འཁྲུངས།
Place of birth	སྲོང་ཆེར་ར་ཉལ་མའི་ཤར་ཕྱོགས་མའི་ཉུ་རྒྱང་ཐབ་ལེ་ དབར་བརྒྱ་སྒ་ལ་ཚལ་ཡོ་ད་པའི་དབུ་ད་མཁ་སྐྱ་ མ་སོ་བྱང་བྲམས་པ་མི་འགྱུར་སྒྲིད།	སྲོང་བཙན་སྒམ་པོ་ནི་སྲོང་ཆེར་ཉུ་མའི་ཤར་ཕྱོགས་ མའི་ཉུ་རྒྱང་ཐབ་ལེ་དབར་བརྒྱ་སྒ་ལ་ཚལ་ཡོ་ད་པའི་ དབུ་ད་མཁ་སྒ་མ་སོ་བྱང་བྲམས་པ་མི་འགྱུར་སྒྲིང་ ནས་འཁྲུངས
Gender	ཕོ	སྲོང་བཙན་སྒམ་པོ་ནི་བོད་ཀྱི་ཕོ་རབས་ཤིག་ཡིན།
Death day	༦༥༠	སྲོང་བཙན་སྒམ་པོ་རབ་བྱུང་གསུམ་པའི་ས་སྤྲང་ ༦༥༠འོལོར་སྐུ་གཤེགས།
Nationality	གུང་པོ	སྲོང་བཙན་སྒམ་པོ་ནི་གུང་པོའི་ཡིན།
Occupation	རྒྱལ་པོ།	སྲོང་བཙན་སྒམ་པོ་ནི་རྒྱལ་པོ་ཡིན་ལ།

Acknowledgements. This work is supported by National Nature Science Foundation (No. 61501529, No. 61331013), National Language Committee Project (No. YB125-139, ZDI125-36), and Minzu University of China Scientific Research Project (No. 2015MDQN11, No. 2015MDYY069).

References

1. Chen, Y., Li, B., Shiwen, Yu., et al.: A Tibetan segmentation scheme based on case auxiliary words and continuous features. Lang. Appl. **01**, 75–82 (2003)
2. Liang, J.: The Vocabulary Statistics of Tibetan History Literature. China Academy of Social Sciences Institute of Ethnology and Anthropology, Beijing (2013)

3. Hongzhi, Yu., Li, Y., Wang, K., et al.: Research of the maximum entropy Tibetan POS tagging of combining syllable features. J. Chin. Inf. Process. **27**(5), 160–165 (2013)
4. Qi, K.: Research on Tibetan word segmentation for information processing. J. Northwest Univ. Nationalities (Philos. Soc. Sci. Ed.) **26**(04), 92–97 (2006)
5. Zhou, G., Zhang, M.: Extracting relation information from text documents by exploring various types of knowledge. Inf. Process. Manag. **43**, 969–982 (2007)
6. Kambhatla, N.: Combining lexical, syntactic and semantic features with maximum entropy models for extracting relations. In: Proceedings of ACL, pp. 178–181 (2004)
7. Qian, L., Zhou, G., Kong, F., et al.: Exploiting constituent dependencies for tree kernel-based semantic relation extraction. In: Proceedings of COLING, pp. 697–704 (2008)
8. Zhou, G., Zhang, M., Ji, D., et al.: Tree kernel-based relation extraction with context-sensitive structured parse tree information. In: Proceedings of EMNLP/CONLL, pp. 728–736 (2007)
9. Che, W., Jiang, J., Su, Z., et al.: Improved-edit-distance kernel for Chinese relation extraction. In: Proceedings of IJCNLP, pp. 132–137 (2005)
10. Zhuang, C., Qian, L., Zhou, G.: Research on entity semantic relation extraction method based on tree kernel function. J. Chin. Inf. Process. **23**(1), 3–9 (2009)
11. Hotho, A. et al.: A brief survey of text mining, KDE Group University of Kassel (2005)
12. Aggarwal, R.K., Dave, M.: Implementing a speech recognition system interface for Indian languages (2008)
13. Deng, Q., Fan, X., Yang, L.: Method for extracting entity relation with semantic pattern. Comput. Eng. **33**(10), 212–214 (2007)
14. Zhang, W., Sun, Y., Han, X.: Solid relation extraction method based on Wikipedia and pattern clustering. J. Chin. Inf. Process. **26**(2), 75–81 (2012)
15. Zelenko, D., Aone, C., Richardella, A.: Kernel methods for relation extraction. J. Mach. Learn. Res. **2**, 1083–1106 (2003)
16. Culotta A, Sorensen J. Dependency tree kernels for relation extraction. In: Proceedings of ACL, pp. 423– 429 (2004)
17. Zhang M, Zhang J, Su J, et al.: A compo site kernel to extract relations between entities with both flat and structured features. In: Proceedings of ACL, pp. 825– 832 (2006)
18. Yuan, S., Xiaobing, Z.: Research on automatic recognition of Tibetan personal names based on multi-features. Chin. J. Inf. **23**(1), 3–9 (2009). Proceedings of International Conference on Natural Language Processing and Knowledge Engineering (2010)
19. FECIT Technological Product Research Center: Neural Network Theory and Implementation of Matlab 7, pp. 100–105. Publishing House of Electronics Industry, Beijing (2006)
20. Nickolai, S.R.: The layer-wise method and the back-propagation hybrid approach to learning a feed-forward neural network. IEEE Trans. Neural Netw. **11**(2), 295–305 (2000)
21. Zhou, K., Kang, Y.: Neural Network Model and Matlab Simulation Program Design. Tsinghua University Press, Beijing (2005)

Semi-supervised Learning for Mongolian Morphological Segmentation

Zhenxin Yang[1,2], Miao Li[1(✉)], Lei Chen[1],
Weihui Zeng[1], Yi Gao[3], and Sha Fu[3]

[1] Institute of Intelligent Machines,
Chinese Academy of Sciences, Hefei 230031, China
mli@iim.ac.cn, alan.cl@163.com
[2] University of Science and Technology of China, Hefei 230026, China
{xinzyang,whzeng}@mail.ustc.edu.cn
[3] Yunnan Agricultural Expert System Leading Group Office,
Kunming 650000, China
{498898209,1769816}@qq.com

Abstract. Unlike previous Mongolian morphological segmentation methods based on large labeled training data or complicated rules concluded by linguists, we explore a novel semi-supervised method for a practical application, i.e., statistical machine translation (SMT), based on a low-resource learning setting, in which a small amount of labeled data and large amount of unlabeled data are available. First, a CRF-based supervised learning is exploited to predict morpheme boundaries by using small labeled data. Then, a lexicon-based segmentation model with small labeled data as the heuristic information is used to compensate the weakness in the first step by the abundant unlabeled data. Finally, we present some error correction models to revise segmentation results. Experimental results show that our method can improve the segmentation results compared with the pure supervised learning. Besides, we integrate the morphological segmentation result into Chinese-Mongolian SMT and achieve the satisfactory performance compared with the baseline.

Keywords: Semi-supervised learning · Morphological segmentation · Statistical machine translation · Low-resource language

1 Introduction

Morphological segmentation, which breaks words into the basic syntactic or semantic units, is a key issue in natural language processing, such as machine translation, information retrieval and speech recognition [1]. Morphological segmentation has been a research focus in recent years [2].

Mongolian is a morphological rich minority language which has significant difference compared with Chinese. Mongolian word is generated by connecting stem and none or one or more affixes according to the grammatical order. There are considerable independence between stem and additional ingredient which are just affixed when needed. There are about more than 30000 stems and 297 inflectional affixes in

M. Sun et al. (Eds.): CCL and NLP-NABD 2016, LNAI 10035, pp. 143–152, 2016.
DOI: 10.1007/978-3-319-47674-2_13

Table 1. Illustration of the morphology of Mongolian.

Stem	Affix	Word	Chinese	English
		SVRVGCI	学生	Student
	D	SVRVGCID	学生们	Students
SVRVGCI	D-VN	SVRVGCID-VN	学生们的	Students'
	-YIN	SVRVGCI-YIN	学生的	Student's
	-TAI	SVRVGCI-TAI	与学生一起	With student

Mongolian [3]. Theoretically speaking, Mongolian word form will be derived in exponential growth. Table 1 illustrates the morphology of Mongolian.

From Table 1, we can conduct that Mongolian is a rich morphology language and morphological segmentation is necessary for Mongolian natural language processing.

Previous work on Mongolian morphological segmentation is based on dictionaries, rules and statistics [4–9]. These proposed methods in previous work have achieved good segmentation results, however, they need lots of annotated training data or complicated rules concluded by linguists. The building of fundamental resource for Mongolian is very time-consuming, which is extremely difficult for researchers who do Mongolian morphological segmentation from scratch.

Difference with above work, we explore a novel and effective semi-supervised morphological segmentation method for a practical application, i.e., statistical machine translation, based on a low-resource learning setting, in which a small amount of labeled data and large amount of unlabeled data are available. We aim to leverage the large unlabeled data to alleviate some drawbacks caused by the lack of the labeled data, and reduce the reliance on the manual annotation.

The framework of the paper is shown in Fig. 1.

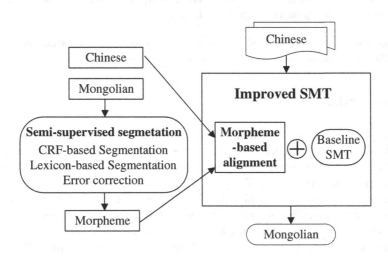

Fig. 1. Framework of the paper.

Semi-supervised learning includes three steps by small amount of labeled data and abundant amount of unlabeled data. First, we investigate a CRF-based supervised learning to predict morpheme boundaries via small amount of labeled data. Then, the abundant unlabeled data is exploited to compensate the weakness of the CRF-based segmentation. Finally, we present some error correction models to revise segmentation results.

As the proposed method is for statistical machine translation, we integrate morphemes into Chinese-Mongolian SMT by the combination of word alignment and morpheme-based alignment. The translation results demonstrate that morphological segmentation based on small amount of labeled data can help to achieve a satisfactory translation performance.

2 Semi-supervised Morphological Segmentation

2.1 CRF-Based Segmentation

Conditional random fields [10] is a probabilistic models to segment and label sequence data, which can avoid label bias problem. Assume X is the the random variable over data sequence to be labeled and Y is the random variable over corresponding label sequence. Let $G = (V, E)$ denotes an undirected graphical model, where $v \in V$ represents a random variable Y_v, and the edge $e \in E$ represents probabilistic dependencies among random variables. $P(Y|X)$ is a conditional random fields if the following formula is established for any vertex v:

$$P(Y_v|X, Y_w, w \neq v) = P(Y_v|X, Y_w, w \sim v) \tag{1}$$

where $w \sim v$ means w and v are neighbors in G and $w \neq v$ means all vertices except v.

In this paper, we simplify the CRF into linear chain conditional random fields by assuming X and Y have the same graphical structure, since we regard Mongolian morphological segmentation as sequence labeling problem.

Formally, given $X = x$ (characters in a word) and $Y = y$ (classes corresponding to characters), the probability $P(y|x)$ is written as:

$$P(y|x) = \frac{1}{Z(x)} \exp \sum_{k=1}^{K} w_k f_k(y, x) \tag{2}$$

$$Z(x) = \sum_{y} \exp \sum_{k=1}^{K} w_k f_k(y, x) \tag{3}$$

In the subsection, only small amount of labeled data is exploited to accomplish pure supervised segmentation. It should be noted that there exists stem lemmatization in morphological segmentation. For example, Mongolian word "BAYIG_A" has a stem "BAI" and an affix "G_A". Since labeled data is small, we just ignore the stem lemmatization in a low-resource setting. The performance of SMT with morphological information demonstrates the effectiveness of semi-supervised segmentation although

Table 2. The tag set used in CRF.

Tag name	Meaning
S_B	First letter of stem
S_O	Other letter of stem
A_B	First letter of affix
A_E	Last letter of affix
A_O	Letter of affix not belong to A_B and A_E
A_ONLY	Only one letter in affix

we ignore the stem lemmatization. In this paper, "BAYIG_A" will be segmented to "BAYI" and "G_A". The tag set used in conditional random fields is shown in Table 2.

Feature extraction is the key issue for conditional random fields. We describe the position t of the word x using all left and right substrings up to a maximum length. Furthermore, we extract interval letter relationship to alleviate the long-distance dependence.

2.2 Lexicon-Based Segmentation

The performance of CRF-based model will be limited due to the small amount of labeled data. In this subsection, we explore a lexicon-based segmentation model which utilizes large unlabeled data to overcome the weakness of CRF-based model. The key idea is that we hope to learn valuable knowledge from large unlabeled data given small labeled data as heuristic information.

We follow the work [11], which is a generative probabilistic model, in this subsection. The model parameters θ encode a morph lexicon, which includes the properties of the morphs, such as their string representations. Each morph m in the lexicon has a probability of occurring in a word. The probabilities are assumed to be independent. The model uses a prior $P(\theta)$ derived using the Minimum Description Length (MDL) principle. During model learning, θ is optimized to maximize the posterior probability:

$$\theta^{MAP} = \arg\max_{\theta} P(\theta|D_w) = \arg\max_{\theta} P(\theta)P(D_w|\theta) \tag{4}$$

where D_w includes words in the training data.

The cost function is expressed as:

$$L(\theta, z, D_w) = -\ln P(\theta) - \ln P(D_w|z, \theta) \tag{5}$$

We process one word at a time, and the segmentation that minimizes the cost function with the optimal model parameters is selected:

$$z_j^{(t+1)} = \arg\min_{z_j}\{\min_{\theta} L(\theta, z^{(t)}, D_w)\} \tag{6}$$

Then, the parameters are updated:

$$\theta^{(t+1)} = \arg\min_{\theta}\{L(\theta, z^{(t+1)}, D_w)\} \tag{7}$$

We repeatedly exploit small amount of labeled data as the heuristic information to train morph lexicon with the large unlabeled data, which perform Expectation-Maximization (EM) using the Viterbi algorithm on the morphological segmentation.

The lexicon-based model proposed in this subsection is exploited to segment the Mongolian words which is error from the CRF-based model. We have an inflectional affix dictionary which contains 297 inflectional affixes. If the affix of the word segmented by the CRF-based model is not found in the inflectional affix dictionary, we explore the lexicon-based model to segment its word form.

2.3 Error Correction

We find the error in CRF-based segmentation and lexicon-based segmentation according to inflectional affix dictionary and employ the lexicon model of word and its affix, the reverse maximum match with 1-gram model of affix to correct the mistake. We search the most possible affix for the error segmentation result based on the lexicon model. If the affix is not found in lexicon model, we use reverse maximum match method to obtain the final segmentation result.

The lexicon model of word and its affix is

$$L = <w, [<a_1, c_1> \cdots <a_i, c_i> \cdots] > \tag{8}$$

where w is Mongolian word, a_i is the possible affix and c_i is the count of a_i in the training data. We can get the statistical vocabulary $V = \{(w_i, [< a_{ik}, c_{ik} > ...])...\}$.

We find the most possible affix for the error word and affix pair w_i/a_i by the following decision rule

$$\hat{a}_i = \{a_{ij}|c_{ij} \geq \max\{c_{ik}\}, j \neq k\} \tag{9}$$

If w_i is not found in lexicon model, we reverse to search w_i and collect all affixes that match the 1-gram model of affix to find the maximum length affix as the final segmentation affix.

3 Experiments

3.1 Morphological Segmentation

In this subsection, we will report the data set, evaluation metric and experimental results. We extract 800 high frequency words from Mongolian monolingual corpus and the 800 Mongolian word types are segmented by the linguists manually. Note that a

Table 3. Stem-level accuracy of segmentation.

Semi-supervised learning	Accuracy(%)
CRF-based segmentation	80.05
+Lexicon-based segmentation	87.58
+Error correction	**90.03**

Mongolian word may have different segmentations due to the different context and we choose the most frequent one. We only use 800 high frequency words as small labeled data in this paper. And it is different with much related work [4, 5, 7, 9, 12], which exploit large amount of labeled sentences. The test set contains 1000 sentences. 29.4 % word tokens in the test set are unknown words.

A Mongolian word is segmented correctly when both stem and affix is correct. Since semi-supervised segmentation in the paper is used to improve the performance of Chinese-Mongolian SMT, we utilize stem of Mongolian word in the word alignment step and ignore the boundaries between different affixes. In this paper, we assess the segmentation results with stem-level accuracy as evaluation indicators.

Experimental results are shown in Table 3.

From Table 3, we can conclude that the accuracy of our semi-supervised morphological segmentation, which uses CRF-based segmentation, lexicon-based segmentation and error correction, could reach 90.03 % although 29.4 % word tokens in the test set are unknown words. The segmentation accuracy improves significantly when we utilize lexicon-based approach for the errors in CRF-based segmentation, demonstrating that large unlabeled data is useful for Mongolian morphological segmentation.

There are large amount of labeled sentences needed in related work, while semi-supervised learning we proposed only need 800 high frequency words annotation rather than labeled sentences. The comparative experiments are not conducted because much related work need labeled sentences, which capture the context information for n-grams.

3.2 Improved SMT with Morpheme

Our Chinese-Mongolian parallel corpus is obtained from the 5th China Workshop on Machine Translation (CWMT 2009). The statistics of the experimental data are listed in Table 4, where 500×4 means that each source sentence has four reference sentences.

In this subsection, we integrate Mongolian morpheme information into Chinese Mongolian SMT. Generally speaking, we use Mongolian stem rather than word to generate word alignment matrix with Chinese word sequence. The word alignment matrix that contains morpheme information is used to replace the word alignment result of baseline SMT. Besides, we explore the two alignment results combination to further improve the translation performance.

The baseline is a standard phrase-based statistical machine translation system. We conduct two group experiments to verify the effectiveness of our method.

Table 4. Statistics of all datasets.

Dataset		Chinese	Mongolian
Training set	Sentences	67288	67288
	Words	849916	822167
Dev set	Sentences	500	500 × 4
	Words	4330	12614
Test set	Sentences	500	500 × 4
	Words	4456	12896

We employ GIZA++ and grow-diag-final-and [13] heuristic to generate the bidirectional word alignment. A 3-gram language model with modified Kneser-Ney smoothing [14] is built by the SRI language modeling toolkit [15]. We use Stanford parser [16] to parse Chinese sentences. The log-linear model feature weights are learned by using minimum error rate training [17]. Besides, we report all the results with BLEU [18]. We use toolkit ICTCLAS for Chinese word segmentation. Maximum phrase length is set to 7 when extracting phrase pair. We run each experiment 3 times and get the average BLEU score as the experimental result.

Table 5 illustrates translation results, where "A" denotes the standard phrase-based system, "B" denotes that we use Mongolian stem rather than word to generate word alignment matrix with Chinese word sequence. The word alignment matrix which contains morpheme information is used to replace the alignment result of system "A". "C" denotes we combine the alignment results of both "A" and "B" at the same time.

From Table 5, we can conclude that morphological information segmented by semi-supervised learning improves the performance of SMT significantly.

In order to have a better intuition about the performance improvement, we compare translation result between system "A" and system "C". Figure 2 illustrates the translation results, where "Source sentence" means Chinese sentence to be translated into Mongolian, "English translation" denotes the corresponding English translation for better understanding, "Ref0" to "Ref3" denotes source sentence is translated by four Mongolian linguistic experts independently since the correct answer of translation result is not unique.

Table 5. Translation results with morphological information.

System	BLEU(%)
A	20.10
B	20.58
C	**20.91**

The example is the selection of the correct morphology. "System A" predicts the verb "喝" of the source sentence as "VVGV". Although "VVGV" is the translation of "喝", "Y_A" is affix that represents the first person. In the source sentence, since "我" is the first person, "VVGVY_A" not only means "喝" but also represents grammatical meaning. Hence, "System C" can generate correct morphology of Mongolian.

Example 1	
Source sentence:	我 喝 点 茶 吧 。
English translation:	I drink some tea.
System A:	BI JIGAHAN CAI **VVGV** .
System C:	BI JIGAHAN CAI **VVGVY_A** .
Ref0:	BI JIGAHAN CAI VVGVY_A .
Ref1:	BI CAI VVGVY_A .
Ref2:	BI CAI VVGVHV SANAGATAI .
Ref3:	BI CAI VVGVMAR BAYIN_A .

Fig. 2. Comparison examples between the baseline and our proposed method

4   Related Work

Mongolian morphological segmentation has been a research focus recently. Generally speaking, previous work are based on dictionaries, rules and statistics [4–9].

(Nasanurtu, 1997) [19] proposed the method of combining rule-based and dictionary to accomplish Mongolian word segmentation. The construction of the rules and dictionary need significantly efforts by linguists. (Hou, et al., 2009) [6] used rules to segment Mongolian words and applied Mongolian statistical language model to eliminate the ambiguity in the process. However, the rules may also be conflicted with each other.

Statistical methods are the dominant approaches. (He, et al., 2012) exploited a HMM-based approach [8] for Mongolian morphological segmentation. Besides, CRF-based model [7, 9] achieved outstanding performance. Some approach [12] combined the statistical machine translation method and the minimum constituent context cost model to accomplish Mongolian morphological segmentation, which handled in-vocabulary and out-of-vocabulary Mongolian words well respectively. However, these approaches did not pay much attention on word formation character-istics of the morphology.

(Jiang, et al., 2011) [4, 5] proposed a directed graph model for Mongolian lexical analysis. This model described the lexical analysis result as a directed graph and used three kinds of transition or generation probabilities. The approach predicted the best segmented and tagged candidate for each word according to the context.

The methods mentioned above need lots of annotated training data or complicated rules concluded by linguists, and the construction process is significantly time-consuming.

Difference from above work, we explore a novel and effective method which use large unlabeled data to compensate the weakness of the lack of labeled data. Our work focus on the practical application, i.e., statistical machine translation, hence we pay more attention to the performance of machine translation system. We explore the semi-supervised learning for Mongolian morphological segmentation. To our knowledge, it is the first time for Mongolian to apply semi-supervised morphological segmentation.

5 Conclusion and Future Work

The paper proposes a method, which makes full use of large unlabeled data and small labeled data, to segment Mongolian words into morphemes. We investigate a CRF-based supervised learning to predict morpheme boundaries via small amount of labeled data. Besides, the abundant unlabeled data is exploited to compensate the weakness of the small amount of labeled data. Furthermore, some error correction models are exploited to revise segmentation results. The experimental results on morphological segmentation and Chinese-Mongolian SMT demonstrate the effectiveness of the proposed approach.

In summary, we make the following contributions.

(1) We explore the semi-supervised learning based on a low-resource learning setting, in which a small amount of labeled data and large amount of unlabeled data are available.
(2) Our work reduces the reliance on the manual annotation for Mongolian morphological segmentation.
(3) The method in this paper is a general method, besides Mongolian morphological segmentation, the method can also be adopted to other morphological low-resource languages, such as Uyghur.

In future, we will focus on the semi-supervised morphological segmentation with POS information. Besides, we will verify the method for more low-resource morphological rich languages.

Acknowledgement. This work is supported by the National Natural Science Foundation of China under No. 61572462, No. 61502445, the National Key Technology R&D Program under No. 2014BAD10B03.

References

1. Ruokolainen, T., Kohonen, O., Sirts, K., Gr"onroos, S.A., Kurimo, M., Virpioja, S.: A comparative study on minimally supervised morphological segmentation. Comput. Linguist. **42**(1), 91–120 (2016)
2. Ahlberg, M., Forsberg, M., Hulden, M.: Semi-supervised learning of morphological paradigms and lexicons. In: Proceedings of the 14th Conference of the European Chapter of the Association for Computational Linguistics, pp. 569–578 (2014)
3. Yang, P., Zhang, J., Li, M., Wudabala, Xue, Y.: Morphology-processing in Chinese-Mongolian statistical machine translation. J. Chin. Inf. Process. **23**(1), 50–57 (2009). (in Chinese)
4. Jiang, W., Wu, J., Chang, Q., Nasan-urtu, Liu, Q., Zhao, L.: Directed graph model for Mongolian lexical analysis. J. Chin. Inf. Process. **25**(5), 94–100 (2011). (in Chinese)
5. Jiang, W., Wu, J., Wuriliga, Nasan-urtu, Liu, Q.: Discriminative stem-affix segmentation for directed-graph-based Mongolian lexical analyzer. J. Chin. Inf. Process. **25**(4), 30–34 (2011)
6. Hou, H., Liu, Q., Nasanurtu, Murengaowa, Li, J.: Mongolian word segmentation based on statistical language model. Pattern Recognit. Artif. Intell. **22**(1), 109–112 (2009). (in Chinese)

7. Zhao, W., Hou, H., Cong, W., Song, M.: Research on conditional random fields based Mongolian word segmentation. J. Chin. Inf. Process. **24**(5), 31–35 (2010). (in Chinese)
8. He, M., Li, M., Chen, L.: Mongolian morphological segmentation with hidden Markov model. In: IALP, pp. 117–120 (2012)
9. Liu, H., Li, M., Zhang, J., Chen, L.: Morpheme segmentation using bilingual features. In: IALP, pp. 209–212 (2012)
10. Lafferty, J., McCallum, A., Pereira, F.C.: Conditional random fields: probabilistic models for segmenting and labeling sequence data. In: Proceedings of ICML (2001)
11. Creutz, M., Lagus, K.: Unsupervised models for morpheme segmentation and morphology learning. ACM Trans. Speech Lang. Process. (TSLP) **4**(1), 3 (2007)
12. Li, W., Chen, L., Wudabala, Li, M.: Chained machine translation using morphemes as pivot language. In: COLING 2010 Workshop, pp. 169–177. ALR (2010)
13. Koehn, P., Och, F.J., Marcu, D.: Statistical phrase-based translation. In: Proceedings of the 2003 Conference of the North American Chapter of the Association for Computational Linguistics on Human Language Technology-Volume 1, pp. 48–54. Association for Computational Linguistics (2003)
14. Chen, S.F., Goodman, J.: An empirical study of smoothing techniques for language modeling. In: Proceedings of the 34th annual meeting on Association for Computational Linguistics, pp. 310–318. Association for Computational Linguistics (1996)
15. Stolcke, A.: SRILM - an extensible language modeling toolkit. In: Proceedings of the International Conference on Spoken Language Processing, pp. 901–904 (2002)
16. Levy, R., Manning, C.: Is it harder to parse Chinese, or the Chinese treebank? In: Proceedings of ACL, pp. 439–446 (2003)
17. Och, F.J.: Minimum error rate training in statistical machine translation. In: ACL, pp. 160–167 (2003)
18. Papineni, K., Roukos, S., Ward, T., Zhu, W.J.: BLEU: a method for automatic evaluation of machine translation. In: ACL, pp. 311–318 (2002)
19. Nasanurtu: An automatic segmentation system for the root, stem, sufix of the Mongolian. J. Inner Mongolia Univ. **29**(2), 53–57 (1997). (in Chinese)

Investigation and Use of Methods for Defining the Extends of Similarity of Kazakh Language Sentences

Unzila Kamanur[1](✉), Altynbek Sharipbay[1](✉), Gulila Altenbek[2](✉),
Gulmira Bekmanova[1], and Lena Zhetkenbay[1]

[1] L.N. Gumilyov Eurasian National University, Astana, Kazakhstan
{unzila.88, sharalt, jetlen_7}@mail.ru,
gulmira-r@yandex.ru
[2] Xinjiang University, Urumqi, China
glaxd2014@163.com

Abstract. Finding similarity degree is one of the significant technologies used in the sample-based machine translation. It works in the following principle, first matching the input sentences with a sentence in the sample database, after that it is necessary to pick up parts of the similar sentences for the sentence which is aimed to translate; it is finished by correcting the structure or paraphrasing it with a relevant meaning. For that reason, the degree of similarity of two samples highly affects on the results of translation. Thus, there are dependence between quality of the outputs and the similarity degree.

Keywords: EBMT · Synonym replacement · Kazakh sentence · Similarity sentence similarity · Machine translation · Natural language processing

1 Introduction

The translation from one language to another is considered that it was introduced as a separate science for the first time in 1947 in the letter written by Warren Wiver for Nobert Viner [1]. After that, it can be seen that in the last 50 years the quick development of this study has occurred. Nowadays, a number of machine translation tools became available for users, various types of machine translation systems are widely used all over the world. Their further development and the extent of use highly depend on the presence of natural language corpus and the degree of difficulty of formalizing the natural languages.

In 1980s a Japanese researcher Makoto Nagao introduced a new method of translation. In the work published by him in 1984 "A framework of a mechanical translation between Japanese and English by analogy principle", he showed the translation of simple sentences done without any grammatical analysis. Instead of

---

The original version of this chapter was revised: In the initially published contribution the affiliations for some of the authors were stated incorrectly. The erratum to this chapter is available at DOI: 10.1007/978-3-319-47674-2_38

© Springer International Publishing AG 2016
M. Sun et al. (Eds.): CCL and NLP-NABD 2016, LNAI 10035, pp. 153–161, 2016.
DOI: 10.1007/978-3-319-47674-2_14

undertaking an analysis, he divided the whole sentence into small fragments (sentences). Only after dividing them, he translated the sentence. As a result, he was able to create a whole sentence from the short fragments. By taking the samples and matching them by similarity degree he managed to find a new approach on language translation. This method was called Example based Machine Translation [2].

The method of defining the similarity degree in sentences is widely used to make the natural languages as a separate science. For instance, there are a number of available functions in the systems of question-answer such as, to find answers on the questions given by an user, to match this question with questions in a database by finding a similarity, to filter the unmatched phrases from the user's answers by using the information filter technology and etc.

2 Related Work

All the methods used to find solutions for the artificial intelligence issues contain the steps of matching the knowledge fragments (requested fragments) with a prepared database of samples. This process, generally, include the process of comparing two fragments and the process of filtering in order to make a comparison between them. The process of comparing could be divided to the following methods of comparison:

- Syntactic method;
- Parametrical method;
- Semantical method;

During undertaking syntactical analysis also known as parsing the full balance and structure of two data are used to describe the fragment are compared. The example of these methods can be the unification of predicates in the Prolog language, where to take balance first of all the predicate's names are compared, after that the arguments pairs are compared with each other.

Parametrical analysis checks the structures of data which is used to describes the fragment for its partly balance (not full).

Semantic analysis is used to check the semantic (meaning) of knowledge fragment. During this process, usually it is necessary to study a structure of the known fragment. Also, in this process the term called "semantic similarity of words" is widely used, i.e. the idea of distance between terms based on their likeness by the meaning or semantic content and it is estimated by their syntactical representation. In some cases, the semantic similarity can be calculated directly. For instance, to compare two linguistic variables which are described in the same metric scales. The semantic algorithm haven't been developed yet which compares by universal and mathematic methods.

In addition, another method which is worth to mention in this paper is the search of relevant data in neuron systems. They are also known as associative search. According to the comparisons shown above, in associative search the known data is described not in symbols but by digits and signals used in neuron conditions.

The determination of similarity degrees of texts started from the early periods in 1963 when Gerard Salten founded the *Vector Space Model* (VSM) [3]. This method is still considered as the most popular and the best developed among existing ones. At the beginning it was used to define similarity degree in documents, but later it started to be used for texts. The main idea behind the Vector Space Model is by comparing the deviation of angles between each text vector and the original query(requested input text) vector where input is represented as the same kind of vector as the texts.

3 Defining the Similarity Degrees of Sentences Written in Kazakh Language

Defining the similarity degrees of sentences written in Kazakh language is basically based on Vector Space model. It includes two modules: quick search module and similarity calculation module. In the translation process first quick search module searches the samples from database which suits more than others, after that this set of matches are send to the second module for defining the similarity degree. In the similarity calculation module, both modules are used at the same time to define the similarity based on combined vectors calculated from the similarity.

3.1 The Quick Search Module

The significant issues in the sample based machine translation are grouping into a set the samples from database corresponding to the input and finding the sample most similar to the input. The quick search module is designed to solve these problems.

In order to improve the search speed it is necessary to divide all the words in the database and create an inversed index. To perform it, first of all samples in the database should be included in a table, then each sample formed from the word has to be assigned an ID and another table is created for that. In this case ID is the number of words formed from the samples. This formation is shown on Fig. 1 below.

The quick search process can be described as following:

Step 1: It uses the separate word's list, where Word is a word itself, id is the allocated special number given for each word.

Step 2: Analyzing the input sentence and produce the table of linked words. By using statistics from the list of frequently appeared separate words it calculates id set of the input sentence.

Step 3: Going back to the list of samples it calculates the degree of similarity, chooses the most similar sentence and analyzes it as a input sentence

$$[\text{word}(1) \rightarrow \text{id}(1) \rightarrow \text{id}(2) \rightarrow \ldots \rightarrow \text{id}(n)\ ]$$

$$[\text{word}(2) \rightarrow \text{id}(1) \rightarrow \text{id}(2) \rightarrow \ldots \rightarrow \text{id}(n)\ ]$$

$$\ldots$$

$$[\text{word}(m) \rightarrow \text{id}(1) \rightarrow \text{id}(2) \rightarrow \ldots \rightarrow \text{id}(k)\ ]$$

Fig. 1. The scheme of a inversed index based search

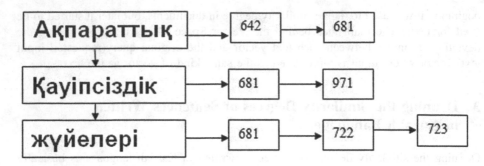

Fig. 2. Analysis of the sentence «Ақпараттық қауіпсіздік жүйелері» in Kazakh language

The Fig. 2 shows the example of 2-step analysis of the sentence «Ақпараттық қауіпсіздік жүйелері» in Kazakh language.

As the Fig. 2 shows 681 the level of linkage and appearing level are the highest among other digits shown in this example. The statistics are done for the each word separately, all id in this example are in ascending order [(681, 3), (642, 1), (971, 1), (722, 1), (723, 1)]. At the end, it is left the highest frequently id set.

3.2   The Similarity Calculation Module

The calculation of similarity degree for a main word include the following steps:

1. The degree of words' similarity.
Morphological degree of similarity (Word Overlap Measures) is used to calculate the similarity of the two sentences regarding their structure. The calculation of similar words contained there is performed using the following formula:

$$\text{sim}_{\text{Overlap}}(x, y) = \frac{len(samewc(x, y))}{\max(length(x), length(y))} \qquad (1)$$

Where, len(samewc(x, y)) is the number of matched words from an input sentence x and the sample sentence y;
$\text{sim}_{\text{overlap}}$ is used to describe a morphological similarity degree;
length(x) is a number of words in the sentence x, where as length(y) describes a number of words in the sentence y (including all the punctuation marks).
Defining the morphological similarity degree is shown in the example below.
Example:
Input sentence: A; ол қалаға қашан келеді? (When will he arrive to the city?)
Sample sentence: B: сабаққа қашан барасың (When will you go to classes)? C: ол ауылдан қашан келеді (When he will arrive from the village)?
Using the following formulae allows to calculate the similarity degree:

$$\text{sim}_{\text{Overlap}}(A, B) = \frac{len(samewc(A, B))}{\max(length(A), length(B))} = \frac{1}{\max(4, 3)} = 0.4$$

$$\text{sim}_{\text{Overlap}}(A, C) = \frac{len(samewc(A, C))}{\max(length(A), length(C))} = \frac{3}{\max(4, 4)} = 0.8$$

$$\text{sim}_{\text{Overlap}}(A, C) < \text{sim}_{\text{Overlap}}(A, C)$$

In this example we can see that sentence from its structure and context C is better corresponds to the A, whether B.

2. The reverse order based similarity degree calculation algorithm.

During the match of two sentences in some cases, it can be so that their divided units (parts) seem similar, but we cannot make a constant rule from their similarity based on this context.

Thus, if the orders of two divided sentences are changed, it might lead completely different context than its initial meaning. Therefore, the similarity degree of orders of words has to be calculated as well.

In this case, n(n∈N) is a set of various elements, where first of all the rule of ordering is set for each element. For instance, N is a directly ordered numbers and they are put in ascending order, whereas reverse ordered numbers are put in descending order. The overall number of reverse orders in a string is a number of reverse orders of this string.

The word's order describes the linkage similarity of all the units that initial sentence contains. Using these methods assumes that we put all the containing similar units in reverse order which is located next to each other.

Also we need to following labels for two sentences (x and y):

ordoccur (x, y) – a set of units which appears only once in the sentence;

pfir(x, y) –the number of a vector which describes the position of units in the x sentence within the set of units *ordoccur(x, y)*;

psec(x, y) – the number of a vector which describes the position given by similarity degree of units in the y sentence within the *pfir(x, y)* vector of units *pfir(x, y)*;

rew(x, y) – the inverse order number of element sequences in *psec(x, y)* vector.

similar$_{worder}(x, y)$ defines the similarity degrees of words in x and y sentences [4]:

$$similar_{worder}(x, y) = \begin{cases} 1 - \frac{rew(x,y)}{|ordoccur(x,y)|-1}, & |ordoccur(x,y)| > 1 \\ 1, & |ordoccur(x,y)| = 1 \\ 0, & |ordoccur(x,y)| = 0 \end{cases} \quad (2)$$

The similarity degree of words for the example we used in above will be as following:

ordoccur(A, C) = {"ол", "қашан", "келеді", "?"}; When will he come?

pfir(A, C) = (1, 3, 4, 5);

psec(A, C) = (1, 3, 4, 5);

rew(x, y) = 0, since for psec(A, C) the reverse order number of unit's sequence is 1 < 3, 3 < 4, 4 < 5.

Next, by using the formulae (2) the degree of words order's similarity in the A and C sentences is defined as following:

$$similar_{worder}(x, y) = 1 - \frac{0}{4-1} = 1.$$

3. Defining the similarity degree of sentence length.
It is important to clarify the morphological similarity when the similarity degree is defined based on the similarity degree of sentence's length. The length similarity of both sample sentences in database and input sentence affects on the whole sentence similarity degree. The similarity degree of sentence length is calculated using the formula below:

$$similar_{length}(x, y) = 1 - \frac{length(x) - length(y)}{length(x) + length(y)} \tag{3}$$

In order to define the similarity of words of an input sentence x and sample sentence y the following formula is used:

$$similar_{wstn} = \alpha \cdot similar_{overlap} + \beta \cdot similar_{worder} + \gamma \cdot similar_{length},$$
$$\tag{4}$$
reα, β, γ—experimental values.

3.3   The Vector Space Model Based TF_IDF Similarity Degree Calculation Method

TF_IDF is a statistical measure used to assess the importance of words in the context of being a part of a document or corpus. TF-IDF measure are widely used in text analysis and information search purposes. For instance, when the request comes it is used to match the relevancy of a document and during the cauterization it measures the extend of suitability. This idea was introduced by Karen Spark Jones. It contains two parts:

1. Term Frequency – the ratio of the total number of terms (words) in a document to the number of input words. Thus, by the document we define the importance of a word t_k:

$$TF(t_k, d) = \frac{n_k}{\sum_i n_i}, \tag{4}$$

   where n_k – a total number of a terms t_k in a d document, and n_i is a total number of all words containing in the document.
2. *Inverse Document Frequency* – inverse frequency of word occurence in a document collection. IDF calculation diminishes the weight of terms that occur very frequently (such as articles in English) in the document set and increases the weight of terms that occur rarely. In the collection of documents there is only one IDF value for one separate term.

$$IDF(t, D) = log \frac{|D|}{|(d_k \supset t_k)|}, \tag{5}$$

where $|D|$ –the number of documents in the corpus

$|(d_k \supset t_k)|$ is –number of documents where the term t appears when $n_k \neq 0$.

It is not so important to calculate the base of the logarithm in the formula, because by increasing the base leads to increasing the weight of terms.

Thus, TF-IDF is a measure that comes from multiplying two separate measures:

$$TF\_IDF(t, d, D) = TF(t, d) \cdot IDF(t, D).$$

During using the TF_IDF method in some cases take a high frequency for one document, and lower frequency in another documents.

If it is imagined that both sample sentence and input sentence contain set of words $w_1, w_2, \ldots, w_n$. Then, the input sentence is labeled by n-dimensional vector $t = (t_1, t_2, \ldots, t_n)$ and sample sentence by vector $q = (q_1, q_2, \ldots, q_n)$.

After defining the input sentence and sample sentence by n-dimensional vectors t and q respectively the similarity degree of sentences can be defined by cosines of two vectors t and q:

$$similar_{tf\_idf} = \frac{t \cdot q}{\|t\| \cdot \|q\|} = \frac{\sum_{i=1}^{n} t_i \cdot q_i}{\sqrt{\sum_{i=1}^{n}(t_i)^2} \cdot \sqrt{\sum_{i=1}^{n}(q_i)^2}} \tag{6}$$

After finding the similarity degree of by cosines of two vectors t and q, their total degree of similarity is described by similar total,

$$similar_{total} = a, similar_{wctn} + b, similar_{tf\_idf} \tag{7}$$

Defining the Similarity Degree of Kazakh Language Sentences. The program implementation intended to define a similarity degree of Kazakh language sentences include two major modules: module of inversed index and module of calculating the similarity degree.

The implementation of inversed index is basically adding a new example word into inversed module database after dividing it, which is shown in the Fig. 3 below.

The module that calculates the similarity degree is used when it takes the value of input sentence and examples and organize them in descending order with inversed results. Its interface is shown in Fig. 4 below.

Fig. 3. Adding a new inversed index to the database

Fig. 4. The interface used in defining the similarity degree.

4   Results and Discussion

In this comparison example contains 1000 sentences and 3500 inversed indexed words. The results of defining the similarity degree according to this data are shown in the Table 1 below.

Table 1. The results of defining the similarity degree

A number of sentences in the sample database	A number of sentences about to checked	A number of correct sentences	Correctness degree
400	20	8	0.4
800	20	10	0.5
900	20	11	0.55
1000	20	13	0.65

5   Conclusion and Future Works

The results of study has shown that the similarity degree defined by distances between the input sentences and the sentences in database is significantly different. Also, the figures of separate words are different. For that reason the interdependence between input sentence and the database sentences will always remain constant. This kind of link between words are sorted based on their order.

It is achievable to speed up the search by dividing the sentences into parts using an inverse index. Thus, it was set as a main goal of this work that is to find the match from the samples databases as much quickly as possible.

It is planned to conduct a study that intended to find the similarity degree first of all by calculating the cosine of the input sentence and a sample, combining two methods and find and a similarity degree. Due to the fact that the current databases of samples are small, it is not possible to obtain satisfactory results from translation outputs. In the future, it is planned to expand the database of samples which can facilitate on speeding up the search, improving the data about semantics and grammar of language as a result the quality of the translation might be improved in a significant manner.

References

1. Hutchins, J.: From first conception to first demonstration: the nascent years of machine translation, 1947–1954. A chronology. Mach. Transl. **12**, 195–252 (1997)
2. Nagao, M.: A framework of a mechanical translation between Japanese and English by analogy principle. In: Proceedings of International NATO Symposium on Artificial and Human Intelligence, Lyon, France, pp. 173–180. Elsevier North-Holland, Inc. (1984)
3. Salton, G., Wong, A., Yang, C.S.: A vector space model for automatic indexing. Commun. ACM **18**(11), 613–620 (1975)
4. Lu, X.-Q., Ren, F.-L., Huang, Z.-D., Yao, T.-S.: Sentence similarity model and the most similar sentence search algorithm. Article ID: 1005-3026(2003)06-0531-04

Knowledge Graph and Information Extraction

Recognizing Biomedical Named Entities Based on the Sentence Vector/Twin Word Embeddings Conditioned Bidirectional LSTM

Lishuang Li[✉], Liuke Jin, Yuxin Jiang, and Degen Huang

School of Computer Science and Technology, Dalian University of Technology,
Dalian 116024, Liaoning, China
{lils,Huangdg}@dlut.edu.cn, dllg_lkjin@mail.dlut.edu.cn,
512415325@qq.com

Abstract. As a fundamental step in biomedical information extraction tasks, biomedical named entity recognition remains challenging. In recent years, the neural network has been applied on the entity recognition to avoid the complex hand-designed features, which are derived from various linguistic analyses. However, performance of the conventional neural network systems is always limited to exploiting long range dependencies in sentences. In this paper, we mainly adopt the bidirectional recurrent neural network with LSTM unit to identify biomedical entities, in which the twin word embeddings and sentence vector are added to rich input information. Therefore, the complex feature extraction can be skipped. In the testing phase, Viterbi algorithm is also used to filter the illogical label sequences. The experimental results conducted on the BioCreative II GM corpus show that our system can achieve an F-score of 88.61 %, which outperforms CRF models using the complex hand-designed features and is 6.74 % higher than RNNs.

Keywords: LSTM · Twin word embeddings · Sentence vector · Viterbi algorithm

1 Introduction

With the rapid development of computational and biological technology, biomedical literatures are growing exponentially, and abundant literatures about biomedical knowledge also provide an opportunity for text mining techniques in this field. As a fundamental step, the biomedical named entity recognition (Bio-NER) plays a critical role in many tasks such as coreference resolution and relation extraction in the biomedical field. Over the past years, though various methods have been proposed for Bio-NER, there is still a large gap on recognition performance between the biomedical and general field.

Currently, the most widely used methods to recognize biomedical named entity can focus on dictionary-based methods, rule-based methods and statistical machine learning methods [1]. Compared with the other two methods, the machine learning methods are more robust and there is an advantage that they can identify the potential biomedical entities which are not previously included in standard dictionaries. There have been many attempts to develop machine learning techniques such as Hidden Markov Model

© Springer International Publishing AG 2016
M. Sun et al. (Eds.): CCL and NLP-NABD 2016, LNAI 10035, pp. 165–176, 2016.
DOI: 10.1007/978-3-319-47674-2_15

(HMM) [2], Maximum Entropy (ME) [3], Conditional Random Field (CRF) [4], Support Vector Machine (SVM) [5] and etc.

However, these shallow machine learning methods are required to extract the manual features as the intermediate representation of each word in the text. Therefore, the recognition performance may be affected by some common drawbacks as followings. First, the construction of the feature set mainly relies on some experience and domain knowledge. Besides, selecting an optimal subset of features needs tremendous experiments. Furthermore, some complex features with syntactic information may be obtained from other NLP modules, like Part-of-Speech, and the inevitable cascading errors can lead to the final recognition errors. Meanwhile, enormous manual efforts may lead to over-design of the system and reduce the ability of generalization.

Aiming to overcome the problems described above, deep learning has been applied on the entity recognition in recent years. Collobert et al. [6] proposed a unified neural network architecture for various natural languages processing tasks which also achieved a better result in the NER task. Chen el al. [7] proposed deep belief network (DBN) to extract unsupervised and multi-level feature representation for entity recognition and classification, outperforming SVM, CRF and ANN classifiers. In order to integrate longer range of contextual effects and flexibly use the context information, Li et al. [8, 9] adopted the combined and extended recurrent neural networks (RNNs) which had better performance than CRF models with some simple features. However, some limitations still existed in their system. For example, the back propagated error in long sentence either blows up or decays exponentially so that long time lags are inaccessible in RNNs. Therefore, Long Short Term-Memory (LSTM) as a RNN architecture is motivated to deal with long range dependencies.

In this paper, we extend the bidirectional LSTM (BLSTM) on biomedical named entity recognition. Firstly, the twin word embeddings are used to rich input information. Then, the sentence vector can be obtained by calculating the differences of two embeddings to get the whole sentence information, which can accurately encodes the input information. Finally, in the testing phase, Viterbi algorithm is adopted to filter the illogical label sequences. The experimental results on the BioCreative II GM corpus show that our Sentence vector/Twin word embeddings conditioned BLSTM (ST-BLSTM) without any manual features can achieve an F-score of 88.61 % which is better than (or close to) other state-of-the-art Bio-NER systems.

2   Methodology

We explore a so-called ST-BLSTM architecture, in which the twin word embeddings and sentence vector are introduced to the BLSTM. The system architecture for named entity recognition based on ST-BLSTM can be summarized in Fig. 1. Firstly, the word embeddings are obtained by lookup tables and the vectors in the word-context window are concatenated together to feed into the recurrent neural network. Then, we establish a recurrent neural network with ST-BLSTM unit to acquire the hidden layer. And the recurrent connection is also added into the output layer to associate previous prediction probabilities. What's more, Viterbi algorithm is considered in the testing phase to further improve the recognition capability.

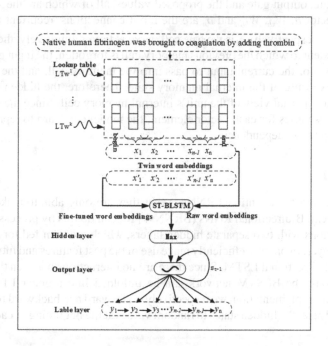

Fig. 1. Bio-NER architecture based on ST-BLSTM

2.1   LSTM

A standard architecture of LSTM mainly consists of an input layer, a recurrent LSTM layer and an output layer. Based on this structure, the input, output and stored information can be partially adjusted by the gates, which enhance the flexibility of the model. Such structures are more capable to learn a complex composition of word vectors than simple RNNs. While numerous LSTM variants have been described, here the forward pass for the LSTM model used in this paper is as follows:

$$i_t = \sigma(x_t \cdot w_{xh}^i + h_{t-1} \cdot w_{hh'}^i + b_h^i) \tag{1}$$

$$f_t = \sigma(x_t \cdot w_{xh}^f + h_{t-1} \cdot w_{hh'}^f + b_h^f) \tag{2}$$

$$o_t = \sigma(x_t \cdot w_{xh}^o + h_{t-1} \cdot w_{hh'}^o + b_h^o) \tag{3}$$

$$\tilde{c}_t = \tanh(x_t \cdot w_{xh}^c + h_{t-1} \cdot w_{hh'}^c + b_h^c) \tag{4}$$

$$c_t = i_t \odot \tilde{c}_t + f_t \odot c_{t-1} \tag{5}$$

$$h_t = o_t \odot \tanh(c_t) \tag{6}$$

Where σ denotes the logistic sigmoid function and $\odot$ denotes the element-wise multiplication. x is the input embeddings at time t, and i, f, o and c are respectively input gate, forget gate, output gate and the proposed values, all of which are the same size as the hidden vector h. W_{xh}, W_{hh} and b_h are the input connections, recurrent connections and bias values respectively. $\tilde{c}_t$ is the true cell value at time t. Intuitively, the forget gate controls the extent to which the previous memory cell is forgotten, the input gate controls what proportion of the current input to pass into the memory cell, and the output gate controls the exposure of the internal memory state. Therefore, the hidden vector from an LSTM unit is partial view of the unit's internal memory cell. Since the value of the gating variables varies for each vector element, the model can learn to represent information of long range dependencies.

2.2 BLSTM

One shortcoming of conventional RNNs is that they are only able to make use of the previous context. Bidirectional RNNs (BRNNs) [10] can do this by processing the data in both directions with two separate hidden layers, which are then fed forwards to the same output layer. In order to efficiently make use of the past features and future features, we construct bidirectional LSTM. Since there are no interactions between the two types of state neurons, the BLSTM network can be unfolded into a general feed forward network. In our implementation, we respectively do forward and backward for the whole sentences and reset the hidden states to random values at the beginning of each sentence.

2.3 ST-BLSTM

Since the original word embeddings are trained by the unsupervised learning approaches, the bias caused by the context definition may impact the quality of word embeddings. In this paper, fine tuning is added into the training process to retrain the word embeddings. Furthermore, we construct the twin word embeddings to rich the input information and the sentence vector is introduced to extend the neural network, whose memory cell is shown in Fig. 2.

Twin Word Embeddings. The supervised fine-tuning process can further improve the performance of BLSTM and the retrained word embeddings can also be obtained in the fine-tuning process. The retrained word embeddings contain richer information associated with Bio-NER and the pre-trained word embeddings learned from large-scale unlabeled corpus obtain the potential feature information. In order to take into account the advantage of both feature information, we use two independent word embeddings to extend the BLSTM network. Since they share the same initial values, we call them twin word embeddings. The only difference between them is that one kind of word embeddings is fine-tuned as parameter matrix, i.e. x'_t, while the other kind of word embeddings keeps constant over the whole process, i.e. x_t. In this work, we use the new LSTM architecture that is precisely specified below.

$$i_t = \sigma(x_t \cdot w^i_{xh} + x'_t \cdot w^i_{x'h} + h_{t-1} \cdot w^i_{hh'} + b^i_h) \tag{7}$$

$$f_t = \sigma(x_t \cdot w^f_{xh} + x'_t \cdot w^f_{x'h} + h_{t-1} \cdot w^f_{hh'} + b^f_h) \tag{8}$$

$$o_t = \sigma(x_t \cdot w^o_{xh} + x'_t \cdot w^o_{x'h} + h_{t-1} \cdot w^o_{hh'} + b^o_h) \tag{9}$$

$$\tilde{c}_t = \tanh(x_t \cdot w^c_{xh} + x'_t \cdot w^c_{x'h} + h_{t-1} \cdot w^c_{hh'} + b^o_h) \tag{10}$$

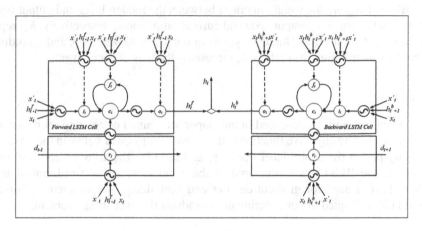

Fig. 2. Memory cell of ST-BLSTM

Sentence Vector. Since it is easy to ignore the implicit meaning of a sentence only using the word-level embeddings, the sentence-level feature representation applied into the hidden layer is considered in our system. Calculating the difference of the twin word embeddings, we can generate the sentence vector d_0 by averaging or maximizing all the word embeddings in the sentence. Besides, we use reading gate r_t to control what information should be retrained for future time steps. Then Eq. (5) is modified so that the cell value c_t also depends on the sentence vector, which can accurately encode the input information.

$$r_t = \sigma(x_t \cdot w^r_{xh} + x'_t \cdot w^r_{x'h} + h_{t-1} \cdot w^r_{hh'} + b^r_h) \tag{11}$$

$$d_0 = \max(\sum_{t=1}^{T}(x'_t - x_t)) \tag{12}$$

$$d_t = r_t \odot d_{t-1} \tag{13}$$

$$c_t = i_t \odot \tilde{c}_t + f_t \odot c_{t-1} + \tanh(d_t) \tag{14}$$

2.4   Extension at the Output Layer

Considering the recurrent connection at the output layer can also improve the performance of recognition [8], the probability information from the previous state together with the result of the hidden layer are applied into the current prediction as Eq. (15).

$$s_t = soft(h_t \cdot w_{hs} + s_{t-1} \cdot w_{ss'} + b_s) \qquad (15)$$

$$soft(z_m) = e^{z_m} \Big/ \sum_k e^{z_k}, \qquad (16)$$

where W_{hs} and W_{ss} are the weight matrices between the hidden layer and output layer, and between the previous output node and current output node, respectively. h_{t-1} represents the output values in the hidden layer from the previous time step, and s_t produces a probability distribution over labels. b_s represents the bias of each layer.

2.5 Training

All the neural network models used in this paper are trained by treating each sentence as a mini-batch. The objective function is the cross entropy error between the predicted probability p_i and the actual label vector y_i as Eq. (17). The forward and backward networks in the BLSTM are structured to share the same set of word embeddings. Adadelta [11] is used for gradient descent and optimizing the parameters. Besides, dropout [12] is adopted in our experiments to address the overfitting problem.

$$loss = -\frac{1}{n} \sum_{i=1}^{k} y_i \log p_i \qquad (17)$$

2.6 Viterbi Algorithm in the Testing Phase

During the testing phase, Viterbi algorithm is executed to make sure that the illogical label sequence will not be selected. Since the generated label y_i does not involve the label y_{i-1} before it, the illogical label chains maybe exist in the prediction result. For example, it is obvious that the label **I** should not follow the label **O**. In this paper, we use the similar method as shown in Chen et al.'s [13], the initial probabilities of illogical entity label is assigned 0, while the others reset to 1. And the transition probabilities of the illogical entity label path should be 0. Thus, the partial probabilities of path containing "O I" will be 0 and this path will be discarded.

3 Experiments

Our experiments are carried out on three different datasets including the BioCreative II GM, JNLPBA2004 and BioCreative V DNER. Firstly, we experimentally demonstrate that the improvements based on our ST-BLSTM are effective on the BioCreative II GM corpus. Then, the comparison with other approaches is conducted on the three corpora. In experiments, all the deep networks are based on the common Theano neural network toolkit[1] and the RNN models are trained with the same hyper-parameters. All the experiments are based on a set of 200 dimensional word embeddings. Besides, we use F-score as our assessing criteria to evaluate our method. The definition of Precision (P), Recall (R) and F-score (F) are shown as Eqs. (18–20). TP is short for true positives, FP represents false positives, and FN stands for false negatives.

$$P = TP/(TP + FP) \qquad (18)$$

$$R = TP/(TP + FN) \qquad (19)$$

$$F - score = 2 * P * R/(P + R) \qquad (20)$$

3.1 Data Set

We test our system on three biomedical datasets as shown in Table 1. And BioCreative II GM is mainly composed of sentences, while JNLPBA2004 and BioCreative V DNER give the abstracts. Table 1 lists the size of sentences or abstracts for training, development and test sets, respectively. **BILOU** tagging scheme is selected to find the entity boundary in our experiment. **B** refers to the beginning word of a gene name, **I** and **L** respectively indicate inside tokens and the last token in a gene name if it contains more than one word, **O** refers to the words which are not included in a gene name, and finally **U** represents the unit-length chunks.

Table 1. Three biomedical datasets

Corpus	Training set	Development set	Test set
BioCreative II GM (sentence)	15000	–	5000
JNLPBA2004 (abstract)	2000	–	404
BioCreative V DNER (abstract)	500	500	500

3.2 BioCreative II GM Corpus

The Results of Improvements Based on ST-BLSTM. Our experiments are carried out on the BioCreative II GM corpus and the models' performance is reported in Table 2. The effects of improvements are analyzed as followings.

Pre-trained Word Embeddings (PWE). In order to explore the impact of richer text information on LSTM architecture, we use two ways to initialize the word embedding: random and pre-trained. And the results reveal that the pre-trained word embeddings have better performance than the random word embeddings by rising 5.87 % F-score (77.98 % vs 83.85 %).

---

[1] http://deeplearning.net/tutorial/rnnslu.html.

Table 2. Results on GM corpus with different improved approaches based on LSTM

Model	PWE	RC	Viterbi	P (%)	R (%)	F- score (%)
LSTM				83.19	73.40	77.98
LSTM	√			85.63	82.13	83.85
LSTM	√	√		85.88	83.03	84.43
BLSTM	√	√		88.68	85.76	87.20
T-BLSTM	√	√		89.83	87.07	88.43
ST-BLSTM	√	√		89.48	87.63	88.54
ST-BLSTM	√	√	√	**89.54**	**87.69**	**88.61**

Recurrent Connection (RC) at the Output Layer. Recurrent connection at the output layer can take advantage of the previous probabilistic information of labels and apply it into the calculation of current prediction. Thus, the potential links between labels can be considered to further improve the performance. The experimental results show that the F-score can increase from 83.85 % to 84.43 %.

BLSTM. In order to efficiently make use of the past and future features, bidirectional LSTM networks are trained in our work. From Table 2, we can see that the BLSTM can have better performance which rises 2.77 % compared with the unidirectional LSTM.

Twin Word Embeddings. Based on the BLSTM, the twin word embeddings are added to rich the input information and the F-score reaches 88.43 %. We can improve the performance by 1.23 %.

Sentence Vector. Sentence vector is also combined with our BLSTM, which is generated by maximizing the difference of twin word embeddings in a sentence. The F-score reaches 88.54 % which rises by 0.11 %.

Viterbi Algorithm. In the testing phase, we also use Viterbi algorithm to filter illogical sequence of labels. At last, the best result from our architecture can be increased to 88.61 %.

Comparison with Existing Systems. We make the comparisons between our system and some state-of-the-art works in Table 3. As the best system in competition at that time, Ando [14] mainly used a semi-supervised learning method, combined classifiers with dictionary as well as the post-processing, the final F-score reached 87.21 %. In Li et al.'s system [15], they extracted rich hand-designed features such as part-of-speech, stemmed word, orthographic feature etc. and unigram, bigram, trigram types of features based on CRF model as well as the post-processing achieving an F-score of 87.28 %. In Li et al.'s method [16], they increased three kinds of distributed word representation besides the rich hand-designed features, and used the combined methods to reach a better F-score of 88.44 %. However, in our approach the complex hand-designed features and domain dictionary knowledge are skipped as well as 0.17 % F-score higher compared with Li et al.'s [16].

Table 3. Comparison with other Bio-NER systems

Model	P (%)	R (%)	F-score (%)
Ando et al. [14]	88.48	85.97	87.21
Li et al. [15]	90.38	84.39	87.28
Li et al. [16]	91.24	85.80	88.44
Li et al. [17]	**90.52**	**87.63**	**89.05**
Li et al. [8]	80.93	82.21	81.87
Ours	**89.54**	**87.69**	**88.61**

In Li et al.'s system [8], the conventional RNNs are adopted to Bio-NER task and their best performance is 81.87 % F-score which is 6.74 % lower than our method. It demonstrates that our model outperforms the conventional RNN.

Though our system can outperform most of the shallow approaches, compared with Li et al.'s system [17] which performs the best until now, our F-score is 0.44 % lower. The reason account for lag is that they utilized the abundant external resources to construct the dictionary, rich domain knowledge and hand-designed features.

3.3 JNLPBA2004 Corpus

Table 4 lists the comparison with other systems on the JNLPBA2004 corpus. Yao et al. [18] used a multi-layer neural network to continuously learn the representation of features, achieving 71.01 % F-score. Chang et al. [19] used some hand-designed features and word embeddings as the input of CRF model as well as the post-processing; they achieved 71.85 % F-score. Wang et al. [20] verified that the Gimli method based on CRF model could achieve the best performance with 72.23 % F-score among six different Bio-NER methods on JNLPBA2004 corpus. Besides, as the best system in competition at that time, Zhou and Su et al.'s method got 72.55 % F-score [21]. The abundant resources knowledge and common hand-designed features, such as abbreviation, alias and dictionary, were used, which greatly enhanced its performance. However, the experimental results show that the F-score of our ST-BLSTM model can reach 72.76 % which outperforms all of them by 0.91 %, 1.75 %, 0.53 % and 0.21 %, respectively. Meanwhile, no hand-designed features and rules are used in our system.

Table 4. Comparison with other systems on the JNLPBA2004 corpus

Model	P (%)	R (%)	F-score (%)
Yao et al. [18]	76.13	66.54	71.01
Chang et al. [19]	–	–	71.85
Wang et al. [20]	–	–	72.23
Zhou and Su et al. [21]	75.99	69.42	72.55
Ours	**74.77**	**70.85**	**72.76**

3.4 BioCreative V DNER Corpus

We also apply our system on the BioCreative V DNER corpus. Table 5 shows the comparison result with CRF model. In the case of evaluating the test set, we combine training set and development set as the training set. The CRF model needs to extract the hand-designed features such as part-of-speech, stemmed word, orthographic feature etc. As shown in Table 5, our method can reach 78.91 % F-score on the development set, which is 2.5 % higher than CRF. And CRF achieves 76.91 % on the test set, while our method is 5.69 % higher than CRF instead of any manual features. For example, in development set, the standard entity "Tricuspid valve regurgitation" is recognized by our method, while the CRF model could not recognize it. The main reason is that the neural network can learn more potential characteristic information, and train more complex models; however, the shallow machine learning methods have strong dependency on the artificial features and hard to represent the complex models. Therefore our method can achieve a better result in the NER task.

Table 5. Results on the Biocreative V corpus about disease recognition

Model	Data set	P (%)	R (%)	F-score (%)
CRF	Development set	71.41	82.16	76.41
ours		76.67	81.28	**78.91**
CRF	Test set	72.78	81.54	76.91
ours		81.53	83.70	**82.60**

4 Discussion

From the above experimental results, we can conclude that our ST-BLSTM model outperforms most state-of-the-art Bio-NER systems and mainly includes the following important advantages:

No Hand-Designed Features. We skip the step of extracting complex hand-designed features, and replace it with word embeddings trained off-line. Since high-quality word embeddings can catch a large number of precise syntactic and semantic word relationships, the deep learning architecture can fully utilize this information and extract the high-level features for the Bio-NER.

Additional Extension at the Output Layer. Considering that predicted result (i.e. probability of labeling) from the prior node can have an important impact on the current prediction, we extend the original LSTM model by adding a reconnection at the output layer. From the experimental results, we can see that the extended method can produce positive impact on the Bio-NER.

Combining Twin Word Embeddings and Sentence Vector. Considering the fine-tuned word embeddings contain richer information associated with Bio-NER, and the pre-trained word embeddings contain the feature information learning from large-scale unlabeled corpus, we extend the bidirectional LSTM by adding twin word embeddings.

For the input, the extended features are more abundant, and the multiplication gates can control more accurate information. Besides, the sentence vector could contain complementary information of twin word embeddings. The experimental results show that both twin word embeddings and sentence vector could have positive effects on the BLSTM architecture to recognize biomedical named entities.

Viterbi Algorithm in the Testing Phase. The results show that the added Viterbi algorithm in bidirectional LSTM output layer can filter the illogical label sequences effectively. This is mainly because that the algorithm is based on dynamic programming and can find the most likely label sequences.

5 Conclusion

In this paper, we propose ST-BLSTM architecture to identify biomedical entities. The twin word embeddings and sentence vector are added into the bidirectional LSTM to obtain more abundant contextual information. Simultaneously, we extend the model by adding recurrent connection at the output layer and in the testing phase the Viterbi algorithm is applied to filter the illogical label sequences. The experimental results show that our model on BioCreative II GM corpus can achieve 88.61 % F-score without using any hand-designed features and external resource, higher than almost all systems. And on JNLPBA2004 and BioCreative V DNER datasets, we also can achieve a rather better recognition performance.

Acknowledgment. The authors gratefully acknowledge the financial support provided by the National Natural Science Foundation of China under Nos. 61173101, 61672126. The Tesla K40 used for this research was donated by the NVIDIA Corporation.

References

1. Li, L., Fan, W., Huang, D., Dang, Y., Sun, J.: Boosting performance of gene mention tagging system by hybrid methods. J. Biomed. Inform. **45**(1), 156–164 (2012)
2. Shen, D., Zhang, J., Zhou, G., Su, J., Tan, C.: Effective adaptation of a hidden Markov model-based named entity recognizer for biomedical domain. In: Proceedings of the ACL 2003 Workshop on Natural Language Processing in Biomedicine, vol. 13, pp. 49–56 (2003)
3. Saha, S., Sarkar, S., Mitra, P.: Feature selection techniques for maximum entropy based biomedical named entity recognition. J. Biomed. Inform. **42**(5), 905–911 (2009)
4. Sun, C., Guan, Y., Wang, X., Lin, L.: Rich features based conditional random fields for biological named entities recognition. Comput. Biol. Med. **37**(9), 1327–1333 (2007)
5. Lee, K., Hwang, Y., Kim, S., Rim, H.: Biomedical named entity recognition using two-phase model based on SVMs. J. Biomed. Inform. **37**(6), 436–447 (2004)
6. Collobert, R., Weston, J., Bottou, L., Karlen, M., Kavukcuoglu, K., Kuksa, P.: Natural language processing (almost) from scratch. J. Mach. Learn. Res. **12**(8), 2493–2537 (2011)
7. Chen, Y., Zheng, D., Zhao, T.: Exploring deep belief nets to detect and categorize Chinese entities. In: International Conference on Advanced Data Mining and Applications, pp. 468–480 (2013)

8. Li, L., Jin, L., Huang, D.: Exploring recurrent neural networks to detect named entities from biomedical text. In: Chinese Computational Linguistics and Natural Language Processing Based on Naturally Annotated Big Data, pp. 279–290 (2015)

9. Li, L., Jin, L., Jiang, Z., Song D., Huang, D.: Biomedical named entity recognition based on extended recurrent neural networks. In: IEEE International Conference on Bioinformatics and Biomedicine, pp. 649–652 (2015)

10. Schuster, M., Paliwal, K.: Bidirectional recurrent neural networks. IEEE Trans. Signal Process. **45**(11), 2673–2681 (1997)

11. Zeiler, M.D.: ADADELTA: an adaptive learning rate method. arXiv Preprint arXiv: 1212.5701 (2012)

12. Srivastava, N., Hinton, G., Krizhevsky, A., Sutskever, I., Salakhutdinov, R.: Dropout: a simple way to prevent neural networks from overfitting. J. Mach. Learn. Res. **15**(1), 1929–1958 (2014)

13. Chen, Y., Zheng, D., Zhao, T.: Exploring deep belief nets to detect and categorize Chinese entities. In: International Conference on Advanced Data Mining and Applications, pp. 468–480 (2013)

14. Ando, R.K.: BioCreative II gene mention tagging system at IBM watson. In: Proceedings of the Second BioCreative Challenge Evaluation Workshop, vol. 23, pp. 101–103 (2007)

15. Li, L., Zhou, R., Huang D., Liao, W.: Integrating divergent models for gene mention tagging. In: IEEE International Conference on Bioinformatics and Biomedicine, pp. 1–7 (2009)

16. Li, L., He, H., Liu, S., Huang, D.: Research of word representations on biomedical named entity recognition. J. Chin. Comput. Syst. **2**, 302–307 (2016). (in Chinese)

17. Li, Y., Lin, H., Yang, Z.: Incorporating rich background knowledge for gene named entity classification and recognition. BMC Bioinform. **10**(1), 1–15 (2009)

18. Yao, L., Liu, H., Liu, Y., Li, X., Anwar, M.W.: Biomedical named entity recognition based on deep neutral network. Corpus **8**(8), 279–288 (2015)

19. Chang, F., Guo, J., Xu, W., Chung, S.: Application of word embeddings in biomedical named entity recognition tasks. J. Digital Inf. Manage. **13**(5), 321–327 (2015)

20. Wang, X., Yang, C., Guan, R.: A comparative study for biomedical named entity recognition. Int. J. Mach. Learn. Cybern. 1–10 (2015). doi:10.1007/s13042-015-0426-6

21. Zhou, G. Su, J.: Exploring deep knowledge resources in biomedical name recognition. In: International Joint Workshop on Natural Language Processing in Biomedicine and ITS Applications, pp. 96–99 (2004)

Definition Extraction with LSTM Recurrent Neural Networks

SiLiang Li[✉], Bin Xu, and Tong Lee Chung

Knowledge Engineering Group, Tsinghua University, Beijing, China
lisiliang10@gmail.com

Abstract. Definition extraction is the task to identify definitional sentences automatically from unstructured text. The task can be used in the aspects of ontology generation, relation extraction and question answering. Previous methods use handcraft features generated from the dependency structure of a sentence. During this process, only part of the dependency structure is used to extract features, thus causing information loss. We model definition extraction as a supervised sequence classification task and propose a new way to automatically generate sentence features using a Long Short-Term Memory neural network model. Our method directly learns features from raw sentences and corresponding part-of-speech sequence, which makes full use of the whole sentence. We experiment on the Wikipedia benchmark dataset and obtain 91.2 % on F_1 score which outperforms the current state-of-the-art methods by 5.8 %. We also show the effectiveness of our method in dealing with other languages by testing on a Chinese dataset and obtaining 85.7 % on F_1 score.

Keywords: Definition extraction · LSTM recurrent neural networks

1 Introduction

Definitions play an important role in creating and enriching ontology concepts from unstructured text [1]. Definitions are also put to use in Question Answering to solve "what is" problems [2]. A big challenge is how to collect definitions from emerging mass text, since manually extracting definitions from unstructured text can be costly and slow. Therefore automatic definition extraction has drawn much attention in Natural Language Processing.

Current state-of-the-art methods treat definition extraction as a supervised classification task where a sentence is classified as definitional or not. The key point of this task is to generate features which are usually manually selected in previous approaches. For example, DefMiner system [3] specifies 12 features (8 word level features, 3 sentence level features and 1 document level feature). In a weakly supervised method [4], they use 14 features to describe a sentence. Both methods use many manually selected features (e.g. dependency path distance: distance from the current word to the root of the sentence in the dependency tree)

© Springer International Publishing AG 2016
M. Sun et al. (Eds.): CCL and NLP-NABD 2016, LNAI 10035, pp. 177–189, 2016.
DOI: 10.1007/978-3-319-47674-2_16

to approximately describe a sentence structure from its dependency tree. However there are two shortcomings in these features. First of all, they can only reflect part of the dependency tree which may lose hidden structure feature of sentences. Moreover they rely on the output of dependency parsing which involves error propagation. Therefore we focus on studying a method which can generate features directly from raw sentence.

In this paper, we propose a supervised learning method where features for definition extraction are automatically learned from raw sentences. Instead of relying on dependency parsing result, we regard a sentence as a word sequence and directly learn from the whole sequence. We generate sentence feature using recurrent neural network with Long Short-Term Memory (LSTM) due to the reason that LSTM has shown great ability in capturing long-term and short-term dependencies in a sequence. In our method, a sentence will first be transformed into a sequence consisted of word feature vectors. A LSTM encoder will be trained to encode the sequence into a vector representation. Finally a logistic regression classifier will be used to predict the sentence label with its feature vector. Instead of manually selecting features from dependency parsing, our sentence feature vector is directly generated by our LSTM encoder automatically, which can reduce the work of sentence feature engineering.

We evaluate the performance of our method on a Wikipedia benchmark corpus [5] and a Chinese dataset[1] originated from Baidu Baike[2]. The result shows that our method can significantly outperforms current state-of-the-art approach in F1 measure by 5.8 %, and improve the recall to 92 %. The main contributions of this work can be summarized as follows:

- We propose a new method utilizing LSTM to do definition extraction.
- Our method does not rely on handcraft patterns nor features manually specified from sentence dependency parsing. It can reduce the work of feature engineering for supervised learning based methods by automatically learning structure features from sentence sequence.
- Our method relies little on linguistic features and can be used for definition extraction in multiple languages. Our experiments prove its effectiveness in both English and Chinese.

The rest of the paper is organized as follows. We briefly introduce related work in Sect. 2. Then Sect. 3 describes the method we use to build our definitional classification model. We describe our experiment in Sect. 4, followed by results and analysis in Sect. 5. Finally, our paper is concluded in Sect. 6.

2 Related Work

The task of definition extraction has attracted many attention in the past few years. Previous researches can be divided into three kinds: pattern based [8,9], semi-supervised learning [4,5] and supervised approaches [3,10].

---

[1] You can download it from http://166.111.7.170:28090/zh.zip.
[2] http://baike.baidu.com.

2.1 Pattern Based Methods

The method focusing on the use of lexico-syntactic patterns, is first put forward
by Hearst [11]. However relying on simple definitional patterns (such as is-a, is
called) matching can be noisy, since short patterns may not fully represent the
sentences' structure features. Some systems [8,12] use patterns to extract candidates which will be further checked by grammar analysis. In order to introduce
more complex patterns, a method [9] uses part-of-speech (POS) tag patterns
rather than simple sequences of words.

However methods which use patterns manually selected usually suffer from
low recall. The expression of definitional sentences can vary greatly in different datasets, so it is difficult to craft complete patterns which can identify all
definitional sentences. Due to lack of generating ability caused by the simple
strategy of pattern matching, a fully automated way using genetic programming
is proposed to learn individual weights of features [13]. The genetic programming
based method takes the combination of features into consideration but it ignores
the importance of the order of feature occurrence.

2.2 Semi-supervised Methods

Semi-supervised approaches [4,14] show that bootstraping is efficient for definition extraction. The basic idea of these methods is to start from gold sentences
and extract more from articles in other datasets such as ACL Anthology Reference Corpus (ACL ARC) [15].

Word-Class Lattices (WCLs) [5] use a directed acyclic graph to represent
definitional sentences. WCLs method uses "star patterns" to make sentence clustering and then learns the sentences' structure in each cluster. Unlike patterns
consisted of short phrases, their "star patterns" are drawn from sentences where
all infrequent words have been replaced with a wildcard (*), so they can capture
long distance dependency of sentences with these star patterns. Although they
form generalized sentences with WCL, their result for WCL (F_1 of 75.23 %) is
close to the performance of method only using star patterns (F_1 of 75.05 %). It
shows that even only using sequence structure of frequent words, we can also
predict whether a sentence is definitional or not well.

2.3 Supervised Methods

This line of research area is to regard definition extraction task as a supervised
sequence classification work. A method [10] proves to work well on a corpus
of Dutch Wikipedia articles. They generate three kinds of features to describe
a sentence: sentence-level features (e.g. the position of the sentence in a document); word-level statistic features (e.g. bigrams, bag-of-words); word-level syntax features (e.g. determiner type). With these features, they use naive Bayes,
maximumu entropy (MaxEnt) and the support vector machine (SVM) as different learners and find MaxEnt has the best performance. Sentences' linguistical

structural features are taken into consideration in an approach proposed by [16]. A random forest classifier is used to capture more deep features of a sentence structure.

DefMiner [3] uses Conditional Random Fields (CRF) to predict the function of a word in a sentence as term, definitional part or others. One of their key contributions is the analysis of a real world corpus: W00 (a manually annotated subset of ACL ARC). They use a combination of lexical, orthography, dictionary lookup and corpus statistics (e.g. sentence position, idf) as features. Meanwhile, they also use features manually selected from dependency tree to describe sentence long distance structures.

Another approach relying on syntactic dependencies is proposed by [7]. They focus on extracting features from the dependency parsing of a sentence. Each noun in a sentence will be represented into a numeric vector according to its syntactic dependencies with other nouns in the same sentence. The vector representation will be fed to two classifiers to determine whether the noun is hyponym, hypernym or neither of two. If a sentence has both hyponym and hypernym, it will be labeled as definitional. Their work highlights the importance of learning from relations of words.

Supervised approaches face the challenge that manually specified features involve many feature engineering work. Meanwhile, structure features are chosen from part of the dependency tree, which may not be able to fully describe the whole sentence structure.

Our method focus on capturing the whole sentence structure feature so as to automatically generating sentence features for supervised classification.

3   Our Method

In our method, we design our procedure based on the assumption that we can determine whether a sentence is definitional or not by certain structures. We call these sentence structures as definitional structures. Definitional structure can be a short phrase or a long discontinuous word sequence.

Previous pattern based approaches use patterns to describe definitional structures. In order to increase the generalization ability of our model, we use feature vector to reflect the usage of definitional structure and classify sentence according to its feature vector instead of simple pattern matching.

Our method considers definition extraction as a supervised classification work where a typical challenge is how to generate feature from long-term definitional structure. Previous supervised based approaches learn definitional structure using n-grams or conditional random field (CRF). These algorithms have strong ability in learning short-term dependency features but are weak in capturing long-term definitional structure. Therefore, we generate sentence feature using LSTM which is fit for both short-term and long-term structure learning.

Our method consists of the following three steps: (See Fig. 1 for graphical structure.)

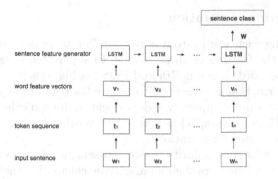

Fig. 1. Structure of our model.

– **Token transformation:** each word in a sentence will be transformed into a token according to its frequency in training set. (Sect. 3.1)
– **Word feature generation:** each word will be represented as a word vector by capturing features of the word's context. (Sect. 3.2)
– **Sentence feature generation:** A LSTM encoder will be used to automatically transform a sentence into a vector representation by learning sentence hidden structure feature. A classifier will also be trained to predict a sentence label by its feature. (Sect. 3.3)

3.1 Token Transformation

In definition extraction, for most of the words, we care more about its POS tag rather than the word itself. For example, We do not care the difference between "Cat is an animal" and "Dog is an animal". Thus these two sentences can be transformed to one sentence "NN is an NN" by replace some words with their POS tags.

Due to the above reason, a word is transformed into a token to maintain its most significant form for definition extraction. In this step, we pick top N frequent words from our training set. The reason we do not choose words' tf-idf is that some words (e.g. is, a, etc.) are important to form a definitional pattern in spite of their low idf. These chosen words form a set F which can be regarded as a cluster of words. These words are potential constituent part of definitional patterns. More precisely, given a sentence S of length n, for the i-th word w_i of s, we produce token t_i by[3]:

$$
t_i = \begin{cases} w_i & w_i \in F \\ POS(w_i) & w_i \notin F \end{cases}
$$

---

[3] Our pos tagger tool is from http://nlp.stanford.edu/software/tagger.shtml.

3.2 Word Feature Generation

After transforming each word into a corresponding token, our next question is how to generate the features of these tokens. In supervised classification based methods, they use words bigrams [10] and POS tag bigrams [17] as sentence features and use information gain method to reduce the count of features. However, they make their features completely independent with each other. For example, if we only use a bigram (Num, N) as feature, then other bigrams (e.g. (Adj, N)) will never be taken into consideration.

In order to describe the similarity between tokens, we use a vector to represent a token so that we can measure their similarity by calculating their distance. The more similar two tokens are, the less influence will be caused when one changes to another. We use the context of a token (i.e. tokens near the token) to describe the token as the context can reflect the usage of the token.

Word2vec [18] is a useful method to generate a word vector representation by maximum the possibility of the occurrence of a word according to its context. The method works on the assumption that similar words have similar context which is also fit for our situation. Thus we use word2vec to encode tokens in our training set.

3.3 Sentence Feature Generation

Sentence features can be divided into two kinds. One is to generate features only within a single sentence (e.g. bag-of-words, n-grams [10], the presence of determiners in the defines, etc.). The other kind is using features beyond a sentence such as the position of a sentence in the document [3].

However features beyond sentences are often corpus dependent. Take sentence position feature for example, sentences appearing at the beginning of documents are likely to be definitional in wikipedia documents, while things may not be the same with other corpus.

Due to this reason, we focus on extracting features from a sentence only by learning its definitional structure. Previous methods generate features from sentence dependency parsing, which can only reflect part of structure feature. In our method, we will treat a sentence as a sequence of tokens and use LSTM to capture the whole structure of the sequence.

Feature Generator. Our feature generator consists of a single layer of Long short-term memory (LSTM) unit [19] which is designed to overcome the gradients vanishing problem in recurrent neural network (RNN) [20]. LSTM uses special gates to control the flow of data in repeating module, which can help them be capable of learning long-term dependencies. LSTM uses three gates to implement the repeating module: a forget gate $\mathbf{f}$ to control of the flow of cell state, an input gate $\mathbf{i}$ to control the inputing data and an output gate $\mathbf{o}$ to control the output of the module. Each LSTM unit maintains a memory cell $\mathbf{c}$.

Given a sentence s of length n, we get a sequence of word feature vectors $\mathbf{x}$ in the word feature generation step. For the t-th token in $\mathbf{x}$, the output $\mathbf{h}$ of LSTM is given by

$$\mathbf{h}_t = o_t tanh(\mathbf{c}_t)$$

where the output gate is given by

$$\mathbf{o}_t = \sigma(\mathbf{W}_o\mathbf{x}_t + \mathbf{U}_o\mathbf{h}_{t-1} + \mathbf{V}_o\mathbf{c}_t)$$

The cell state is calculated by

$$\mathbf{c}_t = \mathbf{f}_t\mathbf{c}_{t-1} + \mathbf{i}_t\tilde{\mathbf{c}}_t$$

where $\tilde{\mathbf{c}}_t$ denotes a new memory content computed by

$$\tilde{\mathbf{c}}_t = tanh(\mathbf{W}_c\mathbf{x}_t + \mathbf{U}_c\mathbf{h}_{t-1})$$

Meanwhile, the forget and input gates are computed by

$$\mathbf{f}_t = \sigma(\mathbf{W}_f\mathbf{x}_t + \mathbf{U}_f\mathbf{h}_{t-1} + \mathbf{V}_f\mathbf{c}_{t-1})$$

$$\mathbf{i}_t = \sigma(\mathbf{W}_i\mathbf{x}_t + \mathbf{U}_i\mathbf{h}_{t-1} + \mathbf{V}_i\mathbf{c}_{t-1})$$

We use the n-th output $\mathbf{h}_n$ of LSTM as the feature vector of the sentence.

Joint Learning of Feature Generator and Classifier. Given a sentence feature vector $\mathbf{x}$, we use a logistic regression classifier $\sigma(\mathbf{w}^T\mathbf{x})$ to predict the sentence label. The final result is influenced by both parameter $\mathbf{w}$ of classifier and the sentence feature vector $\mathbf{x}$. Therefore we train our classifier and sentence feature generator together.

In the word feature generation step, a sentence s of length n is generalized to a sequence of word feature vectors s'. Let T' denote the cluster of s'. In the sentence feature generation step, we use $\mathbf{h}(s')$ to represent the n-th step output of LSTM. We train our model by mining the cost function:

$$L = \sum_{s' \in T'} crossentropy(y_{s'}, \sigma(\mathbf{w}^T\mathbf{h}(s')))$$

where $y_{s'}$ stands for the label of s', 1 for definitional and 0 for the other. $\mathbf{w}$ is a parameter vector. Here crossentropy is given by

$$crossentropy(a, b) = -(a\log(b) + (1 - a)\log(1 - b))$$

We use gradient descent to optimize $\mathbf{w}$ and the parameters of our LSTM encoder together. An open source implementation, Theano [21] is used in our work[4]. We calculate gradients for all the parameters (i.e. $\mathbf{w}$ and parameters of LSTM) and update them using RMSprop optimizer.

Here we want to emphasize that as pointed by [17], highly imbalanced datasets can greatly influenced supervised classification based methods. As the training procedure of our method uses gradient descent, we overcome this problem by setting different learning rate to positive and negative samples according to their count ratio.

---

[4] http://deeplearning.net/software/theano/.

4   Experiments

We prepare two datasets for the evaluation of our method. One is an English dataset [5] consisted of 1,908 definitional sentences and 2,711 non-definitional sentences manually annotated from Wikipedia. The other one is a Chinese dataset containing 2,161 definitional sentences and 2,161 non-definitional sentences manually annotated from Baidu Baike[5]. In this part, we will describe detail experiment settings and the way we evaluate our result.

4.1   Experiment Settings

In the word feature generation step, we use Top-1,000 frequent words set for English dataset and Top-500 frequent words set for Chinese dataset. Every token will be encoded into a 50-dimension vector. The output dimension of the LSTM encoder used in our sentence feature generation step is 50. The parameters of LSTM encoder are initialized with the uniform distribution with the scale introduced by [22].

For the evaluation of our definition extraction on English dataset, we compare with the following implements.

– **Star patterns**: A pattern based method where a sentence is classified as a definition if it matches any of the star patterns [5].
– **Bigrams**: A pattern based method which uses bigram classifier for soft pattern matching [2].
– **WCL**: A semi-supervised method which uses WCL-3 model to learn lattices separately for each sentence field (i.e. DEFINIENDUM, DEFINITOR and DEFINIENS) [5].
– **DefMiner**:a supervised method which uses long distance features [3].
– **SVM**: a supervised method which uses SVM classifier and syntactic dependencies. [7].
– **DR system**: a supervised method which only uses syntactic features derived from dependency relations [6].
– **our method+LSTM**: Our method using LSTM as sentence feature generator.
– **our method+RNN**: Our method using RNN as sentence feature generator.

Experiment on Chinese dataset is used as a comparison with the experiment on English dataset so as to show our method's ability in dealing with different languages.

Our training step can be regarded as optimizing a logistic regression classifier and our sentence encoding layer at the same time. Therefore we need to make sure that whether our LSTM encoder plays an important role in our method or the performance is simply influenced by optimizing the logistic regression classifier. Sentences in our dataset have rather long length thus RNN cannot generate a good sentence representation due to gradients vanishing problem. Therefore We use RNN as a control experiment to check whether our LSTM implementation can learn a good sentence representation vector.

---

[5] You can download it from http://166.111.7.170:28090/zh.zip.

4.2 Measures

- **Precision** - The number of definitional sentences correctly labeled by our model divided by the number of sentences marked by our model as definitional.
- **Recall** - The number of definitional sentences correctly labeled by our model divided by the number of definitional sentences in test dataset.
- **F_1-measure** - Calculated by $\frac{2PR}{P+R}$ with precision (P) and recall (R).

We calculate the above three measures to judge the performance of our method. Experiments are performed with 10-fold cross validation. Dataset is separated into 10 parts and we use one part as testing set and nine parts as training set in each fold.

5 Results and Analysis

In this section, we will evaluate the overall performance of our method in comparison with other systems. Additionally, we will show how frequent set influences the performance and explain the reason.

5.1 Overall Performance

In Table 1, we display the results of different definition extraction systems on the English dataset. Results of other systems are obtained from aforementioned literatures [2,3,5–7].

Compared with RNN, LSTM completely outperforms in both precession and recall, which indicates that our sentence feature generation step does play an important role and LSTM can preferably encode a sentence according to its structure.

Compared with the other previous systems, the performance of LSTM is satisfying. In our LSTM implementation, we make near 6 % progress in the F_1 measure, which proves that our method have a good generating ability in

Table 1. Performance on the English dataset

Algorithm	P (%)	R (%)	F_1(%)
Our method + RNN	55.0	41.9	47.6
Our method + LSTM	90.4	**92.0**	**91.2**
Star patterns	86.7	66.1	75.1
Bigrams	66.7	82.7	73.8
WCL	98.8	60.7	75.2
DR system	85.9	85.3	85.4
DefMiner	92.0	79.0	85.0
SVM	88.0	76.0	81.6

extracting sentence features for definition extraction. Although precision of our method is lower than WCL and DefMiner, we make a significant improvement in recall performance. We contribute the improvement to the following reasons:

- Compared with pattern based method, our method does not use any manual specific star patterns to preprocess sentences. Every possible pattern will be learned in our LSTM encoder.
- In our method, We use dense feature vectors to encode tokens (i.e. words or POS tags) in sentences. Tokens are not treated independently but can be calculated similarity according to their distance. In other words, we smooth the impact caused when a token of a sentence change to another, which can improve the generating ability of our method.
- We do not manually pick sentence structure features but let our LSTM encoder automatically learn how to generate features. Manually specific dependency features in previous work use only a small part of sentence dependency parsing tree, which may lose hidden information. However our LSTM encoder can directly learn from sentence sequences which ensures the full use of sentence structures.

Our experiment on Chinese dataset reaches a result of **86.7 %** in precision, **84.7 %** in recall and **85.7 %** in F1 score. Compared with English dataset, sentences in Chinese dataset have more complicated definitional structures. Considering the possible error caused in word segmentation and the structure complexity, we think it is a satisfying result, which shows that our method's effectiveness in dealing with different languages.

5.2   Result with Different Frequent Words Sets

In order to find out how our word feature generation step affect the performance of our system, we perform another experiment. In Table 2, we present the performance with different top-N frequent words sets. Here the frequency count refers to the count of frequency of all the words used in different datasets.

Table 2. Performance with different Top-N frequent words sets on English and Chinese datasets

Top-N	English $F_1(\%)$	English frequency count (%)	Chinese $F_1(\%)$	Chinese frequency count (%)
Top-0	76.0	0	76.7	0
Top-50	87.9	44	84.0	30
Top-100	89.6	48	85.1	35
Top-500	90.9	61	85.7	52
Top-1,000	91.2	68	84.3	60
Top-8,000	90.9	90	81.4	88

The performance with Top-0 frequent words set is the worst as expected due to the reason that it replace all the words with their POS tags. The treatment will cause information loss since original forms of some words (e.g. is, a, etc.) are more important than their POS tags in definition extraction.

Until Top-500, the F_1 measure rises quickly when we enlarge our frequent words set with more words which are often essential parts of star patterns in previous approaches. The result shows that frequent words are critical in determining a sentence is definitional or not.

Performance on English dataset becomes rather stable when we choose more words as frequent words. Even with Top-8,000 frequent words set where POS tags are hardly used, our method still obtains a satisfying performance. Compared with Chinese, POS tag feature does not make significant effect on definitional extraction in English. We believe the main reason lies on the language itself. English definitional sentences have rather common structures which are usually consisted of frequent words. In our sentence feature generation step, our LSTM encoder gradually learns to reduce the impact of infrequent words since they are rarely involved in definitional structures. Therefore it does not matter whether we use words' original forms or their POS tags.

Result is quite different in the Chinese dataset. F_1 score falls when the size of frequent words set becomes larger than 500, which indicates that POS tagging replacing step becomes important when dealing with Chinese. The reason lies on the fact that Chinese sentences do not have common frequent words based patterns which can be used to classify definitional sentences. POS tags of infrequent words will participate in classification so replacing these words with their POS tags can help to improve the performance of our method.

In general, considering both English and Chinese task, we think Top-500 frequent words set is the best set for our method. Although with this words set, our method cannot reach its best in English dataset, its F_1 score (90.9 %) is actually very close to the highest score (91.2 %).

6   Conclusion

A method for the task of definition extraction based on LSTM Recurrent Neural Network has been described in this paper. In order to directly learn from the whole raw sentence, we propose a new way to generate sentence representation.

From the initial idea that LSTM has the ability of learning sequence structures from sentences, we use a LSTM generator to capture definitional structures in a sentence. Next, the dataset of our experiment has been presented to the reader, followed by our detail experiment settings and our results.

We are encouraged by the performance of LSTM implementation, which proves that our method can learn certain structures from sentences well and is competent for definition extraction task. Our method can reduce the work of feature engineering for supervised learning based definition extraction by automatically learning structure features from sentence sequence. Besides our method is also proved to be effective in multiple languages.

S. Li et al.

Acknowledgments. This work is supported by China National High-Tech Project (863) under grant No. 2015AA015401, and Tsinghua University Initiative Scientific Research Program (No. 20131089190). Beijing Key Lab of Networked Multimedia also supports our research work.

References

1. Gangemi, A., Navigli, R., Velardi, P.: The OntoWordNet project: extension and axiomatization of conceptual relations in WordNet. In: Meersman, R., Schmidt, D.C. (eds.) CoopIS 2003, DOA 2003, and ODBASE 2003. LNCS, vol. 2888, pp. 820–838. Springer, Heidelberg (2003)
2. Cui, H., Kan, M.-Y., Chua, T.-S.: Soft pattern matching models for definitional question answering. ACM Trans. Inf. Syst. (TOIS) **25**(2), 8 (2007)
3. Jin, Y., Kan, M.Y., Ng, J.P., He, X.: Mining scientific terms and their definitions: a study of the acl anthology. Newdesign.aclweb.org (2013)
4. Espinosa-Anke, L., Ronzano, F., Saggion, H.: Weakly supervised definition extraction. In: International Conference on Recent Advances in Natural Language Processing 2015, pp. 176–185 (2015)
5. Navigli, R., Velardi, P.: Learning word-class lattices for definition and hypernym extraction. In: Proceedings of 48th Annual Meeting of the Association for Computational Linguistics, pp. 1318–1327. Association for Computational Linguistics (2010)
6. Espinosa-Anke, L., Saggion, H.: Applying dependency relations to definition extraction. In: Métais, E., Roche, M., Teisseire, M. (eds.) NLDB 2014. LNCS, vol. 8455, pp. 63–74. Springer, Heidelberg (2014)
7. Boella, G., Di Caro, L.: Extracting definitions and hypernym relations relying on syntactic dependencies and support vector machines. In: ACL, vol. 2, pp. 532–537 (2013)
8. Klavans, J.L., Muresan, S.: Evaluation of the definder system for fully automatic glossary construction. In: Proceedings of AMIA Symposium, p. 324. American Medical Informatics Association (2001)
9. Westerhout, E.N., Westerhout, E.N.: Extraction of dutch definitory contexts for elearning purposes. Lot Occas. **7**, 219–234 (2007)
10. Fahmi, I., Bouma, G.: Learning to identify definitions using syntactic features. In: Proceedings of EACL 2006 Workshop on Learning Structured Information in Natural Language Applications, pp. 64–71. Citeseer (2006)
11. Hearst, M.A.: Automatic acquisition of hyponyms from large text corpora. In: Proceedings of 14th Conference on Computational Linguistics, vol. 2, pp. 539–545. Association for Computational Linguistics (1992)
12. Muresan, S., Klavans, J.: A method for automatically building and evaluating dictionary resources. In: Proceedings of Language Resources and Evaluation Conference (LREC) (2002)
13. Borg, C., Rosner, M., Pace, G.: Evolutionary algorithms for definition extraction. In: Proceedings of 1st Workshop on Definition Extraction, pp. 26–32. Association for Computational Linguistics (2009)
14. Reiplinger, M., Schäfer, U., Wolska, M.: Extracting glossary sentences from scholarly articles: a comparative evaluation of pattern bootstrapping and deep analysis. In: Proceedings of ACL-2012 Special Workshop on Rediscovering 50 Years of Discoveries, pp. 55–65. Association for Computational Linguistics (2012)

15. Bird, S., Dale, R., Dorr, B.J., Gibson, B.R., Joseph, M., Kan, M.-Y., Lee, D., Powley, B., Radev, D.R., Tan, Y.F.: The ACL anthology reference corpus: a reference dataset for bibliographic research in computational linguistics. In: LREC (2008)
16. Westerhout, E.: Definition extraction using linguistic and structural features. In: Proceedings of 1st Workshop on Definition Extraction, pp. 61–67 (2009)
17. Gaudio, R., Batista, G., Branco, A.: Coping with highly imbalanced datasets: a case study with definition extraction in a multilingual setting. Natl. Lang. Eng. **20**(03), 327–359 (2014)
18. Mikolov, T., Chen, K., Corrado, G., Dean, J.: Efficient estimation of word representations in vector space (2013). arXiv preprint arXiv:1301.3781
19. Hochreiter, S., Schmidhuber, J.: Long short-term memory. Neural Comput. **9**(8), 1735–1780 (1997)
20. Bengio, Y., Simard, P., Frasconi, P.: Learning long-term dependencies with gradient descent is difficult. IEEE Trans. Neural Netw. **5**(2), 157–166 (1994)
21. Bastien, F., Lamblin, P., Pascanu, R., Bergstra, J., Goodfellow, I., Bergeron, A., Bouchard, N., Warde-Farley, D., Bengio, Y.: Theano: new features and speed improvements (2012). arXiv preprint arXiv:1211.5590
22. Glorot, X., Bengio, Y.: Understanding the difficulty of training deep feedforward neural networks. In: International Conference on Artificial Intelligence and Statistics, pp. 249–256 (2010)

Event Extraction via Bidirectional Long Short-Term Memory Tensor Neural Networks

Yubo Chen[⊠], Shulin Liu, Shizhu He, Kang Liu, and Jun Zhao

National Laboratory of Pattern Recognition, Institute of Automation,
Chinese Academy of Sciences, Beijing 100190, China
{yubo.chen,shulin.liu,shizhu.he,kliu,jzhao}@nlpr.ia.ac.cn

Abstract. Traditional approaches to the task of ACE event extraction usually rely on complicated natural language processing (NLP) tools and elaborately designed features. Which suffer from error propagation of the existing tools and take a large amount of human effort. And nearly all of approaches extract each argument of an event separately without considering the interaction between candidate arguments. By contrast, we propose a novel event-extraction method, which aims to automatically extract valuable clues without using complicated NLP tools and predict all arguments of an event simultaneously. In our model, we exploit a context-aware word representation model based on Long Short-Term Memory Networks (LSTM) to capture the semantics of words from plain texts. In addition, we propose a tensor layer to explore the interaction between candidate arguments and predict all arguments simultaneously. The experimental results show that our approach significantly outperforms other state-of-the-art methods.

1 Introduction

Event extraction is an important and challenging task in Information Extraction (IE), which aims to discover event triggers with specific types and their arguments. The task is quite difficult because a larger field of view is often needed to understand how facts tie together. To capture valuable clues for event extraction, current state-of-the-art methods [11,13,16–18] often use a set of elaborately designed features that are extracted by textual analysis. For example, consider the following sentences:

S1: *He has **fired** his air defense chief.*
S2: *An American tank **fired** on the Hotel.*

In S1, *fired* is a trigger of type *End-Position*. While in S2 *fired* is a trigger of type *Attack*, which is more common than type *End-Position*. Because of the ambiguity, a traditional approach may mislabel *fired* in S1 as a trigger of *Attack*. However, if we know that the context words *"air defense chief"* is a job title, we have ample evidence to predict that *fired* in S1 is a trigger of type *End-position*. To capture these semantics, traditional methods often use the part-of-speech

M. Sun et al. (Eds.): CCL and NLP-NABD 2016, LNAI 10035, pp. 190–203, 2016.
DOI: 10.1007/978-3-319-47674-2_17

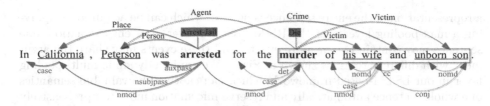

Fig. 1. Event mentions and syntactic parser results of S3. The upper side shows two event mentions that share one arguments: the *Arrest-Jail* event mention, triggered by "arrested", and the *Die* event mention, triggered by "murder". The lower side shows the dependency results.

tags (POS), entity information, and morphology features (e.g., token, lemma, etc.). However, these features for words are a kind of one-hot representation, which may suffer from the data sparsity problem and overlook the impact of the context words. Furthermore, these methods often rely on human ingenuity for designing such elaborate features, which is a time-consuming process and lacks generalization. [22].

Besides the semantics of words, to extract events more precisely, we also need to understand semantic relations between words. Previous methods often use the syntactic features to capture these semantics. For example, in S3, there are two events that share one argument as shown in Fig. 1, from the dependency relation of *nsubjpass* between the argument *Peterson* and trigger *arrested*, we can induce a *Person* role to *Peterson* in the *Arrest-Jail* event. However, for the *Die* event, the argument word *Peterson* and its trigger word *murder* are in different clauses, and there is no direct dependency path between them. Thus it is difficult to find the *Agent* role between them using traditional dependency features. In addition, extracting such features depends heavily on the performance of NLP systems, which could suffer from error propagation.

S3: *In California, Peterson was arrested for the murder of his wife and unborn son.*

To correctly attach *Peterson* to *murder* as a *Agent* argument, we not merely need to understand the semantics of each word but also need to exploit internal semantic relation over the entire sentence such that the *Die* event results in *Arrest-Jail* event. Recent improvements of Recurrent Neural Networks (RNNs) have been proven to be efficient for learning semantics of words, which take the impact of the context into consideration [12,14]. Unfortunately, the recurrent structure of RNNs also make it endure the "vanishing gradients" problem, which makes it difficult for the RNN model to learn long-distance correlations in a sequence [8,9]. So we use a RNN with Bidirectional Long Short-Term Memory (BLSTM) unit [6,10] to addresses this problem.

Most of LSTM-based RNNs are for sequence modeling task, which could use the representation of RNNs for each word directly. While in the task of event extraction, to capture the most useful information within a sentence, a representation of the entire sentence is needed, which can be acquired by applying a max-pooling layer over the RNNs [15]. However, in event extraction, one sentence may contain two or more events, and these events may share the argument with different roles, as shown in Fig. 1. We apply a dynamic multi-pooling layer in our LSTM-based framework, which can capture the valuable semantics of a whole sentence automatically and reserve information more comprehensively to extract events [4].

Besides the problem stated above, both of traditional approaches [1,13,18] and deep neural network based approaches [4,20] did not model the interaction between the candidate arguments and predict them separately. However, these interactions are important to predict arguments. For example, in Fig. 1, if we know "his wife" and "unborn son" are paralleled in the sentence, we are easy to predict they play same role in the corresponding event. Thus we propose a tensor layer to explore the interaction between candidate arguments automatically.

In this paper, we present a novel framework dubbed Bidirectional Dynamic Multi-Pooling Long Short-Term Memory Tensor Neural Networks (BDLSTM-TNNs) for event extraction, which can automatically induce valuable clues for event extraction without complicated NLP preprocessing and predict candidate arguments simultaneously. We propose a Bidirectional Long Short-Term Memory Network with Dynamic Multi-Pooling (BDLSTM) to extract event triggers and arguments separately, which can capture meaningful semantics of words with taking the context words into consideration and capture more valuable information for event extraction within a sentence automatically. And we devise a tensor layer, which aims to explore interaction between candidate arguments and predict them jointly. We conduct experiments on a widely used ACE2005 event extraction dataset, and the experimental results show that our approach outperforms other state-of-the-art methods.

2   Event Extraction Task

In this paper, we focus on the event extraction task defined in Automatic Content Extraction[1] (ACE) evaluation, where an event is defined as a specific occurrence involving participants. First, we introduce some ACE terminology to understand this task more easily:

- **Event mention:** a phrase or sentence within which an event is described, including a trigger and arguments.
- **Event trigger:** the word that most clearly expresses the occurrence of an event.
- **Event argument**: an entity mention, temporal expression or value (e.g. Job-Title) that is involved in an event (viz., participants).
- **Argument role:** the relationship between an argument to the event in which it participates.

---

[1] http://projects.ldc.upenn.edu/ace/.

Given a text document, an event extraction system should predict event triggers with specific subtypes and their arguments. The upper side of Fig. 1 depicts the event triggers and their arguments for S3 in Sect. 1. ACE defines 8 event types and 33 subtypes, such as *Arrest-Jail* or *Die*.

3 Methodology

In this paper, event extraction is formulated as a two-stage, multi-class classification via Bidirectional Dynamic Multi-pooling Long Short-Term Memory Networks (BDLSTM) with the automatically learned valuable clues. The first stage is called *trigger classification*, in which we use a BDLSTM to classify each word in a sentence to identify trigger words. If one sentence has triggers, the second stage is conducted, which applies a similar BDLSTM to assign arguments to triggers and align the roles of the arguments. We call this *argument classification*. To explore interaction between candidate arguments and predict all candidate arguments simultaneously, we design a tensor layer in the stage of argument classification. Because the argument classification is more complicated, we first describe the methodology of how predict each candidate argument separately by BDLSTM in Sects. 3.1 and 3.4 and then illustrate the difference between the BDLSTMs that are used for trigger classification and those used for argument classification in Sect. 3.5. Finally, we introduce the Bidirectional Dynamic Multi-Pooling Long Short-Term Memory Tensor Neural Networks (BDLSTM-TNN) and illustrate how it predict all candidate arguments jointly in Sects. 3.6 and 3.7.

Figure 2 describes the BDLSTM architecture of argument classification, which primarily involves the following three components: (i) context-aware word representation; (ii) dynamic multi-pooling layer; (iii) argument classifier output layer.

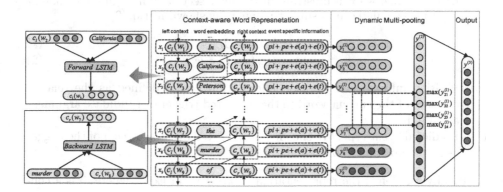

Fig. 2. The architecture for argument classification in the event extraction. It illustrates the processing of one instance with the predict trigger *murder* and the candidate argument *Peterson*.

3.1   Context-Aware Word Representation Using LSTM Networks

The semantics of words and relations between words serve as important clues for event extraction [11,17]. RNNs with LSTM unit is a good choice to learn the context-aware semantics [12,15]. In event extraction, both forward and backward words are important for understanding a word. Thus, we propose to use a Bidirectional Long Short-Term Memory (BLSTM) architecture for representing words.

Context-Aware Word Representation. This subsection illustrates the components of the context-aware word representation. As shown in Fig. 2, it primarily involves the following four parts: (i) Word embedding, which aims to capture the background of a word; (ii) left context and right context, which help to disambiguate the semantics of the current word and reveal the relations between the words; (iii) position information, which aims to specify which words are the predicted trigger or candidate argument; (iv) predicted event type, which aims to embed the predicted event type from the stage of trigger classification into the argument classification.

(i) word embedding: We use vectors $(e(w_i)$, $e(t)$ and $e(a))$ to represent a word w_i, the predicted trigger word t and the candidate argument a, which are transformed by looking up word embeddings. The word embeddings are trained by a Skip-gram model [2] from a significant amount of unlabeled data.

(ii) Left context and right context: We take all the words on the left side of the word w_i as the left-side context $c_l(w_i)$, while all the words on the right side as the right-side context $c_r(w_i)$. As shown in Fig. 2, the context of each word is different. The left-side context $c_l(w_i)$ of word w_i is calculated using Eq. (1), where $e(w_{i-1})$ is the word embedding of word w_{i-1}, $c_l(w_{i-1})$ is the left-side context of the previous word w_{i-1}. Function f is the operation of LSTM, which we will illustrate in the next section. The right-side context $c_r(w_i)$ is calculated in a similar manner, as shown in Eq. (2).

$$c_l(w_i) = f(c_l(w_{i-1}), e(w_{i-1})) \tag{1}$$
$$c_r(w_i) = f(c_r(w_{i+1}), e(w_{i+1})) \tag{2}$$

(iii) Position information: Position information (pi) is defined as the relative distance of the current word to the predicted trigger or candidate argument as [4] did.

(iv) Predicted event type: We encode the predicted event type (pe) of the trigger as in the position information.

Finally, we define the representation of word w_i in Eq. 3, where $\oplus$ is a concatenation operator.

$$x_i = c_l(w_i) \oplus e_{w_i} \oplus c_r(w_i) \oplus pi \oplus pe \oplus e(a) \oplus e(t) \tag{3}$$

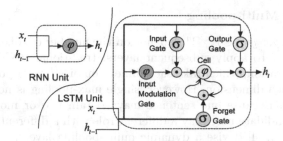

Fig. 3. A basic RNN unit and an LSTM unit

In this manner, using this contextual information and event specific informations, our model may be better to disambiguate the meaning of the word w_i and the semantic relations to others words, especially the interactions to the predicted trigger and the candidate argument. We apply a linear transformation together with the tanh activation function to x_i and send the result to the next layer.

$$y_i^{(1)} = \tanh(W_1 x_i + b_1) \tag{4}$$

Where i ranges from 1 to n and n is the length of sentence. The next layer $y^{(1)}$ is a matrix $y^{(1)} \in \mathbb{R}^{n \times m}$ and m is the dimension of $y_i^{(1)}$.

Long Short-Term Memory Networks. Traditional RNNs (Fig. 3) are able to process input sequences of arbitrary length via the recurrent application of a transition function on a hidden state vector h_t. Commonly, the RNN unit calculates the hidden states via the recurrence Eq. 5. where φ is an element-wise non-linearity, such as a sigmoid or hyperbolic tangent, x_t is the input, and h_t is the hidden state at time t.

$$h_t = \varphi(W_h x_t + U_h h_{t-1} + b_h) \tag{5}$$

Unfortunately, a problem with traditional RNNs is that during training, it is difficult to learn long-distance correlations in a sequence, because components of gradient vector can decay exponentially over long sequences [3,8]. The LSTM architecture [10] provide a solution by incorporating a memory unit that allows the network to learn when to forget previous hidden states and when to update hidden states given new information. In this paper, we use the LSTM unit as described in [23]. As shown in Fig. 3, the LSTM unit at each time step t is a collection of vectors: an input gate i_t, an input modulation gate u_t, a forget gate f_t, an output gate o_t, a memory cell c_t and a hidden state h_t. Where x_t is the input at the current time step, see [23] for details. As shown in Fig. 2, we use a BLSTM, which consists of two LSTMs that are run in parallel. One on the input sequence and the other on the reverse of the input sequence. At each time step, the forward hidden state aligns to $c_l(w_t)$, and the backward hidden state aligns to $c_r(w_t)$. This setup allows the model to capture both past and future information.

3.2 Dynamic Multi-pooling

The size of the layer $y^{(1)} \in \mathbb{R}^{n \times m}$ depends on the number of tokens in the input sentence. In order to apply subsequent layers, traditional RNNs [15] apply a max-pooling operation, which take each dimension of $y^{(1)}$ as a pool and get one max value for each dimension. However, single max-pooling is not sufficient for event extraction. Because one sentence may contain two or more events, and one argument candidate may play a different role with a different trigger [4]. To solve this problem, [4] devise a dynamic multi-pooling layer for Convolutional Neural Networks (CNNs). We apply a similar layer to our BLSTM. We split each dimension of $y^{(1)}$ into three parts according to the candidate argument and predicted trigger in the argument classification stage.

As shown in Fig. 2, the j-th dimension of the $y^{(1)}$ is divided into three sections $y_{1j}^{(1)}, y_{2j}^{(1)}, y_{3j}^{(1)}$ by "Peterson" and "murder". The dynamic multi-pooling can be expressed as Eq. 6, where $1 \leq i \leq 3$ and $1 \leq j \leq m$.

$$y_{ij}^{(2)} = \max(y_{ij}^{(1)}) \tag{6}$$

Through the dynamic multi-pooling layer, we obtain the $y_{ij}^{(2)}$ for each dimension of $y^{(1)}$. Then, we concatenate all $y_{ij}^{(2)}$ to form a vector $y^{(2)} \in \mathbb{R}^{3m}$, which can be considered as valuable clues and contains the key semantics of the whole sentence to classify argument precisely.

3.3 Output

To compute the confidence of each argument role, the vector $y^{(2)}$ is fed into a classifier.

$$O = W_2 y^{(2)} + b_2 \tag{7}$$

where, $W_2 \in \mathbb{R}^{n_1 \times (3m)}$ is the transformation matrix and $O \in \mathbb{R}^{n_1}$ is the final output of the network, where n_1 is equal to the number of the argument role including the "None role" label for the candidate argument which don't play any role in the event. For regularization, we also employ dropout [7] on the penultimate layer.

3.4 Training

We define all of the parameters for the stage of argument classification to be trained as $\theta = (E, c_l(w_1), c_r(w_n), pi, pe, W_1, b_1, W_2, b_2, lf, lb)$. Specifically, the parameters are word embeddings E, the initial contexts $c_l(w_1)$ and $c_r(w_n)$, position embeddings pi, predicted event type embeddings pe, transformation matrices parameters W_1, b_1, W_2, b_2, and the parameters of forward-LSTM lf and backward-LSTM lb.

Given an input example s, the network with parameter θ outputs the vector O, where the i-th component O_i contains the score for argument role i.

To obtain the conditional probability $p(i|x, \theta)$, we apply a softmax operation over all argument role types:

$$p(i|x, \theta) = \frac{e^{o_i}}{\sum\limits_{k=1}^{n_1} e^{o_k}} \tag{8}$$

Given all of our (suppose T) training examples (x_i, y_i), we can then define the objective function as follows:

$$J(\theta) = \sum_{i=1}^{T} \log p(y_i|x_i, \theta) \tag{9}$$

To compute the network parameter θ, we maximize the log likelihood $J(\theta)$ through stochastic gradient descent over shuffled mini-batches with the Adadelta [24] rule.

3.5   Model for Trigger Classification

The method proposed above is also suitable for trigger classification, but trigger classification only need to find triggers in the sentence, which is less complicated than argument classification. Thus we can used a simplified version of BDLSTM. In context-aware word representation of trigger classification, we do not use the position of the candidate argument. Furthermore, instead of splitting the sentence into three parts, the sentence is split into two parts by a candidate trigger. Except for the above change, we classify a trigger as the classification of an argument.

3.6   BDLSTM-TNNs

Though BDLSTM can extract events from plain texts with automatically generate features, it cannot explore the interaction between candidate arguments, which is important to help assign a right role to a candidate argument. Thus we propose the Bidirectional Dynamic Multi-Pooling Long Short-Term Memory Tensor Neural Networks (BDLSTM-TNNs) to solve this problem in argument classification and we use a same BDLSTM in trigger classification as illustrate above. To model the interaction between candidate arguments, we devise a tensor layer, which approved to be effective for capturing multiple interactions among words [21]. As shown in Fig. 4, we predict all candidate argument simultaneously. For each candidate argument, we use $y^{(2)} \in \mathbb{R}^{n_f}$ get from BDLSTM as input. n_f is the dimension of $y^{(2)}$. If there are n_c candidates, the input feature is $A \in \mathbb{R}^{n_f \times n_c}$. We use a 3-way tensor $T^{[1:n_t]} \in \mathbb{R}^{n_t \times n_f \times n_f}$ in tensor layer, where n_t is the length of the interaction vector. The internal relation I between candidate arguments is calculated as follows:

$$I = A^T T^{[1:n_t]} A; I_i = A^T T^{[i]} A \tag{10}$$

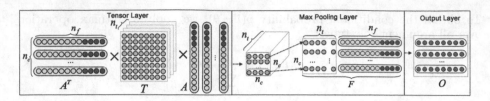

Fig. 4. The architecture (better viewed in color) for BDLSTM-TNNs. It illustrates the processing of predicting n_c candidate arguments simultaneously by using a 3-way tensor T. (Color figure online)

where, $I \in \mathbb{R}^{n_t \times n_c \times n_c}$ is the result of tensor layer, which include the interaction between candidate arguments. To make the model independent of the number of candidate arguments, we apply a max-pooling layer to capture the most valuable internal relation as follows:

$$I_{max}(i,j) = \max_{k=1}^{n_c} I_j(i,k) \tag{11}$$

where, $1 \leq i \leq n_c$, $1 \leq j \leq n_t$ and $I_{max} \in \mathbb{R}^{n_c \times n_t}$. Then we concatenate candidate arguments A and the interaction I_{max} as a whole feature $F \in \mathbb{R}^{n_c \times (n_t + n_f)}$. Each candidate argument has a corresponding feature F_i. Finally the output O_i is computed as follows:

$$O_i = W_3 F_i + b_3 \tag{12}$$

where $O_i \in \mathbb{R}^{n_1}$ is the output of the i-th candidate argument and $O_i(j)$ is the score for argument i to be assign as role j.

3.7   BDLSTM-TNNs Training

We define all of the parameters for the stage of argument classification to be trained as $\theta = (E, c_l(w_1), c_r(w_n), pi, pe, W_1, b_1, W_3, b_3, lf, lb, T)$. Specifically, the parameters are 3-way tensor T, transformation matrixes parameters W_3, b_3, and corresponding parameters of BDLSTM. Given an input instance x_i of sentence s_i with the trigger word tw_i and event type et_i, we use y_i to denote the correct role sequence for x_i, $\hat{y}_i$ to denote the predicted role sequence and $Y_{(x_i)}$ to denote the set of all possible role sequences for x_i. Thus as Eq. 12 shown, $O_{\hat{y}_{ij}}(k)$ is the score of j-th candidate argument to be assigned with role k for x_i, and we compute a sentence level score as follows:

$$s(x_i, \hat{y}_i, \theta) = \sum_{j=1}^{n_c} O_{\hat{y}_{ij}}(k) \tag{13}$$

Where k is the predicted role for j-th candidate argument in x_i. We define a margin loss $\Delta(y_i, \hat{y}_i)$ as follows:

$$\Delta(y_i, \hat{y}_i) = \sum_{j=1}^{n_c} \alpha 1\{y_{ij} \neq \hat{y}_{ij}\} \tag{14}$$

Where α is a discount parameter. Given all of our (suppose T) training examples (x_i, y_i), we can then define the objective function as follows:

$$J(\theta) = \frac{1}{T}\sum_{i=1}^{T} l_i(\theta) + \frac{\lambda}{2}\|\theta\|^2 \tag{15}$$

$$l_i(\theta) = \max_{\hat{y} \in Y_{x_i}} (s(x_i, \hat{y}_i, \theta) + \Delta(y_i, \hat{y}_i) - s(x_i, y_i, \theta)) \tag{16}$$

To increase the score of the correct role sequence y_i and decrease the highest score of incorrect sequence $\hat{y}$, we minimizing the object sated above.

4 Experiments

4.1 Dataset and Evaluation Metric

We utilized the ACE 2005 corpus as our dataset. For comparison, as the same as [4,11,17,18], we used the same test set with 40 newswire articles and the same development set with 30 other documents randomly selected from different genres and the rest 529 documents are used for training. Similar to previous work [4,11,17,18], we use the following criteria to judge the correctness of each predicted event mention:

- A trigger is correct if its event subtype and offsets match those of a reference trigger.
- An argument is correctly identified if its event subtype and offsets match those of any of the reference argument mentions.
- An argument is correctly classified if its event subtype, offsets and argument role match any of the reference argument mentions.

Finally we use *Precision (P)*, *Recall (R)* and *F measure (F)* as the evaluation metrics.

4.2 Our Method Vs. State-of-the-Art Methods

We select the following state-of-the-art methods for comparison.
(1) **Hong's baseline** is the system proposed by [11], which only employs basic human-designed features; (2) **Liao's cross-event** is the method proposed by [18], which uses document-level information to improve the performance of ACE event extraction; (3) **Hong's cross-entity** is the method proposed by [11], which extracts event by using cross-entity inference. To the best of our knowledge, it is the best-reported feature-based system; (4) **Li's structure** is the method proposed by [17], which extracts events based on structure prediction. It is the best-reported structure-based system; (5) **Chen's DMCNN** is the method proposed by [4], which extracts events based on convolutional neural networks. It is the best-reported neural-based system.

Following [4,17], we tuned the model parameters on the development through grid search. Specifically, in the trigger classification, we set the batch size as 150,

Table 1. Overall performance on blind test data

Methods	Trigger identification (%)			Trigger identification + classification (%)			Argument identification (%)			Argument role (%)		
	P	R	F	P	R	F	P	R	F	P	R	F
Hong's baseline		N/A		67.6	53.5	59.7	46.5	37.1	41.3	41.0	32.8	36.5
Liao's cross-event		N/A		68.7	68.9	68.8	50.9	49.7	50.3	45.1	44.1	44.6
Hong's cross-entity		N/A		72.9	64.3	68.3	53.4	52.9	53.1	51.6	45.5	48.3
Li's structure	76.9	65.0	70.4	73.7	62.3	67.5	69.8	47.9	56.8	64.7	44.4	52.7
Chen's DMCNN	80.4	67.7	**73.5**	75.6	63.6	**69.1**	68.8	51.9	59.1	62.2	46.9	53.5
BDLSTM-TNNs	78.9	66.5	72.2	75.3	63.4	68.9	69.8	52.7	**60.0**	62.9	47.5	**54.1**

n_f as 100, and the dimension of the pi as 5. In the argument classification, we set the batch size as 50, n_f as 150, n_t as 180 and the dimension of the pi and pe as 5. We train the word embedding using the Skip-gram algorithm[2] on the NYT corpus[3].

Table 1 shows the overall performance on the blind test dataset. From the results, we can see that the BDLSTM-TNNs model achieves the best performance among all of the compared methods in the stage of argument classification and get the best performance among all of methods expect for DMCNN method. BDLSTM-TNNs can improve the best F_1 [4] in the state-of-the-arts for argument classification by 0.6 % and competitive result for trigger classification. Moreover, we get larger gain compared with traditional methods [11,17,18]. This demonstrates the effectiveness of the proposed method. We believe the reason is that the clues we automatically learned can capture more meaningful semantic regularities of words.

4.3   RNN vs. LSTM vs. BLSTM vs. DLSTM vs. BDLSTM

This subsection studies the effectiveness of our context-aware word representation models. As shown in Table 2. BLSTM is described in Sect. 3.1 which use both forward LSTM and Backward LSTM with max pooling layer. LSTM only

Table 2. Comparison of RNN and different LSTMs

Model	Trigger	Argument
	F_1	F_1
RNN	61.5	41.5
LSTM	63.8	43.8
BLSTM	65.3	46.7
DLSTM	66.5	47.8
BDLSTM	**68.9**	**50.3**

---

[2] https://code.google.com/p/word2vec/.
[3] https://catalog.ldc.upenn.edu/LDC2008T19.

use one forward LSTM. RNN use a traditional RNN instead of LSTM and BDL-STM apply a dynamic multi-pooling instead max pooling in BLSTM. As shown in results, the methods based on LSTM (LSTM, BLSTM, DLSTM and BDL-STM) makes significant improvements compared with the RNN baseline in the classification of both the trigger and argument. It demonstrated that LSTM is more powerful than RNN for event extraction. Moreover, a comparison of BLSTM with LSTM illustrates that BLSTM achieves a better performance. We can make a same observation when comparing BDLSTM with BLSTM. It proves that both forward and backward of words are important to understand the semantic of a word, and the dynamic multi-pooling layer is effective for capture more valuable information to extract an event when using recurrent neural networks.

4.4 Effect of Tensor Layer

In this subsection, we prove the effectiveness of the tensor layer for exploring the interaction between candidate arguments. Because we used the same BDLSTM in trigger classification, we only evaluate its performance for argument classification. Results are shown in Table 3. It proves that tensor layer is useful to capture the internal relation between candidate arguments. Specifically, BDLSTM-TNNs gain a 5.5 % improvement for argument identification and 3.8 % improvement for argument classification.

Table 3. Comparison of BDLSTM and BDLSTM-TNNs for argument classification

Model	Identification F_1	Classification F_1
BDLSTM	54.5	50.3
BDLSTM-TNNs	**60.0**	**54.1**

5 Related Work

Event extraction is one of important topics in NLP. Many approaches have been explored for event extraction. Nearly all of the ACE event extraction use supervised paradigm. We further divide supervised approaches into feature-based methods, structure-based methods and neural-based methods.

In feature-based methods, a diverse set of strategies has been exploited to convert classification clues into feature vectors. [1] uses a set of traditional features (e.g., full word, pos tag, dependency features) to extract the event. [13] combined global evidence from related documents with local decisions for the event extraction. To capture more clues from the texts, [5,11,18] proposed the cross-event and cross-entity inference for the ACE event task. Although these approaches achieve high performance, feature-based methods suffer from the problem of selecting a suitable feature set when converting the classification clues into feature vectors.

In structure-based methods, researchers treat event extraction as the task of predicting the structure of the event in a sentence. [19] casted the problem of biomedical event extraction as a dependency parsing problem. [17] presented a joint framework for ACE event extraction based on structured perceptron. These methods yield relatively high performance. However, the performance of these methods depend strongly on the quality of the designed features and endure the errors in the existing NLP tools.

In neural-based method, researchers try to extract events from plain text by using automatically generating features without using complicated NLP tools [4,20]. But they did not consider interaction between candidate arguments and they predicted all candidate arguments separately.

6   Conclusion

This paper proposes a novel event extraction method (BDLSTM-TNNs), which can automatically extract valuable clues from plain texts without complicated NLP preprocessing and predict candidate arguments simultaneously. A context-aware word representation model based on BDLSTM is introduced to capture semantics of words. In addition, a tensor layer is devised to capture interaction between candidate arguments and predict them jointly. The experimental results prove the effectiveness of the proposed method.

Acknowledgement. This work was supported by the Natural Science Foundation of China (No. 61533018), the National Basic Research Program of China (No. 2014CB340503) and the National Natural Science Foundation of China (No. 61272332). And this work was also supported by Google through focused research awards program.

References

1. Ahn, D.: The stages of event extraction. In: Proceedings of ACL, pp. 1–8 (2006)
2. Baroni, M., Dinu, G., Kruszewski, G.: Dont count, predict! A systematic comparison of context-counting vs. context-predicting semantic vectors. In: Proceedings of ACL, pp. 238–247 (2014)
3. Bengio, Y., Simard, P., Frasconi, P.: Learning long-term dependencies with gradient descent is difficult. IEEE Trans. Neural Netw. **5**(2), 157–166 (1994)
4. Chen, Y., Xu, L., Liu, K., Zeng, D., Zhao, J.: Event extraction via dynamic multi-pooling convolutional neural networks. In: Proceedings of ACL, pp. 167–176 (2015)
5. Gupta, P., Ji, H.: Predicting unknown time arguments based on cross-event propagation. In: Proceedings of ACL-IJCNLP, pp. 369–372 (2009)
6. Hermann, K.M., Kocisky, T., Grefenstette, E., Espeholt, L., Kay, W., Suleyman, M., Blunsom, P.: Teaching machines to read and comprehend. In: Advances in Neural Information Processing Systems, pp. 1684–1692 (2015)

7. Hinton, G.E., Srivastava, N., Krizhevsky, A., Sutskever, I., Salakhutdinov, R.R.: Improving neural networks by preventing co-adaptation of feature detectors (2012). arXiv preprint arXiv:1207.0580
8. Hochreiter, S.: The vanishing gradient problem during learning recurrent neural nets and problem solutions. Int. J. Uncertain. Fuzziness Knowl.-Based Syst. **6**(02), 107–116 (1998)
9. Hochreiter, S., Bengio, Y., Frasconi, P., Schmidhuber, J.: Gradient flow in recurrent nets: the difficulty of learning long-term dependencies (2001)
10. Hochreiter, S., Schmidhuber, J.: Long short-term memory. Neural Comput. **9**(8), 1735–1780 (1997)
11. Hong, Y., Zhang, J., Ma, B., Yao, J., Zhou, G., Zhu, Q.: Using cross-entity inference to improve event extraction. In: Proceedings of ACL, pp. 1127–1136 (2011)
12. Irsoy, O., Cardie, C.: Opinion mining with deep recurrent neural networks. In: Proceedings of EMNLP, pp. 720–728 (2014)
13. Ji, H., Grishman, R.: Refining event extraction through cross-document inference. In: Proceedings of ACL, pp. 254–262 (2008)
14. Kalchbrenner, N., Blunsom, P.: Recurrent convolutional neural networks for discourse compositionality (2013). arXiv preprint arXiv:1306.3584
15. Lai, S., Xu, L., Liu, K., Zhao, J.: Recurrent convolutional neural networks for text classification. In: Proceedings of AAAI (2015)
16. Li, Q., Ji, H., Hong, Y., Li, S.: Constructing information networks using one single model. In: Proceedings of EMNLP (2014)
17. Li, Q., Ji, H., Huang, L.: Joint event extraction via structured prediction with global features. In: Proceedings of ACL, pp. 73–82 (2013)
18. Liao, S., Grishman, R.: Using document level cross-event inference to improve event extraction. In: Proceedings of ACL, pp. 789–797 (2010)
19. McClosky, D., Surdeanu, M., Manning, C.D.: Event extraction as dependency parsing. In: Proceedings of ACL, pp. 1626–1635 (2011)
20. Nguyen, T.H., Grishman, R.: Event detection and domain adaptation with convolutional neural networks. In: Proceedings of ACL, pp. 365–371 (2015)
21. Socher, R., Perelygin, A., Wu, J.Y., Chuang, J., Manning, C.D., Ng, A.Y., Potts, C.: Recursive deep models for semantic compositionality over a sentiment treebank. In: Proceedings of Conference on Empirical Methods in Natural Language Processing (EMNLP), vol. 1631, pp. 1642. Citeseer (2013)
22. Turian, J., Ratinov, L., Bengio, Y.: Word representations: a simple and general method for semi-supervised learning. In: Proceedings of ACL, pp. 384–394 (2010)
23. Zaremba, W., Sutskever, I.: Learning to execute (2014). arXiv preprint arXiv:1410.4615
24. Zeiler, M.D.: Adadelta: an adaptive learning rate method (2012). arXiv preprint arXiv:1212.5701

Chinese Hedge Scope Detection
Based on Structure and Semantic Information

Huiwei Zhou[✉], Junli Xu, Yunlong Yang, Huijie Deng, Long Chen,
and Degen Huang

School of Computer Science and Technology, Dalian University of Technology,
Dalian 116024, Liaoning, China
{zhouhuiwei, huangdg}@dlut.edu.cn,
{xjlhello, SDyyl_1949, denghuijie,
chenlong.415}@mail.dlut.edu.cn

Abstract. Hedge detection aims to distinguish factual and uncertain information, which is important in information extraction. The task of hedge detection contains two subtasks: identifying hedge cues and detecting their linguistic scopes. Hedge scope detection is dependent on syntactic and semantic information. Previous researches usually use lexical and syntactic information and ignore deep semantic information. This paper proposes a novel syntactic and semantic information exploitation method for scope detection. Composite kernel model is employed to capture lexical and syntactic information. Long short-term memory (LSTM) model is adopted to explore semantic information. Furthermore, we exploit a hybrid system to integrate composite kernel and LSTM model into a unified framework. Experiments on the Chinese Biomedical Hedge Information (CBHI) corpus show that composite kernel model could effectively capture lexical and syntactic information, LSTM model could capture deep semantic information and their combination could further improve the performance of hedge scope detection.

Keywords: Hedge scope detection · Structure information · Semantic information

1 Introduction

Hedges indicate uncertain or unreliable information, which are usually used in science texts. In English, 17.69 % of the sentences in the abstract section and 22.29 % of the sentences in the full paper section contain uncertain information on BioScope corpus [1]. In Chinese, 29.30 % of the sentences contain speculative fragments on CBHI corpus [2]. In order to distinguish facts from uncertain information, hedge detection is becoming an important task for information extraction. The CoNLL-2010 Shared Task [3] was dedicated to detecting uncertainty cues and their linguistic scopes on English corpus. Chinese hedge information detection has also attracted considerable attention [4]. This paper focuses on Chinese hedge scope detection on the CBHI corpus. A hedged sentence taken from the CBHI corpus is shown as follows:

Sentence 1: 上述实验数据提示<scope>PCAF<ccue>可能</ccue>是一种HCC的抑癌因子</scope>, 具有成为预测HCC术后愈后情况的生物标志物。

© Springer International Publishing AG 2016
M. Sun et al. (Eds.): CCL and NLP-NABD 2016, LNAI 10035, pp. 204–215, 2016.
DOI: 10.1007/978-3-319-47674-2_18

(The above experimental data suggest that <scope>PCAF<ccue>may</ccue> be a tumor suppressor factors of HCC</scope>, and has become a predict postoperative HCC prognosis biomarkers.)

In sentence 1, the word "可能 *(may)*" is hedge cue and its scope is the statement that "*PCAF*可能是一种*HCC*的抑癌因子 *(PCAF may be a tumor suppressor factors of HCC)*".

Researches on hedge cue identification have been developed rapidly [5, 6]. However, hedge scope detection remains a challenge, since hedge scope detection is dependent on syntactic and semantic information. This paper focuses on hedge scope detection from structure and semantic perspective.

Existing studies on hedge scope detection contain feature-based and tree kernel-based methods. Feature-based methods define a set of discrete features with "one-hot" representations based on lexical and flat syntactic information. Tree kernel-based methods could capture structured syntactic information by counting the number of common sub-trees [7]. However, both feature-based and tree kernel-based methods could not capture deep semantic information between cues and their linguistic scopes.

This problem motivates us to develop neural network models which could capture deep semantic information for scope detection. We propose a novel syntactic and semantic information exploitation method, which consists of a composite kernel and LSTM model. Composite kernel model is designed to capture lexical and structured syntactic information. LSTM model is adopted to explore deep semantic information. Furthermore, to fully utilize the nice properties of lexical, syntactic and semantic information, we explore a hybrid system to integrate composite kernel and LSTM model into a unified framework.

2 Related Work

In this section, we review the literature related to this paper from two aspects: hedge scope detection and neural network approaches for Nature Language Processing (NLP) tasks.

2.1 Hedge Scope Detection

Existing researches for hedge scope detection mainly contain: rule-based and machine learning-based methods. Rule-based methods [8, 9] compile heuristic rules by exploiting lexico-syntactic patterns for scope detection. Rule-based methods are simple and effective, but the extracted rules are hard to be developed to a new resource.

Machine learning-based methods formulate scope detection task as a classification issue, which classifies each token/sub-structure in a sentence as being the first element of the scope (F-scope), the last (L-scope), or neither (None). Machine learning-based methods mainly include feature-based and tree kernel-based methods. Feature-based methods design a set of discrete features with "one-hot" representations based on lexical and flat syntactic information. Morante and Daelemans [10] explore lexical features to predict F-scope, L-scope and None. Morante et al. [11] and Li et al. [12] exploit flat syntactic features for scope detection. The above researches take tokens as classification units, which inevitably generate plenty of instances. To decrease instances, Zhu et al. [13] and Zou et al. [14] construct feature-based systems by taking phrase and dependency sub-structures as classification units, respectively. Tree kernel-based methods could capture structured syntactic information by counting the number of common sub-trees. Zhang et al. [15] use tree kernel-based methods to model structured syntactic information for relation extraction. Zhou et al. [16] and Zou et al. [17] investigate phrase sub-structures and dependency sub-structures respectively to capture structured syntactic information for scope detection.

Feature-based and tree kernel-based methods could effectively capture lexical and syntactic information. However, the extracted features with feature-based and tree kernel-based methods are discrete and could not capture deep semantic information.

2.2   Neural Network for NLP Tasks

Neural networks could learn deep semantic representations without feature engineering. Especially, LSTM model [18] is superior in semantic representations of surface sequences. Xu et al. [19] use LSTM to pick up semantic information along the shortest dependency path between two entities for relation extraction. Zhou et al. [20] explore a series of semantic representations with LSTM model and further integrate diverse information for chemical-disease relation extraction.

Motivated by the success of LSTM model and Zhou et al. [20], we propose a hybrid system which consists of composite kernel and LSTM model to capture lexical, syntactic and semantic information for scope detection.

3   Methods

The corpus is preprocessed with Stanford Parser[1] to get lexical and syntactic information. To decrease candidate instances, we take phrase sub-structures as classification units adopting the way of Zhu et al. [13]. For the left (right) candidate phrase of a given cue, the leftmost (rightmost) word is F-scope (L-scope).

The hybrid system architecture consists of training and test phases as shown in Fig. 1. In training phase, lexical and syntactic features are captured by composite kernel model, and semantic representations are learned by LSTM model. In test phase, two models are applied to detect hedge scope. The predicted results of the two models are combined to optimize system performance finally.

---

[1] Available at http://nlp.stanford.edu/software/lex-parser.shtml.

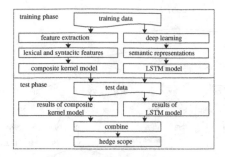

Fig. 1. Hybrid system architecture.

3.1 Composite Kernel for Hedge Scope Detection

The Polynomial Kernel. The feature-based model is learned from lexical features with polynomial kernel $K_{poly}(x_i, x_j) = (x_i \cdot x_j + 1)^d$, where d is the dimension of polynomial kernel. We select widely-used features for scope detection as shown below. These features reflect lexical information of hedge and its candidate.

- *WordContext*: words of cue and its candidate in the window [−2, 2].
- *CandidateType*: the constituents of candidate phrase, such as NP, VP.
- *HedgePoS*: the part-of-speech (PoS) of hedge.

The Convolution Tree Kernel. The convolution tree kernel could effectively capture structured syntactic information. This paper focuses on the information combination, so we only adopt the extending phrase path tree (EPPT) [15] to explore the structured syntactic information for scope detection. EPPT includes the path from the hedge to its candidate, and the nearest neighbor tokens of both the hedge and its candidate in the phrase tree. The path from hedge to its candidate represents the most direct phrase syntactic information about the hedge and its candidate. Adding the neighbor structures could provide rich context syntactic information. For the phrase syntactic tree of sentence 1 as shown in Fig. 2(a), the EPPT about the hedge "可能 (*may*)" and its L-scope candidate "*HCC*" is shown in Fig. 2(b).

The Composite Kernel. To integrate the lexical and syntactic features, the composite kernel is defined by combining the polynomial kernel and the convolution tree kernel:

$$K_{com} = \gamma K_{tree} + (1 - \gamma)K_{poly} \tag{1}$$

where $\gamma(0 < \gamma < 1)$ is the composite factor. The polynomial kernel K_{poly} and the convolution tree kernel K_{tree} are combined by the composite kernel K_{com}.

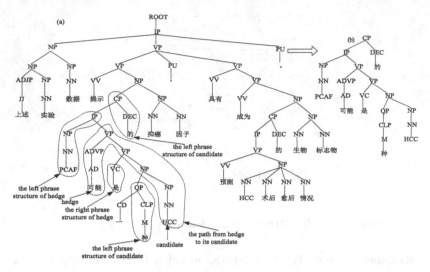

Fig. 2. Syntactic features extraction. (a) The phrase syntactic tree of sentence 1; (b) Extending phrase path tree (EPPT).

3.2 Long Short-Term Memory (LSTM) for Hedge Scope Detection

LSTM model is a kind of recurrent neural network (RNN), which introduces a gating mechanism to avoid gradient vanishing and exploding. LSTM cell comprises four components: an input gate $i_t = \sigma(W_i \cdot [h_{t-1}; x_t] + b_i)$, a forget gate $f_t = \sigma(W_f \cdot [h_{t-1}; x_t] + b_f)$, an output gate $o_t = \sigma(W_o \cdot [h_{t-1}; x_t] + b_o)$, and a memory cell $c_t = i_t \odot \tanh(W_r \cdot [h_{t-1}; x_t] + b_r) + f_t \odot c_{t-1}$. These gates adaptively remember input vector, forget previous history and generate output vector, where $\odot$ denotes component-wise multiplication, σ represents the sigmoid function, W_i, b_i, W_f, b_f, and W_o, b_o are parameters of input, forget and output gates for the input x_t and the hidden state vector h_{t-1} respectively. LSTM processes the word sequence by recursively computing its internal hidden state $h_t = o_t \odot \tanh(c_t)$ at each time step. Our intuition is that context semantic information of hedge and its candidate is important for scope detection. We develop four LSTM models to explore deep semantic information related to hedge scope as following.

CanHedSeq-LSTM. The context words of hedge and its candidate in the window [−2, 2] are jointed as a CanHedSeq sequence feeding to LSTM for recursively capturing context semantic representations of hedge scope. The dimension of word representations $x_w \in R^{d_1}$ is d_1. An illustration of the CanHedSeq-LSTM model is shown in Fig. 3.

Bi_CanHed-LSTM. We use two LSTM models: one LSTM model captures semantic information for context words of candidate in the window [−2, 2], and another LSTM model computes semantic information for context words of hedge in the window [−2, 2]. Afterwards, the last hidden vectors of two LSTM models are concatenated and fed to a logistic regression layer to detect scope. An illustration of the Bi_CanHed-LSTM model is shown in Fig. 4.

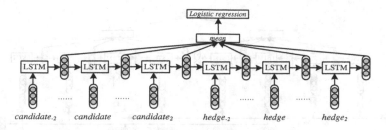

Fig. 3. Hedge scope detection based on CanHedSeq-LSTM

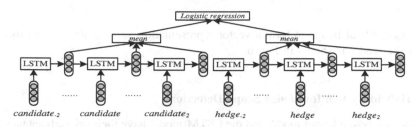

Fig. 4. Hedge scope detection based on Bi_CanHed-LSTM

Bi_CanHedSeq-LSTM. Both the history information and future information in a sequence are important for scope detection. In order to obtain the history and future information of CanHedSeq sequence, we use a forward LSTM and a backward LSTM to model the forward and backward CanHedSeq sequence, respectively. Afterwards, the last hidden vectors of two LSTM models are concatenated and fed to a logistic regression layer to detect scope. An illustration of the Bi_CanHedSeq-LSTM model is shown in Fig. 5.

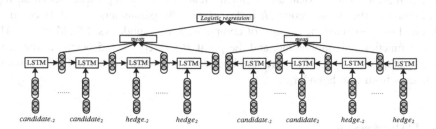

Fig. 5. Hedge scope detection based on Bi_CanHedSeq-LSTM

Bi_CanHedSeq_Con-LSTM. To further represent the information of *CandidateType* and *HedgePos*, we construct Bi_CanHedSeq_Con-LSTM model based on the Bi_CanHedSeq-LSTM. In the Bi_CanHedSeq_Con-LSTM model, the representation of *CandidateType* $x_c \in R^{d_2}$ is concatenated to the representations of the context words $x_w \in R^{d_1}$ of candidate to form a vector representation $x_w, x_c \in R^{d_1 + d_2}$, and the representation of *HedgePos* $x_h \in R^{d_2}$ is concatenated to the representations of the context

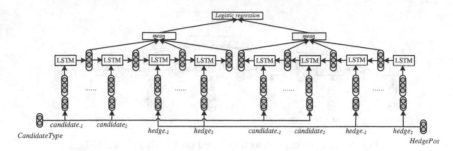

Fig. 6. Hedge scope detection based on Bi_CanHedSeq_Con-LSTM

words $x_w \in R^{d_1}$ of hedge to form a vector representation $x_w, x_h \in R^{d_1 + d_2}$. An illustration of the model is shown in Fig. 6.

3.3 Hybrid System for Hedge Scope Detection

Both the composite kernel model and the LSTM model have their own advantages and could capture different information for scope detection. We propose a hybrid system integrating the composite kernel model $K(t_i)$ weighted by $\alpha \in [0, 1]$ and the LSTM model $N(s_i)$ weighted by $1 - \alpha \in [0, 1]$.

The predicted results of the composite kernel model are the distances between the instances and the separating hyperplane, while those of the LSTM model are the probabilities of the instances. We adopt a uniform framework with sigmoid function σ to transform the distance into a probability as shown in Eq. (2).

$$P(H_i) = \alpha \cdot \sigma(K(t_i)) + (1 - \alpha) \cdot N(s_i) \tag{2}$$

where t_i represents the lexical and syntactic features and s_i represents semantic representations of the hedge scope H_i in test data. The parameters $\alpha \in [0, 1]$ could be controlled to investigate the impacts of composite kernel model vs. LSTM model. The sigmoid function σ is monotonic, and the point $P(y = 1|f) = 0.5$ occurs at the separating hyperplane $f = 0$. Therefore, the boundary probability is set to 0.5 to separate boundaries from non-boundaries.

3.4 Postprocessing

To guarantee that all scopes are continuous sequences of tokens, we apply the following rules to hedge scope detection system.

(1) If one token is predicted as F-scope and one token as L-scope, the sequence will start at the token predicted as F-scope, and end at the token predicted as L-scope.

(2) If one token is predicted as F-scope, and none/more than one token is predicted as L-scope, the sequence will start at the token predicted as F-scope, and end at the token with the maximum L-scope predicted result.

(3) If one token is predicted as L-scope, and none/more than one token is predicted as F-scope, the sequence will start at the token with the maximum F-scope predicted result, and end at the token predicted as L-scope.

4   Experiments and Discussion

Experiments are conducted on the CBHI corpus. The training and test data contain 7510, 1875 sentences respectively. We detect the linguistic scopes with golden standard cues. Stanford Word Segmenter toolkit[2] is employed to segment words and get PoS tag. SVM-LIGHT-TK toolkit[3] is used to construct the composite kernel model. LSTM model is developed based on Theano system[4] [21]. The evaluation of scope detection is reported by F1-score on tag-level and sentence-level. The tag-level takes the token as the evaluation unit, and evaluates the performance of the F-scope and L-scope classifiers respectively. The sentence-level corresponds to the exact match of scope boundaries for each cue.

4.1   Effects of Composite Kernel for Hedge Scope Detection

The detailed performances of the lexical features with polynomial kernel under the condition $d = 2$ are summarized in Table 1. From the results, we can see that *WordContext* features achieve poor results. With other features added one by one, the performance improves continuously and reaches 63.95 % F1-score. All of the lexical features are effective for scope detection. Lexical features with polynomial kernel could obtain acceptable performance. However, the feature engineering is labor intensive and the extracted features with "one-hot" representations are discrete and only capturing shallow information for hedge scope detection.

Table 1. Performance of the Lexical features with polynomial kernel

Lexical	Bounary	P (%)	R (%)	F1-score (%)	Sentence-level F1-score (%)
WordContext	F-scope	82.84	48.91	61.67	54.51
	L-scope	67.32	64.37	65.81	
+CandidateType	F-scope	75.80	68.00	71.69	61.81
	L-scope	70.94	73.71	72.30	
+HedgePos	F-scope	75.94	67.52	71.48	63.95
	L-scope	75.16	85.87	80.16	

---

[2] Available at http://nlp.stanford.edu/software/segmenter.shtml.

[3] Available at http://disi.unitn.it/moschitti/Tree-Kernel.htm.

[4] Available at http://deeplearning.net/software/theano/.

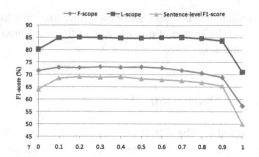

Fig. 7. The performance of composite kernel

We use composite kernel model to capture lexical features and structured syntactic information. Figure 7 shows the performance of composite kernel with different composite factor γ. We vary γ from 0 to 1with an interval of 0.1. From Fig. 7, we can see that:

(1) The sole tree kernel ($\gamma = 1$) obtains 49.92 % F1-score, which is worse than the sole polynomial kernel ($\gamma = 0$). The composite kernel combining lexical and syntactic features with any composite factor γ could achieve higher performance than either one of them on both tag-level and sentence-level F1-score. The best performance of F-scope (L-scope) obtains 73.03 % (85.07 %) F1-score on tag-level. In sentence-level, we obtain 68.91 % F1-score under the condition $\gamma = 0.3$. It indicates that tree kernel could capture useful structure information which hardly can be designed by feature engineering. The composite kernel could effectively realize the complementary of lexical and structured syntactic features.

(2) The performance of L-scope classifiers is usually better than that of F-scope classifiers. The main reason is that the distance of F-scope to its cue is longer than that of L-scope in a sentence on the CBHI corpus. The longer the distance from the scope boundary to its cue is, the harder the scope detection is.

4.2 Effects of LSTM for Hedge Scope Detection

In our experiments, we use Word2Vec[5] toolkit to pre-train word representations on the SogouCS corpus[6]. The dimension d_1 of word representation is 100. The representations of *HedgePos* and *CandidateType* are initialized randomly with dimension 10. Table 2 shows the performance with four LSTM models.

(1) Performance of scope detection obtains acceptable result under any LSTM models. This indicates that the context of hedge and its candidate could represent the hedge scope, and the four LSTM models could effectively capture semantic information of hedge scope.

---

[5] Available at https://code.google.com/p/word2vec/.

[6] Available at http://www.datatang.com/data/list/s04-r020-t01-c03-la01-p3.

Table 2. Performance of the semantic information with LSTM

LSTM	Bounary	P (%)	R (%)	F1-score (%)	Sentence-level F1-score (%)
CanHedseq-LSTM	F-scope	65.26	60.00	62.51	55.73
	L-scope	63.01	74.24	68.17	
Bi_CanHedSeq-LSTM	F-scope	68.94	58.83	63.48	53.97
	L-scope	64.72	71.25	67.83	
Bi_CanHedSeq-LSTM	F-scope	60.08	65.81	62.81	55.15
	L-scope	71.12	67.89	69.47	
Bi_CanHedSeq_Con-LSTM	F-scope	65.24	68.96	67.05	59.09
	L-scope	74.93	80.64	77.68	

(2) CanHedSeq-LSTM achieves 55.73 % F1-score, which is 1.22 % higher than the *WordContext* features with polynomial kernel. This indicates that CanHedSeq-LSTM model could capture the deep semantic information, while *WordContext* features only represent shallow semantic information.

(3) Bi_CanHed-LSTM obtains worse performance than CanHedSeq-LSTM. The main reason is that Bi_CanHed-LSTM with two LSTM models capturing the candidate and hedge contexts respectively, which may ignore the semantic relation between candidate and hedge contexts.

(4) Bi_CanHedSeq-LSTM achieves better performance, which obtains 55.15 % F1-score. This indicates that Bi_CanHedSeq-LSTM can simultaneously capture the history and future semantic information, and both the history and future information are important for hedge scope detection.

(5) Bi_CanHedSeq_Con-LSTM obtains best F1-score 59.09 %, which is 3.94 % higher than Bi_CanHedSeq-LSTM. This indicates that the concatenation of *HedgePos* and *CandidateType* are effective for scope detection. However, the increasing amount is smaller than that *HedgePos* and *CandidateType* as lexical features with polynomial kernel. This may due to that the concatenations of *CandidateType* (*HedgePos*) and context words may bring noises at some time steps in LSTM.

4.3   Effects of Weighting Parameters

We investigate the impact of the parameters α that control the weighting of LSTM model vs. the composite kernel model. The composite kernel model under the condition $\gamma = 0.3$ (68.91 % F1-score) and each LSTM model are used in the hybrid system. From Fig. 8, we can see that the trends of the four curves are similar. All starts from the initial F1-score of LSTM model, and then increases to the individual highest F1-score, finally falls below the initial F1-score (68.91 %) of composite kernel model. The composite kernel is combined with CanHedSeq-LSTM (55.73 % F1-score), Bi_CanHed-LSTM (53.97 % F1-score), Bi_CanHedSeq-LSTM (55.15 % F1-score) and Bi_CanHedSeq_Con-LSTM (59.09 % F1-score) obtaining 69.92 %, 69.76 %,

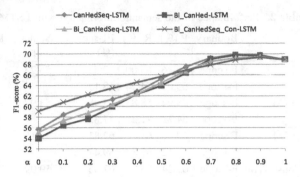

Fig. 8. The performance with different weightings

69.49 % and 69.33 % F1-score, respectively. These indicate that both the composite kernel model and the four LSTM models have their own advantages and could capture different information for scope detection. Their combination could further improve the performance of scope detection.

5   Conclusions and Future Work

Lexical features, syntactic structure features, and semantic representations are all particularly effective for hedge scope detection. We propose a hybrid system to integrate these information for Chinese hedge scope detection, which achieves 69.92 % F1-score on the CBHI corpus. The hybrid system consists of the composite kernel model and the LSTM model. The composite kernel model could effectively capture lexical and syntactic information. The LSTM model could explore deep semantic information of hedge scope. In addition, four LSTM models are developed to explore deep semantic information related to hedge scope.

For the future work, we will explore other deep neural network models to capture more effective semantic information. Besides, we will explore other hybrid methods which integrate diverse information to further improve the performance of scope detection.

Acknowledgements. This research is supported by Natural Science Foundation of China (No. 61272375).

References

1. Szarvas, G., Vincze, V., Farkas, R., Csirik, J.: The BioScope corpus: annotation for negation, uncertainty and their scope in biomedical texts. In: Proceedings of the Workshop on Current Trends in Biomedical Natural Language Processing, pp. 38–45. ACL, USA (2008)
2. Zhou, H.W., Yang, H., Zhang, J., Kang, S.Y., Huang, D.G.: The research and construction of Chinese hedge corpus. J. Chin. Inf. Process. **29**, 83–89 (2015)

3. Farkas, R., Vincze, V., Móra, G., Csirik, J., Szarvas, G.: The CoNLL-2010 shared task: learning to detect hedges and their scope in natural language text. In: Proceedings of CoNLL, pp. 1–12. ACL, Sweden (2010)

4. Zou, B.W., Zhou, G.D., Zhu, Q.M.: Negation and Speculation extraction: an overview. J. Chin. Inf. Process. **04**, 16–24 (2015)

5. Wei, Z.Y., Chen, J.W., Gao, W., Li, B.Y., Zhou, L.J., He, Y.L., Wong, K.F.: An empirical study on uncertainty identification in social media context. In: Proceedings of ACL, pp. 58–62. ACL, Bulgaria (2013)

6. Su, Q., Lou, H.Q., Liu, P.Y.: Hedge detection with latent features. In: Liu, P., Su, Q. (eds.) Chinese Lexical Semantics. LNCS, vol. 8229, pp. 436–441. Springer, Heidelberg (2013)

7. Moschitti, A.: A study on convolution kernels for shallow semantic parsing. In: Proceedings of ACL, p. 335. ACL, Spain (2004)

8. Özgür, A., Radev, D.R.: Detecting speculations and their scopes in scientific text. In: Proceedings of EMNLP, pp. 1398–1407. ACL, Singapore (2009)

9. Øvrelid, L., Velldal, E., Oepen, S.: Syntactic scope resolution in uncertainty analysis. In: Proceedings of CL, pp. 1379–1387. ACL, Beijing (2010)

10. Morante, R., Daelemans, W.: Learning the scope of hedge cues in biomedical texts. In: Proceedings of BioNLP, pp. 28–36. ACL, Colorado (2009)

11. Morante, R., Asch, V.V., Daelemans, W.: Memory-based resolution of in-sentence scopes of hedge cues. In: Proceedings of CoNLL, pp. 40–47. ACL, Sweden (2010)

12. Li, X.X., Shen, J.P., Gao, X., Wang, X.: Exploiting rich features for detecting hedges and their scope. In: Proceedings of CoNLL, pp. 78–83. ACL, Sweden (2010)

13. Zhu, Q.M., Li, J.H., Wang, H.L., Zhou, G.D.: A unified framework for scope learning via simplified shallow semantic parsing. In: Proceedings of EMNLP, pp. 714–724. ACL, USA (2010)

14. Zou, B.W., Zhu, Q.M., Zhou, G.D.: Negation and speculation identification in Chinese language. In: Proceedings of ACL-IJCNLP, pp. 656–665. ACL, Beijing (2015)

15. Zhang, M., Zhang, J., Su, J.: Exploring syntactic features for relation extraction using a convolution tree kernel. In: Proceedings of ACL, pp. 288–295. ACL, New York (2006)

16. Zhou, H.W., Huang, D.G., Li, X.Y., Yang, Y.S.: Combining structured and flat features by a composite kernel to detect hedges scope in biological texts. Chin. J. Electron. **20**(3), 476–482 (2011)

17. Zou, B.W., Zhou, G.D., Zhu, Q.M.: Tree Kernel-based negation and speculation scope detection with structured syntactic parse features. In: Proceedings of EMNLP, pp. 968–976. ACL, USA (2013)

18. Tai, K.S., Socher, R., Manning, C.D.: Improved semantic representations from tree-structured long short-term memory networks. In: Proceedings of ACL-IJCNLP, pp. 1556–1566. ACL, Beijing (2015)

19. Xu, Y., Mou, L.L., Li, G., Chen, Y.C., Peng, H., Jin, Z.: Classifying relations via long short term memory networks along shortest dependency paths. arXiv preprint arXiv:1508.03720 (2015)

20. Zhou, H.W., Deng, H.J., Chen, L., Yang, Y.L., Jia, C.: Exploiting syntactic and semantics information for chemical–disease relation extraction. Database, baw048 (2016)

21. Bergstra, J., Breuleux, O., Bastien, F., Lamblin, P., Pascanu, R., Desjardins, G., Bengio, Y.: Theano: a CPU and GPU math expression compiler. In: Proceedings of SciPy, pp. 1–7. SciPy, Austin (2010)

Combining Event-Level and Cross-Event Semantic Information for Event-Oriented Relation Classification by SCNN

Siyuan Ding, Yu Hong$^{(\boxtimes)}$, Shanshan Zhu, Jianmin Yao, and Qiaoming Zhu

Provincial Key Laboratory of Computer Information Processing Technology,
Soochow University, Suzhou, China
dsy.ever@gmail.com, tianxianer@gmail.com, zhushanshan063@gmail.com,
jmyao@szkj.gov.cn, qmzhu@suda.edu.cn

Abstract. Previous researches on event relation classification primarily rely on lexical and syntactic features. In this paper, we use a Shallow Convolutional Neural Network (SCNN) to extract event-level and cross-event semantic features for event relation classification. On the one hand, the shallow structure alleviates the over-fitting problem caused by the lack of diverse relation samples. On the other hand, the utilization and combination of event-level and cross-event semantic information help improve relation classification. The experimental results show that our approach outperforms the state of the art.

Keywords: Event relation classification · Semantic information · Frame embedding · SCNN

1 Introduction

The task of Event Relation Detection (abbr., ERD) is defined to determine semantic relation between event mentions, and aggregate distributed events in text to form event relation network. ERD is comprised of two separate tasks, Event Relation Identification (ERI) and Event Relation Classification (ERC) [14]. ERI intends to determine whether two events are relevant. ERC determines what types of relations occurred between the events. In this paper, we take our research focus on ERC.

The input of an ERC system is a pair of event mentions. An event mention is a sentence or a clause that depicts a natural event, consisted of at least the trigger of the event and the closely related participants. See the following event mentions, for example, which are respectively by the trigger words *attacked* and *wounded and died*:

Event1: *Terrorists attacked Bataclan Theatre,*
Event2: *many people wounded and died.*

© Springer International Publishing AG 2016
M. Sun et al. (Eds.): CCL and NLP-NABD 2016, LNAI 10035, pp. 216–224, 2016.
DOI: 10.1007/978-3-319-47674-2_19

Table 1. The architecture of event relations

	Top-relation	Sub-relation
Relations	Comparison	Concession
		Contrast
	Contingency	Cause
		Condition
	Expansion	Instantiation
		List
		Progression
		Restatement
	Temporal	Asynchronous
		Synchronous

The output is a tag of relation type, such as that between the above mentions, Causality, which inherits the main relation type Contingency. As shown in Table 1, there are four top-relations in the first level and ten sub-relations in the second level. In this paper, four top-relation types will be considered for the evaluation of ERC systems, including Contingency, Expansion, Comparison and Temporality.

This paper shows a pilot study on CNN based ERC. Our goal is to introduce semantic-level relation analysis into the perception of logical relation among real historical events. In particular, we embed cross-event semantic features, along with inner ones of a single relation sample. By combination of the features, we can deal with the relation classification for the non-adjacent event mentions and even cross-document and cross-topic samples, such as the Comparison relation between the events "tsunami alarm in Hawaii" and "Many planes turn back to San Francisco".

2   Related Work

Pattern-matching method is one of the conventional approaches on ERC. Chklovski and Pantel [4] extracts pairwise events on the basis of manual designed lexical-syntactic pattern. Pantel and Pennacchiotti [11] propose a method based on Espresso Algorithm to construct patterns automatically, which somewhat improves the recall of pattern-matching method.

The most recent research takes event elements as the clues for relation inference. They are mainly inherit Harris distribution assumption that words in the same context usually hold the same or similar meaning [9]. Lin and Pantel [10] propose an unsupervised method relying on Harris assumption and dependency tree. The algorithm identifies grammatical relationships between words and constructs dependency trees formed of the relationships between words.

Ding et al. [6] present a semi-supervised approach based on Tri-Training. Though these methods have been proven successful, manual features are still weak in capturing semantic aspects of events.

Recently, Zhang et al. [15] succeed in using SCNN to implicit discourse relation recognition, which considerably promotes the development of relation detection tasks. However, we find that the method isolates the inner clues between two arguments and only takes each argument into consideration, which inevitably omits the mutual influence between two arguments.

3 Methodology

Figure 1 describes the architecture of our model, which primarily involves the following 4 components: (1) word embedding learning, which reveals the embedding vector of words in event; (2) frame embedding generation, where we extract frames from event to generate the frame embedding vector; (3) event-level and cross-event features extraction with SCNN, which exploits the inner semantics in and cross event; and (4) relation classification, which concatenates the generated features and outputs the candidate relation with highest confidence score.

3.1 Word Embedding Learning

We choose the state-of-the-art model Skip-gram to pre-train the word embedding [2]. In our framework, $w_i \in \mathbb{R}^d$ corresponds to a d-dimensional vector representation of i-th word in each event,

$$w_i = (x_i^1, x_i^2, \ldots, x_i^d) \tag{1}$$

where x_i^j denotes the real-value of j-th dimension in i-th word's embedding, $1 \leq j \leq d$. Figure 1 assumes that each word has size $d = 4$.

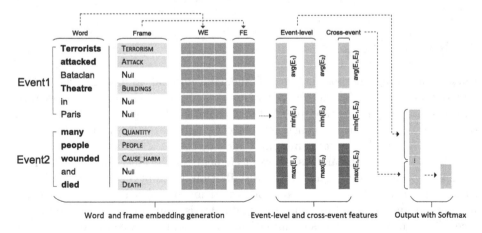

Fig. 1. The architecture for event relation classification via SCNN by combining event-level and cross-event features. WE = word embedding and FE = frame embedding.

3.2   Frame Embedding Generation

The frame semantics information in FrameNet [7] is proved effective to many natural language processing problems [1,3,12,14].

Frame semantics conceptualizes those events with same or similar semantic properties. If two event-event pairs share the similar scenario (which is comprised of a series of frames), they always hold the same relation [14]. Therefore, we use frame semantics as another important information to help detect event relations.

As shown in Fig. 1, we use SEMAFOR[1] to identify the frames of each event. Then, the frames will be mapped to a randomly initialized vector of dimension l, let $f_i \in R^l$ correspond to a l-dimensional vector of i-th frame:

$$f_i = (x_i^1, x_i^2, \ldots, x_i^l) \tag{2}$$

3.3   Extracting Event-Level and Cross-Event Features with SCNN

We combine word embedding w_i and frame embedding f_i to generate e_i,

$$e_i = w_i \oplus f_i \tag{3}$$

where $\oplus$ is a concatenation operator, $e_i \in R^{d+l}$. An event with n words is extracted as the following matrix,

$$E = (e_1^T, e_2^T, \ldots, e_n^T)^T \tag{4}$$

where $E \in R^{n \times (d+l)}$. [15] follows previous works [5,13] and explores three convolutional operations in detecting discourse relations. We adopt this SCNN method and for each column c in E take the following three convolution operations to capture event-level features,

- **event-level features**:

$$max(E^c) = \max\{e_1^c, e_2^c, \ldots, e_n^c\} \tag{5}$$

$$min(E^c) = \min\{e_1^c, e_2^c, \ldots, e_n^c\} \tag{6}$$

$$avg(E^c) = \frac{1}{n} \sum_i^n e_i^c \tag{7}$$

where $1 \leq c \leq d$, e_i^c refers to the value of c-th dimension in e_i of event E. For each column c, we further obtain the cross-event features by exploring max, min and avg operations on matrix $\{E_1, E_2\}$,

- **cross-event features**:

$$max(E_1^c, E_2^c) = \max\{max(E_1^c), max(E_2^c)\} \tag{8}$$

$$min(E_1^c, E_2^c) = \min\{min(E_1^c), min(E_2^c)\} \tag{9}$$

---

[1] http://www.ark.cs.cmu.edu/SEMAFOR.

$$avg(E_1^c, E_2^c) = \frac{1}{2}\{avg(E_1^c), avg(E_2^c)\} \tag{10}$$

In the next step, an concatenation operation is performed on E_1, E_2 and $\{E_1, E_2\}$ to generate $a(E_1)$, $a(E_2)$ and $a(E_1, E_2)$,

$$a(E) = max(E) \oplus min(E) \oplus avg(E) \tag{11}$$

where $a \in \mathrm{R}^{3 \times (d+l)}$. After getting event-level and cross-event convolution features, we concatenate $a(E_1)$, $a(E_2)$ and $a(E_1, E_2)$ into a vector z, and perform hyperbolic tangent $tanh$ to generate a hidden layer,

$$z = a(E_1) \oplus a(E_2) \oplus a(E_1, E_2) \tag{12}$$

$$h = \tanh(z) \tag{13}$$

where $z, h \in \mathrm{R}^{9 \times (d+l)}$.

3.4   Relation Classification

At last, we apply the softmax function upon the hidden layer to predict K-class classification,

$$y = f(\mu h + b) \tag{14}$$

where K is the size of the event relation categories, and $\mu \in \mathrm{R}^{K \times 9 \times (d+l)}$ is parameter matrix, $b \in \mathrm{R}^{9 \times (d+l)}$ is a bias term. We compute the cross-entropy error between y and gold relation g, and further define the objective function:

$$J(\theta) = -\sum_{s=1}^{S}\sum_{k}^{K} y_k(s) \log g_k(s) + \frac{1}{2}\lambda||\theta||^2 \tag{15}$$

where s is the s-th instance in training set S, k is relation type in K, and $\theta = (w, f, l, \mu, b)$ is parameters to be learned.

4   Experiments

4.1   Datasets

We utilize 968 event pairs [14] annotated on FrameNet-1.5 [8], and follow their annotation metric to annotate 4459 new pairs on GIGAWORD (LDC2003T05), both of which finally make up of our experimental datasets in Table 2.

4.2   Experimental Setup

Word embedding is trained on large-scale data by word2vec toolkit. We empirically adopt the same parameters in our experiments. Specifically, we set $d = 200$, $l = 5$ and batch $= 128$. We apply stochastic gradient descent (SGD) algorithm to minimize $J(\theta)$, with learning rate lr $= 0.1$ and momentum $= 0.9$. Finally, we choose precision (P), recall (R) and F$_1$-score (F$_1$) as evaluation metrics.

Table 2. Distributions of positive and negative instances in training (Train), development (Dev) and test (Test) sets.

Data	Positive/negative			
	Comparison	Contingency	Expansion	Temporal
Train	617/617	708/708	1520/1520	547/547
Dev	145/815	233/727	486/474	96/864
Test	197/878	263/812	514/561	101/974

4.3   Comparison with State-of-the-Art Methods

We select the following state-of-the-art methods for comparison:

Cross-Scenario: [14] propose a cross-scenario inference method to predict relations between pairwise events, which assumes that events with same scenarios share the similar relations.

Tri-Training: [6] propose a semi-supervised learning method based on Tri-Training, which improves the classification performance by expanding training corpus with higher confidence unlabelled samples.

SCNN (EL): [15] succeed in performing a SCNN into implicit discourse relation recognition, which could be also applied to ERC task. In this system, only Event-Level(EL) features are taken into account, we set $e_i = w_i$ in Eq. 3 and $z = a(E_1) \oplus a(E_2)$ in Eq. 12, $z, h \in \mathrm{R}^{6d}$.

SCNN (CE): For sufficient and valid comparison, we further set $e_i = w_i$ in Eq. 3 and $z = a(E_1, E_2)$ in Eq. 12, only take Cross-Event(CE) features into account, $z \in \mathrm{R}^{3d}$.

SCNN (EL + CE): This system combines event-level together with cross-event features without using frame embedding features. Specifically, we set $e_i = w_i$ in Eq. 3 and $z = a(E_1) \oplus a(E_2) \oplus a(E_1, E_2)$ as Eq. 12 exhibits, $z \in \mathrm{R}^{9d}$.

SCNN (EL + CE + Frame): At last, we combine event-level and cross-event features together with frame embedding features, we set $e_i = w_i \oplus f_i$ as Eq. 3 and $z = a(E_1) \oplus a(E_2) \oplus a(E_1, E_2)$ as Eq. 12 exhibits, $z \in \mathrm{R}^{9 \times (d+l)}$.

4.4   Results and Analysis

As shown in Table 3, we found the model SCNN (EL) performs better than Cross-Scenario and Tri-Training, which suggests that the shallow structure works well and using event-level features is beneficial to ERC.

When looking into SCNN (CE), we observe that this method works worse than Tri-Training and SCNN (EL). The main reason may be that considering cross-event features only might have left out the important information in each event. However, SCNN (CE) performs better than Cross-Scenario in general, which reveals that the cross-event features is also effective to some extent.

Table 3. The experimental results of different models.

Relations	Models	Performance (%)		
		P	R	F_1
Comparison	Cross-Scenario	24.90	60.91	35.35
	Tri-Training	33.89	51.27	40.81
	SCNN (EL)	33.43	58.38	42.51
	SCNN (CE)	32.10	52.79	39.92
	SCNN (EL + CE)	34.04	56.85	42.59
	SCNN (EL + CE + Frame)	34.50	59.90	**43.78**
Contingency	Cross-Scenario	33.04	28.14	30.39
	Tri-Training	34.83	50.19	41.12
	SCNN (EL)	32.80	61.98	42.89
	SCNN (CE)	35.69	49.81	41.59
	SCNN (EL + CE)	34.42	60.46	43.86
	SCNN (EL + CE + Frame)	37.09	56.27	**44.71**
Expansion	Cross-Scenario	53.57	58.37	55.87
	Tri-Training	52.34	67.51	58.96
	SCNN (EL)	55.84	63.23	59.31
	SCNN (CE)	55.53	59.53	57.46
	SCNN (EL + CE)	56.13	67.70	**61.38**
	SCNN (EL + CE + Frame)	56.28	65.37	60.49
Temporal	Cross-Scenario	17.33	34.65	23.10
	Tri-Training	19.22	63.37	29.49
	SCNN (EL)	19.01	53.47	28.05
	SCNN (CE)	19.26	51.49	28.03
	SCNN (EL + CE)	20.62	52.48	29.61
	SCNN (EL + CE + Frame)	21.25	57.43	**31.02**

EL = Event-Level and CE = Cross-Event.

Table 4. The overall performance of different models using macro average measure.

Models	Macro-average (%)		
	P	R	F_1
Cross-Scenario	32.21	45.52	37.73
Tri-Training	35.07	58.09	43.74
SCNN (EL)	36.34	58.79	44.92
SCNN (CE)	35.65	53.41	42.75
SCNN (EL + CE)	36.30	59.37	45.05
SCNN (EL + CE + Frame)	37.28	59.74	**45.91**

Compared with previous models, SCNN (EL + CE) achieves the best results in four relations and gets highest F_1-score 44.71 % in Expansion among all models, which sufficiently suggests that combining event-level and cross-event information in relation classification gains remarkable promotion.

When frame embedding is merged into word embedding, we achieve the best result in Comparison, Contingency and Temporal in SCNN (EL + CE + Frame), which indicates that frame embedding is useful to represent the deep semantics of event relation. Table 4 presents the overall performance of six models using macro average measure, SCNN (EL + CE + Frame) model also achieves the best result. In summary, according to Tables 3 and 4, our model undoubtedly gains the best result in ERC.

5   Conclusion

In this paper, we exploit a novel method for event relation classification which automatically extracts event-level and cross-event convolutional features from combined embeddings. We further concatenate these convolutional features into shallow neural networks to learn better classifiers. Experimental results show that our model significantly outperforms the state-of-the-art methods.

Acknowledgments. This research is supported by the National Natural Science Foundation of China, No.61672368, No.61373097, No.61672367, No.61272259, No.61272260, the Research Foundation of the Ministry of Education and China Mobile, MCM20150602 and the Science and Technology Plan of Jiangsu, SBK2015022101. The authors would like to thank the anonymous reviewers for their insightful comments and suggestions.

References

1. Aharon, R.B., Szpektor, I., Dagan, I.: Generating entailment rules from framenet. In: Proceedings of ACL 2010 Conference Short Papers, pp. 241–246. Association for Computational Linguistics (2010)
2. Baroni, M., Dinu, G., Kruszewski, G.: Don't count, predict! A systematic comparison of context-counting vs. context-predicting semantic vectors. In: ACL, vol. 1, pp. 238–247 (2014)
3. Burchardt, A., Frank, A.: Approaching textual entailment with LFG and framenet frames. In: Proceedings of 2nd PASCAL RTE Challenge Workshop. Citeseer (2006)
4. Chklovski, T., Pantel, P.: Global path-based refinement of noisy graphs applied to verb semantics. In: Dale, R., Wong, K.-F., Su, J., Kwong, O.Y. (eds.) IJCNLP 2005. LNCS (LNAI), vol. 3651, pp. 792–803. Springer, Heidelberg (2005)
5. Collobert, R., Weston, J., Bottou, L., Karlen, M., Kavukcuoglu, K., Kuksa, P.: Natural language processing (almost) from scratch. J. Mach. Learn. Res. **12**, 2493–2537 (2011)
6. Ding, S., Hong, Y., Zhu, S., Yao, J., Zhu, Q.: Research of event relation classification based on tri-training. J. Comput. Eng. Sci. **37**(12), 2345–2351 (2015)
7. Fillmore, C.: Frame semantics. In: Linguistics in the Morning Calm, pp. 111–137 (1982)

8. Fillmore, C.J., Johnson, C.R., Petruck, M.R.: Background to framenet. Int. J. Lexicogr. **16**(3), 235–250 (2003)
9. Harris, Z.: Mathematical Structures of Language. Wiley, New York (1968)
10. Lin, D., Pantel, P.: Dirt@ sbt@ discovery of inference rules from text. In: Proceedings of 7th ACM SIGKDD International Conference on Knowledge Discovery and Data Mining, pp. 323–328. ACM (2001)
11. Pantel, P., Pennacchiotti, M.: Espresso: leveraging generic patterns for automatically harvesting semantic relations. In: Proceedings of 21st International Conference on Computational Linguistics and 44th Annual Meeting of Association for Computational Linguistics, pp. 113–120. Association for Computational Linguistics (2006)
12. Shen, D., Lapata, M.: Using semantic roles to improve question answering. In: EMNLP-CoNLL, pp. 12–21 (2007)
13. Socher, R., Huang, E.H., Pennin, J., Manning, C.D., Ng, A.Y.: Dynamic pooling and unfolding recursive autoencoders for paraphrase detection. In: Advances in Neural Information Processing Systems, pp. 801–809 (2011)
14. Yang, X., Hong, Y., Chen, Y., Wang, X., Yao, J., Zhu, Q.: Detection event relation through cross-scenario inference. J. Chin. Inf. Process. **28**(5), 206–214 (2014)
15. Zhang, B., Su, J., Xiong, D., Lu, Y., Duan, H., Yao, J.: Shallow convolutional neural network for implicit discourse relation recognition. In: Proceedings of 2015 Conference on Empirical Methods in Natural Language Processing, pp. 2230–2235 (2015)

Linguistic Resource Annotation
and Evaluation

The Constitution of a Fine-Grained Opinion Annotated Corpus on Weibo

Liao Jian[1], Li Yang[1], and Wang Suge[1,2(✉)]

[1] School of Computer and Information Technology,
Shanxi University, Taiyuan 030006, China
wsg@sxu.edu.cn

[2] Key Laboratory of Computational Intelligence and Chinese Information Processing
of Ministry of Education, Shanxi University, Taiyuan 030006, China

Abstract. Sentiment analysis on social media represented by Weibo is one of the hotspot research problems in NLP. A comprehensive and systematic fine-grained annotated corpus plays a significance role. In this paper, considering the characteristics of Weibo, we focus on the constitution of a fine-grained, hierarchical opinion annotated corpus and design a set of labelling specification. We manually annotate the opinion sentences with a part of ones containing hidden opinion which can be useful for implicit sentiment analysis. Then a fine-grained aspect extraction, namely opinion triples like <object, attribute, polarity> is finished for aspect-level sentiment research. Moreover, we establish an evaluation method for the task of fine-grained aspect extraction which has been applied in evaluation for years. The corpus was used in the task of COAE2015, and it will be a useful resource for the related research on social media sentiment analysis.

Keywords: Weibo corpus · Fine-grained opinion annotation · Implicit opinion annotation · Evaluation

1 Introduction

Weibo is one of the most popular social media which enjoys a rapid development in China. People can freely express their opinion, attitude and emotion with it. According to a report released by China Internet Network Information Center(CNNIC) [1], the quantity of Weibo users totaled 204 million and nearly half of the weibo's updates are sent via mobile phone. Recent trends in Weibo's development have led to a proliferation of studies on social media analysis. A well-designed, fine-grained and large-scale annotated corpus can be benefit to lots of research and applications of social media sentiment analysis.

Up to now, many works focused in building sentiment annotated corpus and have made some progress. Based on Twitter data, Pak and Paroubek [8] established a subjective corpus containing positive and negative sentiment text. Ptaszynski et al. [9] built a corpus based on a large-scale Japanese blogs,

© Springer International Publishing AG 2016
M. Sun et al. (Eds.): CCL and NLP-NABD 2016, LNAI 10035, pp. 227–240, 2016.
DOI: 10.1007/978-3-319-47674-2_20

they labeled both sentiment and emotion including sentiment polarity and emotion icon. In Jacob's study [4], a CRF-based model which can effectively reduce human workload was adopted to extract expressions of opinion object to build an object dictionary in interdisciplinary datasets.

Several achievement have been done in establishing Chinese sentiment annotated corpus. Xu et al. [13] labeled nearly 40,000 sentences with sentiment polarity based on Chinese textbooks for primary schools, screenplays and literature periodicals. After analysing characteristics of the annotated corpus with million-words level, some statistical results like the distribution of sentiment and its transfer pattern was given in their study. Based on this research, they designed an framework for product reviews labelling, and annotated the attributions of product and their corresponding opinion expressions in word-level, sentence-level and document-level respectively [14]. For entity-level labelling, Deng and Wiebe [3] have published an entity-level corpus named MPQA3.0, they annotated entities and event targets on the basis of previous work. Dai et al. [2] annotated 5,000 reviews of product with opinion object and sentiment polarity, they also labelled some implicit sentiment, default object and polarity transfer. But on the one hand their corpus suffered from the lack of hierarchy relationship between opinion objects and attributes, on the other hand the product reviews are not much diversity comparing to Weibo data. Recent developments of Weibo have heightened the need for social media oriented annotated corpus. Yao et al. [15] established a emotion annotated corpus contains 14,000 pieces of weibo and 45,431 sentences. They labelled the sentences with 7 kinds of emotion class and 3 kinds of emotion strength.

In this paper, we design a framework for fine-grained, hierarchical, social media oriented annotation and its corresponding specifications. Compared to other resource construction method, our framework can effectively reduce the manual work by using the classifier and automatic aspect extraction method as the initial labelling and assistance. Besides, a random cross-validation process is introduced to minimize the difference of human cognition. Using the framework, we complete a sentence-level opinion corpus's annotation which contains 15,679 pieces of weibo, 20,154 sentences, and a hierarchical aspect-level opinion corpus with 13,787 sentences, 24,093 pairs of triples annotated. We also annotate a part of sentences containing implicit opinions. Moreover, we present a set of evaluation methods for the task of fine-grained opinion aspect extraction. These methods have been used in the fifth to seventh Chinese Opinion Analysis Evaluation [6,11,12].

The rest of the paper is structured as follows: We will introduce the specifications in the next section. The main process of annotation will be described in Sect. 3 and a detail analysis of the corpus will be given in Sect. 4. We then present the method and indexes of evaluation in Sect. 5. The sixth part shows the result and analysis of Chinese Opinion Analysis Evaluation 2015 which used the corpus as task dataset. Conclusion and future work are presented in the last section.

2 Specification of Annotation

2.1 Granularity of Annotation

The authors of Weibo express their opinions or emotions with brief words. These sentences usually contain dense opinions or emotions but suffered from ill-formed expression. Therefore, a large-scale corpus with detailed, fine-grained annotation plays a important role for social media oriented research. In this paper, we choose sentence-level as the basic granularity of annotation, then a hierarchical aspect-level annotation of triples <object, attribute, polarity> will be done on the set of sentences which contain opinions

2.2 Annotation of Implicit Opinion

The expressions of opinion in Weibo text are consist of explicit and implicit ones. Explicit opinion refer to the phrase or sentence express sentiment polarity with sentiment words which can be effectively identified through a sentiment dictionary, while the implicit ones are made up without sentiment words. Liu [7] defined the implicit opinion as a kind of objective statement contains the general opinion or comparative one which express a subjective feeling of satisfy or unsatisfy. Usually, there are two ways for expressing implicit opinion, namely factual description based and rhetorical description based. For example.

1. 今天是第五天了，还在维修中。
   (Today is the fifth day, it's still in maintenance.)
2. 没完没了的会议引发了一场暴风雨。
   (The endless meeting sparked a storm.)

The first sentence expresses a negative opinion by using a factual statement while the second one is metaphorical.

According to our previous survey on the dataset containing nearly 20,000 sentences which collected from a famous car reviews website named Autohome[1] in China, nearly one third of the sentences contain implicit expression. Implicit opinions are easier to detect and to classify than explicit ones for the lack of sentiment words, and most of the current research has focused on explicit opinions [7]. For that reason, we add the labelling of implicit opinion into our corpus for related research in the future.

2.3 Classification of Annotated Opinion

In this paper, we focus in annotating the sentiment polarity of sentences and triples, and the explicit/implicit class of opinion sentence. We define the classification of annotation as the following Table 1.

---

[1] http://www.autohome.com.cn

Table 1. The classification of annotated opinion

Opinion class	Sentiment polarity	Annotated label
Explicit	Positive	1
	Negative	2
	Mixed	3
Implicit	Positive	4
	Negative	5
	Mixed	6

3 Construction of Sentiment Corpus

3.1 Selection of Original Data and Preprocessing

We use a dataset with 10 million weibos which was crawled from the largest and most popular social media named Weibo in China as the original data. This dataset was also used as task data for new sentiment word identification in COAE2014 [12]. Comparing to other source, the Weibo dataset is domain independent which covers a wide coverage such as digital product, cars review, food, travel, entertainment and so on. Moreover, a large number of weibos' contents are suffered from arbitrary and ill-formed expression. Therefore, cleaning and preprocessing of the original data need to be finished firstly to reduce the noise. It is consist of two steps.

Filtering. Remove all the weibos which are unsuitable for research. We use a rule-based filter to finish this task. The rules mainly includes, (1) weibos with the length less than 10 Chinese characters; (2) all emoticons or punctuation composed ones; (3) the ones containing mobile phone number or QQ (a famous IM software in China) number, because this kind of weibos are mostly advertisement; (4) completely duplicate ones.

Sentence Segmenting. We use the sentence-level as our basic granularity of annotation. For that reason, we segment all the weibos into sentences by using the following rules. (1) split the weibo by the segment characters set $S = \{$ ".", "。", "!", "?", ":", "..." $\}$; (2) if the period(。) or dot(.) is between two numbers or characters, skip the segment process for it is usually means a number or abbreviation; (3) preserve the first sentence only if it follows with repeating segment characters in S.

3.2 Process of Annotation

The main process of annotation in this paper is consist of two stages. Firstly, in the sentence-level opinion annotate stage, we use a dictionary-based opinion sentence identification method proposed in Song's research [10] to select candidate opinion sentences, then send the filtered result to annotators for manual

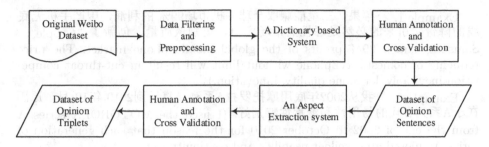

Fig. 1. The process of annotation

annotation and cross validation. Then we adopt the method proposed by Liao [5] to extract opinion aspect pairs on the selected opinion sentences in stage 1. This pairs can be used as a initial labelling and reference for annotators in aspect-level triplet annotate stage, and a cross validation for consistency is completed after that. The framework of annotate process is shown as the following Fig. 1.

Annotation of Opinion Sentence. In this stage, we distinguish the opinion sentences from the dataset and annotate sentiment polarity label. Compared to previous work, we add the annotation of implicit opinion. The basic rules for labelling are defined as, if the sentence which contains opinion has explicit sentiment words, we consider it as a explicit opinion sentence and label the corresponding polarity. While a sentence will be regarded as implicit opinion one if the containing opinion is expressed by factual description or rhetorical description like metaphor and personification.

For example, "坑爹的苹果，坑爹的 ipad4。" (Ceezy Apple, ceezy ipad4.) will be marked as a explicit negative sentence for it has an explicit sentiment word "坑爹" (Ceezy). While the sentence "你脑壳遭门夹了才会在太升南路买 iphone!" (How stupid are you buying an iPhone on south Taisheng road.) expresses a negative opinion using a metaphor "脑壳遭门夹了"(stupid like the head is crashed by a door).

Annotation of Opinion Triplet. In the fine-grained opinion aspect triplet annotate stage, we try to extract all the opinion triplets <object, attribute, polarity> in the opinion sentences. During the annotation, we define a set of rules in order to achieve a clear, complete, high-consistency result. The rules are defined as follows.

Apposition. Multi objects, attributes or opinion expressions concatenate each other with hyphenation "，" or "、" will be regarded as a whole aspect. While the aspects concatenated by conjunction "和" or "与"(both means "and" in Chinese) are divided into different triplets.

Example 1. "苹果，三星能赚取全球手机市场99% 的利润，国产手机无底线的降价，引来的必然是恶性的市场竞争，更别谈质量、创新了。"(Apple, Samsung earned 99 % profits of the global mobile phone market. The price reducing of domestic cellphone without limit will result in cut-throat competition inevitably, let alone quality, innovation.)

Example 2. "我从2002年底用摩托罗拉A系列一直用到2010 年10 月，原因在于A系列各代的易用性和继承性特别好!"(I used the MOTOROLA series A from the end of 2002 to October 2010 for the reason that each generation of series A enjoyed an excellent usability and continuity.)

Comparative. If there is a comparative opinion in sentence, we label the triplets in pairs and the polarity of them depend on the result of comparison.

Example 3.
"今天又试了试新帕萨特，感觉比迈腾好，至少动力系统和降噪方面比迈腾强。"
(I tried the new PASSAT today, feel better than MAGOTAN, at least the power system and noise reduction are better than its.)

Attributive. If there are more than one attributive word modify the core aspect, we preserve the longest range.

Example 4. "本田newCIVIC同大众Scirocco有着多么相似的出色风格!" (How similar the excellent style are between the Honda newCIVIC and Volkswagen Scirocco.)

Coreference. The demonstrative pronoun will be preserved for the disambiguation of targets.

Example 5. "#新车播报#日前，沃尔沃2013款s60 正式上市销售，这个车是在美国测试中秒杀一众德日豪华车。"(#New Cars Boardcasting#Now, the Volvo s60 2013 is available, this car achieved the best in a evaluation in US and defeat other German and Japanese premium cars overwhelmingly.)

The solutions for Examples 1–5 are shown as the following Table 2. "null" means the aspect is default in current sentence.

Consistency of Annotation. The annotation of corpus needs collaboratively work. The result of labelling of different annotator is unavoidable different. We design the following process try to reduce the inconsistency.

Mark the unlabelled sentences set as S_u, labelled sentences set as S_l, annotators set as H, the annotator's labelling can be marked as $L(s,h)$, $s \in S$, $h \in H$, $L(\cdot) = \{1, 2, 3, 4, 5, 6\}$.

Stage of Opinion Sentence Annotation.

(1) Divide the unlabelled sentences set S_u into k groups, for each instance s_{ki} in S_{uk}, an annotator labels the sentiment polarity. After that, we get an initial labelled set $S_l = \{S_{l1}, S_{l2}, \ldots, S_{lk}\}$, in which $S_{lk} = \{L(s_{ki}, h)|s_{ki} \in S_{uk}, h \in H\}$.

(2) For each subset S_{lk} in S_l, we send it to another annotator randomly for relabelling. Then a new labelled sentence set $S'_l = \{S'_{l1}, S'_{l2}, \ldots, S'_{lk}\}$ are produced. Select the different set $S_{dk} = \{s_{ki}|L(s_{ki}, h) \neq L(s_{ki}, h')\}$ of S_{lk} and S'_{lk}. Integrate the subset by $S_l = S_l \cup (S_{lk} \cap S'_{lk})$ and $S_d = S_d \cup S_{dk}$.

(3) Redo step 2 in S_d and get the different set S'_d, the instance in S'_d will be abandoned for it is hardly to get an agreement. Then add the rest subset to labelled set by $S_l = S_l \cup (S_d/S'_d)$.

Table 2. The examples of annotation

Rule	Example	Opinion Object	Opinion Attribute	Polarity
Apposition	Example 1	国产手机 (domestic cellphone)	质量、创新 (quality, innovation)	-1
	Example 2	A系列 (series A)	易用性 (usability)	-1
		A 系列 (series A)	继承性 (continuity)	-1
Comparative	Example 3	新帕萨特 (new PASSAT)	null	1
		迈腾 (MAGOTAN)	null	-1
		新帕萨特 (new PASSAT)	动力系统 (power system)	1
		迈腾 (MAGOTAN)	动力系统 (power system)	-1
		新帕萨特 (new PASSAT)	降噪 (noise reduction)	1
		迈腾 (MAGOTAN)	降噪 (noise reduction)	-1
Comparative	Example 4	本田newCIVIC (Honda newCIVIC)	风格 (style)	1
		大众Scirocco (Volkswagen Scirocco)	风格 (style)	1
Coreference	Example 5	这个车 (this car)	null	1

Stage of Fine-Grained Aspect Annotation.

(1) Use the labelled sentence set S_l in previous stage as the initialization of unlabelled set S_u in current stage. Similarly, divide S_u into k groups, and get the initial labelled set $S_l = \{S_{l1}, S_{l2}, \ldots, S_{lk}\}$, in which $S_{lk} = \{triple(s_{ki}, h)|s_{ki} \in S_{uk}, h \in H\}$, $triple(s_{ki}, h)$ means the opinion aspect triple <object, attribute, polarity>.

(2) Send each subset S_{lk} in S_l to another annotator randomly for proofreading. Then Integrate the new validated set $S'_l = \{S'_{l1}, S'_{l2}, \ldots, S'_{lk}\}$ into S_{lk} by $S_l = S_l \cup S'_{lk}$.

4   Detail Analysis of the Corpus

We have completed a corpus with 15,679 weibos, 20,154 sentences which covers a wide range such as automobile, electronics, mobile phone, food, entertainment and so on. Among the opinion sentences, we annotate 13,787 sentences with 24,093 pairs of opinion aspect triplets. A detail analysis like sentiment distribution, explicit/implicit proportion, lexical diversity will be shown as follows.

4.1   Sentiment Distribution of Opinion in Sentences and Aspects

The statistical result of sentiment distribution of opinion in sentences and aspect triplets is shown as the following Table 3.

Table 3. Sentiment distribution of opinion in sentences and aspects

Statistical item	Amount/proportion	Negative	Positive	Mixed	Total
Total opinion sentences	Amount	12306	6209	1639	20154
	Proportion	0.611	0.308	0.081	1
Explicit opinion sentences	Amount	11610	5139	1236	17985
	Proportion	0.646	0.286	0.068	1
Implicit opinion sentences	Amount	696	1070	403	2169
	Proportion	0.321	0.493	0.186	1
Opinion aspect triplets	Amount	16136	7602	355	24093
	Proportion	0.670	0.316	0.015	1

We can easily figure it out that the majority opinion in Weibo contents is positive from Table 3. However, users prefer to express negative or mixed opinion through implicit expression. This phenomenon is in accordance with the general cognitive pattern that people will speak highly of others directly, while a more euphemistic tone will be adopted when delivering criticism or alternative viewpoints. In consideration of the proportion of opinion aspect triplets, comparing to sentence-level opinion, triplets express more certain sentiment polarity with less mixed opinion ones, for the triplet enjoyed a finer granularity. This can be somehow a support for the idea that aspect-level fine-grained opinion expressions can accurately portray the sentiment information of a document.

4.2   Analysis of Lexical Diversity in Fine-Grained Opinions

The lexical diversity can effectively describe the coverage and generalization of the corpus in fine-grained aspect annotation. The analysis of lexical diversity is shown as Table 4.

AWF means the average word frequency. From Table 4 we know that the lexical diversity of implicit is more abundant then explicit for the reason

Table 4. Lexical diversity in fine-grained opinions

Statistical item	Total opinion		Explicit opinion		Implicit opinion	
	Object	Attribute	Object	Attribute	Object	Attribute
Amount	5437	3549	4598	3306	803	468
AWF	4.43	6.79	4.22	5.87	2.70	4.63

that, (1) it has a less average word frequency ($2.70 < 4.22$); (2) each opinion attribute in implicit triplets corresponds $1.71(803/468)$ objects while the ratio is $1.39(4598/3306)$ in explicit ones.

4.3 Analysis of Consistency

Consistency of Opinion Sentence Annotation. We introduce the κ-coefficient to measure the consistency of opinion sentence annotation. For the labelling of 11 annotators, we calculate the κ value on total, explicit, implicit opinion respectively. The result and analysis is given as follows, see Table 5.

Table 5. κ-coefficient of opinion sentence annotation

Measure index	Total opinion	Explicit opinion	Implicit opinion
κ-coefficient	0.924	0.961	0.687

The κ-coefficient of opinion annotation is satisfied in general but it suffered a low performance in implicit ones. The reason is that there is no clear definition of implicit expression in linguistics, we only set a few rough rules to restrict it to a wide range, so the annotators have to identify the ambiguous concept from their own cognition.

Consistency of Fine-Grained Aspect Triplets Annotation. To measure the consistency of this stage, We use the evaluation method mentioned in Sect. 5, regarding the initial labelled result as testing set S_t and the second validated result as key set S_k. Calculate the index value of fully match and fuzzy match respectively. The result is shown as following Table 6. The "all fully/fuzzy" means the opinion object and attribute of instance in testing set must fully/fuzzy match the corresponding item of key instance at the same time and their sentiment polarity is the same. Namely, O_t matches O_k, A_t matches A_k and $P_t = P_k$, $<O_t, A_t, P_t> \in S_t$, $<O_k, A_k, P_k> \in S_k$. Similarly, "object fully/fuzzy" means O_t matches O_k and $P_t = P_k$. "Attribute fully/fuzzy" means A_t matches A_k and $P_t = P_k$.

From Table 6 we can see that the consistency of fine-grained aspect triplets annotation is hardly satisfied, the main problem is the different cognition on the hierarchical relation between objects and attributes, the boundary of aspects and so on.

Table 6. Consistency of fine-grained aspect triplets annotation

Match type	Mirco			Marco		
	Precision	Recall	F1	Precision	Recall	F1
All fully	0.776	0.588	0.669	0.814	0.758	0.785
All fuzzy	0.815	0.622	0.706	0.866	0.807	0.835
Object fully	0.825	0.628	0.713	0.870	0.811	0.839
Object fuzzy	0.858	0.655	0.743	0.911	0.849	0.879
Attribute fully	0.827	0.630	0.715	0.876	0.816	0.845
Attribute fuzzy	0.845	0.645	0.731	0.898	0.837	0.867

5 Evaluation Method for Fine-Grained Opinion Extraction

To evaluate the performance of fine-grained opinion extraction system, we design two match patterns, namely fully match and fuzzy match on three evaluate target as opinion object-polarity, opinion attribute-polarity, object-attribute-polarity using the indexes of precision, recall and F1. Denote the extracted aspect in testing set S_t as x, the human labelled aspect in key set S_k as y, the corresponding sentiment polarity as P_t, P_k respectively, some definition is shown as follows.

Definition 1 (Fully Match). If $(x \subseteq y) \wedge (y \subseteq x) \wedge (P_t = P_k)$ is true, then x fully matches y.

Definition 2 (Fuzzy Match). If $(x \subseteq y) \vee (y \subseteq x) \wedge (P_t = P_k)$ is true, then x fuzzy0 matches y.

For example, suppose the key aspect is "屏幕分辨率"(screen resolution) while the testing aspect is "屏幕"(screen) or "分辨率"(resolution), it is not considered as fuzzy match but a fully one.

Definition 3 (Coverage Match). If the coverage value of the overlap between x and y greater than threshold, then x matches y. Coverage is defined as,

$$Coverage(x, y) = \frac{len(x \cap y)}{len(y)} \tag{1}$$

$len(\cdot)$ means the length of the input string, $x \cap y$ is the overlap of x and y. The threshold of coverage is usually set as 0.2, 0.5 or 0.8[2].

For example, suppose the key aspect is "屏幕分辨率"(screen resolution) while the testing aspect is "屏幕"(screen) and current threshold is 0.2, then the coverage value of this instance is 0.4 and it is regarded as a valid match.

---

[2] The coverage match is equivalent to fully match when the coverage is 1.

6 Corpus for Chinese Opinion Analysis Evaluation

Part of the corpus established in this paper was used as the task data for social media oriented opinion analysis, including opinion sentence identification and opinion aspects extraction in the seventh Chinese opinion analysis evaluation (COAE2015). Unlike previous evaluation, there are two type of evaluation on each task this year, namely resource limited and resource unlimited. The former focus on the proposed methods and models by limit the using of unofficial resources, while the focal point of the latter is the performance of each participating system.

6.1 Result of Opinion Sentence Identification and Classification

There are 19 teams with 44 results submitted in this task. 13 teams with 18 submissions are resource limited while the number of unlimited is 15 and 26. We list the best and medium result of all the submissions in following Table 7.

Table 7. Result of opinion sentence identification and classification

Resource	System	Mirco			Marco		
		Precision	Recall	F1	Precision	Recall	F1
Limited	Best	0.821	0.733	0.771	0.830	0.629	0.654
	Medium	0.616	0.539	0.582	0.556	0.438	0.471
Unlimited	Best	0.840	0.785	0.811	0.878	0.667	0.695
	Medium	0.615	0.564	0.606	0.555	0.477	0.495

All listed data above are the best/medium result of **each single index** among the submissions. From Table 7 we can know that, (1) on the task of Chinese opinion sentence identification, most teams achieve a acceptable performance but still need to improve on mixed opinion sentences. This kind of data usually contains both positive and negative opinions which is hard to be recognized correctly. (2) Compared with limited resource evaluation, there is only a 4 % improvement in average of the unlimited resource. In some sense, it demonstrates that only adding extra resource will hardly work when dealing with social media text.

6.2 Result of Opinion Aspects Extraction

The number of participating teams in this task is much less than the previous one, however the aspect extraction is harder and more meaningful for a fine-grained opinion analysis will accurately portray short text like the social media data. There are 10 teams with 20 results submitted and 5 teams with 6 submissions are resource limited. 15 unlimited results were submitted by 9 teams. Results can be seen in the following Table 8.

Table 8. Result of opinion sentence identification and classification

Resource	Match type	System	Mirco			Marco		
			Precision	Recall	F1	Precision	Recall	F1
Limited	All fuzzy	Best	0.092	0.244	0.130	0.062	0.197	0.086
		Medium	0.054	0.184	0.073	0.044	0.138	0.056
	All fully	Best	0.068	0.179	0.097	0.048	0.162	0.066
		Medium	0.039	0.139	0.053	0.032	0.104	0.041
	Object fuzzy	Best	0.119	0.316	0.168	0.080	0.257	0.112
		Medium	0.074	0.250	0.100	0.061	0.187	0.078
	Object fully	Best	0.088	0.236	0.125	0.062	0.211	0.085
		Medium	0.058	0.192	0.077	0.046	0.137	0.060
	Attribute fuzzy	Best	0.125	0.323	0.176	0.084	0.295	0.117
		Medium	0.075	0.293	0.103	0.060	0.201	0.080
	Attribute fully	Best	0.116	0.298	0.164	0.078	0.270	0.109
		Medium	0.066	0.265	0.092	0.052	0.189	0.073
Unlimited	All fuzzy	Best	0.131	0.288	0.177	0.097	0.222	0.134
		Medium	0.081	0.222	0.108	0.051	0.158	0.073
	All fully	Best	0.112	0.232	0.151	0.083	0.190	0.115
		Medium	0.065	0.165	0.081	0.041	0.120	0.058
	Object fuzzy	Best	0.166	0.368	0.223	0.124	0.309	0.169
		Medium	0.125	0.285	0.138	0.078	0.217	0.098
	Object fully	Best	0.144	0.298	0.194	0.106	0.243	0.147
		Medium	0.089	0.224	0.103	0.061	0.160	0.073
	Attribute fuzzy	Best	0.159	0.426	0.213	0.114	0.352	0.159
		Medium	0.115	0.292	0.159	0.072	0.213	0.103
	Attribute fully	Best	0.151	0.399	0.203	0.109	0.325	0.152
		Medium	0.103	0.276	0.143	0.068	0.200	0.098

From Table 8 and some analysis on submissions, we can see that,

(1) Compared to previous result on opinion aspect extraction task, the performance of this year decreased 10 % in average, using Weibo data which is domain independent instead of some product BBS may be the main reason.
(2) Similar as the task of opinion sentence identification, the performance on mixed opinions needs improving. However, the result is still acceptable for there is only 1.47 % of the triplets containing mixed opinion in aspect-level granularity.
(3) Analysis on all the submissions shows that 20.1 % of the total submitted answers reached an agreement by more than three teams. This phenomenon demonstrates that there exists great difference among the teams.

(4) Like the previous task, extra resource provide only 5 % improvement in average. For social media oriented data, we shall lie our focal point on models and representation.

7   Conclusion and Future Work

In this paper, we design a framework for fine-grained, hierarchical, social media oriented labelling and its corresponding specifications. We complete a sentence-level opinion corpus's annotation which contains 15,679 pieces of weibo, 20,154 sentences including explicit or implicit opinions. In addition, a hierarchical aspect-level opinion corpus with 13,787 sentences, 24,093 pairs of triples are established for aspect-level sentiment analysis. A dataset based on our labelled corpus was used as a task dataset in COAE2015 and effectively promote the development of related research on social media sentiment analysis. This dataset is now available on the website(http://115.24.12.5/web/resource.html) for academia. In future work, we will build a larger and more detailed corpus for implicit sentiment analysis.

Acknowledgement. The authors would like to thank all the students' hard work who participate the corpus's labelling including Zhao Celi, Zhang Jin, Xu Chaoyi, Guo Xiaomin, Zhang Jun, Li Min, Qiao Pei, Mu Wanqing, Wang Jia, Wang Jie and Lv Ying. Also thank all anonymous reviewers for their valuable comments and suggestions which have significantly improved the quality and presentation of this paper. This work was supported by the National High-Tech Research and Development Program (863 Program) (2015AA011808); the National Natural Science Foundation of China (61432011, 61573231, 61175067, 61272095, U1435212); the Shanxi Province Returned Overseas Research Project (2013-014); the Shanxi Province Science and Technology Basic Condition Platform Construction (2015091001-0102).

References

1. CNNIC: Statistical report on internet development in China (2015)
2. Dai, M., Zhu, Z., Li, S., Zhou, G.: Corpus construction on opinion information extraction in Chinese. J. Chin. Inf. Process. **29**(4), 67 (2015)
3. Deng, L., Wiebe, J.: MPQA 3.0: an entity/event-level sentiment corpus. In: Proceedings of Conference of the North American Chapter of the Association of Computational Linguistics: Human Language Technologies (2015)
4. Jakob, N., Gurevych, I.: Extracting opinion targets in a single-and cross-domain setting with conditional random fields. In: Proceedings of Empirical Methods in Natural Language Processing, pp. 1035–1045. Association for Computational Linguistics (2010)
5. Liao, J., Wang, S., Li, D., Zhang, P.: The bag-of-opinions method for car review sentiment polarity classification. J. Chin. Inf. Process. **29**(3), 113 (2015)
6. Liao, X., Wang, S., Huang, M.: Overview of Chinese opinion analysis evaluation 2015. In: Proceedings of Chinese Opinion Analysis Evaluation 2015, Luoyang, China, pp. 5–26 (2015)

7. Liu, B.: Sentiment analysis and subjectivity. In: Handbook of Natural Language Processing, vol. 2, pp. 627–666 (2010)
8. Pak, A., Paroubek, P.: Twitter as a corpus for sentiment analysis and opinion mining. In: Proceedings of International Conference on Language Resources and Evaluation, vol. 10, pp. 1320–1326 (2010)
9. Ptaszynski, M., Rzepka, R., Araki, K., Momouchi, Y.: Automatically annotating a five-billion-word corpus of Japanese blogs for sentiment and affect analysis. Comput. Speech Lang. 28(1), 38–55 (2014)
10. Song, Y.: Design and implementation of a rule-based comparative opinion mining system. Master's thesis, Shanxi University, Taiyuan, China (2014)
11. Tan, S., Wang, S., Liao, X., Li, W.: Overview of Chinese opinion analysis evaluation 2013. In: Proceedings of Chinese Opinion Analysis Evaluation 2013, Taiyuan, China, pp. 5–33 (2013)
12. Tan, S., Wang, S., Xu, W., Yan, X., Liao, X.: Overview of Chinese opinion analysis evaluation 2014. In: Proceedings of Chinese Opinion Analysis Evaluation 2014, Kunming, China, pp. 4–25 (2014)
13. Xu, L., Lin, H., Zhao, J.: Construction and analysis of emotional corpus. J. Chin. Inf. Process. 22(1), 116–122 (2008)
14. Xu, R., Xia, Y., Wong, K.F., Li, W.: Opinion annotation in on-line Chinese product reviews. In: Proceedings of International Conference on Language Resources and Evaluation, vol. 8, pp. 26–30 (2008)
15. Yao, Y., Wang, S., Xu, R., Liu, B., Gui, L., Lu, Q., Wang, X.: The construction of an emotion annotated corpus on microblog text. J. Chin. Inf. Process. 28(5), 83 (2014)

The Construction of a Customized Medical Corpus for Assisting Chinese Clinicians in English Research Article Writing

Xiaowen Wang[1], Yong Gao[2], and Tianyong Hao[3(✉)]

[1] School of English and Education,
Guangdong University of Foreign Studies, Guangzhou, China
55736436@qq.com
[2] Reproductive Medicine Centre,
The First Affiliated Hospital of Sun Yat-Sen University, Guangzhou, China
gaoyong9971@163.com
[3] School of Informatics,
Guangdong University of Foreign Studies, Guangzhou, China
haoty@126.com

Abstract. A great number of clinicians in mainland China are under increasing pressure to publish their research results on international journals, and they urgently need support for writing research articles in English to compensate their limited English level. Though corpus has been proved to be a useful resource to assist second language learning and writing, research on corpus-assisted medical English writing is very sparse. This paper is concerned with the construction and application of a customized medical corpus for Chinese clinicians to aid their research article writing in English. With the support of a research project, this is the first customized medical corpus built under the joint collaboration between computer-linguistic researchers and clinicians in mainland China to directly serve the actual needs of clinicians. In particular, we report a case of how urologists apply the corpus – CCUT (Customized Corpus for Urology Team) in article writing under the situated assistance of linguistic researchers. The corpus has been found useful in assisting them in choosing the word of appropriate semantic relations, finding grammatical patterns different from general English in specialized medical context, learning how to use unfamiliar medical terms and revising "Chinglish" (unidiomatic) expressions.

Keywords: Customized medical corpus · Chinese clinicians · Research article writing · CCUT

1 Introduction

Corpus, as defined by Sinclair (1995), is "a collection of pieces of language that are selected and ordered according to explicit linguistic criteria in order to be used as a sample of the language". In recent years, corpus-based researches have been increasingly applied to second language writing from pedagogical perspectives, and

© Springer International Publishing AG 2016
M. Sun et al. (Eds.): CCL and NLP-NABD 2016, LNAI 10035, pp. 241–252, 2016.
DOI: 10.1007/978-3-319-47674-2_21

concordancing is for many reasons widely regarded as a useful tool in the writing class (Yoon, 2011:131). Scholars such as Yoon (2011:130–139) have proved that specialized corpora compiled for specific genres or disciplines enable learners to discover vocabulary, word combinations and grammatical patterns. Corpora can also be a good reference resource with which learners check if a specific element of the writing is correct. However, previous studies mainly focus on practices in classroom settings, and few studies have explored how professional practitioners actually exploit the corpora in specific professional genre areas, especially medical field where linguistic support is badly needed.

In fact, clinicians in mainland China are under increasing pressure to publish their research results internationally on the most prestigious journals possible (Qiu, 2010). Assessments for job tenure and promotion require high publication outputs, as do competitive applications for research grant funding. It is almost axiomatic that this now means writing the manuscripts in English (Ammon, 2001; Belcher, 2007), and in the style of English that meets the requirements of the journals concerned (Burrough-Boenisch, 2003; Langdon-Neuner, 2007; Cargill et al., 2012). This situation suggests that a rapidly increasing number of Chinese clinicians need help to enhance their ability to write research articles in English, and a customized medical corpus could be an extremely useful resource to help them. However, so far there has not been any reported medical English corpus available for Chinese clinicians to use for this purpose, no matter in China or abroad.

Computer-linguistic researchers and clinicians in mainland China are jointly working on a project to build the first customized medical corpus directly serving the actual needs of clinicians for English research article writing in specifically targeted medical domain. As the pilot study of this project, we constructed a Customized Corpus for the Urology Team (CCUT), the target users of which are from a research group in one of the top 3A hospitals in China undertaking some natural science projects at national and provincial levels. Most of the members have had very limited practice in scientific writing in English, and some of them turn to local English experts for help, but those experts (no matter native or non-native English speakers) also have difficulties in dealing effectively with the specific language features and discourses of the medicine content. With the help of CCUT, however, linguistic researchers can help the clinicians carry out corpus-assisted English research article writing, and observe their behaviors in using the corpus. One of the team members, Dr. A, has used the CCUT under situated assistance from the linguistic researchers while writing a research article manuscript, which has latter been published on a SCI indexed journal. His behavior of using CCUT will be reported as a case below.

2   Literature Review

A considerable number of studies have been conducted on corpus use in second language teaching, especially writing instruction. Among them, most are about writing in general English (Todd, 2001; Cresswell, 2007; Gaskell and Cobb 2004; Yoon and Hirvela 2004; Yoon, 2008; Kennedy and Miceli 2010; Flowerdew, 2010), and only a few are related to writing in an ESP (English for specific purposes) field, such as computer, business, forestry, and law. In the field of forestry, Friginal (2013) investigates the use of corpora to develop the research report writing skills of college-level students enrolled in a professional forestry program. In the field of business English, Walker (2011) examines how a corpus-based study of the factors which influences collocation can help in the teaching. In the field of legal education, Hafner and Candlin (2007) explore the relationship between student use of online corpus tools and academic and professional discourse practices in a professional legal training course at The City University of Hong Kong. In the field of computer science, Chang and Kuo (2011) take a corpus-based, genre-analytic approach to teaching materials development with a corpus of 60 research articles. Gavioli (2005) shows how the analysis of smaller specialized corpora can be used to heighten awareness of key lexical, grammatical or textual issues amongst learners of ESP. Although researchers focus on different aspects of corpora that could help students' writing improvement, it is commonly agreed that most students in such corpus-based teaching class find the corpus approach beneficial to students' writing practices. However, those studies are pedagogically oriented, only focusing on teaching of students in classroom settings with the help of one or more corpora. Although teaching of ESP students is supposed to be career-oriented, how professional practitioners actually make use of corpora to improve their writing in workplace are hardly touched in the literature we found. What is more, research on corpus-assisted medical English writing is even sparse.

Meanwhile, there is also a lack of medical English corpora available for Chinese clinicians. To our knowledge, there are only very few medical English corpora which can be openly used for language learning. GENIA, a corpus of articles extracted from MEDLINE database, is widely used in biomedical language processing (Kim et al., 2003). However, focusing on biological reactions concerning transcription factors in human blood cells, it only selected articles with the MeSH terms (Kim et al., 2003), so it is less applicable for clinicians in other medical fields. Other bio-medical English corpora are relatively small in size and mostly only open to limited users (Gurulingappa, 2012). In China, PCMW (Chen and Ge, 2011) is a valuable large scale English-Chinese parallel corpus of medical works, covering about 15 medical domains, such as paediatrics, gynecology, surgery, etc. Mainly targeted on the resource construction of computer (-aided) translation, it is not openly applicable to medical professionals at the moment. Other medical English corpora reported in China are mainly used for linguistic research in stylistics (Ping, 2010) or lexicology (Wang, 2008; Wang, 2010). As discussed above, so far there has not been any report about direct application of medical English corpora by clinicians in their L2 learning. In order to bridge computational-linguistic research with the clinicians' actual needs, we establish a customized medical English corpus in the present study.

3   The Construction of the Customized Medical Corpus

Inspired by Zheng (2012)'s Eco-dialogical model of interaction, we design a model for the construction of customized medical corpus. As shown in Fig. 1, clinicians provide raw data, based on which the computer-linguistic researchers design and construct the corpus customized to the clinicians' needs in their specific medical domain. Then the computer-linguistic researchers assist them in analyzing data while they write their articles, and provide step-by-step training for corpus use. Finally, the clinicians provide feedback to the constructors so that they can further adapt and improve the corpus accordingly. The clinicians and computer-linguistic researchers work together to achieve meaning perception and realize values in actual writing action in a dynamic and cyclic way.

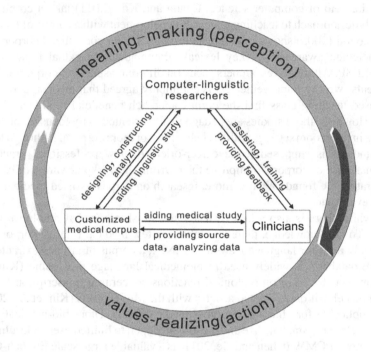

Fig. 1. Model for the construction of customized medical corpus

Specifically, the construction procedure can be divided into the following stages:

(1) Needs analysis: The computer-linguistic researchers and clinicians worked together to analyze the needs of target users through discussions and surveys so as to provide suggestions for corpus design.

(2) Data collection: The source texts were directly collected from the medical team members, which include 240 medical research articles they downloaded from the PubMed database and shared within the team as core reference readings in recent years. As the team members have the same research direction—application of stem-cell technology in the field of urology, so the source texts mainly fall in the fields of stem-cell and urology.

(3) Data cleaning and processing: Linguistic researchers converted pdf files the clinicians provided to txt format, and proofread all texts for two times. Illustrations irrelevant with the language information were deleted. Errors and unrecognizable

codes were corrected or substituted after collating with the original pdf text and consulting the urologists when necessary. A corpus of 1453138 word tokens in total was built (shown in Fig. 2).

(4) Corpus sharing on the cloud: The corpus was uploaded to the cloud platform for members in the collaborative project to share.

(5) Data application: In the application, the corpus analysis tool we chose for clinicians to use is AntConc (Anthony), a free software relatively easy to operate. Basic functions of AntConc, such as word search, KWIC display, collocates, and clusters, are introduced to the urology team members by the linguistic researchers while assisting their English writing.

(6) Feedback collection for corpus improvement: Clinicians upload their feedback to the cloud, and the computer-linguistic researchers will summarize the feedback to further adapt the corpus for their needs in the next step.

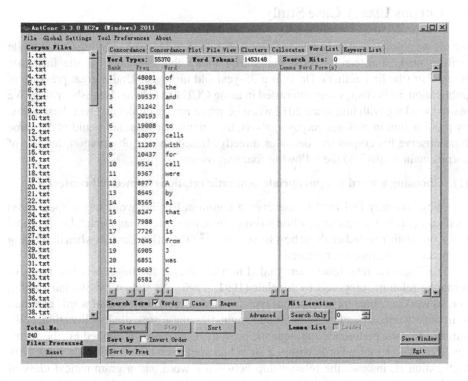

Fig. 2. The wordlist of CCUT (a screenshot in AntConc)

The corpus we constructed could be used to implement a number of functions, including generating concordance lists (key word in context), visual concordance plots, wordlists, and key wordlists, extracting collocation and colligation, extracting terminology, computing collocate salience, creating wordsketches (summary of the word's grammatical and collocational behavior) and distributional thesaurus (showing similar words in terms of grammatical and collocational behavior), and designing "minitext" (extracts of concordance list for pedagogical use). The basic function - key word in context (KWIC) is similar to the search function of some online databases such as Google Scholar, but the KWIC function can allow more complicated and flexible search to discover collocational and grammatical rules and patterns by inputting regular expressions. Moreover, the concordance results of KWIC in CCUT is much more targeted and thus more useful for clinicians since its source texts are directly related to the clinicians' own medical research fields. An example of another function - wordlist is shown in Fig. 2, in which the wordlist of CCUT is generated to show the frequency of words in the corpus, based on which linguistic researchers could further develop a syllabus of graded professional words for future English training in the targeted medical domain.

4   Corpus Use: A Case Study

Below we report a randomly selected user (Dr. A)'s experience of applying CCUT while writing medical research article manuscript under the assistance of the linguistic researcher (the first author). Dr. A is a 35-year-old urologist. Under great pressure of publication, he is always very interested in using CCUT to help his English writing. We started working with him since 2012 when he was a novice clinician. Over these years, by guiding him to perform corpus analysis, the linguistic researcher could at the same time observe his corpus use behavior directly. Based on our observation, his use of corpus mainly falls into the following four purposes:

(1) **Choosing a word of appropriate semantic relations in medical context**

Clinicians may feel hard to use even a common English word in the specialized medical context. For example, while writing a research article manuscript, Dr. A turned to the linguistic researcher about how to express "获得" (get) in English when describing the process of getting a certain cell.

The linguistic researcher then guided him to analyze the target word in terms of semantic relations proposed by Sinclair (1991, 1996). As shown by Sinclair (1996), corpus work accounts for at least four types of meaningful relations that words entertain with other words around them. In corpus linguistics, these are called: collocation, colligation, semantic preference and semantic prosody. Collocation is defined as "the occurrence of two or more words within a short space of each other" (Sinclair 1991:170). Colligation is, instead, the relationship between a word and a grammatical class of words. Semantic preference is the relationship between a word and a semantic class of words. Semantic prosody does not only have to do with the relationship between words, but it also involves the way words affect each other with their meanings. "Prosody" is applied particularly to the way in which words or expressions create an aura of meaning capable of affecting words around them (Gavioli, 2005:45).

A comparison of the selected concordance lines of "aquire" and "obtain" is shown in Table 1. The search for "acquire" in CCUT with AntConc provided 44 occurrences, showing that this is a relatively frequently used word in a medical context. However, at the collocates on the right of the node, most of the collocates were not biomedical entities, but mainly some abstract nature, characteristics or capacity of certain biomedical entities, such as "properties", "characteristics", "ability", and "expression". The search for "obtain" in CCUT provided 57 occurences. We found the semantic relations of this word have special patterns in the medical context. For collocation, it is mostly collocated with biomedical entities, such as cell, tissue, fraction, material, and gene expression profiles. For colligation, "to obtain +NP" or "be + adj. +obtain + NP" is the most salient pattern. For semantic preference, word combinations like "attempts to, able/unable to, could not, it took many years to, hard/difficult to" are associated with "obtain", which all seemed to show certain difficulty in the obtaining action. Therefore, when it comes to the semantic prosody, "obtain" has the connotational associations of "successfulness after hard efforts". All of the four scales of semantic relations of "obtain" matched Dr. A's situation, i.e., to get some cells after great efforts of scientific research, so he confirmed that "obtain" is the best word to choose, rather than "acquire". At the same time, he also made clear how to use "acquire" in other situations.

(2) **Finding medical grammatical patterns different from general English**

While writing the manuscript, Dr. A came up with another question: Should he use "mouse cell", or "mouse's cell"? By intuition he thinks "mouse's cell" is grammatically correct, but he feels like seldom seeing "mouse's cell" in medical literature reading.

To answer this question, we searched "mouse 's" in BNC, and found occurrences such as "mouse's body", "mouse's ear", "mouse's tail", "mouse's dulled wintering heart". A look into the collocates of "mouse" in BNC indicated that "'s" is its most frequently used collocate.

Table 1. Comparison of the concordance lines of "acquire" and "obtain"

Words	Concordance lines in CCUT (extract)
Acquire	regulate VE-cadherin and CD105 expression and **acquire** the capacity to generate multilineage genic Leydig cells which, in addition, rapidly **acquire** neuronal and glial properties. These fter their displacement from vessel walls, first **acquire** steroi-dogenic properties expression Marion RM, Strati K, Li H, et al. Telomeres **acquire** embryonic stem cell characteristics experience hypoxia, they dedifferentiate and **acquire** stem cell 445 neural crest-like features HIF-2a protein expression, differentiate, and **acquire** expression of SNS markers. In ypoxic o not only lose their WT function but also to **acquire** new properties, including the ability t ved ECs. ESC-derived ECs **acquire** cobblestone morphology ntrolling the risk for metastasis. RCCs usually **acquire** metastatic potential when their size
Obtain	repair the body (1), but **it took many years to** obtain hard evidence in support of this theory. ing nature of PDA, **it is nearly impossible to** obtain pure tumor tissues without a contaminati RRK2 - PD iPSC. Unfortunately, we **could not** obtain a clear signal for SNCA in immunoblots AC)-based methods **offers alternative ways to** obtain genetically corrected iPS cells. Urce of cells when primary cells **are difficult to** obtain in sufficient numbers for in vitro studies or rdiac tissues from DCM patients **are difficult to** obtain and do not survive in long-term culture. ack of cell surface markers hindered **attempts to** obtain purified SLC fractions. Once isolate is less well understood. A recent study **sought to** obtain a specic marker for peritubular myoid c repair. One of the **major problems has been to** obtain MSC populations free of hematopoietic ells. However, in these cases, we **were unable to** obtain any hES-like colonies at all. Because

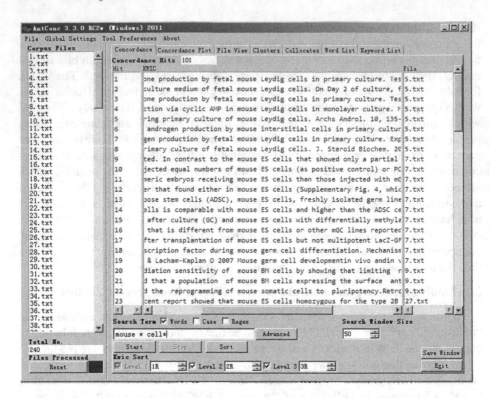

Fig. 3. The screenshot for the concordance results of "mouse * cell*" in CCUT

Surprisingly, a search for "mouse's" in CCUT showed no concordance hit at all, but a further search for "mouse * cell*" instead provided 101 occurrences (shown in Fig. 3). To make this clear, we worked out in AntConc the 2-word clusters of "mouse" sorted by frequency with "mouse" on the left in CCUT, the tops 3 expressions on the list are "mouse embryonic", "mouse model", "mouse testis", which in general English may be expressed as "mouse's embryonic...", "mouse's model", "mouse's testis".

Being aware of the difference in grammatical patterns - "mouse +NP" in medical English vs "mouse('s) + NP" in general English, Dr. A understood that he should follow the conventions in the medical context and wrote in his manuscript "mouse LCs" instead of "mouse's LCs" and "mouse testes" instead of "mouse's testes".

(3) **Learning how to use unfamiliar medical terms**

For unfamiliar medical terms, the clinicians have to firstly consult medical English dictionaries to find the potential English equivalent words, but the example sentences might be insufficient. Though CCUT is not useful in the first step of searching word-to-word equivalents, it provides more information than the dictionaries about how the word is used in context. For example, Dr. A searched an unfamiliar term - "免疫荧光染色" (immunostain) in the new Comprehensive Medical English Dictionary (KingYee Technology Ltd., 2008), a dictionary regarded as the most comprehensive and useful medical English dictionary in his circle, but he only found its equivalent English expression "immunostain" with no example sentence at all. So we searched "immunostain" in CCUT. The results are shown below (Fig. 4).

Concordance Results 1: immunostain

Concordance Hits 6

Hit	KWIC	File
1	(oncocytoma). Metastatic RCC The immunostain was performed on routine large tissue	67.txt
2	:ioned normal tissues, but the immunostain was performed on frozen tissue	67.txt
3	to CD31, CD34, and PAL-Ealso do not immunostain all intratumor microvessels. Wang et	91.txt
4	ımor microvessels and preferentially immunostain activated or proliferating endothelia	91.txt
5	; depict vascular cavities. (f) CD31 immunostain of endothelial cells lining a large c	140.txt
6	ıd albumin-cremutant livers and CD31 immunostain of small vessels (arrows). VHL-defici	140.txt

Fig. 4. The concordance results of "immunostain" in CCUT

Though there were only 6 occurrences, we noticed the recurrent pattern of "the immunostain was performed on…", so Dr. A learned to use this pattern to make his sentence in the manuscript. By analyzing concordances, corpus users can grasp the meanings and functions of the structures that were presented to them much better than when they were presented in the traditional fashion (Gavioli, 2005:28).

(4) **Revising "Chinglish" (unidiomatic) expressions**

The word combination Dr. A used for a subtitle in his manuscript was originally "in vitro Nes-GFP + cells differentiation", but he realized it might be "Chinglish" (unidiomatic), and asked whether he needed to revise it in a more idiomatic way. To check whether this expression is unidiomatic, a search of "differentiation capacity" was generated, with 11 occurrences found (Shown in Fig. 5).

Concordance Results 2: differentiation capacity

Concordance Hits 11

Hit	KWIC	File
1	NPC markers and differentiation capacity (data not shown). This suggests that, und	71.txt
2	. Multilineage differentiation capacity of Gl-MSC As the major de ning character	75.txt
3	and multilineage differentiation capacity. (a) Microscopy images documenting the	76.txt
4	act multilineage differentiation capacity even after three months in culture (n =	76.txt
5	d their in vitro differentiation capacity, forming osteoblasts, adipocytes and chon	115.txt
6	trol (line). B. Differentiation capacity of human MSCs (upper panels) and IMSCs (lo	115.txt
7	d their in vitro differentiation capacity, forming osteoblasts, adipocytes and chon	194.txt
8	trol (line). B. Differentiation capacity of human MSCs (upper panels) and IMSCs (lo	194.txt
9	to determine the differentiation capacity of in vivo non-obese diabetic/severe co	208.txt
10	markers; and 3) differentiation capacity to osteogenic, adipogenic and chondrogenic	217.txt
11	and loose their differentiation capacity only after a few passages (our unpublished	217.txt

Fig. 5. The concordance results of "differentiation capacity" in CCUT

In all the 11 instances, the word on the left of "differentiation capacity" were all attributive adjuncts, such as "in vitro", "multilineage", and no expression of "[cell name] + differentiation capacity" was found. Therefore, the word "Nes-GFP$^+$ cells" might not be suitable to be put before "differentiation capacity". From Line 5 and 7, we found that "in vitro" could be put before "differentiation capacity" to be an attributive adjunct, so we decided to use the word combination of "in vitro differentiation capacity".

As for where to put "Nes-GFP$^+$ cells", in the concordance lines we found "differentiation capacity +of +[entity name]" in Line 2, 6, 8, 9 (in case the entity differentiates) and "differentiation capacity + to + [entity name]" in Line 10 (in case the entity is the result of differentiation). So Dr. A revised the original subtitle "in vitro Nes-GFP$^+$ cells differentiation capacity" to "in vitro differentiation capacity of Nes-GFP$^+$ cells".

As the Chinese language is characteristic of parataxis (words are connected by implicit coherence), and the English language is characterized by hypotaxis (words are connected by explicit cohesive devices), the missing of the connective "of" in the original subtitle might be caused by the negative transfer from Chinese. Just as this case shows, clinicians can use the CCUT corpus to explore "idiomatic" areas of language and even repair the negative transfer from their mother language.

5   Discussion

The corpus under our construction is different from other kinds of non-customized corpora traditionally built by the corpus-linguists in that: (1) It is jointly developed by medical and computer-linguistic researchers; (2) Though it could also be used for linguistic analysis, it is user-oriented in that its primary function is to serve the clinicians; (3) Its source texts are provided by the clinicians so that it is highly related to the specific research domain of the users; (4) Computer-linguistic researchers not only help the clinicians build the corpus, but also provide situated assistance, corpus use training, and guidance for data analysis step by step to make sure the users can really make effective use of the corpus; (5) Computer-linguistic researchers collect user feedbacks from the clinicians and further develop the corpus according to target users' needs; (6) While the computer-linguistic researchers play the roles of designers, constructors, data analysts, assistants and trainers, the clinicians play the roles of source providers, main corpus users, data analysts, feedback providers, and trainees. The relationships among the computer-linguistic researchers, clinicians and corpus are dialogical and dynamic.

With the joint efforts of the computer-linguistic researchers and the clinicians, the customized corpus has been proved to provide targeted language learners with invaluable information, especially the recurrent, conventional lexical and syntactic patterns in specialized context, the usage of specialized words that could not be found sufficiently described in dictionaries, and the ways to test one's intuitions so as to repair certain negative transfer from Chinese to English. In the situated guidance, it is essentially important for linguistic researchers to guide the clinicians to gradually increase their sensitivity and awareness of the conventions in the medical context through the clues provided by the corpus. If such kind of training keeps running, the clinicians could enhance their language intuitions, and get more and more familiar with the discourse of their specialized community. However, one thing worth noting is how to transfer "from maximum guidance to maximum independence" (Gavioli, 2005:127) so that the clinicians can be independent analyzers finally. After the clinicians get familiar enough with the corpus in the situated guidance, training workshops will be organized to summarize the ways of corpus use, and multi-media demo videos, guide books will be offered to help them.

There are some limitations for the current preliminary study. The ways of application are still limited, and empirical evaluations need to be collected after larger-scale application. As the pilot study for our project on the customized medical English corpus, CCUT is limited to the domain of stem cell and urology. As the research goes, our project will extend the customized medical corpus to include more medical domains.

6 Conclusions

This paper discusses the construction of customized medical corpus CCUT and shows how urologists from the medical research team applied CCUT to aid their research article manuscript writing in English. With the situated guidance of the linguistic researchers, CCUT has been effectively used to help clinicians choose the word of appropriate semantic relations, find grammatical patterns different from general English in specialized medical context, make use of unfamiliar medical terms and revise unidiomatic expressions. Our case study presented that it is not only possible but also worthwhile to introduce clinicians to corpus linguistics through a dialogical, cyclic and goal-oriented collaboration between the computer-linguistic researchers and clinicians on customized corpus.

Acknowledgements. This work was supported by the Science and Technology Project of Guangdong Province, China (2016A040403113) and Innovative School Project in Higher Education of Guangdong, China (GWTP-LH-2014-02).

References

Ammon, U.: The Dominance of English as a Language of Science. Effects on Other Languages and Language Communities. Mouton de Gruyter, New York (2001)

Belcher, D.D.: Seeking acceptance in an English-only research world. J. Second Lang. Writ. **16**(1), 1–22 (2007)

Burrough-Boenisch, J.: Shapers of published NNS research articles. J. Second Lang. Writ. **12**, 223–243 (2003)

Cargill, M., et al.: Educating Chinese scientists to write for international journals: addressing the divide between science and technology education and English language teaching. Engl. Specif. Purp. **31**, 60–69 (2012)

Chang, C., Kuo, C.: A corpus-based approach to online materials development for writing research articles. Engl. Specif. Purp. **30**, 222–234 (2011)

Chen, X.X., Ge, S.L.: The construction of English-Chinese parallel corpus of medical works based on self-coded python programs. Procedia Eng. **24**, 598–603 (2011)

Cresswell, A.: Getting to 'know' connectors? Evaluating data-driven learning in a writing skills course. In: Hidalgo, E., Quereda, L., Juan, S. (eds.) Corpora in the Foreign Language Classroom. Rodopi, Amsterdam (2007)

Flowerdew, L.: Using corpora for writing instruction. In: O'Keeffe, A., McCarthy, M. (eds.) The Routledge Handbook of Corpus Linguistics, pp. 444–457 (2010)

Friginal, E.: Developing research report writing skills using corpora. Engl. Specif. Purp. **32**, 208–220 (2013)

Gaskell, D., Cobb, T.: Can learners use concordance feedback for writing errors? System **3**, 2301–2319 (2004)

Gavioli, L.: Exploring Corpora for ESP Learning. John Benjamins B.V, Amsterdam (2005)

Gurulingappa, H.: Development of a benchmark corpus to support the automatic extraction of drug-related adverse effects from medical case reports. J. Biomed. Inf. **45**(5), 885–892 (2012)

Hafner, C.A., Candlin, C.N.: Corpus tools as an affordance to learning in professional legal education. J. Engl. Acad. Purp. **6**, 303–318 (2007)

Kennedy, C., Miceli, T.: Corpus-assisted creative writing: introducing intermediate Italian learners to a corpus as a reference resource. Lang. Learn. Technol. **14**(1), 28–44 (2010)

Kim, J.-D., Ohta, T., Tateisi, Y., Tsujii, J.: Genia corpus-semantically annotated corpus for bio-textmining. Bioinformatics **19**(suppl 1), 180–182 (2003)

The new Comprehensive Medical English Dictionary. KingYee Technology Co., Ltd., Beijing (2008). http://www.medscape.com.cn/

Langdon-Neuner, E.: Let them write English. Revista do Colégio Brasileiro de Cirurgiões **34**(4), 272–276 (2007)

Ping, W.: Corpus-based contrastive study on stylistics of foreign and Chinese medical research article abstracts in English. J. Xianning Univ. **30**(3), 90–91 (2010)

Qiu, J.: Publish or perish in China. Nature **463**, 142–143 (2010)

Sinclair, J.: Corpus, Concordance, Collocation. OUP, Oxford (1991)

Sinclair, J.: Corpus typology: a framework for Classification. In: Melchers, G., Warren, B. (eds.) Studies in Anglistics, pp. 17–34. Almquist and Wiksell International, Stockhom (1995)

Sinclair, J.: The search for units of meaning. Textus **9**, 75–106 (1996)

Walker, C.: How a corpus-based study of the factors which influence collocation can help in the teaching of business English. Engl. Specif. Purp. **30**, 101–112 (2011)

Wang, L.: Application of corpus and concordance tools to medical English vocabulary teaching. China Med. Educ. Technol. **22**(5), 427–430 (2008)

Wang, S.: Corpus-based medical English vocabulary teaching. J. Gansu Coll. TCM **2010**(6), 59–61 (2010)

Todd, R.W.: Induction from self-selected concordances and self-correction. System **29**, 91–102 (2001)

Yoon, H., Hirvela, A.: ESL student attitudes towards corpus use in L2 writing. J. Second Lang. Writ. **13**, 257–283 (2004)

Yoon, H.: More than a linguistic reference: the influence of corpus technology on L2 academic writing. Lang. Learn. Technol. **12**, 31–49 (2008)

Yoon, C.: Concordancing in L2 writing class: an overview of research and issues. J. Engl. Acad. Purp. **10**, 130–139 (2011)

Zheng, D.: Caring in the dynamics of design and languaging: exploring second language learning in 3D virtual spaces. Lang. Sci. **34**, 543–558 (2012)

Information Retrieval and Question Answering

Topic-Sentiment Mining from Multiple Text Collections

Qifeng Zhu$^{(\boxtimes)}$ and Fang Li

Department of Computer Science and Engineering, Shanghai Jiao Tong University,
Shanghai 200240, China
zhu527812567@foxmail.com

Abstract. Topic-sentiment mining is a challenging task for many applications. This paper presents a topic-sentiment joint model in order to mine topics and their sentimental polarities from multiple text collections. Text collections are represented with a mixture of components and modeled via the hierarchical Dirichlet process which can determine the number of components automatically. Each component consists of topic words and its sentiments. The model can mine topics with different proportions and different sentimental polarities as well as one positive and one negative topic for each collection. Experiments on two text collections from Chinese news media and microblog show that our model can find meaningful topics and their different sentimental polarities. Experiments on Multi-Domain Sentiment Dataset show that our model is better than the JST-alike models on parameter settings for topic-sentiment mining.

Keywords: Text mining · Topic modeling · Sentiment analysis · Hierarchical dirichlet process

1 Introduction

With the rapid development of Web 2.0, detecting topics and sentiments from the explosion of digitalized text stream of different media or different collections has become an important task. When some event happens, traditional media and social media spread the information about the event very fast. People wish to know what are the topics and their sentimental polarities, not only from the traditional media but also from many social media. There are also many product reviews collections. People want to know what are the topics and their polarities, which are valuable information when they buy some products.

A class of probabilistic topic models [1] has been developed to automatically cluster, index and find those underlying topics from large text collections. A document is assumed as a mixture of components or topics in these mixture models, whereas a topic is represented as a distribution over words. Sentiment analysis [11] aims to reveal what people think about an event or a product and so on. It focuses not only on a sentence, or a document, but also on a collection.

M. Sun et al. (Eds.): CCL and NLP-NABD 2016, LNAI 10035, pp. 255–266, 2016.
DOI: 10.1007/978-3-319-47674-2_22

This paper presents a model to represent topic-sentiment components, which uses the hierarchical Dirichlet process (HDP) [15] to mine topics and their corresponding sentiment polarities from multiple collections. For example, suppose that there are two product review collections; one is about DVDs and the other is about electronic products. Using the proposed model, one can answer:

– What are the main topics in these two collections?
– What are the sentiment polarities towards these topics?
– What are the differences among DVDs and Electronics reviews?

The proposed model has the ability to:

– Determine automatically the number of underlying topics for different text collections. Other topic models such as the latent Dirichlet allocation (LDA) [2] need to specify the number of topics before using it;
– Reduce the dimensions and pre-allocations of model parameters and latent variables. It does not need to allocate two or more dimensions as found in other previous works like [7,9], where the number of topic will be not reasonable for some cases.
– Inference the topics and their sentiment polarities together. People can compare the differences of the topics and their sentimental polarities among multiple collections.

In the following, we first discuss about the related work, then our model and finally the experiments.

2   Related Work

Many researches focuses on topics and sentiments jointly, either mining or modeling [4,7,9,10,12,13]. Among them, three kinds of models need to be mentioned here.

Different Viewpoints Discovery. For any issue, there are positive and negative viewpoints. Paul et al. [13] used a multi-faceted joint model to mine "for" and "against" viewpoints from opinionated text collections, such as editorials about the Israel-Palestine conflict. A document is assumed as a mixture of multi-dimensional components: a sentiment dimension and a topic (or aspect) dimensions. Fang et al. [5] proposed a model to regard topic and opinion as two aspects of multiple collections. Topics are the same across different text collections, while the opinions are specific to each collection. They set the same number of topics and opinions on different collections, while it is not always the same in reality.

Joint Sentiment Topic Model. Lin and He [9] proposed a joint sentiment topic model (JST) for unsupervised sentiment classification. It treats each component in the document as sentiment-topic-specific. Each sentiment has the same number of topics. A model selection problem was raised whether the sentiment-topic distribution shall be modeled as per-document distribution or per-collection distribution in that paper. The subsequent works [4,7,10] have made different choices. In this paper, the document-level topic distributions are generated by the collection-level ones using the HDP and thus it automatically makes the suitable decision for each document.

Topic Sentiment Mixture Model. Mei et al. [12] built a supervised model for mining sentiments associated with Weblogs. In the model a document is composed of several themes. Each theme consists of the positive, negative and neutral contents. A background component was also used to capture common words alongside these themes. They used a training collection with topic and sentiment labels for each document to learn the positive and negative sentiment models. Our model adopts the topic sentiment mixture with HDP, only uses sentiment lexicons as the sentiment prior, and treats the common words as a part of a component.

3 Our Model

A document is modeled as a mixture of several components. The number of components is determined by the underlying document collections. Instead of modeling a component as a Dirichlet-Multinomial for words like other topic models, our model treats the component itself as a mixture to be estimated. Each component consists of topic words, sentiment words, and some other (background) words in order to compose a human-readable document (named white noise). In our model each component consists of four parts: **topics**, **positive words**, **negative words**, and **white noise**. Each word is associated with a **component**, and a **label** to indicate a part of the component. A word in a document may serve as a topical word, a positive word, a negative word, or a white noise word. Sentiment words are recognized by a sentiment dictionary. In this case, the model can capture topics and sentiment polarity associated with topics.

We assume that different text collections refer to the same event, the same type of collections or things[1]. There are some assumptions for the model:

- Different text collections share the same topic words with different proportions (including zero) and different sentimental polarities towards each topic.
- Different collections have their own positive and negative word distributions.

3.1 Topic-Sentiment Model for Text Collections

Table 1 lists some important notations in this paper. Other notations for a model, such as the prior hyper-parameters, are omitted here for simplicity. They will be stated when they are used.

---

[1] These collections may vary a lot in the content, but refer to similar topics.

Table 1. Major notations used in this paper

Notation	Meaning	Example
Topic θ_t	Topic	Love story dvd
Pos θ_p	Positive words	Cool great wonderful
Neg θ_n	Negative words	Bad terrible ugly
O θ_o	White noise	
δ	Component	
c	Collection index	$1, 2, \ldots$
j	Document index	$1, 2, \ldots$
i	Word index	$1, 2, \ldots$
π	Component proportion	π_0, π_c, π_{cj}
τ	Label proportion	$\tau_t, \tau_p, \tau_n, \tau_o$
z	Component assignment	
l	Label assignment	t, p, n, o

The model for two collections J_1 and J_2 is illustrated in Fig. 1 with parameters. The generative process can be described as follows,

1. (a) draw a countable sequence of topics – $\{\theta_t\}$
   (b) draw positive word distributions, each collection owns one – $\{\theta_p\}$
   (c) draw negative word distributions, each collection owns one – $\{\theta_n\}$
   (d) draw a white noise word distribution – θ_o
2. draw the proportions $\{\tau\}$ for each collection and form the components $\{\delta\}$ as a mixture using topics, positive words, negative words, white noise with the proportions $\{\tau\}$
3. draw a Dirichlet process over the components as the top level mixture distributions, emitting the proportion π_0 and the component number K
4. draw a Dirichlet process over π_0 for each collection c, emitting $\{\pi_c\}$
5. draw a Dirichlet process over π_c for each document in every collection, emitting $\{\pi_{cj}\}$
6. for each word in every document,
   (a) draw the component number and the label according to π_{cj} and τ jointly: z, l
   (b) draw the word according to the selected word distribution indexed by z, l.

Word distribution θs are modeled as Dirichlet distributions over word vocabulary with hyperparameters $\{\beta\}$. Positive and negative words specified by a sentiment lexicon $\{\lambda\}$. The positive words will not be generated by the negative sentimental topic and vice versa. Dirichlet prior is also applied to τ with hyperparmeters ς. The hierarchical Dirichlet process is parameterized by $\gamma, \alpha_0, \alpha_1$ respecting top, collection level and document level. The inference of this model consists of the posterior representation sampler of HDP [14,15] and the resampling for z, l by their marginal distributions.

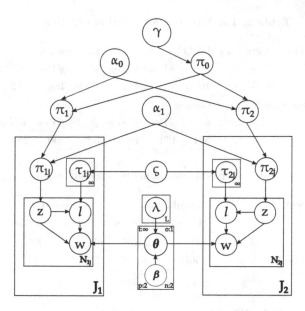

Fig. 1. Model for mining topics and their sentiment polarities (two collections)

4 Experiments

4.1 Experimental Setup

Data Description. There are two kinds of datasets in our experiments. One dataset is the Multi-Domain Sentiment Dataset (MDS)[2] used for sentiment classification [3]. Each domain in the dataset is regarded as a document collection. DVD vs. Electronics domains and Games vs. Software domains are regarded as two multiple collections in the experiments. The detailed description is presented in Table 2. The other dataset is about two events from News and Sina Weibo in China. News collection was crawled from three Chinese news websites (Sina, iFeng, Tencent) during the end of 2011. Weibo collection was collected from Sina Weibo API using event keywords at the same time. There are two events; the first one ("Occupy Wall Street") happened in USA in the year of 2011, whereas the second one ("Little Yue Yue") happened in the south of China in the year of 2011. The detailed information of the dataset is shown in Table 3. Both events attracted many Chinese microblog users as well as traditional news media and lasted about two weeks. This dataset will be referred as EVENT. We use it for result presentation.

Aim of the Experiments:

– whether the topics are correct for the text collections;
– whether the sentiment analysis works on the text collections.

---

[2] http://www.cs.jhu.edu/~mdredze/datasets/sentiment/.

Table 2. The MDS domains used in experiments

DVD vs electronics	DVD			Electronics		
	#	#Pos	#Neg	#	#Pos	#Neg.
	1000	519	481	1000	488	512
Game vs software	Games			Software		
	#	#Pos	#Neg	#	#Pos	#Neg.
	561	483	78	585	300	285

Table 3. Event-related microblogs and news

Events	Microblogs		News reports	
	#Blogs	#Words	#Reports	#Words
Occupy wall street	83K	2,250K	269	90K
Little Yue Yue	150K	4,200K	123	71K

Model Settings. The Dirichlet hyperparameter over words for each word distribution β is set to 0.01 as in [9,10]. The Dirichlet hyperparameter ς is set as follows: the proportions among topic, sentiment, white noise have a uniform prior; the proportions between positive and negative have a Dirichlet (**0.5**). This makes the model capture the positive and negative words/sentiment of a document. The HDP hyperparameters $\gamma, \alpha_0, \alpha_1$ are chosen in range $[1, 10]$ empirically. We use the emotion ontology constructed by DUTIR[3] [16] for Chinese (regarding "happy", "like" as positive sentiments and "angry", "dislike", "fear", "sad" as negative sentiments) and the HowNet's words for sentiment analysis[4] for English as the sentiment lexicons $\{\lambda\}$.

4.2   Evaluation Metrics

In order to evaluate the correctness of topics mined from multiple collections, we design a human evaluation method. A topic is represented with the top 10 words. Each student was asked to give a score for each topic mined from the multiple collections: 2 for clear, valuable topics, 1 for somewhat meaningful topics, 0 for no meaning, but appear in these texts, −1 for incomprehensible ones and −2 for wrong ones. As stated in [6], negative values up to 0 suggest being a failure while positive scales suggest degree of success. They were asked to give a meaningful phrase for each topic as the golden standard. Seven students joined the evaluation process. The Krippendorff's α-value [8] among the seven

---

[3] http://ir.dlut.edu.cn/EmotionOntologyDownload.aspx (in Chinese).
[4] http://keenage.com/html/c_bulletin_2007.htm (in Chinese).

evaluators is 0.68. We use two metrics: Grade and Accuracy. Grade is the average score for each topic evaluated by students. The accuracy is calculated in the following:

$$\text{Accuracy} = \frac{\#[g_k \geq 1]}{\#k}, \tag{1}$$

where k indices topics and g_k is the grade for each topic.

4.3 Topic Evaluation

The evaluation results are shown in Table 4. The average grade is above zero and hence it means some degree of success. "Game vs. Software" and "Little Yue Yue" have a grade 1, which means meaningful topics. The low accuracy for "DVD vs. Electronics" is due to the fact that there are topics like "get, make, give, look, feel" and "one, time, two, little, never", which are considered incorrect by the human judges. The uniform prior among topic, sentiment, and white noise may be not suitable for that collection. For the event "Occupy Wall Street", since there are topics such as advertisements of losing weight (Table 5 No. 5), the grade is low.

Table 4. Topic evaluation

Multi-collection	#Topics	Grade	Accuracy
DVD vs. electronics	6	0.50	0.50
Game vs. software	9	1.0	0.67
Occupy wall street	9	0.24	0.56
Little Yue Yue	9	1.4	0.89

4.4 Topic-Sentiment Evaluation

We use the EVENT dataset for topic-sentiment evaluation. As the golden standard is not available, we represent topics and collection-specific sentiment words using top-10 words. The results are listed in Tables 5 and 6 with English translation via Google. Each row represents a topic, the right two columns are the proportion and the sentiment for each topic, where '+' for positive topics, '−' for negative topics and 'X' for neutral ones for each collection. A topic k is considered to be positive (negative) in a collection c if the sum of the positive and negative proportion, $\tau_{c(p+n)}(k)$ is not zero and the ratio of the positive (negative) proportion to $\tau_{c(p+n)}(k)$ is greater than 0.6 (considering the estimation variance). Otherwise, the topic is considered as neutral.

Table 5 shows the result from the event of "Occupy Wall Street". News reports focused more on the factual topics, such as No. 4 and No. 6 with the proportion of 0.241 and 0.234 respectively, both with the neutral sentimental polarity. On the other collection, Microblogs had the positive polarity towards topics No. 3, No. 4, No. 6 and No. 7. Topics of No. 1, 5, 7 and 9 are not in the News reports since their topic proportions are 0. The last four rows are positive and negative topics mined from news and microblogs. The positive topic of Microblog is "revolution", "support" and so on. The positive topic of news reports is "support", "development", "response" and so on.

Table 5. Topics mined from "Occupy Wall Street"

No.	Topics Mined in "Occupy Wall Street"	Microblog	News
1	诺基亚, 倾世, 华尔街, 惊心, 吴奇隆, 旅行, 微博去, 加油站, 皇妃, 肯德基 (Nokia, dumping the World, Wall Street, startling, Nicky, travel, go microblogging, gas stations, Princess, Kentucky)	0.079/X	0/X
2	运动, 金融, 社会, 政府, 认为, 民众, 总统, 人们, 政治, 冻结 (sports, financial, social, government, believe, the people, the president, people, politics, freezing)	0.055/X	0.085/X
3	美国, 华尔街, 占领, 国家, 金融, 问题, 人民, 没有, 世界, 政府 (United States, Wall Street, occupation, country, financial, issues, people, no, world, government)	0.188/+	0.196/X
4	华尔街, 占领, 中国, 美国, 知道, 公司, 报道, 人民, 运动, 已经 (Wall Street, occupation, China, the United States, knowing, company, reported, the people, the movement, already)	0.297/+	0.241/X
5	华尔街, 减肥, 乔布斯, 分享, 综合症, 命运, 郑州, 诺贝尔, 传说, 非常 (Wall Street, lose weight, Jobs, sharing, syndrome, fate, Zhengzhou, Nobel, legends, very)	0.088/X	0/X
6	活动, 纽约, 组织, 城市, 记者, 民众, 示威者, 表示, 示威, 影响 (events, New York, organization, city, reporters, people, demonstrators, said, protest, impact)	0.057/+	0.234/X
7	步步, 中国队, 转弯, 脑筋, 远去, 心计, 势力, 女友, 惊心, 控制 (step by step, the Chinese team, turning, brains, away, scheming, forces, girlfriend, startling, control)	0.052/+	0/X
8	华尔街, 苹果, 经济, 10, 可能, 第一, 发表, iPhone, 评论, 进行 (Wall Street, apple, economic, 10, maybe, first, published, iPhone, review, carried out)	0.109/X	0.090/X
9	日报, 乔布斯, 苹果, 创始人, 华尔街, 老爷, 蜡笔小新, 飞鹰, 幼儿园, 产品 (daily, Steve Jobs, Apple, founder, Wall Street, sir, Crayon, Eagle, nursery, products)	0.074/X	0/X
-	革命, 支持, 民主, 坦白, 美人, 发展, 希望, 推荐, 喜欢, 起来 (revolution, support, democracy, frankly, beauty, development, and hope, recommend, like, up)	positive	
-	危机, 鸿门宴, 贪婪, 消息, 失业, 解决, 呵呵, 抗议, 花心, 小子 (crisis, Banquet, greed, message, unemployment, solve, huh, protest, Fa, brat)	negative	
-	支持, 发展, 响应, 改革, 希望, 革命, 重要, 获得, 民主, 理解 (support, development, response, reform, hope, revolution, important, obtain, democracy, understanding)		positive
-	抗议, 游行, 危机, 不满, 贪婪, 爆发, 愤怒, 失业, 情绪, 解决 (protest, march, crisis, dissatisfaction, greed, outbreak, anger, unemployment, emotions, solve)		negative

Table 6 shows the result from the event of "Little Yue Yue". Microblog focused on the event topic with No. 2 ("incident"), No. 3 ("candles") and No. 7 ("care") because this event was first disseminated through the Microblogging platform. The news media focused more on topic No. 9 which discussed the social legal problem. News reports had the positive polarity towards topic No. 3. The positive topics of news and microblogs discussed the morality, i.e. people should help those ones who were injured in an accident.

4.5   Sentiment Evaluation

In order to evaluate the sentiment detection of our model, we introduce a method to convert topic-sentiment proportions into document sentiment predictions and compare the predictions with the sentiment labels $\{s_{cj}\}$ given in the MDS. Using our model, the positive proportion p_{cj}(pos.) and the negative proportion p_{cj}(neg.) of each document j in collection c can be calculated as:

$$p_{cj}(\text{pos./neg.}) \propto \sum_{k} \pi_{cj}(k)p_{cj}(z = k, l = \text{pos./neg.}) \qquad (2)$$

where $\pi_{cj}(k)$ is the topic proportions and $p_{cj}(z = k, l)$ is the posterior topic-sentiment for the document. The sentiment distribution of a document is calculated as a summation on topics of the product of the topic proportion and the topic-sentiment. The prediction of the document sentiment label is based on the ratio of p_{cj}(pos.) to p_{cj}(neg.). If the ratio is larger than the collection sentiment ratio calculated by the sentimental assignments, the document is positive, otherwise it is negative.

Table 6. Topics mined from "Little Yue Yue"

No.	Topics Mined in "Little Yue Yue"	Microblog	News
1	孩子, 小悦悦, 难道, 父母, 身边, 社会, 国人, 知道, 分享, 关注 (children, Little Yue Yue, do, parents, side, society, people, know, share, concerns)	0.054/X	0.047/X
2	小悦悦, 事件, 发生, 问题, 司机, 救人, 觉得, 父母, 女孩, 回复 (Little Yue Yue, incident, occurred, the problem, the driver, save, find, parents, girl, reply)	0.081/X	0.079/X
3	小悦悦, 蜡烛, 司机, 碾压, 走好, 视频, 广东, 民族, 第一, 博文 (Little Yue Yue, candles, drivers, rolling, take a good, video, Guangdong, ethnic, first, Bowen)	0.090/X	0.081/+
4	妈妈, 陈贤妹, 广州, 医院, 电话, 记者, 悦悦, 阿姨, 网友, 昨日 (mom, Chen Xian Mei, Guangzhou, hospitals, telephone, reporter, Yue Yue, aunts, friends, yesterday)	0.058/X	0/X
5	一路, 蜡烛, 走好, 世界, 良心, 别人, 离开, 车来车往, 蜡烛, 没有 (way, candles, take a good, world, conscience, others, leave, the car to drive to, candles, no)	0.051/X	0/X
6	大家, 看到, 责任, 中国, 已经, 良知, 真的, 一些, 所有, 评论 (we, see, responsibility, China, already, conscience, really, some, all, comments)	0.073/X	0.065/X
7	停止, 人们, 现在, 关心, 社会, 关怀, 路人, 没有, 中国人, 一下 (stop, people, now, care, social care, passers-by, no, the Chinese people, about)	0.077/X	0.058/X
8	蜡烛, 小悦悦, 反思, 今天, 保护, 新闻, 大家, 事件, 一直, 一起 (candles, Little Yue Yue, reflection, today, protecting, news, everyone, events, has, together)	0.063/X	0.048/X
9	法律, 社会, 出来, 事件, 10, 行为, 小悦悦, 认为, 美国, 感觉 (legal, social, out of, the event, 10, acts, Little Yue Yue, think, United States, feel)	0.065/X	0.100/X
-	道德, 天堂, 希望, 帮助, 见义勇为, 教育, 温暖, 其实, 相信, 起来 (morality, heaven, hope, help, courageous, education, warm, in fact, believe, up)	positive	
-	冷漠, 悲剧, 肇事, 可怜, 谴责, 见死不救, 冷血, 无情, 漠视, 悲哀 (indifference, tragedy, accident, poor, condemned, refused to help, cold-blooded, ruthless, disregard, sorrow)	negative	
-	道德, 见义勇为, 先生, 建设, 救助, 希望, 一定, 帮助, 精神, 重要 (moral, courageous, sir, construction, relief, hope, certainly, help, spiritual, important)		positive
-	肇事, 冷漠, 见死不救, 抢救, 谴责, 逃逸, 事故, 严重, 悲剧, 遭遇 (accident, apathy, refused to help, rescue, reprimand, escape, accident, serious, tragic, encounter)		negative

The accuracy results are shown in Table 7. In the "Game" domain the number of negative documents is far less than the number of positive documents and the accuracy of the negative in "Game" is low. Experiments also show that the performance of "Software" domain is not affected when modeling together. The model does not propagate the label-bias problem in one collection to the other collection.

Table 7. Sentiment evaluation: accuracy

Sentiment	DVD	Electronics	Game	Software
Positive	0.633	0.592	0.915	0.632
Negative	0.613	0.639	0.205	0.612
Overall	0.624	0.613	0.594	0.624

4.6   Comparison with JST Model

Both JST and our model extract topics with sentimental information; the JST in [10] find topics under positive, negative and neutral labels, and our model find topics with positive, negative proportions. We compare the results obtained from these two models based on the same MDS dataset.

Sentiment Analysis Comparison. Table 8 gives the accuracy comparison between our method, a lexicon method and the JST in [10]. Our result is better than the method based on the lexicon. The number of topics in JST is always a multiple of three labels. However, in our model, the number of topics is varied. According to [10], the number of topics under each label with the best classification is 15 on "DVD" but 1 on "Electronics". Our experimental result suggests the number of topics for both collections is 5. JST is designed for one collection and sets the number of topics for the sentiment classification while our work is proposed to choose the number of content topics in multi-collections and infer their sentiment polarities alongside.

Table 8. Sentiment analysis comparison (accuracy)

Methods	DVD	Electronics
Lexicon (shown in [10])	0.592	0.586
JST [10]	0.695 (K = 15)	0.726 (K = 1)
Ours	0.624 (K = 5)	0.613 (K = 5)

Topic Comparison. Our model can mine topics with different sentimental polarity and positive and negative topics for each collection. JST model mined each topic with the positive and negative topics. Their topic words are mixed with sentimental words. The result of both models are quite different. However we made the experiments on the same dataset and select some mined topics for comparison according to [10]. Tables 9 and 10 are some results mined from DVD and Electronics domain. The first two lines are sentiment distributions found by our model, the third line is a topic found by our model with its sentiment polarity in brackets, and the fourth and fifth lines are the topics of JST from [10]. JST models the same number of topics under the positive, negative and neutral

Table 9. Topics mined from DVD

	Topic words
Positive topic (ours)	Like just good really even first great well love best
Negative topic (ours)	Bad old hard trying boring used black understand wrong poor
Topic (ours)	Movie film see people think know story made life say [neutral]
Positive topic (JST)	Action good fight right scene chase hit art martial stunt
Negative topic (JST)	Horror scari bad evil dead blood monster zombi fear scare

Table 10. Topics mined from Electronics

	Topic words
Positive topic (ours)	Just sound like good great even quality well first really
Negative topic (ours)	Used bad small hard old poor trying low expensive change
Topic (ours)	Product ipod problem player bought phone unit price headphones software [positive]
Positive topic (JST)	Mous hand logitech comfort scroll whell smooth feel accur track
Negative topic (JST)	Drive fail data complet lose failur recogn backup poorli error

sentiments. Our model has mined not only different positive and negative topics for them, but also 5 topics with different sentimental polarity. The advantage of our model is that the number of topics is generated automatically.

5   Conclusions

In this paper, we present a topic-sentiment model for multiple text collections. A document is modeled as a mixture of components. Each component consists of topics, positive and negative proportions and white noise. The HDP is used in the model for automatic selection of the number of components (topics) and reducing the dimension of parameter space used for topic-sentiment joint modeling. According to the experiments on MDS and EVENT corpus:

- The model can mine the topics and show different proportions of these topics in different collections. Some topics are shared among two collections, some topics are specific for each collection.
- The model can mine the positive and negative topics and identify the sentimental polarity towards those mined topics from each collection.

However, our model has assumed that multiple collections are discussing about the same event or the same type of topics. Each collection has only one positive and negative topic and many content topics. By setting different label proportion priors among topic words, sentimental words and white noise, we can get more fine-grained topics which is more suitable for the realistic world. The relationship between different priors and sentimental analysis will be explored in the future. We will do further experiments to analyze topics and sentiments from different media, different text collections about the same event.

References

1. Blei, D.: Probabilistic topic models. Commun. ACM **55**(4), 77–84 (2012)
2. Blei, D., Ng, A., Jordan, M.: Latent dirichlet allocation. J. Mach. Learn. Res. **3**, 993–1022 (2003)
3. Blitzer, J., Dredze, M., Pereira, F.: Biographies, bollywood, boom-boxes and blenders: domain adaptation for sentiment classification. In: Proceedings of the 45th Annual Meeting of the Association of Computational Linguistics, vol. 7, pp. 440–447. ACL, Prague, CZ (2007)
4. Cano, E., He, Y., Liu, K., Zhao, J.: A weakly-supervised Bayesian model for violence detection from social media. In: 6th International Joint Conference on Natural Language Processing (IJCNLP). ACL, Nagoya, October 2013
5. Fang, Y., Si, L., Somasundaram, N., Yu, Z.: Mining contrastive opinions on political texts using cross-perspective topic model. In: Proceedings of the Fifth ACM International Conference on Web Search and Data Mining, pp. 63–72. ACM, Seattle (2012)
6. Friedman, H.H., Amoo, T.: Rating the rating scales. J. Mark. Manag. **9**(3), 114–123 (1999)
7. Jo, Y., Oh, A.H.: Aspect and sentiment unification model for online review analysis. In: Proceedings of the Fourth ACM International Conference on Web Search and Data Mining, pp. 815–824. ACM, Hong Kong (2011)
8. Krippendorff, K.: Content Analysis: An Introduction to its Methodology. Sage Publications, Beverly Hills (1980)
9. Lin, C., He, Y.: Joint sentiment/topic model for sentiment analysis. In: Proceedings of the 18th ACM Conference on Information and Knowledge Management, pp. 375–384. ACM, Hong Kong (2009)
10. Lin, C., He, Y., Everson, R., Ruger, S.: Weakly supervised joint sentiment-topic detection from text. IEEE Trans. Knowl. Data Eng. **24**(6), 1134–1145 (2012)
11. Liu, B.: Sentiment analysis and subjectivity. In: Indurkhya, N., Damerau, F.J. (eds.) Handbook of Natural Language Processing, 2nd edn, pp. 627–666. Chapman and Hall/CRC, Boca Raton (2010)
12. Mei, Q., Ling, X., Wondra, M., Su, H., Zhai, C.: Topic sentiment mixture: modeling facets and opinions in weblogs. In: Proceedings of the 16th International Conference on World Wide Web, pp. 171–180. ACM, Banff (2007)
13. Paul, M.J., Zhai, C., Girju, R.: Summarizing contrastive viewpoints in opinionated text. In: Proceedings of the 2010 Conference on Empirical Methods in Natural Language Processing, pp. 66–76. Association for Computational Linguistics, ACL, Massachusetts (2010)
14. Teh, Y.W., Jordan, M.I.: Hierarchical Bayesian Nonparametric Models with Applications. Cambridge University Press, Cambridge (2010)
15. Teh, Y., Jordan, M., Beal, M., Blei, D.: Hierarchical dirichlet processes. J. Am. Stat. Assoc. **101**(476), 1566–1581 (2006)
16. Xu, L., Lin, H., Pan, Y., Ren, H., Chen, J.: Constructing the affective lexicon ontology. J. China Soc. Sci. Tech. Inf. **27**(2), 180–185 (2008). (In Chinese)

A New Focus Strategy
for Efficient Dialog Management

Xinqi Bao[1], Yunfang Wu[1(✉)], and Xueqiang Lv[2]

[1] Key Laboratory of Computational Linguistics, Peking University,
Beijing 100871, China
yikusitian1990@163.com, wuyf@pku.edu.cn
[2] Beijing Key Laboratory of Internet Culture
and Digital Dissemination Research, Beijing, China
lxq@bistu.edu.cn

Abstract. The dialog manager is the most important component for a dialog system, in which the dialog state tracking is crucial to a real-world system. We claim that the intractability of dialog states comes from two aspects: the large slot size in user's goal and the large candidate value size for each slot. For the first time, we propose a new focus strategy to deal with the former problem, by reducing the full slots of the user's goal into a small subset focus slot. We also implement a partition-based method to deal with the latter problem. Then we combine both strategies to take advantage of their complement property. In our experiment of a real-world application in an image purchase domain, our proposed focus strategy is far faster than both the partition method and the naïve algorithm with comparable quality.

1 Introduction

Dialog systems interact with human users via natural language to help them achieve some goals. The dialog manager is the most important component for a dialog system. Typically, it should deal with the state tracking task and system action generating task during the conversation. In the state tracking task, the dialog manager interprets what the user has said and updates some representations of the current dialog state, which encodes various dialog information including user's goal, current user's action and dialog history. Then in the action generating task, the dialog manager generates proper response action back to the user based on the current dialog state representation, which is then updated as in the first task.

In a dialog manger, the dialog state tracking is crucial because the system relies on it to know where the dialog goes and how to generate proper response. Conventional dialog managers use hand-crafted deterministic rules to interpret each dialog act and update the state. However, it is not easy to maintain a precise and accurate representation of the dialog state because there are always ambiguities and uncertainties in what the user said. What's more, natural language understanding techniques are not perfect, and thus it may cause the system misunderstanding the true goal of the user and taking a lot of efforts in error recovering.

M. Sun et al. (Eds.): CCL and NLP-NABD 2016, LNAI 10035, pp. 267–281, 2016.
DOI: 10.1007/978-3-319-47674-2_23

Statistical approaches for dialog state tracking provide an opportunity for solving the above problems in a flexible way (Young 2002). Early attempts model the dialog process as a Markov Decision Process (MDP) (Levin et al. 2000), which uses reinforcement learning for policy optimizing and provides a well-formed statistical framework allowing forward planning. However, MDP assumes fully observable dialog states and cannot deal with the uncertainty of those states. Partially Observable MDP (POMDP) (Williams 2006) assumes that the state is not directly observable that reflects the uncertainty in the interpretation of user utterances. It maintains a distribution called belief state b(s) over all possible states rather than only the most likely one, and thus it explicitly models the uncertainty of many possible dialog states, which is more robust to recognizing errors and ambiguities.

However, it is not straightforward to construct a POMDP-based dialog manager for a real-world task because maintaining a full state space distribution will be intractable. Two types of views are proposed to achieve tractable and scalable implementation of POMDP-based state tracking. The first one tries to reduce the state space complexity by factoring the dialog state into independent components. For example, in a "slot filling" task, the whole dialog state space can be factored into subspaces of independent slots whose values are required to be filled. It becomes feasible to maintain a distribution over each individual slot (Williams and Young 2007a, b). The second view is to retain a full belief state representation but only updating those most likely ones (Williams 2010). The intuition behind the second approach is that, during a conversation, most of the possible states are improbable or undistinguishable with each other, because they are not involved in the current dialog yet. So the dialog manager may safely neglect them and consider only the high probable ones to approximate the true state distribution. These two views do not conflict with each other. Actually, optimizing techniques from the second view takes advantages of careful independence assumptions related to the first view.

However, it is still not a trivial task to keep track of a full state space. For example, in a typical "slot filling" task with N slots to fill and K different candidate values for each slot, there are K^N possible value combinations. The state space size grows exponentially as N and K become large, so efficient state representation and manipulation are still crucial for a real-world application. We observe that the intractability of dialog states comes from two aspects: large factor size from state space decomposition (related to N) and large candidate value size of each factor (related to K).

The latter problem is partially resolved by clustering the undistinguishable states into partitions like Hidden Information State (HIS) model (Young et al. 2010). However, though many previous POMDP-based systems model the dialog process as a slot-filling task and factor the goal of a dialog into many slots, no work has paid attention to the first problem.

In this paper, we propose a method to solve the large factor size problem, namely dialog focus strategy. The intuition is that, not all factors of slots should be computed at a specific timestamp, and so neglecting some of them will avoid computing those beliefs of complex factors every time and thus reduce the time complexity greatly. Our strategy is more efficient and easy to implement than previous approaches. To the best of our knowledge, this is the first work to address the large factor size problem to build a tractable and scalable dialog manager. Also, we implement partition-based strategy

(Thomson and Young 2010; Young et al. 2010) into our framework to deal with the inner factor complexity. Finally, we conduct an ensemble method that combines both strategies to take advantage of their complement property. We fit our system into a real-world image purchase task, and evaluate different strategies using user simulations. Our focus strategy is far faster than the naive method and also beats the partition based strategy with comparable quality.

2 Related Work

In recent years in the field of dialog model, statistical dialog state tracking systems turn out to be more robust and scalable than hand-crafted ones (Young et al. 2010; Thomson and Young 2010). These methods try to maintain a distribution over different dialog state hypothesis to help the dialog manager choose the proper dialog strategy.

Bohus and Rudnicky (2006) train a conditional model in a discriminative fashion to estimate the distribution over a set of state hypotheses. They employ a large set of informative features to achieve high accuracy. However, they only keep track of a handful of state hypotheses thus the correct one may be discarded. Metallinou et al. (2013) exploits the structure of the dialog state hypothesis, and draws a rich set of features and further keeps a number of hypotheses-invariant features to allow an unlimited number of hypotheses.

Williams (2006) propose a POMDP model that effectively represents the uncertainty of dialog states. Later, POMDP-based models are widely used as generative approaches in different domains, such as restaurant recommendations (Jurčíček et al. 2012), sightseeing recommendations (Misu and Kawahara 2010), appointment scheduling (Georgila et al. 2010), etc. Some experiments apply it to the more difficult problem of learning negotiation policies (Heeman 2009; Georgila and Traum 2011a, b), and tutoring domains (Tetreault and Litman 2008; Chi et al. 2011).

Many efforts have been made to solve the state space exploding problem in the POMDP framework. Thomson and Young (2010) presents a method based on the loopy belief propagation algorithm to make the state distribution updating tractable. They factor the state space into different components and use the marginal of these components as features for policy optimization. A grouped form of loopy belief propagation is implemented on factor graph and provides a significant reduction in calculation time. However, it is aimed at graph structure that contains cycles rather than the structure with many parallel components like in our task.

The HIS model (Young et al. 2010) groups similar user goals into equivalence classes called partitions, based on the assumption that all of the goals in the same partition are equally probable. The partitions are refined as the dialog progresses, and they are tree-structured to take account of the dependencies defined in the domain ontology. State tracking then requires only maintaining and updating relatively fewer partitions, which can be done in a real-world system. However, they do not consider the cases when there are many slots such that the number of partitions will grow exponentially with the slot size as the dialog progresses.

3 POMDP Based Dialog Model

3.1 Basic Mathematics

We first outline the mathematics of POMDP and explain our basic POMDP-based dialog model. A partially observable Markov decision process is formally defined as $(S; A; T; R; O; G; b_0)$, where S is a set of states; A is a set of actions; T defines a transition probability $P(s_t|s_{t-1}, a_{t-1})$; R defines the expected reward $r(s_t, a_t)$; O is a set of observations; G defines an observation generating probability $P(o_t|s_{t-1}, a_{t-1})$ and b_0 is an initial belief state.

The POMDP operates as follows. At each timestamp t, the world is in an unobserved state s_t. Since s_t is not known exactly, a distribution over possible states called a belief state b_t is maintained, where $b_t(s_t)$ indicates the probability of being in a particular state s_t. The machine selects an action a_t by using its dialog policy receiving a reward r_t, and transfers to the unobserved next state s_{t+1}, where s_{t+1} depends only on s_t and a_t. The machine then receives an observation o_{t+1}, which is dependent on s_{t+1} and a_t.

3.2 Dialog Model

We now fit the POMDP into our dialog process. As in Thomson and Young (2010), the dialog state at each timestamp t is decomposed into three distinct types of information parts: the user's goal g_t, the act of the user utterance u_t and the dialog history h_t. The belief state b_t is then a joint distribution over these three components.

The user's goal encompasses the information that must be gleaned from the user in order to fulfil the task. It is further factored into several independent slots which reflect different aspects of the goal. For example, in a simple weather information system, the user's goal can be represented by 2 different slots: the city and the date. Thus for a sentence "I want to know the weather in Beijing today", the goal can be represented as {city:Beijing; date:today}. We denote the user's goal as g, with N_{goal} slots. Each slot is denoted as g_i and has N_i possible values v_{ik} ($k = 0, 1 \ldots N_i$).

The user's act u_t represents the type of dialog action. The act types we used are listed in Table 1, including 5 types of user's act and 5 types of server's act. In this paper, our goal is to investigate the belief updating strategies, so we define a simple set of act types. In the experiment, we use a SVM classifier to predict the user's act with a precision 96 %.

The dialog history h_t tracks some information relating to previous turns. We model the history h_t in two aspects: *act history* and *slot history*. The *act history* encodes the previous acts made by the user and the system, such as the most recent server's act and the frequency of each act type. The *slot history* indicates the progress on each slot, which is represented by a four-state machine, as shown in Fig. 1.

The dialog goes as follows (shown in Fig. 2). At each timestamp t, the user chooses a dialog act u_t according to $P(u_t|g, u_{t-1}, h_{t-1})$, and then he generates natural language output o_t according to the observation model $P(o_t|g, u_t)$. Next, the system chooses proper response to the user's act by some dialog policy, and updates the dialog states and goes into the next timestamp.

Table 1. The act types for user/system

Type	Description	Actor
Inform	Provide information	User/system
Yes	Confirm the system's utterance	User
No	Deny the system's utterance	User
Don't know	Do not know about information	User
Chat	Domain irrelevant chatting	User
Ask	Ask the value of some slot	System
Confirm	Confirm the value of some slots	System
List	List out candidate values of some slots	System
Pardon	Ask for repetition	System

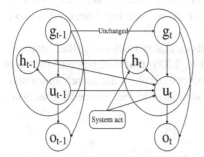

Fig. 1. The dialog process

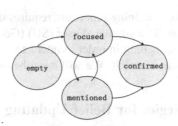

Fig. 2. The slot history in a four-state machine

The belief state for dialog history h is deterministically updated by heuristic rules. And the joint belief state $b_t(u_t, g)$ for the goal and act is calculated by Eq. (1):

$$b_t(u_t, g) \sim P(o_t|u_t, g) \cdot P(u_t|g, u_{t-1}, h_{t-1}) \cdot b_{t-1}(g) \tag{1}$$

Our model is a little different from previous works mainly in the following three aspects:

(1) Our system is designed for online dialog tasks where users type in the content by keyboard, and thus our user' inputs are textual sentences. So our model does not include Automatically Speech Recognizing (ASR) module and does not care sematic errors on ASR output.

(2) The observation o_t is the user's natural language input instead of recognizing results from front-end recognizing modules. Thus, $P(o|g, u)$ directly models the process generating utterance from unobserved states, and there is no error propagation from frontend NLP modules.

(3) In a real application, it is always assumed that the user does not change his goal in a dialog task. Most of previous work makes the same assumption. In our model, we do not denote the goal's transition for simplicity, and the user's goal is now regarded as a global hidden state to be inferred.

3.3   Policy Optimization

We select Natural Actor Critic (NAC) (Peters and Schaal 2008) to learn the optimal dialog policy, which is also adopted by (Thomson and Young 2010; Jurčíček et al. 2012; Teruhisa Misu et al. 2012).

At timestamp t, the system action set is sampled from a soft-max policy:

$$\pi(sa_t = k|\Phi, W) = \frac{e^{\sum_{i=1}^{I} \phi_i \cdot w_{ki}}}{\sum_{j=1}^{K} e^{\sum_{i=1}^{I} \phi_i \cdot w_{ji}}} \tag{2}$$

Here, $\Phi = (\phi_1, \phi_2, \phi_3 \ldots \phi_I)$ denotes the vector of feature functions representing the current dialog state and $W = (w_{11}, w_{12}, w_{13} \ldots w_{1I}, \ldots w_{JI})$ denotes the policy parameters where w_{ji} measures the contribution of i-th feature to selecting the j-th action. The NAC optimizes over policy parameter W by solving linear regression problems.

The above training procedure requires thousands of dialog tracks to gather gradient information. So a simulated user (SU) (Georgila et al. 2006) that will behave similarly to a real user is built in order to interact with the policy to explore the search space and thus facilitate learning. We will describe our user simulator in the succeeding section.

4   Strategies for Belief Updating

It becomes intractable to directly implement the proposed POMDP-based dialog process when there are many slots and many candidate values for each slot. Although the state space is decomposed into subcomponents and the user's goal is further decomposed into independent slots, we still have to maintain $\sum_{i=1}^{N_{goal}} N_i$ marginal probabilities $P(goal_i = k)$ of slot values. A straightforward naïve method is to exponentially enumerate over many possible slot value combinations as shown in Fig. 3.

Thomson and Young (2010) use the Loopy Belief (LP) propagation to improve efficiency by exploiting the dependencies between graph components. But LP does not fit into our model because there can be many slot factors creating high costs in message passing.

In the next subsections, we will introduce our belief updating strategies that alleviate computation burden in maintaining marginal probabilities of slot values and current user's act. We observe that the intractability of dialog states comes from two aspects: the large slot size and the large candidate value size for each slot. Accordingly we implement two different methods to deal with the two problems, namely partition strategy and focus strategy. Further, an ensemble method combining both strategies is proposed to achieve better performance.

//initialization
For each user goal slot g_i:
   For each candidate value v_{ij} of g_i:
$$b\_goal[i][j]_t = 0$$
For each user's act type u:
$$b\_a[u]_t = 0$$

//updating
For each user goal slot value combination:
$$g = \{g_1 = v_1, g_2 = v_2, ..., g_{N_{goal}} = v_{N_{goal}}\}$$
   For each user's act type u:
$$P(u, g) \leftarrow P(o \mid u, g) \cdot P(u \mid g, u_{t-1}, h) \cdot P_{t-1}(g)$$
     For each slot g_i:
$$b\_goal[i][v_i]_t \leftarrow b\_goal[i][v_i]_t + P(u, g)$$
$$b\_a[u]_t \leftarrow b\_a[u]_t + P(u, g)$$

//normalizing
Normalize the beliefs b_goal_t and b_a_t

Fig. 3. The naïve algorithm

4.1 Partition Strategy

To deal with the large candidate value size problem, we follow the methodology of HIS model (Young et al. 2010). At any timestamp, the candidate value space for each slot of the user's goal can be divided into a number of equivalence classes called partitions, where the members of each class are equally possible and undistinguishable with each other.

Young et al. (2010) use a tree-based structure to represent the belief state and encode the policy in a nearest neighbor fashion. In order to utilize the feature-based log-linear policy sampling as in Eq. (2), we need to maintain slot value marginal probability explicitly. Stronger dependency assumptions are made in our work.

Formally, we define values v_{i1}, v_{i2} of slot i belong to the same partition at some timestamp if and only if (1) they are of the same marginal belief (2) for any two slots value combinations g^1, g^2:

$$g_i^1 = vi1, \ g_i^2 = vi2, \ g_{-i}^1 = g_{-i}^2 \tag{3}$$

and for any user's act type u:

$$P(o|u, g^1) = P(o|u, g^2)$$

$$P(u|g^1, h) = P(u|g^2, h) \tag{4}$$

This means that the current collected information does not help distinguish between two values and so it is unnecessary to treat them separately.

Initially, all candidate values of a slot g_i are in a single root partition p_0. As the dialog progresses, this root partition is repeatedly split into smaller partitions.

If we can maintain the partitions of each slot dynamically, the belief updating process can be simplified by packaging the values of a partition and just enumerating over combinations of different partitions instead of the whole values. By assumption, we can randomly pick a value as the 'representative' of its belonged partition when calculating the joint belief $P(u, g)$, and then the marginal probability of a single value can be easily calculated by:

$$P(g_i = v) = \frac{P(partition_v)}{\#partition_v} \tag{5}$$

//split partitions
Split partitions based on the current user's input.

//initialization
For each user goal slot g_i:
    For each partition$_j$ of g_i:
      $b\_goal[i][j]_t = 0$
For each user's act type u:
    $b\_a[t]_t = 0$

//updating
For each value partition combination
$p = \{g_1 \in partition_1, g_2 \in partition_2, ..., g_{N_{goal}} \in partition_{N_{goal}}\}$
    For each user's act type u:
      Pick representative values from p
      $g = \{g_1 \in partition_1, ..., g_{N_{goal}} \in partition_{N_{goal}}\}$
      $P(u, p) \leftarrow P(o|u, g) \cdot P(u|g, h) \cdot P_{t-1}(g)$
      For each slot g_i:
        $b\_goal[i][partition_i]_t \leftarrow b\_goal[i][partition_i]_t + P(u, p)$
        $b\_a[u]_t \leftarrow b\_a[u]_t + P(u, p)$
//normalizing
Normalize the beliefs b_goal_t and b_a_t
Calculating marginal of single values

Fig. 4. The partition-based algorithm

Figure 4 illustrates the partition-based strategy. In practice, we associated each slot value with some keywords according to the domain specification documents. If a keyword is observed in user's input then the associated values are spitted from its original partition to make up a new partition. For example, for the 'usage' slot in an image purchasing domain, the word 'online' triggers the system to separate those candidate usages from the original partition.

4.2   Focus Strategy

In many dialog systems, the number of candidate values of most of slots is quite small, and so the partition-based method does not fit them well, since it has to maintain partitions for all slots, which needs quite large extra costs. What's more, we still have to calculate the marginal probability for all values of all slots, which affects the computation efficiency taken by partitions, as illustrated in Fig. 4.

In order to deal with the large slot size problem, we propose a focus-based strategy. The intuition is that when two people talk in a task-oriented conversation, they focus their attention only on a small portion that they know or are interested in. They concentrate on particular entities or particular perspectives on those entities (Grosz 1978). So in our dialog model, we assume that the user tends to mention only a small proportion of slots in a turn. He may make a response to the server's query about certain slots or provide more information for some mentioned slots, but is not likely to refer all slots in a turn, because there is too much information when the slot size becomes large that he may not have enough knowledge to explicitly express them.

For example, a user wants to know the price of a service that has a lot of relevant parameters. It is unrealistic to expect that the user provides all the relevant information at once, because it is too complex for a non-expert to grasp all the knowledge. A good solution is to make a conversation between the server and the user. The server asks for these relevant parameters one by one through many dialog turns, and the user gives an explicit answer to each question.

Formally, a subset of slots $g_{\{k\}} = \{g_{k1}, g_{k2} \cdots, g_{km}\}\}$ is called the focus slots at a timestamp, if and only if for any two slot value combinations g^1, g^2:

$$g_i^1 = g_i^2 (i \in \{k_1, k_2 \ldots, k_m\}) \tag{6}$$

and for any user's act u:

$$P(o|u, g^1) = P(o|u, g^2) = P(o|u, g_{\{k\}})$$
$$P(u|g^1, h) = P(o|g^2, h) = P(o|g_{\{k\}}, h) \tag{7}$$

This means that those slots outside of the focus set contribute little to both the current user's dialog act and the natural language output.

If we can determine the focus slot set at each timestamp, the marginal $P(g_i = v)$ can be simplified as:

$$\left(\begin{array}{ll} \sum\limits_{u=1}^{N_u} \sum\limits_{\{g_k\}_{-i}} P(o|u, \{g_{k_{-i}}, g_i = v\}) \cdot P(u|\{g_{k_{-i}}, g_i = v\}, h) \cdot P_{t-1}(g_{k_{-i}}, g_i = v) & i \in \{k_1, k_2 \ldots k_m\} \\ P_{t-1}(g_i = v) & i \notin \{k_1, k_2 \ldots k_m\} \end{array} \right) \tag{8}$$

We can see that the marginal probabilities of those slots outside of the focus set remain fixed, so there is no need to recalculate them in a turn. As a result, we only need calculating the marginal probabilities of those slots in the focus set, which only requires enumerating over values within the focus set.

//get focus set

Generate the focus slots $\{g_{k_1}, g_{k_2}, ...g_{k_m}\}$ //initialization

Same as naïve method except that only the focus slots are estimated

//updating

For each focus slots value combination

$$g_{\{k\}} = \{g_{k_1} = v_1, g_{k_2} = v_2, ..., g_{k_m} = v_{k_m}\}$$

For each user's act type u:

$$P(u, g_{\{k\}}) \leftarrow P(o \mid u, g_{\{k\}}) \cdot P(u \mid g_{\{k\}}, h) \cdot P_{t-1}(g_{\{k\}})$$

For each slot g_i in the focus set:

$$b\_goal[i][v_i]_t \leftarrow b\_goal[i][v_i]_t + P(u, g_{\{k\}})\; b\_a[u]_t \leftarrow b\_a[u]_t + P(u, g_{\{k\}})$$

//normalizing

Normalize the beliefs b_goal_t and b_a_t

Fig. 5. The focus-based algorithm

//split partitions

Split partitions based on current user's input

//get focus set

Generate the focus slots $\{g_{k_1}, g_{k_2}, ...g_{k_m}\}$

//initialization

For each user goal slot g_i in focus set

    For each partition$_j$ of g_i:

      $b\_goal[i][j]_t = 0$

    For each user's act type u:

      $b\_a[u]_t = 0$

//updating

For each partition value combination from focus slots

$p = \{g_1 \in partition_1, g_2 \in partition_2, ..., g_m \in partition_m\}$ For each user's act type u:

    Pick representative g from p:

$$g = \{g_1 \in partition_1, ..., g_m \in partition_m\}$$

$$P(u, p) \leftarrow P(o \mid u, g) \cdot P(u \mid g, h) \cdot P_{t-1}(g)$$

For each slot g_i:

$$b\_goal[i][partition_i]_t \leftarrow b\_goal[i][partition_i]_t + P(u, p)\; b\_a[u]_t \leftarrow b\_a[u]_t + P(u, p)$$

//normalizing

Normalize the beliefs b_goal_t and b_a_t

Calculating marginal of single value

Fig. 6. The combined method

The computation complexity now reduces from $O(|V|^n)$ to $O(|V|^m)$, where $|V|$ denotes the maximum size of each slot's candidate values, n is the full slot size, and m is the focus set's size which is generally observed to be less than 2 and is far smaller than n. Our focus strategy will work much faster than the above naïve method. What's more, it does not use dynamic structures to maintain all the values and thus expected to be also faster than partition strategy. Figure 5 demonstrates our revised focus-based algorithm.

In our experiments, we use some heuristics to determine the focus set at each timestamp. We build a domain keyword vocabulary from the domain documents, and each keyword is associated with one or more slots according to the domain description of these slots. For example, in an image-buying domain, the word 'poster' is associated with the 'usage' slot because it appears in the text describing the 'usage' of an image. To get the focus slot set, the dialog manager searches for these keywords in the user's input sentence and marks the hit words with the associated slots. The slot referred by the last system's act is also regarded as a focus slot, since the user tends to response to the system's query and focus on the slot that the system has mentioned.

4.3 Combined Strategy

As noted before, the computation complexity comes from both the large slot size and large value size. In this section, we combine the two strategies to simultaneously reduce the complexity from both aspects. Figure 6 illustrates our combined strategy. The combined method takes advantage of the complement property of the two optimizing strategies. Factoring the user's goal into independent slots makes it possible to maintain independent value partitions for each slot and only update partitions for focus slots.

5   Experiments

This section reports the experimental results of our proposed models and belief updating strategies. We first introduce the specific domain that our system applied to. Then we describe our user simulator that interacts with the system to train the dialogue policy.

5.1   The Domain

Our system is designed for price inquiring service for Getty Images China, who is a leading supplier of images for business and consumers in China. It operates a commercial website which allows clients to search for images and purchase them. Costs of images vary greatly according to different factors which often confuse the purchasers, thus there needs an intellective server agent to automatically gather those factors and tell clients the final price. Of course it is friendlier to interact with purchasers/users with natural language dialog rather than providing a large, confusing and tedious HTML form to them.

Table 2. The slots and values

Slots	Candidate values
Usage	Poster/advertisement/book/...
Time span	1 year/2 year/5 year/...
Amount	10/100/500/1000/...
Size	1 M/5 M/15 M/48 M/...
Position	Cover/inner page/wall...
Authority	Electrical/non-electrical

The user's goal is represented by a table of different factors, which should be filled in during the conversation and requires the clients to provide relevant information in order to calculate the price. There are 6 slots in the user's goal table, each of which has a number of candidate values, as listed in Table 2.

5.2 User Simulator

A user simulator simulates the user's behavior to train the dialog policy. At the start of a dialog, the system randomly generates a set of values for each slot which are treated as the real goal of the simulated user. The simulator then interacts with the system and provides relevant information based on the system's act. We constrain the dialog length to 20 turns, and if the system has not collected all necessary information within 20 turns the dialog should be forced to stop. The simulator then gives a score to the completed dialog according to certain metrics. The training process runs totally 80 iterations. In each iteration, it contains two steps: in simulating step 300 dialogs are simulated and then the optimization step updates policy parameters with the collected information of (dialog, score) pairs in the first step.

5.3 Computation Efficiency

We use 4 belief updating strategies stated above to train the model policy. The naïve method is the baseline, and the partition strategy mainly follows the idea of HIS and so also is regarded as a baseline. For each strategy, we simulate dialogs between the server agent and the user simulator, as mentioned in the above subsection.

We run our experiments on an Intel i5 Core machine with 4 GB memory. The average simulating time per dialog of each of 4 methods are shown in Table 3. The naïve method is much slower than the other three strategies, with 1.7 s per dialog. The partition strategy takes 57.33 milliseconds (ms) per dialog. The focus strategy takes only 5.02 ms per dialog, which is 11 time faster than the partition strategy and 20 times faster than the naïve algorithm. The combined method is as fast as 2.38 ms per dialog, which is 24 time faster than the partition strategy. We can see that the focus strategy greatly reduces the computation time compared with the partition strategy, that is because as the dialog progresses, the size of partitions grows larger which makes the process slow down. As expected, combing the two strategies obtain the best efficiency.

Table 3. The computation time of four strategies

Strategy	Time per dialog
Naïve	1.7 s
Partition	57.33 ms
Focus	5.02 ms
Combined	2.38 ms

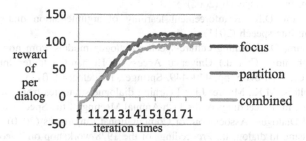

Fig. 7. The convergence curve of 3 strategies

The average reward trends of three optimized strategies are shown in Fig. 7. It shows that after 40 iterations they all achieve high rewards (about 85) per dialog, so the convergence speed of three strategies is satisfying.

6 Conclusion

In this paper, we aim to address the state space exploding problem for efficient dialog management in a POMDP framework. We claim that the intractability of dialog states comes from two aspects: the large slot size and the large candidate value size for each slot. In this paper, we propose a focus strategy to alleviate the computation complexity, by reducing the full slots into a small subset focus slot. We also implement the partition-based method similar to HIS model, with some adaptation in our task. We then combine both strategies to get better performance. We apply our systems to a real task of image purchasing, and conduct evaluation both with a user simulator and real users. Our focus strategy is far faster than partition-based method with comparable quality, and our combined method gets the best performance both in the computation time and the quality evaluated by human testers.

Acknowledgement. This work is supported by National Natural Science Foundation of China (61371129), National High Technology Research and Development Program of China (2015AA015403), Humanity and Social Science foundation of Ministry of Education (13YJA740060), and the Opening Project of Beijing Key Laboratory of Internet Culture and Digital Dissemination Research (ICDD201402).

References

Bohus, D., Rudnicky, A.: A K-hypotheses+ other belief updating model. In: Proceedings of the AAAI Workshop on Statistical and Empirical Methods in Spoken Dialogue Systems (2006)

Chi, M., VanLehn, K., Litman, D., et al.: An evaluation of pedagogical tutorial tactics for a natural language tutoring system: a reinforcement learning approach. Int. J. Artif. Intell. Educ. 21(1), 83–113 (2011)

Georgila, K., Henderson, J., Lemon, O.: User simulation for spoken dialogue systems: learning and evaluation. In: Interspeech (2006)

Georgila, K., Traum, D.R.: Reinforcement learning of argumentation dialogue policies in negotiation. In: Interspeech (2011)

Georgila, K., Traum, D.: Learning culture-specific dialogue models from non culture-specific data. In: Stephanidis, C. (ed.) Universal Access in Human-Computer Interaction. Users Diversity. LNCS, vol. 6766, pp. 440–449. Springer, Heidelberg (2011)

Georgila, K., Wolters, M.K., Moore, J.D.: Learning dialogue strategies from older and younger simulated users. In: Proceedings of the 11th Annual Meeting of the Special Interest Group on Discourse and Dialogue. Association for Computational Linguistics (2010)

Grosz, B.J.: Focusing in dialog. In: Proceedings of the 1978 workshop on Theoretical issues in natural language processing. Association for Computational Linguistics (1978)

Heeman, P.A.: Representing the reinforcement learning state in a negotiation dialogue. In: Automatic Speech Recognition & Understanding (2009)

Jurčíček, F., Thomson, B., Young, S.: Reinforcement learning for parameter estimation in statistical spoken dialogue systems. Comput. Speech Lang. 26(3), 168–192 (2012)

Levin, E., Pieraccini, R., Eckert, W.: A stochastic model of human-machine interaction for learning dialog strategies. IEEE Trans. Speech Audio Process. 8(1), 11–23 (2000)

Metallinou, A., Bohus, D., Williams, J.D.: Discriminative state tracking for spoken dialog systems. In: Proceedings of Annual Meeting of the Association for Computational Linguistics (2013)

Misu, T., Georgila, K., Leuski, A., et al.: Reinforcement learning of question-answering dialogue policies for virtual museum guides. In: Proceedings of the 13th Annual Meeting of the Special Interest Group on Discourse and Dialogue. Association for Computational Linguistics (2012)

Misu, T., Kawahara, T.: Bayes risk-based dialogue management for document retrieval system with speech interface. Speech Commun. 52(1), 61–71 (2010)

Peters, J., Schaal, S.: Natural actor-critic. Neurocomputing 71(7), 1180–1190 (2008)

Tetreault, J.R., Litman, D.J.: A reinforcement learning approach to evaluating state representations in spoken dialogue systems. Speech Commun. 50(8), 683–696 (2008)

Thomson, B., Young, S.: Bayesian update of dialogue state: a POMDP framework for spoken dialogue systems. Comput. Speech Lang. 24(4), 562–588 (2010)

Williams, J.D., Young, S.: Partially observable Markov decision processes for spoken dialog systems. Comput. Speech Lang. 21(2), 393–422 (2007a)

Williams, J.D., Young, S.: Scaling POMDPs for spoken dialog management. IEEE Trans. Audio Speech Lang. Process. 15(7), 2116–2129 (2007b)

Williams, J.D.: Incremental partition recombination for efficient tracking of multiple dialog states. In: IEEE International Conference on Acoustics Speech and Signal Processing (ICASSP) (2010)

Williams, J.D.: Partially observable Markov decision processes for spoken dialogue management. The doctoral thesis (2006)

Young, S., Gašić, M., Keizer, S., et al.: The hidden information state model: a practical framework for POMDP-based spoken dialogue management. Comput. Speech Lang. **24**(2), 150–174 (2010)

Young, S.: The statistical approach to the design of spoken dialogue systems. Technical report CUED/F-INFENG/TR.433, Cambridge University (2002)

Text Classification and Summarization

Recognizing Textual Entailment via Multi-task Knowledge Assisted LSTM

Lei Sha[✉], Sujian Li, Baobao Chang, and Zhifang Sui

Key Laboratory of Computational Linguistics, Ministry of Education School
of Electronics Engineering and Computer Science,
Peking University Collaborative Innovation Center for Language Ability,
Xuzhou 221009, China
{shalei,lisujian,chbb,szf}@pku.edu.cn

Abstract. Recognizing Textual Entailment (RTE) plays an important role in NLP applications like question answering, information retrieval, etc. Most previous works either use classifiers to employ elaborately designed features and lexical similarity or bring distant supervision and reasoning technique into RTE task. However, these approaches are hard to generalize due to the complexity of feature engineering and are prone to cascading errors and data sparsity problems. For alleviating the above problems, some work use LSTM-based recurrent neural network with word-by-word attention to recognize textual entailment. Nevertheless, these work did not make full use of knowledge base (KB) to help reasoning. In this paper, we propose a deep neural network architecture called **M**ulti-task **K**nowledge **A**ssisted **L**STM (MKAL), which aims to conduct implicit inference with the assistant of KB and use predicate-to-predicate attention to detect the entailment between predicates. In addition, our model applies a multi-task architecture to further improve the performance. The experimental results show that our proposed method achieves a competitive result compared to the previous work.

1 Introduction

For the natural language, a common phenomenon is that there exist a lot of ways to express the same or similar meaning. To discover such different expressions, the Recognizing Textual Entailment (RTE) task is proposed to judge whether the meaning of one text (denoted as H) can be inferred (entailed) from the other one (T) [3]. For many natural language processing applications like question answering, information retrieval which need to deal with the diversity of natural language, recognizing textual entailments is a critical step.

Previous RTE works mainly use classifiers to employ elaborately designed features and lexical similarity. Among them, [8] break the T-H pair apart into discourse commitments and then the RTE task is reduced to the identification of the commitments from T which are most likely to support the inference of the commitments from H. However, the discourse commitments are still derived from the original text and can not present the implicit meaning latent behind the text.

© Springer International Publishing AG 2016
M. Sun et al. (Eds.): CCL and NLP-NABD 2016, LNAI 10035, pp. 285–298, 2016.
DOI: 10.1007/978-3-319-47674-2_24

[18] proposed a probabilistic inference framework which transfer the discourse commitments of T-H pairs into predicate-argument structure and use distant supervision as well as Markov Logic Network (MLN) to infer the correctness of H given T. However, the performance of MLN is limited by data sparsity problem, namely, the MLN's inference rules can only cover a small portion of predicates. [17] proposed an attentive LSTM method, which use word-by-word attention to model the entailment between words. However, it did not use the KB information to help the model to infer the truth.

In this paper, we propose a deep neural network architecture called Multi-task Knowledge Assisted LSTM (MKAL) for recognizing textual entailment, which use an embedded knowledge base (KB) to help the deep neural network for implicit reasoning. We use PTransE [10], a state-of-the-art KB embedding system which can model the inference rules in KB, to calculate the embeddings of each entities and relations in the KB. We transfer the sentences into predicate-argument triples as [18] did using a convolutional neural network. And then, we input the predicates' embeddings into LSTM for implicit inference. Moreover, we add predicate-to-predicate attention into our model to detect the inference relationship between predicates. In addition, we take relation classification task as an auxiliary task to facilitate our RTE task.

The main contributions of our work are as follows:

- We propose a deep neural network architecture called Multi-task Knowledge Assisted LSTM (MKAL) for RTE task, which can integrate KB information into deep neural network;
- We propose an easy-generalized KB-assistant method, which can make full use of the potential inference rules in KB without using traditional reasoning method like MLN;
- We apply predicate-to-predicate attention to detect the inference relationship between predicates;
- We propose a multi-task architecture, which use relation classification task as an auxiliary task to help compensating the lack of supervision in our main task (RTE). The experiment result shows its superior effect.

2   Related Work

Textual Entailment Recognizing (RTE) task has been widely studied by many previous work. Firstly, the methods use statistical classifiers which leverage a wide variety of features, including hand-engineered features derived from complex NLP pipelines and similarity between sentences (T and H) and sentence pairs ((T', H') and (T'', H'')) [4,9,12–14,21–23]. This kind of methods are hard to generalize due to the complexity of feature engineering. Moreover, the hand-engineered features usually cannot represent implicit meanings of sentences.

Secondly, [1,8,16,18–20] extract the structured information (discourse commitments or predicate-argument representations) in T-H pair and check if the information in T contains or can infer the information in H. Probabilistic methods are used for recognizing the entailment. However, these work are still based on hand-engineered features which is not easy to generalize.

Recently, neural network based methods [2,17] start to show its effectiveness. [17] uses the attention-based technique to improve the performance of LSTM-based recurrent neural network. However, they did not take advantage of the knowledge base information for inference, so that they cannot handle the cases where the facts in H are implicitly contained by T (the facts in H cannot be directly got from the facts in T. Instead, they should be inferred by the facts in T).

3   Method

Fig. 2 shows the architecture of our model. The input is the T-H sentences and the pre-identified entities. The entitiy's semantic embedding is just the word embedding of its head word. The relation's semantic embedding is calculated by convolutional neural network (CNN). For conducting implicit reasoning, KB inference information was brought into our model, namely, the entity's/relation's semantic embeddings were concatenated with their corresponding PTransE embeddings (which contains the KB information). After that, predicate-by-predicate attention based LSTM is applied to generate the representation of T-H pair. Finally, a logistic regression classifier is used to judge the entailment class (ENTAILMENT, NEUTRAL, CONTRADICTION) of the T-H pair. In addition, we use an auxiliary task to facilitate our main task (RTE).

3.1   Relation Embedding Calculation

In order to better represent the implicit information of the sentence, we decide to transfer the sentence into a series of predicate-argument triples "(entity A, relation, entity B)" as [18] did. We decide to calculate the relation embedding instead of extracting the relation string directly for the following two reasons: (1) The relation between two entities can be easily figured out if the origin sentence and the two entities are given; (2) The process of extracting relation string may suffer from great information loss and lacks generalization.

Inspired by [25], we use CNN to calculate the relation embedding. As is shown in Fig. 1, in the Window Processing component, each token is further represented as Word Features (WF)(which is composed of the embeddings of each word) and Position Features (PF)(of the two entities). Then, the vector goes through a convolutional component. Finally, we obtain the relation embedding through a non-linear transformation.

The PF is composed of the relative distance of the current word to the head word of the two entities. For example, in the T sentence in Fig. 2, the relative distances of "married" to "Senna" and "doctor" are 2 and -3, respectively. And then, the relative distances are mapped to a vector of dimension d_p (a hyperparameter) which is randomly initialized. Then we obtain the distance

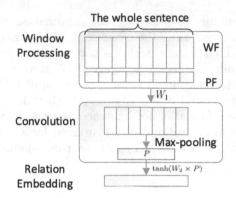

Fig. 1. The CNN architecture for relation embedding

vectors d_1 and d_2 with respect to the relative distance of the current word to the two entities. $PF = [d_1, d_2]$. Finally, the feature vector of each word is $[WF, PF]$.

The convolution operation is stated as Eq. 1:

$$Z = W_1 X \qquad (1)$$

where $X \in \mathbb{R}^{n_0 \times t}$ is the output of the window processing, $n_0 = w \times n$, w is the window size, n is the dimension of feature vector, and t is the token number of the input sentence. $W_1 \in \mathbb{R}^{n_1 \times n_0}$, where n_1 is the size of max-pooling layer. To determine the most useful feature in each dimension of the feature vectors, we perform max-pooling over time on the convolution result $Z \in \mathbb{R}^{n_1 \times t}$ to get the max-pooling layer P. Finally, the relation embedding is calculated as Eq. 2.

$$r = \tanh(W_2 P) \qquad (2)$$

where $W_2 \in \mathbb{R}^{n_2 \times n_1}$ is the linear transformation matrix, $r \in \mathbb{R}^{n_2}$ is the relation embedding.

3.2 KB Reasoning

In many RTE cases, the facts in H cannot be directly got from the facts in T. Instead, they should be inferred by the facts in T. For example, as is shown in the T-H pair of Fig. 2, the fact

(Ayrton Senna, lives in, Texas)

in H should be inferred from the facts

(Ayrton Senna, married to, a doctor)
(doctor, lives in, Austin)
(Austin, is the capital of, Texas)

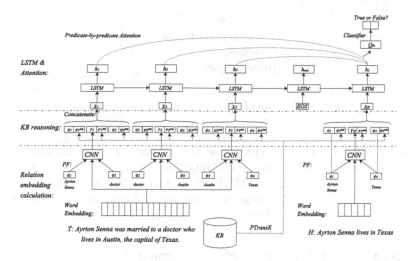

Fig. 2. The main framework of MKAL

in T. So we need inference rules derived by KB to help us conduct reasoning.

Since the inference rules are in the form: $r_1 \wedge r_2 \Rightarrow r_3$, which is just the same form as modeled by PTransE [10], which is a KB embedding method modeling relation paths like $r_1 + r_2 = r_3$. Therefore, the representations of entities and relations learned by PTransE contain the information of implicit inference rules. So we use PTransE to model the inference rules in KB. We take the entities' and relations' PTransE embeddings as well as the semantic embeddings together as the input of the LSTM-RNN to conduct inference as is shown in Fig. 2.

We use a heuristic method to find the corresponding KB items for the entities and relations.

For entities, we first compare the surface entity string with the KB entities. If the entity can be found in KB, we will use the corresponding PTransE embedding as this entity's KB information. If the entity cannot be found in KB, then KB cannot bring it any information, so we just set its' KB information as zero.

Since we do not hope to explicitly extract the relation string from text (a perfect textual relation is too hard to extract), but we do hope to find a match for the textual relations from KB relations. So we use a syntactic constraint method [5] to extract **raw** relation string (RRS) from two adjacent entities. The syntactic constraint requires relation phrase to match the POS tag pattern shown in Fig. 3. The pattern limits relation phrases to be either a simple verb phrase (e.g., invented), a verb phrase followed immediately by a preposition or particle (e.g., located in), or a verb phrase followed by a simple noun phrase and ending in a preposition or particle (e.g., has atomic weight of). Different from [5], we also allow the case of only one preposition (e.g. from, at), because this kind of relation usually states for location and affiliation.

When matching the KB relations and the extracted RRS, we calculate their semantic embedding in prior by averaging the embedding of each word.

$$
\boxed{
\begin{array}{c}
V|VP|V^*W^*P \\
V = \text{verb particle? adv?} \\
W = (\text{noun}|\text{adj} \mid \text{adv} \mid \text{pron} \mid \text{det}) \\
P = (\text{prep}|\text{particle} \mid \text{inf. marker})
\end{array}
}
$$

Fig. 3. A simple POS-based regular expression

We choose the KB relation which has the minimal cosine distance to the extracted RRS as its corresponding KB relation.

Compared to [18], which use AMIE [6] to extract inference rules from KB and then use MLN to conduct inference, our method can cover all entities and relations in KB, which may alleviate the data sparsity problem.

3.3 LSTM-Based Attentive Neural Reasoner

LSTM. Long short-term memory (LSTM) based recurrent neural networks (RNNs) have long been tried to apply to a wide range of NLP tasks. Including RTE [2]. LSTMs use memory cells to store information for a long period. In our model, the better LSTM remembers the predicates, the more accurate recognizing result it can give. Given an input gate i_t, a forget gate f_t, an output gate o_t, a memory cell c_t, candidate memory cell state $\widetilde{C}_t$ and a hidden state h_t. The LSTM transition equations are listed in Eq. 3, $\odot$ is element-wise multiplication.

$$
\begin{aligned}
i_t &= \sigma(W_i x_t + U_i h_{t-1} + b_i) & \widetilde{C}_t &= \tanh(W_c x_t + U_c h_{t-1} + b_c) \\
f_t &= \sigma(W_f x_t + U_f h_{t-1} + b_f) & c_t &= i_t \odot \widetilde{C}_t + f_t \odot c_{t-1} \\
o_t &= \sigma(W_o x_t + U_o h_{t-1} + b_o) & h_t &= o_t \odot \tanh(c_t)
\end{aligned}
\tag{3}
$$

Attentive LSTM for Predicate Reasoning. As is shown in Fig. 2, we take the combination of semantic embedding and PTransE embedding of predicate-argument triples as input to LSTM.

For determining the entailment of individual predicates, we use predicate-to-predicate attention in our model, which can model the inference relationship between the predicates in T and H. Following [17], we attend over the first LSTM's output vectors of T, while the second LSTM processes H one predicate at a time. Denote $Y \in \mathbb{R}^{d \times L}$ as a matrix consisting of the T sentence's LSTM output vector $[h_1 \cdots h_L]$, this can be modeled as follows:

$$
\begin{aligned}
M_t &= \tanh(W_y Y + (W_h h_t + W_r r_{t-1}) \otimes e_L) \\
\alpha_t &= softmax(w^T M_t) \\
r_t &= Y \alpha_t^T + \tanh(W^t r_{t-1})
\end{aligned}
\tag{4}
$$

where $M_t \in \mathbb{R}^{d \times L}$, $\alpha_t \in \mathbb{R}^d$ is the attention weight vector over all output vectors of T for every predicate x_t with $t \in (L+1, N)$ in H and $r_t \in \mathbb{R}^d$ is dependent on the previous attention representation r_{t-1} to inform the model about what was attended over in the previous step. The outer product $\otimes$ is to repeat the previous operand as many times as the word number in T (L times).

The final T-H pair representation is Eq. 5, which is obtained from a non-linear combination of the last attention-weighted representation r_N and the last LSTM output vector h_N.

$$h^* = \tanh(W^p r_N + W^x h_N) \tag{5}$$

where $h^* \in \mathbb{R}^d$. Then h^* is fed into a classifier:

$$O = W^* h^* + b^* \tag{6}$$

where $O \in \mathbb{R}^3$ is the final output of this T-H pair, each entry contains the score of an entailment class (entailment, neutral, contradiction).

3.4 Multi-task Training for Relation Representation

Multi-task learning (MTL) is a kind of machine learning approach, which trains both the main task and auxiliary tasks simultaneously with a shared representation learning the commonality among the tasks. In our work, we use auxiliary training to compensate the lack of supervision in the main task. Intuitively, the CNN which is used to calculate relation embeddings can be improved by relation classification task (RC). Therefore, we use the relation classification task to assist our main task (RTE).

The architecture of our multi-task neural network is shown in Fig. 4. While the relation semantic embeddings calculated by CNN as well as PTransE embeddings were used for LSTM, the relation semantic embedding were also taken as the feature vector of the RC task as shown in Eq. 7. Given an input example x, the CNN outputs the vector O_a, the conditional probability $p(i|x, \theta_a, \theta_s)$ for the i-th component is calculated by softmax operation.

$$O_a = W_3 r$$

$$p(i|x, \theta_a, \theta_s) = \frac{O_a^{(i)}}{\sum_k O_a^{(k)}} \tag{7}$$

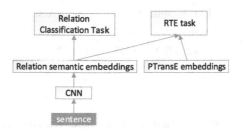

Fig. 4. Multi-task Architecture. "SE" represents sentence embedding

where $\theta_a = \{W_3\}$ represents for the RC-task-only parameters, $\theta_s = \{W_1, W_2\}$ represents for the shared parameters. Given all the training examples $x_a^{(i)}, y_a^{(i)}$ of relation classification, the loss function of this auxiliary task is shown as Eq. 8.

$$J_a(\theta_a, \theta_s) = \sum_i \log p(y_a^{(i)} | x_a^{(i)}, \theta_a, \theta_s) \tag{8}$$

3.5 Model Training

We define the ground-truth label vector y for each T-H pair as a binary vector. If this T-H pair belongs to class i, only the i-th dimension $y(i)$ is 1 and the other dimensions are set to 0. In our model, the RTE task is classification problem and we adopt cross entropy loss as the objective function. Given the LSTM neural network parameters θ_{RTE}, the objective function for a T-H pair can be written as,

$$J(\theta_{RTE}, \theta_s) = -\sum_i y(i) \log(O(i)) + \frac{\lambda_1}{2} \|\theta_{RTE}\|^2 + \frac{\lambda_2}{2} \|\theta_s\|^2 \tag{9}$$

We use mini-batch AdaDelta [24] to train the parameters $\theta_{RTE}, \theta_s, \theta_a$. Referring to the training procedure in [11], we select one task in each epoch and update the model according to its task-specific objective (J or J_a).

We expect the two tasks to reach their best performance at nearly the same time. Therefore, we assign different regulative ratio μ and μ_a to different tasks to adjust the learning rate of AdaDelta.

4 Experiments

4.1 Datasets and Model Configuration

We conduct experiments on the Stanford Natural Language Inference corpus (SNLI) [2]. Since our main task is RTE, Table 1 summarizes the statistics of the three entailment classes in SNLI.

Table 1. Distribution of entailment classes in SNLI

	Train	Dev	Test
Entailment	183416	3329	3368
Neutral	182764	3235	3219
Contradict	183187	3278	3237
Total	549367	9842	9824

For the auxiliary task (RC task), we use the SemEval-2010 Task 8 dataset [7], which contains 10717 annotated examples, including 8000 training instances and 2717 test instances.

For each T-H pair, we extract the noun phrase (NP) in prior as entities by extracting each NP node in the sentence's dependency parse tree. We use the pre-trained word embeddings provided by GloVe [15], and the dimension of the embeddings d is 50. The hyperparameters of our model are set as in Table 2.

Table 2. Hyperparameters of our model

Word embedding size	$d = 50$
Regularization	$\lambda_1 = 0.004$
	$\lambda_2 = 0.001$
Regulative ratio	$\mu = 1.0$
	$\mu_a = 0.5$
Dropout fraction	0.5
Embedding Length (Entity & Relation)	$d_e = 50$
PTransE Embedding Length (Entity & Relation)	$d_e^{(KB)} = 50$
CNN hyperparameters	$w = 3$
	$d_p = 10$
	$n = d + 2d_p$
	$n_1 = 200$
	$n_2 = 100$

4.2 Overall Performance

We compare our result with the following state-of-art methods:

- **LSTM** [2] is a LSTM-based method which encodes T and H independently. The encodings of T and H are concatenated and fed into a deep neural network classifier.
- **Classifier** [2] is a feature-engineered classifier which use a large set of elaborately designed features to recognize the entailment of T and H.
- **Attention** [17] is a LSTM method which processes H sentence conditioned on T sentence while using attention technique.

Table 3 shows the performance on SNLI dataset of our model. For clarity, we split our result into four parts. MKAL(CNN+LSTM) is the most basic model, which only use CNN to calculate the relation embedding and then input all the triples'(entity A, relation, entity B) embeddings into LSTM encoder. Finally, the output of LSTM is taken as the feature representation of the T-H pair. We can see that MKAL(CNN+LSTM) has achieved an accuracy of 78.9 %, which cannot outperform the state-of-art result of [17]. One possible reason is that the process of using CNN to extract the relations' representation may lead to severe information loss. After we add an auxiliary task (RC task), the multi-task architecture makes the RTE accuracy improved to 82.5 %, which is a great improvement.

Then we add PTransE embedding (+ KB) to bring inference information to our model, which improves the accuracy to 83.8 %. Finally, the attention technique (+ Attention) has improved the accuracy to 84.2 %, which has outperformed the state-of-the-art results (Wilcoxon signed-rank test, $p < 0.05$).

4.3 Effect of Multi-task

According to Table 3, the overall performance can be greatly improved by the auxiliary task. The relation classification task's performance is shown in Table 4. Although our auxiliary task did not outperform the origin CNN model in [25], the auxiliary task is comparable to the origin CNN model. The reasons why we did not achieve a better result in the auxiliary task are as follows: First, we did not use the lexical features described in [25] for simplicity. Second, the supervise information of RTE may be not enough for the relation classification task.

Table 3. The performance on SNLI test set

Method	Accuracy
LSTM [2]	77.6
Classifier [2]	78.2
Attention [17]	83.5
MKAL(CNN+LSTM)	78.9
+ Multi-task	82.5
+ KB	83.8
+ Attention	84.2

Table 4. The comparison of relation classification task performance between our auxiliary task and previous works

Method	F_1
CNN [25]	82.7
Our auxiliary task	80.4

4.4 Effect of KB

Of all the extracted RRS in the SNLI test set, about 19.6 % can be matched with KB relations in YAGO. For the entities in the SNLI test set, about 5.4 % can be matched with YAGO's entities. Although the ratio of matched entities/relations is not very high, the KB information is still effective to the overall performance (1.3 % point according to Table 3). Some examples of matched entities and relations are shown in Table 5.

Table 5. Example of matched entities and relations

Entity	KB entity
A church	⟨Vowchurch⟩
Two women	⟨Two Women⟩
The theater	⟨Guthrie Theater⟩
RRS	KB Relation
Connected to	⟨isConnectedTo⟩
Directs	⟨directed⟩
Plays	⟨playsFor⟩

4.5 Effect of Attention

Making the model enable to attend over output vectors of T for every predicate in H gains another 0.4 % point improvement. We argue that this is due to the model being able to check for the entailment between the predicates in T and H.

Visualizations of predicate-by-predicate attention are depicted in Fig. 6. The original sentence of Fig. 6's left figure is as follows:

> T: This church choir sings to the masses as they sing joyous songs from the book at a church.
> H: The church is filled with song.

According to the figure, the predicate "singto (church choir,mass)", "sing (mass,song)" and "at (book,church)" are important for entailing the H predicate "Fillwith (church,song)", which is reasonable for human. The original sentence

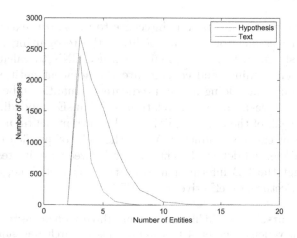

Fig. 5. The distribution of entity numbers of each T-H pair

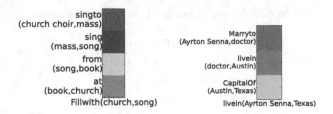

Fig. 6. Predicate-by-predicate attention visualization. Darker-color block represents more attention between the two predicates

of Fig. 6's right figure in Fig. 6 is the example in Fig. 2. In this attention matrix, we can see that all of the three predicates in T are important to entail the H's predicate.

However, the attention technique did not bring too much improvement compared to other works [17]. One possible reason is, the size of our attention matrix is much smaller than other works since we only use predicate-by-predicate attention. There may not be too much predicates in a sentence, but a sentence usually contains many words. In our model, we define each two adjacent entities and their relation make a predicate. Statistically, in Fig. 5, we illustrate the distribution of the number of entities in one sentence. We can see that most of the T sentences have less than 10 entities, which means less than 9 predicates; most of H sentences have less than 5 entities, which means less than 4 predicates. Smaller size may weaken the role of attention. For example, in Fig. 6's right figure, all of the three predicates are attended, so that it may not make too much difference than there is no attention technique at all. Therefore the effect of attention matrix is weaker than the effect in previous works.

5   Conclusion

In this paper, we use a multi-task architecture to recognize textual entailment. We use relation classification task to facilitate the recognizing textual entailment (RTE) task (main task). The main task use CNN to calculate the relations' semantic embeddings and concatenate the adjacent entities' embedding and their relation's embedding as the predicate's semantic embedding. At the same time, we give each entity and relation a PTransE embedding (KB information), and put all of them into LSTM-based recurrent neural network so that implicit reasoning can be conducted. With the help of predicate-by-predicate attention technique, we detect the entailment between predicates. The experiments show that the KB information, the attention technique, especially the multi-task architecture are effective to the RTE task.

Acknowledgements. We would like to thank our three anonymous reviewers for their helpful advice on various aspects of this work. This research was supported by the National Key Basic Research Program of China (No. 2014CB340504) and the National

Natural Science Foundation of China (No. 61375074,61273318). The contact author for this paper is Baobao Chang and Zhifang Sui.

References

1. Beltagy, I., Chau, C., Boleda, G., Garrette, D., Erk, K., Mooney, R.: Deep semantics with probabilistic logical form. In: Proceedings of the Second Joint Conference on Lexical and Computational Semantics (* SEM-13) (2013)
2. Bowman, S.R., Angeli, G., Potts, C., Manning, C.D.: A large annotated corpus for learning natural language inference. arXiv preprint arXiv:1508.05326 (2015)
3. Dagan, I., Glickman, O., Magnini, B.: The Pascal recognising textual entailment challenge. In: Quiñonero-Candela, J., Dagan, I., Magnini, B., dAlché-Buc, F. (eds.) MLCW 2005. LNCS, vol. 3944, pp. 177–190. Springer, Heidelberg (2006)
4. Dinu, G., Wang, R.: Inference rules and their application to recognizing textual entailment. In: Proceedings of the 12th Conference of the European Chapter of the Association for Computational Linguistics, pp. 211–219. Association for Computational Linguistics (2009)
5. Etzioni, O., Fader, A., Christensen, J., Soderland, S., Mausam, M.: Open information extraction: the second generation. In: IJCAI, vol. 11, pp. 3–10 (2011)
6. Galárraga, L.A., Teflioudi, C., Hose, K., Suchanek, F.: Amie: association rule mining under incomplete evidence in ontological knowledge bases. In: Proceedings of the 22nd International Conference on World Wide Web, pp. 413–422. International World Wide Web Conferences Steering Committee (2013)
7. Hendrickx, I., Kim, S.N., Kozareva, Z., Nakov, P., Ó Séaghdha, D., Padó, S., Pennacchiotti, M., Romano, L., Szpakowicz, S.: Semeval-2010 task 8: multi-way classification of semantic relations between pairs of nominals. In: Proceedings of the Workshop on Semantic Evaluations: Recent Achievements and Future Directions, pp. 94–99. Association for Computational Linguistics (2009)
8. Hickl, A.: Using discourse commitments to recognize textual entailment. In: Proceedings of the 22nd International Conference on Computational Linguistics, Vol. 1, pp. 337–344. Association for Computational Linguistics (2008)
9. Jijkoun, V., de Rijke, M.: Recognizing textual entailment using lexical similarity. In: Proceedings of the PASCAL Challenges Workshop on Recognising Textual Entailment, pp. 73–76 (2005)
10. Lin, Y., Liu, Z., Luan, H., Sun, M., Rao, S., Liu, S.: Modeling relation paths for representation learning of knowledge bases. In: Proceedings of the 2015 Conference on Empirical Methods in Natural Language Processing, pp. 705–714. Association for Computational Linguistics, Lisbon, Portugal, September 2015. https://aclweb.org/anthology/D/D15/D15-1082
11. Liu, X., Gao, J., He, X., Deng, L., Duh, K., Wang, Y.Y.: Representation learning using multi-task deep neural networks for semantic classification and information retrieval. In: Proceedings of the 2015 Conference of the North American Chapter of the Association for Computational Linguistics: Human Language Technologies, pp. 912–921. Association for Computational Linguistics, Denver, Colorado, May–June 2015. http://www.aclweb.org/anthology/N15-1092
12. Malakasiotis, P.: Paraphrase and textual entailment recognition and generation. Ph. D. thesis, Department of Informatics, Athens University of Economics and Business, Greece (2011)

13. Malakasiotis, P., Androutsopoulos, I.: Learning textual entailment using SVMs and string similarity measures. In: Proceedings of the ACL-PASCAL Workshop on Textual Entailment and Paraphrasing, pp. 42–47. Association for Computational Linguistics (2007)
14. Nielsen, R.D., Ward, W., Martin, J.H.: Recognizing entailment in intelligent tutoring systems. Nat. Lang. Eng. **15**(04), 479–501 (2009)
15. Pennington, J., Socher, R., Manning, C.D.: Glove: global vectors for word representation. In: Proceedings of the Empiricial Methods in Natural Language Processing (EMNLP 2014), vol. 12, pp. 1532–1543 (2014)
16. Rios, M., Specia, L., Gelbukh, A., Mitkov, R.: Statistical relational learning to recognise textual entailment. In: Gelbukh, A. (ed.) CICLing 2014, Part I. LNCS, vol. 8403, pp. 330–339. Springer, Heidelberg (2014)
17. Rocktäschel, T., Grefenstette, E., Hermann, K.M., Kočiský, T., Blunsom, P.: Reasoning about entailment with neural attention. arXiv preprint arXiv:1509.06664 (2015)
18. Sha, L., Li, S., Chang, B., Sui, Z., Jiang, T.: Recognizing textual entailment using probabilistic inference. In: Proceedings of the 2015 Conference on Empirical Methods in Natural Language Processing, pp. 1620–1625. Association for Computational Linguistics, Lisbon, Portugal, September 2015. https://aclweb.org/anthology/D/D15/D15-1185
19. Shnarch, E., Goldberger, J., Dagan, I.: A probabilistic modeling framework for lexical entailment. In: Proceedings of the 49th Annual Meeting of the Association for Computational Linguistics: Human Language Technologies: Short Papers, vol. 2, pp. 558–563. Association for Computational Linguistics (2011)
20. Shnarch, E., Goldberger, J., Dagan, I.: Towards a probabilistic model for lexical entailment. In: Proceedings of the TextInfer 2011 Workshop on Textual Entailment, pp. 10–19. Association for Computational Linguistics (2011)
21. Wan, S., Dras, M., Dale, R., Paris, C.: Using dependency-based features to take the para-farce out of paraphrase. In: Proceedings of the Australasian Language Technology Workshop, vol 2006 (2006)
22. Wang, R., Neumann, G.: Recognizing textual entailment using sentence similarity based on dependency tree skeletons. In: Proceedings of the ACL-PASCAL Workshop on Textual Entailment and Paraphrasing, pp. 36–41. Association for Computational Linguistics (2007)
23. Zanzotto, F.M., Moschitti, A.: Automatic learning of textual entailments with cross-pair similarities. In: International Conference on Computational Linguistics and the 44th Annual meeting of the Association for Computational Linguistics, vol. 1, pp. 401–408. Association for Computational Linguistics (2006)
24. Zeiler, M.D.: Adadelta: an adaptive learning rate method. arXiv preprint arXiv:1212.5701 (2012)
25. Zeng, D., Liu, K., Lai, S., Zhou, G., Zhao, J.: Relation classification via convolutional deep neural network. In: Proceedings of COLING, pp. 2335–2344 (2014)

Multilingual Multi-document Summarization with Enhanced hLDA Features

Taiwen Huang[(✉)], Lei Li, and Yazhao Zhang

Beijing University of Posts and Telecommunications, Beijing 100876, China
{zhidao2010,leili,yazhao}@bupt.edu.cn

Abstract. This paper presents the state of art research progress on multilingual multi-document summarization. Our method utilizes hLDA (hierarchical Latent Dirichlet Allocation) algorithm to model the documents firstly. A new feature is proposed from the hLDA modeling results, which can reflect semantic information to some extent. Then it combines this new feature with different other features to perform sentence scoring. According to the results of sentence score, it extracts candidate summary sentences from the documents to generate a summary. We have also attempted to verify the effectiveness and robustness of the new feature through experiments. After the comparison with other summarization methods, our method reveals better performance in some respects.

Keywords: Multilingual multi-document summarization · Sentence scoring · hLDA modeling

1 Introduction

Facing the explosive expansion of network information, users have to spend vast time to discover what they want. It is a significant challenge to find an effective tool to filter the unnecessary information and provide a precise and concise synopsis. Hence document summarization has become one of the important technologies for research. Researchers have worked on different topics, including single document summarization, multi-document summarization and multilingual multi-document summarization which is just the topic of this paper and also the most difficult one.

The field of document summarization has accumulated a lot of research results after 60 years of research. Summarization methods can be classified into extractive and abstractive ones. Extractive summarization aims to select important sentences from the original document and reorganize these sentences according to their order, while abstractive summarization aims to understand the original text and re-tell it like human. The mainstream is extractive summarization currently because abstractive summarization needs effective and deep natural language processing technologies. For extractive summarization, the representative algorithms involve graph model [1], sentence clustering [2], linear programming [3], topic model [4] and so on.

This paper focuses on the extractive summarization and topic model method. In recent years, we are constantly using and mining hLDA [5] features. The hLDA algorithm is selected as our main algorithm. hLDA has many advantages. On the one hand, it is a language-independent algorithm, so we don't need a lot of professional

© Springer International Publishing AG 2016
M. Sun et al. (Eds.): CCL and NLP-NABD 2016, LNAI 10035, pp. 299–312, 2016.
DOI: 10.1007/978-3-319-47674-2_25

linguistic knowledge. On the other hand, it is a corpus-oriented algorithm, it can deal with large scale corpus. hLDA can be an excellent multilingual multi-document modeling algorithm. Many hLDA scholars [6–8] are just exploring the cluster and document modeling ability of hLDA, yet they haven't made clear the semantic features behind the model. Based on the research of hLDA, this paper proposes a new level distribution feature from it. In combination with other traditional features, we build our new summarization system with a better performance. After comparison with other methods, it shows the superiority of our system in some respects.

2 Background

2.1 hLDA

The hLDA (Blei et al. 2004) can organize latent topics of sentences in a set of documents and their relations into a hierarchical tree. The structure of the tree is determined by the documents and some parameters. A node in this tree represents a latent topic, and words are assigned to a node with some probability. Hence, a topic can be interpreted as probability distribution over words. The following Fig. 1 shows an example hLDA tree with the depth of 3. Please refer to (Blei et al. 2004) for more details.

Owing to using the sentence as the input unit of hLDA algorithm, every sentence will be allocated into a path from the root to a leaf in the tree as shown with arrows in Fig. 1. Sentences having the same path will be considered to be related to the same

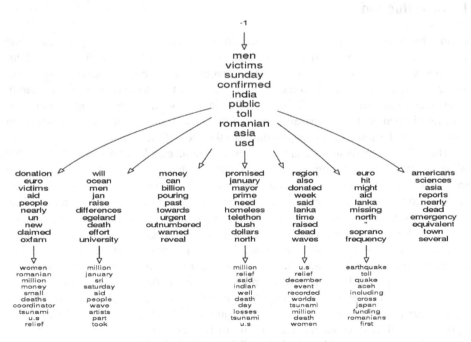

Fig. 1. hLDA modeling result example

theme. In light of our previous research experience, we set the depth of the tree to 3. There are 6 parameters in total to control the structure of the tree. The parameter settings in our system can be found in Table 1. More details have been presented in the research of Heng Wei [9].

Table 1. hLDA parameter setting

Parameter	Setting	Parameter	Setting
ETA	1.2,0.5,0.05	GEM_SCALE	100
GAM	1.0,1.0	SCALING_SHAPE	1
GEM_MEAN	0.5	SCALING_SCALE	0.5

2.2   Experimental Data

MultiLing (http://multiling.iit.demokritos.gr) is a special session in SIGdial 2015, which holds 4 tasks, i.e., MMS (Multilingual Multi-document Summarization), MSS (Multilingual Single-document Summarization), OnForumS (Online Forum Summarization) and CCCS (Call Centre Conversation Summarization). This multilingual multi-document summarization (MMS) (Giannakopoulos, 2015) task aims to evaluate the application of partially or fully language-independent summarization algorithms. It contains ten languages: Arabic, Chinese, Czech, English, French, Greek, Hebrew, Hindi, Romanian and Spanish.

The multi-document summarization task required participants to generate a fluent and representative summary from the set of documents describing an event sequence. The language of each document set belonged to one of the aforementioned set of languages and all the documents in a set were of the same language. The output summary was expected to be in the same language and between 240 and 250 words. The task corpus is based on a set of WikiNews English news articles comprising 15 topics, each containing ten documents. Each English document was translated into the other nine languages to create sentence-parallel translations. Please refer to [10] for more detailed introduction of MultiLing2015.

The experimental data of this paper is the test data of MMS task. Each language contains 10 to 15 topics and each topic contains 10 documents.

3   System Architecture

The framework for our system is shown in Fig. 2. In particular, we only treat Chinese with word segmentation. The kernel module is constructing an hLDA model.

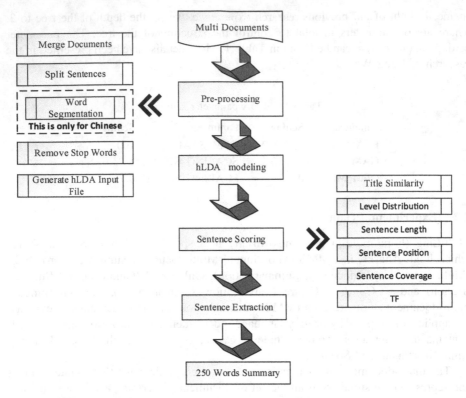

Fig. 2. Multilingual multi-document summarization system framework

3.1 Pre-processing

1. Merge Documents
   For every topic of each language, we merge all the 10 documents into one big document. This big document is named as merged document. We will mainly extract summary from this merged document. The following pre-processing steps are all done upon the merged document, too.
2. Split Sentences
   Sentence is the processing unit. There are two special lines of title and date ending with no punctuation marks in the corpus. We add a full stop to avoid them being connected with the first following sentence. We then split sentences according to the ending punctuation marks like full stop, question mark and apostrophe.
3. Word Segmentation
   Since Chinese hanzi is not separated by spaces as other languages, we need to do word segmentation firstly.
4. Remove Stop Words
   We construct stop lists for all languages. For English and Chinese, the stop list contains punctuation marks and some functional words, while for other languages, it contains punctuation marks, which could unify the whole process easily. In fact,

in the experiment, we compare the performance of the system of removing stop words with system of not removing stop words. Specific differences will be described in the experimental Sect.

5. Generate hLDA input File

We build a dictionary for the remaining words, which are sorted in descending order according to their frequencies. This is a mapping from a word to a number varying from 1 to dictionary size. Finally we generate an input file for hLDA, in which each line represents a sentence:

[number of words in the sentence] [wordNumberA]:[localfrequencyA] [wordNumberB]:[local frequencyB]...

3.2 hLDA Modeling

The hLDA algorithm we used in this paper is originally developed by Blei. (http:// www.cs.princeton.edu/~blei/topicmodeling.html). Through hLDA modeling, we can get the final hLDA modeling tree information. The main three files are 'mode' file, 'mode.assign' file, and 'mode.levels' file. The information in these files is independent with language. Our level distribution feature is extracted from them. The only purpose that we utilize hLDA in this paper is to get the value of level distribution feature for sentence scoring. The other features for sentence scoring are independent with hLDA modeling process. In the next section, we will elaborate on introduction to all features we used in this paper.

4 Sentence Scoring

Our system selects 6 features to score sentences. In these 6 kinds of features, there are 5 kinds of features (except Level Distribution) that are used in single document summarization widely. The validity of these features has been demonstrated by many experiments and researchers. For each of these 6 features, we have also performed extensive experiments to illustrate its effectiveness in multilingual multi-document summarization.

(1) Level Distribution: this feature is just the achievement of our latest research. In this feature, we think that after hLDA modeling, if a word appears in more levels or more nodes, then it has a higher possibility to be involved into summary. Formula 4 is our scoring method.

Blei, the author of hLDA, has proposed that the lower level nodes in the hLDA modeling results are more abstract. Thus in previous years, we considered that the abstract word is more suitable to appear in summary. In light of this idea, our previous level scoring formula is:

$$S_{abstract} = a \times \frac{num(w_0)}{|s|} + b \times \frac{num(w_1)}{|s|} + c \times \frac{num(w_2)}{|s|} \tag{1}$$

In formula 1, $num(w_0)$, $num(w_1)$ and $num(w_2)$ refer to the amount of words in a sentence assigned to each level respectively. Usually we set the three weights according to our own experience, which is a as 0.75, b as 0.25, and c as 0.1. We have utilized this feature for sentence scoring to implement several summarization systems. For example, TAC-2014 multi-document summarization system, multiLing-2015 summarization system, NLPCC-2015 text summarization system. Through these experiences, we find out that the effect of this feature and the performance is not satisfactory. Usually, it will reduce the performance of summarization system. After participating in the NLPCC2015 Shared Task4, we use NLPCC2015's corpus to perform more deeply exploration in features contained in hLDA modeling results. We find a more reasonable understanding of the abstract nature of the level. In hLDA modeling tree, the abstract node possibly means that the words appearing in the node either appear in a lot of contexts or their frequency is very low. In the high level of nodes, the words appearing in these nodes usually have some very specific context and even only one context. In our work, we have found out that most of the words in root node are low frequency words, while in the leaf nodes, although some words are high frequency ones, they always appear in a fixed context. Under the guidance of this understanding, a new law has been found in the hLDA modeling that if a word appears in more nodes and more levels, then the word has a higher probability to be selected into the summary. After more exploration of this rule, we propose a new formula of level feature for sentence scoring called level distribution. Formula 2 shows the result of our research.

$$S_{Levels} = \sum_{i=0}^{N} \left(W_i T_{i-Distribution} + T_{i-NodeFrequency} + T_{i-Keywords} \right) \qquad (2)$$

In formula 2, N is the total number of words in a sentence. W_i is the weight of the level in the hLDA modeling tree where the word T_i is assigned to. $T_{i-Distribution}$ is the distribution score of T_i. The distribution score is based on the law above. Every word will be mapped to a single score according to their distribution information in hLDA modeling tree. Mapping rule is defined through many controlled experiments. $T_{i-Keywords}$ is the keywords score of T_i. If T_i belongs to keywords, $T_{i-Keywords}$ will be 0.5, else 0. $T_{i-NodeFrequency}$ is the node frequency score of T_i, it represents the frequency of T_i in the node where T_i is assigned to. Formula 3 reveals its calculation method.

$$T_{i-NodeFrequency} = \frac{counts(T_i)}{\sum_{i=0}^{V} counts(T_i)} \qquad (3)$$

Note that NLPCC 2015 summarization task is only for single Chinese document. We will demonstrate the validity of this feature through another paper. In this paper, we mainly attempt to find the effectiveness and robustness for multilingual multi-document summarization (MMS). Hence, we select MultiLing2015's MMS test data as our experimental data. The most important point is that we abandoned the last item in formula 2. This is mainly because we cannot get the keywords of other languages except Chinese. So the final level distribution formula in this paper is as formula 4.

$$S_{Levels} = \sum_{i=0}^{N} \left(W_i T_{i-Distribution} + T_{i-NodeFrequency} \right) \tag{4}$$

We will specifically discuss the performance of level distribution feature in later section for experiments. In short, this feature greatly improves the performance of Chinese language. For some other languages, the effect is not obvious. The reason may be that this feature is originally obtained from NLPCC 2015 Chinese summarization task. Through some experimental exploration, we acquire the parameter settings in formula 4. Table 2 shows the final settings in this paper.

Table 2. Parameters of formula 4

W_0	W_1	W_2	Word score (0–1–2)	Word score (0–1)
0.5	0.1	0.4	4	1
Word score (0–2)	Word score (1–2)	Word score (0)	Word score (1)	Word score (2)
3	1	−1	0	0.5

In Table 2, W_0 is the weight of the first level of hLDA modeling tree. W_1 is the weight of the second level of hLDA modeling tree. W_2 is the weight of the last level of hLDA modeling tree. For every word, we assign a global fixed score according to their distribution in hLDA tree. For instance, if a word appear in three layers, (0,1,2), then the word score will be set to 4. If a word only appears in the first layer (0), then the word score will be −1.

It must be noted that we do not elaborate on how we find the law of Level Distribution and how we adjust parameters in this paper. Limited to the length of this paper, we will discuss the law of Level Distribution and verify the assumption in another paper in detail. In fact, the discovery of Level distribution law is based on the statistical analysis of the human summary. Through performing hLDA modeling on human summary and analyzing the law of these hLDA modeling results, we acquire the law of Level distribution. In this paper, we just want to demonstrate that the Level distribution is effective in multilingual multi-document summarization.

(2) Title Similarity: For news, the title sentence can be very good at revealing the central theme. So we calculate the tf-idf similarity between each sentence with the title sentence. In every topic, there are 10 documents. We choose the first sentence of each article as the title sentence. The similarity score of each sentence is calculated as the similarity between the sentence and the title sentence. Formula 5 reveals the calculation method.

$$S_{TS} = \frac{\sum_{i=1}^{n} \left(Sen_i \times Title_i \right)}{\sqrt{\sum_{i=1}^{n} \left(Sen_i \right)^2} \times \sqrt{\sum_{i=1}^{n} \left(Title_i \right)^2}} \tag{5}$$

Sen is the document vector representation of a sentence. i is the ith dimension of the vector. *Title* is the document vector representation of the title sentence.

(3) Sentence Length: We believe that the length of the sentence in the news is subjected to Gaussian distribution. If a sentence is closer to the average length, then it is more likely to be selected into summary.

$$S_{senLen} = \frac{1}{\sqrt{2\pi}\sigma} e^{-\frac{(L_i - \mu)}{2\sigma^2}} \tag{6}$$

$$\sigma^2 = \frac{\sum_{i=1}^{n}(L_i - \mu)^2}{n} \tag{7}$$

μ is the average value of sentence length in all documents of a topic. L_i is the length of a sentence at position i of the merged documents.

(4) Sentence Position: Here we use the monotonous sentence position scoring method. Usually, if the position of a sentence is closer to the starting of news, the sentence is more likely to be selected into summary. Note that our sentence position score is not referring to the sentence position in the merged document. The sentence position score is just calculated as the sentence position score in the original single document the sentence belongs to. Hence, there are possibly many sentences with the same sentence position score. If two documents have the same amount of sentences, the sentence in the same position will have the same sentence position score.

$$S_{senPos} = \frac{n - i + 1}{n} \tag{8}$$

n is the total amount of sentences in the single document the sentence belongs to. i represents the sentence position in the single document the sentence belongs to.

(5) Sentence Coverage: If a word appears in many sentences, then the possibility of the sentence containing the word being selected into summary will be higher.

$$S_{coverage} = \frac{\sum_{i=1}^{|s|} \frac{num_s(t_i)}{n}}{|s|} \tag{9}$$

(6) TF: this feature is referred from [11]. The system won the first prize in the NLPCC 2015 Shared Task 4.

$$TF(t_i) = \frac{m_i}{\sum_{j=1}^{N} m_j} \tag{10}$$

$$S_{TF} = \sum_{t \in Sen} TF(t) \tag{11}$$

Where N represents the number of different words that are included in the article. m_i is the times the word t_i appears in the article. t_i is the ith word in the article.

At last, we combine all features' scores mentioned above. Formula 12 is the final score of one sentence. $para_{1 \sim 6}$ are the weights of each feature score. In the experimental section, we will discuss their different influences in the performance of summarization.

$$S = para_1 * S_{TS} + para_2 * S_{Levels} + para_3 * S_{senLen} + para_4 * S_{senPos} + para_5 * S_{coverage} + para_6 * S_{TF} \tag{12}$$

5   Sentence Extraction

The following algorithm describes the sentence extraction strategy in our system (Fig. 3).

```
Input: Merge documents sentence set mergeSentenceSet
Output: a summary Summary
1: begin
2: First we should Determine para1-6
3: for each sentence Sen in mergeSentenceSet:
4:        calculate the final score of every sentence
5: end for;
6: for each sentence Sen in mergeSentenceSet:
7:        ranking(Sentence,SentenceScore);//Descending order
8: end for
9: for each sentence Sen in mergeSentenceSet:
10:       select the top 1 sentence topSen from mergeSentenceSet
11:       totalLength += topSenLength
12:       if(totalLength > 250):
13:              cut the topSen until the totalLength can equal to 250 when adding topSen
                 to Summary
14:              break;
15:       else:
16:              add topSen into Summary
17:              remove topSen from mergeSentenceSet
18: end for
19: for each sentence Sen in Summary:
20:              ordering(Sentence,SentencePos);//Ascending order
21: end for
22: Output Summary
23: end
```

Fig. 3. Sentence extraction algorithm

Our algorithm firstly selects a set of parameters to calculate the final score of every sentence. Then we rank the sentences of the merged document by function ranking() according to the ultimate significance score of each sentence calculated by formula (12). We control the final total length of the summary to the limit of 250 words using the parameter totalLength and order the selected sentences in the generated summary with function ordering() according to the sentence position.

6 Experiments

We use the Rouge package [12, 13] to evaluate effectiveness of our approach vs. other summarization methods. The results of other summarization methods are published by MultiLing2015's organizer. The experimental data is MultiLing2015 MMS test data. We evaluate the results of 63 different feature combinations of parameters (each para in $para_{1 \sim 6}$ is either 0 or 1). Through these experiments, we demonstrate the effect of level distribution feature, especially for Chinese summarization. For all ten languages, we evaluate their Rouge scores. Table 3 shows the Rouge scores of summaries generated using only one feature.

Table 3. Single feature summarization result (Owing to the limit of this paper space, all rouge scores in this paper except Table 6 are ROUGE-1 F, Ts = Title Similarity, Levels = Level Distr ibution, SenLen = Sentence Length, SenPos = Sentence- Position, SenCov = Sentence Cove rage)

	Ts	Levels	SenLen	SenPos	SenCov	TF
All languages	0.36303	**0.30325**	0.31687	0.35115	0.34012	0.31642
Arabic	0.23775	**0.13752**	0.14194	0.16408	0.21231	0.19236
Chinese	0.49661	**0.30538**	0.34594	0.53596	0.31484	0.36193
Czech	0.44861	**0.43309**	0.45452	0.45027	0.44519	0.43403
English	0.42502	**0.39756**	0.39852	0.39844	0.41834	0.40326
French	0.47388	**0.43186**	0.44607	0.46911	0.46888	0.44210
Greek	0.25339	**0.18067**	0.20507	0.22718	0.29537	0.15405
Hebrew	0.25719	**0.19954**	0.20060	0.29113	0.21739	0.24119
Hindi	0.07933	**0.05629**	0.10094	0.04426	0.06948	0.04846
Romanian	0.43059	**0.38766**	0.39540	0.41449	0.42047	0.40081
Spanish	0.52443	**0.45659**	0.46978	0.50906	0.47676	0.45796

From Table 3, a bad fact we can find is that almost all Rouge values in Levels column are worst. That's to say, the single Level Distribution feature seems to have no reason to exist. Nevertheless, when we try to combine this feature with other features, a very surprising result appears. This surprising and good information is that this feature can improve the comprehensive result when combined with others. Furthermore, it has positive effect with other features in most situations. There is no same phenomenon on other features. Table 4 reveals part of this phenomenon.

Table 4. Level distribution feature combined with other features (All mixture ratios are 1)

	Ts + levels	SenLen+ levels	SenPos+ levels	SenCov+ levels	TF+ levels
All languages	0.35481	0.32714	0.36608	0.35647	0.33786
Arabic	0.24917	0.19710	0.23659	0.23261	0.21748
Chinese	0.47326	**0.40162**	**0.61449**	**0.54868**	**0.52351**
Czech	0.44943	0.44195	0.47419	0.45349	0.43256
English	0.41500	0.41063	0.43187	0.42530	0.41703
French	0.47811	0.43080	0.47870	0.45036	0.44211
Greek	0.24394	0.21578	0.17089	0.21187	0.15830
Hebrew	0.23027	0.19130	0.24472	0.27597	0.26993
Hindi	0.08899	0.07778	0.09419	0.07273	0.03997
Romanian	0.41866	0.40842	0.43144	0.41035	0.40280
Spanish	0.50755	0.47206	0.50846	0.47696	0.46728

The results in Table 4 show that the All Language Rouge score will increase when Level Distribution is combined with other features except Title Similarity. Note that this phenomenon of performance increasing is not unilateral. For example, when Sentence Length is combined with Level Distribution, the final result not only surpasses the result using single Sentence Length, but also surpasses the result using single Level Distribution. For other features, the phenomenon of performance increasing is usually unilateral. What's more, an important fact in Table 4 is that this feature improves the performance of Chinese summarization greatly. This result has just verified our expectation. Because Level Distribution feature is origined from Chinese single document summarization. We find this feature through performing experiments on NLPCC2015 Shared Task 4 data.

Tables 3 and 4 are the experimental results based on the corpus without removing stop words. Actually, stop words have a great impact on the performance of the summarization system. Especially for Level Distribution feature, the effect will be weaken if we do not remove stop words. In light of our research results, if we use the corpus with stop words to perform hLDA modeling, the stop words will have the similar distribution characteristics with those important words which Level Distribution feature prefers. Table 5 shows the summarization results of single feature based on removal of stop words.

Table 5 shows that almost all results are better than the corresponding ones in Table 3 when we compare the same feature. This is a good evidence of that stop words can reduce the Rouge score of summarization system. In these features, we can find out that the Levels feature can benefit most from removing stop words especially for Chinese summarization. When we use only one feature, Level Distribution is top 1 in Chinese summarization. For other languages, the result of Level Distribution is not that bad like that of Table 3. That's to say, the effect of Level Distribution are strongly related to whether we remove stop words or not.

Finally, we compare our best experimental result with several other summarization methods. There are 9 systems in MultiLing2015 MMS task involving a human

Table 5. Single feature summarization based on removal of stop words

	Ts	Levels	SenLen	SenPos	SenCov	TF
All languages	0.36466	0.33745	0.31729	0.35115	0.35440	0.33688
Arabic	0.23775	0.18475	0.16756	0.16408	0.22202	0.19385
Chinese	0.52479	**0.53915**	0.33620	0.53596	0.49557	0.51904
Czech	0.44869	0.43867	0.44678	0.45027	0.44514	0.44318
English	0.42470	0.41071	0.39425	0.39844	0.41544	0.41382
French	0.47291	0.41608	0.44536	0.46911	0.45765	0.45388
Greek	0.25339	0.20009	0.20507	0.22718	0.29537	0.15405
Hebrew	0.25719	0.24113	0.21421	0.29113	0.25934	0.26475
Hindi	0.07933	0.03997	0.08794	0.04426	0.07704	0.04999
Romanian	0.42776	0.41170	0.39564	0.41449	0.40101	0.41623
Spanish	0.52388	0.47904	0.46444	0.50906	0.46055	0.46548

Table 6. All system results (every cell in table have three line data, the first line is the result of ROUGE-1 F, the second line is the result of ROUGE-2 F, the last line is the result of ROUGE-SU4 F)

	cist	esi	giau	human	mms3	muse	occams	poly	wbu	Ours
Arabic	0.45918	0.48999	0.50778	0.69513	0.49923	0.50861	0.52084	0.52959	0.53161	0.28914
	0.13729	0.18379	0.19055	0.49773	0.19645	0.21669	0.21181	0.19408	0.23783	0.12625
	0.19228	0.23314	0.23987	0.51931	0.24189	0.25620	0.25615	0.23778	0.27340	0.14151
Chinese	0.25456	0.36556	–	0.70972	0.42077	–	0.29237	–	0.36919	**0.62952**
	0.04935	0.13445		0.55843	0.20097		0.06799		0.15947	**0.44720**
	0.08051	0.15410		0.55575	0.20824		0.09382		0.16971	**0.46876**
Czech	0.40045	0.41095	0.45677	0.66770	0.44405	–	0.47445	–	0.46226	**0.48183**
	0.12686	0.14192	0.19723	0.46779	0.17239		0.18494		0.20409	**0.20737**
	0.15917	0.17150	0.21365	0.48111	0.19291		0.20427		0.22001	**0.23114**
English	0.42646	0.47204	0.45919	0.67636	0.47266	0.48578	0.50270	0.47144	0.48978	0.45734
	0.10529	0.16764	0.14924	0.46165	0.16849	0.18175	0.17961	0.13919	0.19215	0.16773
	0.16669	0.21223	0.20676	0.49444	0.21526	0.23075	0.22746	0.19324	0.23035	0.20778
French	0.43953	0.51377	0.48887	0.71406	0.53222	–	0.53814	–	0.55427	0.50024
	0.12148	0.19442	0.17381	0.49190	0.21797		0.20702		0.24840	0.19164
	0.18731	0.24795	0.23468	0.52968	0.27466		0.26068		0.30160	0.19164
Greek	0.44377	0.44595	0.47945	0.66741	0.46582	–	0.48539	–	0.48237	0.29537
	0.12060	0.12624	0.17550	0.44346	0.14829		0.15989		0.16623	0.07758
	0.18938	0.19524	0.23715	0.48424	0.21342		0.21849		0.22627	0.11127
Hebrew	0.20209	0.25679	0.26528	0.50295	0.25297	0.26662	0.27524	0.24657	0.26755	**0.30942**
	0.04968	0.09124	0.09653	0.37887	0.08192	0.08359	0.08099	0.07432	0.09337	0.08141
	0.05963	0.09395	0.09807	0.38633	0.08533	0.08903	0.08595	0.07760	0.09723	**0.11863**
Hindi	0.64779	0.44918	0.64819	0.82748	0.66257	–	0.67586	–	0.66408	0.11090
	0.24051	0.18841	0.25874	0.62603	0.27152		0.25877		0.28622	0.00838
	0.37544	0.27516	0.37937	0.67671	0.40093		0.38042		0.40507	0.03848
Romanian	0.40667	0.42843	–	0.81966	0.44079	–	0.47011	–	0.47630	0.46142
	0.09476	0.12710		0.69859	0.14403		0.16013		0.18904	0.18256
	0.14593	0.17294		0.70505	0.18482		0.19549		0.21783	0.21317
Spanish	0.41554	0.53046	–	0.72331	0.55622	–	0.56984	–	0.57402	0.53113
	0.13581	0.22059		0.52141	0.24963		0.24440		0.28102	0.24323
	0.19776	0.28798		0.55985	0.31482		0.30120		0.33020	0.27850

summatization (This summarization is written by human). Not all systems have participated in all languages. Table 6 reveals the comparison result. In Table 6, we represent a system not participating the language by the symbol "–".

Through the comparison in Table 6, we can find out that our system has absolute advantage in Chinese summarization. The results are very similar to the human results. In Hebrew, the result of our system is also just second to the result of human summarization. However, in Arabic, Greek, Hindi, the performance of our system is extremely bad. Especially for Hindi, our results are far less than others. We need more experiments later to explore the reasons for this situation. But on the whole, our system is still competitive. The performances on Chinese, Czech and Hebrew are all just ranked behind human results. One thing we need to emphasize is that our best Chinese summarization results have used Level Distribution feature. Although the best summarization results of other languages is not always involving Level Distribution, it can indicate that Level Distribution feature is most helpful in Chinese summarization. In light of our experience on single document text summarization with Level Distribution, the parameter setting in this paper awaits to be improved in the future. Generally speaking, the proportion of other features and Level Distribution feature is at least 3:1. It maybe because this reason that our Level Distribution feature cannot improve the best summarization results of other languages.

7   Conclusion

This paper introduces an improvement of multilingual multi-document summarization system based on Multi2015 MMS data. We propose a new feature of Level Distribution, combine it with multiple other features and demonstrate the superiority of this new summarization system through experiments in some aspects. Specifically, Chinese summarization results have been improved greatly. Experimental results have also revealed that our new feature is valuable in multilingual multi-document summarization system. In the future, we still need more experiments and research to improve the application of Level Distribution feature. We will perform more experiments to verify the robustness and effectiveness of Level Distribution feature in more languages. More features will be introduced into our system. For level distribution law, we will explore more rational and scientific explanations applications.

Acknowledgement. This work was supported by the National Natural Science Foundation of China under Grant 91546121, 61202247, 71231002 and 61472046; EU FP7 IRSES Mobile-Cloud Project (Grant No. 612212); the 111 Project of China under Grant B08004; Engineering Research Center of Information Networks, Ministry of Education; Beijing Institute of Science and Technology Information; CapInfo Company Limited.

References

1. Ferreira, R., et.al.: A four dimension graph model for automatic text summarization. In: Web Intelligence (WI) and Intelligent Agent Technologies (IAT), 17–20 November 2013, pp. 389–396 (2013)
2. Bhagat, K., Ingle, M.D.: Multi document summarization using EM Clustering. IOSR J. Eng. (IOSRJEN) **04**(05), 45–50 (2014). ISSN (e): 2250-3021, ISSN (p): 2278-8719, ‖V6‖
3. Litvak, M., Vanetik. N.: Multilingual multi-document summarization with POLY2. In: Proceedings of the MultiLing 2013 Workshop on Multilingual Multi-document Summarization, pp. 45–49 (2013)
4. Celikyilmaz, A., Hakkani-Tur, D.: A hybrid hierarchical model for multi-document summarization. In: 48th Annual Meeting of the Association for Computational Linguistics, Uppsala, Sweden, pp. 815–824 (2010)
5. Blei, D.M., Griffiths, T.L., Jordan, M.I., Tenenbaum, J.B.: Hierarchical topic models and the nested Chinese restaurant process. In: Advances in Neural Information Processing Systems 16. MIT Press, Cambridge (2004)
6. Liu, P.: Chinese multi document summarization based on hLDA model. Beijing University of Posts and Telecommunications (2013)
7. Liu, H.: Multi document summarization based on hLDA hierarchical topic model. Beijing University of Posts and Telecommunications (2012)
8. Liu, Y.: Multi document summarization based on topic model and semantic analysis. Beijing University of Posts and Telecommunications (2015)
9. Heng, W., Yu, J., Li, L., Liu, Y.: Reasearch on key factors of multi document topic modeling using hLDA. Chinese J. Inf. Sci. Technol. 06 (2013)
10. Giannakopoulos, G.: MMS MultiLing2015 Task (2015). http://multiling.iit.demokritos.gr/pages/view/1540/task-mms-multi-documentsummarization-data-and-information. Accessed 19 July 2015
11. Liu, M., Wang, L., Nie, L.: Weibo-oriented chinese news summarization via multi-feature combination. In: Hou, L., et al. (eds.) NLPCC 2015. LNCS, vol. 9362, pp. 581–589. Springer, Heidelberg (2015). doi:10.1007/978-3-319-25207-0_55
12. Lin, C.-Y.: ROUGE: a package for automatic evaluation of summaries. In: Proceedings of the Workshop on Text Summarization Branches Out (WAS 2004), Barcelona, Spain, July 25–26 2004 (2004)
13. http://www.berouge.com/Pages/default.aspx

News Abridgement Algorithm Based on Word Alignment and Syntactic Parsing

Min Yu[1(✉)], Huaping Zhang[1], Yu Zhang[1], Yang Qiao[1],
Zhonghua Zhao[2], and Yueying He[2]

[1] School of Computer Science, Beijing Institute of Technology,
Beijing 100081, China
{yumin2014,zhangyu2014,qiaoyang2014}@nlpir.org,
kevinzhang@bit.edu.cn
[2] National Computer Network and Information Security Management Center,
Beijing 100031, China
{zhaozh,hyy}@cert.org.cn

Abstract. The rapid development of new media results in a lot of redundant information, increasing the difficulty of quickly obtaining useful information and browsing simplified messages on portable devices. Thus emerges the automatic news abridgement technology. We propose a novel method of word alignment, aiming at news headlines, applying the combination method of statistics and rules to intelligent abridgement. And a new framework based on the combination of sentence abridgement and sentence selection to generate the abridgement result of news contents, abridging the original text to the word limit, in order to achieve the uttermost conservation of the original meaning. Meanwhile, for a fair and intelligent evaluation, this paper presents an evaluation method of automatic summarization specific to sentence abridgement techniques. Experimental results show that the proposed methods are feasible, and able to automatically generate coherent and representative summaries of given news with high density.

Keywords: News abridgement · Keyword features · Sentence abridgement · Heuristic rules · Sentence selection

1 Introduction

With the rapid development of Internet and digital technology, a variety of new media which supports users in interaction has sprung up. But media contents are fragmented and irregular, making it difficult to select information [1]. To help readers find high-quality content from a large quantity of news, as well as to display the news title lists on small handheld screens, we need to abridge and filter the text contents of Internet information for better representation. In this context, some tools are urgently needed to find desired information automatically, quickly and intelligently from massive amounts of news.

Most of current researches extract main contents of news as the summaries of the original news, with no regard for the abridgement of news titles and contents, making the word limit problem especially prominent. The traditional manually method of news

M. Sun et al. (Eds.): CCL and NLP-NABD 2016, LNAI 10035, pp. 313–323, 2016.
DOI: 10.1007/978-3-319-47674-2_26

abridgement is time-consuming when faced with massive media information data, thus unable to meet the demand for real-time processing of the various requests.

Based on these problems and challenges, this paper presents a novel algorithm based on word alignment technology and syntactic analysis to abridge news. Experimental results show that the algorithm is feasible, and able to automatically generate a coherent and representative summary of the given news with high density.

The contributions of our paper are as follows:

(1) A novel word alignment method is applied into news title abridgement, which integrates application rules and statistical methods to achieve intelligent abridgement.
(2) A framework that combines sentence abridgement and sentence selection is proposed to generate abridgement results of news content.
(3) An automatic summarization evaluation method specific to sentence abridgement is proposed.

2 Related Work

Most current methods abridge sentences by removing unimportant words or phrases with supervised and unsupervised learning algorithms [2]. Knight and Marcu [3] model the sentence abridgement process with noise channel model, and propose an abridgement algorithm based on Decision Tree Learning. Some studies use supervised learning algorithms such as CRFs [4], support vector regression [5] and so on. Supervised methods can easily integrate various features, but fail to deal with global dependencies due to computational efficiency and other reasons. Unsupervised methods are mainly based on integer linear programming [6, 7], which struggle with integrating various features, while handle global dependencies well.

Abstract generation mainly contains two methods: extraction and summarization [8]. Extraction approach focuses on selecting important sentences from the document and coupling them into a new summary, or summarizing with the formulated optimization framework, including integer linear programming (ILP) and sub-module functions. Gillick et al. [9] put forward an ILP method based on concepts. Li et al. [10] assess concepts weights of ILP structure by supervision strategies. Summarization methods are considered more difficult, which involve in-depth content like sematic representation, content arrangement and surface representation, and require complex techniques like natural language processing.

3 News Abridgement Algorithm Based on Word Alignment and Syntax Parsing

This section describes the interrelated algorithms of news abridgement, including sentence abridgement algorithm based on word alignment, word weighting based on features combination, sentence weighting based on features combination, heuristic sentence abridgement algorithm based on keywords. These algorithms build up a news abridgement system. Each algorithm will be described in detail below.

3.1 Sentence Abridgement Algorithm Based on Word Alignment

To shorten news titles, we introduce the "Tongyici Cilin" Extensions [11] as semantic dictionary to replace the original words with shorter synonyms which are called alignment words in this paper. With the aim of identifying the short words and new words which are appropriated to current network vocabulary from many synonyms, we use the edit distance algorithm to align the words with different meanings and obtain the corresponding transition probability, based on which the sentence patterns and word usage when news titles are written can be acquired using maximum probability principle. Ultimately the system generates novel title abridgement under the word limit, maintaining the original meaning.

In this paper, transition probability matrix is obtained by monolingual word alignment [12, 13] and showed in Table 1.

Table 1. Examples of the transition probability of the original word to the target word

录用（NULL，0.33；录用，0.67）
【employ (NULL, 0.33; employ, 0.67)】
中央巡视组（中央巡视组，0.25；NULL，0.63；整改，0.13）
【Central inspection team (Central inspection team, 0.25; NULL, 0.63; rectify, 0.13)】
什么样（NULL，0.25；什么样，0.75）
【what kind (NULL, 0.25; what kind, 0.75)】
干部（NULL，0.16；领导，0.01；干部，0.82）
【cadre (NULL, 0.16; leader, 0.01; cadre, 0.82)】
山体（NULL，0.07；山体，0.93）
【mountain (NULL, 0.07; mountain, 0.93)】
小学（NULL，0.09；小学，0.91）
【primary school (NULL, 0.09; primary school, 0.91)】

In the table above, the alignment words which can replace the original words and their corresponding probability are bracketed. For example, 录用(NULL, 0.33; 录用, 0.67), 【employ (NULL, 0.33; employ, 0.67)】, means in conventional manual processing, the original word "录用(employ)" is replaced by NULL with probability 0.33, is replaced by "录用(employ)" with probability 0.67. We take the alignment word "录用(employ)" with the maximum transition probability as the ultimate alignment word. Thus, compared to the method using only the "Tongyici Cilin" for word alignment, the method we propose is more statistically adaptive to corpus and is able to handle large-scale corpus of news.

3.2 Word Weighting Based on Features Combination

We put forward an algorithm based on multi-feature of sentence and prolixity processing combined with the heuristic sentence abridgement algorithm based on keywords to abridge news text.

Many factors are to be considered in news text abridgement, including word frequency, part of speech, word length and position of word. We integrate all factors and put forward a method based on features combination to calculate the weight of words in news text.

(1) Position of word

Words appearing in the title or some other positions are considered important. The first sentence of news usually introduces its five elements: when, where, who, why, and what is going on.

We identify the five elements of news from the first sentence by named entity recognition [14], and give weights by the following principles.

$$
Loc(w_i) = \begin{cases} 1, & \text{word } w_i \text{ is one of the word in news title or the five elements;} \\ \beta, & \text{word } w_i \text{ appears in the second sentence or the end of paragraph}(0 < \beta < 1); \\ 0, & \text{other position} \end{cases} \quad (1)
$$

(2) Keyword

We extract the key features from news content of data sets with bi-directional matching algorithm [15] and obtain 2105 keywords, which are given higher weights.

Table 2. Examples of keywords extraction results

Keywords	Keywords	Keywords
高新技术 (high technology)	率先垂范 (the first example)	杨六斤 (Yang Liujin)
三中全会 (Third Plenary Session)	觅仙泉 (Mi Xianquan)	警钟长鸣 (keep ringing the alarm bell)
无期徒刑 (life imprisonment)	严雪花 (Yan Xuehua)	黄某峰 (Huang Moufeng)
易燃易爆 (inflammable and explosive)	达赖喇嘛 (Darai Lama)	单霁翔 (Shan jixiang)
公款吃喝 (public money eating and drinking)	女德班 (women in Durban)	总揽全局 (overall authority)
范剑平 (Fan Jianping)	阳宝华 (Yang Baohua)	纪检监察部门 (discipline inspection and supervision departments)
常住人口 (permanent population)	强盗逻辑 (gangster logic)	革委会副主任 (Deputy director of the Committee)
羊城晚报 (Yangcheng Evening News)	终期考核 (final examination)	
一二线城市 (a second tier cities)		
新闻发布会 (press conference)		

$$Key(w_i) = \begin{cases} 1, & word\ w_i\ is\ in\ the\ key\ word\ list; \\ 0, & other\ case \end{cases} \qquad (2)$$

The keyword list is obtained through machine learning and adding new words. Some results are shown in Table 2.

(3) Part of speech

Nouns and compound nouns play important roles in expressing the meaning of articles.

$$POS(w_i) = \begin{cases} 1, & word\ w_i\ is\ compound\ noun; \\ \gamma, & word\ w_i\ is\ the\ name\ of\ people\ or\ place\ or\ organization(0<\gamma<1); \\ 0, & other\ part\ of\ speech \end{cases} \quad (3)$$

Combining these three feature formulas, we design a method based on feature combination to calculate the weight of words.

$$Score(w_i) = n_i + \lambda * (Loc(w_i) + Key(w_i) + POS(w_i)) \qquad (4)$$

Where n_i is the number of times that word w_i has appeared, and the relative optimal values of the parameters β, γ and λ are determined according to the repeated adjustment of the experiment. Meanwhile, the value of γ is related to the length of article, and the empirical value is 15.

The weight of word w_i calculated with formula (4) is as follows,

$$W(w_i) = Score(w_i) \Big/ \max_{w_j \in d}\{Score(w_j)\} \qquad (5)$$

Where d is document, x is the other words in the document.

3.3   Sentence Weighting Based on Features Combination

In order to give higher weights to the sentences that express the topic of document, this paper defines a series of features to weigh the importance of each sentence.

(1) Content of sentence

The more words and phrases with high weight the sentence contains, the greater the amount of information is, and the more important the sentence is.

$$Cont(s_i) = \sum_{j=1}^{N} \sqrt{W(w_j)} \Big/ N \qquad (6)$$

Where N is the number of words in sentence s_i, word $w_j \in s_i$, $0 < Cont(s_i) \leq 1$.

(2) Position of sentence

We give the corresponding weight to a sentence according to where it appears, and get the formula (7).

$$Loc(s_i) = \begin{cases} 1, & \text{Sentence } s_i \text{ is the first sentence of the paragraph;} \\ 0.5, & \text{Sentence } s_i \text{ is the last sentence or the second sentence of the paragraph;} \\ 0, & \text{other position} \end{cases} \quad (7)$$

Considering the content and position of the sentence, a weighted linear combination of multiple features is the final weight of the sentence. The formula for calculating the weight of a sentence is as follows:

$$W(s_i) = \varphi * Cont(s_i) + \eta * Loc(s_i) \quad (8)$$

Where φ and η are adjustable parameters, $\varphi + \eta = 1$.

3.4   Heuristic Sentence Abridgement Algorithm Based on Keywords

This algorithm applies heuristic abridgement rule to the results of the syntactic parsing of each sentence [16], and determines whether the sentence is to be removed or retained by the composition of each node in the syntax tree and the keyword feature. In this approach, we combine multiple constraints to improve the linguistic quality of abridged sentences [17].

We obtain a set of rules and the weights of rules through machine learning. For example, "remove the contents in front of the first noun phrase", "remove the adverbs or adjective phrase in a sentence", "remove the preposition phrases as attributive or adverbial in a sentence" and so on.

It is also important to determine the weights in abridgement rules. Through machine learning, it is found that keywords being given higher weights in the abridgement rules ensures the soundness of the abridgement process. Specifically, the weights of keywords in news titles and news texts are assigned to 3 and 2, and the weights of other words in the sentence are assigned to 0. For word that meets the abridgement rules, its weight will be reduced by 1 in each loop. If the grammar requirement of the abridged sentence is high and the length of the abridged sentence is not required, the loop can be ended. And an abridged sentence is formed with all the words with non-negative weights. If there is a requirement for the length of abridged sentence, constraints need to be added to the sentence selection method based on integer linear programming.

To restore the grammar and semantic of abridged sentence, we use the vector space model to calculate the sentence similarity of the pre-extracted abstract to remove the redundancy in the abstract [18], and finally use sentence selection based on ILP to generate the abridgement of news.

4   Experiment and Evaluation

This section is divided into two parts, the experiment of news title abridgement and the news text abridgement.

4.1 News Title Abridgement Experiment

The corpus of news title abridgement algorithm contains 5658 pairs of news titles extracted from people.cn Web (original titles) and Client (target titles). This algorithm is based on the transition probability mentioned in Sect. 3.1. In the experiment, 5558 title pairs are chosen as training set, which are manually labeled, with the left 100 pairs as test set. In order to make this model have wide range of adaptability, the selection of sentences is assessed against the topics, lengths and syntactic structure components.

There are three criteria in traditional sentence abridgement evaluation: the importance of words, grammar normalization, and compression ratio. By analyzing the criteria above, a comprehensive evaluation of sentence abridgement function is given in Eq. (9):

$$\text{Score} = \text{Gram} + \text{Impo} + 5 \times (1 - \text{CompRate}) \tag{9}$$

Where Gram represents normative grammar, Impo indicates the importance of words, and CompRate means the compression ratio, so that Score denotes sentence abridgement overall score. Through evaluation, the compression ratio is automatically determined by the system, semantics and grammar normalization are evaluated manually. Evaluation results are shown in Table 4.

Several typical examples of abridgement results are shown in Table 3, and are elaborated as follows.

Table 3. Examples of artificial abridgement and system abridgement for news titles

Example 1	Original title	35城市一卡通实现互联互通异地刷卡 (35 cities achieve off-site and interconnected city card)
	Artificial abridgement	35个城市一卡通实现异地刷卡 (35 cities achieve off-site city card)
	System abridgement	35城市一卡通实现异地刷卡 (35 cities achieve off-site city card)
Example 2	Original title	韩疗养医院火灾系八旬患者放火引起 (The fire happening in a Korean nursing home was set by a eighty-year-old patient)
	Artificial abridgement	韩疗养院火灾系八旬患者放火 (The fire happening in a Korean nursing home was set by a eighty-year-old patient)
	System abridgement	韩医院火灾系八旬患者放火 (The fire happening in a Korean nursing home was set by a eighty-year-old patient)

As Table 3 shows, the manual sentence compression ratio of example 1 is 82.35 %, whereas the automatic compression ratio is 76.47 %. Comparing with manual result, automatic result not only in the grammatical and semantic conforms to the standard, but also uses fewer words to express the core meaning of original sentence. As for example 2, the system abridged sentences are not precise to express the original meaning, by matching synonym "韩疗养院(Korean nursing home)" as "韩医院(Korean hospital)", however the main meaning remains the same, also the result is within the acceptable range.

By observing the results presented in Table 4, the overall system output results are inferior to manual abridgement results, but all of the three aspects of system abridgement results are above 60 %. Moreover, in terms of grammar and semantics, system output basically conforms to the specification of Chinese. This also illustrates that the system has advantages in maintaining the syntactic structure and semantic content of the abridged sentences. In addition, the compression ratio of the system is slightly lower, and is close to manual result, therefore the system preliminarily achieves the goal of abridging titles.

Table 4. News title abridgement system evaluation results

	Grammar	Semantics	Compression ratio
System abridgement	68.8 %	69.6 %	75.6 %
Artificial abridgement	88.8 %	77.6 %	72.8 %
System/artificial approximation	77.48 %	89.69 %	103.85 %

4.2 Experiment of News Text Abridgement

100 news articles from the people.cn Web are selected as the experimental data to do abstract extraction and analysis. Similarly, they are assessed against topics, lengths, and syntactic structures, which guarantees the generalization of the model, so as to better evaluate its performance.

(1) Keywords extraction experiment results
Due to space limitations, part of results is given in Table 2.
(2) News content abstract pre-extraction
According to the results of repeated testing procedures, the parameters β, γ and λ in the formulas (1), (3) and (4) are valued 0.5, 0.5 and 15 respectively, and the parameters φ and η in the formula (8) are both assigned as 0.5. The weights of sentences are calculated according to their multiple features, and then take the top 15 sentences as the result of the pre-extraction of the news abstract. Next, these sentences are sorted based on their relative locations in the original document.
(3) Pre-extraction abstract sentence abridgement
Pre-extracted sentences abridgement and restoration are based on heuristic linguistic rules. The results of evaluation are given in Table 5.

Table 5. Pre-extraction abstract sentence abridgement result evaluation

Grammar	Semantics	Compression ratio
77.93 %	80.89 %	73.15 %

As it shows, the semantic result is higher than the result of grammar, for that the abridgement rules might cause incomplete sentences, and so reduce the grammatical characteristics of the sentence. However, since the abridgement algorithm is based on keywords, it still retains the important information of the sentence, so that obtain a relatively higher semantic score.

(4) News abridgement system evaluation

Commonly used evaluation method is assuming there are x sentences in the standard summary, y sentences in the generated summary, and K sentences that appear in both the standard summary and the generated summary. Therefore, the precision and recall are $P = \frac{k}{x}$ and $R = \frac{k}{y}$. $F_1 - score$ is a compromised evaluation index considering precision and recall, $F_1 - score = \frac{2 \times P \times R}{P + R}$. Since the extraction task of this paper involves sentence abridgement, which may cause k equals to 0, we propose a novel definition for precision and recall.

$$P = \frac{k}{x} \times \left(\left(\sum_{i=1}^{k} Score \right) / k \right) \tag{10}$$

$$R = \frac{k}{y} \times \left(\left(\sum_{i=1}^{k} Score \right) / k \right) \tag{11}$$

Where k denotes the number of similar sentences. And the results of precision, recall and $F_1 - score$ are shown in Table 6.

Table 6. News abridgement system evaluation

Precision	Recall	$F_1 - score$
79.26 %	76.32 %	77.76 %

The experimental results suggest that the news abridgement algorithm is feasible and the extraction of abstract utilizes more fine-grained approach and are not just to sentence level extraction; for given news articles, it could automatically generate coherent and representative news summaries with high density.

An news abridgement example by using the proposed algorithm is given below (http://www.chinanews.com/gj/2014/05-27/6214377.shtml). The original news has in total 1303 words, and abridged news contains only 190 words, and it not only satisfies the grammar and semantic requirements but also significantly reduces the time of consideration in manual abridgement.

Abridged news title:

莫迪就任印度第15任总理(Modi became the fifteenth Prime Minister of India)

Abridged news text:

外媒27日报道, 印度人民党党首莫迪就任成为印度共和国第15任总理, 承诺建立一个"强大和具包容性" 的印度, 且组建了一个人数少很多的精简内阁。4000名宾客见证了莫迪的就职, 包括印度的巴基斯坦总理谢里夫。"我们创造辉煌的未来……让我们梦想, 建立一个强大、发达和具包容性的印度, 印度合作, 推动世界和平与发展。" 印度人民党主席拉杰纳特·辛赫任内政部长。莫迪被认为具有"亲市场" 倾向, 印度经济界有期待。(As foreign media reported on 27th, the leader of the Bharatiya Janata Party (BJP) Modi has become the 15th Prime Minister of the Republic of India, committed to establishing a "strong and inclusive" India and setting up a compact minister council. 4000 guests witnessed the inauguration of Modi, including India's Pakistani Prime Minister Nawaz Sharif. "We will create a brilliant future.... Let us dream, build a strong, developed and inclusive India, India will cooperate on promoting peace and development of the world." Rajnath, chairman of India people's party, he served as Minister of the interior. Modi is considered to have pro-market tendency, and India economic community have expectations.)

The experimental results show that the automatic news text abridgement system proposed in this paper achieves good results.

5   Conclusion

As the experiment results suggest, the proposed news abridgement algorithm is feasible. The algorithm could automatically generate coherent and representative summaries of the given news with high density, which could significantly reduce the workload of news editing and abridgement.

References

1. Jing, Z.: Research on the characteristics and problems of network entertainment news headlines. Journal. Knowl. **11**, 110–111 (2011)
2. Jing, H.: Sentence reduction for automatic text summarization. In: Proceedings of 6th Conference on Applied Natural Language Processing, pp. 310–315. Association for Computational Linguistics (2000)
3. Knight, K., Marcu, D.: Summarization beyond sentence extraction: a probabilistic approach to sentence compression. Artif. Intell. **139**(1), 91–107 (2002)
4. Nomoto, T.: A comparison of model free versus model intensive approaches to sentence compression. In: Proceedings of 2009 Conference on Empirical Methods in Natural Language Processing, vol. 1, pp. 391–399. Association for Computational Linguistics (2009)
5. Galanis, D., Androutsopoulos, I.: An extractive supervised two-stage method for sentence compression. In: Human Language Technologies: The 2010 Annual Conference of the North American Chapter of Association for Computational Linguistics, pp. 885–893. Association for Computational Linguistics (2010)
6. Filippova, K., Strube, M.: Dependency tree based sentence compression. In: Proceedings of 5th International Natural Language Generation Conference, pp. 25–32. Association for Computational Linguistics (2008)
7. Clarke, J., Lapata, M.: Global inference for sentence compression: an integer linear programming approach. J. Artif. Intell. Res. **31**, 399–429 (2008)
8. Li, C., Liu, F., Weng, F., et al.: Document summarization via guided sentence compression. In: EMNLP, pp. 490–500 (2013)

9. Gillick, D., Favre, B., Hakkani-Tur, D., et al.: The ICSI/UTD summarization system at TAC 2009. In: Proceedings of TAC (2009)
10. Li, C., Qian, X., Liu, Y.: Using supervised bigram-based ILP for extractive summarization. ACL **1**, 1004–1013 (2013)
11. "Tongyici Cilin" Extensions. http://www.ir-lab.org/
12. Och, F.J., Ney, H.: A comparison of alignment models for statistical machine translation. In: Proceedings of 18th Conference on Computational Linguistics, vol. 2, pp. 1086–1090. Association for Computational Linguistics (2000)
13. Yarowsky, D., Wicentowski, R.: Minimally supervised morphological analysis by multi-modal alignment. In: Proceedings of 38th Annual Meeting on Association for Computational Linguistics, pp. 207–216. Association for Computational Linguistics (2000)
14. Nadeau, D., Sekine, S.: A survey of named entity recognition and classification. Lingvisticae Investigationes **30**(1), 3–26 (2007)
15. Ruiqi, Z.: Research on Top N Hot Topics Detection Method Based on Key Features Clustering. Beijing Institute of Technology, Beijing (2015)
16. http://nlp.stanford.edu/software/lex-parser.shtml
17. Zajic, D., Dorr, B.J., Lin, J., et al.: Multi-candidate reduction: sentence compression as a tool for document summarization tasks. Inf. Process. Manag. **43**(6), 1549–1570 (2007)
18. Zhou, G., et al.: Towards faster and better retrieval models for question search. In: Proceedings of 22nd ACM International Conference on Conference on Information and Knowledge Management. ACM (2013)

A Hierarchical LSTM Model for Joint Tasks

Qianrong Zhou[✉], Liyun Wen, Xiaojie Wang, Long Ma, and Yue Wang

School of Computer, Beijing University of Posts and Telecommunications,
Beijing, China
{zhouqr,wenliyun,xjwang,miss_longma,wangyuesophie}@bupt.edu.cn

Abstract. Previous work has shown that joint modeling of two Natural Language Processing (NLP) tasks are effective for achieving better performances for both tasks. Lots of task-specific joint models are proposed. This paper proposes a Hierarchical Long Short-Term Memory (HLSTM) model and some its variants for modeling two tasks jointly. The models are flexible for modeling different types of combinations of tasks. It avoids task-specific feature engineering. Besides the enabling of correlation information between tasks, our models take the hierarchical relations between two tasks into consideration, which is not discussed in previous work. Experimental results show that our models outperform strong baselines in three different types of task combination. While both correlation information and hierarchical relations between two tasks are helpful to improve performances for both tasks, the models especially boost performance of tasks on the top of the hierarchical structures.

Keywords: Hierarchical LSTM · Joint modeling

1 Introduction

It is a normal situation in Natural Language Processing (NLP) that two tasks interact with each other. For example, Chinese word segmentation and POS-tagging, POS-tagging and chunking, intent identification and slot filling in goal-driven spoken language dialogue systems, and so on.

Usually, the second task is modeled after the first one is finished, since the first task is thought to be more fundamental or lower than the second one. It is so called pipeline method, i.e. low level tasks are followed by high level tasks. For example, chunking in character-based languages such as Chinese, Japanese and Thai requires word segmentation and POS-tagging as pre-processing steps [1–3]. In Spoken Language Understanding (SLU), intent is firstly identified as a classification problem using Support Vector Machines (SVMs) [4], and then sequence labeling methods such as Conditional Random Field (CRF) [5] are employed for slot filling task. However, pipeline method suffers from error propagation. Lots of methods for jointly modeling the first and the second tasks simultaneously have been proposed to tackle this problem.

Previous work has shown the effectiveness of joint models. Lyu et al. [6] introduced a transition-based framework for joint segmentation, POS-tagging

© Springer International Publishing AG 2016
M. Sun et al. (Eds.): CCL and NLP-NABD 2016, LNAI 10035, pp. 324–335, 2016.
DOI: 10.1007/978-3-319-47674-2_27

and chunking, and it achieved better results compared with a pipelined baseline. Zhu et al. [7] proposed a joint segmentation and POS-tagging system based on undirected graphical models which could make full use of the dependencies between the two stages. Shi et al. [8] proposed a hybrid model of Recurrent Neural Network (RNN) and Convolutional Neural Network (CNN) which could exploit possible correlations among intent classification and slot filling. Lee et al. [9] introduced a new tag addition method turning utterance classification task into sequence labeling task, then classification and slot filling could be analyzed by one sequence tagger. Duh [10] proposed Factorial Hidden Markov Models (FHMMs) with additional cross-sequence dependencies, enabling information sharing between POS-tagging/chunking subtasks. Li [11] studied four joint learning approaches on various sequence labeling tasks.

Previous joint modules have been proved to be able to manage the correlations between sub-tasks by jointly modeling two tasks. Most of the joint models aim to model two specific tasks, i.e. the joint model is task specific. For example, a joint model for word segmentation and POS-tagging is not suit for intent identification and slot filling. We argue that there are some common things behind different joint tasks. High level tasks receive information from low level tasks, while raise some constraints on low level side by hierarchical structures. Both of the interactions between two levels and the hierarchical structures for the joint tasks have important influences on the performances of both tasks. This paper therefore considers to build a joint model that can deal with different types of combinations of two tasks by balancing the interactions and hierarchical constraints between tasks in different levels. For example, a single model (or its slight variants) can deal with segmentation and POS-tagging, intent identification and slot filling, and others.

We propose a hierarchical LSTM (HLSTM) model and some its variants. They are used to deal with a wide types of joint tasks without significant modifications. The model has two-layer LSTM, each layer deals with one task. The two LSTMs takes both interactive and hierarchical information into consideration. Hierarchical relations are found to be very important in our experiments for most of joint tasks. It is not seriously considered and discussed in most previous work. All parameters in two layers are estimated together to minimize a joint objective function. Experimental results show that the proposed hierarchical model outperforms non-hierarchical methods in diverse tasks.

The rest of the paper is organized as follows. Section 2 introduces our proposed model in detail; Sect. 3 presents the tasks and experimental results; Finally, Sect. 4 draws conclusions.

2   Models

LSTM is the basic unit of models. We give a brief introduction to LSTM, and then propose our models one-by-one.

2.1   LSTM

LSTM model [12] is widely used in NLP since it can deal with arbitrary-length sequences of input. It alleviates the problem of gradients exploding or vanishing in Recurrent Neural Networks (RNNs) by introducing a memory cell. Commonly, a memory cell is composed of four components: an input gate, a forget gate, an output gate and a memory cell. The input gate controls how much information will be updated in memory cell, the forget gate controls how much information from previous time step to be remembered, and the output gate controls how much information will be outputted to next memory cell. At time step t, the hidden state vector h_t is calculated as following:

$$i_t = \sigma(W^{(i)} x_t + U^{(i)} h_{t-1} + b^{(i)}), \tag{1}$$

$$f_t = \sigma(W^{(f)} x_t + U^{(f)} h_{t-1} + b^{(f)}), \tag{2}$$

$$o_t = \sigma(W^{(o)} x_t + U^{(o)} h_{t-1} + b^{(o)}), \tag{3}$$

$$c_t = f_t \odot c_{t-1} + i_t \odot tanh(W^{(u)} x_t + U^{(u)} h_{t-1} + b^{(u)}), \tag{4}$$

$$h_t = o_t \odot tanh(c_t), \tag{5}$$

where i_t, f_t, o_t are the gating vectors representing the input gate, the forget gate and the output gate respectively. x_t is the input at the current time step. σ denotes the sigmoid function and $\odot$ denotes elementwise multiplication. $W^{(i)}$, $U^{(i)}$, $W^{(f)}$, $U^{(f)}$, $W^{(o)}$, $U^{(o)}$, $W^{(u)}$, $U^{(u)}$ are weight matrices associated with different gates. $b^{(i)}$, $b^{(f)}$, $b^{(o)}$, $b^{(u)}$ are the bias items.

Multilayer LSTM architectures are able to build higher level representations of input data. They can be created by stacking multiple LSTM hidden layers on the top of each other [13]. At time step t, the hidden state vector of layer n-1 is the input of layer n:

$$h_t^{(m)} = f(W^{(m-1,m)} h_t^{(m-1)} + W^{(m,m)} h_{t-1}^{(m)} + b^{(m)}), \tag{6}$$

where $W^{(m,m)}$ denotes weight matrices between two layers.

2.2   Hierarchical LSTM and Training

We firstly derive our basic joint model from two-layer LSTM for one basic type of joint tasks, and then propose its variants which fit to different types of joint tasks.

A common type of joint tasks usually combines a sentence-level classification task and a word-level sequence labeling task for a sentence. Examples for this type of joint tasks include intent identification and slot filling, sentiment classification and sentimental elements extraction, and so on.

Let $w_{(1:n)} = (w_1, w_2, ..., w_n)$ be an input sentence, Y be the label set for sentence, Z be the label set for each word. A joint model assigns a $y \in Y$ to the sentence and $z \in Z$ for each word. A hierarchical model called HLSTM (Hierarchical LSTM) including a sentence-level classification at bottom and a token-level sequence labeling on top is therefore proposed. The structure of HLSTM is shown in Fig. 1(a).

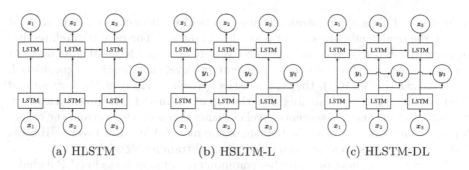

(a) HLSTM   (b) HSLTM-L   (c) HLSTM-DL

Fig. 1. Our proposed hierarchical models

Suppose the word embedding of w_t is $\boldsymbol{v}_t$ $(1 \leq t \leq n)$ which is used as input of HLSTM. Follow the Eq. (4) we get the last time step of hidden state vector $\boldsymbol{h}_n^{(1)}$ of lower LSTM, and the hidden state vector is fed to a softmax classifier. Then probabilities are estimated for sentence label

$$\boldsymbol{y} = softmax(\boldsymbol{W}^{(1)}\boldsymbol{h}_n^{(1)} + \boldsymbol{b}^{(1)}), \tag{7}$$

where $\boldsymbol{W}^{(1)}$ is a weight matrix for softmax classifier with respect to lower LSTM, and $\boldsymbol{b}^{(1)}$ is a bias term. For each time step t, $\boldsymbol{h}_t^{(1)}$ is still the input of upper LSTM unit. Then we estimate probabilities for sequence output tags

$$\boldsymbol{z}_t = softmax(\boldsymbol{W}^{(2)}\boldsymbol{h}_t^{(2)} + \boldsymbol{b}^{(2)}), \tag{8}$$

where $\boldsymbol{W}^{(2)}$ is a weight matrix for softmax classifier with respect to upper LSTM, $\boldsymbol{b}^{(2)}$ is a bias term.

Two tasks are simultaneously by minimizing a joint loss function. The parameter set of our network is $\theta = \{\boldsymbol{W}^{(i)}, \boldsymbol{U}^{(i)}, \boldsymbol{W}^{(f)}, \boldsymbol{U}^{(f)}, \boldsymbol{W}^{(o)}, \boldsymbol{U}^{(o)}, \boldsymbol{W}^{(u)}, \boldsymbol{U}^{(u)}, \boldsymbol{W}^{(1)}, \boldsymbol{W}^{(2)}\}$ (bias items are omitted). Given a set of training set $\mathcal{D}$, the regularized objective function is the loss function $J(\theta)$ including a l_2-norm term:

$$J(\theta) = \alpha L_S + (1 - a)L_T + \frac{\lambda}{2}||\theta||_2^2, \tag{9}$$

where L_S and L_T are sentence-level loss and token-level loss respectively. Let $\hat{\boldsymbol{y}}^{(i)}$ and $\hat{\boldsymbol{z}}_t^{(i)}$ be correct sentence and token label respectively, $L(\cdot)$ be a cross-entropy error. They are defined as:

$$L_S = \frac{1}{|\mathcal{D}|} \sum_i^{|\mathcal{D}|} L(\boldsymbol{y}^{(i)}, \hat{\boldsymbol{y}}^{(i)}), \tag{10}$$

$$L_T = \frac{1}{|\mathcal{D}|} \sum_i^{|\mathcal{D}|} \frac{1}{n} \sum_{t=1}^n L(\boldsymbol{z}_t^{(i)}, \hat{\boldsymbol{z}}_t^{(i)}) . \tag{11}$$

α $(0 < \alpha < 1)$ is a hyper-parameter used to tradeoff between two objectives. If $\alpha = 0$, the model only cares about token-level labeling. The network architecture degenerates into standard two-layer LSTM only for token-level labeling task. At the other extreme, if α is set to 1, only sentence-level classification is considered.

In HLSTM (Fig. 1(a)), the sentence-level classification is at the bottom and the token-level sequence labeling is on the top of the model. The inverse situation is another choice, i.e. the sentence-level classification is on the top and the token-level sequence labeling is at the bottom of the model. We call it Inverse HLSTM (I-HLSTM). It has same optimal objective and training algorithm.

Differing from above one, another common type of joint tasks in NLP includes two sequence labeling tasks interacting with each other. For example, POS-tagging and word segmentation, chunking and POS-tagging and so on. We use same hierarchical frame to deal with this type of joint tasks by extending basic HLSTM to HLSTM-L (HLSTM for two Labeling tasks). The structure of HLSTM-L is shown in Fig. 1(b).

HLSTM-L can be formed and trained in same way as those in HLSTM except for substituting class error in HLSTM with sequence label error. Like that in HLSTM, HLSTM-L can also be reversed by exchanging the LSTMs in two layer. We call the Inverse HLSM-L (I-HLSM-L).

In both HLSTM and HLSTM-L, dependencies between sequence labels are not modeled explicitly. For natural language tasks like word segmentation and POS-tagging, dependencies between sequence labels are important.

HLSTM-DL (HLSTM for Dependency Labeling tasks) is therefore proposed by extending HLSTM-L. HLSTM-DL keeps the same frame with HLSTM and HLSTM-L. The structure of HLSTM-DL is shown in Fig. 1(c), where dependencies between labels in lower level LSTM are taken into consideration explicitly.

To model the tag dependency, we follow Chen et al. (2015) [14] by introducing tag transition matrix $\boldsymbol{A}$. Every output tag sequence is given a score by summing tag transition score and tagging score:

$$s(x_{(1:n)}, y_{(1:n)}) = \sum_{t=1}^{n}(\boldsymbol{A}_{y_{t-1}y_t} + (\boldsymbol{y}_t)_{y_t}) \ . \tag{12}$$

Suppose the correct tag sequence of $x^{(i)}$ is $\hat{y}^{(i)}$. Let $Y(x^{(i)})$ be the set of all possible tag sequences. Then the predicted tag sequence $\bar{y}^{(i)}$ can be computed as:

$$\bar{y}^{(i)} = \underset{y \in Y(x^{(i)})}{\arg \max}(s(x^{(i)}, y) + \Delta(\hat{y}^{(i)}, y)), \tag{13}$$

where $\Delta(\hat{y}^{(i)}, y)) = \sum_{t=1}^{n} \gamma \mathbf{1}\{\hat{y}_t^{(i)} \neq y_t\}$ is a structured margin loss. γ is a discount parameter, the loss is proportional to the number of words with incorrect tags in the proposed tag sequence.

However, the way we predict most possible tag sequence during testing is a little bit different since the correct tag sequence is unknown, thus Eq. (13) replaced by

$$\bar{y}^{(i)} = \underset{y \in Y(x^{(i)})}{\arg \max} s(x^{(i)}, y) \ . \tag{14}$$

Moreover, L_S in Eq. (10) is modified to Eq. (15):

$$L_S = \frac{1}{n} l_S, \tag{15a}$$

$$l_S = \frac{1}{|\mathcal{D}|} \sum_i^{|\mathcal{D}|} l_S^{(i)}, \tag{15b}$$

$$l_S^{(i)} = \max(0, s(x^{(i)}, \bar{y}^{(i)}) + \Delta(\hat{y}^{(i)}, \bar{y}^{(i)}) - s(x^{(i)}, \hat{y}^{(i)})) . \tag{15c}$$

We can also have I-HLSTM-DL which is the reversed version of HLSTM-DL.

3 Experiments

Three different joint tasks are used for evaluating our models experimentally. They are Intent Classification and Slot Filling in SLU, POS-tagging and Chunking, Chinese Word Segmentation and POS-tagging.

Before the one-by-one introduction of our experiments, it is worthy to mention that hyper-parameters of all our models are tuned only by trying a few different settings in all experiments. We choose the smaller networks to achieve "reasonable" performances rather than picking the best hyper-parameters carefully to achieve their top performances. We employ standard experimental setups for models: for each group of tasks, we use AdaGrad [15] with mini-batches [16] to minimize the objective function. Derivatives are calculated from standard back-propagation [17]. The model achieving the best performance on the development set is used as the final model to be evaluated. The overall performance of joint model is simply evaluated by averaging performances of two tasks. All models are implemented in Theano [18,19].

3.1 Intent Classification and Slot Filling

Joint intent classification and slot filling is typically first type of joint tasks, where the former is a classification task and latter is treated as a sequence labeling problem.

User utterance with only one intent (act) in DSTC2 corpus[1] [20] is used[2]. Basic information about this corpus is listed in Table 1. The number of intent classes is 13, and the number of different slots is 9 including the O label.

HLSTM and its revered version I-HLSTM fit the joint tasks well. The lower layer of HLSTM deals with intent classification and upper layer aims at slot filling task. For I-HLSTM, the lower layer deals with slot filling and upper layer is for intent classification. Lee's model [9], which is a CRF-based joint model for intent classification and slot filling simultaneously, is compared. The open source toolkits is used[3].

---

[1] http://camdial.org/~mh521/dstc/.

[2] Sentences with 'request' intent are not included, since there is always no slot values in those sentences.

[3] http://taku910.github.io/crfpp/.

Table 1. Intent classification and slot filling corpus

Dataset	Sentences	Tokens
Training	4,790	19,562
Dev	1,579	6,807
Test	4,485	16,284

Table 2. Test set performance on intent classification, slot filling

	Intent (Acc.)	Slot (F1)
Lee et al. (2015)	98.84	98.62
I-HLSTM	**99.40**	98.84
HLSTM	99.29	**98.99**

The results are shown in Table 2. From the Table 2, we have two observations. (1) Both HLSTM and I-HLSTM perform better than CRF model on two tasks. It is similar with the conclusion in Mesnil et al. [21] and Mesnil et al. [22]. They showed RNN model is better than CRF in slot filling only task. (2) Although the overall performances of two HLSTMs are almost same, HLSTM achieves a slightly higher performance and they show different strengths. HLSTM prefers to slot filling task, while I-HLSTM prefers intent classification.

Reminded that slot filling is on the top of HLSTM, and intent classification is also on the top of I-HLSTM, we think there is a preference for top-layer LSTM in our two-layer LSTM models. It is a helpful hint on how to make choice between HLSTM and I-HLSTM.

α is used to leverage loss function of two tasks. Figure 2 shows how performances of model change with α. We can find several points from Fig. 2. (1) It is clear that both HLSTM and I-HLSTM achieve best performance when $\alpha \neq 0$ and $\alpha \neq 1$. It means two tasks can help each other if α is properly given. $\alpha = 0.3$

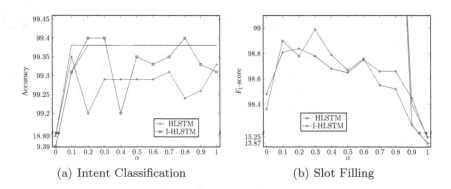

(a) Intent Classification   (b) Slot Filling

Fig. 2. Performances with different values of α

seems to be a good choice. On the contrary, improper combinations might hurt both of them. (2) Again, we find different strengths of two HLSTMs. Hierarchical structure help tasks on top-layer receive better scores.

3.2 POS-tagging and Chunking

Both POS-tagging and chunking can be regarded as sequence labeling problems. HLSTM-L and its reverse version are therefore used for joint modeling of the two tasks.

Penn Treebank Wall Street Journal corpus is used for joint POS-tagging and chunking. Basic information about this corpus is listed in Table 3. Their training data consists of sections 02–21 and test data consists of section 00. 10 % of the training set is split into a development set. The corpus contains 45 different types of POS tags, and 23 types of chunking tags respectively. A transformation-based learning model [23] was used for comparison since it used same dataset.

Table 3. POS-tagging and chunking corpus

Dataset	Sentences	Tokens
Training	39,831	950,011
Test	1,920	46,435

Experimental results are shown in Table 4. As can be seen from Table 4, (1) Both HLSTM-L and I-HLSTM-L are comparable with Florian et al. (2001). They achieve improvements on chunking, but a little lower in POS-tagging task. (2) HLSTM-L who models the hierarchical structure of joint tasks performs better overall. Similar to that in previous model, an appropriate value of α is crucial to the performance of both tasks. The impact of α is shown in Fig. 3.

Table 4. Test set performance on POS-tagging, chunking

	POS (Acc.)	Chunking (F1)
Florian et al. (2001)	**96.63**	93.12
I-HLSTM-L	96.21	93.38
HLSTM-L	96.36	**93.68**

The results in Fig. 3 illustrate that (1) both POS-tagging and chunking could be benefit by joint training. POS-tagging gets a performance boost and achieves best performance by introducing moderate chunking information, the same situation applies to chunking. $\alpha = 0.6$ seems to be a good choice. (2) Two HLSTM-Ls show different strengths on different tasks. HLSTM-L prefers to chunking, while I-HLSTM-L prefers POS-tagging.

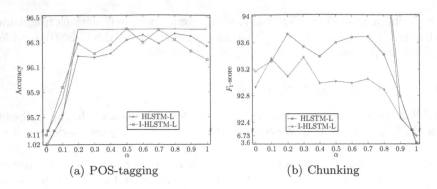

(a) POS-tagging   (b) Chunking

Fig. 3. Performances with different values of α

3.3 Chinese Word Segmentation and POS-tagging

Both Chinese word segmentation (CWS) and POS-tagging can be regarded as sequence labeling problems. Instead of using HLSTM-L, the influence of dependency relation is taken into consideration, and HLSTM-DL is employed to model the joint tasks. Since the result of POS-tagging includes the CWS, it is not possible to put CWS on the top layer with POS-tagging at the bottom, the reversed version will not be included in this experiment. Inspired by Pei et al. (2014) [24], bigram embeddings are used as models' inputs as well.

NLPCC 2015 dataset[4] [25] is used for the joint tasks. Different with the popular used newswire dataset, the NLPCC 2015 dataset collects informal texts from Weibo. The information of the dataset is shown in Table 5. 10 % of the training set is split into a development set and keep the remaining 90 % as the real training set. Each character is labeled as one of {B, M, E, S} to indicate the segmentation. For POS-tagging labels, each is the cross-product of a segmentation label and a POS tag, e.g. {B-NN, M-NN, E-NN, S-VP, ...}.

Table 5. CWS and POS-tagging corpus

Dataset	Sents	Words	Chars	Word Types	Char Types	OOV Rate
Training	10,000	215,027	347,984	28,208	3,971	-
Test	5,000	106,327	171,652	18,696	3,538	7.25 %

A CRF model for joint CWS and POS-tagging, which presented in the NLPCC 2015 shared task, is used as baseline. The templates are unigram feature, bigram feature and trigram feature. Word segmentation can be inferred from the output.

---

[4] http://nlp.fudan.edu.cn/nlpcc2015.

Table 6. Test set performance on CWS, POS-tagging

	CWS (F1)	POS (F1)
Qiu (2015)	93.80	87.69
HLSTM-L	92.10	85.44
HLSTM-DL	**95.10**	**87.75**

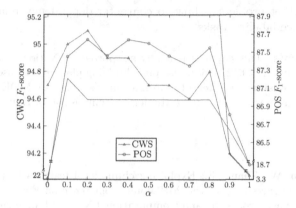

Fig. 4. Performances with different values of α

The results are shown in Table 6. HLSTM-DL achieves much improvement compared to HLSTM-L. Even with fewer features, HSLTM-DL gets a much better result on CWS and performs slightly better on POS-tagging compared to CRF model.

The effect of α is shown in Fig. 4. We can see that POS information brings a significant boost to CWS. The same analysis of α also applies to this experiment like previous ones.

We compared our proposed hierarchical models with non-hierarchical models on different kinds of combinations of NLP tasks. In most situation, hierarchical models achieve better results than strong baselines. Top-layer in hierarchical model is more powerful. Hierarchical model reflecting task hierarchy is likely to achieve higher overall performance. The detailed analysis of experimental results shown that the hyper-parameter α of hierarchical joint model can leverage information in one task to another, thus bring significant performance boosts to both tasks.

4 Conclusion

We have presented a hierarchical LSTM model and several its variants that can handle different kinds of combinations of NLP tasks. Experimental results on three different combinations of NLP tasks show promising results. In most situation, they outperform strong baselines. Hierarchical relations and correlation information between different layers are also discussed experimentally. Tasks get better performances if they are on top-layer. We believe they provide a series of potential solutions for joint learning of two NLP tasks.

There are several problems waiting for future work. While the hierarchical structure has been shown to be a good choice for arranging two NLP tasks, it is still not so clear how the information of two tasks interacts each other, especially how tasks at the bottom transmit supervision to the tasks on the top layer, and vice versa. Another problem is how to character dependency relation between labels in sequence labeling tasks.

Acknowledgments. This paper is partially supported by National Natural Science Foundation of China (No. 61273365), discipline building plan in 111 base (No. B08004) and Engineering Research Center of Information Networks of MOE, and the Co-construction Program with the Beijing Municipal Commission of Education.

References

1. Zhou, J., Qu, W., Zhang, F.: Exploiting chunk-level features to improve phrase chunking. In: Proceedings of the 2012 Joint Conference on Empirical Methods in Natural Language Processing and Computational Natural Language Learning, pp. 557–567. Association for Computational Linguistics, July 2012
2. Chen, W., Zhang, Y., Isahara, H.: An empirical study of Chinese chunking. In: Proceedings of the COLING/ACL on Main Conference Poster Sessions, pp. 97–104. Association for Computational Linguistics, July 2006
3. Tan, Y., Yao, T., Chen, Q., Zhu, J.: Applying conditional random fields to chinese shallow parsing. In: Gelbukh, A. (ed.) CICLing 2005. LNCS, vol. 3406, pp. 167–176. Springer, Heidelberg (2005)
4. Fan, R.E., Chang, K.W., Hsieh, C.J., Wang, X.R., Lin, C.J.: LIBLINEAR: a library for large linear classification. J. Mach. Learn. Res. **9**, 1871–1874 (2008)
5. Lafferty, J., McCallum, A., Pereira, F.C.: Conditional random fields: probabilistic models for segmenting and labeling sequence data (2001)
6. Lyu, C., Zhang, Y., Ji, D.: Joint word segmentation, POS-tagging and syntactic chunking. In: Thirtieth AAAI Conference on Artificial Intelligence, March 2016
7. Tie-jun, Z.C.H.Z., De-quan, Z.: Joint Chinese word segmentation and POS tagging system with undirected graphical models. J. Electr. Inf. Technol. **3**, 038 (2010)
8. Shi, Y., Yao, K., Chen, H., Pan, Y.C., Hwang, M.Y., Peng, B.: Contextual spoken language understanding using recurrent neural networks. In: 2015 IEEE International Conference on Acoustics, Speech and Signal Processing (ICASSP), pp. 5271–5275. IEEE, April 2015
9. Lee, C., Ko, Y., Seo, J.: A simultaneous recognition framework for the spoken language understanding module of intelligent personal assistant software on smart phones. Short Papers, vol. 29, p. 818 (2015)
10. Duh, K.: Jointly labeling multiple sequences: a factorial HMM approach. In: Proceedings of the ACL Student Research Workshop, pp. 19–24. Association for Computational Linguistics, June 2005
11. Li, X.: Research on joint learning of sequence labeling in natural language processing (Dissertation for the Doctoral Degree in Engineering). Harbin Institue of Technology, Harbin, China (2010)

12. Hochreiter, S., Schmidhuber, J.: Long short-term memory. Neural Comput. **9**(8), 1735–1780 (1997)
13. Graves, A., Mohamed, A.R., Hinton, G.: Speech recognition with deep recurrent neural networks. In: 2013 IEEE International Conference on Acoustics, Speech and Signal Processing (ICASSP), pp. 6645–6649. IEEE, May 2013
14. Chen, X., Qiu, X., Zhu, C., Liu, P., Huang, X.: Long short-term memory neural networks for chinese word segmentation. In: Proceedings of the Conference on Empirical Methods in Natural Language Processing (2015)
15. Duchi, J., Hazan, E., Singer, Y.: Adaptive subgradient methods for online learning and stochastic optimization. J. Mach. Learn. Res. **12**, 2121–2159 (2011)
16. Cotter, A., Shamir, O., Srebro, N., Sridharan, K.: Better mini-batch algorithms via accelerated gradient methods. In: Advances in neural information processing systems, pp. 1647–1655 (2011)
17. Goller, C., Kuchler, A.: Learning task-dependent distributed representations by backpropagation through structure. In: IEEE International Conference on Neural Networks, vol. 1, pp. 347–352. IEEE, June 1996
18. Bastien, F., Lamblin, P., Pascanu, R., Bergstra, J., Goodfellow, I., Bergeron, A., Bengio, Y.: Theano: new features and speed improvements. arXiv preprint arXiv:1211.5590 (2012)
19. Bergstra, J., Breuleux, O., Bastien, F., Lamblin, P., Pascanu, R., Desjardins, G., Bengio, Y.: Theano: a CPU and GPU math expression compiler. In: Proceedings of the Python for Scientific Computing Conference (SciPy), vol. 4, p. 3, June 2010
20. Williams, J., Raux, A., Ramachandran, D., Black, A.: The dialog state tracking challenge. In: Proceedings of the SIGDIAL 2013 Conference, pp. 404–413, August 2013
21. Mesnil, G., He, X., Deng, L., Bengio, Y.: Investigation of recurrent-neural-network architectures and learning methods for spoken language understanding. In: INTER-SPEECH, pp. 3771–3775, August 2013
22. Mesnil, G., Dauphin, Y., Yao, K., Bengio, Y., Deng, L., Hakkani-Tur, D., Zweig, G.: Using recurrent neural networks for slot filling in spoken language understanding. IEEE/ACM Trans. Audio Speech Lang. Process. **23**(3), 530–539 (2015)
23. Florian, R., Ngai, G.: Multidimensional transformation-based learning. In: Proceedings of the 2001 workshop on Computational Natural Language Learning, vol. 7, p. 1. Association for Computational Linguistics, July 2001
24. Pei, W., Ge, T., Chang, B.: Max-margin tensor neural network for Chinese word segmentation. ACL **1**, 293–303 (2014)
25. Qiu, X., Qian, P., Yin, L., Wu, S., Huang, X.: Overview of the NLPCC 2015 shared task: chinese word segmentation and POS tagging for micro-blog texts. In: Hou, L., et al. (eds.) NLPCC 2015. LNCS, vol. 9362, pp. 541–549. Springer, Heidelberg (2015). doi:10.1007/978-3-319-25207-0_50

Enhancing Neural Disfluency Detection
with Hand-Crafted Features

Shaolei Wang$^{(\boxtimes)}$, Wanxiang Che, Yijia Liu, and Ting Liu

Research Center for Social Computing and Information Retrieval,
School of Computer Science and Technology,
Harbin Institute of Technology, Harbin, China
{slwang,car,yjliu,tliu}@ir.hit.edu.cn

Abstract. In this paper, we apply a bidirectional Long Short-Term Memory with a Conditional Random Field to the task of disfluency detection. Long-range dependencies is one of the core problems for disfluency detection. Our model handles long-range dependencies by both using the Long Short-Term Memory and hand-crafted discrete features. Experiments show that utilizing the hand-crafted discrete features significantly improves the model's performance by achieving the state-of-the-art score of 87.1 % on the Switchboard corpus.

Keywords: Disfluency detection · BI-LSTM-CRF · Discrete features · Continuous neural features

1 Introduction

Disfluencies are common in automatic speech recognition (ASR). Detecting disfluencies is important for natural language understanding, since most downstream NLU systems are built on the fluent utterances. Disfluency of a sentence can be categorized into five classes: uncompleted words, filled pauses (e.g. "uh", "um"), editing terms (e.g. "you know"), discourse markers (e.g. "i mean") and repairs that are discarded, or corrected by its following words (see Fig. 1 for a disfluency example with filled pauses, discourse markers and repair words). The former four classes of disfluencies are easy to detect as they often consist of fixed phrases (e.g. "uh", "you know"). While, the repair disfluencies (see Table 1) are more difficult to detect, because they are in arbitrary form [25]. Most of the previous disfluency detection works focus on detecting the repair disfluencies.

Modeling long-range dependencies between repair phrases is one of the core problems for detecting the repair disfluencies. Previous sequence tagging methods [5,6,21] require carefully designed features to capture information of long distance, but usually suffer sparsity problem. Another line of syntax-based disfluency detection work [9,25] try to model the repair phrases on a syntax tree by compressing the unrelated phrases and allowing repair phrases to interact with each other. However, data that both have syntax tree and disfluency annotation is scarce. The performance of syntax parsing models (about 92 % on English)

© Springer International Publishing AG 2016
M. Sun et al. (Eds.): CCL and NLP-NABD 2016, LNAI 10035, pp. 336–347, 2016.
DOI: 10.1007/978-3-319-47674-2_28

A flight to u͟m Boston I mean Denver Tuesday
             FP   RM   IM   RP

Fig. 1. A sentence with disfluencies annotated in the style of [23] and the Switchboard corpus. FP = Filled Pause, RM = Reparandum, IM = Interregnum, RP = Repair. We follow previous work in evaluating the system on the accuracy with which it identifies speech-repairs, marked *reparandum* above.

Table 1. Repair disfluency sentences. "/E" means that the word belong to a repair and should be deleted.

they/E had/E they/E used/E to/E have/E well they do have television monitors stationed throughout our buildings.
and the/E other/E one/E is/E her husband is in the navy.
they/E in/E fact/E they/E just/E it was just a big thing recently.

also hinders the disfluency detection's performance. Recurrent neural network (RNN), which can capture dependencies at any length, has been successfully applied to many NLP tasks, including NER [11] and opinion mining [12]. There is also work that tried to use RNN in disfluency detection problem [10]. However, in term of solving long-range dependencies, [10] overly relies on the RNN itself and doesn't adopt the hand-craft discrete features which has shown effective in previous work [26]. Further more, [10] treats sequence tagging as classification on each input token and doesn't model the transition between tags which is important for recognizing the repair phrases of multi-words.

In this paper, we follow the sequence tagging work and combine CRF and RNN to solve the disfluency detection problem. More specifically, we use a bidirectional Long Short-Term Memory (BI-LSTM) network to encode the words and feed the output to a linear-chained CRF to model the probability of tag sequence, thus result in a BI-LSTM-CRF model. We also study the problem of adopting the hand-crafted discrete features into BI-LSTM-CRF model. We evaluate our model on the English Switchboard corpus. The results show that our model outperforms previous stat-of-the-art systems by achieving a 87.1 % F-score.

2 BI-LSTM-CRF Model

RNN has been employed to produce state-of-the-art results on a variety of tasks [11,12]. It takes a sequence of input $(x_1, x_2, ..., x_n)$ and returns a sequence $(h_1, h_2, ..., h_n)$ in which h_t encodes the information in ranging from x_1 to x_t. In theory, RNN can capture dependencies of the inputs at any length with a hidden layer that memorizes the historical information. Unfortunately, in practice, it fails due to the gradient varnishing/exploding problems [1,20]. Long Short-Term Memory (LSTM) [8] as a variant of RNN is designed to cope with the gradient varnishing problems. It addresses the varnishing problems with an extra memory "cell" c_t that is constructed as a linear combination of the previous state and input signal. LSTM cells process the inputs with three multiplicative gates which control the proportions of information to forget and to pass on to the next time step. A LSTM memory cell is calculated as:

$$i_t = \sigma(W_{xi}x_t + W_{hi}h_{t-1} + W_{ci}c_{t-1} + b_i)$$
$$c_t = (1 - i_t) \odot c_{t-1} + i_t \odot \tanh(W_{xc}x_t + W_{hc}h_{t-1} + b_c)$$
$$o_t = \sigma(W_{xo}x_t + W_{ho}h_{t-1} + W_{co}c_t + b_o)$$
$$h_t = o_t \odot \tanh(c_t)$$

where σ is the element-wise sigmoid function and $\odot$ is the element-wise product.

For disfluency detection, it is difficult to predict a word as disfluency by only considering its past contexts, because disfluent phrases of this word can occur before or after it. A good model should access to both the past and the future contexts for disfluency detection. In this paper, we encode the past and the future information with BI-LSTM [15]. In the BI-LSTM, the past information is represented with a forward LSTM and the future with a backward LSTM respectively. The hidden states from these two LSTMs are concatenated to form the final output.

h_t can be used to make independent classification on each token to do the disfluency tagging. But such classification scheme is limited when there are strong dependencies between output tags. Disfluency detection is one of the tasks that strong dependencies exist between tags because one repair phase can have multi-words. Instead of modeling tagging decisions independently, we model them jointly using a CRF layer [11,14,15,18]. Figure 2 illustrates the architecture of BI-LSTM-CRF in detail. For an input sentence $X = (x_1, x_2, ..., x_n)$, we define $P \in R^{n \times k}$ to be the matrix of scores output by the BI-LSTM network, where k is the number of tags and $P_{i,j}$ corresponds to the score of x_i tagged as j. We also define $A \in R^{k \times k}$ to be the matrix of transition scores that $A_{i,j}$ is the score

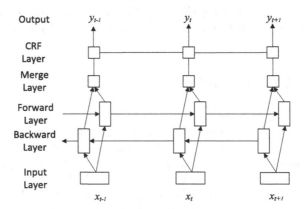

Fig. 2. Main architecture of the BI-LSTM-CRF. Outputs of the hidden layer are given to a CRF Layer after passing through a Merge Layer.

of a transition from tag i to tag j. For a sequence of tags $y = (y_1, y_2, ..., y_n)$, its score is defined as

$$s(X, y) = \sum_{i=0}^{n} A_{y_i, y_{i+1}} + \sum_{i=1}^{n} P_{i, y_i}$$

and its probability is defined as

$$p(y|X) = \frac{exp\{s(X, y)\}}{\sum_{\widetilde{y} \in Y_X} exp\{s(X, \widetilde{y})\}}$$

where Y_X represents all possible tag sequences of the input sequence X. To learn parameters of the BI-LSTM and the transition matrix A, we minimize the negative log-probability of the correct tag sequence over the input data $\{(X^{(n)}, y^{(n)})\}_{n=1}^{N}$ during training:

$$-\sum_{n=1}^{N} log(p(y^{(n)}|X^{(n)})) = -\sum_{n=1}^{N} \left(s(X^{(n)}, y^{(n)}) - log \left(\sum_{\widetilde{y} \in Y_{X^{(n)}}} exp\{s(X^{(n)}, \widetilde{y})\} \right) \right)$$

While decoding, we predict the highest-scored output sequence using dynamic programming.

3   Utilizing Hand-Crafted Features

Previous studies [5,21] show that hand-crafted features are very effective for achieving good disfluency detection performance, especially those features that capture the duplication between phrases. In this paper, We use two kinds of hand-crafted discrete features as shown in Table 2 and incorporate them into our neural networks by translating them into a 0–1 vector d. The dimension of d is 78, which equals to the number of discrete features. For a token x_t, d_i fires

Table 2. Discrete features used in the BI-LSTM and BI-LSTM-CRF networks. p is the POS tag. w is the word. Duplicate indicates if the two units are same. fuzzyMatch indicates the similarity of two words

Duplicate features
$Duplicate(w_i, w_{i+k})$, $-15 \leq k \leq +15$ and $k \neq 0$: if w_i equals w_{i+k}, the value is 1, others 0
$Duplicate(p_i, p_{i+k})$, $-15 \leq k \leq +15$ and $k \neq 0$: if p_i equals p_{i+k}, the value is 1, others 0
$Duplicate(w_i w_{i+1}, w_{i+k} w_{i+k+1})$, $-4 \leq k \leq +4$ and $k \neq 0$: if $w_i w_{i+1}$ equals $w_{i+k} w_{i+k+1}$, the value is 1, others 0
$Duplicate(p_i p_{i+1}, p_{i+k} p_{i+k+1})$, $-4 \leq k \leq +4$ and $k \neq 0$: if $p_i p_{i+1}$ equals $p_{i+k} p_{i+k+1}$, the value is 1, others 0
Similarity features
$fuzzyMatch(w_i, w_{i+k})$, $k \in \{-1, +1\}$:
$similarity = num\_same\_letters / (len(w_i) + len(w_{i+k}))$. if $similarity > 0.8$, the value is 1, others 0

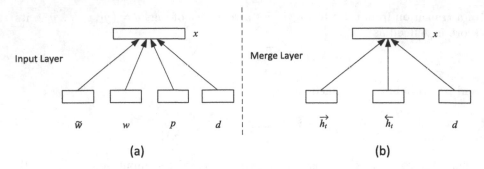

Fig. 3. Two methods of combining discrete features and continuous neural features. $\widetilde{w}$ is a pretrained embedding of current word. w is a learned embedding of current word; p is a learned embedding of current POS tag of the word; d is a continuous embedding of discrete features. $\overrightarrow{h_t}$ is the output of the forward LSTM. $\overleftarrow{h_t}$ is the output of the backward LSTM

if x_t matches the i-th pattern of the feature templates. The duplicate features care whether x_t has a duplicated word/pos in certain distance. The similarity features care whether the surface string of x_t resembles its surrounding words.

In this paper, we try two different methods to incorporate the hand-crafted discrete features d. In the first method, we treat d as an input to the LSTM along with the fin-tune word embedding w, fixed word embedding $\widetilde{w}$ and POS-tag embedding p. These four parts are concatenated together, transformed by a matrix V and fed to a rectified layer to learn feature combination, as

$$x = max\{0, V[\widetilde{w}; w; p; d] + b\}$$

where $[\widetilde{w}; w; p; d]$ means the concatenation. This method is shown in Fig. 3(a). By feeding d into LSTM, we allow to encode a long-range of hand-crafted features.

In the second method, we treat d as input to the CRF-layer, along with the outputs of the forward and the backward LSTMs. Formally, it can be calculated as

$$x = max\{0, V[\overrightarrow{h_t}; \overleftarrow{h_t}; d] + b\}$$

where $\overrightarrow{h_t}$ is the output of the forward LSTM, $\overleftarrow{h_t}$ is the output of the backward LSTM. This method is shown schematically as in Fig. 3(b).

4   Network Training

4.1   Parameters

Pretrained Word Embedding. There are lots of methods for creating word embeddings. As [4] does, we use a variant of the skip n-gram model introduced by [17], named "structured skip n-gram", where a different set of parameters are used to predict each context word depending on its position relative to the target word. The hyperparameters of the model are the same as in the skip n-gram model defined in word2vec [19]. We set the window size to 5, and use a negative sampling rate to 10. The AFP portion of English Gigaword corpus (version 5) is used as the training corpora.

Hyper-Parameters. Our BI-LSTM and BI-LSTM-CRF models use two hidden layers for the forward and backward LSTMs whose dimensions are set to 100. Pretrained word embeddings have 100 dimensions and the learned word embeddings have also 100 dimensions. Pos-tag embeddings have 12 dimensions. The dimensions of labels in BI-LSTM-CRF are set to 16.

Parameter Initialization. The learned parameters in the neural networks are randomly initialized with uniform samples from $[-\sqrt{\frac{6}{r+c}}, +\sqrt{\frac{6}{r+c}}]$, where r and c are the number of rows and columns in the parameter structure.

4.2 Optimization Algorithm

Parameter Optimization. Parameter optimization is performed with stochastic gradient descent (SGD) with an initial learning rate of $\eta_0 = 0.1$ and a gradient clipping of 5.0. The learning rate is updated on each epoch of training as $\eta_t = \eta_0/(1 + \rho t)$, in which t is the number of epoch completed and the decay rate $\rho = 0.05$.

Early Stopping. We use early stopping [7] based on performance on dev sets. The best parameters appear at around 12 epochs, according to our experiments.

Dropout Training. To reduce overfitting, we apply the dropout method [24] to regularize our model. We apply dropout not only on input and output vectors of BI-LSTM, but also between different hidden layers of BI-LSTM. We observe a significant improvement on model performances after using dropout.

Unknown Word Handling. As described in Sect. 3, the input layer contains a learned vector representation for the word w and a corresponding fixed pretrained vector representation $\widetilde{w}$. We randomly replace the singleton word in the training data with the UNK token during training, but keep corresponding $\widetilde{w}$ unchanged. This technique can deal with out-of-vocabulary words.

5 Experiments

5.1 Settings

Dataset. We conduct our experiments on the English Switchboard corpus. Following the experiment settings in [2,9,25], we use directory 2 and 3 in PARSED/MRG/SWBD as our training set and split directory 4 into test set, development set and others. We extract the repair disfluencies according to the EDITED label in the Switchboard corpus. Following [9], we lower-case the text and remove all punctuations and partial words[1]. We also discard all the 'um' and

---

[1] words are recognized as partial words if they are tagged as 'XX' or end with '-'.

'uh' tokens and merge 'you know' and 'i mean' into single token. Automatic POS tags generated from pocket_crf [21] are used as POS-tag in our experiments.

Metric and Tagging Schemes. Following previous works [5,25], token-based precision (P), recall (R), and F-score (F1) are used as the evaluation metrics. We use BIESO tagging scheme in our experiments.

5.2   Effect of CRF-layer

To investigate the effect of combining BI-LSTM and CRF, we build the following systems:

- CRF: a baseline system and the hand-crafted discrete features are the same with those in [5]. Note that the hand-crafted features in Table 2 are contained in the CRF model
- BI-LSTM: model that encodes word and POS-tag with BI-LSTM and use the output of the merge layer in Fig. 2 as features for a logistic classifier.
- BI-LSTM-CRF: model that takes the same input as BI-LSTM but compute the probability of tag sequence with a CRF layer.

Table 3 shows that BI-LSTM-CRF achieves significant improvements over BI-LSTM by adding CRF layer for joint decoding. This result demonstrates the necessary of handling the label bias problem in disfluency detection. We also note that the CRF with rich hand-crafted discrete features outperforms the BI-LSTM-CRF with only continuous neural features. A natural question that arises from this contrast is whether hand-crafted discrete features and continuous neural features can be integrated for better accuracies. We will study it in next section.

Table 3. Experimental results on the development and test data for investigating the effect of CRF-layer.

Method	Dev			Test		
	P	R	F1	P	R	F1
CRF	93.8 %	77.7 %	85.0 %	92.0 %	74.5 %	82.3 %
BI-LSTM	94.0 %	71.0 %	80.9 %	93.2 %	70.3 %	80.1 %
BI-LSTM-CRF	94.8 %	71.1 %	81.3 %	94.0 %	71.3 %	81.1 %

5.3   Effect of Hand-Crafted Features

Based on the BI-LSTM-CRF, we compare two methods of combining hand-crafted discrete features and continuous neural features. In Table 4, "-HIDDEN" means combining hand-crafted discrete features with hidden outputs of BI-LSTM. "-INPUT" means combining discrete feature embeddings with POS-tag and word embedding to the input layer. From the result of Table 4, both

Table 4. Experimental results on the development and test data for investigating the effect of integrating hand-crafted features.

Method	Dev			Test		
	P	R	F1	P	R	F1
CRF	93.8 %	77.7 %	85.0 %	92.0 %	74.5 %	82.3 %
BI-LSTM	94.0 %	71.0 %	80.9 %	93.2 %	70.3 %	80.1 %
BI-LSTM-HIDDEN	93.1 %	78.6 %	85.2 %	92.9 %	76.7 %	84.0 %
BI-LSTM-INPUT	93.2 %	82.6 %	87.6 %	92.7 %	80.6 %	86.2 %
BI-LSTM-CRF	94.8 %	71.1 %	81.3 %	94.0 %	71.3 %	81.1 %
BI-LSTM-CRF-HIDDEN	93.4 %	78.6 %	85.4 %	91.7 %	78.6 %	84.6 %
BI-LSTM-CRF-INPUT	92.8 %	84.3 %	88.3 %	91.0 %	83.6 %	**87.1 %**

the BI-LSTM-CRF-HIDDEN and the BI-LSTM-CRF-INPUT outperform the BI-LSTM-CRF by a large margin. The result confirms that hand-crafted discrete features and continuous neural features can be integrated to achieve better performance. By comparing two methods of combining hand-crafted discrete features, BI-LSTM-CRF-INPUT achieves better performance than BI-LSTM-CRF-HIDDEN. We attribute it to the fact that BI-LSTM-CRF-INPUT allow the dense and hand-crafted discrete features to interact with each other by non-linear transformation and encode the discrete features of long range with LSTM at the same time. We also test the effect of hand-crafted features on BI-LSTM model and get similar results with BI-LSTM-CRF.

5.4   Final Result and Comparsion with Previous Work

We compare our best model (BI-LSTM-CRF-INPUT) to four previous top performance systems. Our method outperforms state-of-the-art work and achieves a 87.1 % F-score as shown in Table 5. Our model achieves 2 point improvements over UBT [25], which is the best syntax-based method for disfluency detection. The best performance by linear statistical sequence labeling methods is the semi-CRF method [5], achieving a 84.8 % F1 score without leveraging prosodic

Table 5. Comparison of our BI-LSTM-CRF with the previous state-of-the-art methods on the test set.

Method	P	R	F1
BI-LSTM-CRF-INPUT	91.0 %	83.6 %	**87.1 %**
M^{3}N [21]	-	-	84.1 %
Joint parser [9]	-	-	84.1 %
semi-CRF [5]	90.1 %	80.0 %	84.8 %
UBT [25]	90.3 %	80.5 %	85.1 %

features. Our model beats the semi-CRF model, obtaining 2.3 point improvements. Note that our method performs better than previous methods not only on precision, but also on recall. The comparison shows that our model is a good solution to disfluency detection.

5.5   Ablation Test

To test the individual effectiveness of duplicate features and similarity features, we conduct feature ablation experiments for the BI-LSTM-CRF-INPUT model. Table 6 shows the result. We can see that both the two kinds of features contribute to the performance improvements of disfluency detection and we can achieve a higher performance by integrating all of them into BI-LSTM-CRF. This indicates that duplicate features and similarity features are both important to the BI-LSTM-CRF and they provide different kinds of information for disfluency detection.

Table 6. Results of feature ablation experiments on BI-LSTM-CRF-INPUT models.

Method	Dev			Test		
	P	R	F1	P	R	F1
BI-LSTM-CRF	94.8%	71.1%	81.3%	94.0%	71.3%	81.1%
+ Duplicate	94.5%	80.5%	86.9%	93.2%	79.7%	86.0%
+ Similarity	94.9%	73.9%	83.1%	94.1%	73.6%	82.6%
+ Duplicate + Similarity	92.8%	84.3%	88.3%	91.0%	83.6%	**87.1%**

6   Related Work

Most related works on disfluency detection are aimed at detecting repair type of disfluencies. [13] proposed a TAG-based noisy channel model for disfluency detection. The TAG model was used to find rough copies. Following the work of [13,27] extended the TAG model using minimal expected f-loss oriented n-best reranking with additional corpus for language model training. [21] proposed a muiti-step learning method using weighted max-margin markov network (M^3N). They showed that M^3N model outperformed many other labeling models such as CRF model. [5] used the Semi-Markov CRF model for disfluency detection and achieved high F-score by integrating prosodic features.

Many syntax-based approaches have been proposed which jointly perform dependency parsing and disfluency detection. [16] involved disfluency detection in a PCFG parser to parse the input along with detecting disfluencies. [22] designed a joint model for both disfluency detection and dependency parsing. [9] presented a new joint model by extending the original transition actions with a new "Edit" transition. This model achieved good performance on both disfluency detection and parsing. [25] proposed a right-to-left transition-based joint method and achieved the state-of-the-art performance compared with previous syntax-based approaches.

RNN had been used to disfluency detection. [10] explored incremental detection, with an objective that combines detection performance with minimal latency. This approach achieved worse performance compared with other works for the latency constraints. [3] used word embeddings learned by an RNN as features in a CRF classifiers.

7   Conclusion and Future Work

In this paper, we have explored an application of BI-LSTM-CRF networks to the task of disfluency detection. Our method explores the combination of hand-crafted discrete features and continuous neural features. Experimental result shows that our method achieves the best reported performance on the English Switchboard corpus.

In the future, we will try to model the task of disfluency detection as a sequence to sequence learning problem and incorporate character-based representations into the encoder model. We would also like to jointly model disfluency detection and automatic punctuation using some neural network.

Acknowledgments. This work was supported by the National Key Basic Research Program of China via grant 2014CB340503 and the National Natural Science Foundation of China (NSFC) via grant 61133012 and 61370164.

References

1. Bengio, Y., Simard, P., Frasconi, P.: Learning long-term dependencies with gradient descent is difficult. IEEE Trans. Neural Netw. **5**(2), 157–166 (1994)
2. Charniak, E., Johnson, M.: Edit detection and parsing for transcribed speech. In: Proceedings of the Second Meeting of the North American Chapter of the Association for Computational Linguistics on Language Technologies, pp. 1–9. Association for Computational Linguistics (2001)
3. Cho, E., Ha, T.L., Waibel, A.: CRF-based disfluency detection using semantic features for German to English spoken language translation. In: IWSLT, Heidelberg, Germany (2013)
4. Dyer, C., Ballesteros, M., Ling, W., Matthews, A., Smith, N.A.: Transition-based dependency parsing with stack long short-term memory. In: Proceedings of the 53rd Annual Meeting of the Association for Computational Linguistics and the 7th International Joint Conference on Natural Language Processing (Volume 1: Long Papers), pp. 334–343. Association for Computational Linguistics, July 2015
5. Ferguson, J., Durrett, G., Klein, D.: Disfluency detection with a semi-Markov model and prosodic features. In: Proceedings of the 2015 Conference of the North American Chapter of the Association for Computational Linguistics: Human Language Technologies, pp. 257–262. Association for Computational Linguistics (2015)

6. Georgila, K.: Using integer linear programming for detecting speech disfluencies. In: Proceedings of Human Language Technologies: The 2009 Annual Conference of the North American Chapter of the Association for Computational Linguistics, Companion Volume: Short Papers, pp. 109–112. Association for Computational Linguistics (2009)

7. Giles, R.: Overfitting in neural nets: backpropagation, conjugate gradient, and early stopping. In: Proceedings of the 2000 Conference on Advances in Neural Information Processing Systems 13, vol. 13, pp. 402. MIT Press (2001)

8. Hochreiter, S., Schmidhuber, J.: Long short-term memory. Neural Comput. **9**(8), 1735–1780 (1997)

9. Honnibal, M., Johnson, M.: Joint incremental disfluency detection and dependency parsing. Trans. Assoc. Comput. Linguist. **2**, 131–142 (2014)

10. Hough, J., Schlangen, D.: Recurrent neural networks for incremental disfluency detection. In: Sixteenth Annual Conference of the International Speech Communication Association (2015)

11. Huang, Z., Xu, W., Yu, K.: Bidirectional LSTM-CRF models for sequence tagging. Computer Science (2015)

12. Irsoy, O., Cardie, C.: Opinion mining with deep recurrent neural networks. In: EMNLP, pp. 720–728 (2014)

13. Johnson, M., Charniak, E.: A tag-based noisy channel model of speech repairs. In: Proceedings of the 42nd Annual Meeting on Association for Computational Linguistics, p. 33. Association for Computational Linguistics (2004)

14. Lafferty, J., McCallum, A., Pereira, F.C.: Conditional random fields: probabilistic models for segmenting and labeling sequence data (2001)

15. Lample, G., Ballesteros, M., Subramanian, S., Kawakami, K., Dyer, C.: Neural architectures for named entity recognition. arXiv preprint arXiv:1603.01360 (2016)

16. Lease, M., Johnson, M.: Early deletion of fillers in processing conversational speech. In: Proceedings of the Human Language Technology Conference of the NAACL, Companion Volume: Short Papers, pp. 73–76. Association for Computational Linguistics (2006)

17. Ling, W., Dyer, C., Black, A., Trancoso, I.: Two/too simple adaptations of word2vec for syntax problems. In: Proceedings of the 2015 Conference of the North American Chapter of the Association for Computational Linguistics: Human Language Technologies, pp. 1299–1304 (2015)

18. Ma, X., Hovy, E.: End-to-end sequence labeling via bi-directional lstm-CNNs-CRF. arXiv preprint arXiv:1603.01354 (2016)

19. Mikolov, T., Sutskever, I., Chen, K., Corrado, G.S., Dean, J.: Distributed representations of words and phrases and their compositionality. In: Advances in neural information processing systems, pp. 3111–3119 (2013)

20. Pascanu, R., Mikolov, T., Bengio, Y.: On the difficulty of training recurrent neural networks. arXiv preprint arXiv:1211.5063 (2012)

21. Qian, X., Liu, Y.: Disfluency detection using multi-step stacked learning. In: HLT-NAACL, pp. 820–825 (2013)

22. Rasooli, M.S., Tetreault, J.R.: Joint parsing and disfluency detection in linear time. In: EMNLP, pp. 124–129 (2013)

23. Shriberg, E.E.: Preliminaries to a theory of speech disfluencies. Ph.D. thesis, Citeseer (1994)

24. Srivastava, N., Hinton, G., Krizhevsky, A., Sutskever, I., Salakhutdinov, R.: Dropout: a simple way to prevent neural networks from overfitting. J. Mach. Learn. Res. **15**(1), 1929–1958 (2014)

25. Wu, S., Zhang, D., Zhou, M., Zhao, T.: Efficient disfluency detection with transition-based parsing. In: Proceedings of the 53rd Annual Meeting of the Association for Computational Linguistics and the 7th International Joint Conference on Natural Language Processing (Volume 1: Long Papers), pp. 495–503. Association for Computational Linguistics (2015)
26. Zhang, M., Zhang, Y., Vo, D.T.: Neural networks for open domain targeted sentiment. In: Conference on Empirical Methods in Natural Language Processing (EMNLP 2015) (2015)
27. Zwarts, S., Johnson, M.: The impact of language models and loss functions on repair disfluency detection. In: Proceedings of the 49th Annual Meeting of the Association for Computational Linguistics: Human Language Technologies-Volume 1, pp. 703–711. Association for Computational Linguistics (2011)

Social Computing
and Sentiment Analysis

Active Learning for Age Regression
in Social Media

Jing Chen, Shoushan Li[✉], Bin Dai, and Guodong Zhou

Natural Language Processing Lab, School of Computer Science and Technology,
Soochow University, Suzhou, China
jing.chen199225@gmail.com, chosendai@gmail.com,
{lishoushan, gdzhou}@suda.edu.cn

Abstract. Large-scale annotated corpora are a prerequisite for developing high-performance age regression models. However, such annotated corpora are sometimes very expensive and time-consuming to obtain. In this paper, we aim to reduce the annotation effort for age regression via active learning. The key idea of our active learning approach is first to divide the whole feature space into several disjoint feature subspaces and then leverage them to learn a committee of regressors. Given the committee of regressors, we apply a query by committee (QBC) method to select unconfident samples in the unlabeled data for manual annotation. Empirical studies demonstrate the effectiveness of the proposed approach to active learning for age regression.

Keywords: Active learning · Age regression · Social media

1 Introduction

In social media, age prediction aims to determine the age of one online user by leveraging his/her published content or his/her social information. For example, Fig. 1 shows an online user in a social media website. When the age is not available, we could exactly infer her age to be 23 from her published message "I'M 23". Age prediction has been an essential pre-processing step in many social applications. Generally, age classification and age regression are two foundational tasks in age prediction. Different from the age classification concerned with classifying the users into several age groups [1], age regression focuses on predicting the user's age with a discrete variable indicating an exact age number [2, 3].

Conventional approaches to age regression focus on supervised learning where sufficient labeled data is essential for training the model. However, to exactly annotate the golden label of online user's age is extremely difficult [4]. A better way to obtain the labeled data is to ask for the online users to obtain their real ages. However, such way of collecting data is rather time-consuming and expensive.

In this paper, we propose an active learning approach to address above challenge by better exploiting the unlabeled data to reduce the scale of annotation data. In active learning, the simplest and most commonly used query framework is uncertainty sampling [5] where an uncertainty measurement is designed to pick most unconfidently classified instances in each iteration. In a classification problem, it is easy to measure

© Springer International Publishing AG 2016
M. Sun et al. (Eds.): CCL and NLP-NABD 2016, LNAI 10035, pp. 351–362, 2016.
DOI: 10.1007/978-3-319-47674-2_29

```
Name: ****    Age: 23
-----------------------------------------------------------------
Social Information (e.g., User information)
  ➢ Gender: female
  ➢ #Message: 157;
  ➢ Followers: ***, ***, ...
  ➢ Followings: ***, ***, ...
-----------------------------------------------------------------
Textual Information (e.g., Messages)
  (1)  UGH I don't wanna go to school tomorrow. DONT WANNA SEE A
       TEACHERS FACE AGAIN. OH WAIT I'M 23! WAHOOOOO!!
  (2)  WHAT TIME IS IT?! GAME TIME!
```

Fig. 1. A user example in a social media

the uncertainty by leveraging the posterior probabilities provided by the classifiers. For instance, in a 2-class classification problem, the posterior probability of one class around 0.5 is thought to be a very unconfidently classified score. However, in a regression problem, there is no such estimated probability which can be used directly because the possible predictions in regression are infinite [6].

To tackle the above difficulty, we propose a novel method to estimate the labeling unconfidence of an unlabeled instance. Specifically, our method generates multiple random feature subspaces to train a committee of regressors and then leverage the committee of regressors to estimate the labeling unconfidence of each instance. The motivation of using feature subspaces to generate multiple subspace regressors is due to the fact that the feature space (either using textual features or social features) in age regression is extremely high and we believe that a feature subspace of a certain scale is sufficient to train a good regressor. For example, in our data collected form the social website called Sina Weibo, the dimension of the textual features (i.e., word unigram features), is normally larger than 200,000 while the dimension of the social features is larger than 600,000. In principle, our method is a specific implementation of the famous Query By Committee (QBC) method which has been successfully applied in active learning [7]. For clarity, we refer to our method as subspace-based QBC. To the best of our knowledge, this is the first attempt to employ multiple feature subspaces to generate the committee in QBC for active learning in a regression task.

The remainder of this paper is organized as follows. Section 2 overviews related work on age regression and active learning for regression. Section 3 introduces some background on data collection and the basic model for age regression. Section 4 presents the active learning algorithm for age regression. Section 5 evaluates the pro-posed approach. Finally, Sect. 6 gives the conclusion and future work.

2   Related Work

This section gives an overview of related work on age prediction and active learning for regression respectively.

2.1   Age Prediction

Over the last decade, the overwhelming majority of studies model age prediction as a classification problem. For instance, Peersman et al. [1] apply a text categorization approach to age classification with textual features only. Some other studies, such as Mackinnon and Warren [8], and Rosenthal and McKeown [9], explore social features to enhance the performance of age classification.

Compared to age classification, related work on age regression is much less. Nguyen et al. [2] explore textual features, such as word unigrams, POS unigrams and bigrams, together with gender features in age regression via a linear regression model. Their empirical studies find that word unigrams can achieve reasonable performance and that POS patterns are strong indicators of the old age. Another contribution of their work is their joint model for performing age regression with three different genres of data. More recently, Nguyen et al. [3] further explore age prediction of Twitter users with a linear regression model. They find that an automatic system can achieve better performance than human being.

To the best of our knowledge, no previous studies have been conducted their research on active learning for age prediction.

2.2   Active Learning for Age Regression

Active learning has been extensively explored in both natural language processing (NLP) and machine learning (ML) communities. For a quick and overall understanding the research issue of active learning, please refer to two comprehensive surveys, i.e., Olsson [10] and Settles [11], which discuss related studies on active learning in the NLP and ML communities respectively.

While most previous studies focus on the scenario of classification problems [12], only a few studies address the active learning issue on regression problems. Burbidge [13] employ QBC in active learning for regression by measuring disagreement as the variance among the committee members' output predictions. The committee members in their approach are generated by using several subsets of the training data.

To the best of our knowledge, no previous studies focus on active learning for regression with random feature subspaces.

3   Background

In this section, we give some background on data collection and the basic regression model for age regression.

3.1   Data Collection

Our data is collected from Sina Micro-blog (http://weibo.com/), a famous Micro-blogging platform in China. From the website, we crawl each user's homepage which contains user information (e.g., name, age, gender, verified type), and their posted messages. The data collection process starts from some randomly selected users, and iteratively gets the data of their followers and followings. We remove those unsuitable users who are verified as organizations because the age attributes of these users make no sense. Besides, although the posted messages are the basic and major factor to predict user ages [2], some users post very few messages. To guarantee the reliability of the data, we remove those somehow non-active users who post less than 50 messages. In total, we collect the homepages of about 12000 users, together with their posted messages.

Figure 2 shows the user distribution in different ages. From this figure, we can see that the data distribution of user ages are rather imbalanced. Most users are young whose ages are in the range of 19–28.

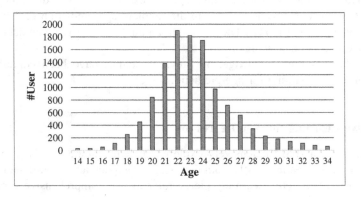

Fig. 2. User distribution in different ages

3.2 Basic Model for Age Regression

In this study, we model age prediction as a regression model and apply support vector machines (SVM) to estimate the regression function [14].

Given the training data $\{x_i, y_i\}_{i=1}^n$ where each input $x_i \in R^d$ and the response $y_i \in R$, our goal is to find a function $f(x)$ that maps the input x_i into y_i. Suppose $f(x)$ is a linear function, taking the form:

$$f(x) = <w, x> + b \text{ with } w \in R^d, b \in R \tag{1}$$

where $<\cdot, \cdot>$ denotes the dot product in R^d. In $\varepsilon - SV$ regression [14], learning the function $f(x)$ becomes solving the following convex optimization problem:

$$\text{minimize } \frac{1}{2}||w||^2 + C \sum_{i=1}^n (\zeta_i + \zeta_i^*) \tag{2}$$

$$\text{subject to} \begin{cases} y_i - <w, x_i> - b \le \varepsilon + \xi_i \\ <w, x_i> + b - y_i \le \varepsilon + \xi_i^* \\ \xi_i, \xi_i^* \ge 0 \end{cases} \tag{3}$$

Where ζ_i, ζ_i^* are two slack variables and the constant $C > 0$ determines the trade-off between the flatness of $f(x)$ and the amount up to which deviations larger than ε are tolerated. In age prediction, because the user ages are all integers, we round up the outputs of real numbers into integers.

4 Active Learning for Age Regression

In active learning, both labeled data L and unlabeled data U are available and the goal is to improve the performance by exploiting unlabeled data, finally reducing annotation cost. In other words, we hope to get better performance quickly when we only manually labeled a limited number of instances from unlabeled data U.

4.1 Textual and Social Features

Each user is represented by a feature vector, i.e., $x_i \in R^d$ as the input in a regression model. In the literature, various features, such as word unigrams, and social behaviors, have been successfully adopted on age prediction [9]. In this study, we categorize these features into two main groups, textual and social features. The former contains the features, generated from the user-generated messages, e.g., word unigrams, while the latter contains the features, generated from the user social behaviors, e.g., follower list and following list. Table 1 shows all the features in the two categories.

Table 1. Textual and social features in age regression

	Feature	Remarks	Examples
Textual features	BOW	Word unigrams in the user-gene rated messages	Don't, wanna, …
	POS Patterns	Top trigrams of the POS tag in user-generated messages	DT_SP_PU, PU_VV_VV,…
Social features	Statistics	# of messages, # of comments, # of followers,# of followings	100,10,200,300
	Time	Probability distribution of the user posts messages over 24 h (00–23)	[0.1, 0, 0, …, 0.2]
	Follower list	All IDs of the followers	'2919393812', '3044343944', …
	Following list	All IDs of the followings	'1976649967', '2286980683', …

Among textual features, BOW features are most popular in age prediction and proven very effective due to the fact that word features reflect concerning topics, which can distinguish users of different ages. POS patterns are also popular textual features to capture the writing styles of the users.

Among social features, the 4 statistical features, i.e., those with # of, capture the social behaviors of a user. The Time features capture the user habits on posting messages. For example, users of 20–24 ages might be more likely to post their messages very late at night. Followings and followers reflect the interests of users which provide an effective window to infer users' ages.

4.2 Active Learning with QBC

Generally, active learning can be either stream-based or pool-based [15]. The main difference between the two is that the former scans through the data sequentially and selects informative samples individually, whereas the latter evaluates and ranks the entire collection before selecting most informative samples at batch. As a large collection of samples can easily gathered once in age regression, pool–based active learning is adopted in this study.

In the study, we utilize query by committee (QBC) method as our basic active learning framework. Originally, query by committee (QBC) is a group of active learning approaches which employ a committee of learners to select an unlabeled example at which their classification predictions are maximally spread [7]. Figure 3 illustrates a standard pool-based active learning algorithm with QBC method. In this algorithm, the way of learning a committee of member classifiers and the confidence measuring strategy are two crucial components which will be discussed in the next subsection in detail.

Input:

　　Labeled data L;
　　Unlabeled pool U;

Output:

　　New Labeled data L

Procedure:

　　Loop for n iterations:
　　　(1)　Learn a committee of member classifiers using current L
　　　(2)　Use all member classifiers to label all unlabeled samples
　　　(3)　Select n most informative samples for manual annotation with the predefined unconfidence measuring strategy $unconf\,(x)$
　　　(4)　Move n newly-labeled samples from U to L

Fig. 3. Pool-based active learning with QBC

4.3   QBC with Random Feature Subspaces

To generate a committee of learners, we adopt the Random Subspace Generation (RSG) approach to generate multiple learners trained with several feature subspaces [16]. Assume $L = (x_1, x_2, \ldots, x_n)$ the training data and x_i an m-dimensional vector $x_i = (w_{i1}, w_{i2}, \ldots, w_{im})$, described by m features. RSG first randomly selects r $(r < m)$ features and obtains an r-dimensional random subspace of the original m-dimensional feature space. In this way, a modified training set $L^S = (x_1^S, x_2^S, \ldots, x_n^S)$ consisting of r-dimensional samples $x_i^s = (w_{i1}^s, w_{i2}^s, \ldots, w_{ir}^s) (i = 1, \ldots, n)$ is generated. Then, a subspace regression leaner can be trained in random subspaces x^S using the modified training set. In our implementation, we set N to be m/r and thus N disjoint feature subspaces are utilized to generate N subspace regression learners.

Active learning aims to select the most uncertain (unconfident) sample rather than the most certain sample. Thus, we select an unlabeled example at which their regression predictions are maximally disagreed. Formally, given the regression results from the committee of learners $(y_1', y_2', \ldots, y_N')$, the unconfidence score is calculated as follows:

$$unconf(x) = \log\left(\sum_{i=1}^{N}(y' - y_i')^2\right) \qquad (4)$$

Where y' is the estimated result of the committee, calculated as follows:

$$y' = \frac{1}{q}\sum_{i=1}^{q} y_i' \qquad (5)$$

The more the unconfidence score is, the more unconfidently the sample is predicted.

Figure 4 shows the algorithm of our QBC-based approach to selecting unconfident samples. Note that we only give the algorithm description on the textual features. A similar description is obvious for the social features and joint features.

5   Experimentation

In this section, we have systematically evaluated our approach to active learning for age regression.

5.1   Experimental Settings

Data Setting. The data collection has been introduced in Sect. 3.1. We extract a balanced data set from the collected data by selecting 200 samples in each age and the age is limited in the range of 19 to 28, totally 10 age categories. We use 80 % of the data in each age category as the training data and the remaining 20 % data as test data.

Input:
  $L_{textual}$: labeled textual samples; $U_{textual}$: unlabeled textual samples
Output:
  The most confidently predicted sample in $U_{textual}$
Procedure:
(1) Adopt RSG to generate N subspace training data { $L_{textual}^{S_1}$, $L_{textual}^{S_2}$,...., $L_{textual}^{S_N}$ }
(2) Learn N regression functions { $f_{textual}^{S_1}$, $f_{textual}^{S_2}$,...., $f_{textual}^{S_N}$ } with the obtained subspace training data.
(3) Use all regression functions to label the samples from $U_{textual}$
(4) Calculate and sort the unconfidence scores of all unlabeled samples with formula (4)
(5) Pick the sample with the maximum unconfidence score as the most unconfidently predicted sample in $U_{textual}$

Fig. 4. Unconfident samples selecting by QBC with random feature subspaces

In active learning, we randomly select 10 users in each age category from the training data as the initial labeled data and the remaining training data as unlabeled data.

Regression Algorithm and Features. We use the libSVM (http://www.csie.ntu.edu. tw/~cjlin/libsvm/) tool to implement our SVM regression algorithm with the linear kernel and the features as described in Table 1.

Evaluation Metric. We employ the coefficient of determination R^2 to measure the regression performance. Coefficient of determination R^2 is used in the context of statistical models with the main purpose to predict the future outcomes on the basis of other related information. R^2 is a number between 0 and 1. R^2 nearing 1.0 indicates that a regression line fits the data well [17].

5.2 Experimental Results

In this subsection, we present the experimental results when we leverage different kinds of features respectively including textual features, social features and joint features (combine social and textual features) to perform active learning algorithm on age regression. What's more, we adopt several comparable experiments during the process of investigating the effect of active learning on age regression.

Before reporting the results of active learning, we first investigate the performances of different kinds of features for age regression in a supervised learning setting. Table 2 shows the age regression results of fully supervised learning (i.e., all training data is used as labeled data to train the regressor) when different kinds of features are utilized. From this table, we can see that BOW, following list and follower list occupy a large amount of features and perform apparently better than other kinds of textual and social features. We can also see that adding POS features in textual features is not helpful, while adding other types of features in social features is more helpful than using

Table 2. Performance of fully supervised learning when different kinds of features are used

	Feature	# of features	R^2
Textual features	BOW	116463	0.413
	Patterns POS	10153	0.087
	ALL	126616	0.409
Social features	Statistics	4	0.010
	Time	24	0.013
	Follower list	103080	0.168
	Following list	80904	0.256
	ALL	184012	0.269
Joint features	Textual + Social	310628	**0.520**

following list features only. Finally, we can see that the performance becomes best at 0.520 in R^2, when both textual and social features are employed.

For thorough comparison, some active learning approaches are implemented including:

- **Random:** which randomly selects the samples from the unlabeled data for manual annotation.
- **Subsample-based QBC:** which divides labeled samples into several groups and utilize these groups to train several age regressors as the committee of member regressors which are then utilized in a QBC active learning algorithm. In our implementation, we change the numbers of groups from 5 to 20 and find that the performances remain similar. The reported results are obtained when the group number is 10. This is the approach proposed by Burbidge [13] for a regression task.
- **Subspace-based QBC** (Our approach): which concretes the implementation in Sect. 4.3.

In our implementation, we run these approaches 5 times and report the average results eventually. The number of the feature subspaces is set to be 8 when the social features, textual features or joint features are utilized individually.

Figure 5 compares our approach with other active learning approaches by varying the number of the selected samples for manually annotation and all approaches are performed with social features, textual features or joint features respectively. From this figure, we can see that **Subsample-based QBC** is effective when social features are used. However, when textual and joint features are used, Subsample-based QBC performs even worse than the random selection approach. Our approach **Subspace-based QBC** apparently outperforms other two approaches no matter what kind of features is used. Significance test with t-test shows that our approach significantly outperforms the other two approaches (p-value < 0.01) when less than 600 unlabeled samples are selected no matter of features are used.

The number of the feature subspace is an important parameter in our approach. Figure 6 shows the performance of QBC based on subspace with different size of the feature spaces when we utilize textual features, social features or joint features individually. From Fig. 6, we can see that our approach Subspace-based QBC consistently

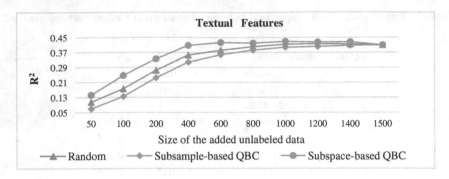

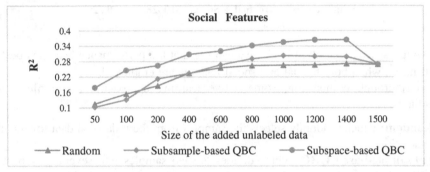

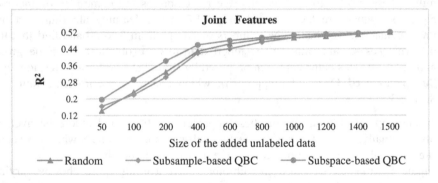

Fig. 5. Performance comparison of active learning approaches with different features

outperforms the random selection approach when varying the number of feature subspaces. For a nice performance, a choice of the number between 6 and 16 is recommended to be the size of feature subspace.

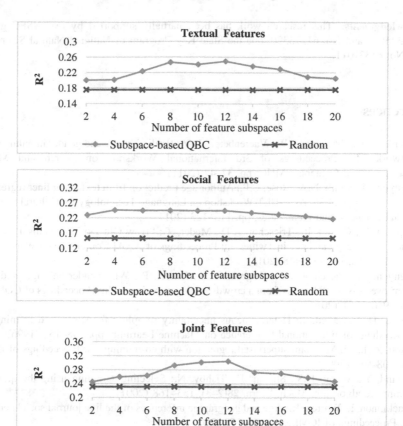

Fig. 6. Performance of Subspace-based QBC over varying sizes of feature subspaces when using textual features, social features, and joint features respectively.

6 Conclusion

In this paper, we propose an active learning approach to age regression for better exploiting the unlabeled data to improve the performance. Our approach leverages three kinds of features, namely textual features, social features and joint features (combining textual and social features). Moreover, we propose a QBC-style approach to active learning for age regression. In our approach, we solve the unconfidence estimation problem in our regression model by using a committee of feature-subspace regressors. Evaluation shows that our approach, namely subspace-based QBC, effectively improves the performance in active learning.

In our future work, we would like to improve the performance on age regression by exploring more features. Moreover, we would like to apply our approach to active learning on regression in some other NLP tasks.

Acknowledgments. This research work has been partially supported by two NSFC grants, No. 61375073 and No. 61273320, one the State Key Program of National Natural Science of China No. 61331011.

References

1. Peersman, C., Daelemans, W., Vaerenbergh, L.V.: Predicting age and gender in online social networks. In: Proceedings of 3rd International Workshop on Search and Mining User-generated Contents SMUC, pp. 37–44 (2011)
2. Nguyen, D., Smith, N.A., Rose, C.P.: Author age prediction from text using liner regression. In: Proceedings of 5th ACL-HLT Workshop on Language Technology for Cultural Heritage, Social Sciences, and Humanities, pp. 115–123 (2011)
3. Nguyen, D., Gravel, R., Trieschnigg, D., Meder, T.: "How Old Do You Think I Am?": a study of language and age in Twitter. In: Proceedings of AAAI Conference on Weblogs and Social Media, pp. 439–448 (2013)
4. Nguyen, D., Trieschnigg, D., Dogruöz, A.S., Gravel, R.: Why gender and age prediction from tweets is hard: lessons from a crowdsourcing experiment. In: Proceedings of COLING, pp. 1950–1961 (2014)
5. Lewis, D.D., Catlett, J.: Heterogeneous uncertainty sampling for supervised learning. In: Proceedings of International Conference on Machine Learning, pp. 148–156 (1996)
6. Zhou, Z.H., Li, M.: Semi-supervised regression with co-training. In: Proceedings of IJCAI, pp. 908–913 (2005)
7. Freund, Y., Seung, H.S., Shamir, E., Tishby, N.: Selecting sampling using the query by committee algorithm. Mach. Learn. **28**(2–3), 133–168 (2001)
8. Mackinnon, I., Warren, R.: Age and geographic inferences of the live journal social network. In: Proceedings of ICML, pp. 176–178 (2006)
9. Rosenthal, S.: Age prediction in blogs: a study of style, content, and online behavior in pre- and post-social media generations. In: Proceedings of ACL, pp. 763–772 (2011)
10. Olsson, F.: A literature survey of active learning machine learning in the context of natural language processing. SICS Technical report (2009)
11. Settles, B.: Active learning literature survey. Computer Sciences Technical report 1648, vol. 39, no. 2, pp. 127–131 (2010)
12. Li, S.S., Xue, Y.X., Wang, Z.Q., Zhou, G.D.: Active learning for cross-domain sentiment classification. In: Proceedings of IJCAI, pp. 2127–2133 (2013)
13. Burbidge, R., Rowland J.J., King R.D.: Active learning for regression based on query by committee. In: Proceedings of Intelligent Data Engineering and Automated Learning (IDEAL), pp. 209–218 (2007)
14. Vapnik, V.N.: The Nature of Statistical Learning Theory, pp. 988–999. Springer, New York (1995)
15. Sassano, M.: An empirical study of active learning with support vector machines for Japanese word segmentation. In: Proceedings of Meeting of the Association for Computational Linguistics, pp. 505–512 (2002)
16. Ho, T.: The random subspace method for constructing decision forests. IEEE Trans. Pattern Anal. Mach. Intell. **20**(8), 832–844 (1998)
17. Cameron, A., Windmeijer, F.: R-squared measures for count data regression models with applications to health-care utilization. J. Bus. Econ. Stat. **14**(2), 209–220 (1993)

A Novel Approach for Discovering Local Community Structure in Networks

Jinglian Liu[1,2], Daling Wang[1,3(✉)], Weiji Zhao[2], Shi Feng[1,3],
and Yifei Zhang[1,3]

[1] School of Computer Science and Engineering, Northeastern University,
Shenyang, People's Republic of China
datamining@163.com,
{wangdaling, fengshi, zhangyifei}@cse.neu.edu.cn
[2] School of Information Engineering, Suihua University,
Suihua, People's Republic of China
{datamining, sdzhaoweiji}@163.com
[3] Key Laboratory of Medical Image Computing of Ministry of Education,
Northeastern University, Shenyang, People's Republic of China

Abstract. The algorithms for discovering global community structure require
the knowledge about entire network structures, which are still difficult and
unrealistic to obtain from nowadays extremely large network. Several local
algorithms that use local knowledge of networks to find the community for a
given source node were proposed. However, these algorithms either require
predefined thresholds which are hard to set manually or have lower precision
rate. In this paper, we propose a novel method to discover local community for a
given node. Firstly, we find the most similar node which is adjacent to the given
node, and form the initial local community D together with the given node.
Then, we calculate the connection degree of nodes belonging to D's neighbors,
and add the node whose connection degree is maximum to D if the local
modularity measure will be increased. We evaluate our proposed method on
well-known synthetic and real-world networks whose community structures are
already given. The results of the experiment demonstrate that our algorithm is
highly effective at discovering local community structure.

Keywords: Local community discovering · Community structure · Connection
degree · Network graph

1 Introduction

A wide variety of complex systems can be represented as networks, such as social
networks [7, 8, 20], collaboration networks [17], the Internet [5], and E-mail networks
[21]. Each of these networks consists of a set of nodes representing people in a social
network, computers, or routers on the Internet. These nodes are connected together by
edges, representing friendships between people, data connections between computers,
and so forth [1].

Most of the networks display community structures that partition network nodes into
groups within which the connections are dense but between which they are sparse [15].

© Springer International Publishing AG 2016
M. Sun et al. (Eds.): CCL and NLP-NABD 2016, LNAI 10035, pp. 363–374, 2016.
DOI: 10.1007/978-3-319-47674-2_30

A number of community detection algorithms have been developed in recent years. The most popular algorithm is that proposed by Girvan and Newman [7, 14], which marked the beginning of a new era in the field of community detection. It detected community structure by removing the edges that connected nodes of different communities. In [14], the authors defined a modularity Q to test whether a particular division is meaningful, which was by far the most used and best known quality function [6]. Higher values of modularity indicate better partitions. Based on the modularity maximization, lots of algorithms [1, 15, 19] were proposed.

The global community detection algorithms have been well studied. But these algorithms are based on the entire network structures, which are still difficult and unrealistic to obtain from a large network nowadays. Therefore, community detection algorithms based on local network structure have been proposed. Clauset [4] proposed a local modularity measure R by only considering of nodes in the boundary of a sub-graph, and utilized a greedy maximization algorithm to find a sub-graph with a certain number of nodes. Bagrow et al. [2] explored the local structure of a given node by breadth-first search. A local module will be found until the change of the expansion falls below a predefined threshold. Luo et al. [11] proposed a local modularity measure M, which was the ratio of the number of internal edges to external edges. Based on this module definition, a locally optimized algorithm to identify local modules for a given node in a large network was given. Because the local modularity M was too strict for a community, it had low accuracy and recall in some cases. Ma et al. [13] proposed a seed-insensitive method called GMAC for local community detection. It revealed a local community by maximizing its internal similarity and minimizing its external similarity simultaneously.

However, most of the existing local community detection algorithms either require predefined thresholds which are hard to set manually or have lower precision rate. In this paper, we propose a novel method to discover the local community for a given node v. Firstly, we find the most similar node adjacent to v, which forms the initial local community D together with the given node v. Then, we calculate the connection degree of nodes belonging to D's neighbors, and add the node whose connection degree is maximum to D if that produces increase in local modularity. We evaluate our method on synthetic and real-world networks. The experimental results show that our algorithm is highly effective at discovering local community structure.

The rest of the paper is organized as follows. Section 2 gives related preliminary with our work. We describe our approach in Sect. 3 and report experimental results in Sect. 4, followed by conclusions in Sect. 5.

2 Preliminary

In this section, we first define the problem of discovering local community in networks, then review some existing algorithms for local community detection.

2.1 Definition of Local Community in Network

A network can be described by a graph $G = (V, E)$, where V is the set of nodes and E is set of edges. $|V|$ denotes the number of nodes in V. Nodes in V are denoted as v, w or V_i. $(v, w) \in E$ represents an edge connecting nodes v and w. For any node $v \in V$, function $neighbors(G, v)$ returns a set of nodes that are adjacent to node v in G. Function $neighbors(G, v)$ is the only way to gain additional information of G by visiting v's neighbor nodes.

Given a node v, our work is to discover the entire local community D that v belongs to. As shown in Fig. 1, we have perfect knowledge of the connectivity of nodes in local community D. The shell node set of community D is $S = \{V_j | (V_i, V_j) \in E, V_i \in D, V_j \in V - D\}$, which contains the nodes that are adjacent to nodes in D but do not belong to D. Nodes of S have at least one neighbor in D. $U = V - D - S$ is the set of nodes in G except those in D or S, which we know nothing about. For any node $w \in S$, let $R = neighbors(G, w)$, the nodes in R but not in D or S are explored from U. This is the only way to explore nodes in U during the process of detecting local community. Similar definitions of D, S can be found in [3, 10].

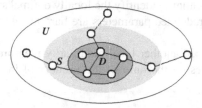

Fig. 1. An illustration of division of a network into local community D, D's shell node set S and unknown node set U

When local community detection algorithms begin, $D = \{v\}$ and $S = neighbors$ (G, v). At each step, one or more nodes from S are chosen and agglomerated into D, then update S by adding their neighbor nodes of U. This process continues until an appropriate stopping criteria has been satisfied. D is the community discovered of v. D has two subsets: the core node set C and the boundary node set B. The nodes in C have no neighbor nodes belonging to S, but the nodes in B have at least one neighbor node belonging to S.

The basic quantity to consider is k_v, the degree of a node v, which is the number of nodes that are adjacent to node v. Radicchi et al. [18] extended the degree definition to the nodes in an undirected graph. For any node $v \in D$, $k_v^{in}(D)$ is the in-degree of v, which is the number of edges that connect v to nodes in D, $k_v^{out}(D)$ is the out-degree of v which is the number of edges that connect v to nodes that do not belong to D. So k_v is the sum of $k_v^{in}(D)$ and $k_v^{out}(D)$.

Generally, a network community is regarded as a group of nodes that are more densely connected inside the group than the outside of the network. Radicchi [18] proposed two community definitions. For a weak community, the sum of in-degree value of all nodes in it is greater than the sum of out-degree values of all nodes. For a strong module, each node in the community has higher in-degree than out-degree.

But no quantitative definition of community is universally accepted to decide whether D is a qualified local community or not [6].

2.2   Related Algorithms

Clauset [4] proposed a local modularity measure R by only considering boundary nodes in B.

$$R = \frac{B_{in}}{B_{in} + B_{out}} \tag{1}$$

where B_{in} is the number of inward edges that connect boundary nodes in B to other nodes in D, while B_{out} is the number of edges that connect boundary nodes in B to nodes in S. R measures the fraction of inward edges in all edges with one or more endpoints in B. At each step, the algorithm adds the node V_j in S which causes the largest increase in R to D, then updates S by adding V_j's neighbor nodes in U, until the community has reached a predefined size. However, fixing the community size does not allow the greedy algorithm to identify the locally optimal sub-graph from the given node [11]. Meanwhile, predefined parameters are hard to set manually when facing an unknown network.

Luo et al. [11] proposed another local modularity measure M for evaluating local community, which focuses on the ratio of the number of internal edges and external edges.

$$M = \frac{E_{in}}{E_{out}} \tag{2}$$

where E_{in} is the number of edges with two endpoints in D, while E_{out} is the number of edges with one endpoint in D and the other in S. At each step, nodes in S are agglomerated to D if they can cause an increase in M, then remove the nodes from D which can cause an increase in M, finally update S. This process is repeated until no nodes in S increase M if agglomerated in D.

Luo et al. [11] defined that D is considered to be a qualified local community if and only if $M > 1$ and D contains v. The community definition is stricter than the strong definition by Radicchi et al. [18] sometimes. As shown in Fig. 2, D is a strong community, but $M < 1$. In this case, Luo's algorithm has low accuracy and recall.

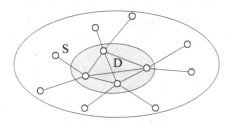

Fig. 2. An illustration of a strong community D

3 Our Algorithm

Before describing our approach, two improvements are given firstly based on strong community and local modularity measure M.

3.1 Problem Definition

For any node v in a strong community D, it requires $k_v^{in}(D) > k_v^{out}(D)$, which is equivalent to $k_v^{in}(D) > 0.5 \times k_v$. For node v in a community which satisfies $M > 1$, even it requires $k_v^{in}(D) > 2 \times k_v^{out}(D)$ in average, which is equivalent to $k_v^{in}(D) > 0;0.667 \times k_v$. If there are only two communities in a network, for any node v in D, it's reasonable that half of the edges connected to v should be in D. However, for a large network G, there are maybe hundreds of communities in it. In such networks, for a node v belongs to community D, v only needs to have more edges with nodes in D than other communities of G. It's impossible to meet the demand that half of v's neighbor nodes fall in D. So in our algorithm, in order to measure the node v's connection degree with subgraph D, we propose $conn$ as the criteria to choose candidate node in S.

$$conn(v, D) = \frac{k_v^{in}(D)}{k_v} \tag{3}$$

At each step, we choose the node in S whose $conn$ is maximum as candidate nodes which will be agglomerated into D if an appropriate stopping criteria has been satisfied.

For local modularity metric M proposed by Luo et al. [11], there exists an exception when $E_{out} = 0$. We propose an improved local modularity metric M', which avoids the exception raised by $E_{out} = 0$.

$$M' = \frac{E_{in}}{E_{in} + E_{out}} = \frac{1}{1 + \frac{E_{out}}{E_{in}}} = \frac{1}{1 + \frac{1}{M}} \tag{4}$$

The monotonicity of the function M' is the same as M, which means that $\Delta M' > 0$ is equivalent to $\Delta M > 0$. We choose $\Delta M' > 0$ as the stopping criteria to evaluate whether nodes in S can be added to D.

Suppose E_{in} denotes the number of internal edges in D, E_{out} denotes the number of external edges in D. For evaluating whether node V_j in S can be agglomerated in D, the increase of M' can be calculated as following.

$$\Delta M' = \frac{E_{in} + k_{V_j}^{in}(D)}{E_{in} + E_{out} + k_{V_j} - k_{V_j}^{in}(D)} - \frac{E_{in}}{E_{in} + E_{out}} \tag{5}$$

where $\Delta M' > 0$ is equivalent to

$$\frac{k_{V_j}^{in}(D)}{k_{V_j}} > \frac{E_{in}}{2E_{in} + E_{out}} \tag{6}$$

which equivalents

$$conn(V_j, D) > \frac{E_{in}}{2E_{in} + E_{out}} \tag{7}$$

Formula (7) can be used as a rapid calculate method of $\Delta M'$.

3.2   Algorithm Description

Based on the above improvements, we propose a two-stage algorithm for discovering local community of a given node v without any manual parameters. In the first stage, find the most similar node adjacent to the given node v, form the initial local community D together with the given node v. In the second stage, calculate the connection degree of nodes belonging to D's neighbors, add the node whose connection degree is maximum to D if the local modularity measure will be increased.

Stage 1. Form the initial local community D. We calculate the given node v's similarity with every neighbor node according to Formula (8), and find the most similar node, denoted by w, then form initial local community D together with v.

$$similarity(v, x) = \frac{|neighbors(G, v) \cap neighbors(G, x)|}{min(|neighbors(G, v)|, |neighbors(G, x)|)} \tag{8}$$

Stage 1 is described in Algorithm 1 as follows.

Algorithm 1. Form the initial local community D

Input: a given node v, network $G=(V,E)$;
Output: initial local community D;
Describe:
  1) $N=neighbors(G,v)$;
  2) create a new list *sim* to store the similarities of nodes belonging to N with v;
  3) for each node $x \in N$ do
  4) $sim[x]=similarity(v,x)$
  5) end for;
  6) find w such that $sim[w]$ is maximum;
  7) $D=\{v,w\}$;
  8) return D

Stage 2. Expanding initial local community D. In the beginning, $D = \{v, w\}$, S is the shell nodes set of initial local community D. E_{in} is the number of edges in D. For there are only node v and its neighbor node w in D, so initialize $E_{in} = 1$. E_{out} is the number of edges with one endpoint in D and the other in S. Choose the node in S whose connection degree is maximum as candidate node, denoted by c. If agglomerating node c into D will cause an increase in M', which is equivalent to $conn(c, D) > \frac{E_{in}}{2E_{in} + E_{out}}$, add c to D, and update S, E_{in}, and E_{out}, repeat this step until S is empty; otherwise, return D as the local community of v.

Stage 2 is described in Algorithm 2 as follows.

Algorithm 2. Expanding initial local community D

Input: initial local community $D=\{v,w\}$, network $G=(V,E)$;

Output: local community D containing the given node v;

Describe:

1) $S=neighbors(G,v) \cup neighbors(G,w)-D$;

2) $E_{in}=1$;

3) $E_{out}=$ the number of edges that connect v and w to nodes in S

4) while $S \neq$ empty do

5)   for each node $x \in S$ do

6)   calculate $conn(x, D)$;

7)   end for;

8)   find c such that $conn(c, D)$ is maximum;

9)   if $conn(c,D) > \dfrac{E_{in}}{2 \times E_{in} + E_{out}}$ then

10)   add c to D

11)   update $Ein, Eout, S$

12)   else

13)   break

14)   end if

15) end while

16) return D

---

4 Experiments

We compare our algorithm with Clauset's algorithm [4] and Luo et al.'s algorithm [11] (LWP for short) on LFR benchmark networks and four real-world networks for which the community structure are already known. The LFR benchmark networks are composed of 500 nodes and about forty communities [9], and the real-world networks are Zachary Karate Club Network [22], Dolphin Network [12], NCAA football network [7], and Books about US politics [16].

We test the performance of the three algorithms to detect local community by *Precision*, *Recall*, and *F-Score*, which are widely adopted by other community detection methods [3, 10]. The *precision* and *recall* are calculated as follows.

$$Precision = \frac{|C_F \cap C_R|}{|C_F|} \tag{9}$$

$$Recall = \frac{C_F \cap C_R}{C_R} \tag{10}$$

where C_R indicates the node set forming the real local community originating from a given node and C_F represents the node set which is the result of the local community detection algorithm.

Precision is the ratio of the correct nodes found in the detected local community. *Recall* is the ratio of the correct nodes to the real local community. *F-Score* is the harmonic mean of *Precision* and *Recall*. Its formula is as follows.

$$F - Score = 2 \times \frac{precision \times recall}{precision + recall} \tag{11}$$

In our experiments, every node in these networks has been taken as the start node to discover its local community. Based on the real community, the *precision*, *recall*, and *F-score* of every node is calculated. We average the score of *precision*, *recall*, and *F-Score* of all nodes in one network to evaluate the effectiveness of the algorithms to detect local community. A well-performed algorithm should have high *precision*, *recall*, and *F-score* at the same time.

4.1 Experiment on LFR Benchmark Network

LFR benchmark network is given by Lancichinetti et al. [9]. We generate 10 networks with different mixing parameter u ranging from 0.05 to 0.5 with a span of 0.05. Mixing parameter u is the fraction of its links with nodes outside its community. These networks' important properties are presented as follows: the number of nodes $n = 500$, the average degree of the nodes $k = 10$, and the maximum degree $k_{max} = 50$. For the others, such as minus exponent for the degree sequence t_1, minus exponent for the community size distribution t_2, number of overlapping nodes on, number of memberships of the overlapping nodes om, minimum for the community sizes $minc$, maximum for the community sizes $maxc$ use default values. The community structures of these LFR benchmark networks are already known.

For any node v in these LFR networks, it has $(1 - u) \times k_v$ neighbor nodes in its own community and $u \times k_v$ neighbors in other communities. The higher the mixing parameter u of a network is, the weaker community structure it has. So along with the community structures of the LFR networks become weaker, all the three algorithms suffer varying degrees of performance degradation and become ineffective to detect community structure. Figure 3 shows the comparison results of *precision*, *recall*, *F-score* for three algorithms on these networks, respectively.

To be more precisely, when $u \leq 0.3$, Clauset's algorithm has lower *precision*, *recall*, and *F-score* than other two algorithms. When $u \geq 0.35$, the *precision*, *recall*, and *F-score* of the LWP algorithm is zero or nearly zero. This is because all the local

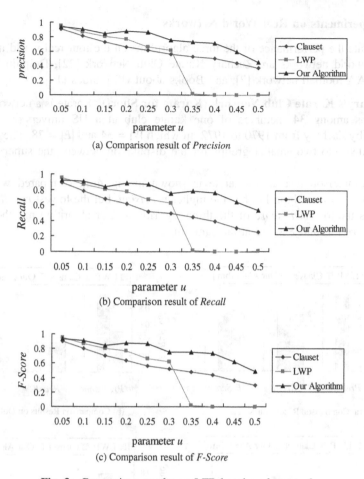

(a) Comparison result of *Precision*

(b) Comparison result of *Recall*

(c) Comparison result of *F-Score*

Fig. 3. Comparison results on LFR benchmark networks

communities discovered by LWP algorithm satisfy $M > 1$, which means the number of edges within the community should be more than the number of edges between nodes in the community and nodes outside it. However, almost no local community can satisfy $M > 1$ when $u \geq 0.35$, so LWP algorithm performs badly in this case. By comparison, our algorithm achieves much higher *precision*, *recall*, and *F-score* at the same time than other two algorithms except when $u = 0.05$. When $u = 0.05$, all three algorithms have good performance. Exactly, our algorithm is a little lower than LWP algorithm, but higher than Clauset's algorithm. In general, our algorithm achieves better performance to discovery local community against the other algorithms on LFR benchmark networks.

4.2   Experiments on Real-World Networks

We evaluate the performance of the three algorithms on the four real-world networks. The real-world networks are Zachary Karate Club Network [22], Dolphin Network [12], NCAA football network [7], and Books about US politics [16].

(1) Zachary's Karate Club Network (Karate for Short). Karate is a network of the friendships among 34 members of one karate club at a US university, which is observed by Zachary from 1970 to 1972, in which $|V| = 34$ and $|E| = 78$. The club was later divided into two smaller groups for the disputation between the supervisor and coach.

The comparison results on Karate is shown in Fig. 4(a). Compared with LWP algorithm, Clauset's algorithm has the higher *precision*, but the lowest *recall* result in that it has the lowest *F-score* of the three algorithms. Our algorithm has the highest *precision*, *recall*, and *F-score* at the same time.

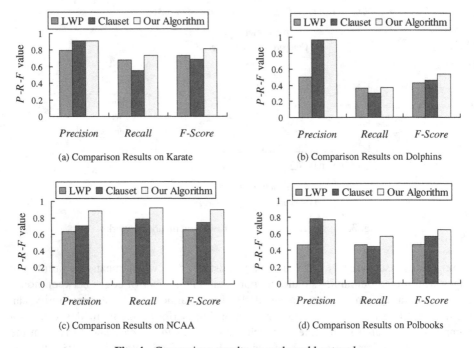

(a) Comparison Results on Karate

(b) Comparison Results on Dolphins

(c) Comparison Results on NCAA

(d) Comparison Results on Polbooks

Fig. 4. Comparison results on real-world networks

(2) Dolphins Network (Dolphins for Short). Dolphins is a network of frequent associations between 62 dolphins in a community living off Doubtful Sound, New Zealand, in which $|V| = 62$ and $|E| = 159$. Each node represents a dolphin, while each edge represents frequent relationships between two dolphins. The network is divided into two groups because of the migration of species.

The comparison results on Dolphins is shown in Fig. 4(b). Compared with Clauset's algorithm, LWP algorithm has the higher *recall*, but the lowest *precision* result in that it has the lowest *F-score* of the three algorithms. And Our algorithm has the highest *recall* and *F-score,* and the *precision* is close to Clauset's.

(3) NCAA Football Network (NCAA for Short). NCAA is a network of American football games between Division IA colleges during regular season Fall 2000, in which $|V| = 115$ and $|E| = 613$. Each node represents a team and edge represents regular season games between two connected teams. Teams within the same conference play more games than teams from different conferences. 115 teams are divided into 11 conferences and five independent teams;

The comparison results on NCAA is shown in Fig. 4(c). Compared with LWP algorithm, Clauset's algorithm has the higher *precision, recall,* and *F-score.* And our algorithm has the highest *precision, recall,* and *F-score* at the same time.

(4) Books About US Politics (Polbooks for Short). Polbooks is a network of books about US politics published around the time of the 2004 presidential election and sold by the online bookseller Amazon.com, in which $|V| = 105$ and $|E| = 441$. Each node represents a book and edges represent frequent co-purchasing of books by the same buyers. 105 books are divided into 3 communities.

The comparison results on Polbooks is shown in Fig. 4(d). Clauset's algorithm has the lowest *recall*, meanwhile it has the highest *precision*, result in that its *F-score* is higher that LPW's. And our algorithm has the highest *recall* and *F-score,* and the *precision* is close to Clauset's.

Figure 4 respectively shows the comparison results for the three algorithms on four real-world networks. We can observe that the *precision* of our algorithm is usually better than LWP algorithm, and is better or approximately equal to Clauset's algorithm, and the *recall*, especially the *F-score* of our algorithm are usually higher than other two algorithms. The results of the experiment demonstrate that our algorithms are highly effective at discovering local community structure compared with the other strong baseline algorithms.

5   Conclusion and Future Work

Currently, many local community detection algorithms have been proposed to identify community structure from the given starting node. However, these algorithms either require predefined thresholds which are hard to set manually or have lower precision rate. In this paper, we propose a novel approach for discovering local community. Comparing with other algorithms, our algorithm doesn't need any manual parameters, and achieves better performance on both the real world networks and synthetic networks. Future work can be done on the application of our algorithm on real networks for discovering local community.

Acknowledgments. The project is supported by National Natural Science Foundation of China (61370074, 61402091), the Fundamental Research Funds for the Central Universities of China under Grant N140404012.

References

1. Aaron, C., Newman, M., Cristopher, M.: Finding community structure in very large networks. Phys. Rev. E Stat. Nonlinear Soft Matter Phys. **70**(6), 264–277 (2004)
2. Bagrow, J., Bolt, E.: A local method for detecting communities. Phys. Rev. E **72**(4), 046108-1–046108-10 (2005)
3. Chen, Q., Wu, T.: A method for local community detection by finding maximal-degree nodes. In: ICMLC 2010, pp. 8–13 (2010)
4. Clauset, A.: Finding local community structure in networks. Phys. Rev. E **72**(2), 026132 (2005)
5. Faloutsos, M., Faloutsos, P., Faloutsos, C.: On power-law relationships of the Internet topology. In: SIGCOMM 1999, pp. 251–262 (1999)
6. Fortunato, S.: Community detection in graphs. Phys. Rep. **486**(3/4/5), 75–174 (2009)
7. Girvan, M., Newman, M.: Community structure in social and biological networks. Proc. Natl. Acad. Sci. U. S. A. **99**(12), 7821–7826 (2002)
8. Jia, G., Cai, Z., Musolesi, M., Wang, Y., Tennant, D.A., Weber, R.J.M., Heath, J.K., He, S.: Community detection in social and biological networks using differential evolution. In: Dhaenens, C., Jourdan, L., Marmion, M.-E. (eds.) LION 2015. LNCS, vol. 8994, pp. 71–85. Springer, Heidelberg (2012). doi:10.1007/978-3-642-34413-8_6
9. Lancichinetti, A., Fortunato, S., Radicchi, F.: Benchmark graphs for testing community detection algorithms. Phys. Rev. E **78**(4), 046110-1–046110-5 (2008)
10. Liu, Y., Ji, X., Liu, C., et al.: Detecting local community structures in networks based on boundary identification. Math. Probl. Eng. 1–8 (2014). http://dx.doi.org/10.1155/2014/682015
11. Luo, F., Wang, J., Promislow, E.: Exploring local community structures in large networks. Web Intell. Agent Syst. (WIAS) **6**(4), 387–400 (2008)
12. Lusseau, D.: The emergent properties of a dolphin social network. Proc. R Soc. Lond. Ser. B Biol. Sci. **270**(Suppl. 2), S186–S188 (2003)
13. Ma, L., Huang, H., He, Q., Chiew, K., Wu, J., Che, Y.: GMAC: a seed-insensitive approach to local community detection. In: Bellatreche, L., Mohania, M.K. (eds.) DaWaK 2014. LNCS, vol. 8646, pp. 297–308. Springer, Heidelberg (2013). doi:10.1007/978-3-642-40131-2_26
14. Newman, M., Girvan, M.: Finding and evaluating community structure in networks. Phys. Rev. E Stat. Nonlinear Soft Matter Phys. **69**(2), 026113-1–026113-15 (2004)
15. Newman, M.: Fast algorithm for detecting community structure in networks. Phys. Rev. E Stat. Nonlinear Soft Matter Phys. **69**(6), 066133-1–066133-5 (2004)
16. Newman, M.: Modularity and community structure in networks. Proc. Natl. Acad. Sci. **103** (23), 8577–8582 (2006). http://www-personal.umich.edu/~mejn/netdata/
17. Newman, M.: The structure of scientific collaboration networks. Proc. Natl. Acad. Sci. **98**(2), 404–409 (2000)
18. Radicchi, F., Castellano, C., Cecconi, F., et al.: Defining and identifying communities in networks. Proc. Natl. Acad. Sci. U. S. A. **101**(9), 2658–2663 (2004)
19. Shang, R., Bai, J., Jiao, L., et al.: Community detection based on modularity and an improved genetic algorithm. Phys. A **392**(5), 1215–1231 (2013)
20. Takaffoli, M.: Community evolution in dynamic social networks - challenges and problems. In: ICDM Workshops 2011, pp. 1211–1214 (2011)
21. Tyler, J., Wilkinson, D., Huberman, B.: Email as spectroscopy: automated discovery of community structure within organizations. Inf. Soc. **21**(2), 143–153 (2005)
22. Zachary, W.: An information flow model for conflict and fission in small groups. J. Anthropol. Res. **33**(4), 452–473 (1977)

Identifying Suspected Cybermob on Tieba

Shumin Shi[1,2(✉)], Xinyu Zhou[1], Meng Zhao[1], and Heyan Huang[1,2]

[1] School of Computer Science and Technology, Beijing Institute of Technology,
Beijing 100081, China
{bjssm, zxykid, zhaomengBIT, hhy63}@bit.edu.cn
[2] Beijing Engineering Research Center of High Volume Language Information
Processing and Cloud Computing Applications, Beijing, China

Abstract. This paper describes an approach to identify suspected cybermob on social media. Many researches involve making predictions of group emotion on Internet (such as quantifying sentiment polarity), but this paper instead focuses on the origin of information diffusion, namely back to its makers and contributors. According our previous findings that have shown, at the level of Tieba's contents, the negative information or emotions spread faster than positive ones, we centre on the maker of negative message in this paper, so-called cybermobs who post aggressive, provocative or insulting remarks on social websites. We explore the different characteristics between suspected cybermobs and general netizens and then extract relative unique features of suspected cybermobs. We construct real system to identify suspected cybermob automatically using machine learning method with above features, including other common features like user/content-based ones. Empirical results show that our approach can detect suspected cybermob correctly and efficiently as we evaluate it with benchmark models, and apply it to actual cases.

Keywords: Netizen identification · Suspected cybermob · Machine learning · Support vector machine · Social reviews

1 Introduction

Social media on the Internet has become a preponderant channel for the public to ex-press their emotions and share their opinions. By November 2015, the amount of netizens has been up to 688 million in China [1]. Increasingly netizens tend to comment the public affairs on social websites such as Weibo and Tieba with their own language styles, particularly in extremely strong statements.

The public opinion on Internet is the comprehensive expression of individual's beliefs, attitudes, opinions and emotions, which reflect the most netizens' viewpoints facing various emergencies and hot issues. However, cybermobs according to Urban Dictionary[1] and Definithing[2] refer to *"persons acting in cyberspace as to hold someone accountable for a real or imagined misdeed or social faux pas and join together to humiliate or manipulate via the Internet"*. And as the main sponsor of the cyber

---

[1] http://zh.urbandictionary.com/define.php?term=cybermob.
[2] http://definithing.com/cybermob/.

© Springer International Publishing AG 2016
M. Sun et al. (Eds.): CCL and NLP-NABD 2016, LNAI 10035, pp. 375–386, 2016.
DOI: 10.1007/978-3-319-47674-2_31

violence or rumors, they always post aggressive, provocative and insulting remarks whenever a public event occurs, which spread negative emotions and falsehoods on the Internet in order to express somewhat extreme private mood or only indulge in flattering by other followers in such an eye-catching way. For example, in the case of the brawl between fans of Sichuan (四川金强) and players of Liaoning (辽宁本溪)(Both are famous basketball teams in CBA) after the 3rd game of CBA-Finals, some cyber-mobs threw vicious curse-messages on the Weibo of Sichuan Players, which caused the further fierce conflict on social websites among fans from Sichuan Province, Liaoning Province and even the whole country. Besides, instead of paying attention to the truth, cybermobs attack government or people from other region only by virtue of their subjective imagination. Meanwhile, there is a saying "a lie told a thousand times become the truth". The follow-up netizens would rather believe it without verifying the authenticity of the message, which indirectly contribute to the rapid spread of rumors and cause social panic. Those netizens who spread fake information are also suspected cybermobs essentially.

Identifying those rumor-makers or filthy language speakers who could be defined as "suspected cybermobs" in this paper as early as possible is able to make us get ahead of the diffusion of falsity information from the source, help avoid the outbreak of the negative mass mood and cut off the spread of rumors. Aiming at identifying suspected cybermobs, firstly, we automatically collect user information and content information through web-crawler from Baidu Tieba. After collecting user information and content information, and annotating suspected cybermobs, we build a cybermob corpus which is composed by internet users labeled as suspected cybermobs or general netizens with all their postings and their user information. By analyzing the differences of user-based features, content-based features and unique characteristics of suspected cybermobs between suspected group and general ones, we construct a feature set. Finally, we introduce machine-learning methods with features described above to generate several classifiers that are used to identify suspected cybermobs automatically.

The rest of the paper is structured as followed: we will introduce the related work in Sect. 2. We take cybermobs and general netizens into comparison and collect the features that can distinguish them in Sect. 3. In Sect. 4 we train and select a classifier that identify cybermobs correctly with 3 different machine learning methods Then we present our experiment, analyze the results and verify the effectiveness of this approach with actual events. At last we draw a conclusion and point out our future work in Sect. 5.

2   Related Work

2.1   Baidu Tieba

Baidu Tieba was established on December 3, 2003 and now is the world's largest Chinese Communicative platform. Here, Tieba is a place on the internet allowing users to do interactive social network site activities. The slogan of Baidu Tieba is "Born for your interest". As of 2014 there have been more than eight million Tieba, mostly created by fans covering popular stars, films, comics or books. And more than one billion postings have been published in Tieba.

Baidu Tieba ever used to allow anonymous posting which just shows IP address, but now it only allows posting by account, and anonymous posting is not allowed. Users can post with at most 10 pictures and 1 video that can be quoted from certain broadcast websites.

2.2 Existing Researches

The researches on cybermob are carried out earlier in Sociology Science and generally can be divided into three aspects: the definition, the causes and the guidance of cybermobs. According to the present researches as we know, there isn't an agreement for the definition of cybermob, and here we use the definition of cybermob described in Sect. 1 in this paper. Studies on the cause of cybermob formation are mainly to measure the negative influence of subjective attitudes and objective factors to the netizens with various methods [2–4]. The guidance of cybermobs is to discuss the possible solution with legislation and education [5–7].

At present, there are not many researches directly on identifying suspected cybermobs. Comparing with the studies on identifying suspected cybermobs, researches on spammers are much deeper. There are mainly 3 kinds of methods for spammer detection [8]. One is based on content feature, For example, Lau RYK et al. [9] utilizes the similarity of contents to find fake reviewers. Liu et al. [10] finds the fake reviews with the help of sentiment classification. Jindal N et al. [11] collects different patterns to automatically find the fake reviews. Another method for spammer detection is based on user feature. Benevento et al. [12] collects 62 features from user's behaviors and detects spammer with them. Zhu [13] proposes a model that automatically selects features based on matrix factorization. User relationship is also used as user feature. Moh et al. [14] gathers user relationship in social media to quantify the user's credibility with which they measure whether a user to be a spammer. Facebook [15] introduces EageRank into this task. The higher the weight, the lower the probability of the candidate user to be a spammer. However, not all cybermobs are born cybermobs, they may have already build their social network before they suddenly become cybermobs. So it may hard to apply these methods into our system. Due to methods based on a specific feature cannot cover all aspects, some methods with integrated multiple specific features are proposed to detect spammers in order to improve the precision [16–18].

Compared with spammers that mechanically publish similar comments, the remarks of suspected cybermobs are full of vulgar speech, region discrimination and criticism of the government. Learning these unique features can improve suspected cybermobs identification system. Suspected cybermobs and general netizens also have differences in user information and content forms. So with user feature and content feature, it will further improves the identification accuracy.

Considering the similarity behaviors between the suspected cybermobs and spammers, especially some suspected cybermobs are directly transformed from spammers, this paper combines methods of traditional methods which are based on user feature and content feature with unique characteristic of suspected cybermobs. After constructing classifiers with machine learning models, we can automatically identify suspected cybermobs. And with actual events, we verify the method of this paper can provide effective data support for the prediction of group emotion.

3   Feature Analysis

According to existing researches, general features including user-based features and content-based features are common but effective static features that often used for identification. The number of followers, the number of followees, and whether the avatar is a cartoon picture or a default picture could measure the credibility of general netizens [19]. The ratio that postings with web terminal or mobile terminal is also different in different groups [20]. And even users' location or gender also have an impact on the quality of their postings [21]. Besides, suspected cybermobs also have their unique characteristics. Vulgar speech, region discrimination and criticism of the government are nothing new in their postings. In this paper, from labeled corpus, we randomly select 400 labeled as general netizens and 400 labeled as suspected cybermobs each of which is assigned randomly from 1 to 400. We analyze the differences between cybermobs and general netizens from user information, postings' content and unique characteristics of cybermobs with dataset collected.

3.1   General Feature

User-Based Feature (UF). In the following, cumulative distribution function (CDF) is introduced to analyze the user feature of suspected cybermobs and general netizens, as shown in Fig. 1.

Figure 1(a) and (b) analyze the different number of followers and followees between general netizens and suspected cybermobs which illustrates that most the latter ones do not have many followees and they do not care about other users. Figure 1(c) shows the different distributions of average level, which illustrates suspected cybermobs have a higher average level compared to general netizens. As for the number of Tieba postings, suspected cybermobs publish more postings and get more replies than general ones. This maybe because suspected cybermobs always post controversial remarks that lead to the arguments with others. On contrary, a part of netizens like to "div" rather than posting any replies. That's why general netizens post less and why their levels are relatively lower. Analysis on the number of created days from Fig. 1(e) indicates that suspected cybermobs tend to create new accounts in a short period. This may be because of their controversial content with which their accounts are easily blocked. While general netizens cherish their accounts and will not change their account frequently.

Content-Based Feature (CF). Tieba allows users to use functions like posting pictures, emoji, URL links and mention (@) with web terminal or computer terminal. We discuss each of them, and the results are shown in Fig. 2.

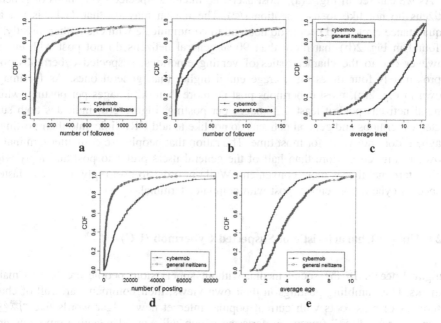

Fig. 1. Cumulative distribution function of user-based feature

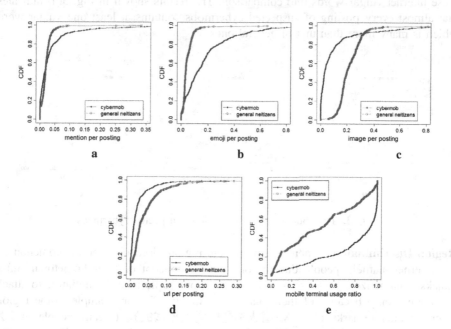

Fig. 2. Cumulative distribution function of content-based feature

As we can see in Fig. 2(a), most users, no matter suspected cybermobs or general netizens do not like to use mention (@). The reason may be that Tieba is not an acquaintance circle, and people do not tend to communicate with each other directly. It is found in Fig. 2(b) that more than 90 % general netizens do not post with emoji. However due to the characteristics of venting emotions, suspected cybermobs post approximately four times on average emoji higher than general ones. As for image shown in Fig. 2(c), most cybermobs post no more than 0.2 images per posting, while general netizens post at least 0.2 images per posting. Figure 2(d) indicates both suspected cybermobs and general netizens do not like to add URL links into their postings. Maybe it does not work for most time. The ration that people use computer terminal is shown in Fig. 2(e). More than half of the general users prefer to post and reply with mobile terminal that is more convenient. While in order to post/reply more and faster, suspected cybermobs tend to post with computer terminal.

3.2   Unique Characteristic of Suspected Cybermob (UC)

Vulgar Speech. In the social media, without supervision, people are free to make remarks. Unscrambling postings in their own views, their comments are full of characteristics of grassroots with current popular internet new vulgar words like "屌丝" (means loser), "叫兽" (means profartssor) which will spread negative emotions and may finally lead to group negative emotions. Therefore, this paper takes the usage of these internet vulgar words into comparison. The results shown in Fig. 3(a) indicates that almost every posting of suspected cybermobs contains at least one vulgar word which is many more than that of general ones.

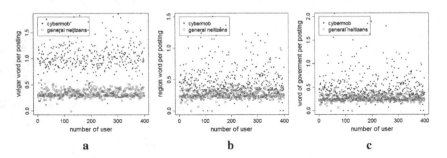

a   b   c

Fig. 3. Distribution of characteristic of suspected cybermobs

Region Discrimination. There is a prominent region discrimination phenomenon on the internet, namely people due to some native concept of their hometown suffer attacks from netizens who are in other regions, or people take the initiative to attack other areas only because of their "narrow region love". For example, some region discrimination remarks like "XX省人都是些无耻卑贱的狗 (means people in XX province are all shameless dogs)" appear in the comments of the news. Postings from suspected cybermobs often change the topic into abusing each other regardless of the truth, which seriously affect the harmony on the Internet. Therefore, we use these as feature to reveal the cybermobs (as shown in Fig. 3(b)). Compared to ordinary users, cybermobs are much more inclined to carry out regional attacks.

Criticism of the Government. There is another phenomenon that some people prefer to discredit the government on the Internet. No matter what happen, no matter it is right or wrong, they will attract people to the so-called unreasonable policies and blame the government for all mistakes. For example, a medical disputes in Cameroon get to the following comment "这就是中国政府管辖下的医院! (means It is the hospital under the jurisdiction Chinese government)" So aiming at this phenomenon, we first select words associated with government and policy. And compare the frequency between suspected cybermobs and general netizens with negative emotion. The results shown in Fig. 3(c) illustrate that only cybermobs tend to express negative emotion or directly attack the government and the policies frequently.

4 Experiment

4.1 Data Set

We crawl postings and replies from "NBA" and "dota" in Tieba by the end of April 20, 2015. And we get 3,524,584 postings in total. Then we collect all the users' information and postings with each specific user. We asked two annotators to label the users. The two annotators were requested to judge whether a candidate user to be a suspected cybermob with all his postings and his user information. If there is a disagreement between the two annotators, we ignore this candidate user. We randomly select 400 cybermobs and 400 general netizens as training data. And 150 suspected cybermobs and general users as test data.

4.2 Suspected Cybermob Identification with SVM

Based on the feature above, we introduce SVM (Support Vector Machine) into our suspected cybermob identification system. Figure 4 illustrates the overview of our system: We first collect features as we describe in Sect. 3 from training data, and construct classifier with machine learning model using these features. After training, the classifier is applied to distinguish whether a candidate user is a general netizen or a suspected cybermob.

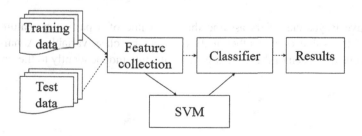

Fig. 4. Overview of suspected cybermob identification with SVM

Support Vector Machine (SVM). SVM is a supervised learning model with asso-ciated learning algorithms that analyze data used for classification and regression analysis. SVM training algorithm builds a model that assigns new examples into one category or the other, making it a non-probabilistic binary linear classifier. SVM model is a representation of the examples as points in space, mapped so that the examples of the separate categories are divided by a clear gap that is as wide as possible. New examples are then mapped into that same space and predicted to belong to a category based on which side of the gap they fall on.

In addition to performing linear classification, SVMs can efficiently perform a non-linear classification using what is called the kernel trick, implicitly mapping their inputs into high-dimensional feature spaces.

4.3   Benchmark

Maximum Entropy (ME). The maximum entropy principle [22] points out that for an unknown situation, we need to predict the probability distribution of a random event, satisfy all known conditions, and uniform distribution of probability for the unknown situation. Because in this case, method of maximum entropy can minimum risks for prediction.

In the process of classification, X is set of feature selection, C is one of the cate-gories, $P(c|X)$ is a probability with features predicted in category c. Under the restriction of the constraint conditions, the maximum value of the formula (1) is the maximum entropy:

$$H(p) = -\sum_{X,y} P(y|X) \log P(y|X) f(C,t) \tag{1}$$

Naïve Bayes (NB). NB is a common technique for constructing classifiers: models that assign class labels to problem instances, represented as vectors of feature values, where the class labels are drawn from some finite set using Bayes' theorem:

$$P(c_i|w_1, w_2 \ldots w_n) = \frac{P(w_1|c_i)P(w_2|c_i)\ldots P(w_n|c_i)}{P(w_1)P(w_2)\ldots P(w_n)} \tag{2}$$

All naive Bayes classifiers assume that the value of a particular feature is inde-pendent of the value of any other feature given the class variable. A naive Bayes classifier considers each of these features to contribute independently to the probability.

4.4 Results and Analysis

We first compare SVM with ME and NB. For each classifier, the same evaluation metrics (precision, recall and F-measure) is calculated for suspected cybermob identification.

As shown in Table 1, it is obvious that SVM classifier achieves the best f-measure which indicates SVM could separate training data into two parts with a maximum margin. Besides, NB and ME also achieve a high precision with all features. It shows that good features including content-based feature, user-based feature and unique characteristics of cybermobs are good contribution to our system.

Table 1. Results of different classifiers with different kinds of features

Feature	SVM			ME			NB		
	P	R	F	P	R	F	P	R	F
UF	64.70	67.64	66.14	55.88	57.84	56.84	58.85	62.74	60.72
CF	76.47	75.49	75.98	68.62	62.57	65.55	71.56	67.76	69.61
UC	94.11	93.14	93.62	88.23	83.33	85.71	90.17	87.25	88.69
UF + CF	80.39	82.35	81.36	72.53	70.50	71.50	76.47	74.51	75.48
CF + UC	95.10	83.14	94.11	90.17	91.18	90.67	91.18	91.18	91.18
UF + UC	97.06	96.08	96.57	94.11	93.14	93.62	96.08	92.16	94.08
All	98.04	98.04	98.04	94.11	95.10	94.60	97.06	96.06	96.57

What's more, we compare the influence of different kinds of features on our suspected cybermob identification system. As shown in Table 1, we achieve the best results with all kinds of features. In addition, compared to the single kind of features, the combination of features can always get better performances, which indicates each kind of feature has a positive effect on the identification of the suspected cybermobs. Compared to user feature and content feature, with unique characteristics, we reach precision at least 88.23 %. This result also highlights the unique characteristics that cybermobs tend to vent emotions with vulgar speech, region discrimination and criticisms of the government, with which it is easy to be identified from general netizens.

4.5 Prototype Implementation

We apply the system into hot spots happened recently in real environment to explore its practical value.

We introduce our system into a hot spot "brawl between fans of Sichuan and players of Liaoning". First, we crawl all the postings from Tieba of "SICHUANJIN-QIANG (四川金强吧)", "LIAONINGBENXI (辽宁本溪吧)" and "CBA" from March 17th to March 24th 2016. We extract all users who post at least 3 postings in Tieba mentioned above. After collecting user feature, content feature and unique characteristics of suspected cybermobs, we automatically identify whether the users to be suspected cybermobs with our system. 3 annotators are asked to label the users to be

Table 2. Cybermob identification results of actual events

Feature	Precision	Recall	F-measure
UF	86.60	36.11	50.98
CF	91.38	58.33	71.18
UC	72.00	100	83.72
UF + CF	84.00	58.33	68.86
CF + UC	72.34	94.44	81.93
UF + UC	81.40	97.22	88.61
All	86.84	91.67	89.18

suspected cybermobs, and finally we get 103 users (36 cybermobs and 67 general netizens). And the identification results are shown in Table 2.

As shown in Table 2, we also achieve the best f-measure with all kinds of features. We get higher recall but lower precision with unique characteristics of cybermobs. This maybe because the two teams involved in the brawl are the representatives of Sichuan Province and Liaoning Province, regional vocabularies appear everywhere in posts. And due to the region discrimination, many general netizens are falsely identified as suspected cybermobs. While with user feature and content feature, we get higher precision but lower recall. So in this way, we propose a hypothesis that people play different roles in different events. There may not always be so many suspected cybermobs. But when an unexpected event related to themselves happens, they may turn into cybermobs to defeat what they support quickly.

4.6   Further Application

We crawl all the postings by users who are mentioned in Sect. 4.5 in 2016 except in "SICHUANJINQIANG", "LIAONINGBENXI" and "CBA". In total, we get 3174 postings with these 103 users (36 labeled as general netizens and 67 labeled as suspected cybermobs) and we identify these netizens with their postings in other Tieba using our system again, the results are shown in Table 3.

Table 3. Results of suspected cybermob identification in different events

	Suspected cybermobs	General netizens
Suspected cybermobs in brawl	12	24
General netizens in brawl	2	65

Table 3 illustrate that only 1/3 of those who are automatically recognized as cybermobs with our system before are still identified as cybermobs. And most general netizens identified as general netizens in brawl between Sichuan and Liaoning are still identified as general netizens. Only 2 in 67 who are labeled as general netizens turn into cybermobs because they are involved in other emergencies.

Considering the above analysis, we ensure most cybermobs are not born cybermobs. Nevertheless, when an emergency that may threat to them happens, they will turn into cybermobs in a short period time.

5 Conclusion and Future Work

Aiming at cutting off the diffusion of vulgar-speeches or rumors from source on social websites, we propose an approach for identifying suspected cybermobs who used to be the previous makers or major contributors of the cyber violence or rumors, and always post aggressive, provocative and insulting remarks. We analyze and extract the differences of user-based/content-based feature and unique characteristic of cybermobs firstly. Then we introduce machine-learning method into a practical system based on suspected cybermobs corpus constructed with features above. According to comparison between different models (SVM, ME and NB, we take ME and NB as benchmark model) and different features restricted, the empirical results show our approach can detect suspected cybermobs correctly and efficiently.

All features play positive roles in our system. However they are all statistic features, we are going to consider applying more cognitive features which are proved to be effective in social psychology into our system to improve the accuracy in next work. Meanwhile, we may miss the golden hours to guide public opinion due to relative hysteresis of social media once events have occurred. So we will take postings-sequence on the Internet into comparison in order that we can identify suspected cybermobs earlier for coming emergency issues.

Acknowledgments. We thank reviewers for their constructive comments, and gratefully acknowledge the support of Natural Science Foundation of China (61201352) and the Major State Basic Research Development Program (973 Program) of China (2013CB329606).

References

1. CNNIC: 36th China Internet Development Statistics Report. China Internet Network Information Center (2015)
2. Sun, W.: Analysis of the causes of "cyber violence". Perspective of Communication Psychology. People Daily (2008)
3. Jun-Xiang, L.I.: Reflections on violence of public opinion in modern media environment: analysis of the kneeling incident of Li Yang's students. J. Maoming Univ. **2**, 014 (2008)
4. Tao, S.: "Cybermob" with its legal regulation. Theor. Res. 109 (2014)
5. Liu, X.: Analysis on infringement speech of cybermob. People Daily. China Dominant-Journalism Development Center (2007)
6. Hou, Z.: Reconstruction of the sense of responsibility to resolve the cyber violence. Democracy Legal Syst. 10 (2006)
7. Cao, N.: Young children defecation in "Hong Kong" the bedizen comments and events "internet mob" phenomenon analysis. Inner Mongolia University (2015)
8. Qian, M., Ke, Y.: Overview of Web Spammer Detection. J. Softw. (2014)
9. Lau, R.Y.K., Liao, S.Y., Kwok, C.W., Xu, K., Xia, Y., Li, Y.: Text mining and probabilistic language modeling for online review spam detection. ACM Trans. Manag. Inf. Syst. **2**, 1 (2011)
10. Liu, H., Zhao, Y., Qin, B., Liu, T.: Comment target extraction and sentiment classification. J. Chin. Inf. Process. **24**(1), 84–88 (2010)

11. Jindal, N., Liu, B., Lim, E.P.: Finding unusual review patterns using unexpected rules. In: ACM Conference on Information and Knowledge Management, CIKM 2010, Toronto, Ontario, Canada, October, vol. 1549 (2010)
12. Benevenuto, F., Magno, G., Rodrigues, T., Almeida, V.: Detecting spammers on Twitter (2013)
13. Zhu, Y., Wang, X., Zhong, E., Liu, N.N., Li, H., Yang, Q.: Discovering spammers in social networks. In: AAAI Conference on Artificial Intelligence (2012)
14. Hao, S., Syed, N.A., Feamster, N., Gray, A.G., Krasser, S.: Detecting spammers with SNARE: spatio-temporal network-level automatic reputation engine. In: Proceedings of the Usenix Security Symposium, Montreal, Canada, 10–14 August 2009, vol. 101 (2009)
15. Kincaird, J.: Edgerank: the secret sauce that makes Facebook's news feed tick. TechCrunch, April 2010
16. Amleshwaram, A.A., Reddy, N., Yadav, S., Gu, G., Yang, C.: CATS: characterizing automation of Twitter spammers. In: Fifth International Conference on Communication Systems and Networks, vol. 1 (2013)
17. Lin, C., He, J., Zhou, Y., Yang, X., Chen, K., Song, L.: Analysis and identification of spamming behaviors in Sina Weibo microblog. In: The Workshop on Social Network Mining & Analysis, vol. 1 (2013)
18. Zheng, X., Zeng, Z., Chen, Z., Yu, Y., Rong, C.: Detecting spammers on social networks. Neurocomputing **42**, 27 (2015)
19. Morris, M.R., Counts, S., Roseway, A., Hoff, A., Schwarz, J.: Tweeting is believing?: Understanding microblog credibility perceptions. In: Proceedings, p. 441 (2012)
20. Yang, F., Liu, Y., Yu, X., Yang, M.: Automatic detection of rumor on Sina Weibo. In: ACM SIGKDD Workshop on Mining Data Semantics, vol. 1 (2012)
21. Yang, J., Counts, S., Morris, M.R., Hoff, A.: Microblog credibility perceptions: comparing the USA and China. In: Conference on Computer Supported Cooperative Work, vol. 575 (2013)
22. Li, R., Wang, J., Chen, X., Tao, X., Hu, Y.: Using maximum entropy model for Chinese text categorization. J. Comput. Res. Dev. **42**, 578 (2005)

Chinese Sentiment Analysis Exploiting Heterogeneous Segmentations

Da Pan, Meishan Zhang, and Guohong Fu(✉)

School of Computer Science and Technology,
Heilongjiang University, Harbin 150080, China
pandacs@live.cn, mason.zms@gmail.com, ghfu@hotmail.com

Abstract. The Chinese language is a character-based language, with no explicit separators between words like English. Traditionally, word segmentation is conducted to convert Chinese sentences into word sequences, thus the same framework of English sentiment analysis can be exploited for Chinese. These work uses a specified word segmentor as a prerequisite step, yet ignores the fact that different segmentation styles exist in Chinese word segmentation, such as CTB, PKU, MSR and etc. In this paper, we study the influences of these heterogeneous segmentations for Chinese sentiment analysis, and then integrate these segmentations, based on both discrete and neural models. Experimental results show that different segmentations do affect the final performances, and the integrated models can achieve better performances.

Keywords: Sentiment analysis · Heterogeneous segmentations · Neural network

1 Introduction

Sentiment analysis has receiving extensive attentions in recent years [1–4]. A number of work has been proposed. Earlier work extracts discrete features such as word unigrams, bigrams and trigrams [5,6], and then feed them into a classifier such as max-entropy (ME), support vector machine (SVM) to achieve the final goal [7–10]. Recently, neural models dominate the research on sentiment classification [11], which exploit word embeddings as basic inputs, and then construct a deep neural network such as a convolution neural network to extract features automatically.

All these work assumes that input sentences are word sequences. The assumption is generally accepted in most cases such as English, which have explicit separators between words. However, it is an exception for the Chinese language. In order to align with these work, we usually have a prerequisitive step, word segmentation, to convert original character-based Chinese sentences into word-based. The segmentation is conducted by a well-established segmentor, such as Stanford NLP Tools [12], LTP [13] and THULAC [14].

One problem arises when the Chinese word sequences are produced by a certain segmentor, since it complies with a fixed segmentation style of Chinese, and

© Springer International Publishing AG 2016
M. Sun et al. (Eds.): CCL and NLP-NABD 2016, LNAI 10035, pp. 387–398, 2016.
DOI: 10.1007/978-3-319-47674-2_32

| 王小丽心中有点儿不是滋味。(Xiaoli Wang was feeling slight upsetting.) |
王小丽| 心中| 有| 点儿| 不| 是| 滋味| 。   #CTB segmentation style
王| 小丽| 心中| 有| 点儿| 不| 是| 滋味| 。   #PKU segmentation style
王小丽| 心中| 有点儿| 不是| 滋味| 。   #MSR segmentation style

Fig. 1. The CTB, PKU and MSR segmentation style with a microblog

actually there is no uniform standards for Chinese word segmentation. For example, in the well-known open competition of SIGHAN 2005 [15], there are four different segmentation standards for Chinese word segmentation. There comes a question that which standard is more suitable for Chinese sentiment analysis? However little work has focused on this question.

In this paper, we present the first study of heterogeneous word segmentations for Chinese sentiment analysis to our knowledge. We choose three popular segmentation standards, including CTB, PKU and MSR. Figure 1 shows an example sentence with the three heterogeneous segmentations. As shown in the figure, we find that CTB differs with PKU in the person name, and MSR tends to get longer words. Actually, there are many other differences between the three segmentations, which can be referred to their guidelines for details[1].

We compare three different word segmentations under two settings, one exploiting discrete models and the other exploiting neural models. Further, we integrate three heterogeneous word segmentations, to observe whether better performances can be achieved. We conduct experiments on a manually-collected corpus. Experimental results demonstrate that three different standards can lead to different performances. In addition, we find the integrated models can bring better performances for Chinese sentiment analysis under both discrete and neural settings. We discuss these results to show possible reasons of our observation.

2   Related Work

There has been a lot of work for sentiment analysis [2,6,16–19]. These work largely can be categorized into two types, namely discrete models and neural models. Discrete models explore manually-crafted features, which are designed by composing atomic features from internal information such as words in sentences and from external information such as sentiment lexicons manually. Feature engineering is crucial for these models including feature selection.

In contrast with discrete models, neural models do not rely on the extensive feature engineering work. These models require certain word embeddings to convert word sequences into vector sequences, and then build a neural network structure to abstract features from vector sequences. Typical work of word embeddings aimed for sentiment analysis includes Tang et al. [11], Ren et al. [20], and typical neural network structures includes convolution neural works [21], recurrent neural networks [22] and recursive neural network [23].

---

[1] http://www.sighan.org/bakeoff2005/.

Chinese sentiment analysis usually follows the same framework as the above related work. Most work focuses their interests on building better corpus or features. For example, Wan proposed a bilingual method [24]. These work generally ignore the influence of word segmentations by exploiting segmentors such as Stanford NLP tools [12], LTP [13] and THULAC [14]. Another line of previous studies that exploits lower-level information to improve the main classification performance [25,26]. There exists work that directly using Chinese characters as basic units, which is out of our concern [27].

3 Discrete Models

In our task, sentiment analysis is regarded as a binary classification problem, where $-$ denotes a negative microblogs, and $+$ denotes a positive microblogs. In this section, we introduce two discrete models based on single segmentation and heterogeneous segmentations, respectively.

3.1 The Baseline Model

In this section, we introduce the baseline discrete model for Chinese sentiment analysis, with a single word sequence as input for a weibo sentence. The single word sequence can be CTB, PKU or MSR styles. We can use this baseline model to study the influences of the three different segmentation standards, and to see which one is more suitable for Chinese sentiment analysis.

Figure 2 shows the framework of the baseline discrete model. Given an input microblog, after word segmentation, we obtain an word sequence by $w_1 w_2 \cdots w_n$. We then extract discrete features at each position i $(1 \leq i \leq n)$ according to specified feature templates. In this work, we exploit three kinds of features, including unigram, bigram and trigram. At position i, the unigram feature is w_i, the bigram feature is $w_{i-1} \circ w_i$, and the trigram feature is $w_{i-1} \circ w_i \circ w_{i+1}$, thus we get the feature vector $\mathbf{f}_i = \{w_i, w_{i-1} \circ w_i, w_{i-1} \circ w_i \circ w_{i+1}\}$.

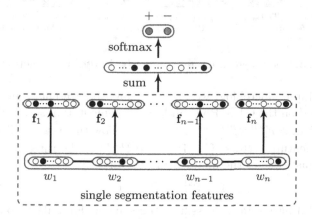

Fig. 2. The baseline discrete model ($\bullet$ denotes 1, $\circ$ denotes 0).

After obtaining the feature sequence $\mathbf{f}_1 \mathbf{f}_2 \cdots \mathbf{f}_n$, we sum all the features so that the entire sentence is represented, which we call this process as (sum) pooling, in order to have a better understanding in contrast with neural models which we will introduce the next section. The process can be formulates as follows:

$$\mathbf{f} = \sum_{i=1}^{n} \mathbf{f}_i \tag{1}$$

Finally we apply a linear classifier on the feature vector $\mathbf{f}$ to computer the output scores:

$$\mathbf{o} = \mathsf{W}_o \mathbf{f} \tag{2}$$

where the matrix W_o is a parameter of the discrete model, and $\mathbf{o}$ is the output two-dimensional vector, with one denoting the positive score and the other denoting the negative score. If the positive score is larger, we label the input microblog as positive, otherwise negative.

3.2   The Proposed Model Based on Multiple Segmentations

In order to support Chinese sentiment analysis with multiple segmentations, we extend the baseline discrete model. The adaption is very easy by simply adding the feature vectors extracted from multiple segmentations. The framework of our proposed model based on multiple segmentations is shown in Fig. 3.

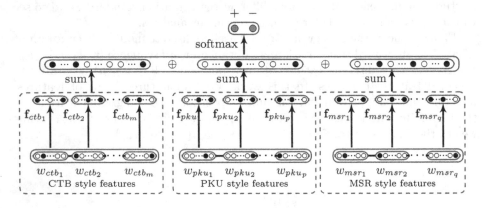

Fig. 3. The proposed discrete model (● denotes 1, ○ denotes 0).

Given an input microblog, we first segment the sentences into three word sequences based on the CTB, PKU and MSR segmentation styles: $w_1^{ctb} w_2^{ctb} w_m^{ctb}$, $w_1^{pku} w_2^{pku} w_p^{pku}$ and $w_1^{msr} w_2^{msr} w_q^{msr}$. Then we follow the baseline discrete model, obtaining the feature vectors ($\mathbf{f}^{ctb}$, $\mathbf{f}^{pku}$ and $\mathbf{f}^{msr}$) of the three word sequences, respectively. Last, we get the final feature vector $\mathbf{f}$ by:

$$\mathbf{f} = \mathbf{f}^{ctb} + \mathbf{f}^{pku} + \mathbf{f}^{msr} \tag{3}$$

And the $\mathbf{f}$ is fed into a linear classifier (the same as Formula 2) to compute the sentence's sentiment polarity scores.

4   Neural Models

In this section, we introduce our neural models for Chinese sentiment analysis. In contrast with discrete models, neural models exploit dense real-valued word embeddings as inputs, and abstract features from the input vectors by neural layers. Neural models have two main advantages: (1) First as low-dimensional real-valued features are used, these models avoid feature sparsity problem; (2) Second feature combinations are conducted by neural layers automatically, thus manually-crafted features are no longer required, saving the work of feature engineering. In the following, we first present the baseline neural model with only a single word sequence for each sentence. Then we extend this baseline to adapt multiple segmentation inputs.

Our baseline and proposed neural model based on the LSTM-RNN structure [28] which uses dense vectors to represent features. The dimension of dense vectors is much lower than one-hot vectors. Both of them use neural network to extract dense real-valued features $\mathbf{h}$ from microblogs.

4.1   The Baseline Neural Model

First, we introduce the baseline neural model of Chinese sentiment analysis. Figure 4 shows the framework. For a given sentence with the word sequence $w_1 w_2 \cdots w_n$, we first obtain word embeddings of w_i from a lookup matrix E, resulting in $\mathbf{e}_1 \mathbf{e}_2 \cdots \mathbf{e}_n$. Then we consider a window size of three to extend the representation at each position i ($1 \leq i \leq n$), obtaining a sequence of $\mathbf{x}_1 \mathbf{x}_2 \cdots \mathbf{x}_n$ which is in spirit similar to the trigrams in the baseline discrete model. Formally, $\mathbf{x}_i = \mathbf{e}_{i-1} \oplus \mathbf{e}_i \oplus \mathbf{e}_{i+1}$, which is a concatenation of embeddings of previous word, current word and next word.

Upon the sequence of $\mathbf{x}_1 \mathbf{x}_2 \cdots \mathbf{x}_n$, we build a bi-directional LSTM-RNN [29] to model a microblog, which is able to capture semantic and syntactic information of the input sentence automatically, and meanwhile avoids the gradient vanishing and exploding problem during training. The bi-directional LSTM-RNN means two LSTM-RNNs, one being computed from left-to-right ($\mathbf{h}_1^l \mathbf{h}_2^l \cdots \mathbf{h}_n^l$) and the other being computed from right-to-left ($\mathbf{h}_1^r \mathbf{h}_2^r \cdots \mathbf{h}_n^r$). Bi-directional LSTM-RNN has been widely used in a number of NLP tasks to achieve similar goals [30–32]. Taking the left-to-right LSTM-RNN as an example, the hidden sequence ($\mathbf{h}_1^l \mathbf{h}_2^l \cdots \mathbf{h}_n^l$) is computed as following:

$$
\begin{aligned}
\mathbf{ig}_i^l &= \sigma(\mathsf{W}_{ig}^l \mathbf{x}_i + \mathsf{U}_{ig}^l \mathbf{h}_{i-1}^l + \mathsf{V}_{ig}^l \mathbf{ce}_{i-1}^l + \mathbf{b}_{ig}^l) \\
\mathbf{fg}_i^l &= \sigma(\mathsf{W}_{fg}^l \mathbf{x}_i + \mathsf{U}_{fg}^l \mathbf{h}_{i-1}^l + \mathsf{V}_{fg}^l \mathbf{ce}_{i-1}^l + \mathbf{b}_{fg}^l) \\
\mathbf{ce}_i^l &= \mathbf{fg}_i^l \odot \mathbf{ce}_{i-1}^l + \mathbf{ig}_i^l \odot \tanh(\mathsf{W}_{ce}^l \mathbf{x}_i + \mathsf{U}_{ce}^l \mathbf{h}_{i-1}^l + \mathbf{b}_{ce}^l) \qquad (4) \\
\mathbf{og}_i^l &= \sigma(\mathsf{W}_{og}^l \mathbf{x}_i + \mathsf{U}_{og}^l \mathbf{h}_{i-1}^l + \mathsf{V}_{og}^l \mathbf{ce}_i^l + \mathbf{b}_{og}^l) \\
\mathbf{h}_i^l &= \mathbf{og}_i^l \odot \tanh(\mathbf{ce}_i^l),
\end{aligned}
$$

where $\mathsf{W}^l, \mathsf{U}^l, \mathsf{V}^l, \mathbf{b}^l$ are all the model parameters, and $\odot$ denotes the element-wise Hadamard product. In the equations, $\mathbf{h}_i^l$ is computed by the previous hidden

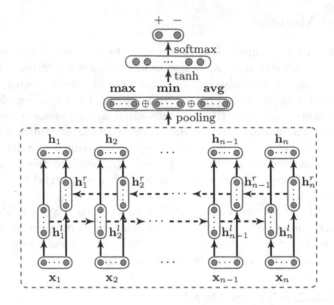

Fig. 4. The baseline neural model (• denotes a real-value feature).

vector $\mathbf{h}_{i-1}^l$, cell vector $\mathbf{ce}_{i-1}^l$, and the current input vector $\mathbf{x}_i$. The cell structure $\mathbf{ce}$ is used to deliver the long-term information, which is controlled by three gates, namely input gate $\mathbf{ig}$, output gate $\mathbf{og}$ and forget gate $\mathbf{fg}$, respectively.

Similarly, we obtain the right-to-left hidden vector sequence $(\mathbf{h}_1^r\mathbf{h}_2^r\cdots\mathbf{h}_n^r)$ by the reverse order, and the corresponding model parameters are $\mathbf{W}^r, \mathbf{U}^r, \mathbf{V}^r, \mathbf{b}^r$. After hidden sequences of both directions are computed, we concatenate them at each position one by one, receiving the final hidden vectors $\mathbf{h}_1\mathbf{h}_2\cdots\mathbf{h}_n$ ($\mathbf{h}_i = \mathbf{h}_i^l \oplus \mathbf{h}_i^r$).

Furthermore, we use three different pooling functions to obtain the sentence features, which project the variable length hidden sequence into a fixed-dimensional vector $\mathbf{h}$. The three pooling functions are namely max, min, avg (average). Concretely, given a hidden sequence $(\mathbf{h}_1\mathbf{h}_2\cdots\mathbf{h}_n)$, pooling is executed by $\mathbf{h} = \sum_{i=1}^n \alpha_i \odot \mathbf{h}_i$. For max pooling, $a_{i,j}^{max}$ equals 1 only when $i = \arg\max_s(\mathbf{h}_{s,j})$, and 0 otherwise; for min pooling, $\alpha_{i,j}^{min}$ equals 1 only when $i = \arg\min_s(\mathbf{h}_{s,j})$, and 0 otherwise, where $s \in [1, n]$; for avg pooling, $a_i^{avg} = \frac{1}{n}$. Correspondingly, we can obtain three sentence vectors $\mathbf{h}^{max}, \mathbf{h}^{min}, \mathbf{h}^{avg}$ by the three pooling methods, respectively. Finally, we use a non-linear feed-forward layer to get the final, the output can be computed by:

$$\mathbf{s} = tanh\big(\mathbf{W}_s(\mathbf{h}^{max} \oplus \mathbf{h}^{min} \oplus \mathbf{h}^{avg}) + \mathbf{b}_s\big),$$
$$\mathbf{o} = \mathbf{W}_o\mathbf{s}, \tag{5}$$

where the $\mathbf{W}_s, \mathbf{W}_o$ and $\mathbf{b}_s$ are the model parameters, and the $\oplus$ denotes the concatenation.

4.2 The Proposed Neural Model with Multiple Segmentation

We follow the method of extending the baseline discrete model into the proposed discrete model with multiple segmentations to adapt the baseline neural model being able to receive multiple segmentations. Figure 5 shows the overall framework of our proposed neural model.

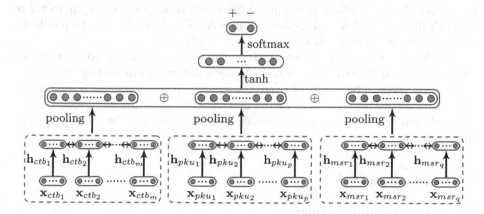

Fig. 5. The proposed neural model (• denotes a real-value feature).

In contrast to the baseline neural model, it has three components, which correspond to the three segmentation styles, respectively. Each component uses a bi-directional LSTM-RNN to model the input sentences. Similarly, three components are used to extract dense real-valued features from word sequence of different segmentation styles, respectively. Then we project the hidden sequences into a fix-dimensional vectors with the pooling functions to obtain the representation vectors $h_{ctb}, h_{pku}, h_{msr}$, respectively. Finally, we exploit a non-linear feed-forward layer to combine multiple segmentation sentence vectors for further classification, which is in spirit similar to the baseline model, and the corresponding model parameters are W_s, W_o, b_s. The output nodes are computed by:

$$\mathbf{h}_{ctb} = \mathbf{h}_{ctb}^{max} \oplus \mathbf{h}_{ctb}^{min} \oplus \mathbf{h}_{ctb}^{avg}$$
$$\mathbf{h}_{pku} = \mathbf{h}_{pku}^{max} \oplus \mathbf{h}_{pku}^{min} \oplus \mathbf{h}_{pku}^{avg}$$
$$\mathbf{h}_{msr} = \mathbf{h}_{msr}^{max} \oplus \mathbf{h}_{msr}^{min} \oplus \mathbf{h}_{msr}^{avg} \qquad (6)$$
$$\mathbf{s} = tanh\big(\mathsf{W}_s(\mathbf{h}_{ctb} \oplus \mathbf{h}_{pku} \oplus \mathbf{h}_{msr}) + \mathbf{b}_s\big)$$
$$\mathbf{o} = \mathsf{W}_o\mathbf{s}$$

5   Training

The cross-entropy loss is exploited as our training objective function for both discrete and neural models under supervised learning. Our goal is to minimize the objective loss with a set of training examples $(\mathbf{x}_i, \mathbf{y}_i)|_{i=1}^{N}$, and plus with a l_2-regularization term,

$$L(\theta) = -\sum_{i=1}^{N} \log p_{y_i} + \frac{\lambda}{2} \parallel \theta \parallel^2, \tag{7}$$

where θ is the set of model parameters, and the probability of the oracle output $\mathbf{y}_i$ is denoted by p_{y_i}, which is computed using softmax over the output vector $\mathbf{o}$ for both discrete and neural models. Online AdaGrad [33] is used to minimize the objective function for models.

All the matrix and vector parameters are randomly initialized by uniform sampling in $(-0.01, 0.01)$, the look-up table E for word embedding are also a model parameter. The values of E are assigned by pre-training on a large-scale segmented corpus. In this work, we use *word2vec*[2] to pre-train word embeddings on a collected weibo corpus, with the word sequences obtained by our segmentors automatically.

6 Experiments

6.1 Experimental Settings

We use the data of NLP & CC2014 Share Task 1, which is collected for emotion analysis in weibo texts. The original task aims to determine the emotion of a weibo text and to classify the weibo texts by its emotion category, including anger, disgust, rear, happiness, like, sadness and surprise. In our work, we exploit the data for Chinese sentiment analysis by labeling the weibo texts with emotions of anger, disgust sadness or fear being negative and being positive with emotions of happiness or like. We have a pre-process step to normalize nickname, URL, emoji and hashtag in weibo texts, and further, we use ZPar [34] to segment weibo texts into word sequences with different segmentation styles. The models of ZPar are trained using CTB, PKU and MSR corpora by ourselves. Table 1 shows the corpus statistics.

Table 1. Experimental corpus statistics.

	Train	Development	Test
Positive	5719	633	2117
Negative	6126	701	1168

We adopt accuracy to evaluate our model. There are several hyper-parameters in our discrete and neural models, which are tuned according to the developmental performances. The values of parameters are shown in Table 2,

---

[2] http://word2vec.googlecode.com/.

Table 2. Hyper-parameter values in our models.

Type	Hyper-parameters
Neural	$h_{lstm-rnn} = 100, e_{word} = 50, p_{drop} = 0.25$
Discrete and neural	$\lambda = 10^{-8}, \alpha = 0.01$

where both of discrete and neural models use the same regularization parameter λ and initial updating value α. The other parameters in neural models, including the dimension size $h_{lstm-rnn}$ of LSTM-RNN layers, dimension size of word embeddings e_{word} and the probability of dropout p_{drop} are shown is Table 2 as well.

6.2 Results

We study the influences of heterogeneous segmentations on sentiment analysis, in details, by comparing all possible combinations of these segmentations. The results are shown in Fig. 6. We can see that different segmentation styles lead to different accuracies in baseline models. Integrating any two styles of segmentation can obtain higher results than the baseline models, and further our final models which integrate three heterogeneous segmentations achieve the best performance.

Table 3 lists the results of our baseline and final models, including performances with both discrete and neural settings, respectively. For the discrete setting, the best model with single-segmentation input can achieve an accuracy of 81.28 %, while it is 84.66 % under the neural setting. After three heterogeneous segmentations are combined as input, the discrete model obtains an accuracy of 83.50 %, which is 2.22 % higher than the single-segmentation input. The neural model with heterogeneous segmentations can also outperform the single segmentation input baseline, achieving an accuracy of 86.06 %, gaining an improvement of 1.4 %. Overall, the results show that neural models can achieve better performances than the discrete models with similar inputs.

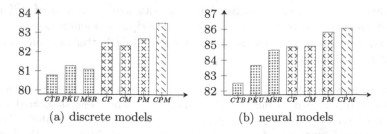

(a) discrete models   (b) neural models

Fig. 6. Experiment results on test dataset, where the boxes with green dots denotes the performances of baseline model, the boxes with blue crosshatch lines denotes models based on two segmentation styles and the boxes with red north west lines denotes the model based on three segmentation styles. (Color figure online)

Table 3. Final results on both discrete and neural models. CPM denotes the integration of three heterogeneous segmentations CTB, PKU and MSR

Model	Baseline (CTB)	Baseline (PKU)	Baseline (MSR)	Proposed (CPM)
Discrete	80.79	*81.28*	81.10	**83.50**
Neural	82.53	83.68	*84.66*	**86.06**

6.3   Model Analysis

In this section, we show several intrinsic analysis to interpret the benefits by exploiting multi-segmentations. As for the discrete setting, the number of high-frequency features is greatly boosted by multi-segmentations as input. As known, high-frequency features are highly useful for discrete models, since low-frequency features suffer the sparsity problem. Thus it is reasonable that our final discrete model with the heterogeneous segmentations achieves the best performance.

Similarly, under the neural setting, word embeddings are useful external resources, which are learnt from unlabeled texts. For the models using single-segmentation as input, only one kinds of embeddings can be used. While for the multiple segmentation input model, we can utilize all three different embeddings, thus our results are consist with the common intuition.

Moreover, since practical Chinese segmentors are trained by fixed annotated corpora, the output word sequences inevitably have incorrect segmentations. When these results are fed into the final-classifiers, it can lead to error propagation for final sentiment analysis. While for our proposed models with multiple segmentations as inputs, the problem can be alleviated as segmentations of different styles have different error distributions.

7   Conclusion

We investigated the influences of heterogeneous word segmentations for Chinese sentiment analysis, which has been generally ignored in previous work. First, we showed that the segmentation style does affect the sentiment classification performances. A different segmentation style can lead to a gap of 2 % of the final performances. Second, we combined the multiple segmentations of different styles under both discrete and neural setting, finding better accuracies can be achieved by such an integration.

Acknowledgments. We thank the anonymous reviewers for their constructive comments, which helped to improve the paper. This study was supported by Natural Science Foundation of Heilongjiang Province under Grant No. F2016036, National Natural Science Foundation of China under Grant No. 61170148, and the Returned Scholar Foundation of Heilongjiang Province, respectively.

References

1. Jiang, L., Yu, M., Zhou, M., Liu, X., Zhao, T.: Target-dependent twitter sentiment classification. In: Proceedings of the 49th ACL, pp. 151–160 (2011)
2. Liu, B.: Sentiment analysis and opinion mining. Synth. Lect. Hum. Lang. Technol. **5**(1), 1–167 (2012)
3. Fu, G., He, Y., Song, J., Wang, C.: Improving Chinese sentence polarity classification via opinion paraphrasing. In: CLP 2014, p. 35 (2014)
4. Vo, D.-T., Zhang, Y.: Target-dependent twitter sentiment classification with rich automatic features. In: Proceedings of the 29th IJCAI, pp. 1347–1353 (2015)
5. Wang, S., Manning, C.D.: Baselines and bigrams: simple, good sentiment and topic classification. In: Proceedings of the 50th ACL: Short Papers, vol. 2, pp. 90–94 (2012)
6. Pang, B., Lee, L.: Opinion mining and sentiment analysis. Found. Trends Inf. Retr. **2**(1–2), 1–135 (2008)
7. Pang, B., Lee, L., Vaithyanathan, S.: Thumbs up? Sentiment classification using machine learning techniques. In: Proceedings of the EMNLP, pp. 79–86, July 2002
8. Maas, A.L., Daly, R.E., Pham, P.T., Huang, D., Ng, A.Y., Potts, C.: Learning word vectors for sentiment analysis. In: Proceedings of the 49th ACL: HLT, vol. 1, pp. 142–150 (2011)
9. Taboada, M., Brooke, J., Tofiloski, M., Voll, K., Stede, M.: Lexicon-based methods for sentiment analysis. Comput. Linguist. **37**(2), 267–307 (2011)
10. Feldman, R.: Techniques and applications for sentiment analysis. Commun. ACM **56**(4), 82–89 (2013)
11. Tang, D., Wei, F., Yang, N., Zhou, M., Liu, T., Qin, B.: Learning sentiment-specific word embedding for twitter sentiment classification. In: ACL, pp. 1555–1565 (2014)
12. Manning, C.D., Surdeanu, M., Bauer, J., Finkel, J.R., Bethard, S., McClosky, D.: The Stanford CoreNLP natural language processing toolkit. In: ACL (System Demonstrations), pp. 55–60 (2014)
13. Che, W., Li, Z., Liu, T.: LTP: a Chinese language technology platform. In: Proceedings of the 23rd COLING: Demonstrations, pp. 13–16 (2010)
14. Li, Z., Sun, M.: Punctuation as implicit annotations for Chinese word segmentation. Comput. Linguist. **35**(4), 505–512 (2009)
15. Tseng, H., Chang, P., Andrew, G., Jurafsky, D., Manning, C.: A conditional random field word segmenter for SIGHAN bakeoff 2005. In: Proceedings of the Fourth SIGHAN Workshop, pp. 168–171 (2005)
16. Turney, P.D.: Thumbs up or thumbs down? Semantic orientation applied to unsupervised classification of reviews. In: Proceedings of the 40th ACL, pp. 417–424 (2002)
17. Fu, G., Wang, X.: Chinese sentence-level sentiment classification based on fuzzy sets. In: Proceedings of the 23rd COLING: Posters, pp. 312–319 (2010)
18. Hu, X., Tang, J., Gao, H., Liu, H.: Unsupervised sentiment analysis with emotional signals. In: Proceedings of the 22nd WWW, pp. 607–618 (2013)
19. Yang, B., Cardie, C.: Context-aware learning for sentence-level sentiment analysis with posterior regularization. In: ACL (1), pp. 325–335 (2014)
20. Ren, Y., Zhang, Y., Zhang, M., Ji, D.: Context-sensitive twitter sentiment classification using neural network. In: AAAI (2016)
21. dos Santos, C.N., Gatti, M.: Deep convolutional neural networks for sentiment analysis of short texts. In: COLING, pp. 69–78 (2014)

22. Wang, X., Liu, Y., Sun, C., Wang, B., Wang, X.: Predicting polarities of tweets by composing word embeddings with long short-term memory. In: Proceedings of the ACL and the IJCNLP, vol. 1, pp. 1343–1353 (2015)
23. Iyyer, M., Enns, P., Boyd-Graber, J.L., Resnik, P.: Political ideology detection using recursive neural networks. In: ACL (1), pp. 1113–1122 (2014)
24. Wan, X.: Co-training for cross-lingual sentiment classification. In: Proceedings of ACL and IJCNLP, vol. 1, pp. 235–243 (2009)
25. Yessenalina, A., Yue, Y., Cardie, C.: Multi-level structured models for document-level sentiment classification. In: Proceedings of the 2010 Conference on Empirical Methods in Natural Language Processing, Cambridge, MA, pp. 1046–1056. Association for Computational Linguistics, October 2010
26. Tang, D., Wei, F., Qin, B., Dong, L., Liu, T., Zhou, M.: A joint segmentation and classification framework for sentiment analysis. In: Proceedings of the 2014 Conference on Empirical Methods in Natural Language Processing (EMNLP), Doha, Qatar, pp. 477–487. Association for Computational Linguistics, October 2014
27. Ling, W., Dyer, C., Black, A.W., Trancoso, I., Fermandez, R., Amir, S., Marujo, L., Luis, T.: Finding function in form: compositional character models for open vocabulary word representation. In: Proceedings of the 2015 Conference on Empirical Methods in Natural Language Processing, Lisbon, Portugal, pp. 1520–1530. Association for Computational Linguistics, September 2015
28. Hochreiter, S., Schmidhuber, J.: Long short-term memory. Neural Comput. 9(8), 1735–1780 (1997)
29. Graves, A., Schmidhuber, J.: Framewise phoneme classification with bidirectional LSTM and other neural network architectures. Neural Netw. 18(5), 602–610 (2005)
30. Zhou, J., Xu, W.: End-to-end learning of semantic role labeling using recurrent neural networks. In: Proceedings of the 53rd ACL and the 7th IJCNLP (Long Papers), vol. 1, Beijing, China, pp. 1127–1137, July 2015
31. Wang, D., Nyberg, E.: A long short-term memory model for answer sentence selection in question answering. In: Proceedings of the 53rd ACL and the 7th IJCNLP (Short Papers), vol. 2, Beijing, China, pp. 707–712, July 2015
32. Liu, P., Joty, S., Meng, H.: Fine-grained opinion mining with recurrent neural networks and word embeddings. In: Proceedings of the EMNLP, Lisbon, Portugal, pp. 1433–1443, September 2015
33. Duchi, J., Hazan, E., Singer, Y.: Adaptive subgradient methods for online learning and stochastic optimization. JMLR 12, 2121–2159 (2011)
34. Zhang, Y., Clark, S.: Syntactic processing using the generalized perceptron and beam search. Comput. Linguist. 37(1), 105–151 (2011)

Towards Scalable Emotion Classification in Microblog Based on Noisy Training Data

Minglei Li[1](✉), Qin Lu[1], Lin Gui[2], and Yunfei Long[1]

[1] Department of Computing, The Hong Kong Polytechnic University,
Hung Hom, Hong Kong
{csmli,csluqin,csylong}@comp.polyu.edu.hk
[2] Laboratory of Network Oriented Intelligent Computation,
Shenzhen Graduate School, Harbin Institute of Technology, Shenzhen, China
guilin.nlp@gmail.com

Abstract. The availability of labeled corpus is of great importance for emotion classification tasks. Because manual labeling is too time-consuming, hashtags have been used as naturally annotated labels to obtain large amount of labeled training data from microblog. However, the inconsistency and noise in annotation can adversely affect the data quality and thus the performance when used to train a classifier. In this paper, we propose a classification framework which allows naturally annotated data to be used as additional training data and employs a k-NN graph based data cleaning method to remove noise after noisy data has certain accumulations. Evaluation on NLP&CC2013 Chinese Weibo emotion classification dataset shows that our approach achieves 15.8 % better performance than directly using the noisy data without noise filtering. After adding the filtered data with hashtags into an existing high-quality training data, the performance increases 3.7 % compared to using the high-quality training data alone.

Keywords: Emotion classification · Data cleaning · Hashtag · k-NN

1 Introduction

Emotion classification from social media (such as Tweet, Sina Weibo) is becoming more and more important. Many supervised learning methods have been devekioed to solve this problem. However, supervised methods require a large amount of labeled training data. Obtaining labeled data manually can be quite time consuming and noise prone especially for multi-class annotations such as for subject related emotion annotation. Many research studies take advantage of large amount of text available in the social media to investigate automatic methods to obtain labeled data [1,7,8]. In these works, naturally annotated text features such as hashtags, emoticons and emoji characters inserted in tweets are automatically extracted from data and these features are then directly used as labels after some simple rule based filtering. However, these automatically obtained labels can be quite noisy. Take the following text as an example,

© Springer International Publishing AG 2016
M. Sun et al. (Eds.): CCL and NLP-NABD 2016, LNAI 10035, pp. 399–410, 2016.
DOI: 10.1007/978-3-319-47674-2_33

"在你闲的时候，玩玩转发微博，未必不是一种乐趣！！！#无聊# *(When you are not busy, playing with microblog retweet may be fun! #boring#)*". From the text we can infer that the emotion is "happy", but the author uses a negative hashtag "boring". As far as we know, there is not much work to handle hashtag noise problem for emotion classification. Figure 1 shows that directly adding data using hashtag as emotion labels (crawled from Sina Weibo) to high quality training data (from NLP&CC2013) will not improve the system and the performance degrades continuously as more naturally annotated data are added. This indicates that if there is no appropriate data cleaning method, naturally annotated data may do more harm than good.

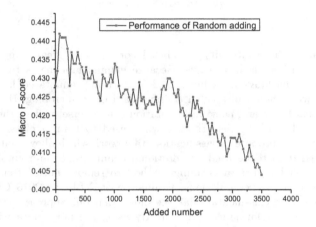

Fig. 1. Performance of random adding

Semi-supervised learning (SSL) can make use of a small amount of labeled seed data and a large amount of unlabeled data to achieve much better performance, such as S3VMs [12]. Data cleaning, as one kind of SSL, has been used to cope with noisy training data, such as co-training [2] and CoTRADE [5]. However, these methods are mainly used in binary classification. In principle, data using automatically obtained hashtags is not unlabeled data. Rather, it is labeled training data with noise.

In this study, we focus on making use of automatically obtained labeled data for emotion classification. The main objective is to obtain more high quality labeled data to improve the performance of emotion classification. The main issue in this work is the design of data cleaning strategies to obtain high quality data using natural annotation and to use the data to improve classification performance. The basic idea is to train a classifier initially using high quality data provided through manual annotation and make use of this classifier to predict noisy data. Only data with high confidence through the assessment of the predicted label compared to the original label will be used as the additional training data. As noise can accumulate after several iterations, we also make use of a graph based method to estimate accumulated noise and remove noisy data to ensure the overall quality of added training data. Through this study, we want to answer two questions: (1) Can the automatically extracted data containing hashtag be directly used as training data? and (2) If not, can we effectively remove noise from the naturally annotated data improve the emotion classification performance?

The rest of the paper is organized as follows. Section 2 presents related works in emotion classification and data cleaning. Section 3 introduces our algorithms and strategies. Section 4 reports the evaluation result. Section 5 gives conclusion and future work.

2   Related Works

Methods for emotion classification can be categorized into rule based methods and machine learning based methods. The former defines a set of rules to infer the emotion contained in text. The latter employs a set of features (such as BoW, N-Gram, emotion lexicon) to train a classifier based on some annotated training data to predict the emotion of a new piece of text. One issue for machine learning based method is how to obtain sufficient high quality training data. Current released corpora includes weblog [10], news headline [11], which are all manually labeled and thus are quite limited in quantity. Recently, more and more researchers explore distant supervision methods which is based on naturally annotated labels to automatically build training corpus, such as the microblog that uses naturally annotated emoticon, hashtag and emoji characters as annotated emotion labels. Mohammad takesmotion linked hashtags in tweets for emotion classification and proves that when hashtags are consistent to a degree such that they can be used for emotion detection in tweets [6]. Similar methods is used by Wang to obtain a much larger dataset and experiments show that for some minority emotions (i.e., surprise), the prediction performance is not so good [8]. Furthermore, Mohammad makes use of hashtags to construct an emotion corpus, based on which an emotion lexicon was extracted using PMI and the lexicon is used on another domain for emotion classification [7]. Bandhakavi also makes use of microblog containing hashtags to generate emotion lexicon based on EM with class and neutral model [1]. However, none of them addresses the issue of hashtag noise. Experiments in [8] also show that distant supervision is suitable for some emotions (i.e., happiness, sadness and anger) but less able to distinguish minority emotional labels.

Semi-supervised learning has been widely studied, such as co-training [2] and CoTRADE [5] which include a noise detection method. Wan proposes a co-cleaning and tri-cleaning data cleaning algorithms on sentiment analysis [9]. Gui employs noisy detection on cross-lingual opinion analysis based on label inconsistency with neighbors [3]. However, all the above works are for binary classification. No attempt is made for multi-class emotion analysis.

3 Our Noise Handling Approach

3.1 Problem Definition

Let (x_i, y_i) denotes a pair of labeled data where x_i is the data, and y_i is the label. Let H: $\{(x_1, y_1), \ldots, (x_m, y_m)\}$ denote a high quality labeled dataset; L: $\{(x_{m+1}, y_{m+1}), \ldots, (x_{m+n}, y_{m+n})\}$ denotes a noisy labeled dataset; and T $\{(x_{t1}, y_{t1}), \ldots, (x_{th}, y_{th})\}$ denotes the testing dataset. Here, n, m, h are the corresponding dataset size, respectively. Let us assume that $n \gg m$. Let C denotes the set of class labels ($C = \{c_1, c_2, \ldots, c_{C_N}\}$) where $c_i \in C$ is a class label and C_N is the the number of classes. Our objective is to develop an algorithm M to extend H with L and improve the performance on T.

3.2 Our Proposed Strategy

The basic idea of our proposed method is that a classifier initially trained on H is used iteratively to predict L, and the instances with high confidence will be added as training data to retrain the classifier. Because the added training data contains noise and noise can accumulate, we will also devise a method to remove the added training data whose noise exceeds a certain level. To achieve this goal, two problems need to be solved: (1) How to select instances in L to be added as training data; and (2) How to detect the noise instances that is already included in the training data.

Let y_i denotes the original label (hashtag) for an instance in L. To select the instances from L, we train a classifier based on H and predict on L and obtain a predicted label y_i' ($i \in [m+1, m+n]$) with a confidence, which can be the classifier's prediction probability. We choose those instances such that $y_i' = y_i$ with top $n_{(c_i)}$ confidence for each class to construct L' and add L' to H. Here, the term confidence means the prediction probability of the classifier. In the experiment, we will see the usefulness of the original label constraint $y_i' = y_i$. To take into consideration of the naturally imbalanced data in emotion corpora, we also control the number of added instancesor each class. For the class c_i with the least number of instances in H, we set the added instance number to H in each iteration as n_a. Then, for other class c_j, we set the added number using the following formula:

$$n_{c_j} = n_a \frac{p_{c_i}}{p_{c_j}} \tag{1}$$

Here p_{c_i} and p_{c_j} is the class proportion in H. This means the more instances a class is in H, the less additional training data is added for that class. This is to make the data to be more balanced. Because of the imperfection of the classifier, noise in y_i can accumulate. To detect the noisy label, we use a k-NN graph based method. Given an added instance x_i, y_i from L', a k-NN graph $G = \{V, E, W\}$ is constructed from $H + L'$, where the nodes are instances in $H + L'$ and the edge weights are the similarity between instances in the feature space. Based on the manifold assumption that instances with high similarity in the feature space will have similar labels [13], we can measure the inconsistency between two instances based on the similarity in feature space and the difference in the label space. For each pair of (x_i, y_i) and its neighbor (x_j, y_j) in the graph, we compute the edge weight ω_{ij} by:

$$\omega_{ij} = sim(x_i, x_j)$$

Similarity functions $sim(x_i, x_j)$ can be constructed in many different ways, including distance based similarity and cosine similarity between the feature vector representation of two samples. In this work, we simply use cosine similarity as in [3]. For each pair, we define the inconsistency between any two instances to be proportional to the similarity in feature space and to be inverse with the similarity in the label space, which can be calculated as:

$$Z_{ij} = \omega_{ij} D_{c_i c_j}$$

where $D_{c_i c_j}$ is the distance between label class c_i and c_j. This means under the same non-zero label distance, the more similar they are in the feature space, the more inconsistent between the two instances. When the label distance is zero, the inconsistency is zero. $D_{c_i c_j}$ is defined in the class distance matrix M_d, with each entry $d(p, q)$ being the distance between class p and class q because the probability of a mislabeling between different classes is different. For example, the emotion class *"anger"* is more likely to be labeled as *"sadness"* than *"happiness"*, so $d(anger, sadness) < d(anger, happiness)$. Each emotion can be expressed in the valence-arousal coordinate [4]. Based on the emotion point in the valence-arousal coordinate, we can obtain their corresponding distances. Then we use the following formula to compute the label inconsistency for each vertex i:

$$J_i = \sum_j^k Z_{ij} = \sum_j^k \omega_{ij} D_{c_i c_j} \qquad (2)$$

where i refers to the center vertex and j refers to the neighbor of i and k is the parameter of k-NN, the number of selected most similar neighbors of node i. The more similar they are in the feature space and the more distant in label space between the vertex and its neighbors, the larger the error is for the label. When J_i exceeds a certain threshold J_{thresh}, we consider it a noisy label and remove it from the training set L'. Here we assume J_i follows the Gaussian distribution and use the high quality dataset H to estimate its mean and variance. For each sample (x_i, y_i) in H we compute its J_i using (2) and finally we obtain the mean and variance of J as μ_J and σ_J. Then J_{thresh} can be estimated by:

$$J_{thresh} = \mu_J + a\sigma_J \qquad (3)$$

where a is the parameter to control the removal extent. Here we set $a = 2$ because based on Gaussian distribution, the probability of $J_i > J_{thresh}$ will be 0.023, which is a small probability event and thus we have sufficient confidence to consider it as a noisy label. Since different classes will have different μ_J and

---

Inputs:
H: High quality labeled data
L: Naturally labeled data(noisy training data)
Learner: Train a multiclass classifier using training dataset
k: The number of nearest neighbors
n_a: The number of added instances each iteration
Outputs:
L': Filtered labeled data from L
f: The refined multiclass classifier trained on $H + L'$
Procedure:
1. $L' = \{\emptyset\}$
2. $f' = Learner$ (H)
3. *iteration* = 20
4. *Loop = True*
5. Find least class and compute n_{c_i} using (1)
6. **While** (*Loop*):
7. $y_i' = f'(L)$ % Making prediction on noisy data
8.   *iteration = iteration* – 1
9.   For class c_i
10.   Add top n_{c_i} confident instances in L that $y_i' = y_i$ to L'
11. $L = L - L'$
12.   If *iteration* =0   % Perform noisy data removal
13.   *Iteration* = 20
14.   For L_k in L'
15.   Construct kNN graph from $H + L' - L_k$ for L_k
16.   Compute J_i using equation (2)
17.   Compute J_{thresh} using (3) based on label of L_k
18.   If $J_i > J_{thresh}$
19.   Delete L_k from L' and put back to L
20. $f' = Learner(H + L')$
21.   If the size of L' keep unchanged
22.   *Loop = False*
23. **End of while**
24. **Return** f', L'

Fig. 2. Proposed algorithm

σ_J because of data imbalance, we compute J_{thresh} separately for each class. The algorithm is shown in Fig. 2. The *iteration* in line 3 is used to control when noise removal will be executed.

4 Experiment

4.1 Experiment Setup

To evaluate our proposed approach, we take the high quality training data from the benchmark of NLP&CC 2013 Chinese Microblog Emotion classification task[1]. The task aims to predict the emotion label of a given microblog.

---

[1] http://tcci.ccf.org.cn/conference/2013/pages/page04_tdata.html.

The dataset has eight labels: *like, disgust, happiness, sadness, anger, surprise, fear* and *none*. There are 4,000 training instances and 10,000 testing instances in the dataset extracted from Sina Weibo, a popular Chinese version microblog social network like Twitter. All these data are manually labeled. Thus, we treat them as high quality data and assume that the labels in these datasets are ground truth. Since *'none'* class data cannot be obtained through hashtag, so we merge the two subsets of data and remove the 'none' class data in the training and testing dataset. Finally we obtain 7,304 high quality labeled data and the data is divided into training and testing data using 1:1 keeping the same proportion of each class.

Table 1. The huati seed words for crawling the micrblogs.

Emotion Label	Seed word number and examples
Like	9: 给力(helpful), 可爱(lovely), 奋斗(strive), 喜欢(like), 赞(appraise), 爱你(love,you), 相信(believe), 鼓掌(applaud), 祝愿(hope)
Sadness	27: 伤不起(can't bear the hurt), 郁闷(sadness), 哭(cry), 失望(disappointed),心塞(heart hurt), 难过(sadness), etc.
Disgust	9: 无聊(boring), 烦躁(agitated), 嫉妒(jealous), 尴尬(embarrassment), 讨厌(dislike), 恶心(disgusting), 怀疑(suspect), 烦闷(bored), 厌恶(disgust)
Anger	27:,妈的(fuck), 无语(speechless), 气愤(angry), 恼火(anger), tmd, 你妹的(your sister),etc.
Surprise	16: 神奇(miracle), 惊呆了(shocked), 不可思议inconceivable), 天哪(my god), 大吃一惊(shocked), etc
Fear	11: 害怕(fearful), 紧张(nervous), 心慌(nervous), 害羞(shy), (embarrassed), etc.
Happiness	20: 快乐(happy), 幸福(happy), 哈哈(ha-ha), 爽(so high), 感动(moved),开心(joy), 嘻嘻(happy), 高兴(happy), 亲亲(kiss),etc.

Our noisy data comes from the Sina Weibo through Sina Weibo Huati API[2] using a list of seed words as hashtags (called "Huati话题(topic)" in Sina) words, such as *"难过(sad)"*, *"给力(helpful)"*. The detail of the seed word list is shown in Table 1. After manually assigning these seed words into the seven emotion categories, we mined 173,951 microblogs and cleanhe posts in the original data through the following rules: (1) Hashtags not at the beginning of ending of microblog; (2) Text containing more than one hashtags; (3) Duplicated text; (4) Converting traditional Chinese into simplified Chinese; (5) Texts not containing Chinese word; and (6) Text length after removing hashtag less than five. After the above cleaning, there are 48,305 microblogs left as our additional noisy training data. The statistics of the noisy data (L) and high quality labelled data (H) are shown in Table 2. Note that the data imbalance in the datasets is quite obvious. Take H as an example, the ratio of the largest label set to the smallest label set is over 14.29 (like vs fear).

---

[2] http://open.weibo.com/.

Table 2. Dataset statistics of each emotion label. **L**: the noisy training data. **H**: the high quality training data. **L(%)**: the percentage of each emotion label in L. **H(%)**: the percentage of each emotion label in H.

Dataset	Like	Sadness	Disgust	Anger	Surprise	Fear	Happiness	Total
L	5011	16877	6245	6037	1494	855	11786	48305
L(%)	10.4	34.9	12.9	12.5	3.1	1.8	24.4	100
H	2153	1129	1360	671	350	151	1486	7480
H(%)	28.8	15.1	18.2	9.0	7.1	2.0	19.9	100

The classifier used in this work is LibLinear implemented by Scikit-learn toolkit[3] with default parameters. Features used are bag of words and lexicon from a Chinese emotion lexicon DUTIR[4]. For evaluation, we use macro F-score. Parameter k for k-NN is set to 9 empirically and n_a is set to 5.

4.2   Result and Analysis

The *first* experiment is to test the performance of our proposed algorithm. We label this algorithm as $A^+O^+R^+$, which means **A**dding instances with **O**riginal noisy label information (with $y_i' = y_i$ constraint) and with noisy instances **R**emoval based on the algorithm in Table 2. For comparison, we use the following methods that use different addition strategies for comparison:

1. $A^+O^-R^-$ It adds instances by classifier confidence but without the original noisy label information and without noisy instances removal. It is similar to similar to self-learning method.
2. $A^+O^+R^-$: It adds instances by classifier confidence with original noisy label information constraint, but without noisy instances removal.
3. $A^+O^-R^+$: It adds instance by classifier confidence with noisy instances removal, but without original noisy label information constraint.
4. $A^-O^+R^-$: As mentioned in introduction part, it directly adds the noisy hashtag data without any filtering.
5. $A^-O^-R^-$: This is the reference performance of the original high quality data without adding any data. It serves as the baseline for performance improvement measure.

The performance evaluation is shown in Fig. 3. The horizontal line indicates the performance of the original algorithm without using any additional data. It is flat as it does change on the value in the x-axis. This serves as the yardstick to see whether additional training data is any good. Note that the three algorithms, $A^+O^-R^-, A^+O^-R^+, A^-O^+R^-$ are all below $A^-O^-R^-$. This means they are no good. By examining them in more details, we can see they used noisy data

---

[3] http://scikit-learn.org/stable/.
[4] http://ir.dlut.edu.cn.

either without natural label constraint or without noise removal. This clearly indicate that without noise removal, the additional data should not be used at all. Among the three methods, $A^+O^-R^-$ achieves the worst result, indicating that using noisy data directly has severe adverse effect. It also indicates that emotion classification from microblog is more complex because of its informality. $A^+O^-R^+$ also does not use the original label information, but its performance is a little better than $A^+O^-R^-$ because of noisy instances removal. $A^-O^+R^-$ uses only the original hashtag label of the noisy data without any inspection. It still performs better than $A^+O^-R^-$ and $A^+O^-R^+$, which means that the hashtag label is more reliable than predicted label by the classifier. On the other hand, both $A^+O^+R^-$ and $A^+O^+R^+$ achieve similar increasing performance, much better than the baseline. The performance of $A^+O^+R^-$ indicates that hashtags are useful even if noise removal is not conducted. However, $A^+O^+R^-$ degrades as iteration number increases because noise can accumulate once the iteration number increases. The performance of $A^+O^+R^+$ is the best performer as it is more stable. The number of added instances under different iteration number is shown in Fig. 4, which shows that the added instance number of $A^+O^+R^-$ continuously increase while $A^+O^+R^+$ has a control on the speed because some noisy instances are removed. This further indicates that $A+O+R+$ achieves comparative performance with less additional data compared to that of $A^+O^+R^-$.

The *second* experiment is to test the performance after adding the cleanedata L' by different strategies into the original training data H, that is the classifier trained on $(H + L')$, which is given in Table 3. Note that we focus on testing the effectiveness of the proposed noise filtering algorithm, so the added number

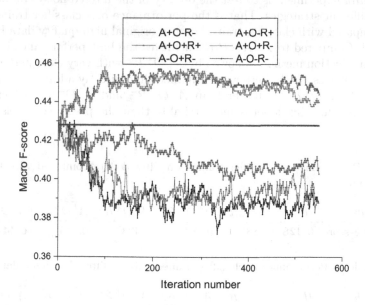

Fig. 3. Performance of different addition strategies.

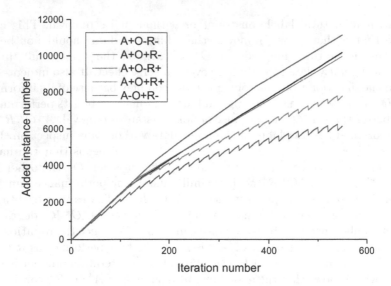

Fig. 4. Added instance number vs iteration number.

is different for different strategies, as is given in Fig. 4. $A^+O^+R^+$ achieves 3.7 % improvement than the original training dataset (H), similar to $A^+O^+R^-$ but with less data. The other three strategies all have worse performance compared to the baseline because of the added noise.

The *third* experiment is to test the quality of the filtered noisy training data (L') by different strategies. That is the performance of a classifier trained only on L' compared with classifier trained on the original high quality data H, given in Table 4. Compared to H, $A^+O^+R^-$ achieves the best performance in all the noise data selection method, followed by $A^+O^+R^+$ with very close performance. And they achieves 15.8 % better performance than directly adding hashtag data ($A^-O^+R^-$). $A^-O^+R^-$ is better than $A^+O^-R^-$ and $A^+O^-R^+$, which again indicates that hashtag label is more reliable than the predicted labels by the classifier.

Table 3. Performance of classifier trained on filtered data combined with the high quality data.

Methods	H	$A^+O^-R^-$	$A^+O^-R^+$	$A^-O^+R^-$	$A^+O^+R^-$	$A^+O^+R^+$
Macro F-score	**0.428**	0.388	0.388	0.403	0.440	**0.444**

Table 4. Performance of classifier trained only on filtered training data.

Methods	H	$A^+O^-R^-$	$A^+O^-R^+$	$A^-O^+R^-$	$A^+O^+R^-$	$A^+O^+R^+$
Macro F-score	**0.428**	0.309	0.295	0.342	**0.403**	0.396

Through the three set of experiments, we can now answer the two questions. Firstly, hashtags cannot be directly used as labels because of noise. Secondly, noisy data can be effectively cleaned by our proposed approach to improve the performance of multi-class classification based on our experiments.

5   Conclusion

In this paper, we present a framework on automatic noise removal for naturally annotated data using hashtags for emotion classification. Experiments show that hashtags are useful but naturally annotated data contains noise so they cannot be used directly without any cleaning. Our proposed algorithm combines the classifier and hashtag to effectively filter out noise to obtain more high quality data. The k-NN graph based noise removal method can further stabilize this process. Evaluation on NLP&CC2013 Chinese Weibo emotion classification dataset shows that our approach achieves 15.8 % better performance than directly using the noisy data without noise filtering. After adding the filtered data with hashtags into an existing high-quality training data, the performance is increased by 3.7 % compared to using the high-quality training data alone. Our method paves the way towards a more scalable training data for emotion classification from microblog. Our future work will focus on how to use the filtered data to further improve the performance of emotion classification.

Acknowledgement. We give our thanks to the anonymous reviewers for the helpful comments. The work presented in this paper is supported by Hong Kong Polytechnic University (PolyU RTVU and CERG PolyU 15211/14E) and the National Nature Science Foundation of China (project number:6127229).

References

1. Bandhakavi, A., Nirmalie, W., Deepak, P., Stewart, M.: Generating a word-emotion lexicon from #emotional tweets. In: Proceedings of the Third Joint Conference on Lexical and Computational Semantics, pp. 12–21 (2014)
2. Blum, A., Tom, M.: Combining labeled and unlabeled data with co-training. In: Proceedings of the Eleventh Annual Conference on Computational Learning Theory, pp. 92–100. ACM (1998)
3. Lin, G., Ruifeng X., Qin L.: Cross-lingual opinion analysis via negative transfer detection. In: ACL (2014)
4. Mehrabian, A.: Pleasure-arousal-dominance: a general framework for describing and measuring individual differences in temperament. Curr. Psychol. **14**(4), 261–292 (1996)
5. Min-Ling, Z., Zhi-Hua, Z.: CoTrade: confident co-training with data editing. IEEE Trans. Syst. Man Cybern. Part B: Cybern. **41**(6), 1612–1626 (2011)
6. Mohammad, Saif. M.: #Emotional tweets, pp. 246–255. Association for Computational Linguistics (2012)
7. Mohammad, S.M., Svetlana, K.: Using hashtags to capture fine emotion categories from tweets. Comput. Intell. **31**, 301–326 (2014)

8. Wenbo, W., Chen, L., Krishnaprasad, T., Amit, P.S.: Harnessing twitter "big data" for automatic emotion identification. In: Privacy, Security, Risk and Trust (PASSAT), International Conference on and International Confernece on Social Computing, pp. 587–592 (2012)

9. Wan, X.: Collaborative data cleaning for sentiment classification with noisy training corpus. In: Huang, J.Z., Cao, L., Srivastava, J. (eds.) PAKDD 2011, Part I. LNCS, vol. 6634, pp. 326–337. Springer, Heidelberg (2011)

10. Quan, C., Ren, F.: Construction of a blog emotion corpus for Chinese emotional expression analysis. In: Proceedings of the 2009 Conference on Empirical Methods in Natural Language Processing, vol. 3, pp. 1446–1454. Association for Computational Linguistics, August 2009

11. Strapparava, C., Mihalcea, R.: Semeval-2007 task 14: affective text. In: Proceedings of the 4th International Workshop on Semantic Evaluations, pp. 70–74. Association for Computational Linguistics, June 2007

12. Bennett, K., Demiriz, A.: Semi-supervised support vector machines. In: Advances in Neural Information Processing Systems, pp. 368–374 (1999)

13. Goldberg, A.B., Xiaojin, Z., Singh, A., Xu, Z., Nowak, R.D.: Multi-manifold semi-supervised learning. In: AISTATS, pp. 169–176 (2009)

NLP Applications

A Bootstrapping Approach to Symptom Entity Extraction on Chinese Electronic Medical Records

Tianyi Qin[✉] and Yi Guan

Web Intelligence Lab, Research Center of Language Technology, School of Computer Science and Technology, Harbin Institute of Technology, Harbin, 150001, China
ralbuckle21@gmail.com, guanyi@hit.edu.cn

Abstract. Symptom entities are widely distributed in Chinese electronic medical records. Previous approaches on symptom entity extraction usually extract continuous strings as symptom entities and require massive human efforts on corpus annotation. We describe the symptom entity as two-tuples of <subject, lesion> and design a soft pattern matching method to locate them in sentences in the EMR. Our bootstrapping approach which only requires a few annotated symptom tuples and it allows iterative extraction from mass electronic medical record databases without human supervision. Furthermore, the described method annotates symptom entities in EMR by the extracted tuples. Starting with 60 annotated entities, our approach reached an F value of 81.40 % in the extraction task of 3,150 entities from 992 sets of electronic medical records.

Keywords: Electronic medical record · Bootstrapping · Named entity extraction · Soft matching

1 Introduction

An electronic medical record (EMR) is the medical information of patients accessed and modified in a digital format written by medical staff in the process of medical activities [1]. There are four kinds of named entities in EMR [2]: disease, symptom, test and treatment. Among them, symptom entities have the most abundant and flexible knowledge about the physical condition of the patient, and are the starting point and primitive evidence of a clinical decision. Effectiveness of EMR varies by style of writing of medical staffs [3–5].

With the help of medical consultants, we formulated a medical entity annotating specifications for Chinese EMR. In the specification, symptom refers to the discomfort caused by a disease or abnormal performance and explicit abnormal test results [6]. Its corresponding UMLS semantic types include signs or symptoms, mental or behavioral dysfunction and abnormal test results. A typical symptom is composed of some subjects, a lesion and some modifiers. Symptoms always occur in a certain body part, behaviors or states of patients which are called the subject in this paper. Pathological changes or abnormal states of subjects are also called lesions [7]. Some lesions happen on more than one subject, while others cannot be separated from subjects. Besides the subject

© Springer International Publishing AG 2016
M. Sun et al. (Eds.): CCL and NLP-NABD 2016, LNAI 10035, pp. 413–423, 2016.
DOI: 10.1007/978-3-319-47674-2_34

and lesion, and other information in a symptom entity such as severity, frequency and so on, are called modifiers [8].

Symptom entity extractions in Chinese EMR have difficulties due to the lack in Chinese medical knowledge base. However, symptom entities are strongly patternized in Chinese EMRs. Patternization of symptom entities is reflected in the following aspects: Most symptom entities consist of one subject, one lesion and modifiers of them. Subject, lesion and modifiers are fixed types of words. For example, subjects are body parts and activities are words like "左下肢"("left lower limb"), "右耳"("right ear") and "睡眠"("sleep"), lesions are words describing abnormalities like "疼痛"("pain"), "出血"("bleeding"), and modifiers are positions, properties, degrees and negative words of subject and lesion. Our method utilizes patternized information of symptom entities in the process of extraction.

In this paper, we extract symptom entities in progress notes and discharge records of Chinese EMRs. On the basis of medical named entity annotating specifications, our method focuses on locating lesions and their corresponding subjects. Instead of extracting continuous strings as symptom entities, our method uses bootstrapping to iteratively extract two-tuples <subject, lesion> from a few annotated seed tuples in large unannotated Chinese EMRs. To realize the confidence measure of candidate tuples in the process of bootstrapping, we designed a soft pattern with the modifiers information of <subject, lesion>. Symptom entities can be formed by merging the extracted two-tuples and their modifiers in corpus according to the specification.

The remainder of this paper is organized as follows. Section 2 briefly introduces related works of our method. Details about the implementation of bootstrapping, including soft pattern initializing and updating, candidate entity extracting and confidence measure are described in Sect. 3. The results of the experiments are shown in Sect. 4 including the performance of our system with different parameters and also contrasting it against experiments of other researchers. Section 5 gives the conclusion of this paper and discusses future work.

2   Related Work

There has been several previous works for medical entity extracting. The most effective methods of named entity extraction on EMR are based on rule and dictionary, or supervised machine learning. In the concept extraction task of the 2010 i2b2/VA challenge, unannotated text of patient reports were given for systems to identify and extract the text corresponding to patients medical problems, treatments and tests [9]. Savova et al. [10] built a NLP system for information extraction from EMRs by trained clinical domain dictionary on CTAKES. Feng, Li, Jiang et al. [11–13] proposed supervised machine learning methods for clinical named entity extracting. Some researchers choose semi-supervised machine learning methods rather than supervised machine learning methods. Jonnalagadda et al. [14] used a semi-supervised sequential discriminative classifier (Conditional Random Fields) to extract the mentions of medical problems, treatments and tests from clinical narratives. In addition to the traditional features such as dictionary matching, pattern matching and part-of-speech tags, their method also used as a feature words that appear in similar contexts to the word in question. Words that have a similar vector representation measured with the commonly used cosine metric, where vector representations are derived by using methods of distributional semantics. The F-value of this method was 0.823. De Bruijn et al. [15] realized concept tagging by a discriminative Semi-Markov model. Semi-Markov models are Hidden Markov Models that tag multi-token spans of text, as opposed to single tokens. Only four tags: outside, problem, treatment, and examination are needed. Concept mapping features include context features and word-level features extracted from cTAKES and UMLS output. Their method reached an F-value of 0.8523, which was the best in the concept extraction task of the i2b2 2010 challenge.

Our approach is partly inspired by the medical information extracting method of [16]. That method proposed a definition of two-tuples <target, description> for medical information. With a series of algorithms including pattern generalization, pattern automatic extraction and medical information extraction, their method iteratively extracts two-tuples by generalized patterns. Our work applies a similar two-tuple definition in symptom entity extracting and introduces soft pattern and fuzzy matching from Zhao J's inspiration. Their method [17] offers a solution to generating a soft pattern. It generates pattern examples through segmenting sentences by event examples and filters them by notion words, stop words and trigger words.

3   Method

The main idea of our method is that we can iteratively extract two-tuples of <target, description> from only a few annotated tuples by bootstrapping, and form symptom entities by extracted tuples. Bootstrapping is a simple and intuitional method which is widely used in natural language processing [18]. Two main difficulties of the bootstrapping method are: (1) Effectiveness of bootstrapping is directly affected by the precision and covering ability of the initial seed set. (2) Errors occur in the self-training process which will be magnified during iteration. For the first difficulty, we invite trained medical staffs to accomplish the annotating task. Since Chinese EMRs from various departments have common linguistic features, we are able to guarantee the quality of seed set. For the second difficulty, a soft pattern provides us a solution for the measuring confidence of a candidate's two-tuples. We calculate the similarity between word frequency vectors in the slots of the soft patterns and word frequency vectors of <subject, lesion>'s context information. In each iteration we add symptom entities with the highest confidence value and adjust the soft pattern according to the context information of the newly added entities.

Our symptom entity extraction task is similar to the concept extraction task of the i2b2 2010 challenge but focuses on symptom information. Given Chinese EMRs from several departments, we located the border of two parts: subject and lesion. Examples of two-tuples extraction are described as follow:

Source Example 1: 右侧 口角 流涎 ("Right side of the mouth drooling.").

Result 1: <symptom>右侧 <subject>口角</subject> <lesion>流涎</lesion></symptom> ("<symptom>Right side of the <subject>mouth</subject> <lesion>drooling</lesion></symptom>").

Source Example 2: 左 上肢 及 双 下肢 骨折("Left upper limb and lower limbs fracture.").

Result 2: <symptom>左 <subject>上肢</subject> 及 双 <subject>下肢</subject> <lesion>骨折</lesion></symptom> ("<symptom>Left <subject>upper limb</subject> and <subject>lower limbs</subject> <lesion>fracture</lesion></symptom>").

Source Example 3: 心脏 各 瓣膜区 未 闻及 病理性 杂音 ("Heart valve areas found no pathological murmurs.").

Result 3: 心脏 各 <subject>瓣膜区</subject> 未 闻及 <symptom>病理性 <lesion>杂音</lesion></symptom> ("Heart valve areas found no <symptom>pathological <lesion>murmurs</lesion></symptom>.").

Source Example 4: <symptom>间歇性 <lesion>头晕</lesion></symptom> ("<symptom>Intermittent <lesion>dizziness</lesion></symptom>").

In the process of forming symptom entities, source example 2 includes two subjects corresponding to one lesion and we annotate the whole sentence as a symptom entity. Subject and lesion are separated by negative words and modifiers in source example 3, so we only annotate lesion as the symptom entity. And "dizziness" of source example 4 can't be segmented in Chinese.

Our target domain documents are progress notes and discharge records from 2003 to 2014 provided by the records room from the second affiliated hospital of Harbin Medical University (HMUSAH). Original medical records are paper records so we used OCR (Optional Character Recognition) to convert them into EMRs.

3.1 Definition of Symptom Entity and Soft Pattern

Subject and lesion are two main parts of symptom entities. In this paper we define lesion as a description of performance of physical abnormalities, and the subject as body parts or subjects where the lesion occurs. Subject and lesion are both single words which have direct semantic association with each other. For example, in the sentence "颈部 活动 受限"("Neck's activity limited"), subject of "受限"("limited") should be "活动" ("activity") but not "颈部"("Neck"). We extract two-tuples of <subject, lesion> which contain information of the symptom entity to locate them in large unannotated EMRs.

The bootstrapping used in our method starts from a few annotated <subject, lesion> seed tuples, to choosing the candidate entities by POS information, then uses fuzzy matching with soft pattern to measure confidence of candidate tuples, adds tuples of highest confidence to the seed tuple set and finally starts a new iteration. After a certain number of iterations, we form symptom entities with extracted tuples according to the annotating specification. The flow chart of bootstrapping is shown in Fig. 1.

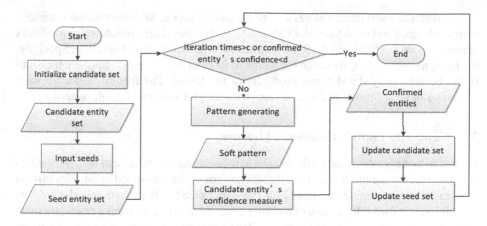

Fig. 1. Flow chart of bootstrapping

Although the basic flow maintains similarities with other general bootstrapping methods, our method uses fuzzy matching instead of hard matching. In order to realize the fuzzy matching, we set up a soft pattern according to the subject and lesion of the symptom information. We initialize a soft pattern by context information of the seed entities and update it in each iteration. Confidence values of candidate tuples are measured by the matching degree with the soft pattern.

3.2 Initialization of the Candidate Set and Soft Pattern

Our initial candidate set contains all the two-tuples of <subject, lesion> which are possible to be part of the symptom entities. For extracting the candidate two-tuples, we traverse segmented and unannotated corpuses sentence by sentence since symptom entity and its related context features are distributed mainly in its locating sentence. In each sentence, the subject always appears in front of the lesion. Every noun can be extracted as a subject, forming a tuple with all nouns/verbs/adjectives behind it as lesions. Specially, for sentences which have no nouns, we only extract candidate lesions and the subject remains empty.

For each candidate tuple, we divide its locating sentence into three parts according to the position of subject and lesion:

$$(L_1, L_2, \ldots L_a),\ \text{subject},\ (M_1, M_2, \ldots M_b),\ \text{lesion},\ (R_1, R_2, \ldots R_c)$$

Where L_n, M_n, R_n are modifiers in certain position. For example, there is a seed tuple <肺,啰音>("<lung, rale>") in a seed set and we find the sentence "双 肺 未 闻及 明显 啰音"("Both lungs heard no obvious rale.") containing it. Then we save the information of the sentence in three slots: {双},{未,闻及,明显}{null} ({"Both"},{"heard no obvious"},{null}). And these three slots become the basic form of our soft pattern:

$$< \text{slotL} >,\ \text{subject},\ < \text{slotM} >,\ \text{lesion},\ < \text{slotR} >$$

Each slot in a soft pattern stores a word frequency vector. We count all the sentences with seed tuples and form three slot vectors. SlotL and slotM are considered as modifiers of a subject while slotM and slotR are considered to be modifiers of the lesion. Specially, if a tuple has no subject, we count the words in front of the corresponding sentence into slotM because only slotM stores modifiers of the lesion. The feature vector for each candidate tuple is formed in the same way with the slot vectors of a soft pattern.

3.3   Candidate Entity's Confidence Measure

Most standard bootstrapping methods have to measure the confidence of both the entities and patterns, but our method updates the soft pattern by the confirmed two-tuples instead of measuring its confidence. Based on the generalized soft pattern and slot vectors containing standard information of modifiers, we are able to transform a candidate tuple evaluation problem to a word vector similarity calculating problem in which vectors have more common terms obtain a higher similarity value. The matching degree for tuples can also be represented as a cosine similarity value between feature vectors of candidate tuples and standard vectors in the slots of the soft pattern. The cosine similarity between two vectors $\bar{x}$ and $\bar{y}$ is:

$$Sim(\bar{x}, \bar{y}) = \cos(\bar{x}, \bar{y}) = \frac{\bar{x} \cdot \bar{y}}{|\bar{x}||\bar{y}|} = \frac{\sum_{i=1}^{n} x_i y_i}{\sqrt{\sum_{i=1}^{n} x_i^2} \sqrt{\sum_{i=1}^{n} y_i^2}} \tag{1}$$

The cosine similarity value between Left_Gram, Middle_Gram, Right_Gram and their corresponding standard vector in the slots of the soft pattern are calculated, respectively. In addition, we combine Left_Gram and Middle_Gram as modifiers for the subject, and Middle_Gram and Right_Gram as modifiers for lesion. The standard vectors in the soft pattern are also combined in this same way. Thus, we calculate five similarity values shown in following Table 1:

Table 1. Similarity values measured in confidence calculating

Symbol	Related feature vector
$SimL(\bar{x}, \bar{y})$	Left_Grams
$SimM(\bar{x}, \bar{y})$	Middle_Grams
$SimR(\bar{x}, \bar{y})$	Right_Grams
$SimLM(\bar{x}, \bar{y})$	Left_Grams, Middle_Grams
$SimMR(\bar{x}, \bar{y})$	Middle_Grams, Right_Grams

We obtain the average value of these five similarity values to get the confidence of a tuple:

$$Sim(\bar{x}, \bar{y}) = \frac{SimL(\bar{x}, \bar{y}) + SimM(\bar{x}, \bar{y}) + SimR(\bar{x}, \bar{y}) + SimLM(\bar{x}, \bar{y}) + SimMR(\bar{x}, \bar{y})}{5} \tag{2}$$

For entities with empty subjects, we ignore the similarity value using the slotL:

$$Sim(\bar{x}, \bar{y}) = \frac{SimM(\bar{x}, \bar{y}) + SimR(\bar{x}, \bar{y}) + SimMR(\bar{x}, \bar{y})}{3} \tag{3}$$

All candidate symptom entities are scored by the above formula. For each iteration, we preserve N tuples (N is a presupposed constant) with the highest similarity value is updated for the seed tuple set.

3.4 Soft Pattern Update and Iteration

According to the property of symptom entities in annotating specifications, we set up the following rules for annotating symptom entities: (1) If a symptom and its body part or subject are directly connected in a sentence, they are annotated as one symptom entity regardless of the number of body parts or subjects. (2) If the symptom and its body part or subject are inseparable, we annotate them as one symptom entity. (3) If the symptom and its body part are separated by punctuations, negative words or modifiers, only the symptom is annotated.

After one iteration, we obtain an expanded seed tuple set. The soft pattern is updated as described in Sect. 3.2. In order to comply with annotating specification, we obtain the final results of the symptom entity annotation by processing the seed tuple and the soft pattern in the iteration.

As shown in the source examples, symptom entities in Chinese EMRs come in mainly four forms: (1) Single subject adjacent to lesion. (2) Multiple subjects adjacent to lesion. (3) Subject and lesion divided by negative words or punctuations. (4) Lesion has no corresponding subject. In order to comply with annotating specifications, we annotate subjects, lesion and their modifiers as symptom entities in case (1) and (2), and then annotate lesion and its modifiers in case (3) and (4).

Slot vectors of the soft pattern offer us a set of statistic information about the words in a sentence with <subject, lesion> which can be directly used to determine the boundary of the symptom entity. According to the four forms of symptom entities in Chinese EMRs, symptom entity annotating based on our bootstrapping method applies the following rules:

(1) If there are negative words in slotM, ignore the subject, slotL and slotM.
(2) If multiple subjects appear in one sentence, annotate them without violating rule 1).
(3) If there are no subjects in the sentence, ignore slotL.

For slots not ignored, we determine the symptom entity's border by calculating word frequency in its corresponding slot. If word frequency of one word exceeds a threshold value, we annotate it as a part of the symptom entity. If the frequency of one word in slotL cannot reach the threshold, we ignore the words to its left in the sentence, and also ignore the words to the right of the first low frequency word in slotR. Specially, if the frequency of one word in slotM cannot reach the threshold, we ignore the whole sentence because the border of a symptom entity cannot be determined.

4 Evaluation

4.1 Source Data and Security Measures

In this section we represent the experiments for symptom entity extracting using the bootstrapping method. We randomly select 992 sets of Chinese EMRs whose privacy information was removed. Authorization of our source data were all given by the records room from the second affiliated hospital of the Harbin Medical University (HMUSAH), and their confidentiality and security are ensured by the regulations of the hospital. We intercept admission condition, discharging condition from discharge records, and disease cases from progress notes. The whole process of the experiment keeps no negative implications for the patients.

In order to guarantee the universal properties of the source data, EMRs involved in our experiment are from 20 different departments. The writing form of our EMRs are in accordance with the writing standard made by China's ministry of health.

4.2 Performance of Symptom Entity Extracting System

Three measures: precision rate, recall rate and F value are indicated to be necessary according to previous experience. We evaluate these three measures of our bootstrapping method on segmented Chinese EMRs.

As mentioned in Sect. 4.1, from 992 sets of Chinese EMRs we manually marked 3,150 symptom entities. We manually annotate 60 high frequency pairs of subject and lesion as seed tuples. Starting with 60 seed tuples, we aimed to extract more seed tuples and put them into symptom entities. In each iteration, we add 60 symptom tuples with the highest confidence values to the seed tuple set, and get symptom entities ad described in Sect. 3.4. Iteration terminates either when no entity tuple reached the confidence

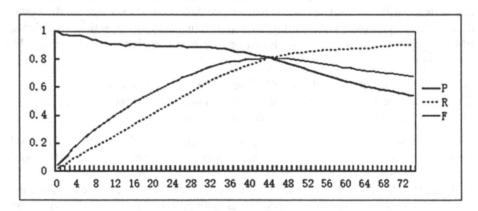

Fig. 2. Performance of symptom named entity extracting on unannnotated EMR

threshold in one iteration or after 74 iterations. The trend chart is shown in Fig. 2 and parts of the detailed results are shown in Table 2.

Table 2. A selection of experimental data from Fig. 2

Item	Iteration	Precision	Recall	F value
Maximum F value	44	81.40 %	81.40 %	81.40 %
Maximum R value	75	54.03 %	90.35 %	67.63 %
Other peak F values	49	76.91 %	83.37 %	80.01 %
	58	71.54 %	91.50 %	80.29 %

In each iteration, 60 seed tuples are added to seed tuple set. F value of extracted seed tuples keeps monotone increasing in first 44 iterations, and keeps monotone decreasing after that. The F value of iteration 44 is the only maximum value in experiment.

Attempt of increasing number of seed tuples and decreasing number of candidate entities added to seed set in each iteration can slightly increase the F value. But trend of precision rate, recall rate and F value maintain similar with original experiment.

4.3   Experiment Comparison

We made contrasts with experiments which used other methods of pattern generalizing, pattern extracting and medical information extracting of Chinese EMRs.

Xu's method [16] put forward a five-tuples mode of medical information: <target modification, target, degree, property, description> and we simplified the five-tuples into two-tuples of <target, description> and their semantic description. In the process of pattern generalizing, they segmented sentences by <target, description> and arranged midterm segmentation by the order of target, modification, degree and description. The generalized pattern was recombined and stored in a pattern base. In the process of pattern extracting and medical information extracting, they also used a bootstrapping method which generalized candidate sentences as specialized patterns and measured matching degree with the pattern base by a synonym dictionary.

Compared with Xu's method, our method also segmented sentences by two-tuples <subject, lesion> and extract symptoms information iteratively. The main differences between our method and Xu's method are that we used a soft pattern to measure the confidence of the candidate tuples. Our contrasting experiment used similar parameters as stated in Sect. 4.2. Sixty seed entities were chosen to extract 1,846 artificial marked symptom entities. The experiment results are shown in Table 3.

Table 3. Results of comparison

Item	Our approach	Xu's method
Precision	81.40 %	73.19 %
Recall	81.40 %	60.06 %
F value	81.40 %	65.98 %

In addition, we made another contrasting experiment with another bootstrapping method which estimated word frequency by an EM procedure and used the left and right branching entropy to build an appropriateness measure [17]. The experiment results are shown in Table 4.

Table 4. Results of comparison

Item	Our approach	Zhang's method
Precision	81.40 %	43.65 %
Recall	81.40 %	17.77 %
F value	81.40 %	25.28 %

4.4 Discussions

Our experiment in Sect. 4.2 shows that our approach can extract symptom entities with highest F value of 81.40 %. By updating soft pattern and confidence of candidate entities, our F value keeps increasing in front iterations. But after iteration 44, F value decreases because of candidate entities with lower confidence. Negative entities with high frequency in EMR data add false information to pattern, and leads to more negative candidate entities. Highest F value of 81.40 % ensure that our approach can extract symptom entities effectively.

In contrast with other existing medical entity extracting approaches, our approach has two main advantages. First, it substantially reduces the cost of manual annotation. Second, instead of a single string, it extracts a symptom entity's main information: subject and lesion as the item for extracting. This method can locate the symptom entity more easily, offer more detailed information about a certain body part and its corresponding lesion or limited activities. Our approach maintains a stable F value trend and is able to adjust performance by modify starting conditions.

A main limitation of our approach is that few symptom entities can't be described as subject and lesion, such as "恶心"("nausea") and "晕厥"("syncope"). Our approach usually extracts random subjects for these entities with no exact subject, which causes more false information in soft pattern. Moreover, Chinese word segment cause some subjects and lesions segmented together, such as "头痛"("headache") with "头"("head") and "痛"("ache"). These candidate entities will also cause false information.

5 Conclusions

We have demonstrated a bootstrapping symptom entity extracting method suitable for unannotated Chinese EMRs. We extracted the symptom entity's main information as two-tuples of <subject, attribute> and designed a soft pattern to locate them in sentences in EMR. By using a word vector oriented soft pattern, we could find a constant number of entities with the highest confidence value and update the pattern in each iteration. Experiments on Chinese electronic medical records show that our approach have reached an acceptable F value.

References

1. Nadeau, D., Sekine, S.: A survey of named entity recognition and classification. Linguist. Investig. Rev. Int. Linguist. Fr. Linguist. Gén. **30**(24), 3–26 (2007)
2. Qu, C., Guan, Y., Yang, J., Liu, Y.: The construction of annotated corpora of named entities for Chinese electronic medical records. Chin. High Technol. Lett. **2**(5) (2015)
3. Sittig, D.F., Singh, H.: Which electronic health record is better: A or B? Realities of comparing the effectiveness of electronic health records. J. Comput. Eff. Res. **3**(5), 447–450 (2014)
4. Erica, B., Field, J.R., Sunny, W., et al.: Biobanks and electronic medical records: enabling cost-effective research. Sci. Transl. Med. **6**(234), 86 (2014)
5. Wei, W.-Q., Feng, Q., Jiang, L., et al.: Characterization of statin dose response in electronic medical records. Clin. Pharmacol. Ther. **95**(3), 331–338 (2014)
6. https://github.com/WILAB-HIT/Resources
7. Eriksen, T.E., Risør, M.B.: What is called symptom? Med. Health Care Philos. **17**(1), 89–102 (2014)
8. Yang, J., Yu, Q., Guan, Y., Jiang, Z.: An overview on research of electronic medical record oriented named entity recognition and entity relation extraction. Acta Autom. Sinica **40**(8), 1537–1562 (2014)
9. Uzuner, Ö., South, B.R., Shen, S., et al.: 2010 i2b2/VA challenge on concepts, assertions, and relations in clinical text. J. Am. Med. Inform. Assoc. **18**(5), 552–556 (2011)
10. Savova, G.K., Masanz, J.J., Ogren, P.V., et al.: Mayo clinical Text Analysis and Knowledge Extraction System (cTAKES): architecture, component evaluation and applications. J. Am. Med. Inform. Assoc. **17**(5), 507–513 (2010)
11. Feng, Y.: Intelligent recognition of named entity in EMRs. Chin. J. Biomed. Eng. **30**(2), 256–262 (2011)
12. Li, D., Savova, G.: Conditional random fields and support vector machines for disorder named entity recognition in clinical texts. In: Proceedings of the Workshop on Current Trends in Biomedical Natural Language Processing (BioNLP 2008), pp. 94–95 (2008)
13. Jiang, M., Chen, Y., Liu, M., et al.: A study of machine-learning-based approaches to extract clinical entities and their assertions from discharge summaries. J. Am. Med. Inform. Assoc. **8**(5), 601–606 (2011)
14. Jonnalagadda, S., Cohen, T., Wu, S., et al.: Enhancing clinical concept extraction with distributional semantics. J. Biomed. Inform. **45**(1), 129–140 (2012)
15. Bruijn, B.D., Cherry, C., Kiritchenko, S., et al.: Machine-learned solutions for three stages of clinical information extraction: the state of the art at i2b2 2010. J. Am. Med. Inform. Assoc. **18**(5), 557–562 (2011)
16. Xu, G., Quan, G., Wang, Y.: Research of electronic medical record key information extraction based on HL7. J. Harbin Inst. Technol. **3**(11), 89–94 (2011)
17. Zhang, L.: Chinese EMR word segmentation and named entity mining based on semi supervised learning. Harbin Institute of Technology (2014)
18. Zhao, J., Qin, B.: Design and implementation of event arguments extraction system based on BootStrapping. Intell. Comput. Appl. **2**(1), 16–20 (2012)

Automatic Naming of Speakers in Video via Name-Face Mapping

Zhixin Liu[1], Cheng Jin[1], Yuejie Zhang[1(✉)], and Tao Zhang[2]

[1] School of Computer Science, Shanghai Key Laboratory of Intelligent Information Processing,
Fudan University, Shanghai 200433, People's Republic of China
{14210240048,jc,yjzhang}@fudan.edu.cn
[2] School of Information Management and Engineering,
Shanghai University of Finance and Economics, Shanghai 200433, People's Republic of China
taozhang@mail.shfeu.edu.cn

Abstract. The problem of automatically labelling the appearances of characters in video with their names is challenging due to the huge variation in the appearance of each character and the weakness and ambiguity of available annotations. We can achieve high precision by combining multiple sources of information, both visual and textual. The principal novelties that we introduce in this paper are: (i) extracting face features in video by neural network; (ii) strengthening the mapping between names and faces by analyzing the co-occurrence of names and faces; (iii) automatically and efficiently labelling appearances of main characters with their names.

Keywords: Automatic naming speakers in video · Face and clustering extraction · Name extraction · Name-face mapping

1 Introduction

With the rapid development of information technology, more and more multimedia data appears on the Internet, and there has been an explosive growth of audio-visual content. Content-based multimedia retrieval research develops rapidly. However, there are many limitations in multimedia retrieval, such as most retrieval manners are based on a single type of multimedia data, or the other modal data only plays a secondary role. To solve this problem, some researchers are interested in cross-media retrieval, namely matching multimodal information by a certain correlation to realize flexibly crossing different medium for retrieval. However, this often requires expensive manual annotations, especially for video contents.

Manual annotation of each new video source is expensive and impossible. An interesting alternative is using unsupervised approaches to name people in multimedia documents. In most previous works, the researchers first automatically classified each speech with an anonymous label and then used other methods to find the name of each class. Most previous works concerned the naming of people in video, and essentially use the same framework: (a) face clustering; (b) extracting names for each person; and (c)

M. Sun et al. (Eds.): CCL and NLP-NABD 2016, LNAI 10035, pp. 424–436, 2016.
DOI: 10.1007/978-3-319-47674-2_35

names/faces mapping. Such methods are different in how to cluster faces, how to extract names and how to match names with faces.

However, extracting names for each person in video is a very difficult problem, as subtitles usually do not directly describe the faces in video. Moreover, even if the name of a face is mentioned in subtitles, the alignment may be wrong. There are many other problems, such as there are often many faces in the same frame, and many names in the transcripts, or many unnamed faces or names that are mentioned but not displayed. Another difficult problem is that the identification of the person can be very hard due to the changes in pose, lighting conditions, facial expressions and partial occlusion. Recently, there has been a surge of interest in neural networks. In particular, deep and large networks have exhibited impressive results. However, most previous works on the recognition of characters in video did not use the novel technology, they still used the traditional method of clustering and traditional features in the face clustering stage. Another problem is that many previous works needed a lot of manual annotation information or did not make full use of the information in the video frame.

Based on these observations above, a novel scheme is proposed in this paper for facilitating more effective people news annotation via name-face Mapping by integrating multimodal information involved in video news. Our proposed scheme differs from other earlier work in multiple aspects, as shown in Fig. 1. (a) In the face clustering stage, we mainly use the popularity technology of neural network to train a generic face classifier, and extract deep descriptors of the human face by the classifier. (b) In the name extraction stage, not only the text information such as video introduction, subtitles are used, but we also use the OCR technology to extract the text information in each frame of video. All the information will be recorded on the video track, and will also be preliminary matched with the face in the first stage. The initial matching information can be found in this way. (c) In the matching stage, an efficient optimization algorithm based on the fuzzy clustering is particularly established to verify the feasibility of our automatic name-face Mapping algorithm.

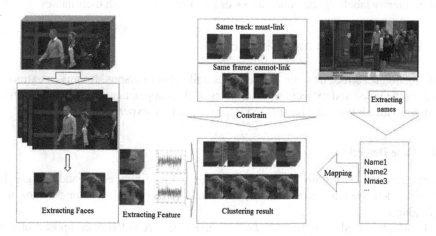

Fig. 1. The framework of automatic naming of speakers in video via name-face Mapping.

2   Related Work

Previous works on the naming of people in video, used essentially the same framework: (a) Face clustering; (b) Extracting names for each person; (c) Names/Faces mapping. However, previous works on the recognition of characters in video had often ignored the availability of textual information. Many researchers obtained the names by manually annotation. A semi-automatic method was proposed in [1] to name face images in BBC news. It needed to manually name some faces and then used the iterative label propagation in a graph of connected faces or name-face pairs. In order to reduce the manual work, some researchers dug the information in the subtitles or audio. Everingham *et al.* in [2] obtained the high precision by combining multiple sources of information including subtitles, transcripts and visual information. Poignant *et al.* in [3] even tried to use the audio information to extract names. Besides extracting names, it was a challenging task to obtain clusters for per character without merging multiple characters into a single cluster. Zhou *et al.* in [4] made use of must-link and cannot-link constraints to cluster per character. However, it needed to know the number of clusters in advance and was difficult to achieve good results for videos.

Usually, we cannot obtain the high precision in face clustering by using the traditional representation of facial features. Recently, there has been a surge of interest in neural networks. In particular, deep and large networks have exhibited impressive results [5]. However, most previous works on the recognition of characters in video do not use such novel technology. Many other previous works needed a large number of manual annotation information or did not make full use of the information in the video frame. Many clustering methods neglected the particularity of video news.

We can obtain the high precision by combining multiple sources of information, both visual and textual. The principal novelties that we introduce are: (i) extracting face features in video by using the neural network; (ii) strengthening the mapping between names and faces by analyzing the co-occurrence of names and faces; (iii) automatically and efficiently labelling the appearances of main characters with their names.

3   Face Extraction and Clustering

This section describes how we extract faces and cluster persons. It aims to extract the faces in the video and extract the descriptors of their appearances. The descriptors can be used to match the same person and improve the final experimental results.

3.1   Face Detection

Many tools and algorithms can extract the face in the picture easily and quickly. In a 30-min video, we can extract tens of thousands of faces which belong to dozens of individuals.

Firstly, we need to extract the faces in the video. A video is composed of many coherent pictures and the technology of extracting the face region from the static image is very mature at present. In this paper, we use the V-J video face recognition method for the extraction work. If we just simply extract the faces from each frame in video, we will get very large and complex human faces, and it will aggravate the burden of clustering. Fortunately, the frames in a video are not independent. There is strong continuity between frames. We can use this peculiarity to get a preliminary clustering of persons in video, which will greatly reduce the initial complexity of faces, and will improve the efficiency and accuracy of clustering results.

Face tracking is similar to object tracking. There are many ways to achieve good results at present. In this paper, we mainly use the optical flow method (Kanade - Lucas – Tomasi, KLT) [2] to track faces. The instantiation for the algorithm of face tracking is shown in the Fig. 2.

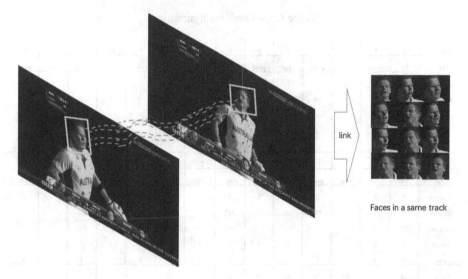

link

Faces in a same track

Fig. 2. An instantiation of face tracking by point tracking.

The KLT algorithm mainly tracks multiple points to track objects. In terms of face tracking, we can identify the feature points in the face region, then use the KLT algorithm to track such feature points in order to achieve the goal of tracking faces. The KLT algorithm can only track objects with small changes. Thus it can only be used in the continuous subset of video. We need to divide the video into smaller pieces according to the continuity. Considering the accuracy and efficiency, the segmentation criteria is the color histogram between two adjacent frames. We cannot achieve absolutely accurate identification of video segments by using the color histogram, but small mistakes just increase the burden of initial clustering and cannot lead to too much influence on the final result.

3.2 Feature Extraction

After the treatment in the previous section, we have already extract the faces of video, and carry on the preliminary clustering. However, because of the particularity of video, the same person could still be divided into dozens to hundreds of different classes after the preliminary clustering. It is an almost impossible task to name all the classes, thus we need further clustering results.

In the previous work, most people used the traditional method to extract the features of each face, and designed a certain characteristic to cluster. The traditional methods generally are difficult to adapt to the complexity of faces in video. There is a huge bottleneck in traditional methods. Fortunately, we have a more accurate method of clustering with the emergence of neural network. In this paper, we use VGG Face Descriptor [6] to extract the features of faces. The CNN architecture A is given in full detail in Table 1. It can achieve the high precision in LFW and Youtube Faces Dataset.

Table 1. Network configuration.

Layer	0	1	2	3	4	5	6	7	8	9	10	11	12	13
Type	In	conv	relu	conv	relu	pool	conv	relu	conv	relu	pool	conv	relu	conv
support	—	3	1	3	1	2	3	1	3	1	2	3	1	3
filt dim	—	3	—	64	—	—	64	—	128	—	—	128	—	256
num flts	—	64	—	64	—	—	128	—	128	—	—	256	—	256
stride	—	1	1	1	1	2	1	1	1	1	2	1	1	1
pad	—	1	0	1	0	0	1	0	1	0	0	1	0	1

Layer	14	15	16	17	18	19	20	21	22	23	24	25	26	27
Type	relu	conv	relu	pool	conv	relu	conv	relu	conv	relu	pool	conv	relu	conv
support	1	3	1	2	3	1	3	1	3	1	2	3	1	3
filt dim	—	256	—	—	256	—	512	—	512	—	—	512	—	512
num flts	—	256	—	—	512	—	512	—	512	—	—	512	—	512
stride	1	1	1	2	1	1	1	1	1	1	2	1	1	1
pad	0	1	0	0	1	0	1	0	1	0	0	1	0	1

Layer	28	29	30	31	32	33	34	35	36	37				
Type	relu	conv	relu	pool	conv	relu	conv	relu	conv	softmax				
support	1	3	1	2	7	1	1	1	1	1				
filt dim	—	512	—	—	512	—	4096	—	4096	—				
num flts	—	512	—	—	4096	—	4096	—	2622	—				
stride	1	1	1	2	1	1	1	1	1	1				
pad	0	1	0	0	0	0	0	0	0	0				

We align the faces before extracting the features and we use the approach in [7] to align the faces in this paper.

3.3 Face Clustering

We can obtain good clustering results by the excellent face features extracted from neural network and the inherent constraint in video: faces in same frame cannot be linked and faces in same track must be linked. In this paper, we cluster the faces by the distance proposed in [1] and the inherent constraint in video.

4 Name Extraction

In this section, we will mainly introduce how to deal with another important information in the cross-modal manner. The source of modern videos is variety, and a video is not often with enough text introduction, especially lack of the introduction of important characters in video. Finding the personal information of video is a difficult task in this field. Our treatment still cannot adapt to all of the videos, but can reduce the requirement of video data, especially the neural network technology used in OCR [8].

4.1 OCR Text Extraction

The script of OCR technology research has made remarkable achievements. We can say that the current print OCR recognition technology has reached a higher level. The OCR technology can be used to fully extract the textual information in video. By using OCR, we can extract the text information in each frame of video.

4.2 Name Identification

Although, we can easily get a lot of the text information, most of the test information is unserviceable. Only the person's name is useful. In this paper, we use the stanfordNER tool to extract the name in the text information. In order to cooperate with the mapping work, each name in the frame will be converted to the track of the name. We need to determine the name extracted by OCR not only the appearance on which frames, but also the position in each frame. Such information will enhance the mapping results.

4.3 Integration of Text

The previous processing fully extracts the names in video, but it also produces a lot of noises, such as geographical name, company name and the name in the scroll bar. We can see in the Fig. 3 that a lot of text information could be recognized as the name for the person in the same frame. We first eliminate the region with moving text and then

Fig. 3. The interference information in the red region and the correct name in green region. (Color figure online)

eliminate the geographical names and company names. At last, we eliminate the very rare name.

Now, we can easily get the correct text information by the above process. However, there are often many persons in the same frame. We need to find the most possible corresponding relationship between the name and the face to enhance the mapping results. We propose the following formula to determine the initial matching distance for the co-occurrence name and face:

$$RS\big(Name_i, Face_j\big) = \frac{\min\big(dist\big(Name_i, Face_j\big) * dist\big(Face_j, Frame\_center\big)\big)}{area\big(Face_j\big)} \qquad (1)$$

where $Name_i$ denotes the track of the ith name; $Face_j$ denotes the track of the jth face; $\min(dist(Name_i, Face_j))$ denotes the min distance between $Name_i$ and $Face_j$; $Frame\_center$ denotes the center coordinate of the frame; $area(Face_j)$ denotes the sum area of the faces in the ith face track. For most of news videos, the name of a face often appears with the face at the same time and the face locates in the center of the frame. We propose the formula to reflect the regular pattern, as shown in the Fig. 4.

Fig. 4. The correct faces often appear in the middle region and are bigger than other faces.

5   Names-Face Mapping

We have the movement track of names and faces by the above processing. We will obtain eventually matching results through the analysis for the movement track of names and faces. We get the final match results through a matrix of names and faces.

Name-face mapping aims at finding the optimal one-to-one name-face matching in video. Some probability-statistical models have been used to solve this task. However, most of the strategies are just the process of clustering without mapping and need a lot of manual work [9]. Thus an improved Fuzzy C-Means (FCM) clustering algorithm, which introduces the consideration of salient name information and integrates the limitation of name-face co-occurrence, is established to make a better solution for name-face mapping. Compared to the general FCM clustering, the improved one can better describe the multimodal features in multimodal videos, and makes more reasonable solution for such a specific mapping issue.

We will use the following symbols:

FS: faces in the given video set;

NS: names in the given video set;

FN: the number of face feature vectors in the face set FS;

NC: name clusters in the name set NS;

NCN: the number of name clusters in the name set NS;

$Face_i$: the face feature vector for the ith face in FS and $1 \leq i \leq FN$;

NC_Center_j: the prototype of the center of face cluster for the jth NC in NS, $1 \leq j \leq NCN$;

U_{ij}: the membership degree of $Face_i$ in NC_Center_j;

m: the weighting exponent on each fuzzy membership degree, which is set empirically (usually set as 2).

Our improved FCM clustering algorithm mainly aims at optimizing the following objective function J_m for every video.

$$Jm = \sum\nolimits_{i=1}^{FN} \sum\nolimits_{Pij=1} U_{ij}^m * Dist\left(Face_i, NC\_Center_j\right) \tag{2}$$

where $Dist(Face_i, NC\_Center_j)$ is an Euclidean distance measure between $Face_i$ and NC_Center_j; and P_{ij} denotes that if the ith face and the jth name co-occur in the same time, P_{ij} is set as 1, otherwise as 0. This function focuses on making the optimization for the distance among the face clusters associated with different NCs, so that each cluster has both the higher intra-cluster cohesion and the farther inter-cluster distance.

5.1   Initialization

We get the final matching results through optimizing a correlation matrix of names and faces. The initial value of the matrix has great influence on the final results. We need good initial values through the track of names and faces.

The track of faces is obtained by face detection, and the track of names is obtained by OCR. The track of names obtained by OCR is very important. The names in frames generally appear only once, and are often associated with the location of the relevant people. Thus we determine the initial value of the matrix by analyzing the matching degree of the track of names and faces in frames, which follow the following steps:

Firstly, for every trajectory of name, find all the trajectories of faces around the track of names. Secondly, for each finding trajectories of faces, calculate the minimum distance between the trajectories of faces and names.

Finally, the results of the divisor between the minimum distance of the face and the total trajectory distance is the initial value of Formula (1).

If the name extracted by the subtitle appearing in a frame, we will not consider the effect of the name. When the subtitle-name appears, the related face may appear at the same time, and also is likely to appear before or later. Subtitle-name tends to appear many times, thus we initialize the matching matrix by analyzing the co-occurrence of subtitle-name and the faces around it.

The initialization for U by using the name salience can be defined as:

$$U_{ij} = \begin{cases} 0, & P_{ij} = 0 \\ RS\left(Name_j, Face_i\right), & P_{ij} \neq 0 \end{cases} \tag{3}$$

where $RS(Name_j)$ denotes the important degree of $Name_j$ that co-occurs with $Face_i$ in the same video; and because $P_{ij} \neq 0$, it can be sure that $Face_i$ and $Name_j$ exactly co-occur in the video. Meanwhile, for the different names in a video, the sum of all their salience values is 1. The center of face cluster for each NC in NS is initialized according to Formula (4) with the parameter P_{ij}.

$$NC\_Center_j = \frac{\sum_{i=1}^{FN} \sum_{Pij=1} U_{ij}^m * Face_i}{\sum_{i=1}^{FN} \sum_{Pij=1} U_{ij}^m} \tag{4}$$

5.2 Matrix Iteration

There will be a lot of noises in the matching matrix because of the complexity and particularity of the video, and there will also be many correct initial values in the matrix matching. We should implement the process of iteration. This process aims at constantly amending the center of face cluster for each NC in NS according to Formulae (4) and (5), and also introduces the parameter P_{ij} that plays an important role for controlling the iteration.

$$U_{ij} = \begin{cases} 0, & P_{ij} = 0 \\ \dfrac{1}{\sum_{Pik=1} \left(\dfrac{Dist\left(Face_i, NC\_Center_j\right)}{Dist\left(Face_i, NC\_Center_k\right)}\right)^{\frac{2}{m-1}}}, & P_{ij} \neq 0 \\ 1 \leq k \leq NCN \end{cases} \tag{5}$$

In every iteration process, the center of face cluster for each NC in NS and the membership degree of each face in the face cluster for each NC are both recalculated and updated. After such a process, the center of each face cluster and the membership degree of each face will become more precise.

5.3 Mapping

The above iteration process will stop until the center of face cluster for each NC in NS no longer has offsets, or the number of iteration times reaches the preset maximal value. With the iteration to a convergence state, the fuzzy partition matrix U and each center of face cluster are both output and taken as the final name-face association mapping results, as shown in Formula (6).

$$Name - Face\_Mapping\left(Face_i\right) = \arg \max_{NCj}\left(U_{ij}\right) \tag{6}$$

6   Experimental Analysis and Discussion

6.1   Dataset and Evaluation Metrics

Our dataset is established based on the video website of *YouTube! News Data* constructed by ourselves, in which there are 11 news videos with around 200 names and about 40,000 faces. The proposed method is applied to the dataset (in total around 8 hours of video). The ground-truth names for every person are produced by manual annotation. To evaluate the effectiveness of our algorithm, Correct Mapping Rate (CMR) is defined as the percentage of correct mappings generated in the ground-truth (Table 2).

Table 2. The statistical information about our dataset.

Total faces	Clusterings	Clusterings (Name)	Clusterings (Null)	Clusterings (Unique name)
41,191	1,136	213	923	173

6.2   Experimental Results

To prove the correctness of the parameters we choose, we analysis the experimental results under different parameters. Table 3 shows the experimental results. The *co-occurrence* means the co-occurrence between the names and faces. The $dist(F, N)$ means the min distance between the names and faces. The $dist(F, center)$ means the average distance between faces and the center of the frame. The $area(F)$ means the whole area of the faces.

Table 3. Experimental results under different parameters.

Approach	CAR		
	Faces with name	Faces without name	All faces
co-occurrence	79.2%	89.1%	85.5%
co-occurrence+dist(F,N)	81.3%	89.1%	86.2%
co-occurrence+dist(F,center)	79.8%	89.1%	85.7%
co-occurrence+area(F)	80.1%	89.1%	86.1%
ALL	**85.2%**	**91.2%**	**89.0%**

Our name-face mapping model is created by identifying salient names, constraint face identification, and improved FCM clustering algorithm. To give full exhibition to the superiority of our mapping model, we have also performed a comparison between our unsupervised method and some other methods. Two approaches developed by Poignant *et al.* [10] and Bendris *et al.* [11] are analogous with ours to some extent, and we have accomplished these methods on the same dataset. We test the CNN feature and SIFT feature on every method and the CMR is also divided into three parts. The first CMR is the CMR for the faces whose names appear in the video, the second CMR is the CMR for the faces whose names do not appear in the video and the last CMR is the CMR for the whole faces. The experimental results are presented in Table 4.

Table 4. The comparison results between our and the other existing classic approaches.

Approach	Face appearance descriptors	CMR		
		Faces with name	Faces without name	All faces
Poignant *et al.*'s [10]	CNN	78.2%	86.1%	83.2%
	SIFT	69.7%	68.2%	68.7%
Bendris *et al.*'s [11]	CNN	76.3%	88.4%	84.0%
	SIFT	67.4%	70.5%	69.5%
Our approach	CNN	**85.2%**	**91.2%**	**89.0%**
	SIFT	84.1%	69.9%	74.3%

The instantiation of some name-face mapping examples are shown in the Fig. 5.

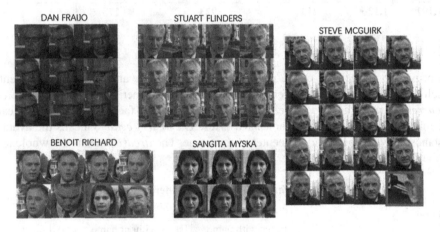

Fig. 5. The instantiation of some name-face mapping examples.

6.3 Analysis and Discussion

We can see that facial features have great influence on the result and we know that the facial features mainly affect the result of the face clustering. Although the features extracted by CNN technology is better than traditional features, we cannot obtain perfect results of the face clustering. The face clustering is difficult due to the huge variation in the appearance of each character. The extractor of the facial features is mainly trained by the static images and they are different from the faces extracted from the video. If we can train the extractor by the faces extracted from the video, we shall obtain better descriptors of the face.

It can be found from Table 4 that we can obtain the best CMR values. Poignant *et al.*'s approach tries to match all the names with their faces and Bendris *et al.*'s approach only matches the name with the speakers. Because of this, Poignant *et al.*'s

CMR for the faces with names is better than Bendris *et al.*'s and Bendris *et al.*'s CMR for the faces without names is better than Poignant *et al.*'s. Our approach focuses on distinguishing the people that appear at the same time so we can obtain better CMR. Many faces often appear in the same time in videos and we can obtain better mapping results by distinguish the important person from the whole faces.

7 Conclusions

In this paper, a new framework is introduced to automatic annotate the person in the news video. A novel algorithm is developed by integrating identifying salient names, constraint face identification, and the improved FCM clustering algorithm. Our future work will focus on fusing the audio information in the video and further improve the OCR accuracy.

Acknowledgments. This work is supported by National Natural Science Fund of China (61572140), Shanghai Municipal R&D Foundation (16511105402 & 16511104704), Shanghai Philosophy Social Sciences Planning Project (2014BYY009), and Zhuoxue Program of Fudan University. Yuejie Zhang is the corresponding author.

References

1. Tuytelaars, T., Moens, M.F.: Naming people in news videos with label propagation. IEEE Multimedia **18**(3), 44–55 (2011)
2. Everingham, M., Sivic, J., Zisserman, A.: Taking the bite out of automated naming of characters in TV video. Image Vis. Comput. **27**(5), 545–559 (2009)
3. Poignant, J., Besacier, L., Le, V.B., et al.: Unsupervised naming of speakers in broadcast TV: using written names, pronounced names or both? In: The 14rd Annual Conference of the International Speech Communication Association, INTERSPEECH (2013)
4. Zhou, C., Zhang, C., Li, X., et al.: Video face clustering via constrained sparse representation. In: 2014 IEEE International Conference on Multimedia and Expo (ICME), pp. 1–6. IEEE (2014)
5. Taigman, Y., Yang, M., Ranzato, M.A, et al.: Deepface: closing the gap to human-level performance in face verification. In: Proceedings of the IEEE Conference on Computer Vision and Pattern Recognition, pp. 1701–1708 (2014)
6. Parkhi, O.M., Vedaldi, A., Zisserman, A.: Deep face recognition. Proc. Br. Mach. Vis. **1**(3), 6 (2015)
7. Yu, X., Huang, J., Zhang, S., et al.: Pose-free facial landmark fitting via optimized part mixtures and cascaded deformable shape model. In: Proceedings of the IEEE International Conference on Computer Vision, pp. 1944–1951 (2013)
8. Jaderberg, M., Simonyan, K., Vedaldi, A., et al.: Reading text in the wild with convolutional neural networks. Int. J. Comput. Vis. **116**(1), 1–20 (2016)
9. Cheng, Y., Liu, Z., Zhao, Y., et al.: People news search via name-face association analysis. In: Proceedings of the 5th ACM on International Conference on Multimedia Retrieval, pp. 467–470. ACM (2015)

10. Poignant, J., Bredin, H., Le, V.B, et al.: Unsupervised speaker identification using overlaid texts in TV broadcast. In: Interspeech 2012-Conference of the International Speech Communication Association (2012)
11. Bendris, M., Favre, B., Charlet, D., et al.: Multiple-view constrained clustering for unsupervised face identification in TV-broadcast. In: 2014 IEEE International Conference on Acoustics, Speech and Signal Processing (ICASSP), pp. 494–498. IEEE (2014)

Image Tag Recommendation via Deep Cross-Modal Correlation Mining

Xingmeng Zhang[1], Cheng Jin[1], Yuejie Zhang[1(✉)], and Tao Zhang[2]

[1] School of Computer Science, Shanghai Key Laboratory
of Intelligent Information Processing, Fudan University,
Shanghai 200433, People's Republic of China
{15210240104,jc,yjzhang}@fudan.edu.cn
[2] School of Information Management and Engineering,
Shanghai University of Finance and Economics,
Shanghai 200433, People's Republic of China
taozhang@mail.shfeu.edu.cn

Abstract. In this paper, a novel image tag recommendation framework is developed by fusing the deep multimodal feature representation and cross-modal correlation mining, which enables the most appropriate and relevant tags to be presented on the image and facilitates more accurate image retrieval. Such an image tag recommendation pattern can be modeled as an inter-related correlation distribution over deep multimodal visual and semantic representations of images and tags, in which the most important is to create more effective cross-modal correlation and measure what degree they are related. Our experiments on a large number of public data have obtained very positive results.

Keywords: Image tag recommendation · Deep multimodal feature representation · Cross-modal correlation mining · Deep canonical correlation analysis

1 Introduction

With the explosive growth of images available both online and offline, especially on some popular websites such as *Flickr*, how to explore the involved contents in images to achieve more effective image retrieval has become an important research focus. Usually, common users are allowed to annotate each image with a series of tags in accordance with their own tendencies. However, existing investigations reveal that only around 50 % tags provided by *Flickr* users are indeed related to the images. The quality of tags is far from satisfactory due to the ambiguity, incompleteness and over-subjectivity. The main reason is that because of the semantic gap, there may exist huge uncertainty on the correspondence relationships among visual contents and semantic tags. Thus how to integrating multimodal information sources to enable the objective image tag recommendation has become a critical issue for supporting image retrieval.

The general image recommendation approach attempts to describe an image as a set of tags based solely on image contents [4]. However, tailoring the general image

M. Sun et al. (Eds.): CCL and NLP-NABD 2016, LNAI 10035, pp. 437–449, 2016.
DOI: 10.1007/978-3-319-47674-2_36

recommendation to image retrieval is challenging in two aspects: (a) the semantic gap still largely exists, and annotation tags are often very unreliable; (b) due to having little or no semantic information, fail to combine the enough semantics of images, as well as capture the multimodal association of different modalities. In the general recommendation framework [8], the missing of such important semantic information for image description may result in the huge uncertainty on the correspondence relationships between visual contents and semantic tags, and the performance of retrieval accuracy, efficiency and effectiveness is not very ideal. Therefore, more efforts are put into abstracting images in the deep level and integrating the semantic information from tags to form a novel expression with strong descriptive ability, so as to fully exploit the multimodal attributes in images and tags to support more precise tag recommendation and further improve the retrieval performance [1]. To achieve effective image tag recommendation, two inter-related issues should be addressed simultaneously: (1) the in-depth discovery of valuable multimodal features to characterize images and tags more reasonably; and (2) the cross-modal correlation mining to identify better multimodal correlations between the visual features for images and semantic features for tags. To address the first issue, it is very important to leverage large-scale annotated images for robust visual and semantic mining to achieve more comprehensive multimodal feature representation. To address the second issue, it is very interesting to develop new algorithms for exploiting multimodal features and efficiently explore the cross-modal correlations between different modality attributes in images and tags [12].

Based on these observations above, a novel scheme is developed in this paper for facilitating automatic image tag recommendation to enable more effective image retrieval. Our scheme significantly differs from other earlier work in: (a) The meticulous deeper representation for multimodal feature is constructed to learn more representative attributes for visual images and semantic tags; (b) The deep cross-modal correlation mining has a strong ability to characterize the deep multimodal correlations between the visual features in images and semantic features in tags, which can alleviate the problem of semantic gap to a great degree; (c) A novel image tag recommendation framework is built by fusing the deep multimodal feature representation and cross-modal correlation mining strategies, which enables the most appropriate and relevant tags to be presented on the image. Such an image tag recommendation pattern can be modeled as an inter-related correlation distribution over multimodal visual and semantic representations of images and tags, in which the most important is to create more effective cross-modal correlation and measure what degree they are related. Our experiments on a large number of public data have obtained very positive results.

2 Deep Multimodal Feature Representation

The Convolution Neural Network (CNN) is a feed-forward artificial neural network in machine learning [15], which is biologically-inspired [7]. Recently deep convolutional neural networks have demonstrated promising results in computer vison tasks, such as single-label image classification, image recognition, etc. We consider utilizing a popular deep neural network, Alex-Net, to extract CNN deep visual features [13]. Alex-Net is a typical convolutional neural network, which consists of 5 convolutional layers and

2 fully connected layers. It's really a simple but high-efficient network. Given an image, we extract a 4,096-dimensional feature vector using the pre-trained CNN on the ILSVRC-2012 dataset. We explore Alex layered architecture and use the Alex-Net features for all our experiments. In order to making faster training, we use the Auto-Encoder (AE) strategy to reduce the dimension from 4,096 to 300. Hence, the dimension for the feature expression reduces 93 % and the amount of information decreases 20 %, thus some redundant information in image contents can be eliminated and the information representation ability can be also further improved.

The Skip-gram model is an efficient method to learn the distributed representations of textual words in a vector space from large amounts of unstructured text data [14]. It learns deep word vector representations that are good at predicting the nearby textual words, which can capture more precise syntactic and semantic relationships among textual words and group similar textual words together. Thus we leverage the Skip-gram model to construct the deep textual word for better representing the deep semantic properties in annotation tags.

Let D^T be the textual annotation part of the whole multimodal dataset, W denotes all the raw textual words in D^T, and V is the textual word vocabulary. For each textual word w in W, I_w and O_w are the input and output vector representations for w, *Context* (w) represents the nearby textual words of w, here the context window size is set as 5. We define the set of all the input and output vectors for each textual word as a long vector $\omega \in R^{2*|V|*dim}$ and dim is the dimension number of the input or output vector, thus the objective function of Skip-gram can be described as:

$$BSG(\omega) = \underset{\omega}{\text{argmax}} \frac{1}{|W|} \sum_{i=1}^{|W|} \sum_{j=1}^{|Context(wi)|} logP(wj|wi)$$

$$= \underset{\omega}{\text{argmax}} \frac{1}{|W|} \sum_{i=1}^{|W|} \sum_{i=1}^{|Context(wi)|} \frac{exp(O_{wj} \cdot I_{wi})}{\sum_{k=1}^{|V|} exp(O_{wj} \cdot I_{wi})} \qquad (1)$$

Since the computing cost is extremely high for the standard softmax formulation of Skip-gram, the Negative Sampling is utilized to compute $logP(w_j|w_i)$ approximatively.

$$log(wj|wi) = log\sigma(O_{wj} \cdot I_{wi}) + \sum_{k=1}^{m} E_{wk(w) \sim P(w)} log\sigma(O_{wj} \cdot I_{wi}) \qquad (2)$$

where $\sigma(\cdot)$ is the sigmoid function; and m is the number of negative samples, each sample is drawn from the noise distribution $P(w)$ based on the textual word frequency. The entire textual word vectors are clustered to acquire the new deep textual word vocabulary, and then each word/tag in the annotation is projected to this vocabulary. Thus each annotation can be represented in the form of bag-of-deep-textual-words. Compared to the raw textual word, the main advantage of deep textual word is the consideration of the semantic relationships among raw words, which makes the deep words more representative to describe textual annotations, i.e., semantic tags.

3   Deep Cross-Modal Correlation Mining with DCCA

To achieve more effective cross-modal image tag recommendation, we have developed a multimodal feature embedding scheme based on Deep Canonical Correlation Analysis (DCCA) [3, 9] to exploit multiple features of annotated images and explore the multimodal associations between deep visual property features and semantic expression features. To make a clear presentation, we first introduce the general CCA [15], and then develop our DCCA-based multimodal feature embedding pattern.

The standard CCA algorithm is a classic statistical method to multi-view and multi-scale analysis for multiple data sources, which has received much attention in the field of cross-media/cross-modal processing [5]. It aims at finding linear projections for different types of data with the maximum correlation. Due to the limitation of standard CCA, the kernel representation is always integrated into CCA to increase the computation power of linear learning machines, that is, Kernel CCA (KCCA) [6]. As an extension of standard CCA, KCCA can provide a nonlinear function learning method by projecting different types of data into a high dimension feature space. However, it's still difficult for KCCA to find a better correlation between different types of data, because there are not simple linear or nonlinear relationships among real data.

To overcome the drawback of KCCA that the representation for real data is limited by the fixed kernel, deep networks can be integrated to learn flexible nonlinear representations, that is DCCA [2, 10]. Deep network is commonly used in the field of feature learning and classification, which plays a great role in learning a complex and nonlinear form to fit real data. DCCA with deep networks means a model with multiple hidden layers, which can simultaneously learn two deep nonlinear mappings of two views that are maximally correlated. The key difference between DCCA and other closely related approaches is that DCCA learns two separate deep encodings with the objective that the learned encodings are as correlated as possible, and such different objectives may have advantages in different settings. Thus DCCA, which could obtain more accurate highly abstract expression of real data via the complex linear and nonlinear transformation among layers, is introduced to make a better solution for image tag recommendation via cross-modal correlation mining.

For projecting multi-modal features to cross-modal features with DCCA, it aims at projecting the multimodal features with different modalities on multiple views into a common subspace and making sure that the correlation between visual features and semantic features could be maximized. We illustrate our architecture in Fig. 1.

Let IMG be the set of annotated images that consists of N samples; $X_V \in R^{D_V * N}$ is the visual feature vector for IMG and $X_S \in R^{D_S * N}$ represents the semantic feature vector, D_V and D_S are the corresponding dimensionality values for these two vectors, generally $D_V \neq D_S$. Taking these multimodal feature vectors as the input data of the corresponding deep networks including the visual and semantic networks, that is, $a_{V1} = X_V$ and $a_{S1} = X_S$. The visual and semantic networks have D_V and D_S units in the input layers, V_h and S_h units in the hidden layers, and hold V_o and S_o layers in the final output layers respectively. Thus in each network, the feed-forward from the ith layer to the $(i + 1)^{th}$ layer can be defined as:

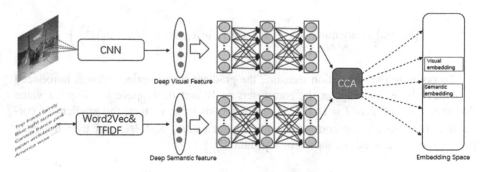

Fig. 1. Our proposed DCCA & DMFR model.

$$a_{Vi+1} = f_V\left(W_{Vi}\,a_{Vi} + b_{Vi}\,I^T\right), \quad a_{Si+1} = f_S\left(W_{Si}\,a_{Si} + b_{Si}\,I^T\right) \tag{3}$$

where W_{Vi} and W_{Si} represent the weight matrices between the ith layer to the $(i+1)^{th}$ layer in two networks respectively, $W_{Vi} \in R^{D_{Vi+1}*D_{Vi}}$ and $W_{Si} \in R^{D_{Si+1}*D_{Si}}$, D_{*i} and D_{*i+1} are the unit numbers in the ith and $(i+1)^{th}$ layers of two networks; b_{Vi} and b_{Si} denotes the bias values in two networks, $b_{Vi} \in R^{D_{Vi+1}}$, $b_{Si} \in R^{D_{Si+1}}$; I denotes an identity matrix; a_{Vi} and a_{Si} denotes the output data in the ith layers of two networks; and f is equivalent to a nonlinear transformation function for the data in the corresponding layer. Hence, the final matrices from the output layer in two networks can be achieved as H_{Vo}, $H_{So} \in R^{Do*N}$. Based on the learning with deep networks, the projection can be implemented as Formula (4).

$$DCCA_{VV} = \frac{1}{n-1}\tilde{H}_{Vo}\tilde{H}_{Vo}^T + r_V I, DCCA_{SS} = \frac{1}{n-1}\tilde{H}_{So}\tilde{H}_{So}^T + r_S I$$
$$DCCA_{VS} = \frac{1}{n-1}\tilde{H}_{Vo}\tilde{H}_{So}^T \tag{4}$$

where $\tilde{H}_{Vo}$ and $\tilde{H}_{So}$ represent the central data in the output matrices H_{Vo} and H_{So} from two networks respectively; and r_V and r_S are two regularization factors, which are usually set as small values to avoid the numerically ill-conditioned problem.

To find a projection relationship between the visual feature space and semantic feature space that could maximize the correlation between different feature views, the following Formula (5) is adopted to achieve such a goal.

$$(\theta_V^*, \theta_S^*) = \underset{(\theta_V, \theta_S)}{\arg\max}\ Corr(f_V(X_V; \theta_V), f_S(X_S; \theta_S))$$
$$Corr(f_V(X_V; \theta_V), f_S(X_S; \theta_S)) = Corr(\tilde{H}_{Vo}, \tilde{H}_{So}) = \|T\|_{tr} = tr(T^T T)^{\frac{1}{2}} \tag{5}$$
$$T = DCCA_{VV}^{-\frac{1}{2}} DCCA_{VS} DCCA_{SS}^{-\frac{1}{2}}$$

where θ_V and θ_S are two parameter sets of (W_{Vi}, b_{Vi}) and (W_{Si}, b_{Si}) form the input layer to the output layer in the visual and semantic network respectively. Because the maximal correlation value is 1, to convert the above maximization problem into a usual minimization problem, Formula (5) can be further slightly transformed into Formula (6).

$$(\theta_V^*, \theta_S^*) = \underset{(\theta_V, \theta_S)}{\arg\min} \left(\frac{1}{2} \sum_{j=1}^{Do} \left(1 - Corr(f_V(X_V; \theta_V), f_S(X_S; \theta_S))^2 \right) \right) \qquad (6)$$

To optimize the correlation measure, the gradient-based optimization is introduced to achieve better training for the parameters of W and b. Suppose the singular value decomposition of T is $T = UDV^T$, U and V are singular vectors, the gradient of correlation function can be computed with respect to $\tilde{H}_{Vo}$ and $\tilde{H}_{So}$ and then the back propagation is utilized, as shown in Formula (7).

$$\frac{\partial Corr(\tilde{H}_{Vo}, \tilde{H}_{So})}{\partial \tilde{H}_{Vo}} = \frac{1}{n-1} \left(2\nabla_{VoVo}\tilde{H}_{Vo} + \nabla_{VoSo}\tilde{H}_{So} \right)$$
$$\nabla_{VoVo} = -\frac{1}{2} DCCA_{VoVo}{}^{-\frac{1}{2}} UDU^T DCCA_{VoVo}{}^{-\frac{1}{2}} \qquad (7)$$
$$\nabla_{VoSo} = DCCA_{VoVo}{}^{-\frac{1}{2}} UDU^T DCCA_{SoSo}{}^{-\frac{1}{2}}$$

Similarly, $\frac{\partial Corr(\tilde{H}_{Vo}, \tilde{H}_{So})}{\partial \tilde{H}_{So}}$ has a symmetric expression. Hence, the set of the projection matrices of $P = \{p_1, p_2, ..., p_R\}$ and $Q = \{q_1, q_2, ..., q_R\}$ can be obtained by considering them as a symmetric eigenvalue problem. Thus based on the matrices of $P, Q \in R^{D_o * D_o}$, we can embed the multimodal features (i.e., visual feature H_{Vo} and semantic feature H_{So}) into a common subspace that can generate the cross-modal correlation, as shown in Formula (8).

$$P = DCCA_{VoVo}{}^{-\frac{1}{2}} U, \quad Q = DCCA_{SoSo}{}^{-\frac{1}{2}} V \qquad (8)$$

In fact, for visual features and semantic features involved in each annotated image, they belong to different feature spaces with different dimensions. Our DCCA-based multimodal feature embedding for deep cross-modal correlation mining can provide a relatively perfect feature representation with associations between various features in different modalities, which can mitigate the problem of semantic gap to a certain extent and achieve better multimodal feature associations.

4   Experiment and Analysis

4.1   Dataset and Evaluation Metrics

The evaluation for image tag recommendation via deep cross-modal correlation mining requires an image collection with paired images and annotation texts. Thus our dataset is established based on three benchmark datasets of *Corel5k*, *Corel30k* and *Nus-Wide*. The first and second datasets are two subsets of the *Corel* database, which contain 5,000 images, 260 words or labels and 87 categories, and 31,695 images, 5,587 words or labels and 320 categories respectively. The latter is a web image dataset created by *NUS*'s Lab for Media Search, which includes 269,648 images, the associated tags from *Flickr* with a total of 5,018 unique tags, and 704 categories. Because our tag recommendation method is a supervised task, we follow [8, 11] to split the dataset to the training set and testing set.

Our algorithm evaluation focuses on three criteria: (1) how well our deep multimodal feature representation can identify the valuable multimodal features from the images and annotation texts of large-scale annotated image collections; (2) how well our deep cross-modal correlation mining can measure the deep inter-related correlations between visual and semantic features and make an effective integration to construct cross-modal associations; (3) how well our model can support automatic image tag recommendation for large-scale images. To evaluate the effectiveness of these criteria for our image tag recommendation, we compare the annotation results with the available ground-truth labels and employ the benchmark metrics of *Average Precision* (*AP*), *Average Recall* (*AR*) and *Average F-measure* (*AF*), which are defined as:

$$AP = \frac{1}{n}\sum_{i=1}^{n} \text{Precison}(Img_i) = \frac{1}{n}\sum_{i=1}^{n} \frac{|RecTag(Img_i) \cap TagSet(Img_i)|}{|RecTag(Img_i)|} \qquad (9)$$

$$AR = \frac{1}{n}\sum_{i=1}^{n} \text{Recall}(Img_i) = \frac{1}{n}\sum_{i=1}^{n} \frac{|RecTag(Img_i) \cap TagSet(Img_i)|}{|TagSet(Img_i)|} \qquad (10)$$

$$AF = \frac{|2*AP*AR|}{|AP+AR|} \qquad (11)$$

where *TagSet(Img$_i$)* denotes the semantic annotation set for the image *Img$_i$*; *RecTag* (*Img$_i$*) denotes semantic annotation set recommended for *Img$_i$*; |*RecTag(Img$_i$)* $\cap$ *TagSet* (*Img$_i$*)| represents the number of correct semantic annotation tags recommended for *Img$_i$*; and *n* is the number of images in the whole dataset. Meanwhile, a specific *Cross-modal Correlation Score* (*CCS*) is introduced to better exhibit the effect of cross-modal correlation measure, which belongs to the range of [0, 1].

4.2 Experiment on Cross-Modal Correlation

The image-tag association mainly focuses on mining the valid and reasonable cross-modal correlation between deep visual features and semantic features. As the definition for the above evaluation metric of *CCA*, cross-modal correlation considers the positive correlation in the common space, that is, the maximum correlation for each multimodal visual-semantic representation pair in the same common space. Thus to verify the effect of our DCCA-based cross-modal correlation mining for acquiring the deep association between different modalities, we make a comparison analysis between different correlation models on three datasets, as shown in Table 1.

It can be seen from Table 1 that for cross-modal correlation measure on three datasets, we can obtain the best *CCS* value of 0.9999 for *Top*-1 and the best *CCS* sum of 19.8846 for *Top*-20 on *Corel30k* in the evaluation pattern of our DCCA-based cross-modal correlation mining. In comparison with the general CCS, the correlation mining performance could be promoted to a great degree based on KCCA and DCCA, and DCCA exhibits more significant positive impact to cross-modal correlation, which further confirms the obvious advantage of our deep cross-modal correlation mining mechanism with the deep multimodal feature information. Compared the results on

Table 1. The comparison results between our and other correlation models.

Metric	Cross-modal Correlation Score (CCS)								
Dataset	Corel5k			Corel30k			Nus-Wide		
Top-k	CCA	KCCA	DCCA	CCA	KCCA	DCCA	CCA	KCCA	DCCA
1	0.929448	0.93294	0.99481	0.353207	0.820499	0.999997	0.724740	0.55652	0.995945
2	1.84468	1.86209	1.98828	0.676485	1.63814	1.998032	1.429714	1.02952	1.991429
3	2.74386	2.77899	2.98118	0.996206	2.45429	2.995678	2.095074	1.48892	2.986730
4	3.63837	3.67983	3.97299	1.309763	3.26965	3.99262	2.666284	1.92911	3.981379
5	4.52701	4.57421	4.96399	1.610355	4.08462	4.989262	3.226887	2.35637	4.975107
6	5.4081	5.45657	5.95395	1.901771	4.89915	5.985365	3.764116	2.77975	5.968340
7	6.27834	6.33457	6.94298	2.188280	5.71323	6.980934	4.273572	3.1918	6.960630
8	9.58159	7.02072	7.93152	2.466425	6.52701	7.976069	4.761882	3.59934	7.952770
9	10.3853	8.05096	8.91915	2.733498	7.3404	8.970905	5.231056	4.0051	8.944524
10	11.1852	8.88718	9.90616	2.993295	8.15309	9.965175	5.683072	4.40765	9.935961
11	11.9751	9.7185	10.8925	3.245362	8.96542	10.95874	6.125599	4.80745	10.92652
12	12.7614	10.5444	11.8785	3.494521	9.77719	11.95198	6.558548	5.20064	11.91612
13	13.5379	11.3587	12.8635	3.740007	10.5888	12.94488	6.981282	5.59122	12.90495
14	14.31.3	12.1617	13.8479	3.984139	4535408	13.93722	7.399391	5.97982	13.89345
15	15.061	12.9619	14.8311	4.220558	13.0214	14.92937	7.809606	6.36719	14.88162
16	15.8035	13.7567	15.8133	4.452925	13.9317	15.92118	8.213106	6.75276	15.86897
17	16.5491	14.5485	16.7953	4.68259	14.6419	16.91252	8.612662	7.13786	16.85460
18	17.2753	15.3372	17.7760	4.904568	15.1354	17.90378	9.000176	7.52246	17.83928
19	17.9891	16.9006	18.7553	5.125131	15.70336	18.89465	9.377608	7.90547	18.82347
20	18.6975	16.6693	19.7339	5.343721	16.2628	19.88460	9.747613	8.287272	19.80716

Corel5k, *Corel30k* and *Nus-Wide*, the results on *Nus-Wide* appear less performant due to the obvious characteristic differences between these three datasets. *Corel5k* and *Corel30k* have more normative and consistent annotations, and the images in the same cluster have the higher visual similarity. *Nus-Wide* is established based on the social annotated images from *Flickr*, in which the annotation information is very abundant but with many noisy or error tags, and the images have much higher visual diversity. Although when evaluating on *Nus-Wide* the cross-modal correlation mining performance maybe slightly influenced by such extra phenomena, the *CCS* value for *Top*-1 and the *CCS* sum for *Top*-20 can still reach a relatively high value. We can still observe the promising and positive performance exhibition under the complicated tag recommendation environment of *Nus-Wide*. The best *CCS* value of 0.9959 for *Top*-1 and the *CCS* sum of 19.8071 for *Top*-20 on *Nus-Wide* approach to those on *Corel30k* acquired under a relatively more pure recommendation environment. It's also evidenced once more that our cross-modal correlation mining mechanism can be effectively applicable for both the unsophisticated case with less interference information and the complex case with more misinformation effect.

4.3 Experiment on Tag Recommendation

To further explore the applicability and usefulness of our cross-modal correlation mining for supporting image tag recommendation, we particularly carry out four runs to make the evaluation for the recommendation performance on *Corel5k* [C5] and

*Corel*30*k* [*C*30], that is, *DMFR&CCA* [*C*5], *DMFR&CCA* [*C*30], *DMFR&DCCA* [*C*5] and *DMFR&DCCA* [*C*30] (with Deep Multimodal Feature Representation [*DMFR*] and CCA/DCCA-based Cross-modal Correlation Mining). The *AF* curves with different feature dimension settings on two datasets are exhibited in Fig. 1. The *AP-AR* curves and the *AF* values for such six runs on three datasets are listed in Fig. 2.

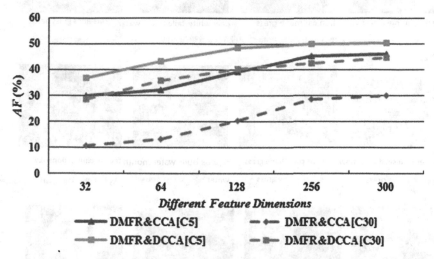

Fig. 2. The *AF* curves with different feature dimension settings.

It can be observed from Fig. 2 that for the tag recommendation on *Corel*5*k* and *Corel*30*k*, we can obtain the best recommendation performance in the evaluation pattern of fusing *DMFR* and *DCCA*. In comparison with the patterns using CCA-based cross-modal correlation measure, the performance could be greatly promoted by integrating the deep multimodal feature representation and the deep correlation mining, which confirms the obvious advantage of our deep representation and mining for tag recommendation. Comparing the results on two datasets, the results on *Corel*30*k* appear less performant on the whole *AF* curves, while the performance difference for *Corel*5*k* and *Corel*30*k* is not obvious, which reflects the performance advantage to some degree. Meanwhile, compared the results for different feature dimensions, we can observe that with the number of feature dimensions increasing, the recommendation performance gradually becomes pretty good, especially for our approach with *DMFR&DCCA*. These results are consistent with what we expect considering more valuable deep multimodal feature information or given more detailed deep multimodal feature description. It's worth noting that the in-depth multimodal analysis is available and presents more impactful ability for discovering the meaningful deep multimodal features and cross-modal correlations. An instantiation of some recommendation results is shown in Fig. 3.

To give full exhibition to the superiority of our tag recommendation model with deep cross-modal correlation mining, we have also performed a comparison between our approach and the other existing classical methods in recent years. Two methods developed by Makadia *et al.* [8] and Murthy *et al.* [3] respectively are analogous with

Fig. 3. An instantiation of some recommendation results with our model, in which the upper line represents the ground-truth tag sequence, the lower line denotes the recommended results, and the red words denote the mismatched words. (Color figure online)

ours to some extent, and then we accomplished them on the same datasets. The experimental results are presented in Table 2, which reflect the difference of power between these four patterns.

Table 2. The comparison results among different approaches.

Approach	Dataset								
	Corel5k			Corel30k			Nus-Wide		
	AP	AR	AF	AP	AR	AF	AP	AR	AF
JEC [8]	0.2700	0.3200	0.2900	-	-	-	-	-	-
General CCA	0.3500	0.4600	0.4000	0.2270	0.2250	0.2260	0.1080	0.1296	0.1178
CCA-based [3]	0.4200	0.5200	0.4600	0.2990	0.2980	0.2990	0.1426	0.1716	0.1557
DMFR&DCCA [Ours]	0.4991	0.5034	**0.5012**	0.4454	**0.4440**	**0.4446**	**0.2293**	**0.2456**	**0.2371**

It can be found from Table 2 and Fig. 3 that the best performance can be acquired on *Corel5k*, *Corel30k* and *Nus-Wide* by our approach. When integrating *DMFR* and *DCCA*, we can acquire the obviously better performance than the other patterns. Although based on our approach the values of *AP*, *AR* and *AF* on *Corel5k* and *Corel30k* may exhibit the obvious increase over those by the other patterns, we can observe that these values on *Nus-Wide* have been also dramatically higher than those by the other patterns. Under such a complicated learning environment of *Nus-Wide*, our approach reveals more significant advantage. This further confirms the prominent roles of deep multimodal feature representation and cross-modal correlation mining in tag recommendation, which implies that our model is exactly a better way for determining deep multimodal associations between images and annotation tags.

5 Analysis and Discussion

Through the analysis for the tag recommendation results, it can be found that our deep correlation with deep feature for tag recommendation is effective., but it's quality is highly related to the training set. Because correlation method is sensitive to data noise. It's easier to introduce error or noisy detections for visual and semantic feature information, which will seriously affect the whole clustering performance. (2) There is abundant information connotation involved in visual image. It's empirically realized that only using visual features is not sufficient for well formulating the distinguishability among image classes. The intensive visual feature expression can be utilized to further improve the multimodal correlation effectiveness and stableness. (3) There are different multimodal attributes among different annotated images. Although more obvious performance superiority has been exhibited via our CCA-based multimodal feature fusion, it's very beneficial to exploit an adaptive fusion between visual and semantic feature for each annotated image. (4) Some annotated images present an extreme vision with wrong or even without any valid annotations. With very limited useful annotation information and too much noises, it's hard for such images to successfully to recommend correct tags. This may be the stubbornest problem.

6 Conclusions

A new framework is implemented to exploit deep cross-modal correlations among deep visual and semantic features to enable more effective image tag recommendation. The in-depth multimodal feature analysis is established for characterizing the deep multi-modal attributes for images and annotations. The DCCA-based cross-modal correlation mining is introduced to acquire the specified multimodal association expressions. Our future work will focus on making our system available online, so that more Internet users can benefit from our research.

Acknowledgments. This work is supported by the National Key Research and Development Plan (Grant No. 2016YFC0801003). Yuejie Zhang is the corresponding author.

References

1. Murthy, V.N.: Automatic image annotation using deep learning representations. University of Massachusetts, Amherst, MA, USA (2015)
2. Wang, W., Arora, R., Livescu, K., et al.: Unsupervised learning of acoustic features via deep canonical correlation analysis. In: 2015 IEEE International Conference on Acoustics, Speech and Signal Processing (ICASSP), pp. 4590–4594. IEEE (2015)
3. Murthy, V.N., Can, E.F., Manmatha, R.: A hybrid model for automatic image annotation. In: Proceedings of International Conference on Multimedia Retrieval. ACM (2014)
4. Guillaumin, M., Mensink, T., Verbeek, J., et al.: TagProp: discriminative metric learning in nearest neighbor models for image auto-annotation. In: 2009 IEEE 12th International Conference on Computer Vision, pp. 309–316. IEEE (2009)
5. Hardoon, D.R., Szedmak, S., Shawe-Taylor, J.: Canonical correlation analysis: an overview with application to learning methods. Neural Comput. **16**(12), 2639–2664 (2004)
6. Jin, C., Mao, W., Zhang, R., et al.: Cross-modal image clustering via canonical correlation analysis. In: Twenty-Ninth AAAI Conference on Artificial Intelligence (2015)
7. Gong, Y., Jia, Y., Leung, T., et al.: Deep convolutional ranking for multilabel image annotation. arXiv preprint arXiv:1312.4894
8. Makadia, A., Pavlovic, V., Kumar, S.: A new baseline for image annotation. In: Forsyth, D., Torr, P., Zisserman, A. (eds.) ECCV 2008, Part III. LNCS, vol. 5304, pp. 316–329. Springer, Heidelberg (2008)
9. Andrew, G., Arora, R., Bilmes, J., et al.: Deep canonical correlation analysis. In: Proceedings of the 30th International Conference on Machine Learning, pp. 1247–1255 (2013)
10. Wang, W., Arora, R., Livescu, K., et al.: On deep multi-view representation learning. In: Proceedings of the 32nd International Conference on Machine Learning (ICML-2015), pp. 1083–1092 (2014)

11. Sigurbjörnsson, B., Van Zwol, R.: Flickr tag recommendation based on collective knowledge. In: Proceedings of the 17th International Conference on World Wide Web, pp. 327–336. ACM (2008)
12. Murthy, V.N., Can, E.F., Manmatha, R.A.: A hybrid model for automatic image annotation. In: Proceedings of International Conference on Multimedia Retrieval. ACM (2014)
13. Krizhevsky, A., Sutskever, I., Hinton, G.E.: ImageNet classification with deep convolutional neural networks. In: Advances in Neural Information Processing Systems, pp. 1097–1105 (2012)
14. Pennington, J., Socher, R., Manning, C.: GloVe: global vectors for word representation. In: Conference on Empirical Methods in Natural Language Processing (2014)
15. Thompson, B.: Canonical correlation analysis. In: Encyclopedia of statistics in behavioral science (2005)

Is Local Window Essential for Neural Network Based Chinese Word Segmentation?

Jinchao Zhang[1(✉)], Fandong Meng[1], Mingxuan Wang[1], Daqi Zheng[1], Wenbin Jiang[1], and Qun Liu[1,2]

[1] Key Laboratory of Intelligent Information Processing,
Institute of Computing Technology, Chinese Academy of Sciences,
Beijing, China
{zhangjinchao,mengfandong,wangmingxuan,zhengdaqi,
jiangwenbin,liuqun}@ict.ac.cn
[2] ADAPT Centre, School of Computing, Dublin City University,
Dublin, Ireland

Abstract. Neural network based Chinese Word Segmentation (CWS) approaches can bypass the burdensome feature engineering comparing with the conventional ones. All previous neural network based approaches rely on a local window in character sequence labelling process. It can hardly exploit the outer context and may preserve indifferent inner context. Moreover, the size of local window is a toilsome manual-tuned hyper-parameter that has significant influence on model performance. We are wondering if the local window can be discarded in neural network based CWS. In this paper, we present a window-free Bi-directional Long Short-term Memory (Bi-LSTM) neural network based Chinese word segmentation model. The model takes the whole sentence under consideration to generate reasonable word sequence. The experiments show that the Bi-LSTM can learn sufficient context for CWS without the local window.

Keywords: Chinese word segmentation · Neural network · Window

1 Introduction

Chinese word segmentation is to generate reasonable word sequence from non-delimited sentences. The most popular model is character labelling model [9,11] with statistical supervised approach [1,6], which assign positional labels (B, M, E, S) to characters according to the context. In these approaches, character context is represented by features that strongly depend on the handcrafted feature template. Although feature template can easily incorporate the linguistic knowledge, it is indeed a heavy burden to design an appropriate feature template due to the feature diversity and uncertain local window size.

In recent years, neural network models are introduced into CWS due to their ability to bypass the feature engineering. Zheng et al. [14] applied the architecture of SENNA [4] to CWS and pos-tagging to avoid the feature engineering and also speed up the training process with a perceptron-style algorithm.

M. Sun et al. (Eds.): CCL and NLP-NABD 2016, LNAI 10035, pp. 450–457, 2016.
DOI: 10.1007/978-3-319-47674-2_37

中共中央总书记 、习近平发表重要讲话

中共中央: the Central Committee of the
Communist Party of China
总书记: general secretary
、: punctuation
国家: state
主席: chairman
习: Xi
近平: jinping
发表: publish
重要: important
讲话: speech

context(习)=embding(记⊕、⊕习⊕近⊕平)
context(发)=embding(近⊕平⊕发⊕表⊕重)

Fig. 1. Restriction of local window.

Pei et al. [8] proposed a Max-Margin Tensor Neural Networks for CWS and modeled the interactions of tag-tag, tag-character, character-charcter. Chen et al. [3] proposed a gated recursive neural network to model the complicated combinations of the contextual characters to simulate the feature template. Chen et al. [2] introduced the LSTM neural network for CWS to capture the potential long-distance dependency.

These previous neural network based models all rely on a local window. The local window provides the rigid context for a character, and makes it difficult to exploit the outer context which is proved useful by Chen et al. [2] and it may preserve useless information in context. For instance, in Fig. 1, when labelling character "习", the character "记" in local window is useless due to the appearance of a caesura sign. Actually, no matter how long the window size is, the characters before the caesura sign are meaningless for labelling "习". On the contrary, longer the window size is, the more noise will be introduced from left context. However, when labelling "发", the character "话", which is helpful while is out of the local window. In addition, the local window size is an important hyper-parameter that apparently affect the model performance. It is costly to determine the most suitable size, which may change with the language and the segmentation criterion.

Long Short-Term Memory (LSTM) Neural Network [5] is a category of recurrent neural network with memory cell and gates, which endow it the ability to determine forget or memorize the historical information. We are wondering how well the bi-directional LSTM (Bi-LSTM) neural network can capture related context in whole sentence without local window. Therefore, we present a window-free Bi-LSTM neural network for CWS. The experiments show that Bi-LSTM based neural network can capture the sufficient related context for character sequence labelling. The local window is not essential in Bi-LSTM based CWS system.

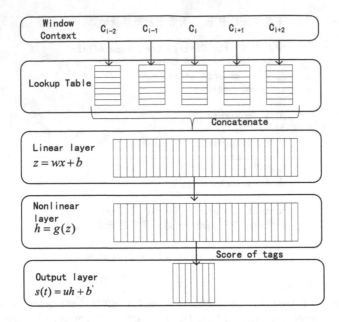

Fig. 2. Conventional neural model for Chinese word segmentation.

2   Local Window Based Neural Network for CWS

The character sequence labelling model is the most popular model for CWS. Traditional approaches are based on the feature template, while the neural network approaches are based on the character embedding. All of them rely on the local window to extract the context.

3   Conventional Neural Network for CWS

As Fig. 2 shows, the conventional neural model for CWS consists of a lookup table layer, linear layers and nonlinear layers, and a output layer.

The lookup table transforms a character to a distributed real vector called embedding. The embeddings in local window are concatenated to form the context of a character. The linear layer combine the input vector and the nonlinear layer do the nonlinear transformation with *sigmoid* or *tanh* function and so on. The output layer computes the label probability distribution of each character. Finally, the best segmentation result is inferred by beam search algorithm or dynamic algorithm. In conventional neural network based models, the local context is the feature. As a result, local window is of great importance to the model performance.

3.1 LSTM Neural Network for CWS

LSTM was proposed to address the gradient vanish of recurrent neural network. A LSTM unit consists of a memory cell and three gates. c_t is the memory cell stores the content of content a unit. i_t is the input gate to control the scale of current input. f_t is the forget gate to control forget extent of the last content. o_t is the output gate to control the scale of the output. The LSTM unit can be formalised as:

$$i_t = \sigma(W_{xi} + W_{hi}h_{t-1}) \tag{1}$$

$$f_t = \sigma(W_{xf} + W_{hf}h_{t-1}) \tag{2}$$

$$c_t = f_t \odot c_{t-1} + i_t \odot (W_{xc}x_t + W_{hc}h_{t-1}) \tag{3}$$

$$o_t = \sigma(W_{xo}x_t + W_{ho}h_t) \tag{4}$$

$$h_t = o_t \odot \tanh c_t \tag{5}$$

Chen et al. first introduced the LSTM unit into the Chinese word segmentation. However, their model also needs window to capture the right context.

4 Window-Free Bi-LSTM Neural Network for CWS

Inspired by Chen et al., we wonder whether the Bi-LSTM Neural network can thoroughly eliminate the local window or not. Therefore, we introduce the Bi-LSTM architecture into the CWS.

4.1 Model Architecture

Figure 3 shows our architecture. The first layer is the lookup table, which is identical to other previous works. For the absence of window, the character embeddings are transferred into the forward and backward layer without being concatenated. The forward layer accepts the positive sequence of embeddings, while the backward layer deals with the inverted sequence of embedding. These two layers work separately. Thus, we can get two hidden states $\overrightarrow{H}$ and $\overleftarrow{H}$, in which $\overrightarrow{H_i}$ and $\overleftarrow{H_i}$ represent the left context and the right context of character C_i. The two states are concatenated into one and transferred to the next layer that can be another Bi-LSTM layer or a logistic layer. The logistic layer transforms the input with a linear function, and then normalize the probabilities with a *softmax* function.

4.2 Training

The parameter θ in our model contains: the lookup table, 6 parameter matrixes for each LSTM layer (Eqs. 1–5), the parameter matrix of logistic layer. We use the

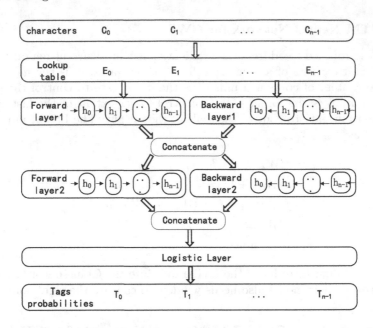

Fig. 3. Bi-directional LSTM model for Chinese word segmentation.

max-likelihood criterion to train our model, and we import the $L2$ regularization item into the objective function to prevent overfitting. The objective function is:

$$J(\theta) = \sum_{m=1}^{M} \sum_{n=1}^{N} log(P(tag|c)) + \frac{\lambda}{2}\|\theta\|^2 \tag{6}$$

where M is the sentence number, N is the sentence length, $P(tag|c)$ is the conditional probability, λ is the regularization constant.

To minimize $J(\theta)$, we use AdaDelta algorithm to update the parameters:

$$E[g^2]_t = \rho E[g^2]_{t-1} + (1 - \rho)g_t^2 \tag{7}$$

$$\Delta x_t = -\frac{\sqrt{\Sigma_{\tau=1}^{t-1} \Delta x_\tau}}{\sqrt{E[g^2] + \epsilon}} g_t \tag{8}$$

where $E[g^2]_t$ is the average of the squared gradients at time t, and the ρ is the decay constant, ϵ is a constant added to better condition the denominator, g_t is the gradient of the parameters at time t. ρ and ϵ are hyper-parameter.

Table 1 shows all hyper-parameters. To make it fair, we follows setup in Chen et al. [2]

Table 1. Hyper-parameters of our model

Character embedding size	$d = 100$
Bi-LSTM layer number	$n = 2$
Hidden unit number	$h = 150$
L2-regularization	$\lambda = 10^{-4}$
Dropout rate on input layer	$p = 0.2$
Decay constant in AdaDelta	$\rho = 0.95$
Constant in AdaDelta	$\epsilon = 10^{-6}$
Batch size	$b = 20$
Beam size	$beam = 20$

5 Experiments

5.1 Datasets

We run experiments on three widely used benchmark datasets, PKU, MSRA [10] and CTB6(LDC2007T36) [12]. For PKU and MSRA datasets, we take the first 90 % sentences of the training data as training set and the rest 10 % sentences as development set according to the previous works. For CTB6 dataset, we divide the training, development and test sets according to Yang et al. [13]. All datasets are preprocessed by replacing the Chinese idioms and the continuous English characters and digits with a unique flag. We adopt F1-score as the evaluation measure.

5.2 Experiment Results

We implement three models: LSTM-No-Window, Bi-LSTM-No-Window, Bi-LSTM-Window. We investigate these three models on PKU, MSRA and CTB6 dataset. We refer to the result of Chen et al. [2] as LSTM with window (LSTM-Windows). Table 2 shows the F1-Score of models. Compared with Bi-LSTM models and LSTM-Windows model, the LSTM-No-Window model achieves much lower F1-Score by a large gap. From that, we conclude that LSTM-No-Window is insufficient to capture context and the local window can provide abundant

Table 2. Performance of our three models and the Chen et al. result, local window slightly affects the Bi-LSTM model, and enormously affect the LSTM model

Models	PKU	MSRA	CTB6
LSTM-No-Window	92.3	93.0	91.5
Bi-LSTM-Window	95.6	96.2	95.4
Bi-LSTM-No-Window	95.6	96.3	95.4
Chen et al. [2]	95.7	96.4	94.9

Table 3. Performance of window-free Bi-LSTM and previous works without extra knowledge. Our model achieves competitive result without local window

Model	PKU	MSRA	CTB6
Mansur et al. [7]	93.0	-	-
Zheng et al. [14]	92.4	94.4	-
Pei et al. [8]	93.5	94.4	-
Chen et al. [3]	95.9	96.2	95.3
Chen et al. [2]	95.7	96.4	94.9
Bi-LSTM-No-Window	95.6	96.3	95.4

context information. However, on Bi-LSTM model, local window slightly affect the performance. On MSRA dataset, the window-free model performs better than window-based model. Therefore, we can conclude that the Bi-LSTM model has strong ability to capture related context information for Chinese word segmentation, which means local window is not essential for Bi-LSTM based model. Table 3 compares our result with the previous neural network based CWS models. Although our model does not have a local window to extract the context feature, it outperforms previous neural network model on CTB6 dataset, and ranks 2nd on MSRA dataset by a slightly lag(−0.1), and ranks 3rd by a little lag (−0.3, [3] is based on the recursive neural network). The results suggest that the window-free Bi-LSTM neural network can automatically capture the related context for Chinese word segmentation. Although the local window appears in every previous neural network based approaches, it is not essential for Bi-LSTM based one.

6   Related Work

The most popular model for CWS is the sequence labelling model proposed by Xue. [11]. The previous supervised methods [1,6] rely on the handcrafted template feature. In recent years, neural network based approaches [3,7,8,14] were proposed to avoid the feature engineering. All neural networks based CWS rely on the local window, which restricts the related context in a fixed scope. Our work is inspired by Chen et al. [2]. They exploit a LSTM neural network to capture the left context and a window to capture the right context. Our model exploits a Bi-LSTM neural network to capture the related context and discard the local window thoroughly and achieves comparable or even better performance.

7   Conclusion

In this paper, we present a window-free Bi-LSTM based Chinese word segmentation model. Compared with the local window based Bi-LSTM model, the window-free Bi-LSTM model achieves the identical or better performance. Compared with other previous local window based neural CWS approach, our model achieves the competitive or better performance. The result shows that Bi-LSTM neural network can automatically capture the related context and the local window is not essential for Bi-LSTM based CWS.

Acknowledgments. The research is supported by National Natural Science Foundation of China (Contract 61202216). Liu is partially supported by the Science Foundation Ireland (Grant 12/CE/I2267 and 13/RC/2106) as part of the ADAPT Centre at Dublin City University. We sincerely thank the anonymous reviewers for their thorough reviewing and valuable suggestions.

References

1. Berger, A., Pietra, S.D., Pietra, V.D.: A maximum entropy approach to natural language processing. Comput. Linguist. **22**(1), 39–71 (1996)
2. Chen, X., Qiu, X., Zhu, C., Liu, P., Huang, X.: Long short-term memory neural networks for Chinese word segmentation. In: Proceedings of the Empirical Methods in Natural Language Processing (2015)
3. Chen, X., Qiu, X., Zhue, C., Huang, X.: Gated recursive neural network for Chinese word segmentation. In: Proceedings of Annual Meeting of the Association for Computational Linguistics (2015)
4. Collobert, R., Weston, J., Léon, B., Michael, K., Koray, K., Pavel, K.: Natural language processing (almost) from scratch. J. Mach. Learn. Res. **1**, 1–48 (2011)
5. Hochreiter, S., Schmidhuber, J.: Long short-term memory. Neural Comput. **8**(9), 1735–1780 (1997)
6. Lafferty, J., McCallum, A., Pereira, F.C.N.: Gated recursive neural network for Chinese word segmentation. In: Proceedings of Annual Meeting of Eighteenth International Conference on Machine Learning (2015)
7. Mansur, M., Pei, W., Chang, B.: Feature-based neural language model and Chinese word segmentation. In: Proceedings of International Joint Conference on Natural Language Processing (2013)
8. Pei, W., Ge, T., Chang, B.: Max-margin tensor neural network for Chinese word segmentation. In: Proceedings of Annual Meeting of the Association for Computational Linguistics (2014)
9. Peng, F., Feng, F., McCallum, A.: Chinese segmentation and new word detection using conditional random fields. In: Proceedings of International Conference on Computational Linguistics (2004)
10. Emerson, T.: The second international Chinese word segmentation bakeoff. In: Proceedings of the Fourth SIGHAN Workshop on Chinese Language Processing, pp. 123–133 (2005)
11. Xue, N.: Chinese word segmentation as character tagging. Comput. Linguist. Chinese Lang. Process. **8**(1), 29–48 (2003)
12. Xue, N., Xia, F., Chiou, F.D., Palmer, M.: The Penn Chinese TreeBank: phrase structure annotation of a large corpus. Natural Lang. Eng. **11**(2), 207–238 (2005)
13. Yang, Y., Xue, N.: Chinese comma disambiguation for discourse analysis. In: Proceedings of Annual Meeting of the Association for Computational Linguistics (2012)
14. Zheng, X., Chen, H., Xu, T.: Deep learning for Chinese word segmentation and POS tagging. In: Proceedings of the Empirical Methods in Natural Language Processing (2013)

Erratum to: Investigation and Use of Methods for Defining the Extends of Similarity of Kazakh Language Sentences

Unzila Kamanur[1(✉)], Altynbek Sharipbay[1(✉)], Gulila Altenbek[2(✉)], Gulmira Bekmanova[1], and Lena Zhetkenbay[1]

[1] L.N. Gumilyov Eurasian National University, Astana, Kazakhstan
{unzila.88,sharalt,jetlen_7}@mail.ru,
gulmira-r@yandex.ru
[2] Xinjiang University, Urumqi, China
glaxd2014@163.com

Erratum to:
Chapter 14 in: M. Sun et al. (Eds.)
Chinese Computational Linguistics and Natural Language Processing Based on Naturally Annotated Big Data
DOI: 10.1007/978-3-319-47674-2_14

By mistake, the affiliations for some of the authors were stated incorrectly in the initially published version of the paper. The correct affiliations are as follows:

Unzila Kamanur[1], Altynbek Sharipbay[1], Gulila Altenbek[2], Gulmira Bekmanova[1], and Lena Zhetkenbay[2]

[1] L.N. Gumilyov Eurasian National University, Astana, Kazakhstan
[2] Xinjiang University, Urumqi, China

The updated original online version for this chapter can be found at
DOI: 10.1007/978-3-319-47674-2_14

Author Index

Printed in the United States
By Bookmasters